Contents

1st Story 5

2nd Story 43

3rd Story 79

4th Story 105

5th Story 135

6th Story 165

Final Story 199

The Story of Their
First Night Together 235

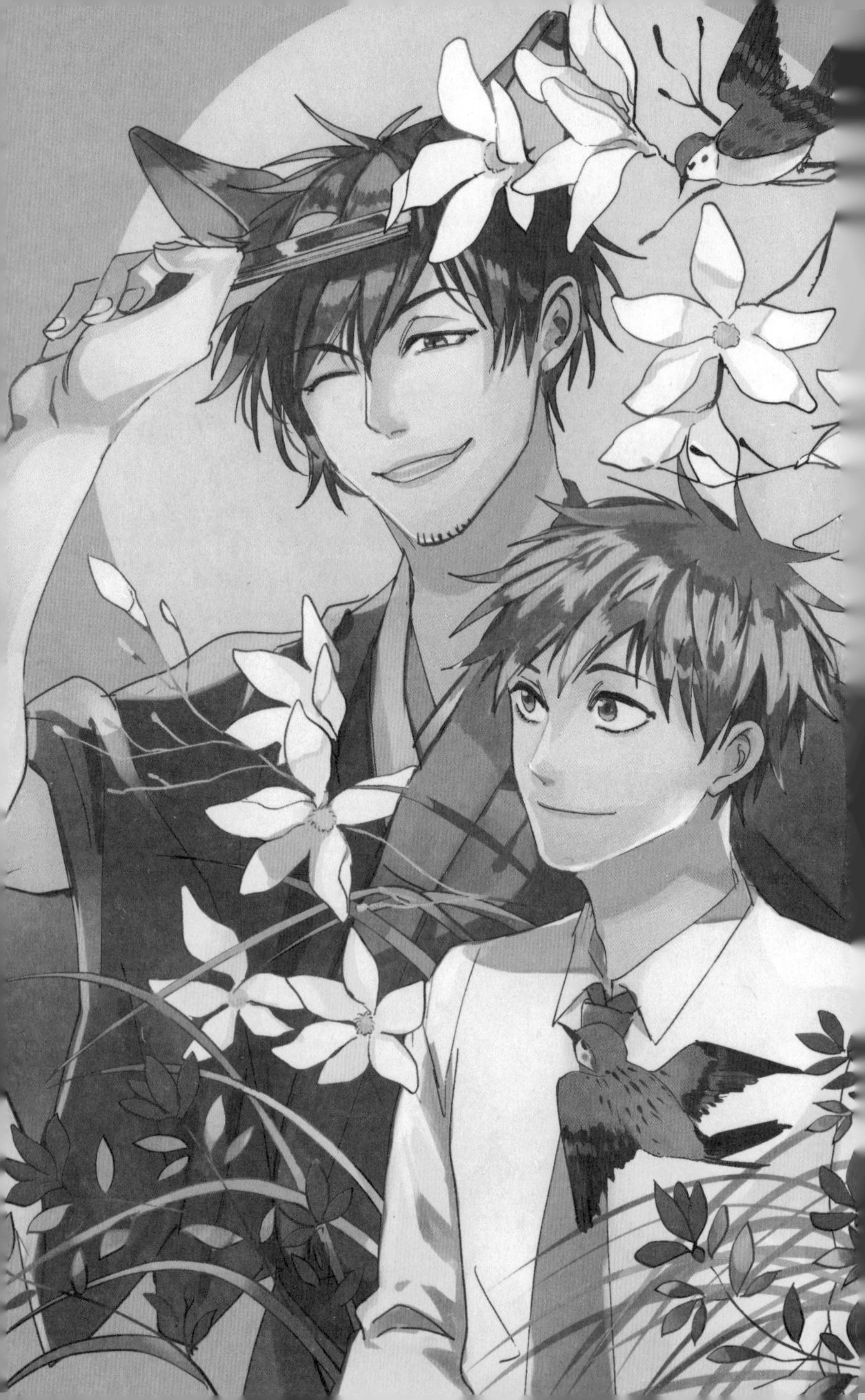

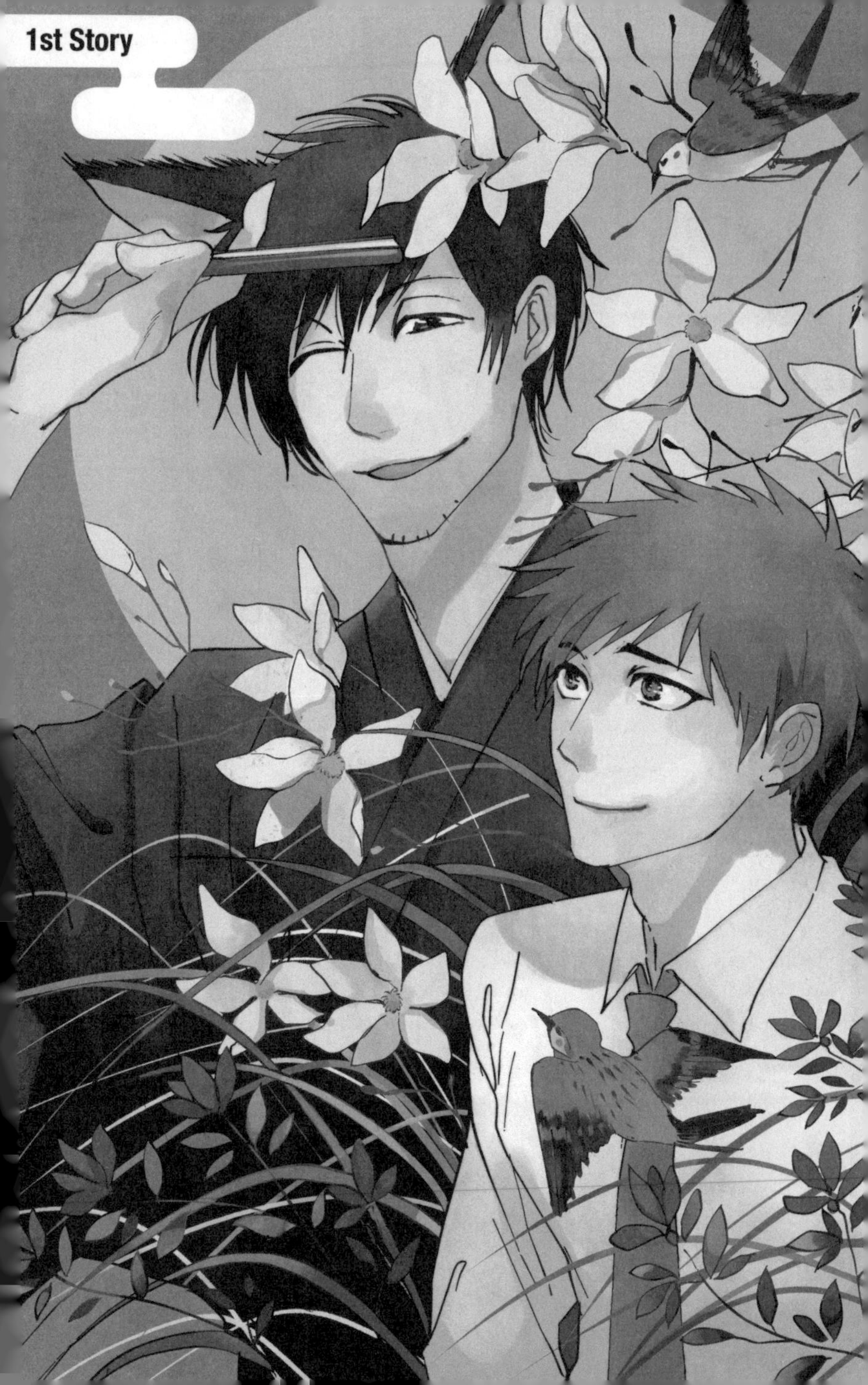
1st Story

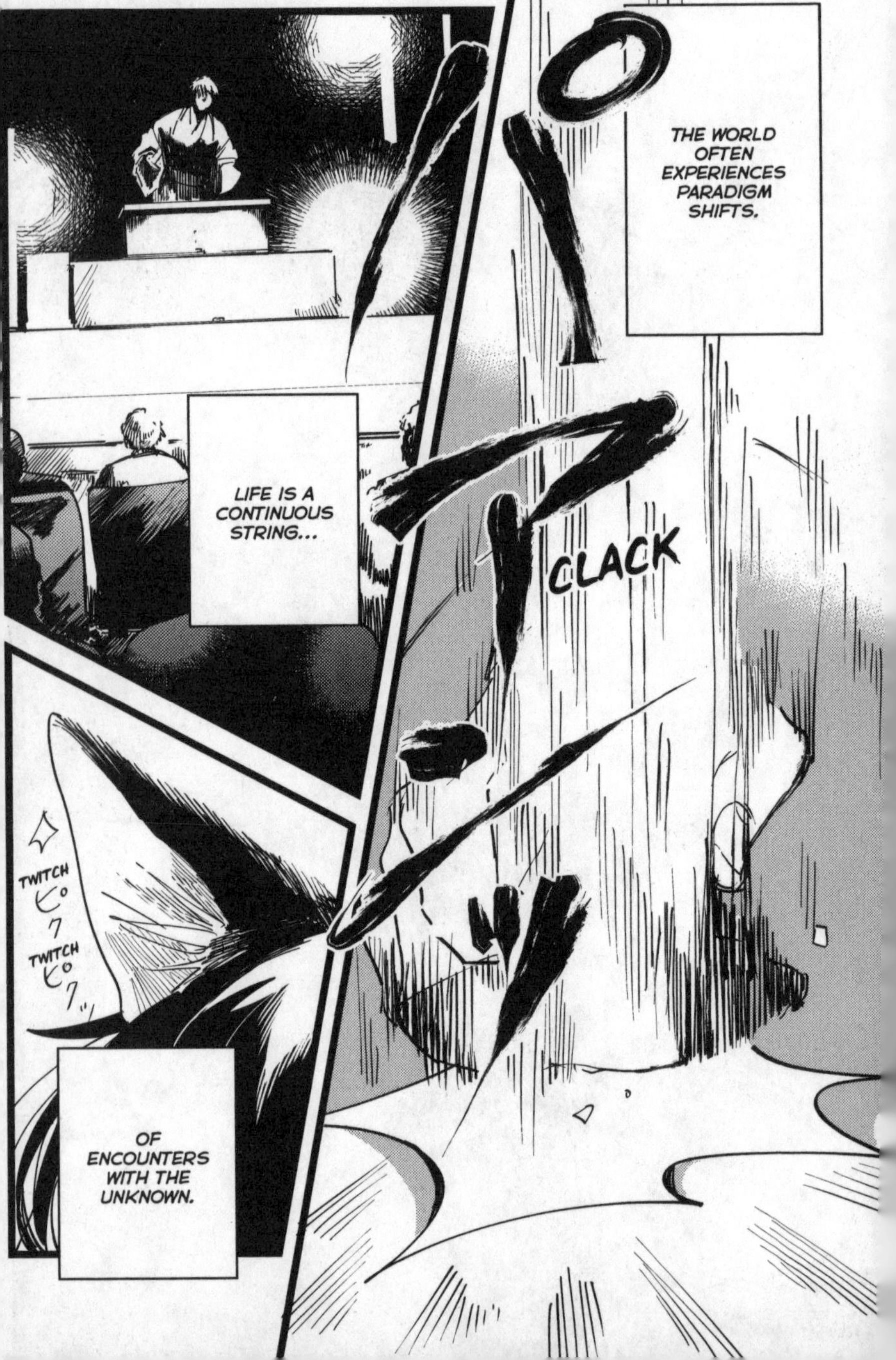
THE WORLD OFTEN EXPERIENCES PARADIGM SHIFTS.
CLACK
LIFE IS A CONTINUOUS STRING...
TWITCH
ピク
TWITCH
ピクッ
OF ENCOUNTERS WITH THE UNKNOWN.

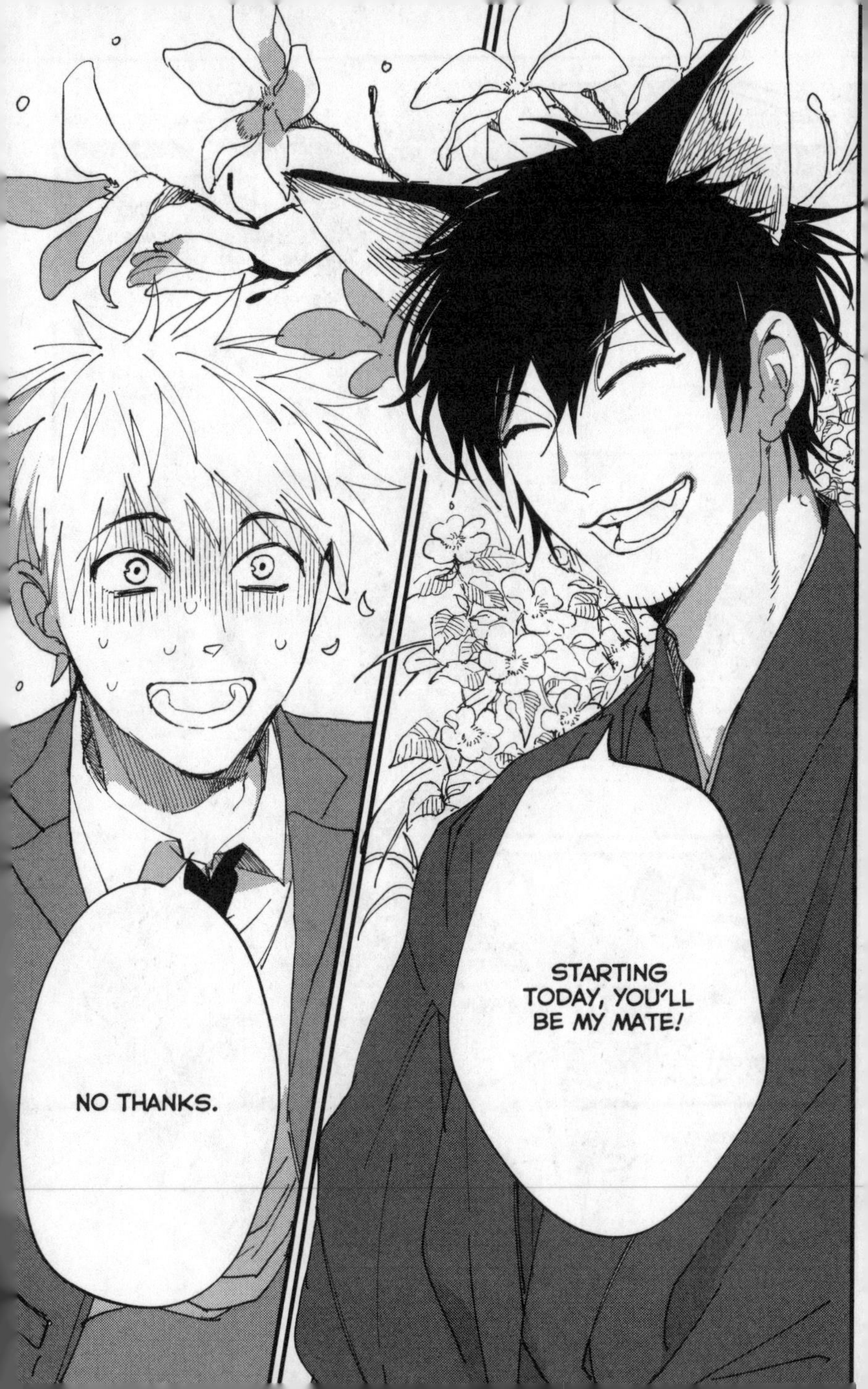
STARTING TODAY, YOU'LL BE MY MATE!
NO THANKS.

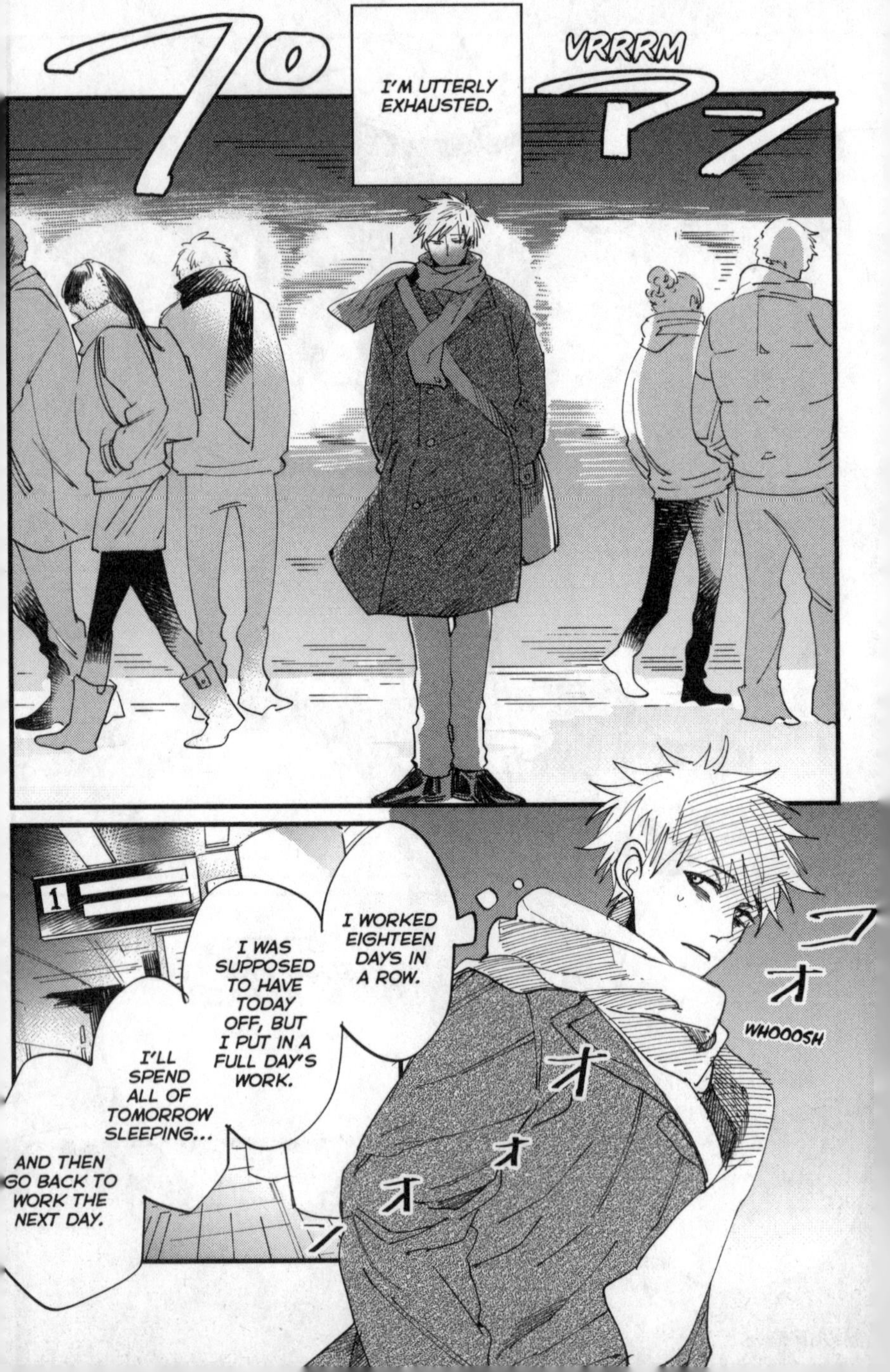
VRRRM
I'M UTTERLY EXHAUSTED.
WHOOOSH
I WORKED EIGHTEEN DAYS IN A ROW.
I WAS SUPPOSED TO HAVE TODAY OFF, BUT I PUT IN A FULL DAY'S WORK.
I'LL SPEND ALL OF TOMORROW SLEEPING...
AND THEN GO BACK TO WORK THE NEXT DAY.

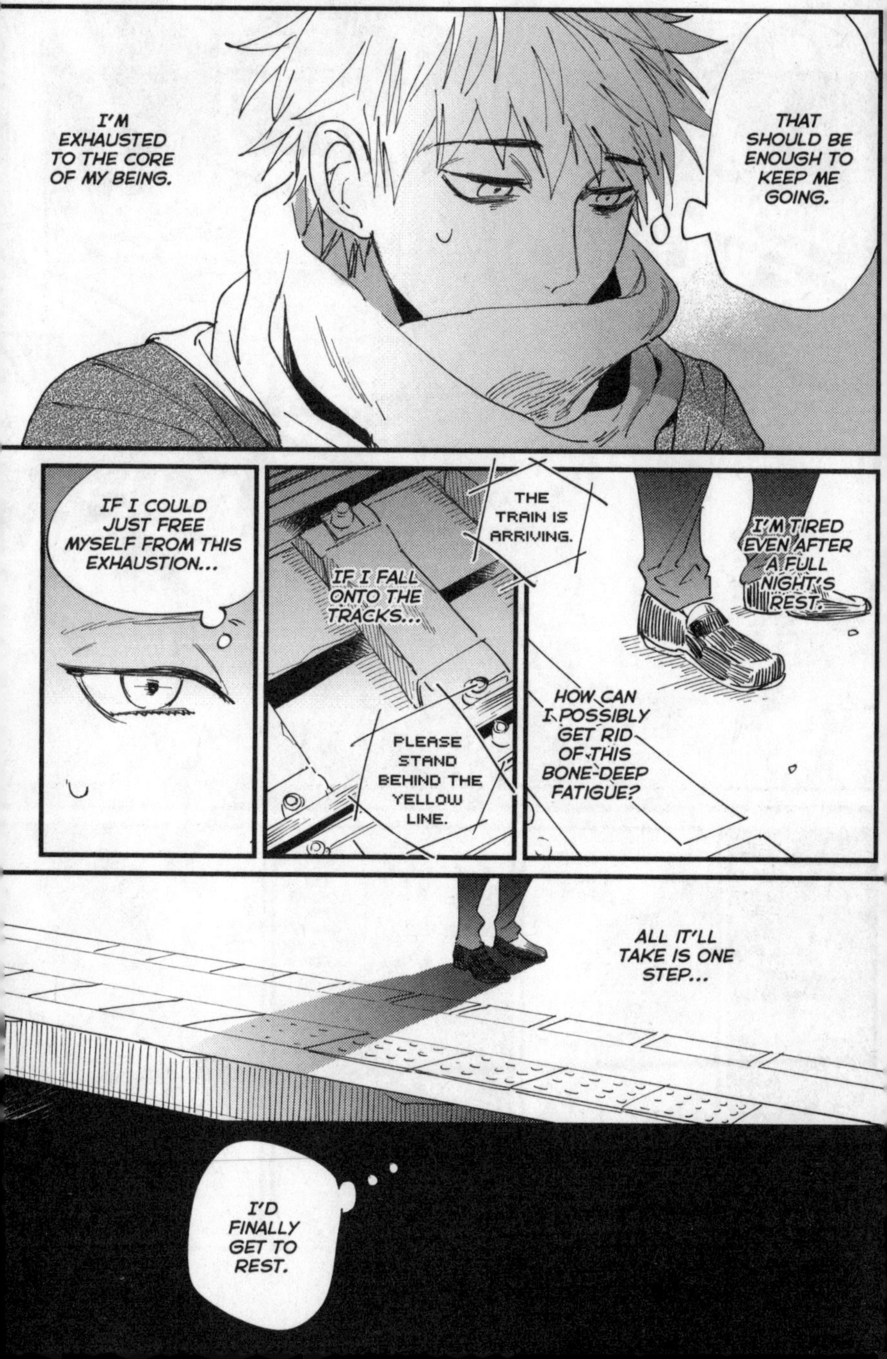
THAT SHOULD BE ENOUGH TO KEEP ME GOING.
I'M EXHAUSTED TO THE CORE OF MY BEING.
I'M TIRED EVEN AFTER A FULL NIGHT'S REST.
HOW CAN I POSSIBLY GET RID OF THIS BONE-DEEP FATIGUE?
THE TRAIN IS ARRIVING.
IF I FALL ONTO THE TRACKS...
PLEASE STAND BEHIND THE YELLOW LINE.
IF I COULD JUST FREE MYSELF FROM THIS EXHAUSTION...
ALL IT'LL TAKE IS ONE STEP...
I'D FINALLY GET TO REST.

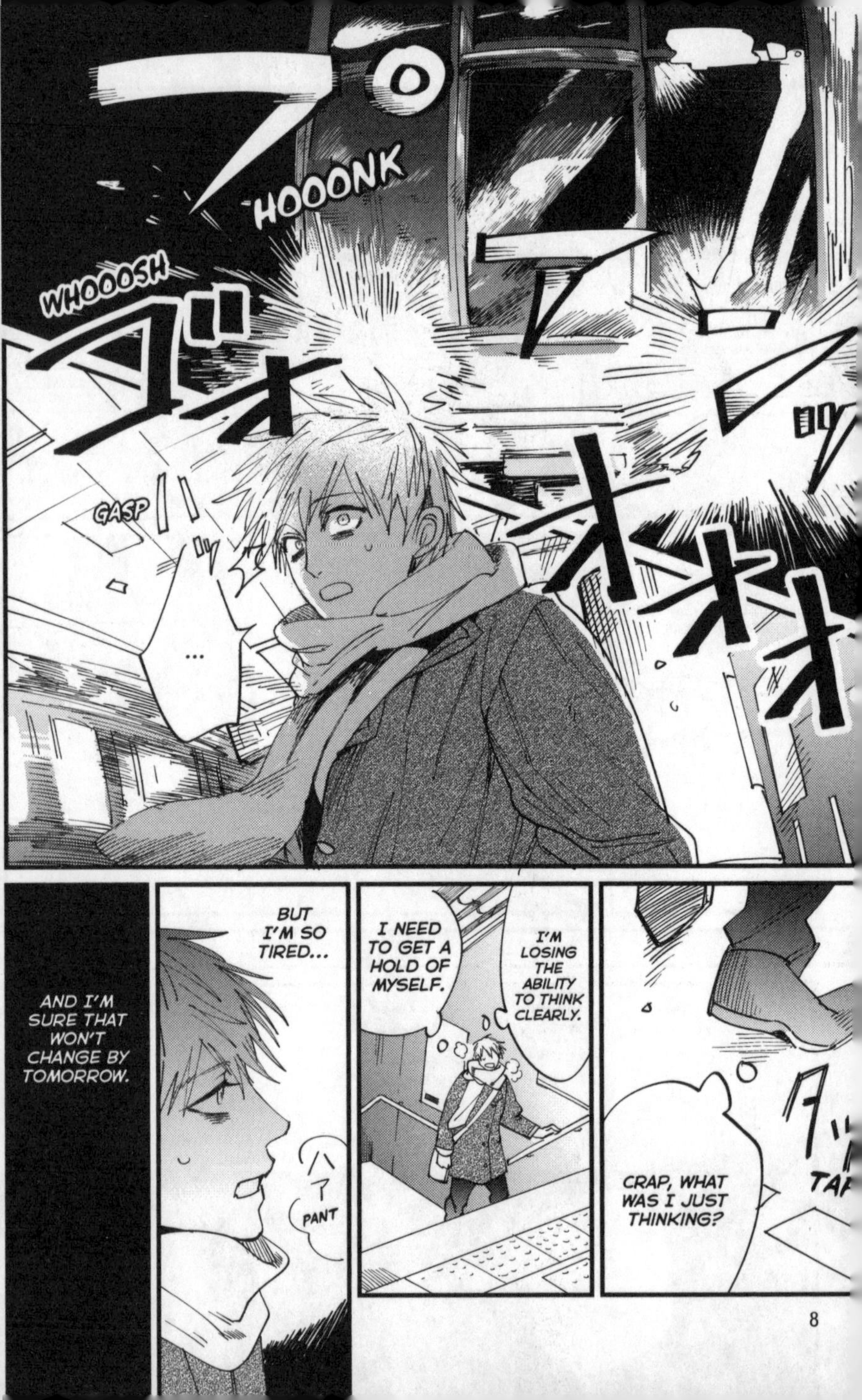
HOOONK
WHOOOSH
GASP
...
CRAP, WHAT WAS I JUST THINKING?
I NEED TO GET A HOLD OF MYSELF.
I'M LOSING THE ABILITY TO THINK CLEARLY.
BUT I'M SO TIRED...
PANT
AND I'M SURE THAT WON'T CHANGE BY TOMORROW.

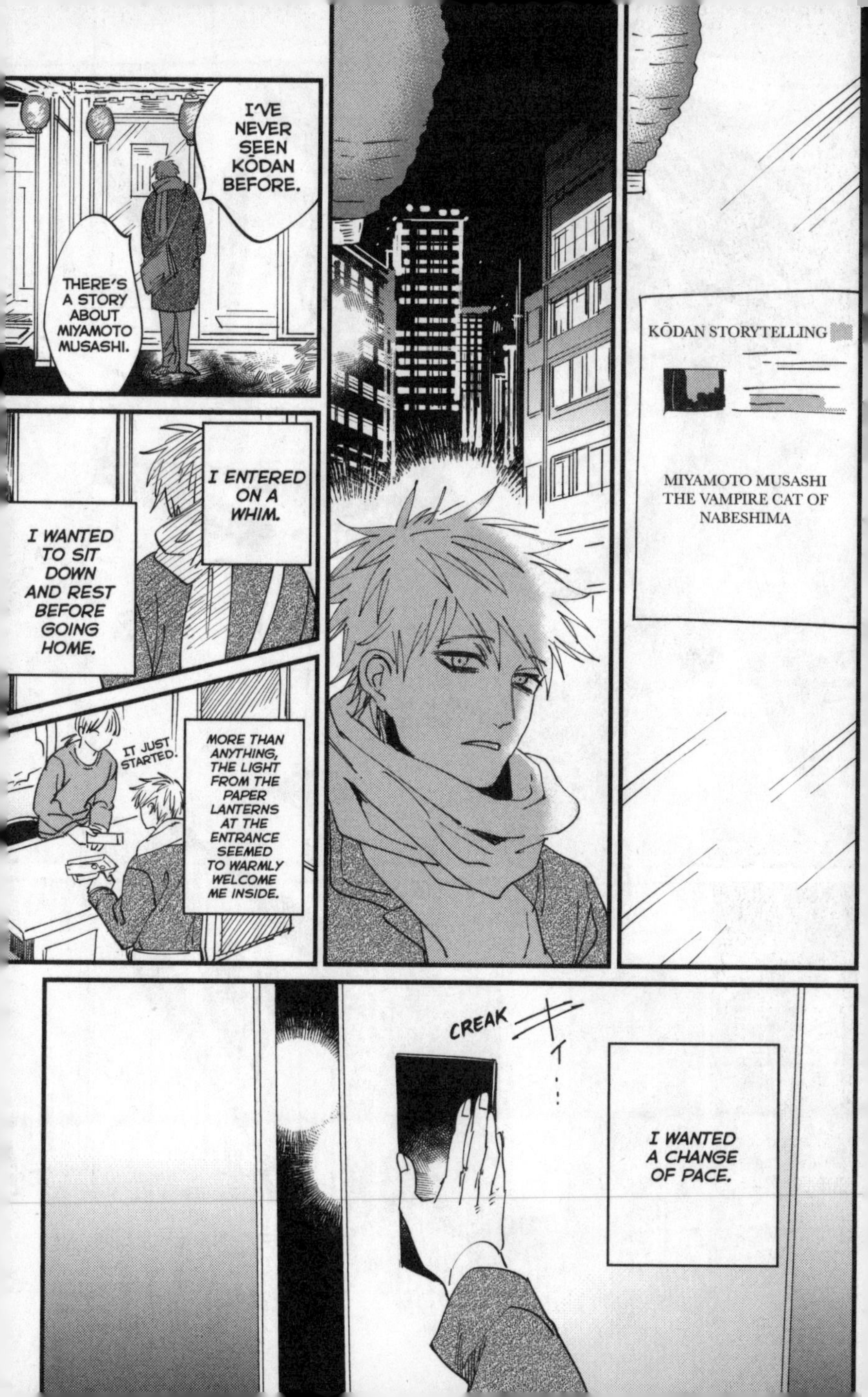
KŌDAN STORYTELLING
MIYAMOTO MUSASHI THE VAMPIRE CAT OF NABESHIMA
I'VE NEVER SEEN KŌDAN BEFORE.
THERE'S A STORY ABOUT MIYAMOTO MUSASHI.
I ENTERED ON A WHIM.
I WANTED TO SIT DOWN AND REST BEFORE GOING HOME.
MORE THAN ANYTHING, THE LIGHT FROM THE PAPER LANTERNS AT THE ENTRANCE SEEMED TO WARMLY WELCOME ME INSIDE.
IT JUST STARTED.
CREAK
I WANTED A CHANGE OF PACE.

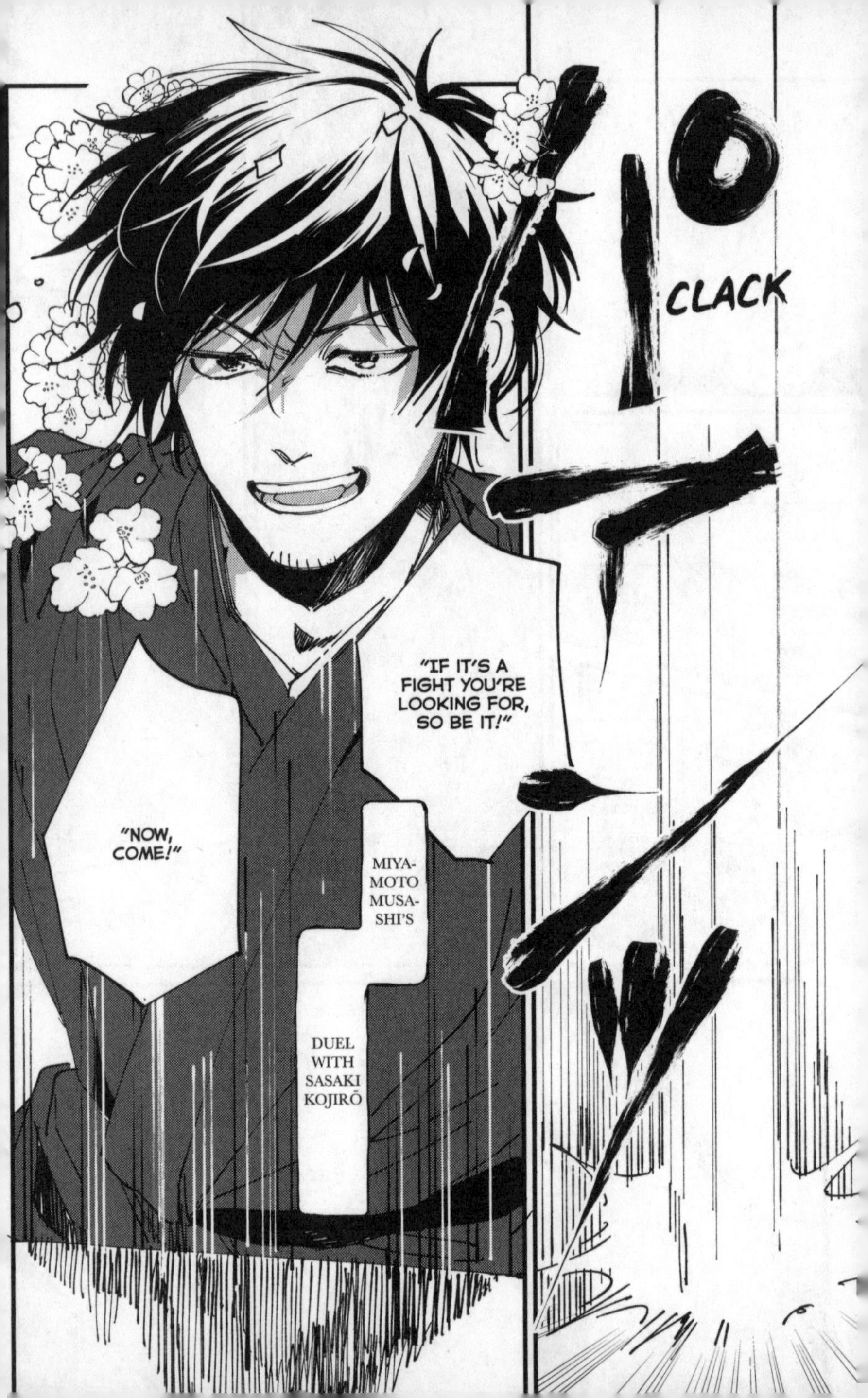
CLACK
"IF IT'S A FIGHT YOU'RE LOOKING FOR, SO BE IT!"
"NOW, COME!"
MIYAMOTO MUSASHI'S DUEL WITH SASAKI KOJIRŌ

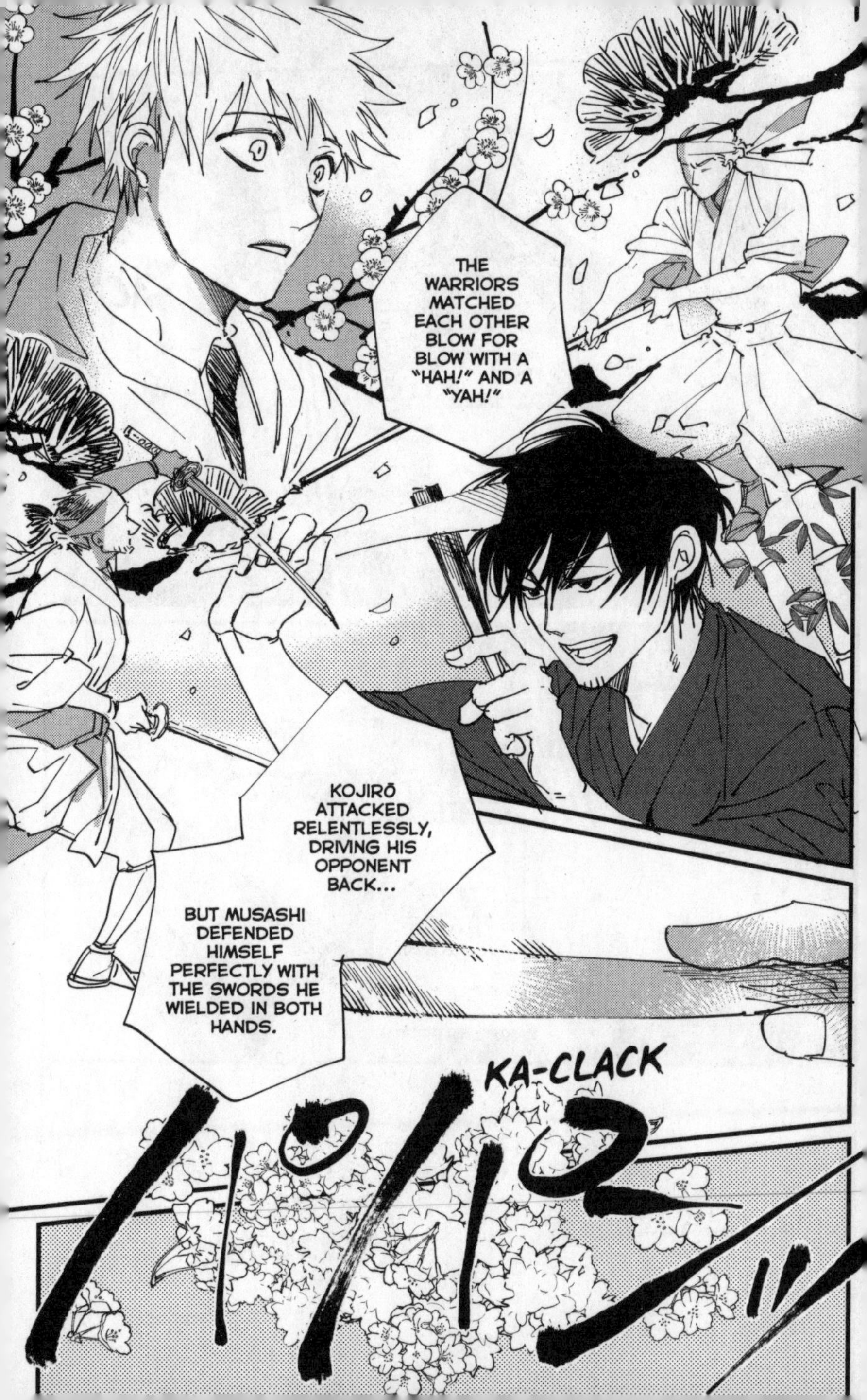
THE WARRIORS MATCHED EACH OTHER BLOW FOR BLOW WITH A "HAH!" AND A "YAH!"
KOJIRŌ ATTACKED RELENTLESSLY, DRIVING HIS OPPONENT BACK...
BUT MUSASHI DEFENDED HIMSELF PERFECTLY WITH THE SWORDS HE WIELDED IN BOTH HANDS.
KA-CLACK

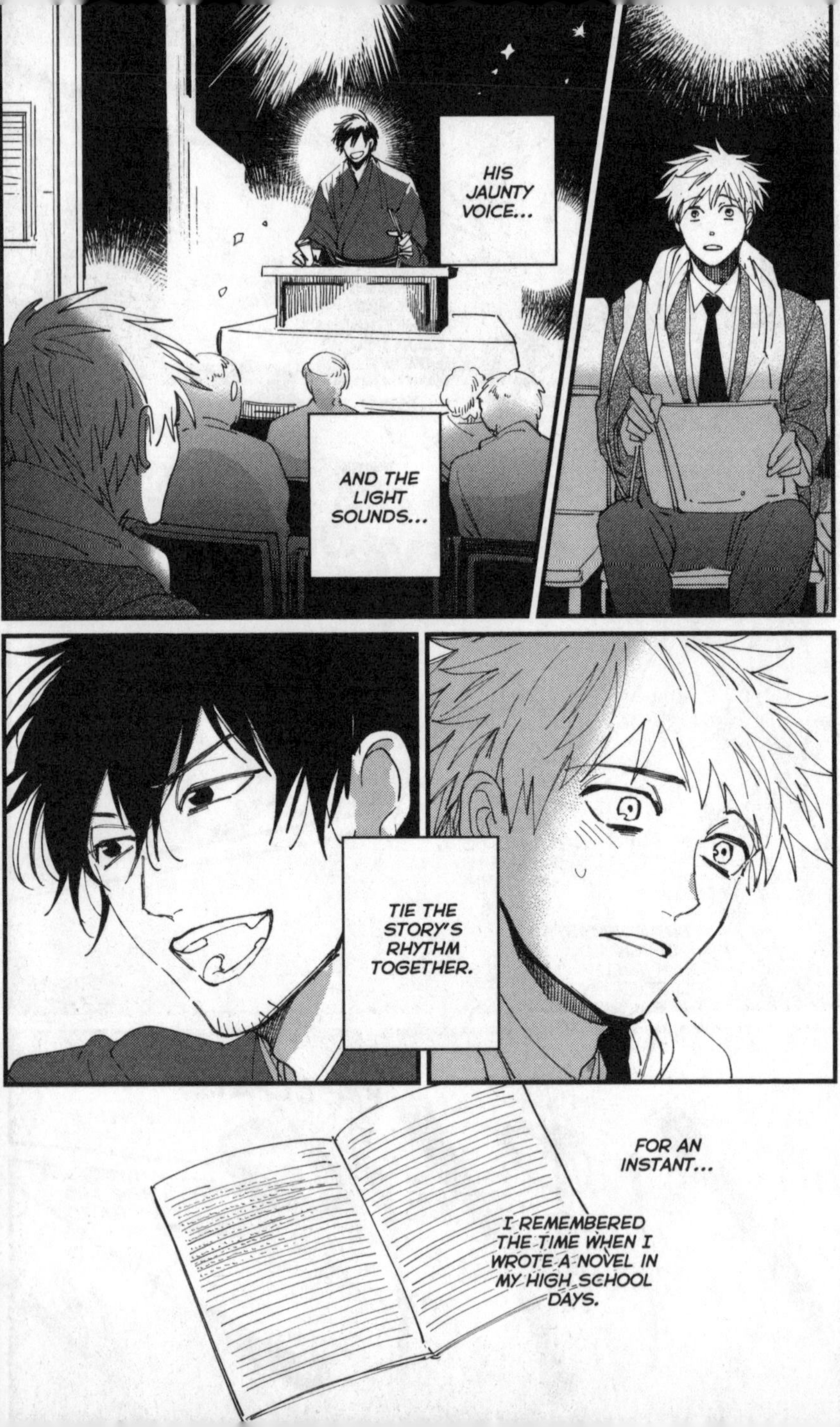
HIS JAUNTY VOICE...
AND THE LIGHT SOUNDS...
TIE THE STORY'S RHYTHM TOGETHER.
FOR AN INSTANT...
I REMEMBERED THE TIME WHEN I WROTE A NOVEL IN MY HIGH SCHOOL DAYS.

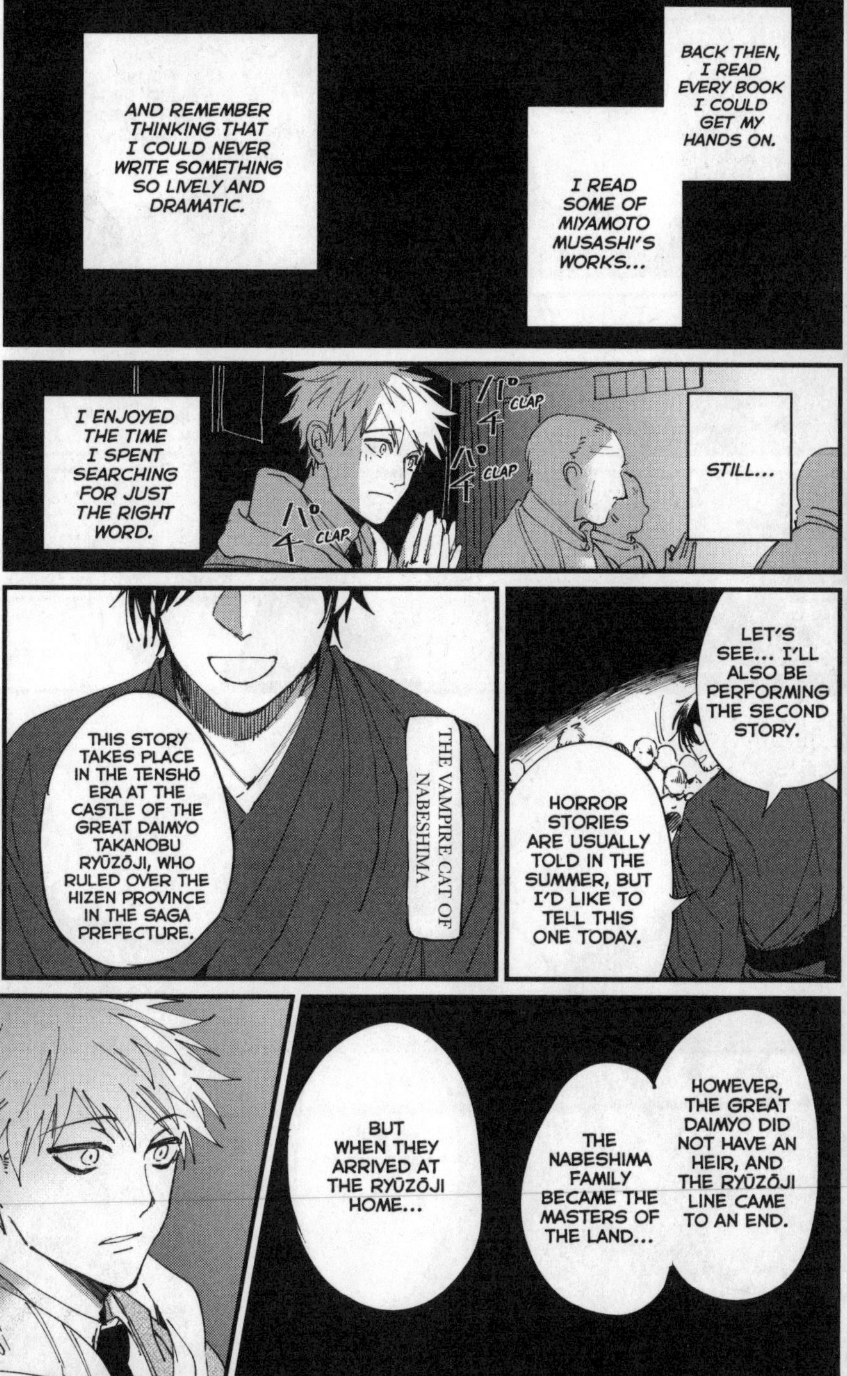
BACK THEN, I READ EVERY BOOK I COULD GET MY HANDS ON.
I READ SOME OF MIYAMOTO MUSASHI'S WORKS...
AND REMEMBER THINKING THAT I COULD NEVER WRITE SOMETHING SO LIVELY AND DRAMATIC.
STILL...
パチ CLAP
パチ CLAP
パチ CLAP
I ENJOYED THE TIME I SPENT SEARCHING FOR JUST THE RIGHT WORD.
LET'S SEE... I'LL ALSO BE PERFORMING THE SECOND STORY.
HORROR STORIES ARE USUALLY TOLD IN THE SUMMER, BUT I'D LIKE TO TELL THIS ONE TODAY.
THE VAMPIRE CAT OF NABESHIMA
THIS STORY TAKES PLACE IN THE TENSHŌ ERA AT THE CASTLE OF THE GREAT DAIMYO TAKANOBU RYŪZŌJI, WHO RULED OVER THE HIZEN PROVINCE IN THE SAGA PREFECTURE.
HOWEVER, THE GREAT DAIMYO DID NOT HAVE AN HEIR, AND THE RYŪZŌJI LINE CAME TO AN END.
THE NABESHIMA FAMILY BECAME THE MASTERS OF THE LAND...
BUT WHEN THEY ARRIVED AT THE RYŪZŌJI HOME...

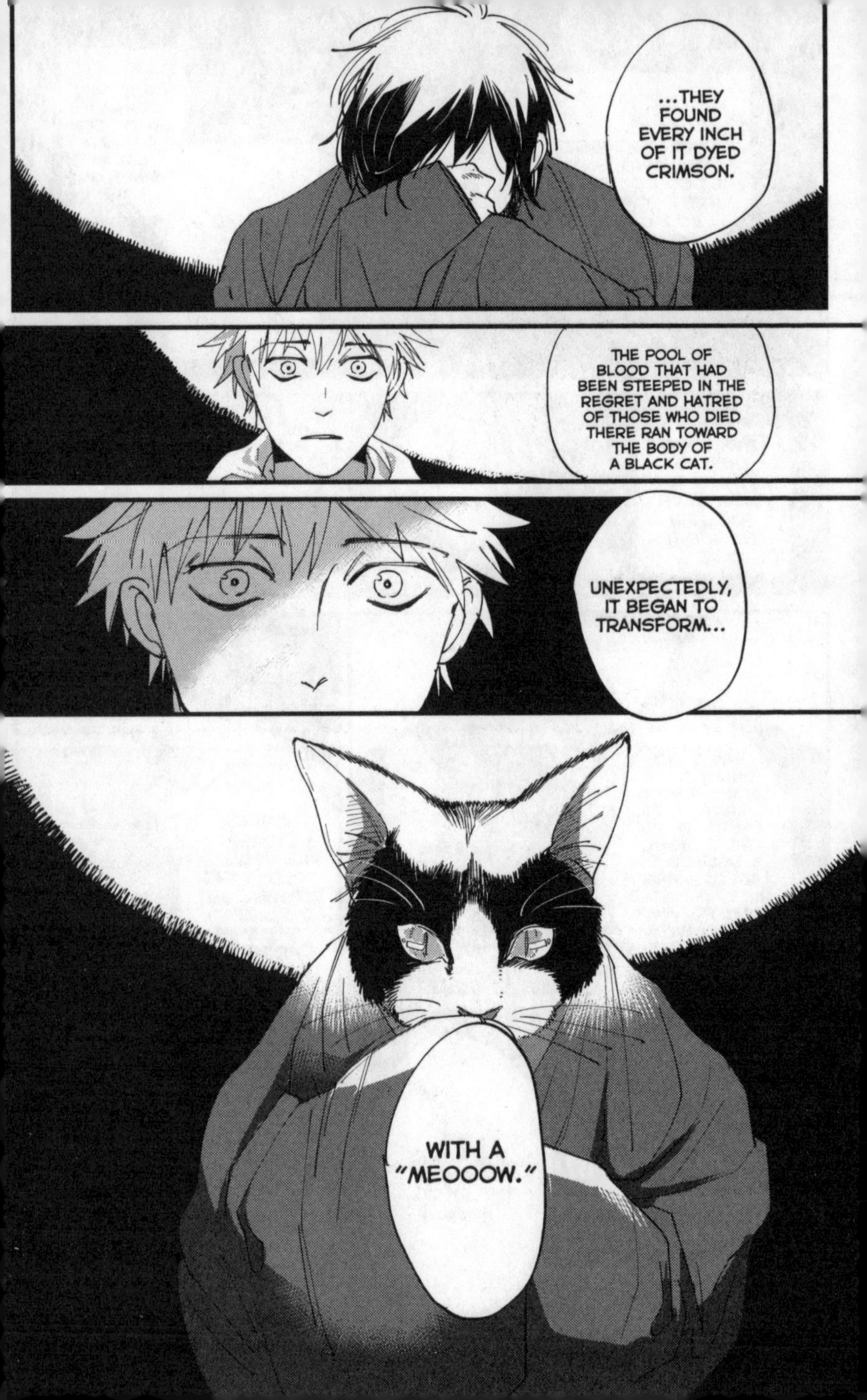
...THEY FOUND EVERY INCH OF IT DYED CRIMSON.
THE POOL OF BLOOD THAT HAD BEEN STEEPED IN THE REGRET AND HATRED OF THOSE WHO DIED THERE RAN TOWARD THE BODY OF A BLACK CAT.
UNEXPECTEDLY, IT BEGAN TO TRANSFORM...
WITH A "MEOOOW."

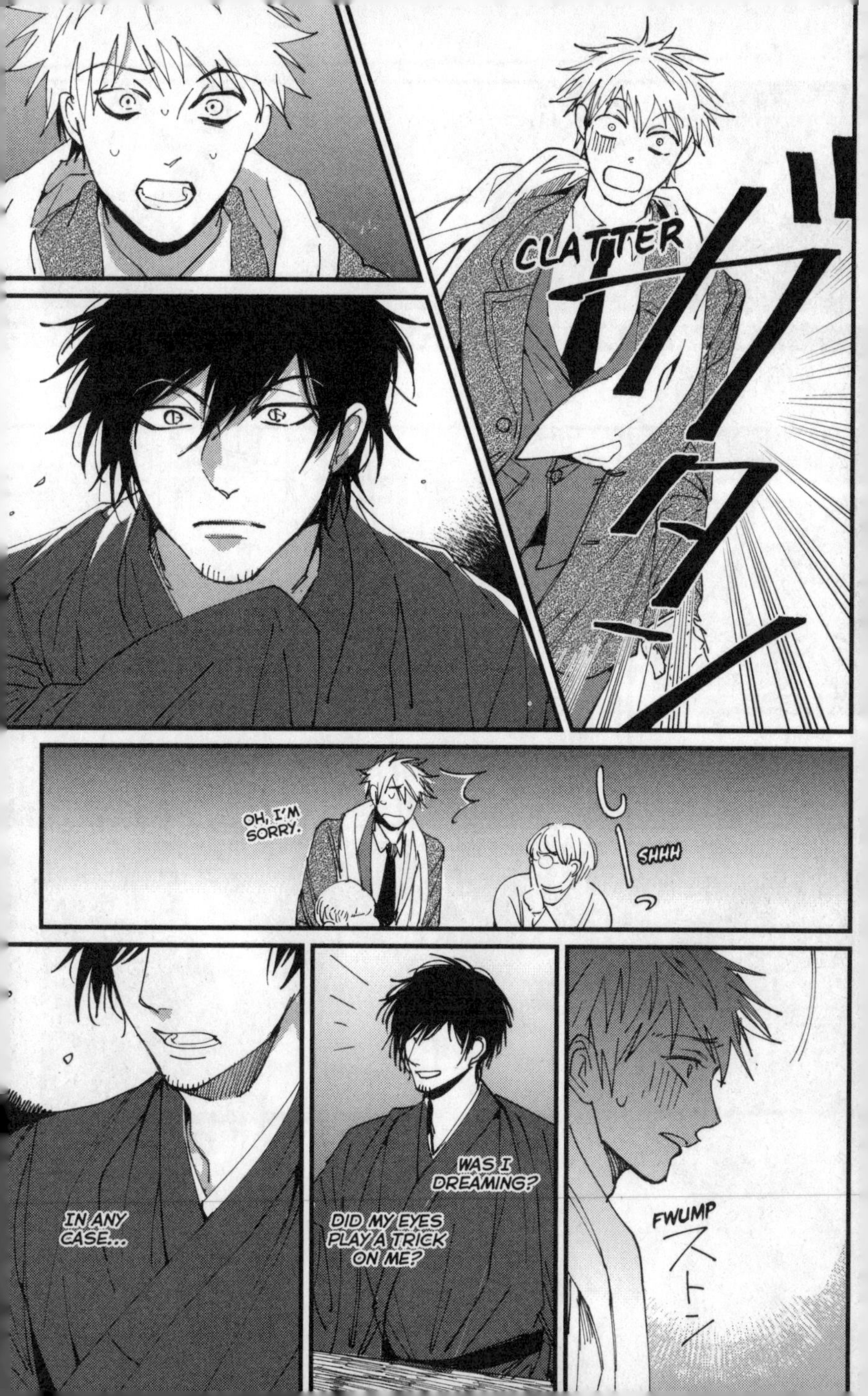
CLATTER
SHHH
OH, I'M SORRY.
FWUMP
WAS I DREAMING?
DID MY EYES PLAY A TRICK ON ME?
IN ANY CASE...

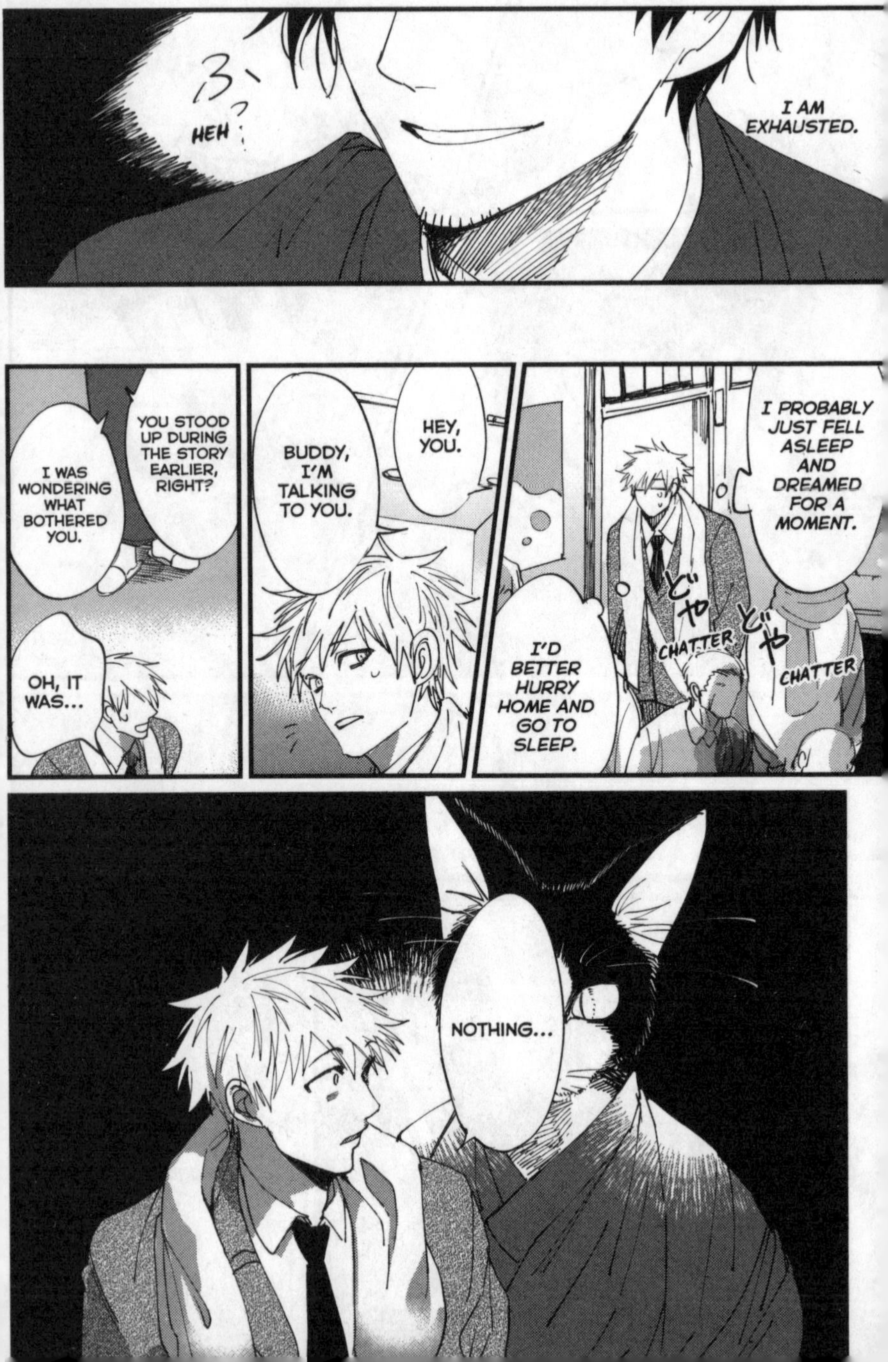
I AM EXHAUSTED.
ふ、
HEH?
I PROBABLY JUST FELL ASLEEP AND DREAMED FOR A MOMENT.
どや
CHATTER
どや
CHATTER
I'D BETTER HURRY HOME AND GO TO SLEEP.
HEY, YOU.
BUDDY, I'M TALKING TO YOU.
YOU STOOD UP DURING THE STORY EARLIER, RIGHT?
I WAS WONDERING WHAT BOTHERED YOU.
OH, IT WAS...
NOTHING...

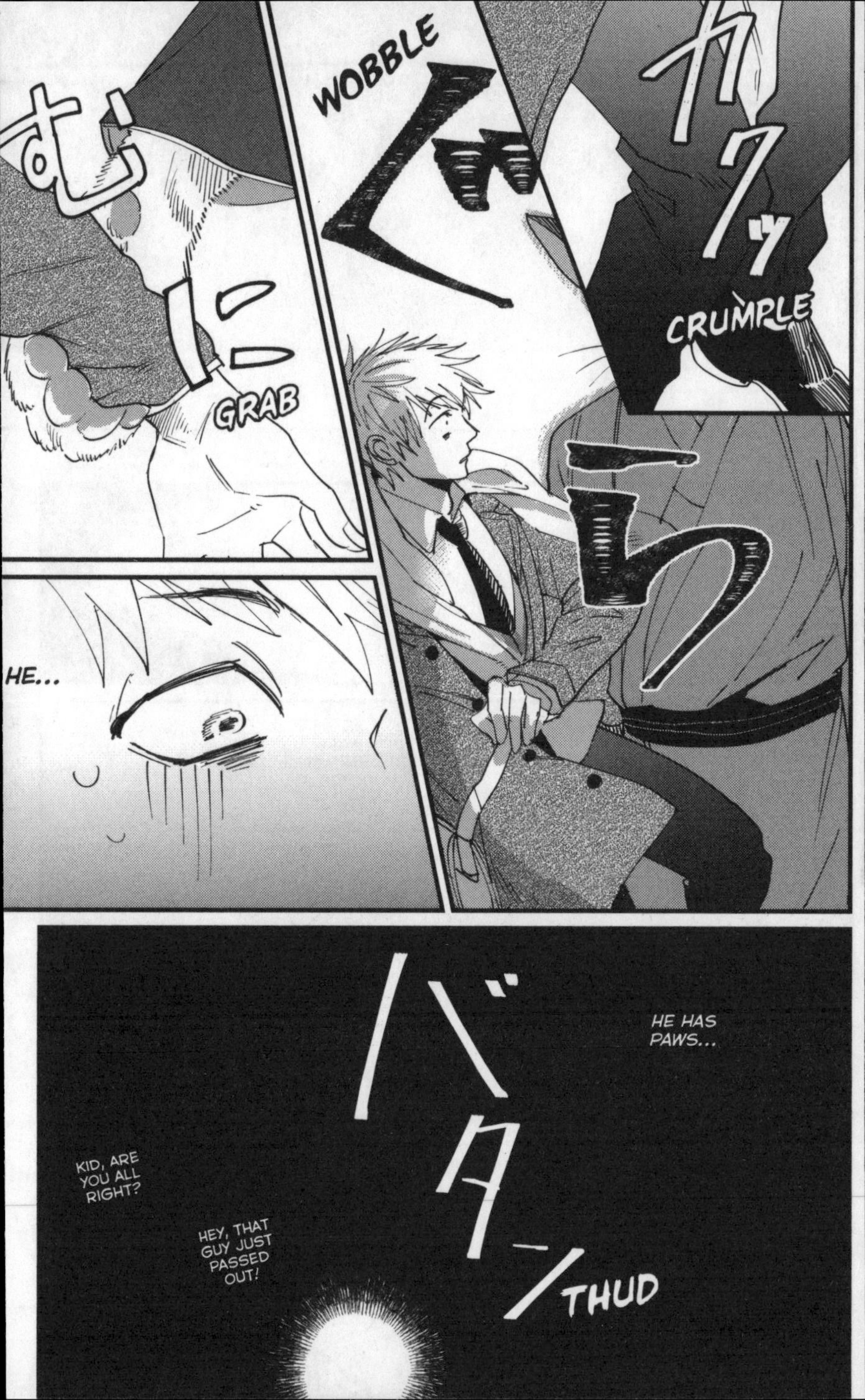
CRUMPLE
WOBBLE
GRAB
HE...
HE HAS PAWS...
THUD
KID, ARE YOU ALL RIGHT?
HEY, THAT GUY JUST PASSED OUT!

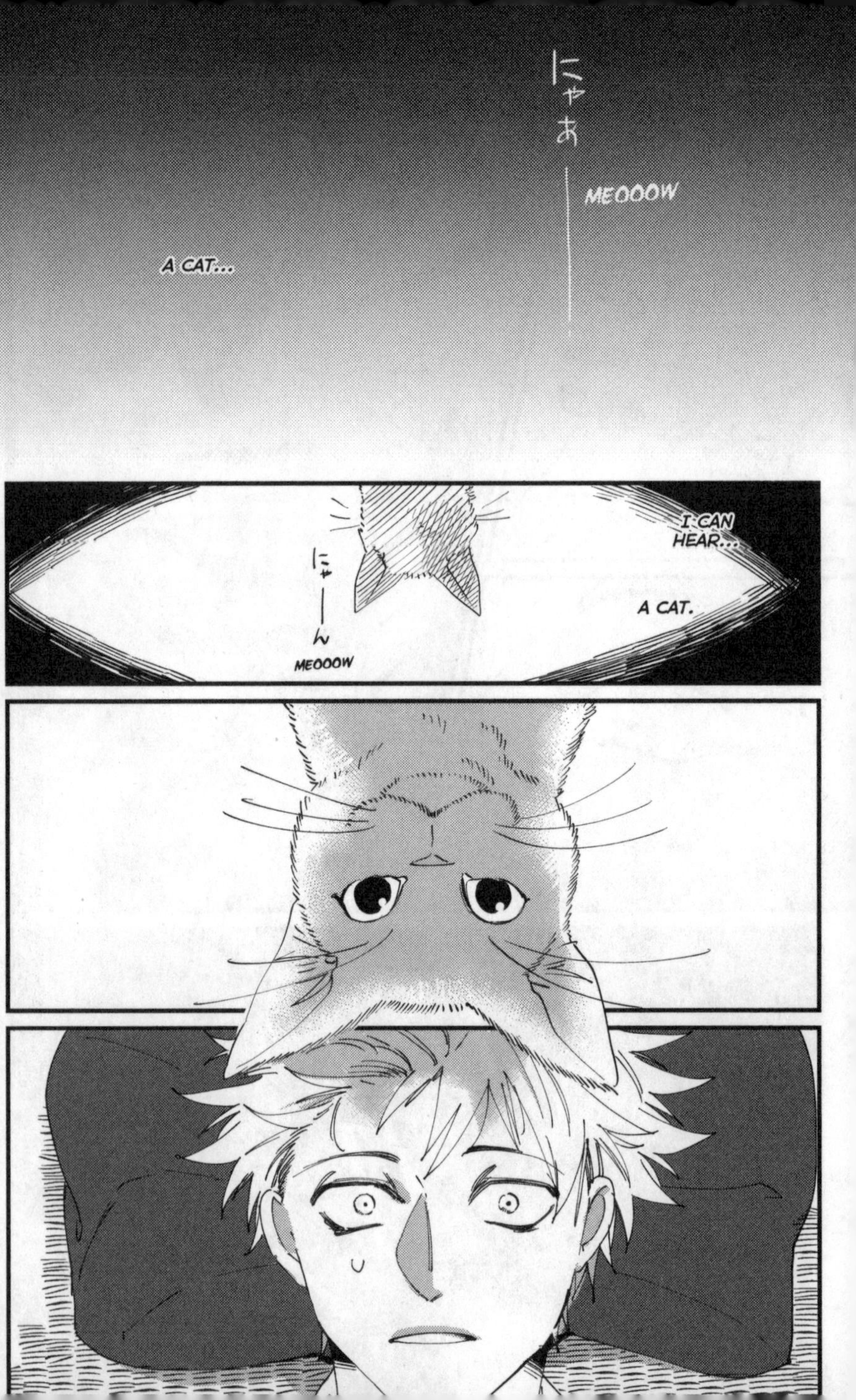
にゃあ——
MEOOOW
A CAT...
I CAN HEAR...
A CAT.
にゃーん
MEOOOW

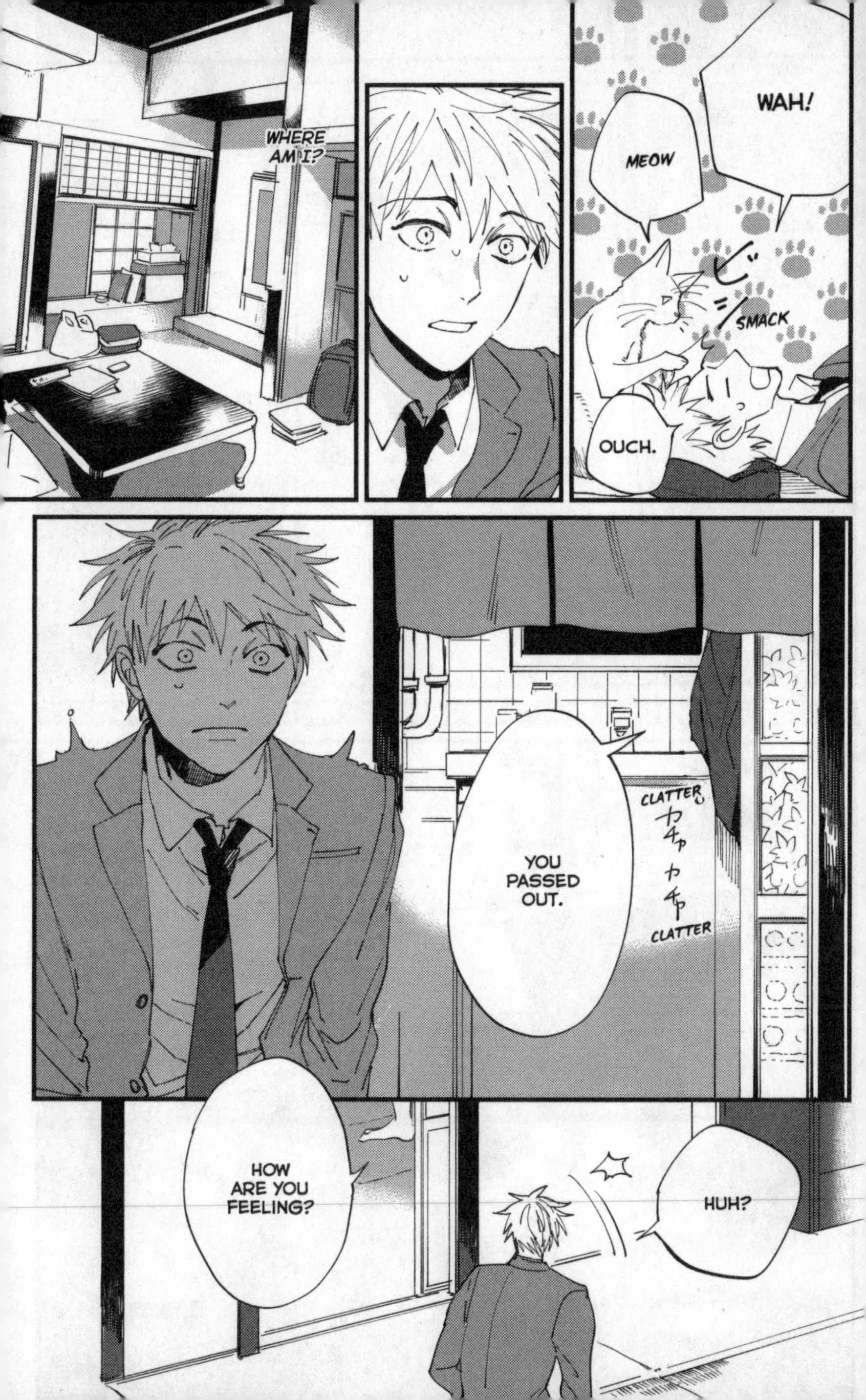
WAH!
MEOW
ビ
SMACK
OUCH.
WHERE AM I?
YOU PASSED OUT.
CLATTER
カチャ カチャ
CLATTER
HUH?
HOW ARE YOU FEELING?

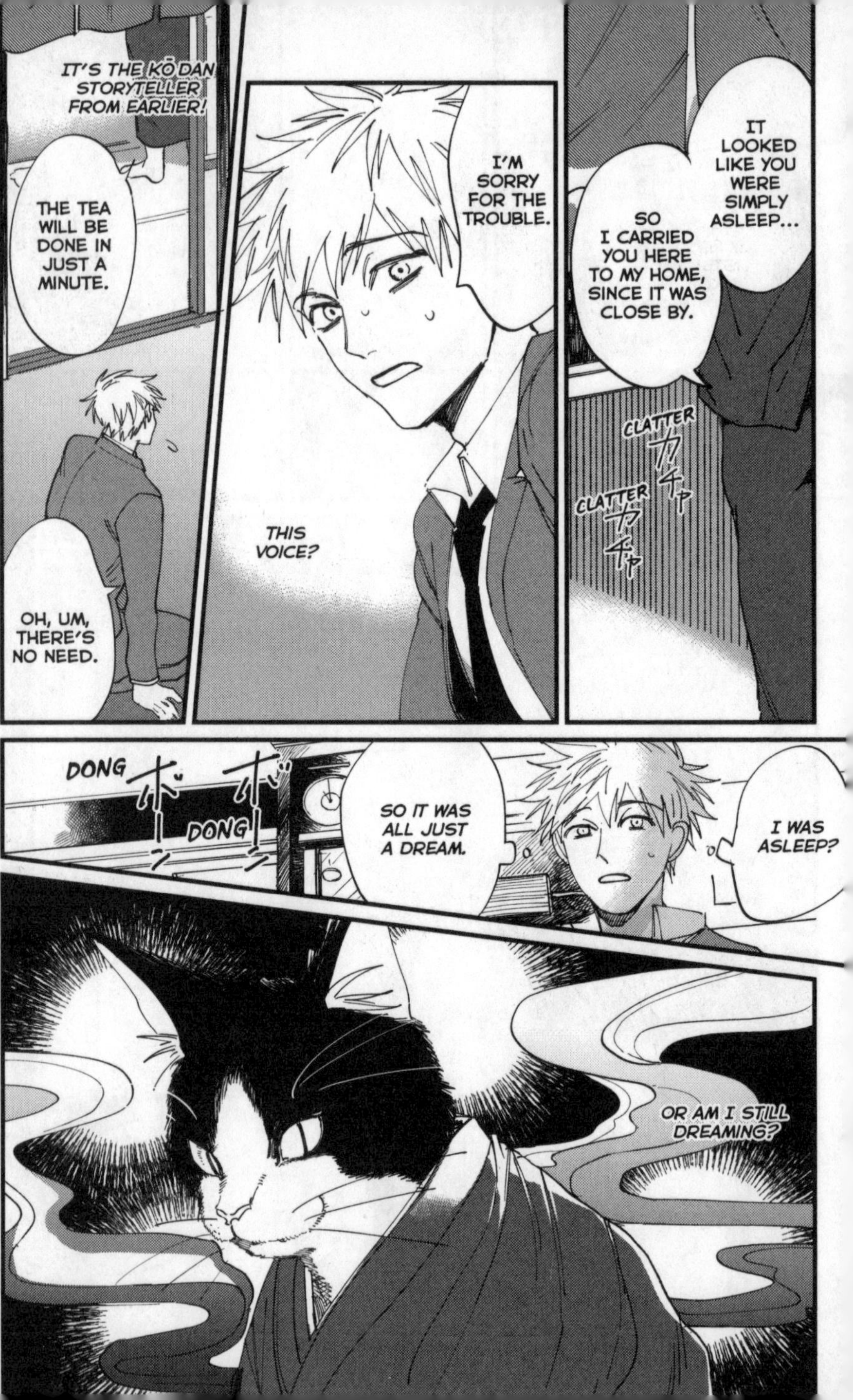
IT LOOKED LIKE YOU WERE SIMPLY ASLEEP...
SO I CARRIED YOU HERE TO MY HOME, SINCE IT WAS CLOSE BY.
CLATTER カチャ
CLATTER カチャ
I'M SORRY FOR THE TROUBLE.
THIS VOICE?
IT'S THE KŌDAN STORYTELLER FROM EARLIER!
THE TEA WILL BE DONE IN JUST A MINUTE.
OH, UM, THERE'S NO NEED.
I WAS ASLEEP?
SO IT WAS ALL JUST A DREAM.
DONG ボーーン
DONG ボーーン
OR AM I STILL DREAMING?

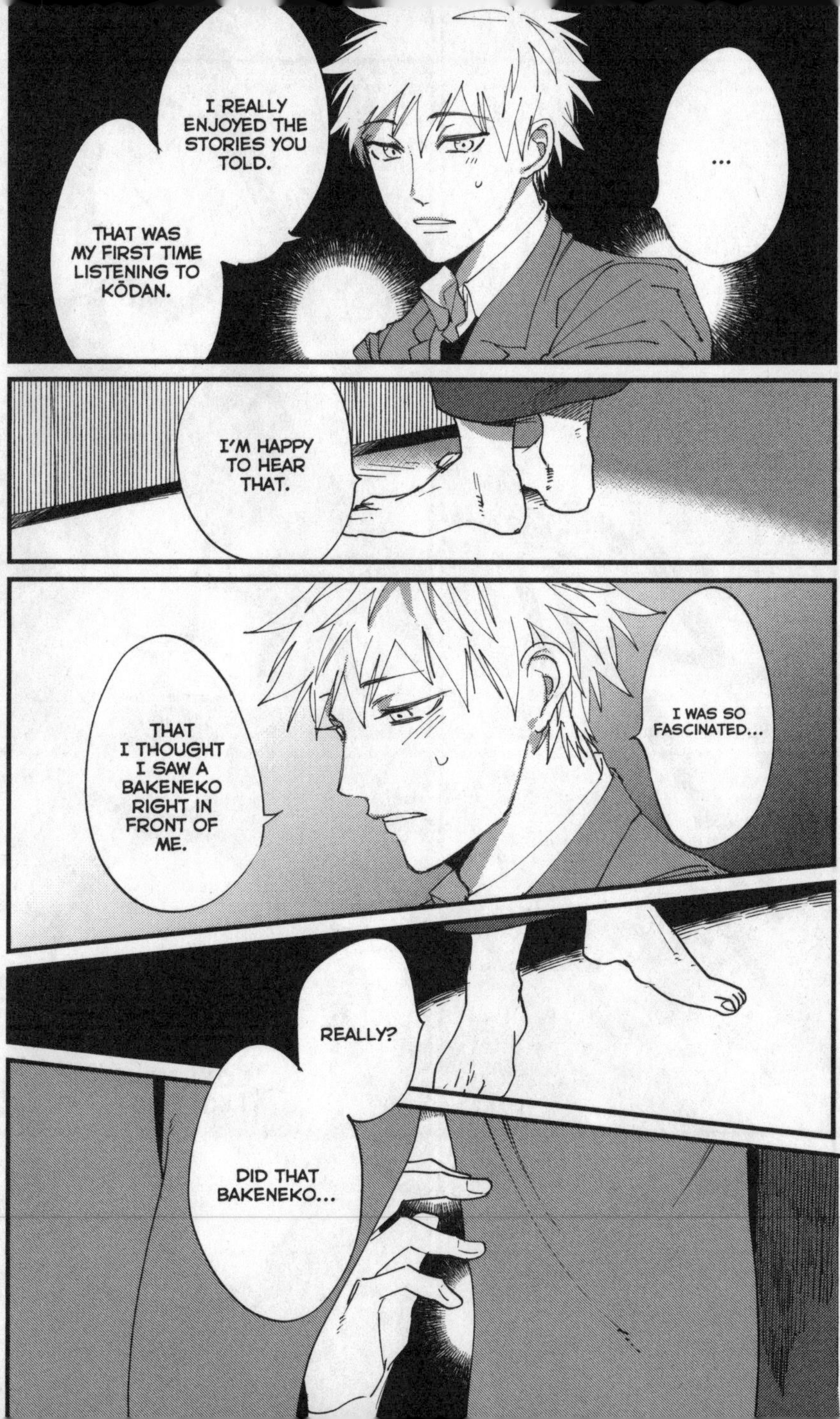
...
I REALLY ENJOYED THE STORIES YOU TOLD.
THAT WAS MY FIRST TIME LISTENING TO KŌDAN.
I'M HAPPY TO HEAR THAT.
I WAS SO FASCINATED...
THAT I THOUGHT I SAW A BAKENEKO RIGHT IN FRONT OF ME.
REALLY?
DID THAT BAKENEKO...

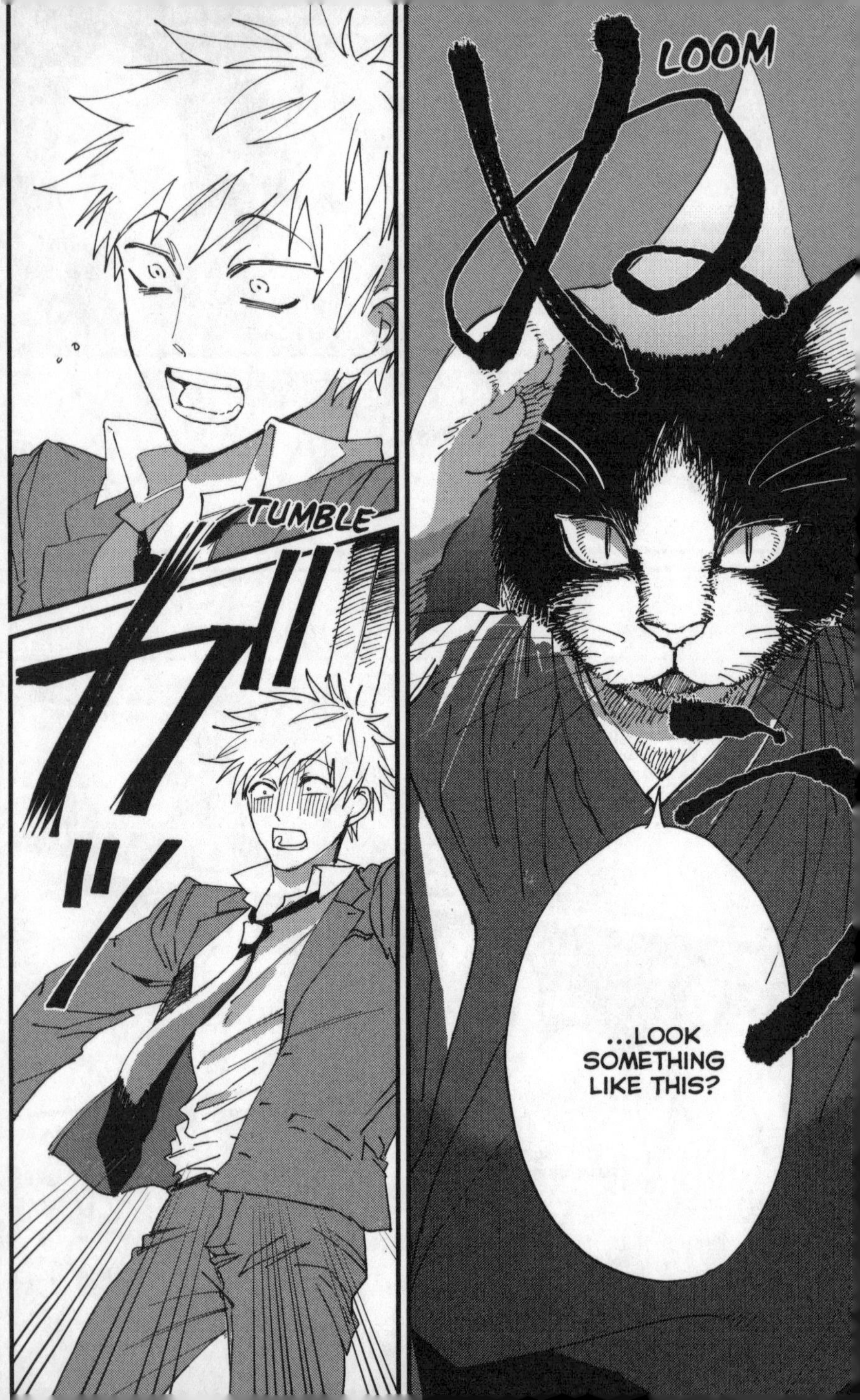
LOOM
...LOOK SOMETHING LIKE THIS?
TUMBLE

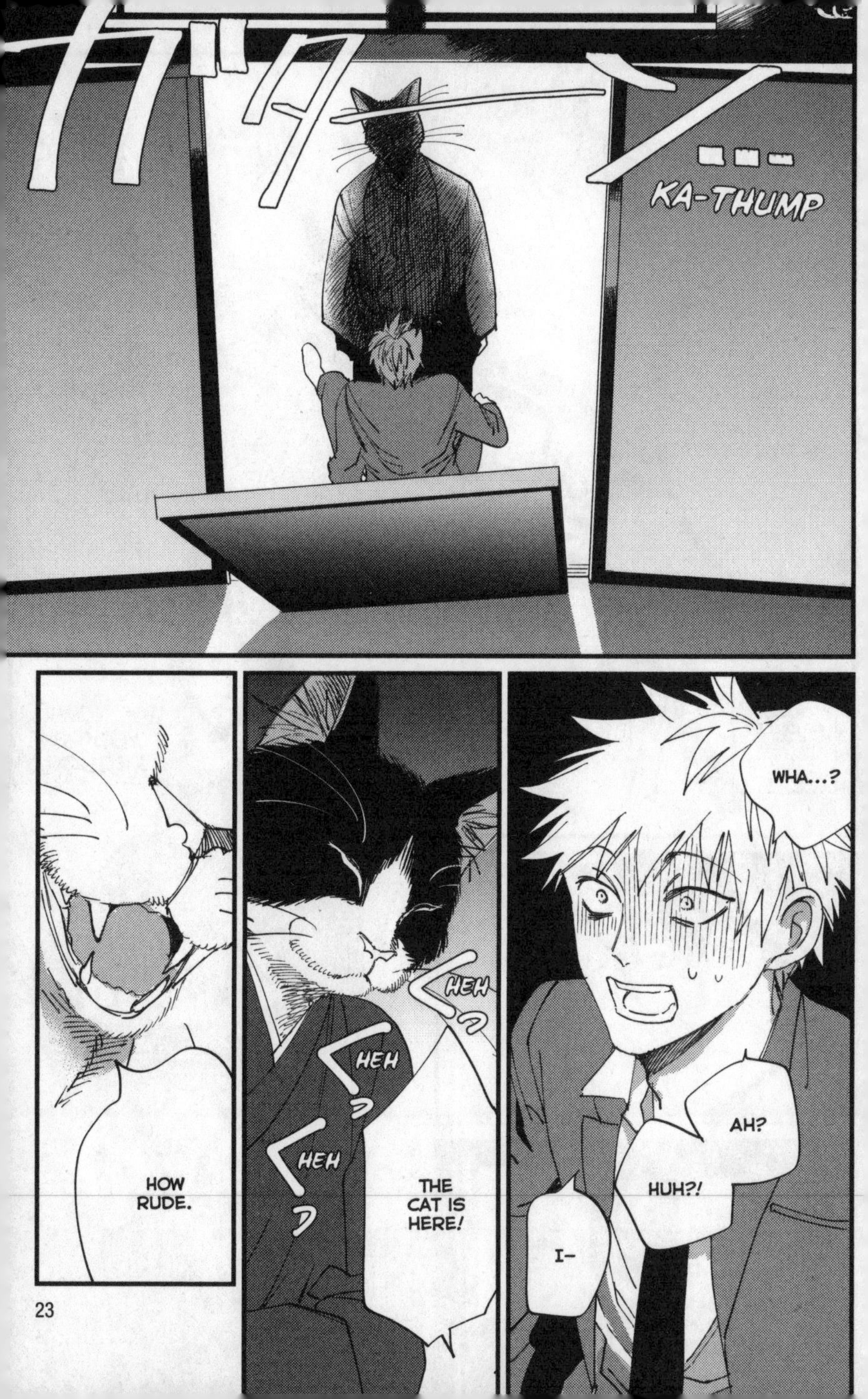
KA-THUMP
WHA...?
AH?
HUH?!
I–
HEH
HEH
HEH
THE CAT IS HERE!
HOW RUDE.

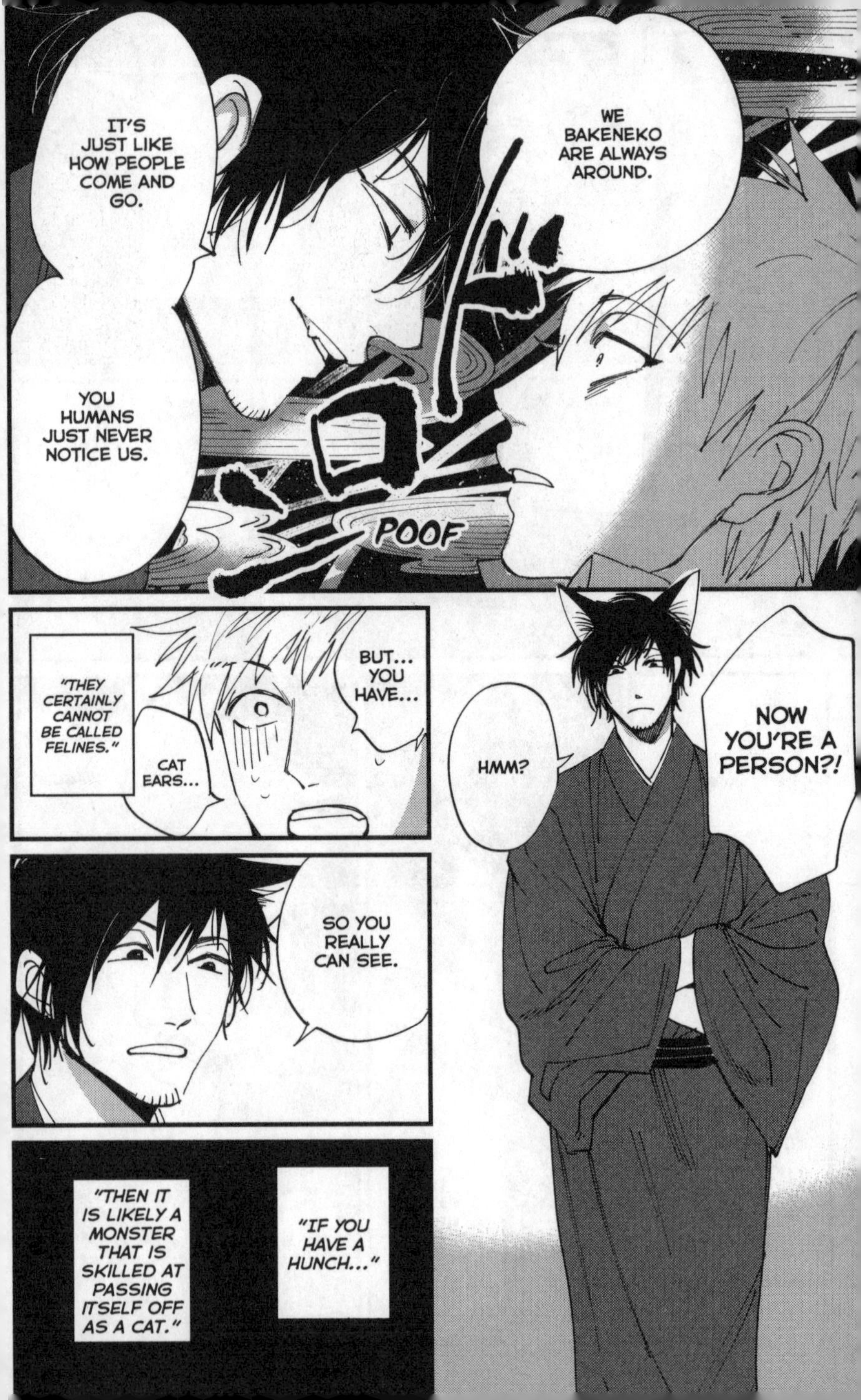
WE BAKENEKO ARE ALWAYS AROUND.
IT'S JUST LIKE HOW PEOPLE COME AND GO.
YOU HUMANS JUST NEVER NOTICE US.
POOF
NOW YOU'RE A PERSON?!
HMM?
BUT... YOU HAVE...
CAT EARS...
"THEY CERTAINLY CANNOT BE CALLED FELINES."
SO YOU REALLY CAN SEE.
"IF YOU HAVE A HUNCH..."
"THEN IT IS LIKELY A MONSTER THAT IS SKILLED AT PASSING ITSELF OFF AS A CAT."

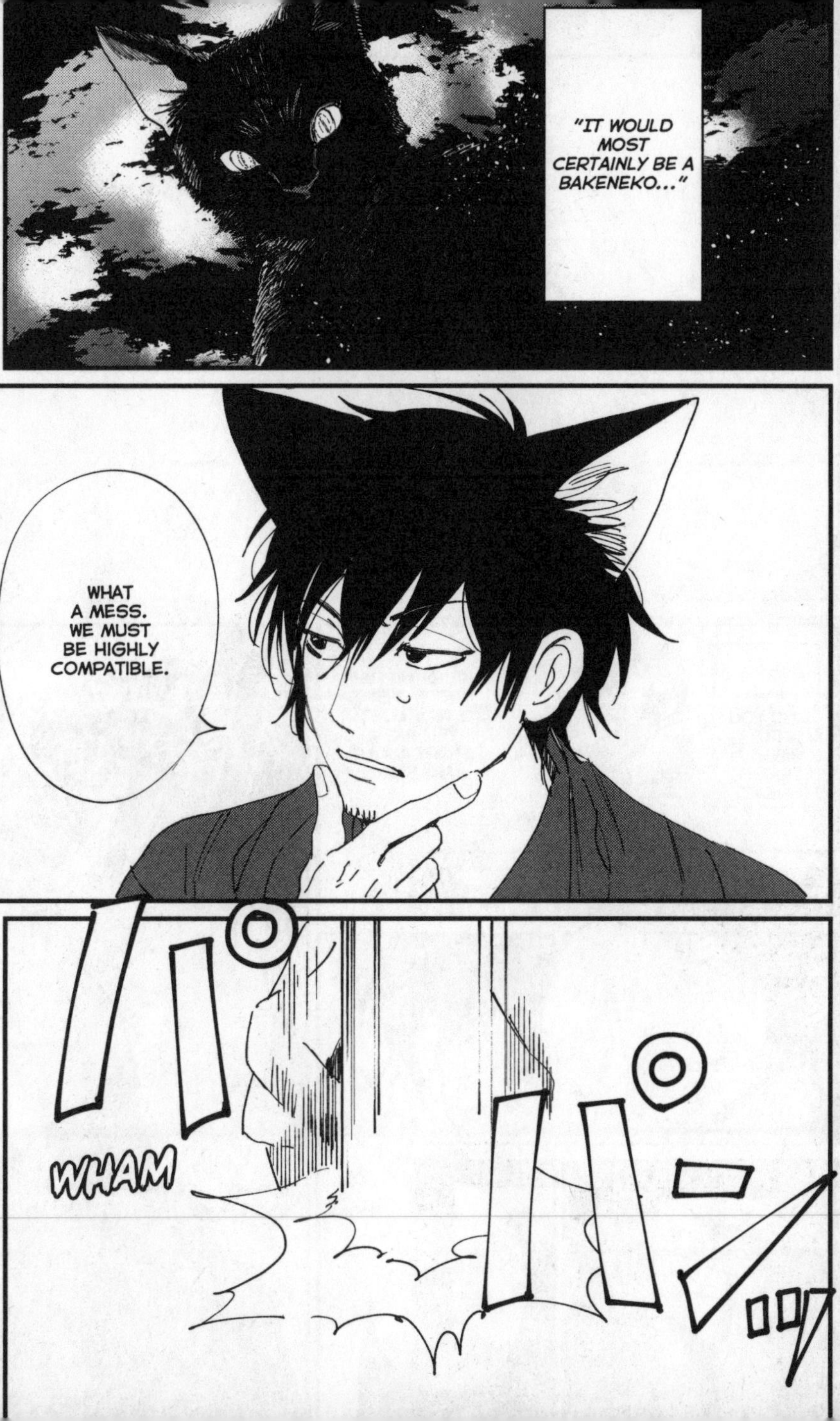
"IT WOULD MOST CERTAINLY BE A BAKENEKO..."
WHAT A MESS. WE MUST BE HIGHLY COMPATIBLE.
パ
WHAM
パーンッ

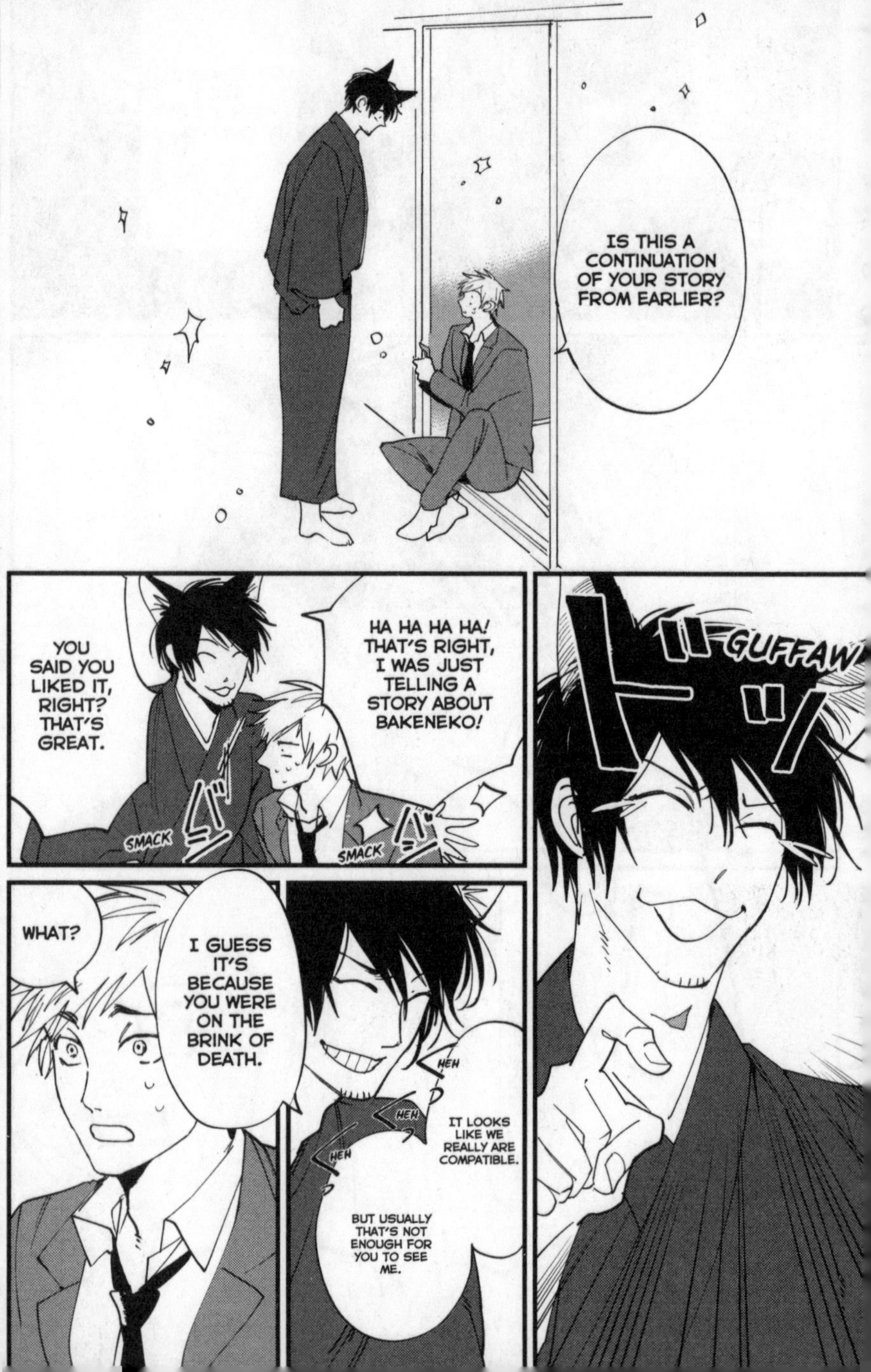
IS THIS A CONTINUATION OF YOUR STORY FROM EARLIER?
GUFFAW
HA HA HA HA! THAT'S RIGHT, I WAS JUST TELLING A STORY ABOUT BAKENEKO!
YOU SAID YOU LIKED IT, RIGHT? THAT'S GREAT.
SMACK
SMACK
HEH
HEH
HEH
IT LOOKS LIKE WE REALLY ARE COMPATIBLE.
BUT USUALLY THAT'S NOT ENOUGH FOR YOU TO SEE ME.
WHAT?
I GUESS IT'S BECAUSE YOU WERE ON THE BRINK OF DEATH.

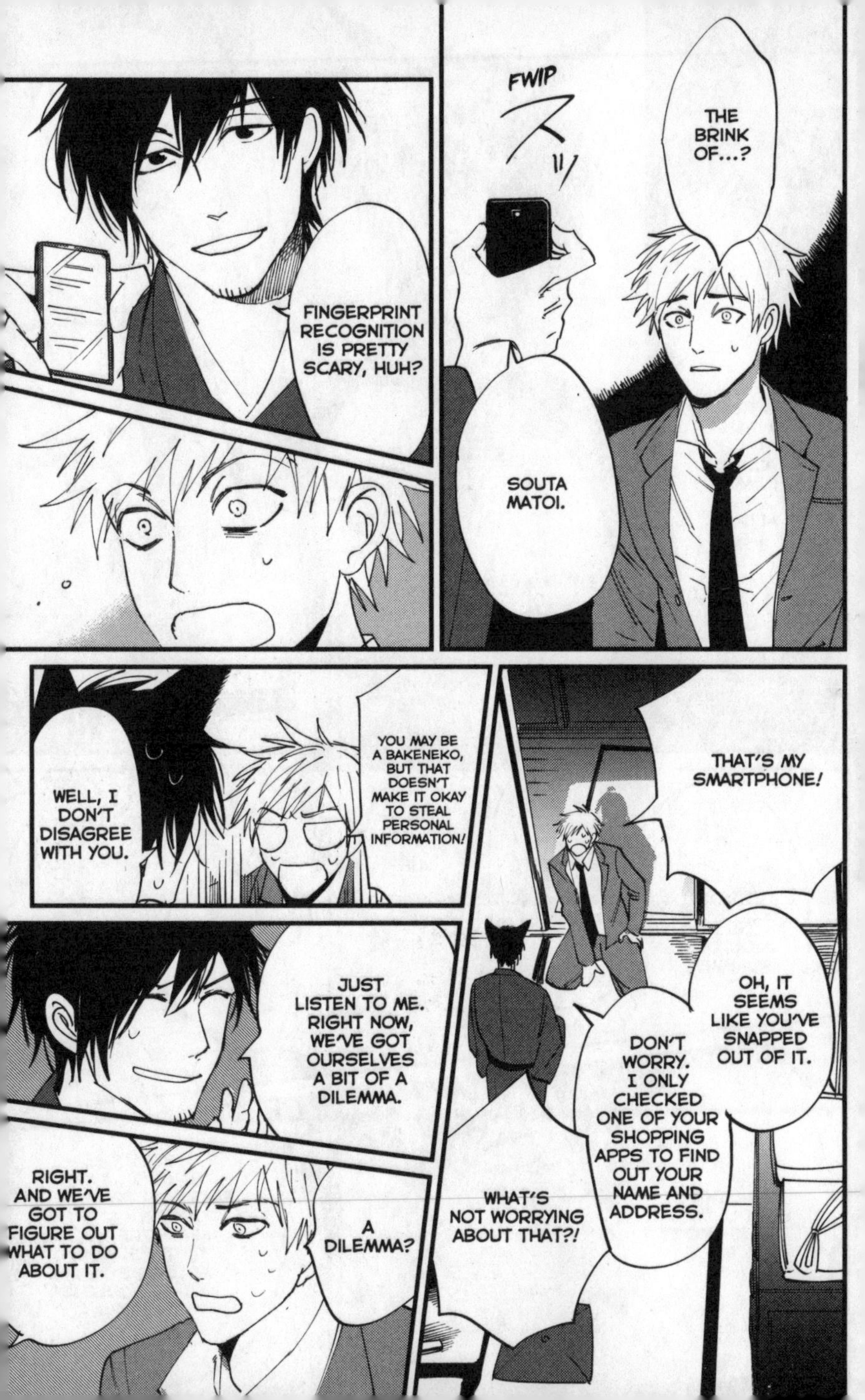

THE BRINK OF...?
FWIP
SOUTA MATOI.
FINGERPRINT RECOGNITION IS PRETTY SCARY, HUH?
THAT'S MY SMARTPHONE!
OH, IT SEEMS LIKE YOU'VE SNAPPED OUT OF IT.
DON'T WORRY. I ONLY CHECKED ONE OF YOUR SHOPPING APPS TO FIND OUT YOUR NAME AND ADDRESS.
WHAT'S NOT WORRYING ABOUT THAT?!
YOU MAY BE A BAKENEKO, BUT THAT DOESN'T MAKE IT OKAY TO STEAL PERSONAL INFORMATION!
WELL, I DON'T DISAGREE WITH YOU.
JUST LISTEN TO ME. RIGHT NOW, WE'VE GOT OURSELVES A BIT OF A DILEMMA.
A DILEMMA?
RIGHT. AND WE'VE GOT TO FIGURE OUT WHAT TO DO ABOUT IT.

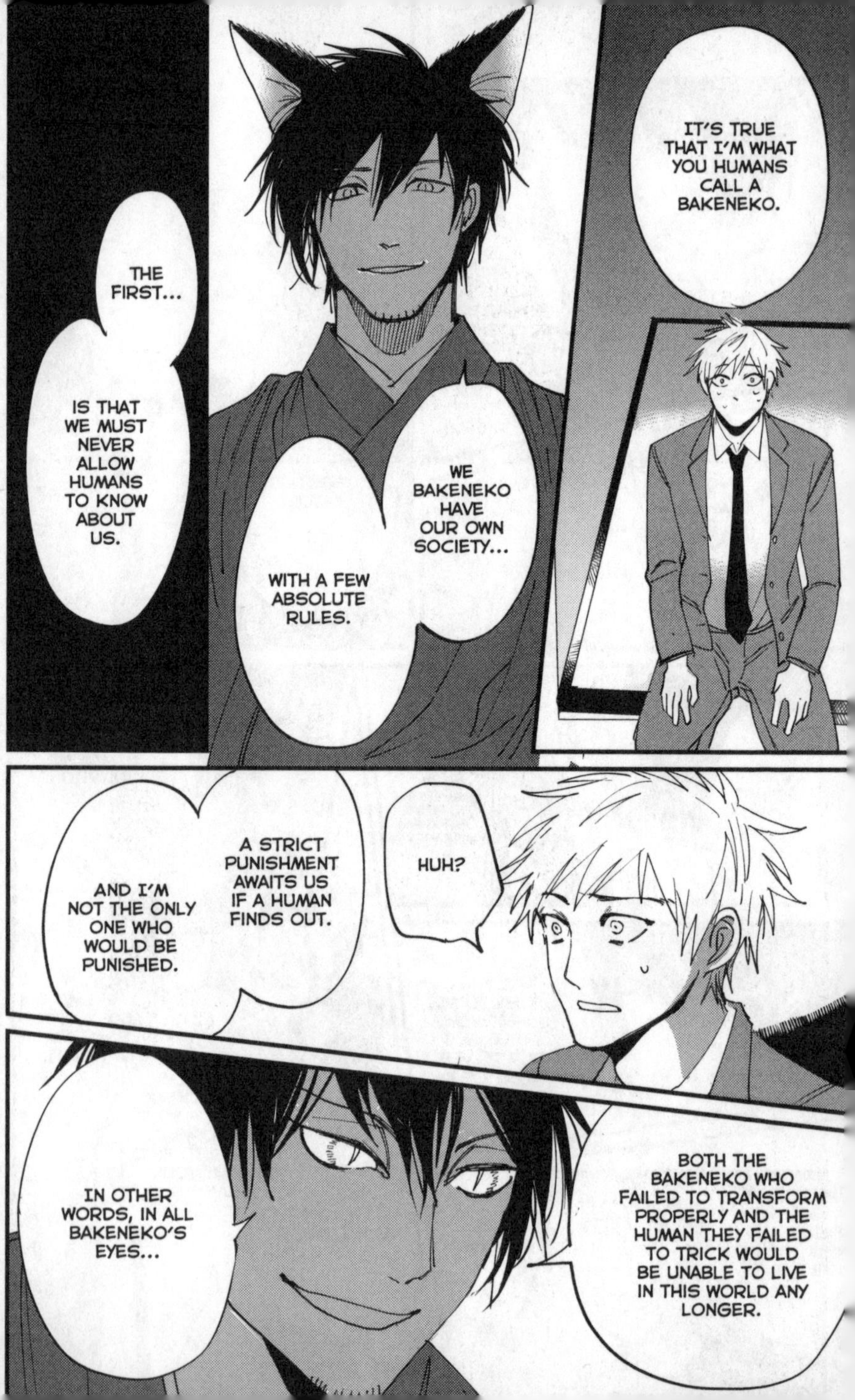
IT'S TRUE THAT I'M WHAT YOU HUMANS CALL A BAKENEKO.
WE BAKENEKO HAVE OUR OWN SOCIETY...
WITH A FEW ABSOLUTE RULES.
THE FIRST...
IS THAT WE MUST NEVER ALLOW HUMANS TO KNOW ABOUT US.
HUH?
A STRICT PUNISHMENT AWAITS US IF A HUMAN FINDS OUT.
AND I'M NOT THE ONLY ONE WHO WOULD BE PUNISHED.
BOTH THE BAKENEKO WHO FAILED TO TRANSFORM PROPERLY AND THE HUMAN THEY FAILED TO TRICK WOULD BE UNABLE TO LIVE IN THIS WORLD ANY LONGER.
IN OTHER WORDS, IN ALL BAKENEKO'S EYES...

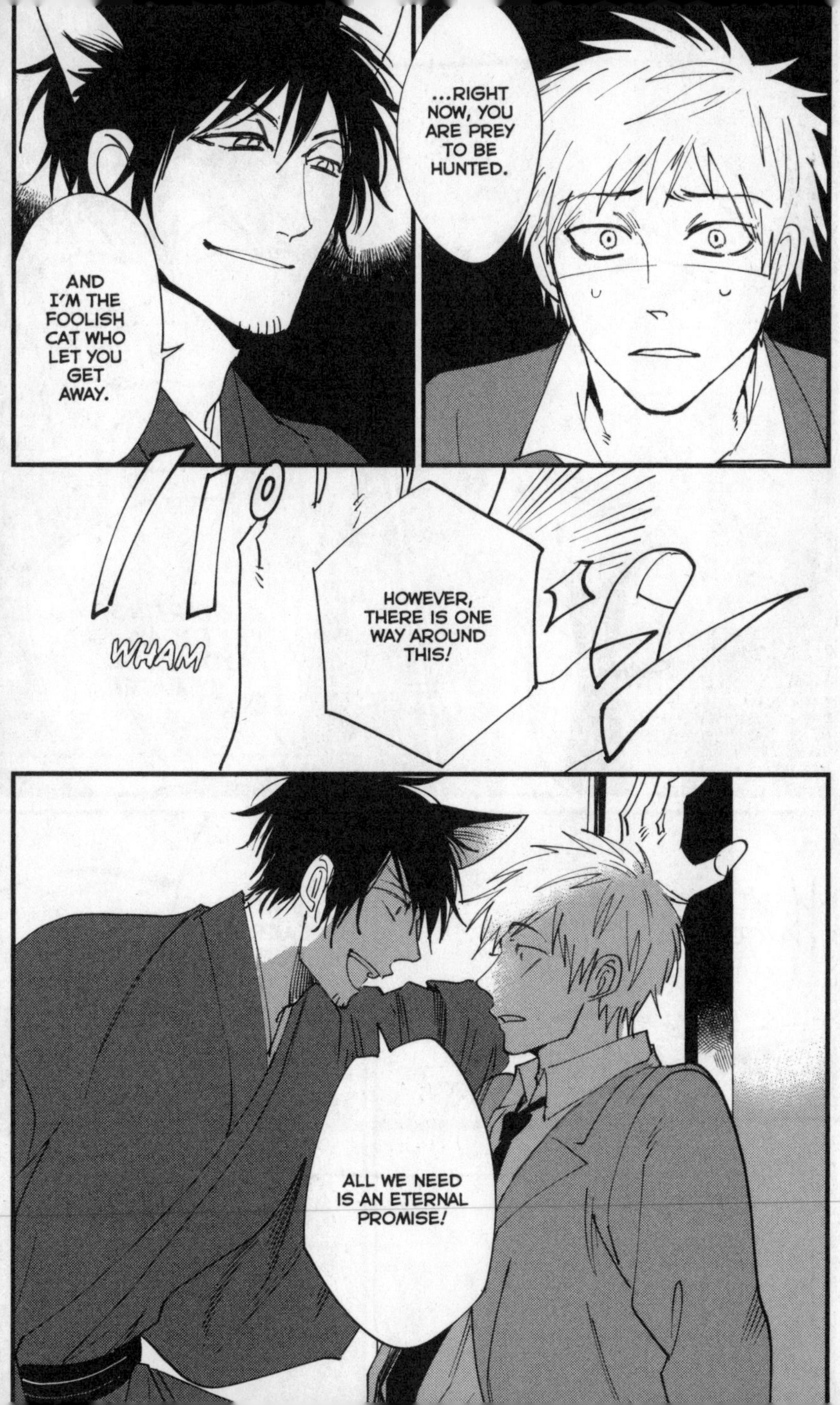
...RIGHT NOW, YOU ARE PREY TO BE HUNTED.
AND I'M THE FOOLISH CAT WHO LET YOU GET AWAY.
HOWEVER, THERE IS ONE WAY AROUND THIS!
WHAM
ALL WE NEED IS AN ETERNAL PROMISE!

NO THANKS.

STARTING TODAY, YOU'LL BE MY MATE!

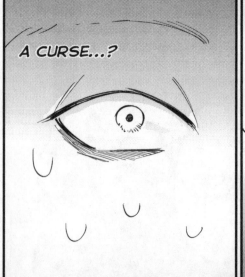

A CURSE...?

THEN I'LL PLACE A CURSE ON YOU.

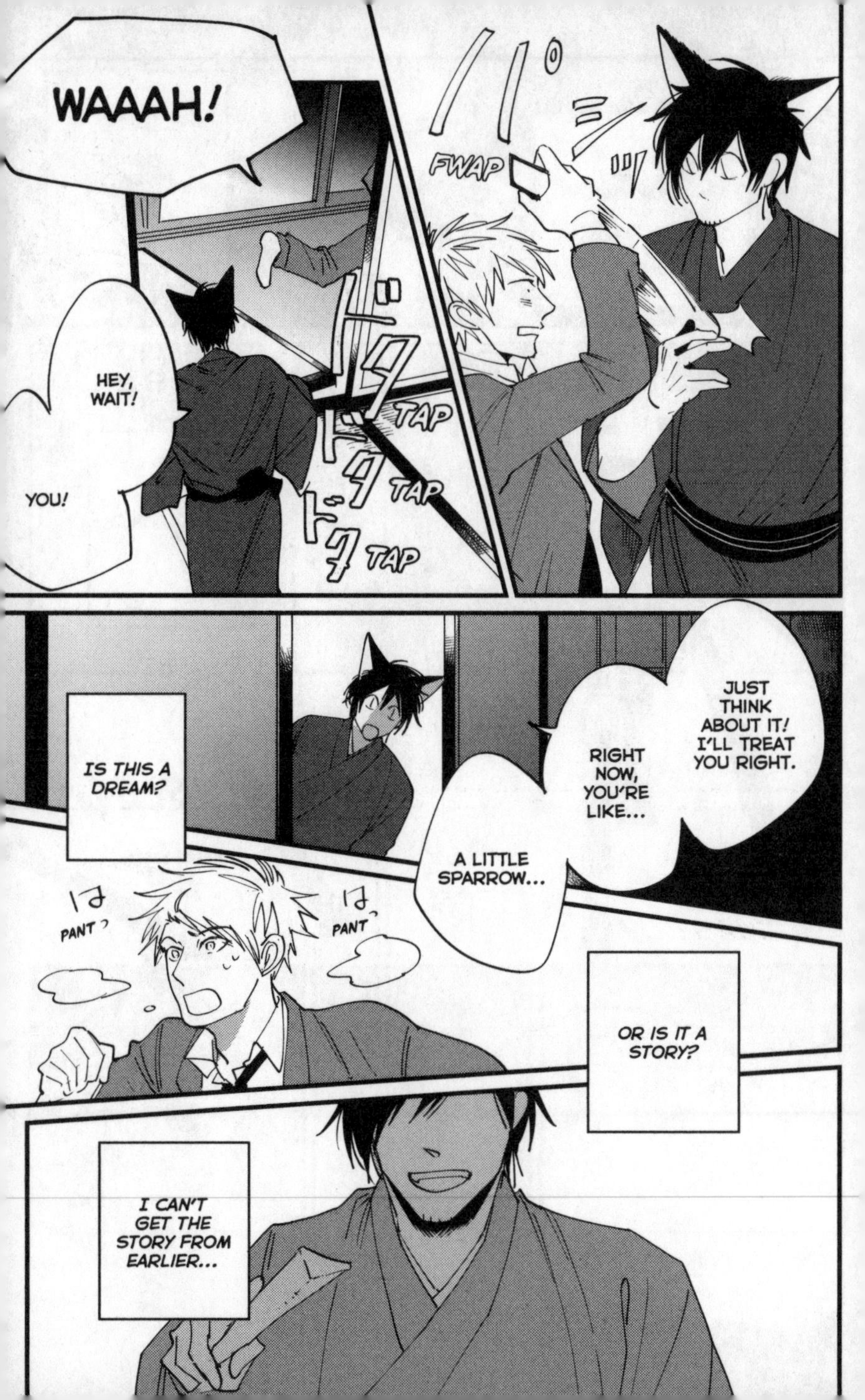
FWAP
WAAAH!
TAP
TAP
TAP
HEY, WAIT!
YOU!
JUST THINK ABOUT IT! I'LL TREAT YOU RIGHT.
RIGHT NOW, YOU'RE LIKE...
A LITTLE SPARROW...
IS THIS A DREAM?
PANT
PANT
OR IS IT A STORY?
I CAN'T GET THE STORY FROM EARLIER...

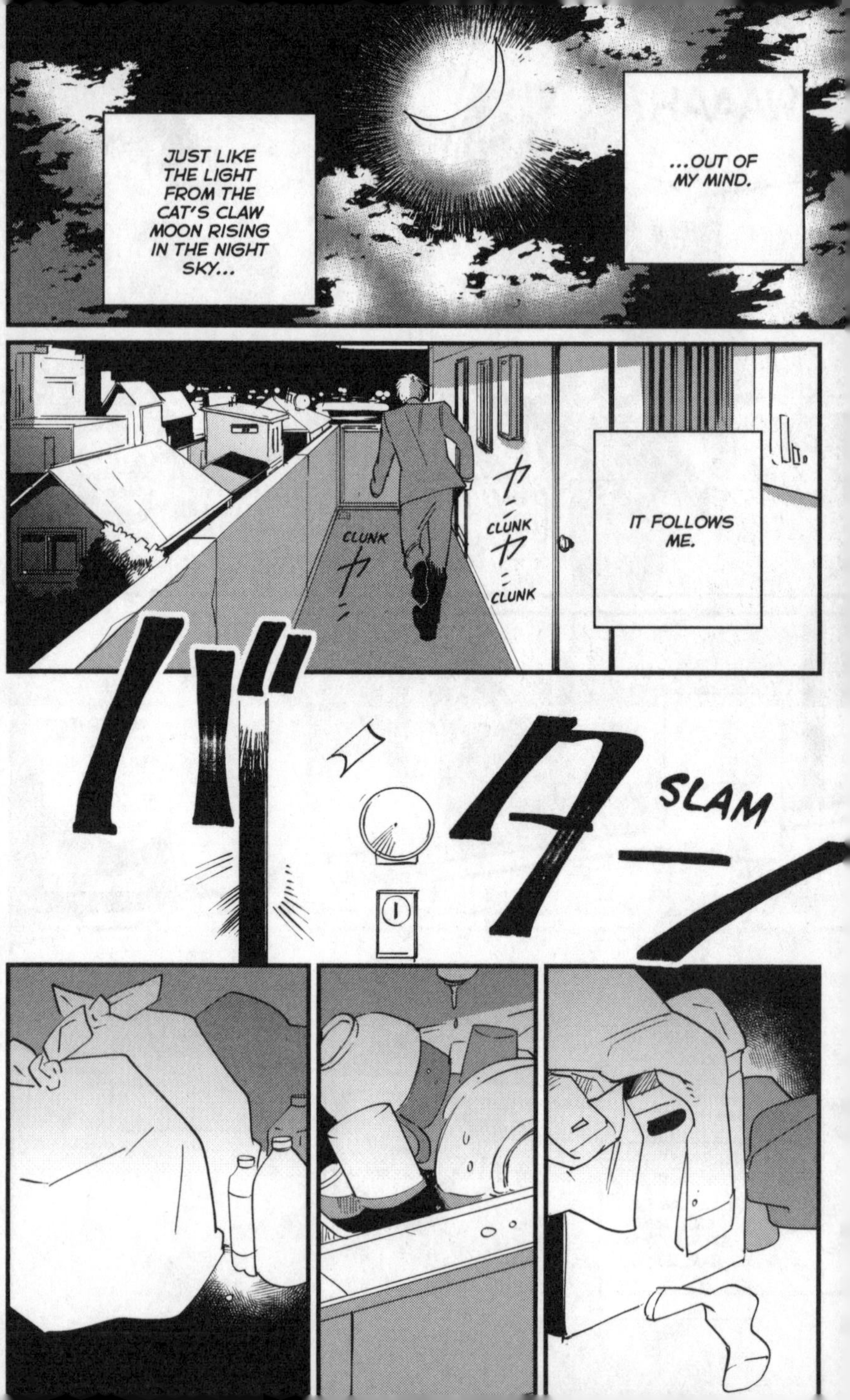
...OUT OF MY MIND.
JUST LIKE THE LIGHT FROM THE CAT'S CLAW MOON RISING IN THE NIGHT SKY...
IT FOLLOWS ME.
CLUNK
CLUNK
CLUNK
SLAM

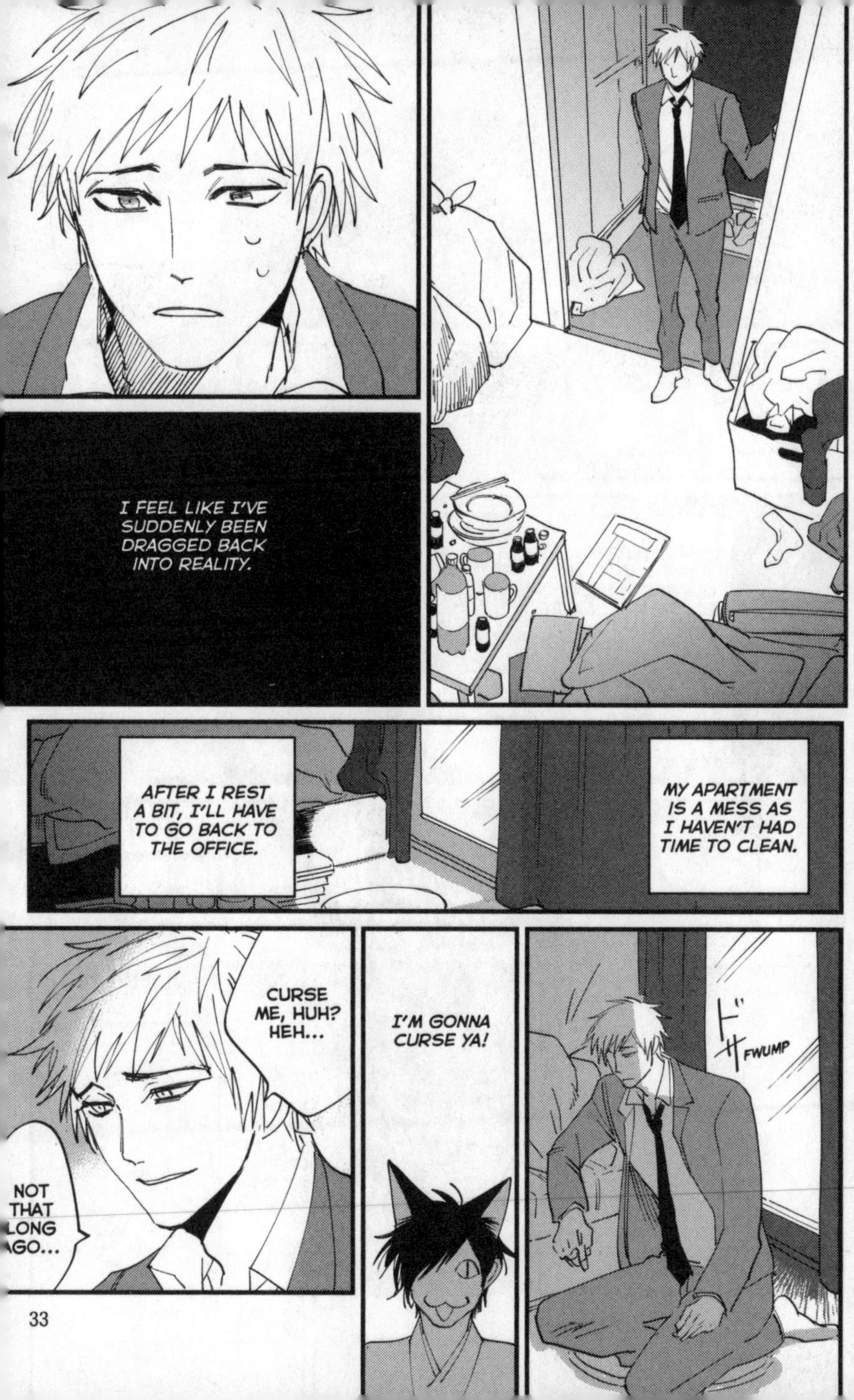
I FEEL LIKE I'VE SUDDENLY BEEN DRAGGED BACK INTO REALITY.
MY APARTMENT IS A MESS AS I HAVEN'T HAD TIME TO CLEAN.
AFTER I REST A BIT, I'LL HAVE TO GO BACK TO THE OFFICE.
ドサ
FWUMP
I'M GONNA CURSE YA!
CURSE ME, HUH? HEH...
NOT THAT LONG AGO...

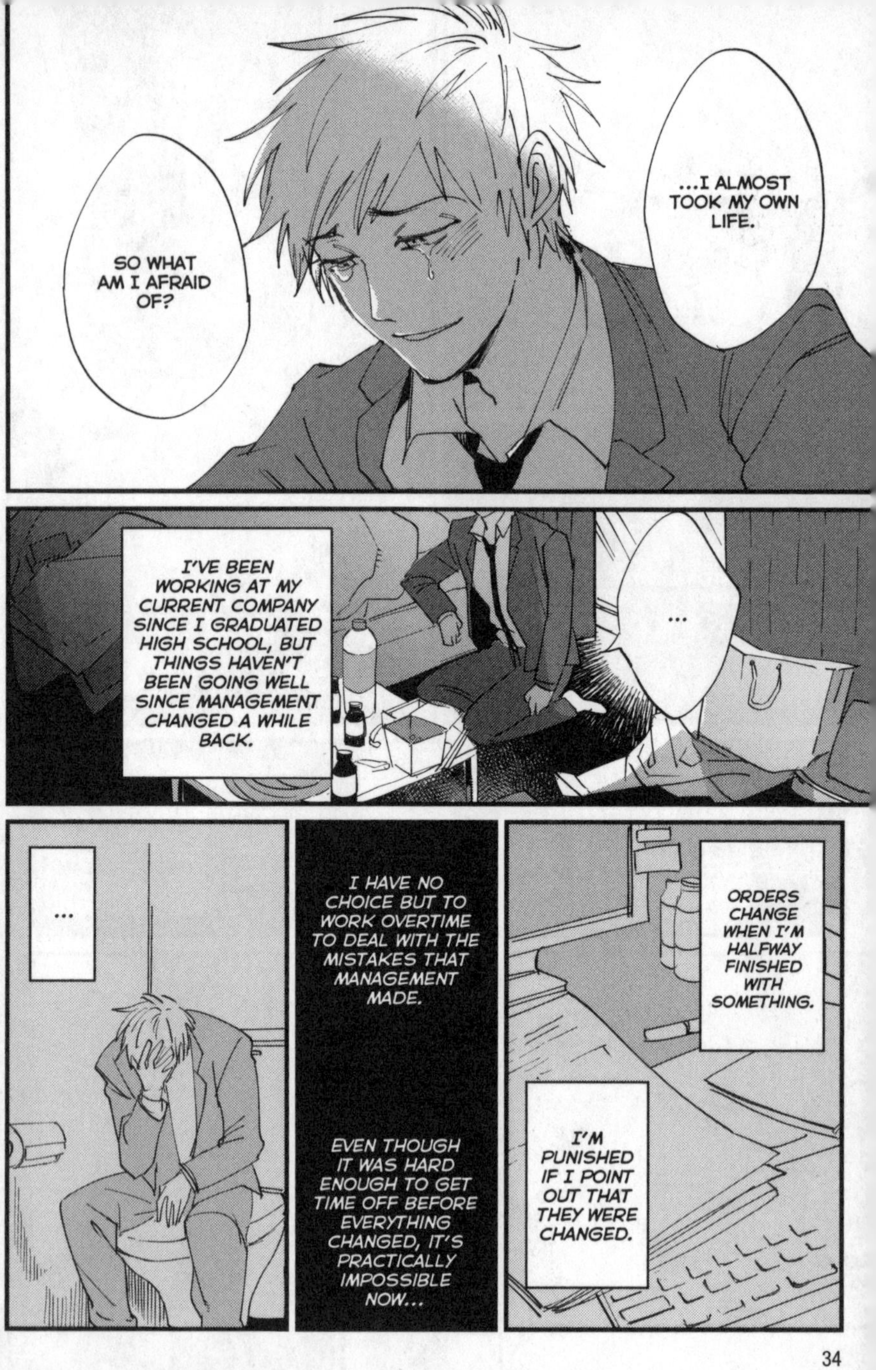
...I ALMOST TOOK MY OWN LIFE.
SO WHAT AM I AFRAID OF?
...
I'VE BEEN WORKING AT MY CURRENT COMPANY SINCE I GRADUATED HIGH SCHOOL, BUT THINGS HAVEN'T BEEN GOING WELL SINCE MANAGEMENT CHANGED A WHILE BACK.
ORDERS CHANGE WHEN I'M HALFWAY FINISHED WITH SOMETHING.
I'M PUNISHED IF I POINT OUT THAT THEY WERE CHANGED.
I HAVE NO CHOICE BUT TO WORK OVERTIME TO DEAL WITH THE MISTAKES THAT MANAGEMENT MADE.
EVEN THOUGH IT WAS HARD ENOUGH TO GET TIME OFF BEFORE EVERYTHING CHANGED, IT'S PRACTICALLY IMPOSSIBLE NOW...
...

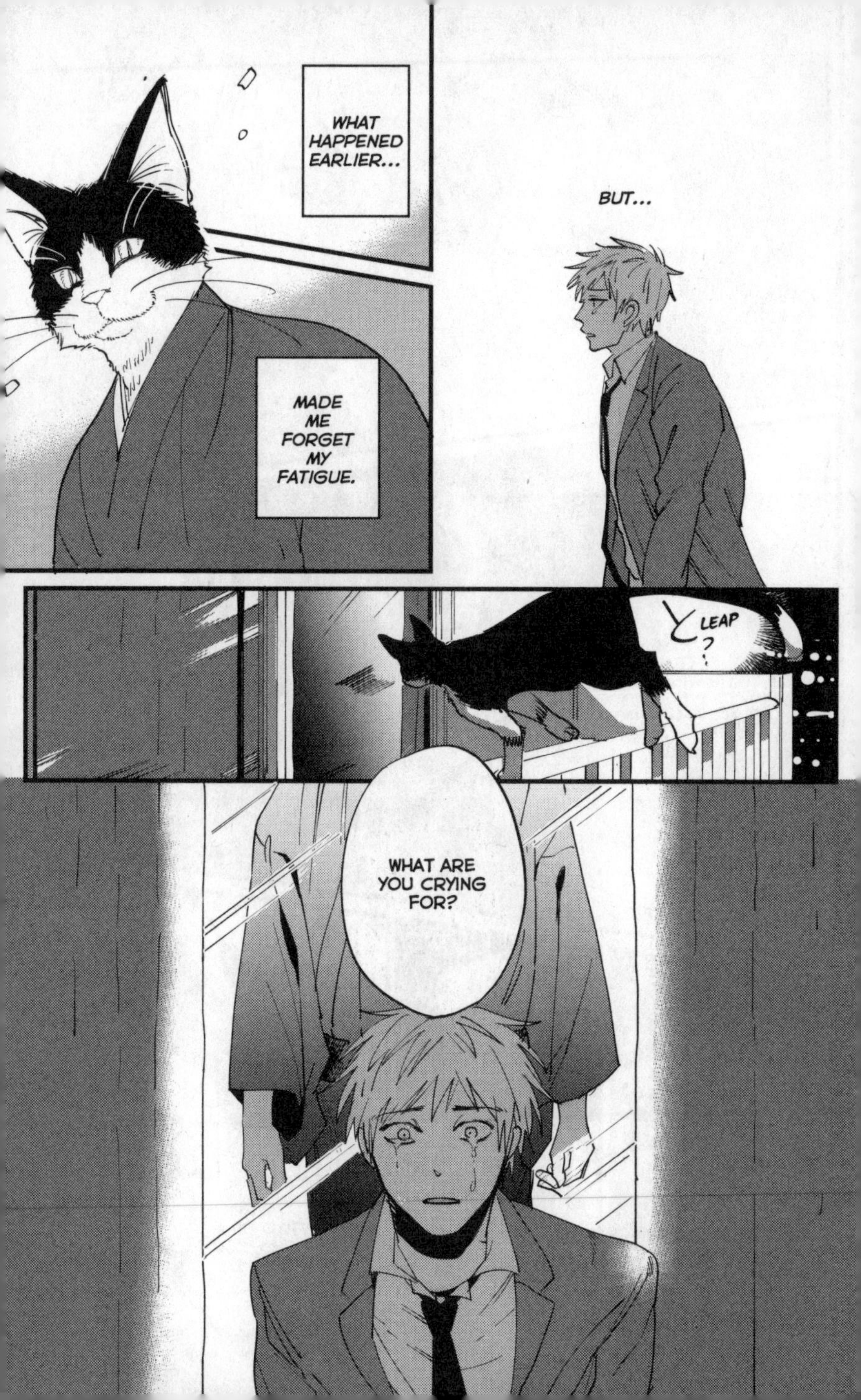
BUT...
WHAT HAPPENED EARLIER...
MADE ME FORGET MY FATIGUE.
LEAP
WHAT ARE YOU CRYING FOR?

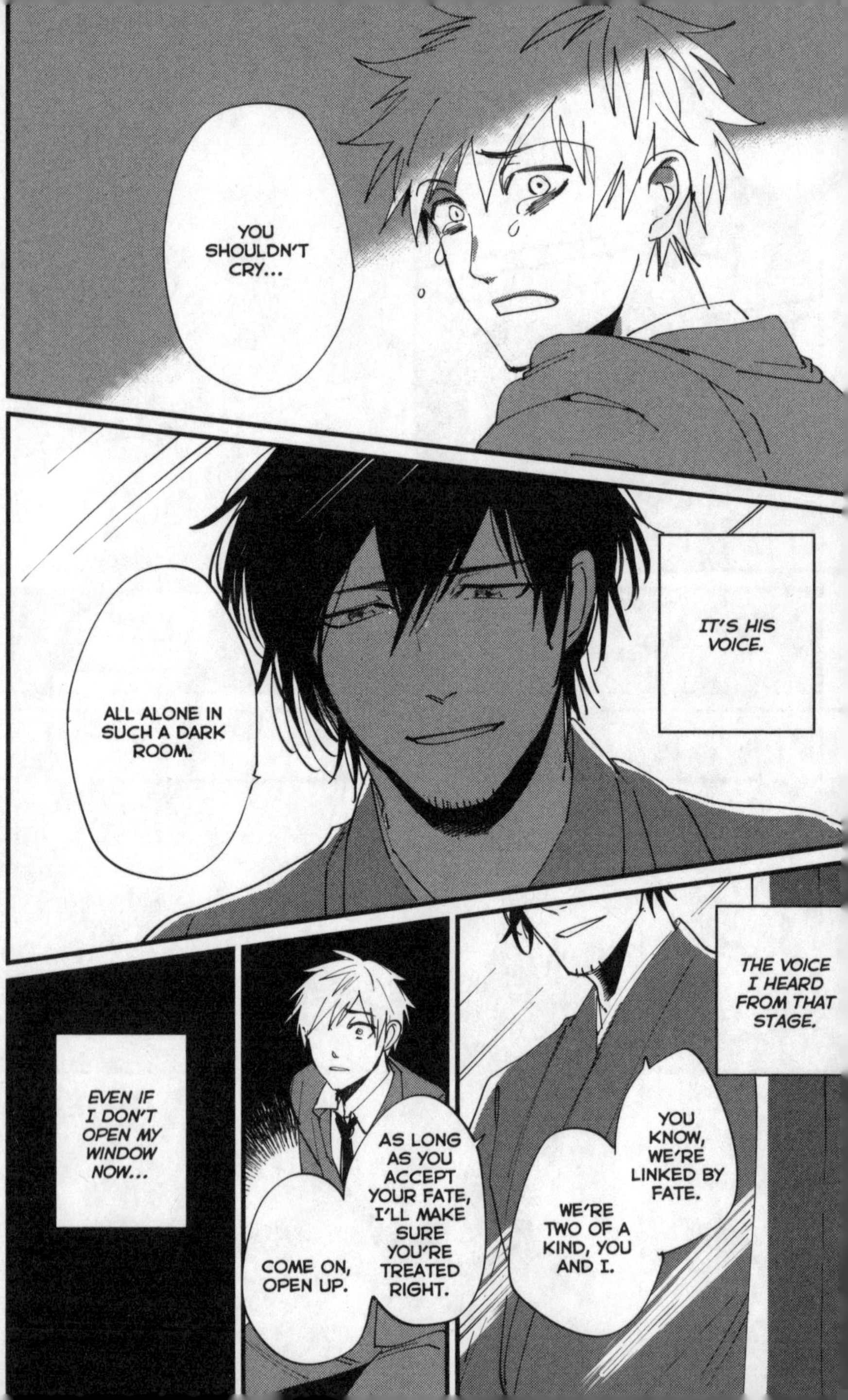
YOU SHOULDN'T CRY...
IT'S HIS VOICE.
ALL ALONE IN SUCH A DARK ROOM.
THE VOICE I HEARD FROM THAT STAGE.
YOU KNOW, WE'RE LINKED BY FATE.
WE'RE TWO OF A KIND, YOU AND I.
AS LONG AS YOU ACCEPT YOUR FATE, I'LL MAKE SURE YOU'RE TREATED RIGHT.
COME ON, OPEN UP.
EVEN IF I DON'T OPEN MY WINDOW NOW...

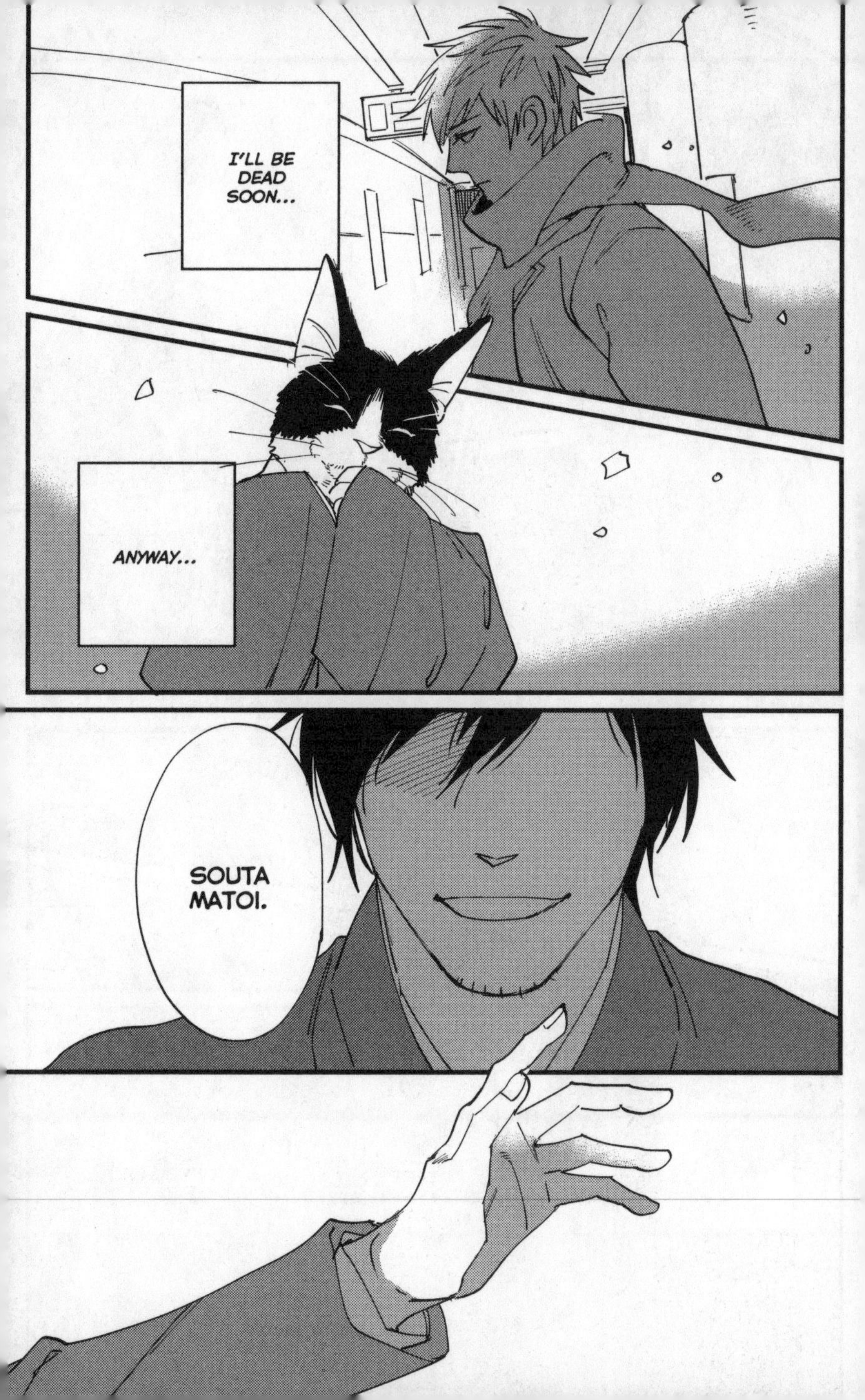
I'LL BE DEAD SOON...
ANYWAY...
SOUTA MATOI.

RATTLE

I CAN'T...

TAKE MY EYES OFF HIM.

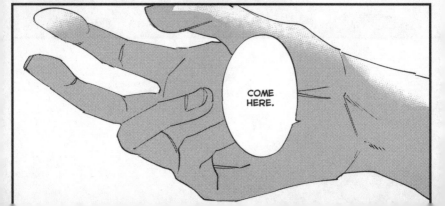

COME HERE.

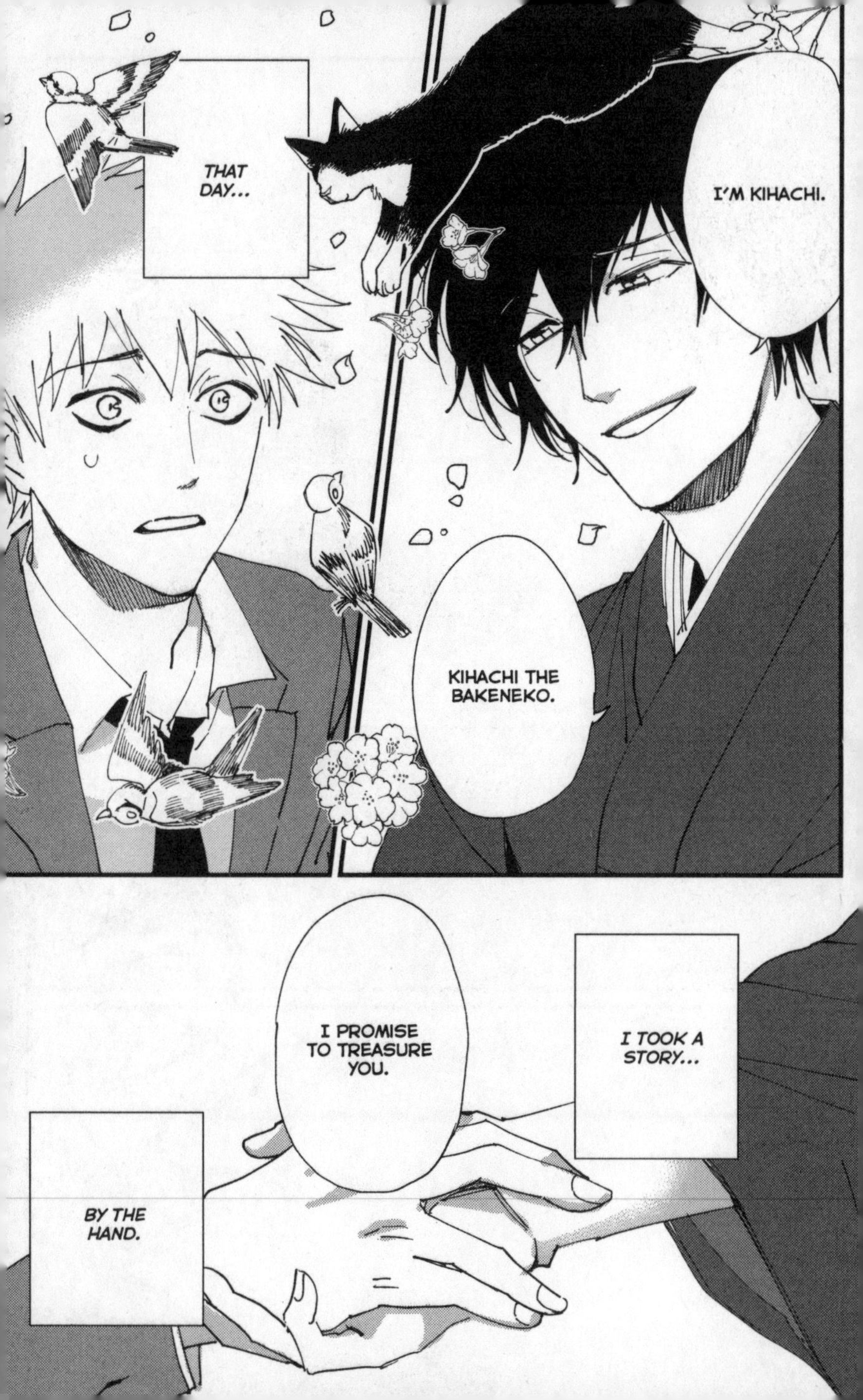
I'M KIHACHI.
KIHACHI THE BAKENEKO.
THAT DAY...
I TOOK A STORY...
I PROMISE TO TREASURE YOU.
BY THE HAND.

2nd Story

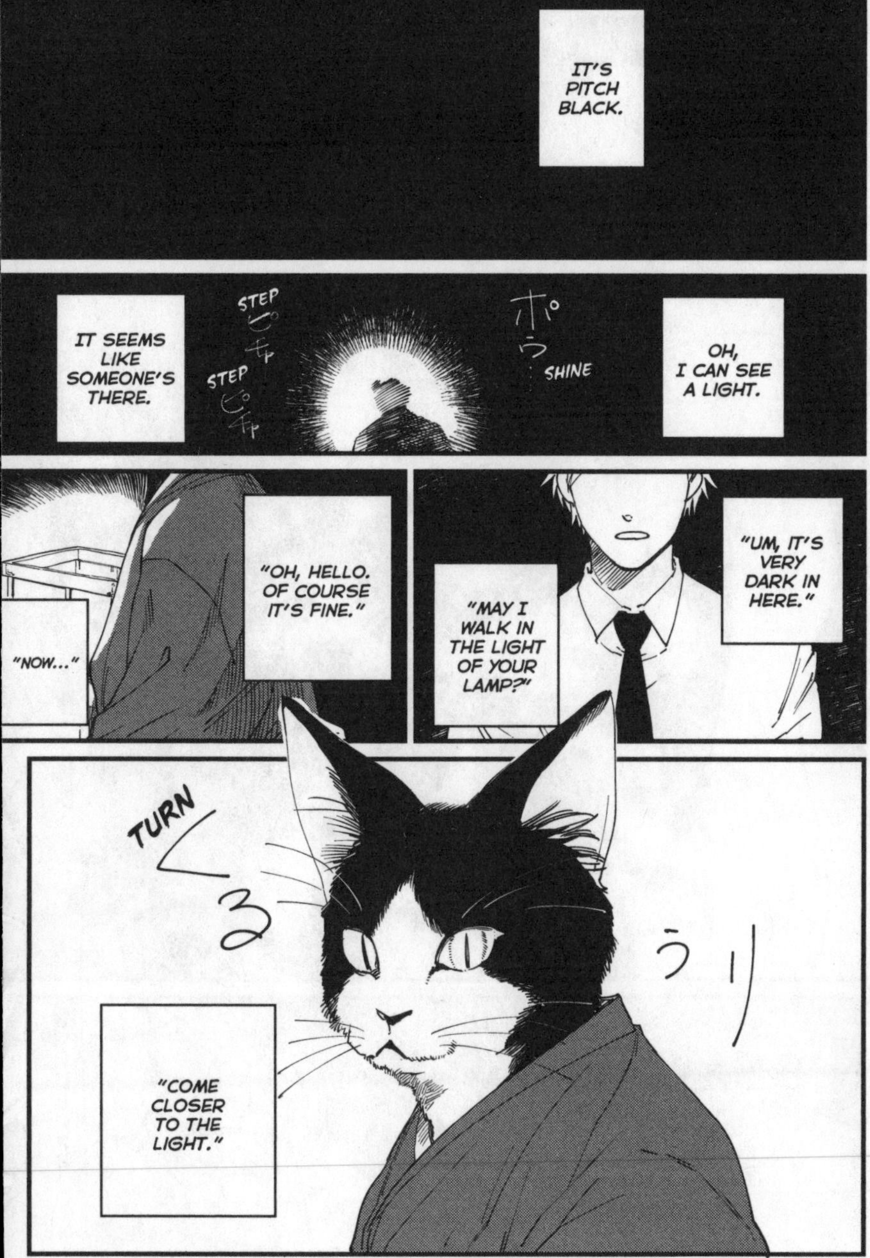
IT'S PITCH BLACK.
OH, I CAN SEE A LIGHT.
ポウ
SHINE
STEP
ピチャ
STEP
ピチャ
IT SEEMS LIKE SOMEONE'S THERE.
"UM, IT'S VERY DARK IN HERE."
"MAY I WALK IN THE LIGHT OF YOUR LAMP?"
"OH, HELLO. OF COURSE IT'S FINE."
"NOW..."
くる
うり
TURN
"COME CLOSER TO THE LIGHT."

2nd Story

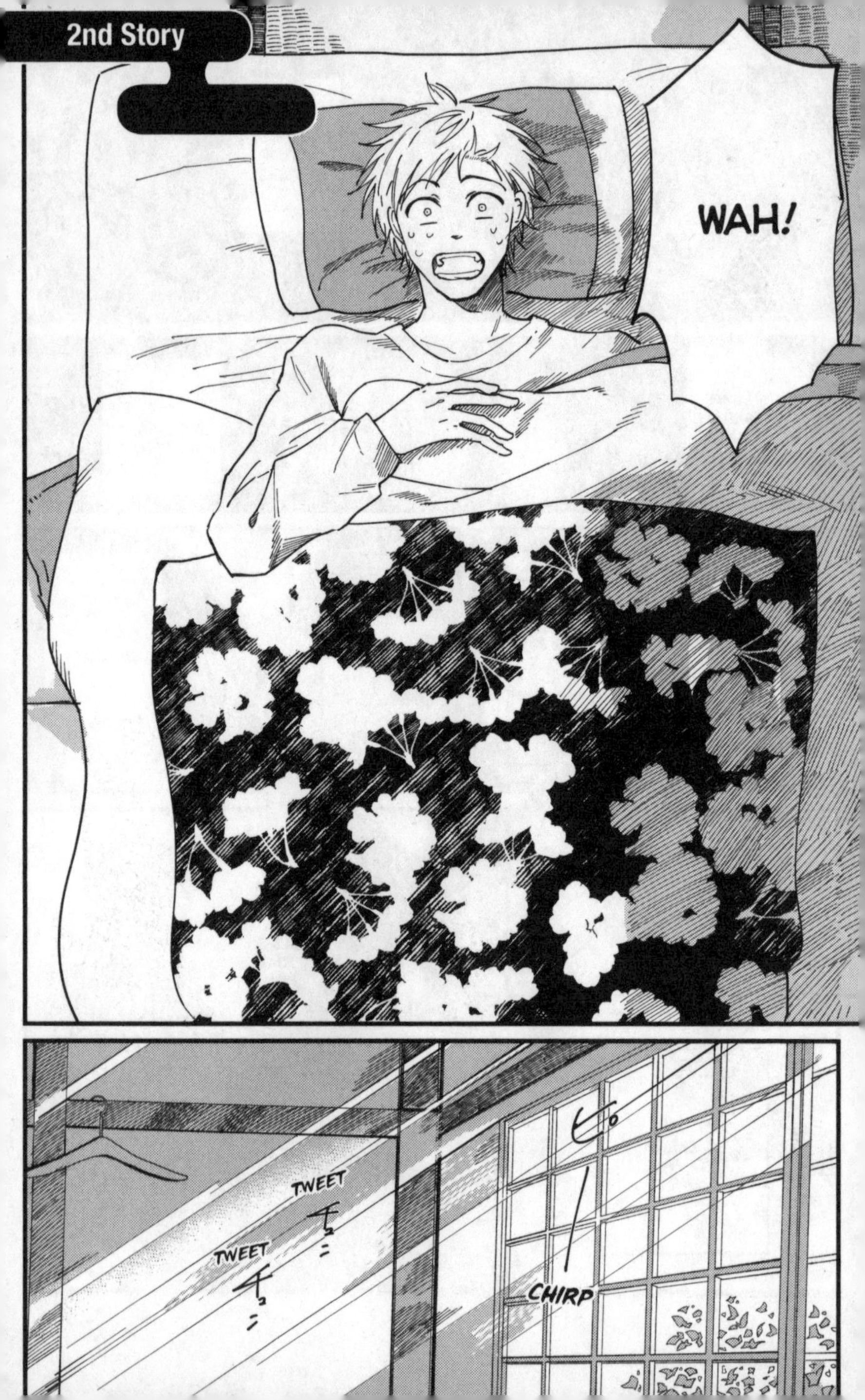
WAH!
CHIRP
TWEET
TWEET

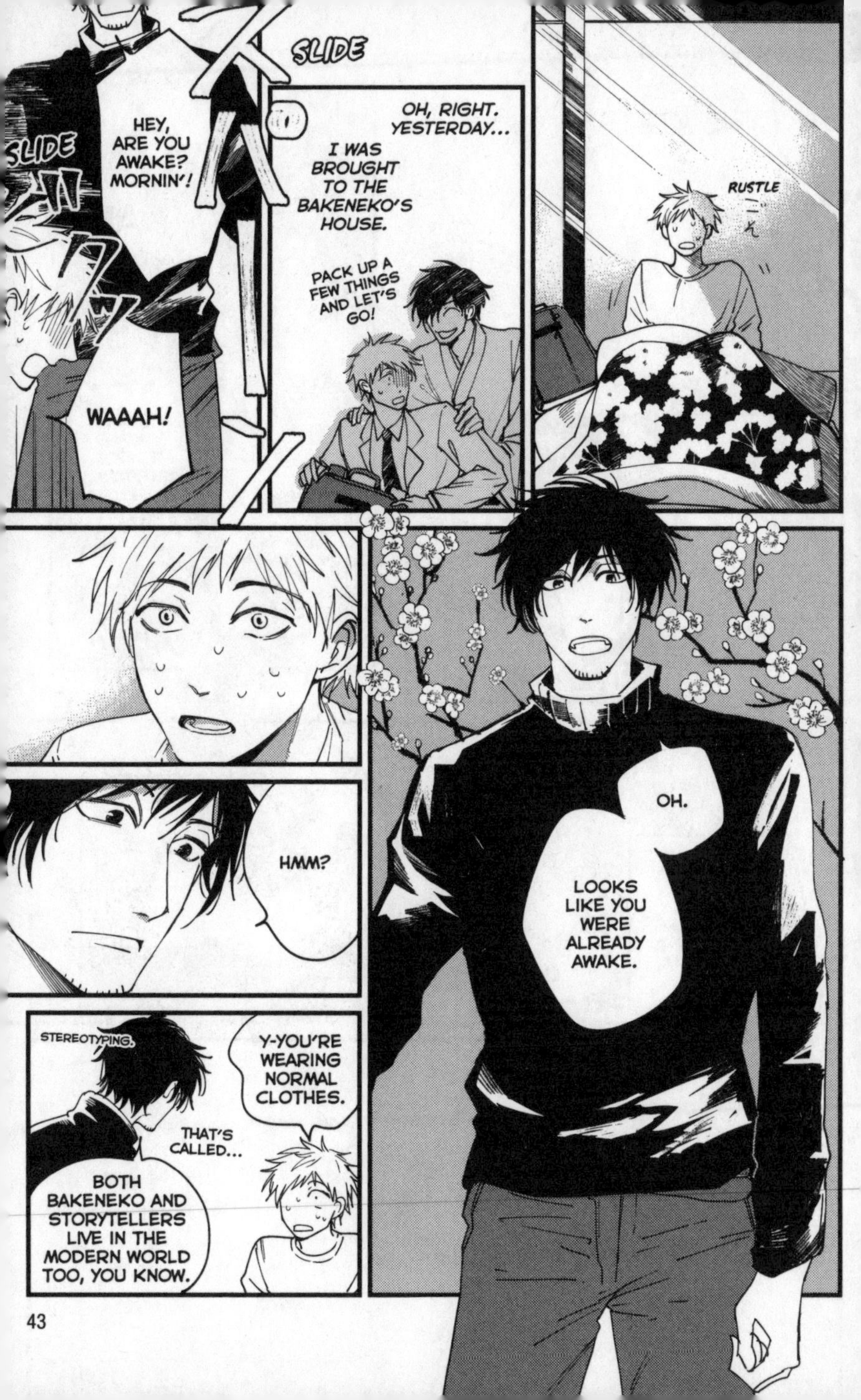
RUSTLE
OH, RIGHT. YESTERDAY...
I WAS BROUGHT TO THE BAKENEKO'S HOUSE.
PACK UP A FEW THINGS AND LET'S GO!
SLIDE
SLIDE
HEY, ARE YOU AWAKE? MORNIN'!
WAAAH!
OH.
LOOKS LIKE YOU WERE ALREADY AWAKE.
HMM?
Y-YOU'RE WEARING NORMAL CLOTHES.
THAT'S CALLED...
STEREOTYPING.
BOTH BAKENEKO AND STORYTELLERS LIVE IN THE MODERN WORLD TOO, YOU KNOW.

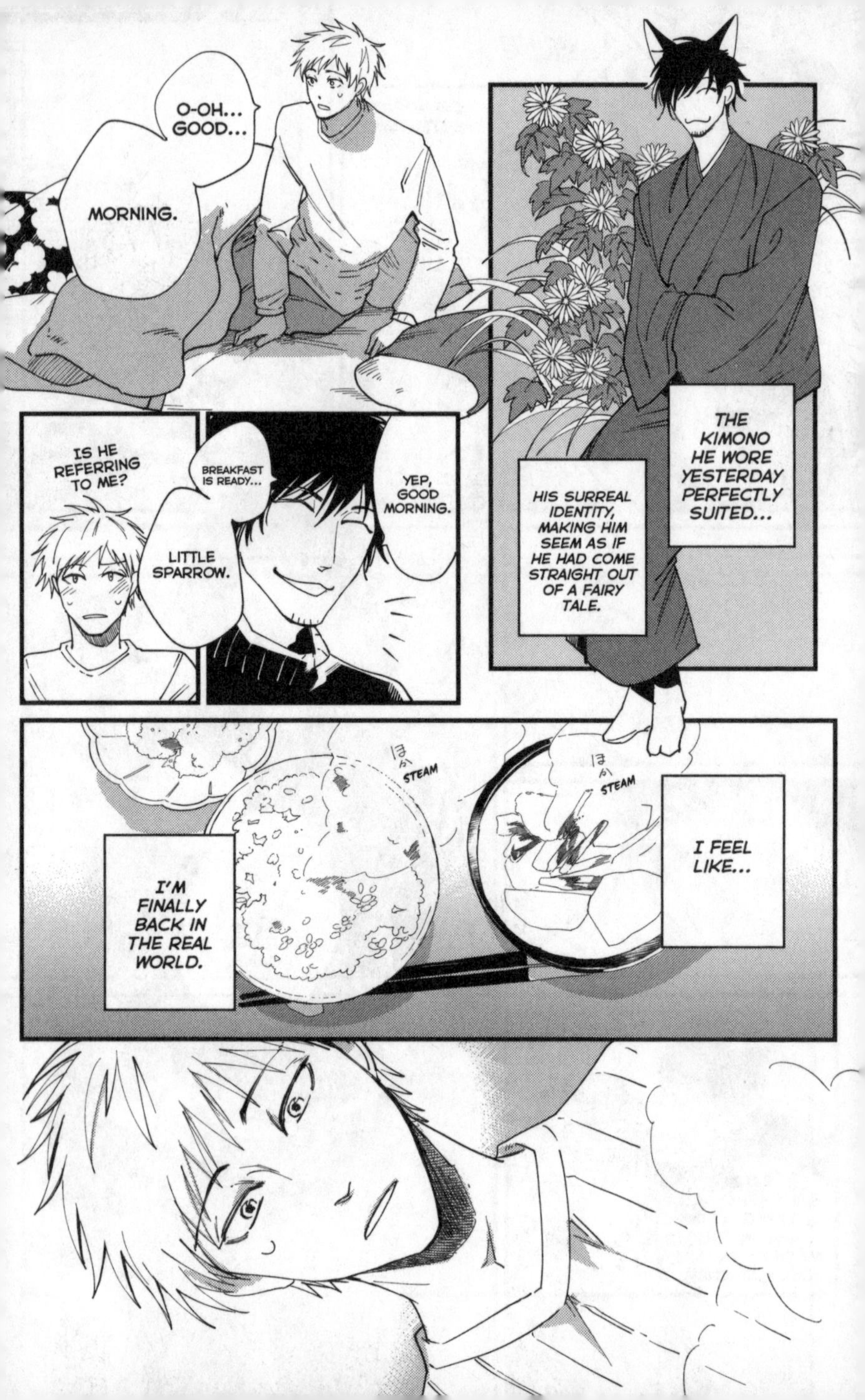
THE KIMONO HE WORE YESTERDAY PERFECTLY SUITED...
HIS SURREAL IDENTITY, MAKING HIM SEEM AS IF HE HAD COME STRAIGHT OUT OF A FAIRY TALE.
O-OH... GOOD...
MORNING.
YEP, GOOD MORNING.
BREAKFAST IS READY...
LITTLE SPARROW.
IS HE REFERRING TO ME?
ほか STEAM
I FEEL LIKE...
ほか STEAM
I'M FINALLY BACK IN THE REAL WORLD.

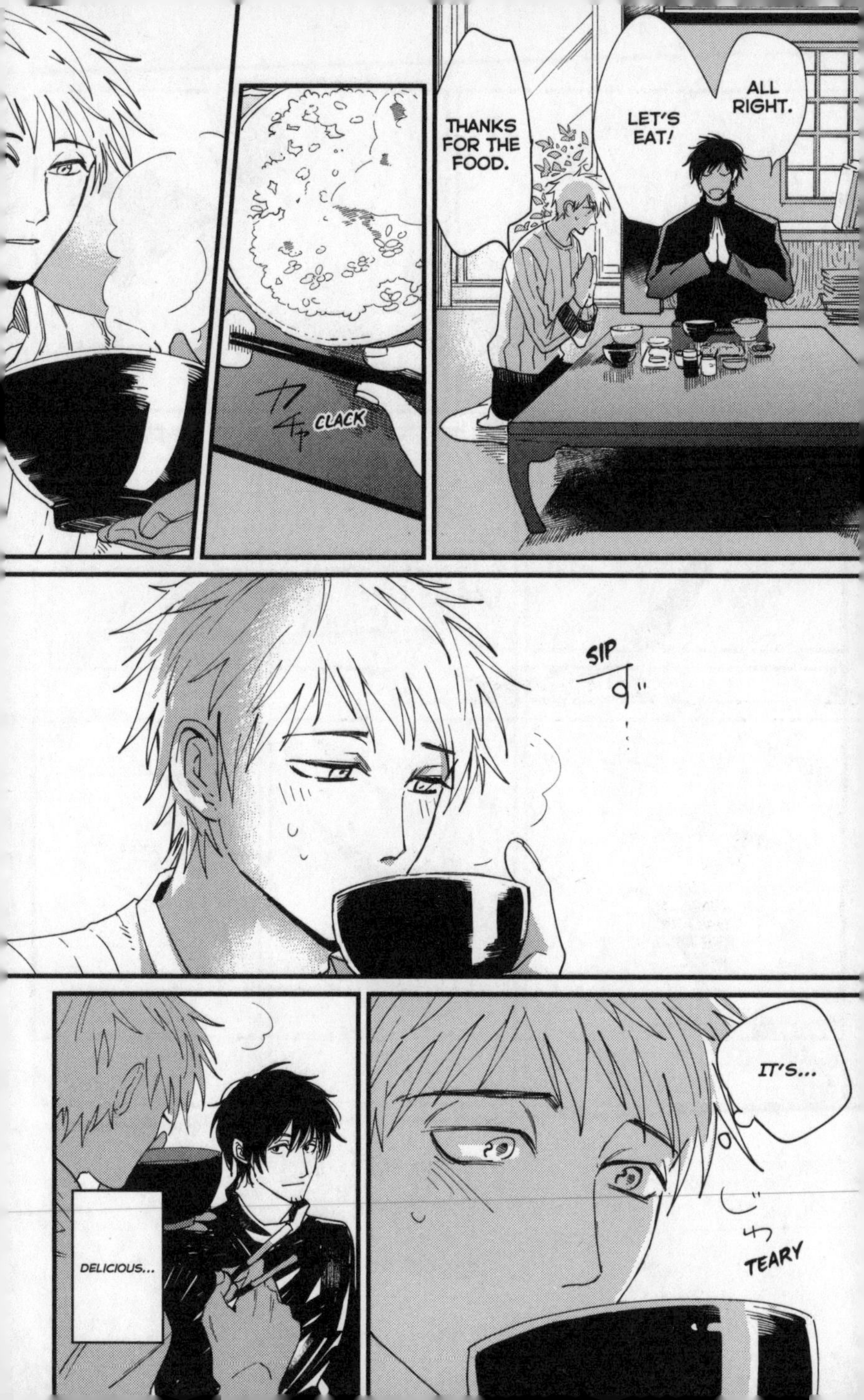
ALL RIGHT.
LET'S EAT!
THANKS FOR THE FOOD.
CLACK
SIP
IT'S...
TEARY
DELICIOUS...

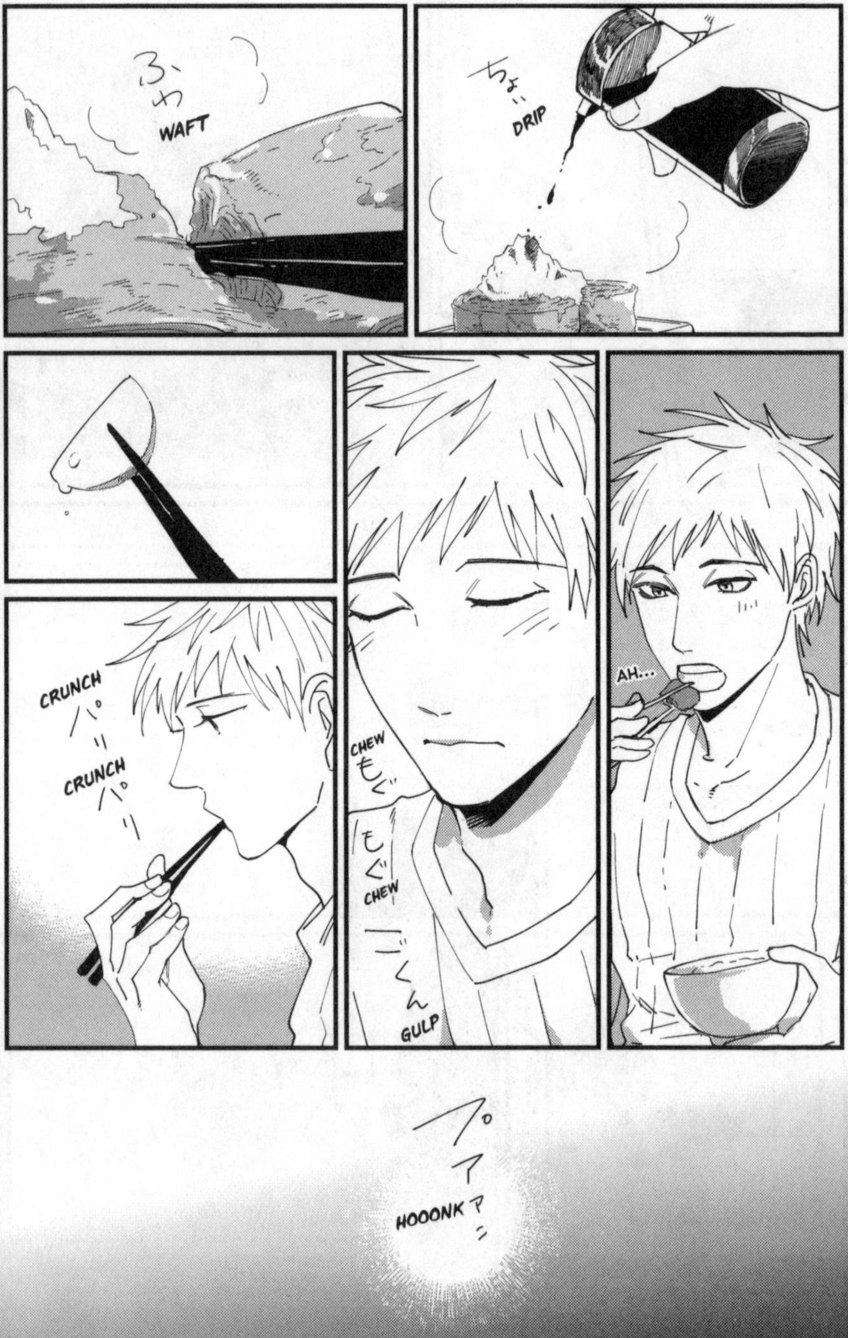
ちょい
DRIP
ふわ
WAFT
AH...
もぐ
CHEW
もぐ
CHEW
ごくん
GULP
CRUNCH
パリ
CRUNCH
パリ
プアァ
HOOONK

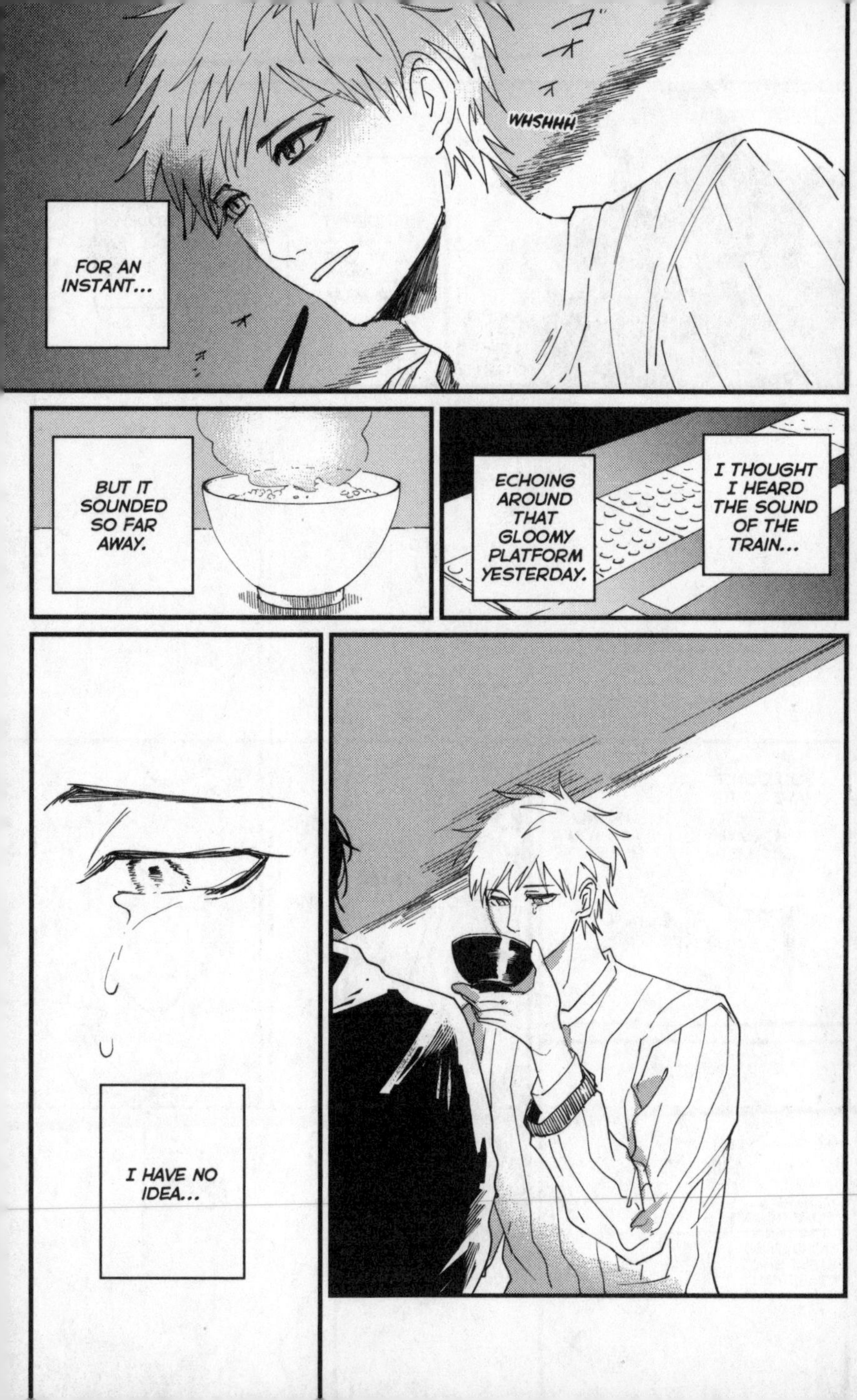
WHSHHH
FOR AN INSTANT...
I THOUGHT I HEARD THE SOUND OF THE TRAIN...
ECHOING AROUND THAT GLOOMY PLATFORM YESTERDAY.
BUT IT SOUNDED SO FAR AWAY.
I HAVE NO IDEA...

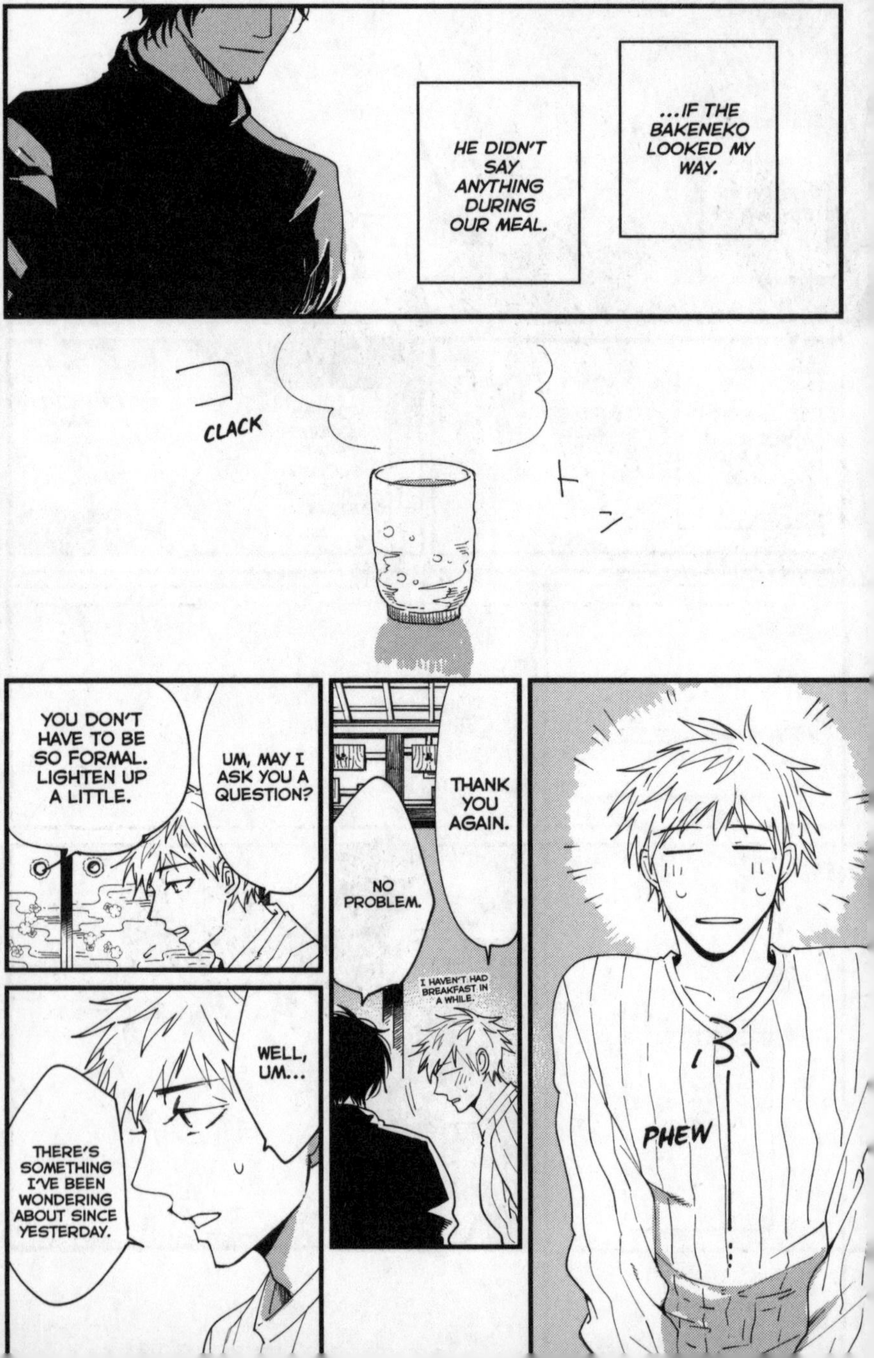
...IF THE BAKENEKO LOOKED MY WAY.
HE DIDN'T SAY ANYTHING DURING OUR MEAL.
CLACK
PHEW
THANK YOU AGAIN.
NO PROBLEM.
I HAVEN'T HAD BREAKFAST IN A WHILE.
UM, MAY I ASK YOU A QUESTION?
YOU DON'T HAVE TO BE SO FORMAL. LIGHTEN UP A LITTLE.
WELL, UM...
THERE'S SOMETHING I'VE BEEN WONDERING ABOUT SINCE YESTERDAY.

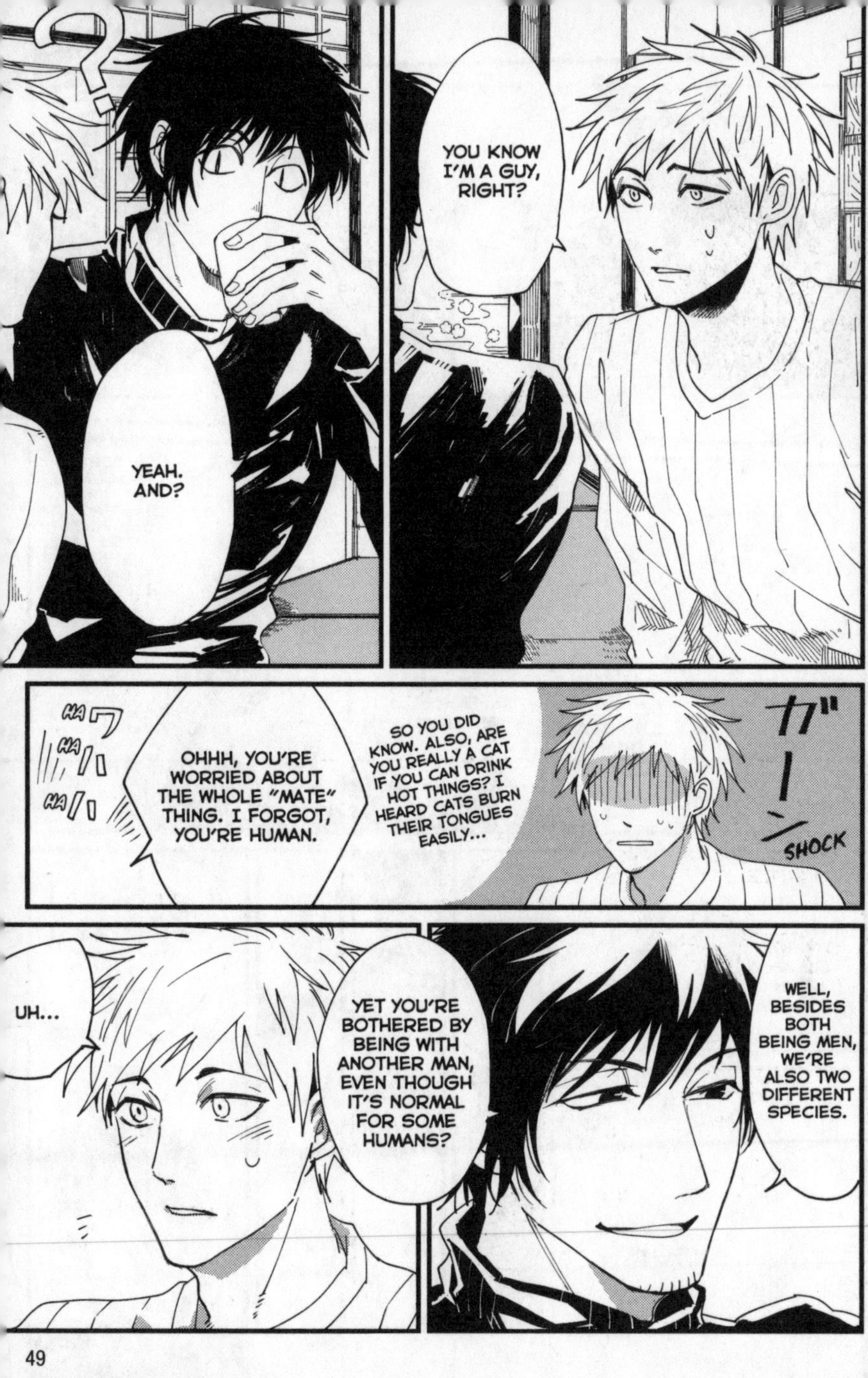
YOU KNOW I'M A GUY, RIGHT?
YEAH. AND?
ガーン
SHOCK
SO YOU DID KNOW. ALSO, ARE YOU REALLY A CAT IF YOU CAN DRINK HOT THINGS? I HEARD CATS BURN THEIR TONGUES EASILY...
OHHH, YOU'RE WORRIED ABOUT THE WHOLE "MATE" THING. I FORGOT, YOU'RE HUMAN.
HA ワ
HA ハ
HA ハ
WELL, BESIDES BOTH BEING MEN, WE'RE ALSO TWO DIFFERENT SPECIES.
YET YOU'RE BOTHERED BY BEING WITH ANOTHER MAN, EVEN THOUGH IT'S NORMAL FOR SOME HUMANS?
UH...

*NOTE: IN JAPAN, PEOPLE WHO CAN'T HANDLE HOT DRINKS ARE SAID TO HAVE A "CAT'S TONGUE."

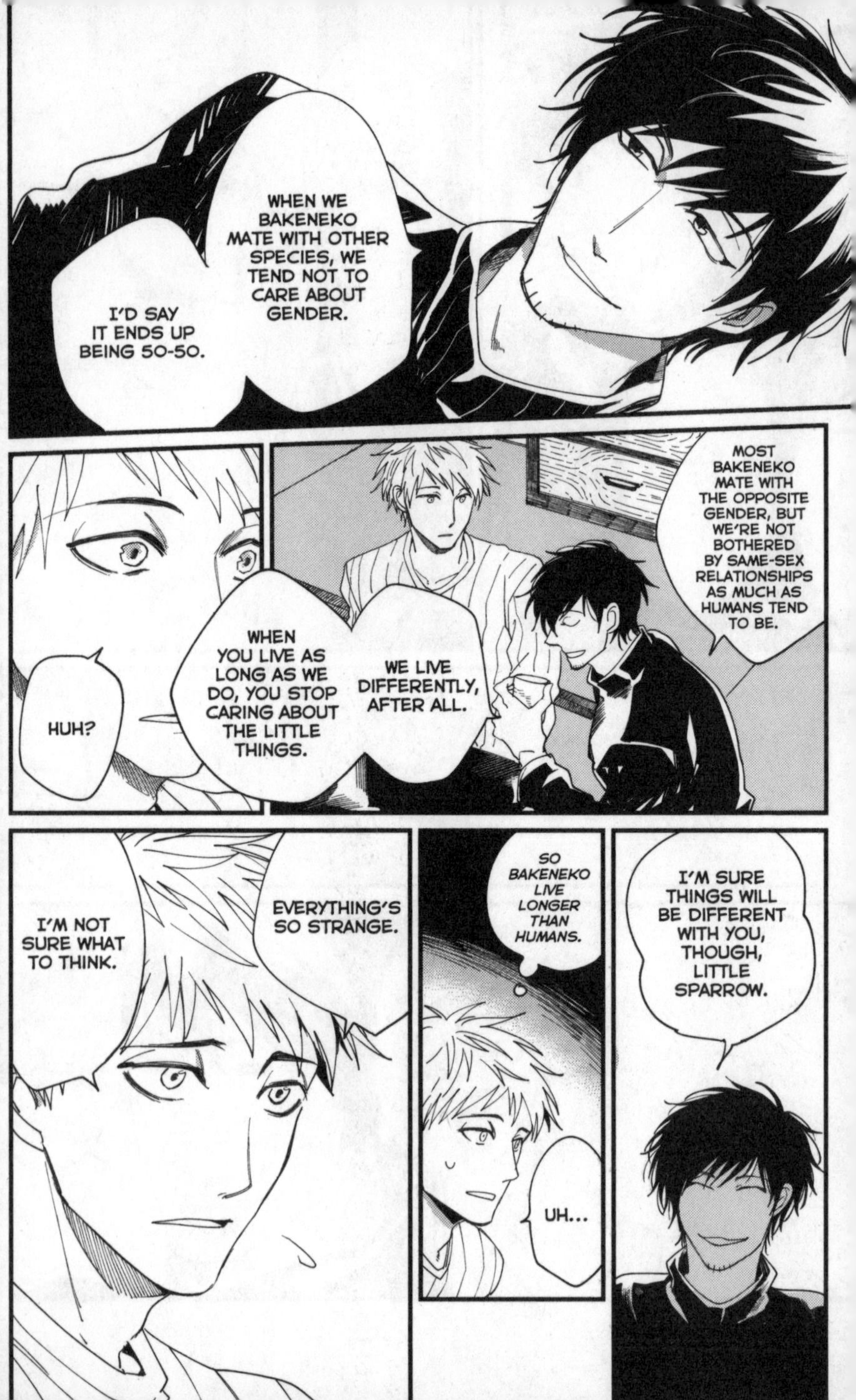
WHEN WE BAKENEKO MATE WITH OTHER SPECIES, WE TEND NOT TO CARE ABOUT GENDER.
I'D SAY IT ENDS UP BEING 50-50.
MOST BAKENEKO MATE WITH THE OPPOSITE GENDER, BUT WE'RE NOT BOTHERED BY SAME-SEX RELATIONSHIPS AS MUCH AS HUMANS TEND TO BE.
WE LIVE DIFFERENTLY, AFTER ALL.
WHEN YOU LIVE AS LONG AS WE DO, YOU STOP CARING ABOUT THE LITTLE THINGS.
HUH?
I'M SURE THINGS WILL BE DIFFERENT WITH YOU, THOUGH, LITTLE SPARROW.
SO BAKENEKO LIVE LONGER THAN HUMANS.
UH...
EVERYTHING'S SO STRANGE.
I'M NOT SURE WHAT TO THINK.

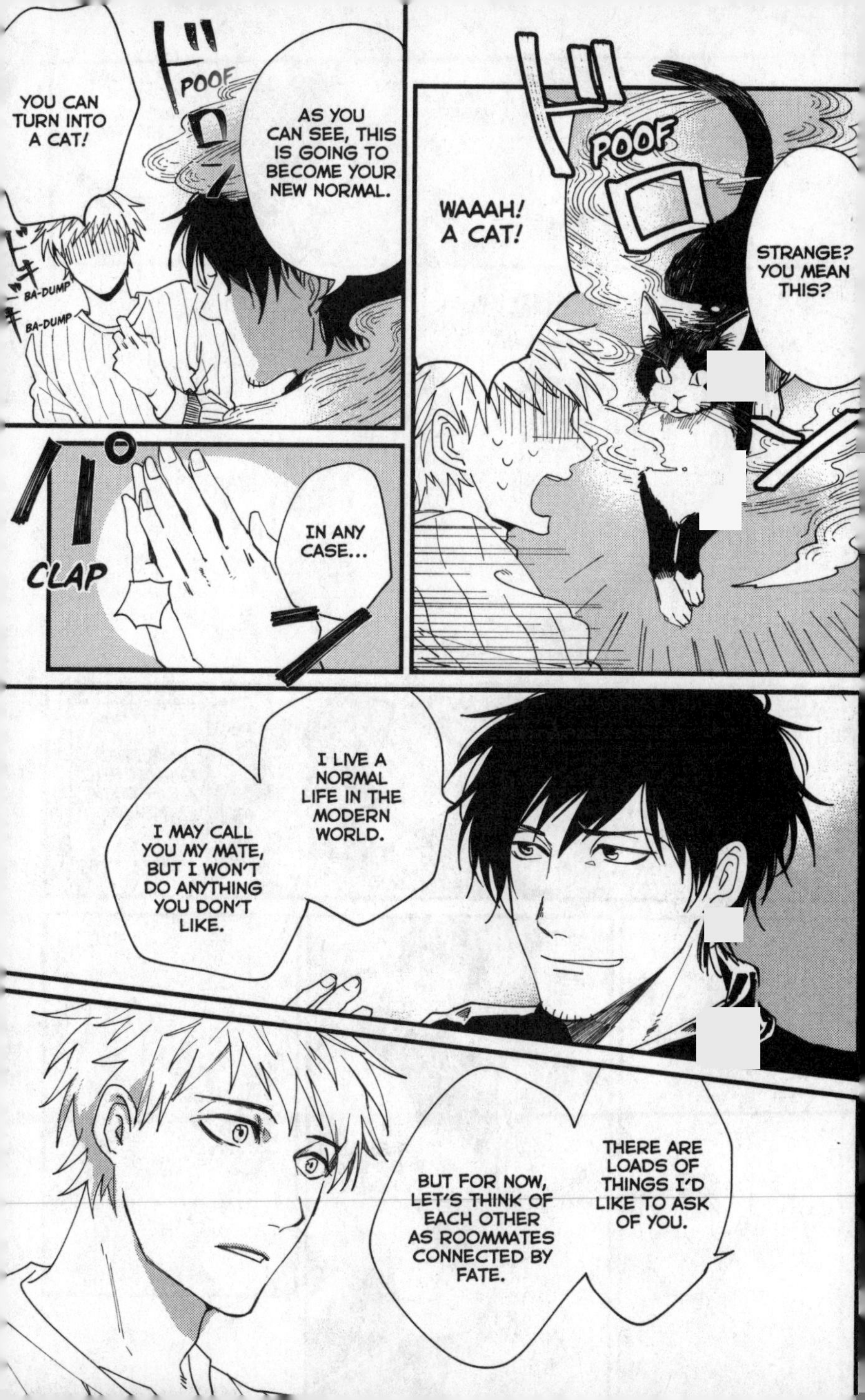
STRANGE? YOU MEAN THIS?
POOF
WAAAH! A CAT!
AS YOU CAN SEE, THIS IS GOING TO BECOME YOUR NEW NORMAL.
POOF
YOU CAN TURN INTO A CAT!
BA-DUMP
BA-DUMP
IN ANY CASE...
CLAP
I LIVE A NORMAL LIFE IN THE MODERN WORLD.
I MAY CALL YOU MY MATE, BUT I WON'T DO ANYTHING YOU DON'T LIKE.
THERE ARE LOADS OF THINGS I'D LIKE TO ASK OF YOU.
BUT FOR NOW, LET'S THINK OF EACH OTHER AS ROOMMATES CONNECTED BY FATE.

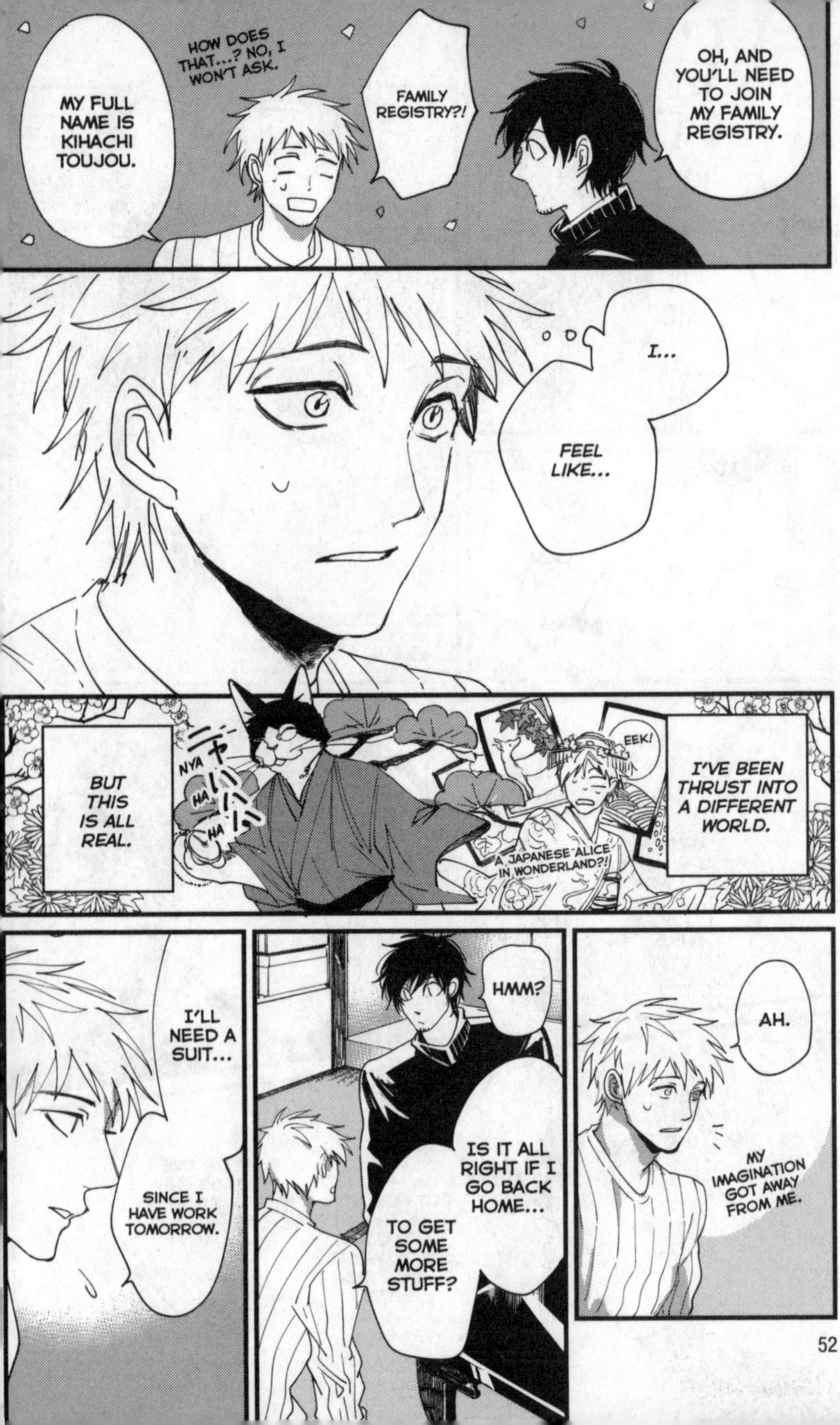
OH, AND YOU'LL NEED TO JOIN MY FAMILY REGISTRY.
FAMILY REGISTRY?!
HOW DOES THAT...? NO, I WON'T ASK.
MY FULL NAME IS KIHACHI TOUJOU.
I...
FEEL LIKE...
I'VE BEEN THRUST INTO A DIFFERENT WORLD.
EEK!
A JAPANESE ALICE IN WONDERLAND?!
NYA HA HA HA
BUT THIS IS ALL REAL.
AH.
MY IMAGINATION GOT AWAY FROM ME.
HMM?
IS IT ALL RIGHT IF I GO BACK HOME...
TO GET SOME MORE STUFF?
I'LL NEED A SUIT...
SINCE I HAVE WORK TOMORROW.

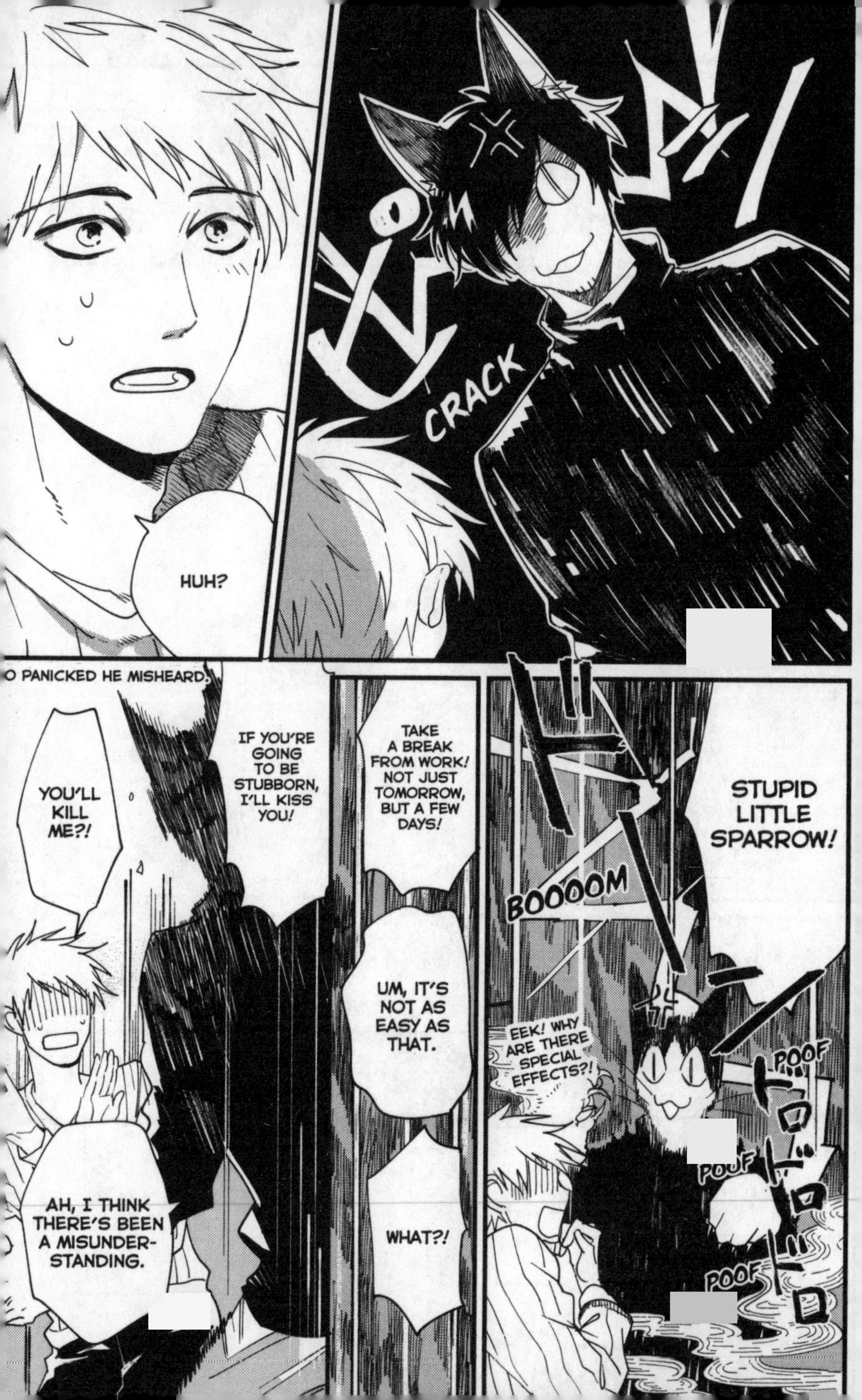
CRACK
HUH?
STUPID LITTLE SPARROW!
BOOOOM
EEK! WHY ARE THERE SPECIAL EFFECTS?!
POOF
POOF
POOF
TAKE A BREAK FROM WORK! NOT JUST TOMORROW, BUT A FEW DAYS!
UM, IT'S NOT AS EASY AS THAT.
WHAT?!
IF YOU'RE GOING TO BE STUBBORN, I'LL KISS YOU!
O PANICKED HE MISHEARD.
YOU'LL KILL ME?!
AH, I THINK THERE'S BEEN A MISUNDERSTANDING.

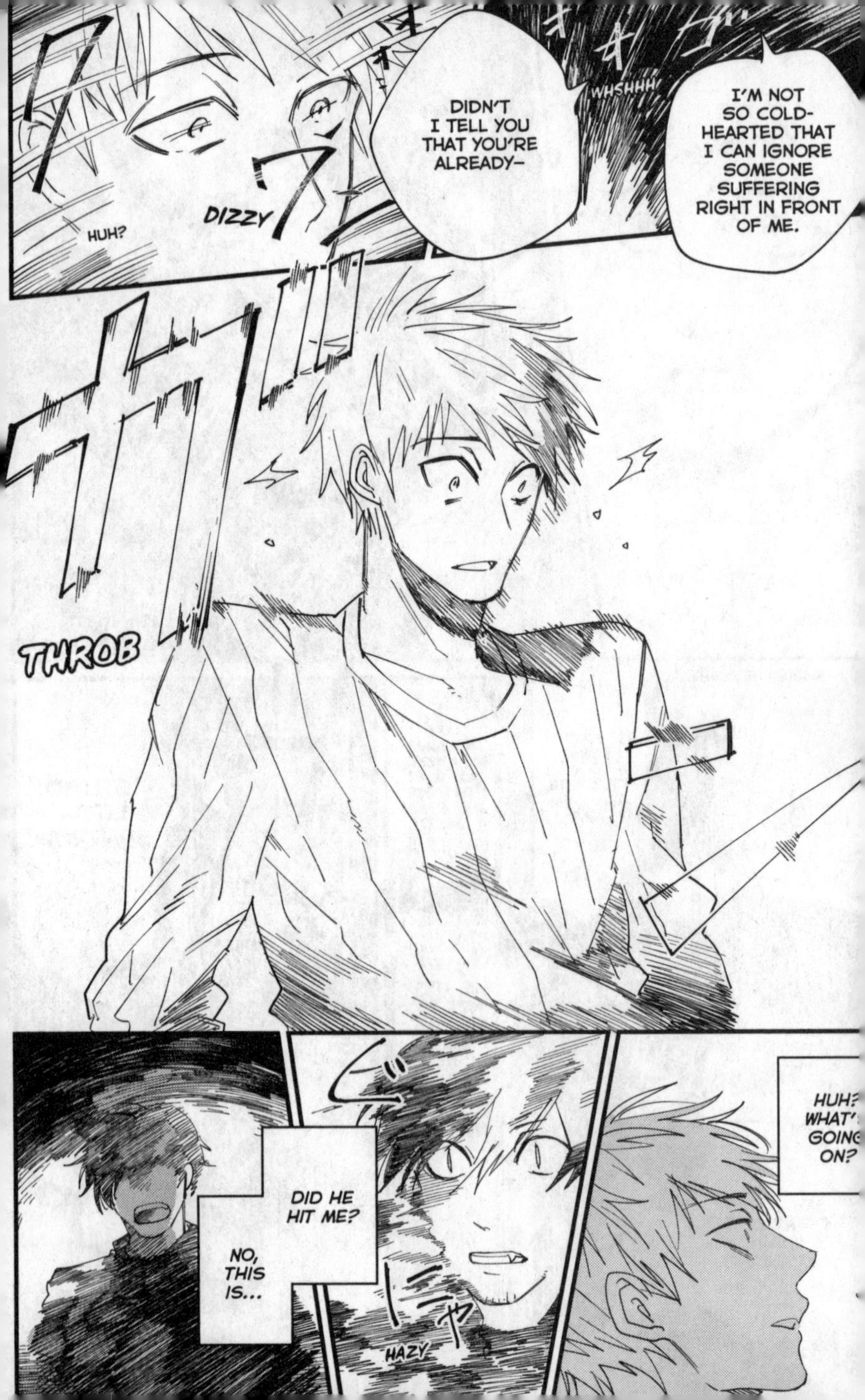
WHSHHH
I'M NOT SO COLD-HEARTED THAT I CAN IGNORE SOMEONE SUFFERING RIGHT IN FRONT OF ME.
DIDN'T I TELL YOU THAT YOU'RE ALREADY–
DIZZY
HUH?
THROB
HUH? WHAT'
GOING ON?
DID HE HIT ME?
NO, THIS IS...
HAZY

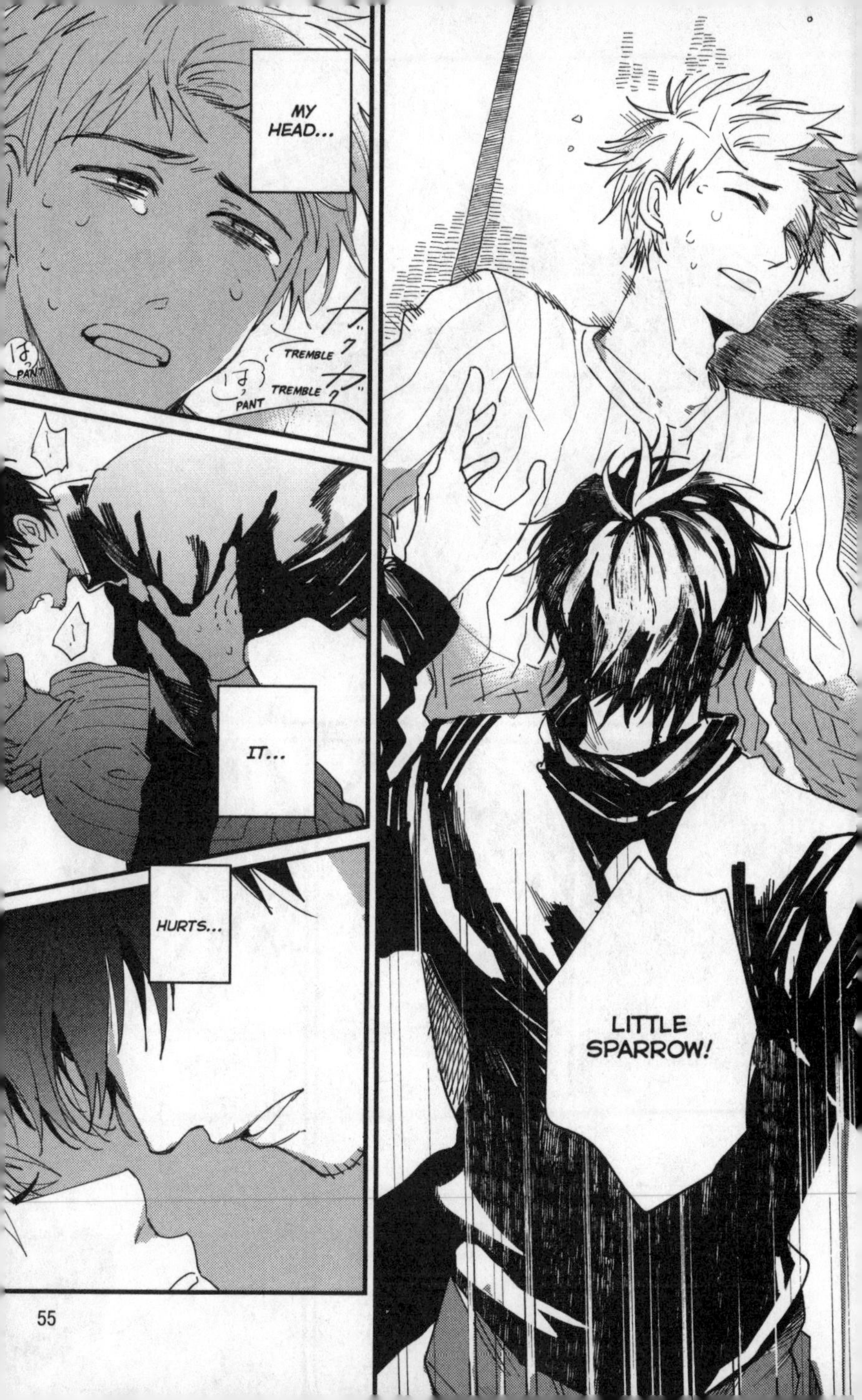
LITTLE SPARROW!
MY HEAD...
TREMBLE
TREMBLE
PANT
PANT
IT...
HURTS...

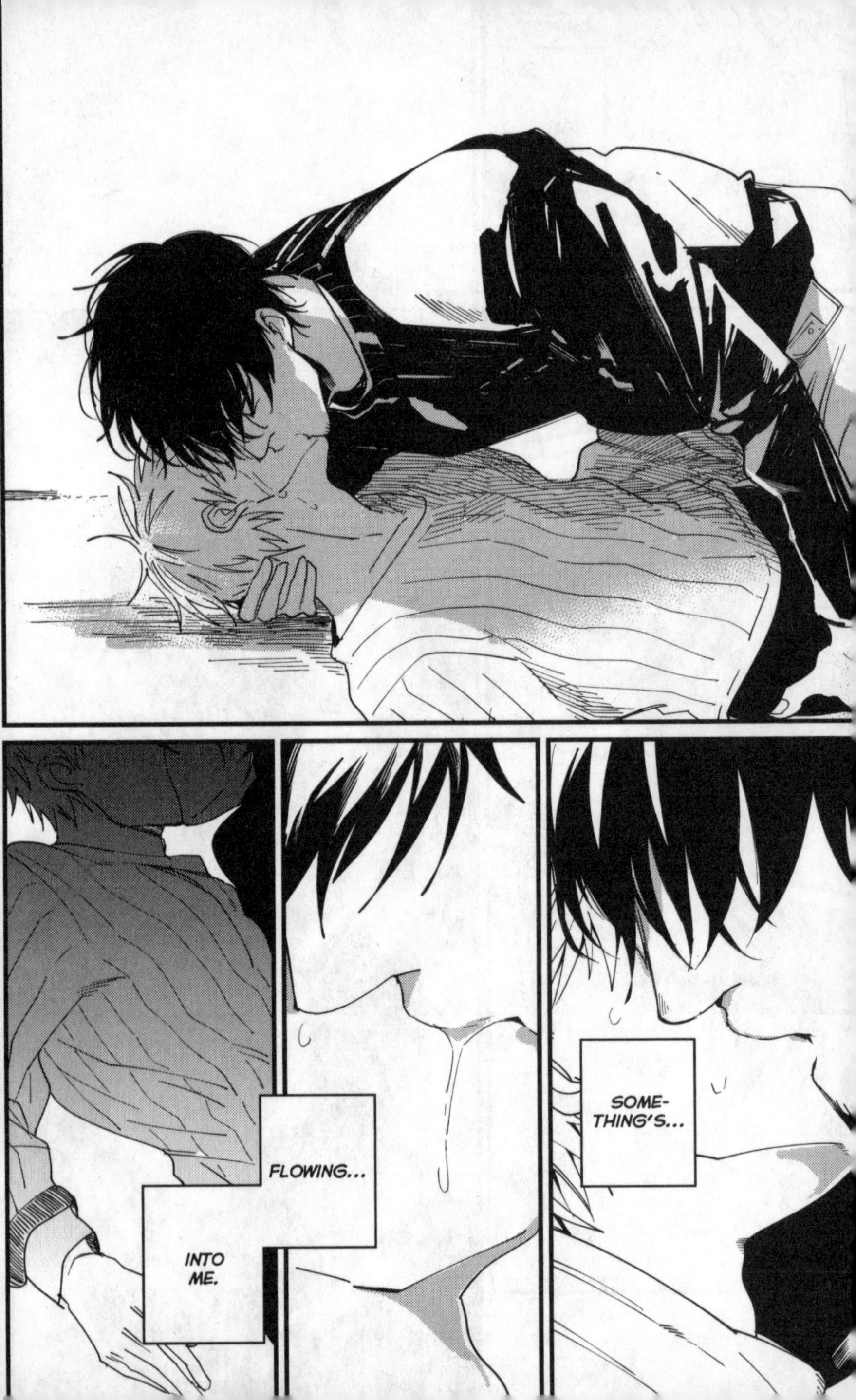
SOME-THING'S...
FLOWING...
INTO ME.

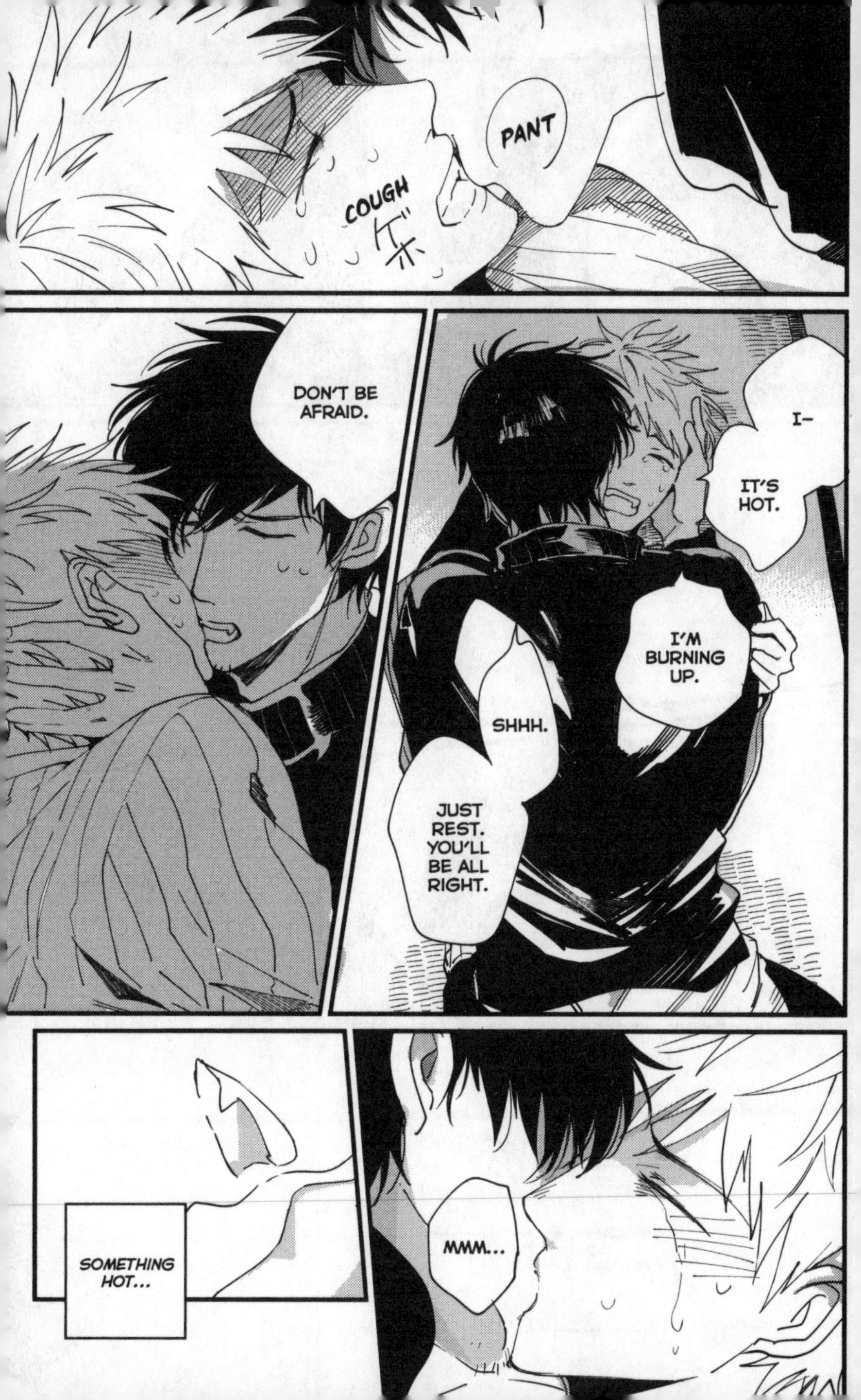
PANT
COUGH
ゲホ
I–
IT'S HOT.
I'M BURNING UP.
SHHH.
JUST REST. YOU'LL BE ALL RIGHT.
DON'T BE AFRAID.
MMM...
SOMETHING HOT...

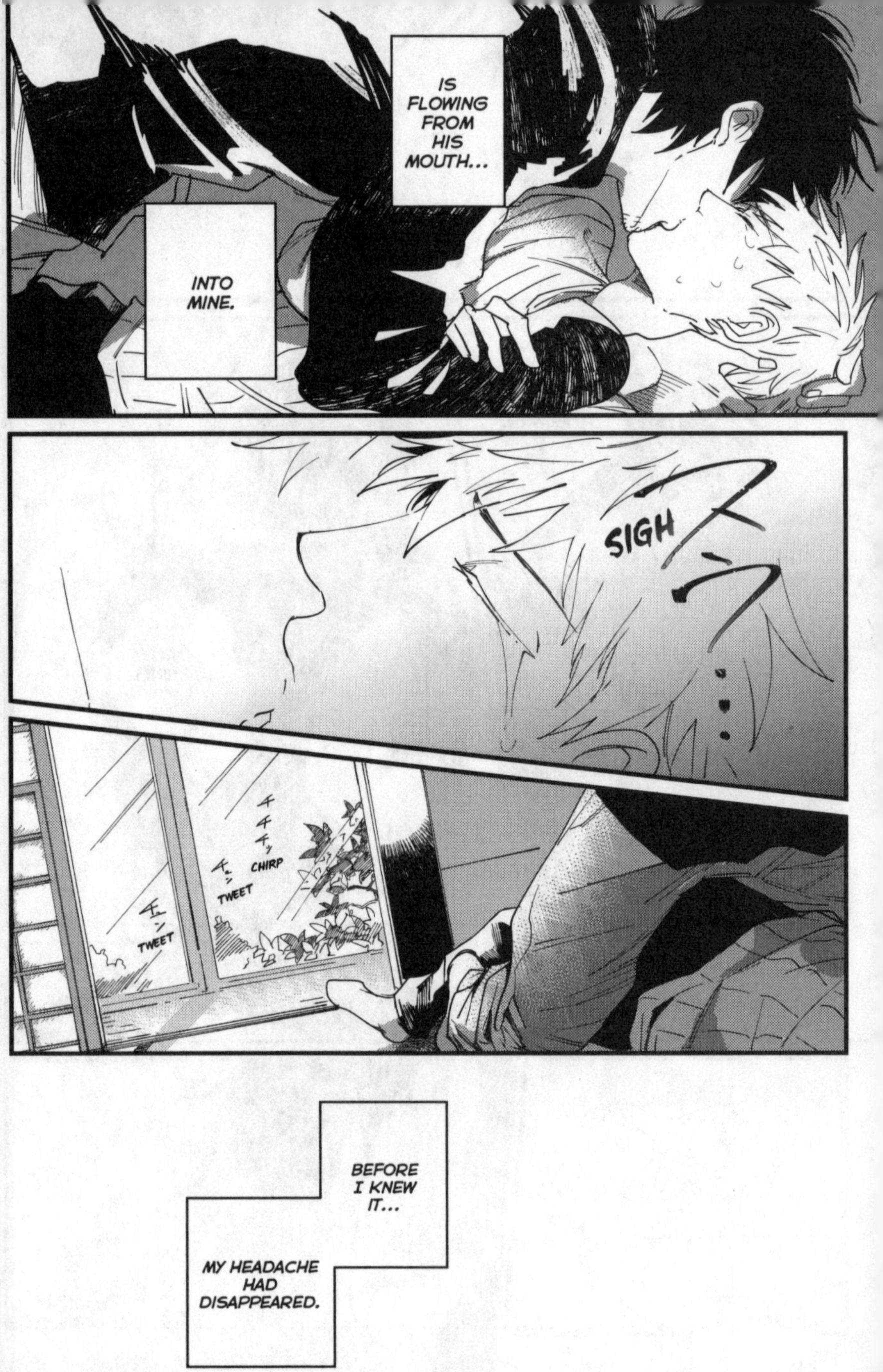
IS FLOWING FROM HIS MOUTH...
INTO MINE.
SIGH
CHIRP
TWEET
TWEET
BEFORE I KNEW IT...
MY HEADACHE HAD DISAPPEARED.

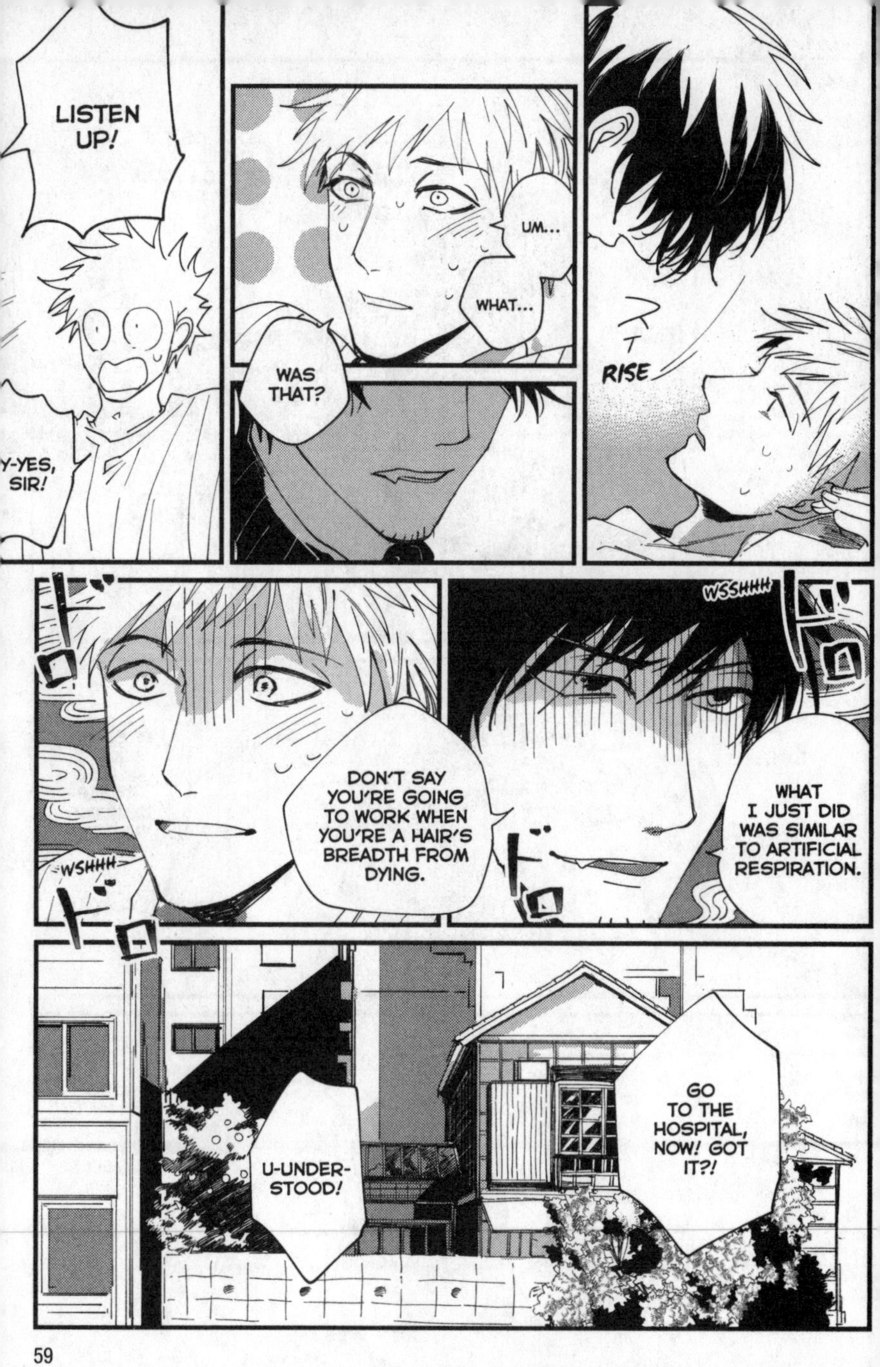
RISE
UM... WHAT...
WAS THAT?
LISTEN UP!
Y-YES, SIR!
WSSHHH
WHAT I JUST DID WAS SIMILAR TO ARTIFICIAL RESPIRATION.
DON'T SAY YOU'RE GOING TO WORK WHEN YOU'RE A HAIR'S BREADTH FROM DYING.
WSHHH
GO TO THE HOSPITAL, NOW! GOT IT?!
U-UNDER-STOOD!

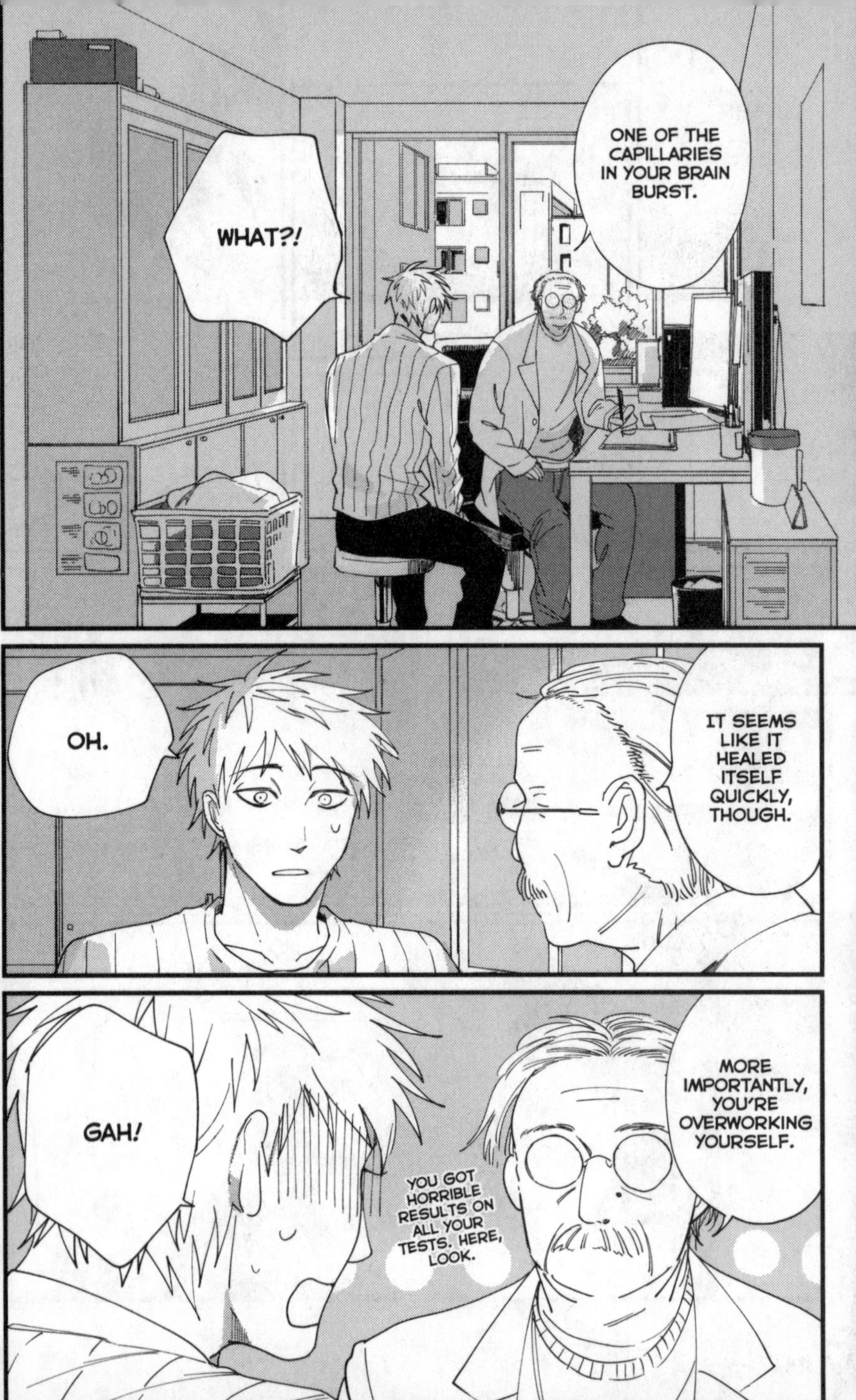
ONE OF THE CAPILLARIES IN YOUR BRAIN BURST.
WHAT?!
IT SEEMS LIKE IT HEALED ITSELF QUICKLY, THOUGH.
OH.
MORE IMPORTANTLY, YOU'RE OVERWORKING YOURSELF.
YOU GOT HORRIBLE RESULTS ON ALL YOUR TESTS. HERE, LOOK.
GAH!

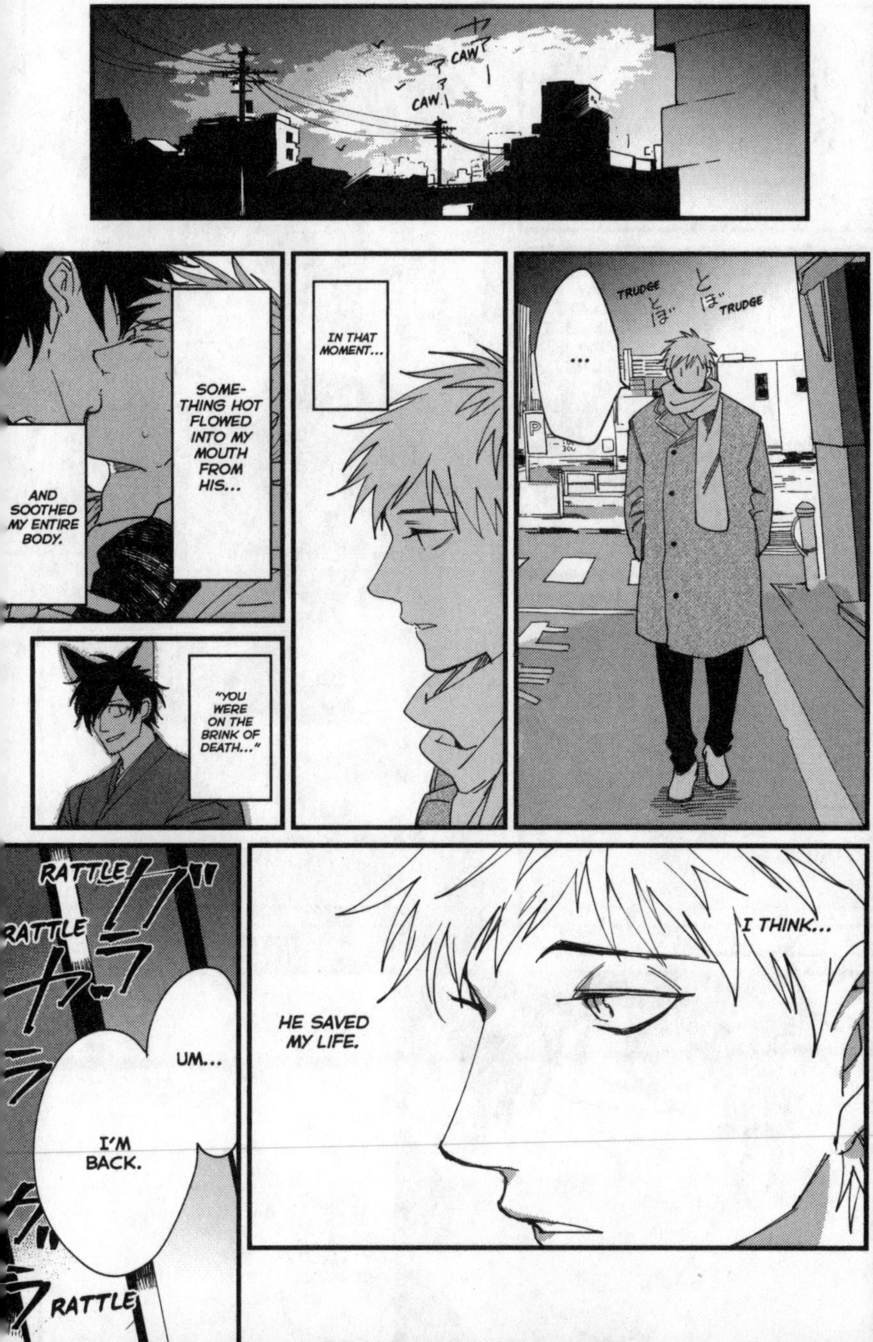
CAW
CAW
TRUDGE
TRUDGE
...
IN THAT MOMENT...
SOME-THING HOT FLOWED INTO MY MOUTH FROM HIS...
AND SOOTHED MY ENTIRE BODY.
"YOU WERE ON THE BRINK OF DEATH..."
I THINK...
HE SAVED MY LIFE.
RATTLE
RATTLE
UM...
I'M BACK.
RATTLE

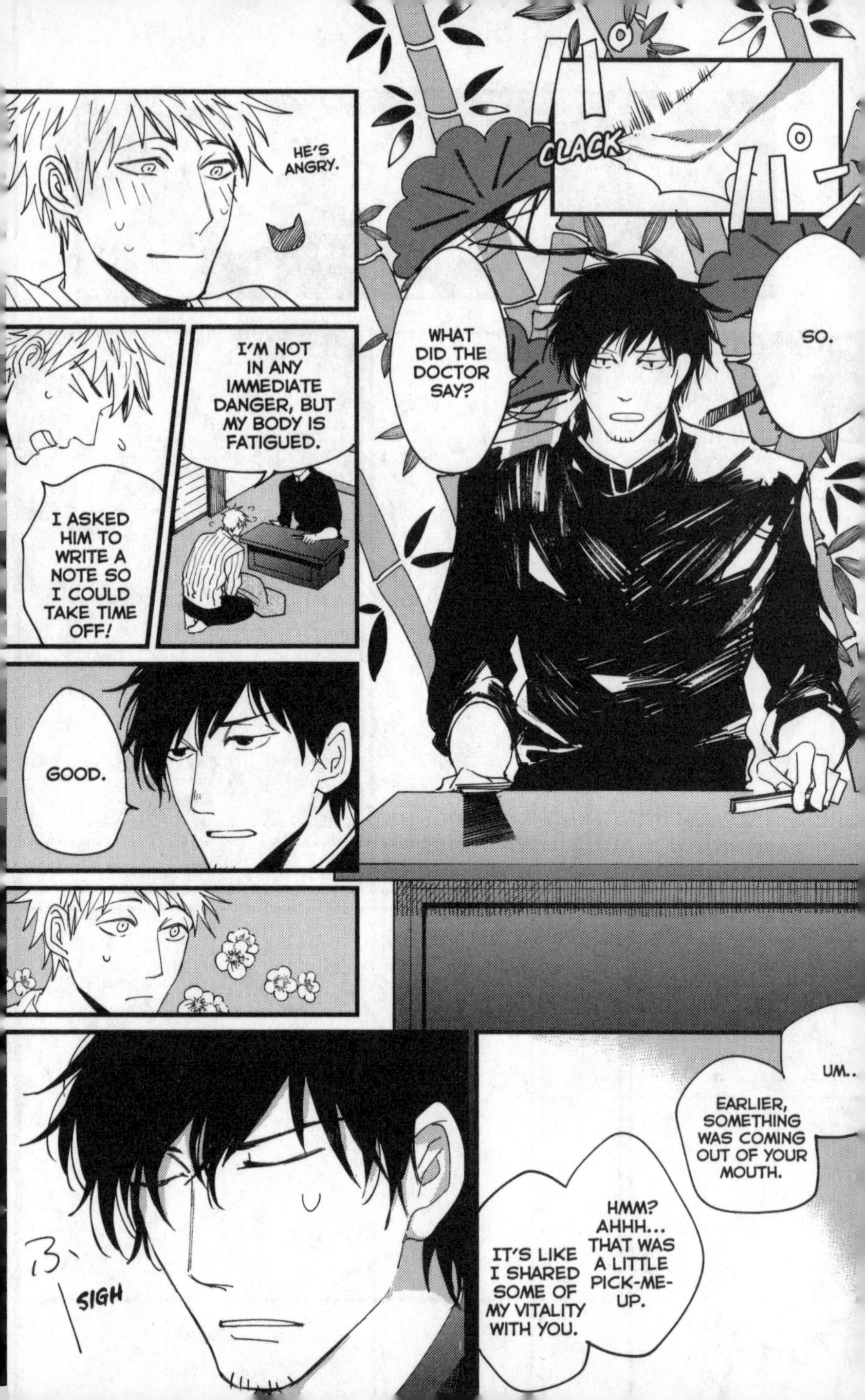
CLACK
SO.
WHAT DID THE DOCTOR SAY?
HE'S ANGRY.
I'M NOT IN ANY IMMEDIATE DANGER, BUT MY BODY IS FATIGUED.
I ASKED HIM TO WRITE A NOTE SO I COULD TAKE TIME OFF!
GOOD.
UM..
EARLIER, SOMETHING WAS COMING OUT OF YOUR MOUTH.
HMM? AHHH... THAT WAS A LITTLE PICK-ME-UP.
IT'S LIKE I SHARED SOME OF MY VITALITY WITH YOU.
SIGH

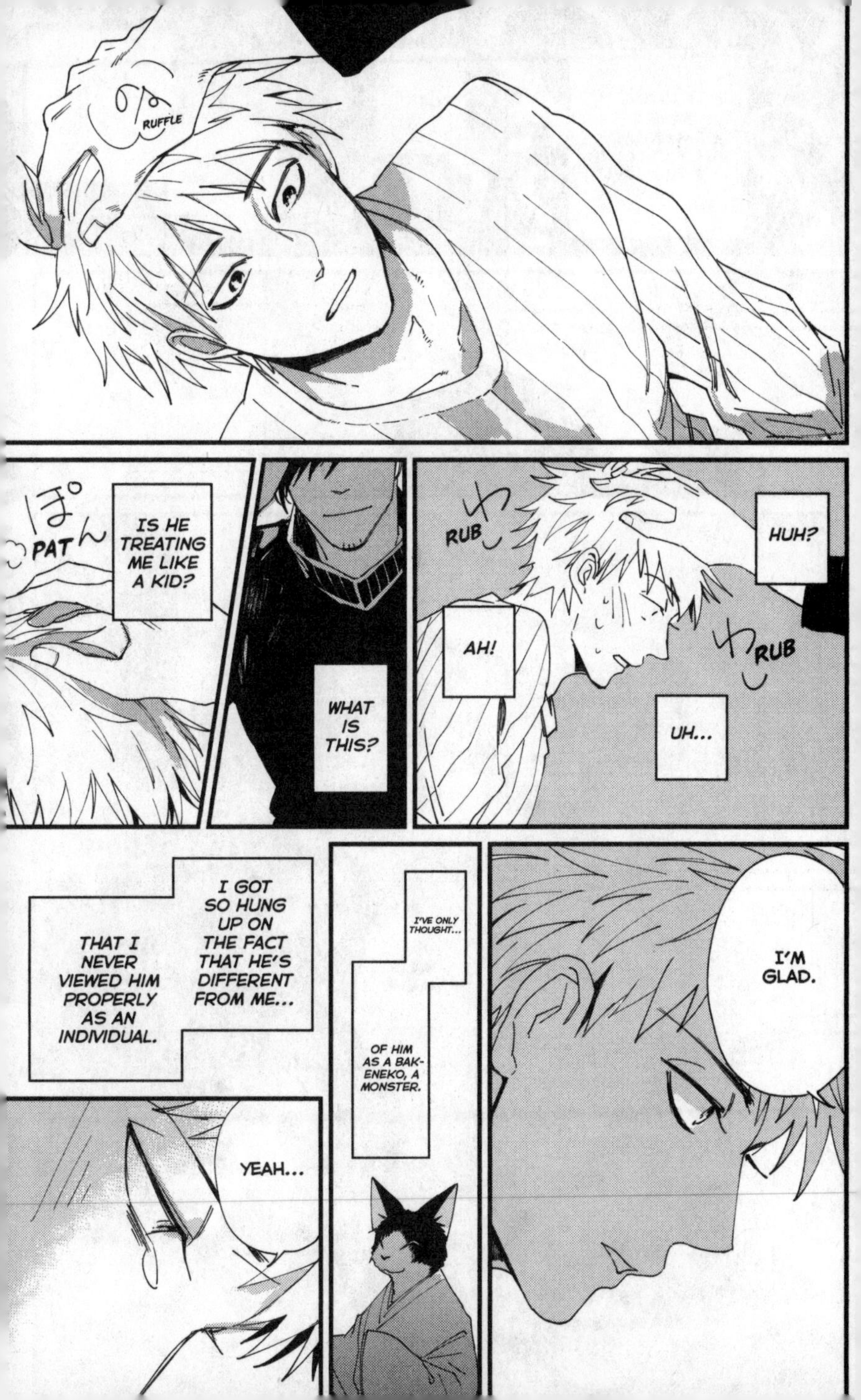

RUFFLE
HUH?
RUB
AH!
RUB
UH...
WHAT IS THIS?
ぽん
PAT
IS HE TREATING ME LIKE A KID?
I'M GLAD.
I'VE ONLY THOUGHT...
OF HIM AS A BAKE-NEKO, A MONSTER.
I GOT SO HUNG UP ON THE FACT THAT HE'S DIFFERENT FROM ME...
THAT I NEVER VIEWED HIM PROPERLY AS AN INDIVIDUAL.
YEAH...

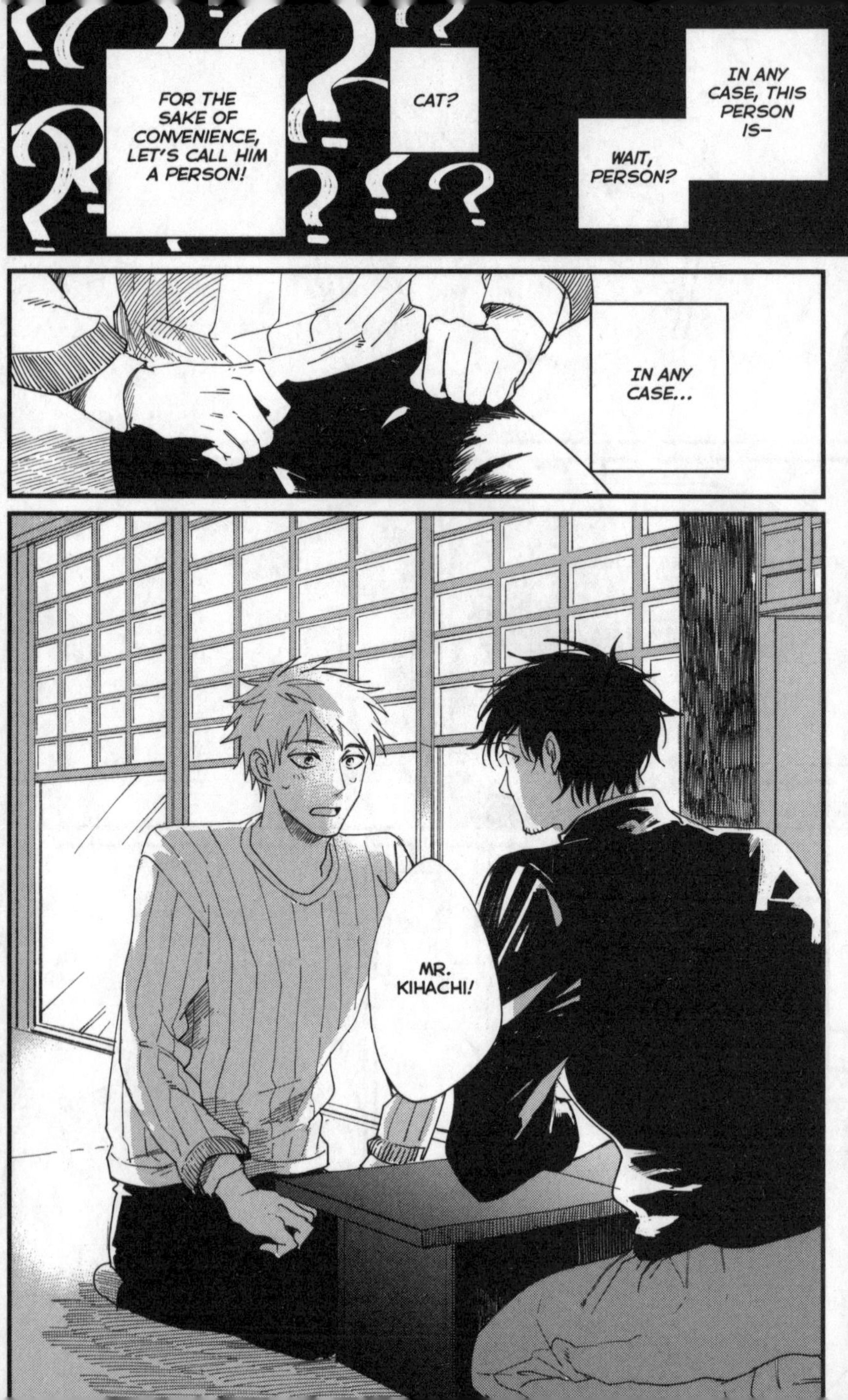
IN ANY CASE, THIS PERSON IS—
WAIT, PERSON?
CAT?
FOR THE SAKE OF CONVENIENCE, LET'S CALL HIM A PERSON!
IN ANY CASE...
MR. KIHACHI!

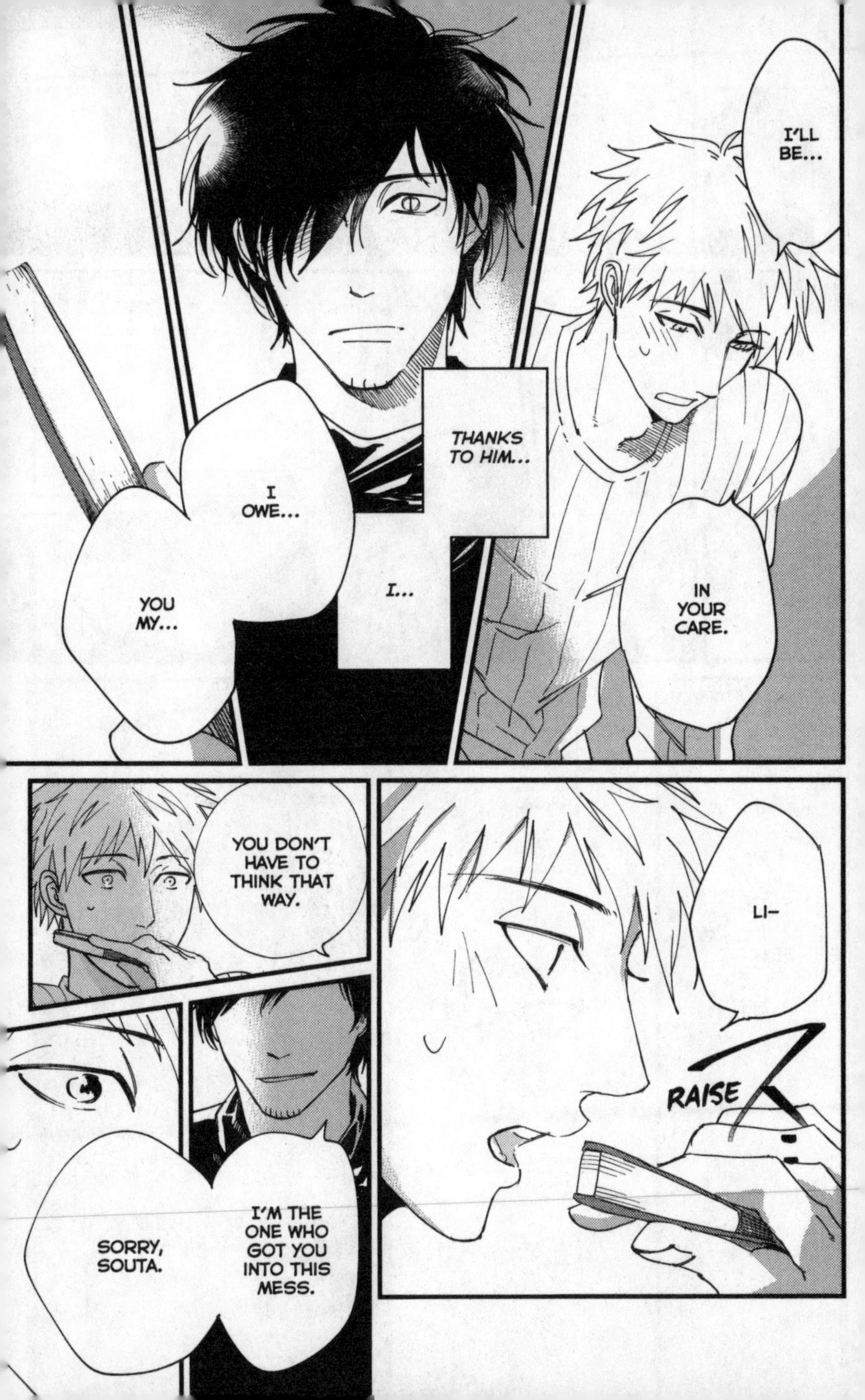
I'LL BE...
IN YOUR CARE.
THANKS TO HIM...
I...
I OWE...
YOU MY...
LI–
RAISE
YOU DON'T HAVE TO THINK THAT WAY.
I'M THE ONE WHO GOT YOU INTO THIS MESS.
SORRY, SOUTA.

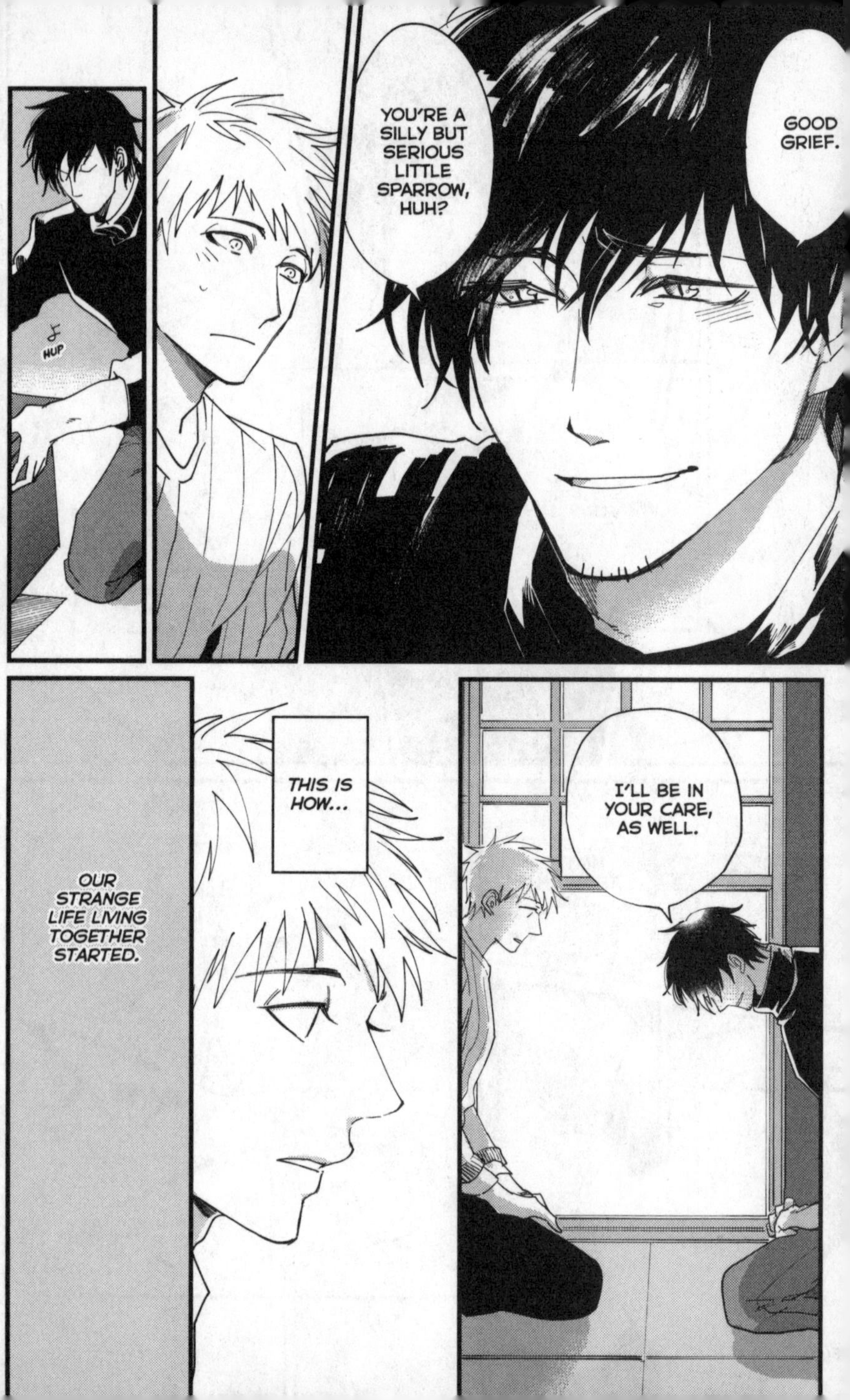
GOOD GRIEF.
YOU'RE A SILLY BUT SERIOUS LITTLE SPARROW, HUH?
HUP
I'LL BE IN YOUR CARE, AS WELL.
THIS IS HOW...
OUR STRANGE LIFE LIVING TOGETHER STARTED.

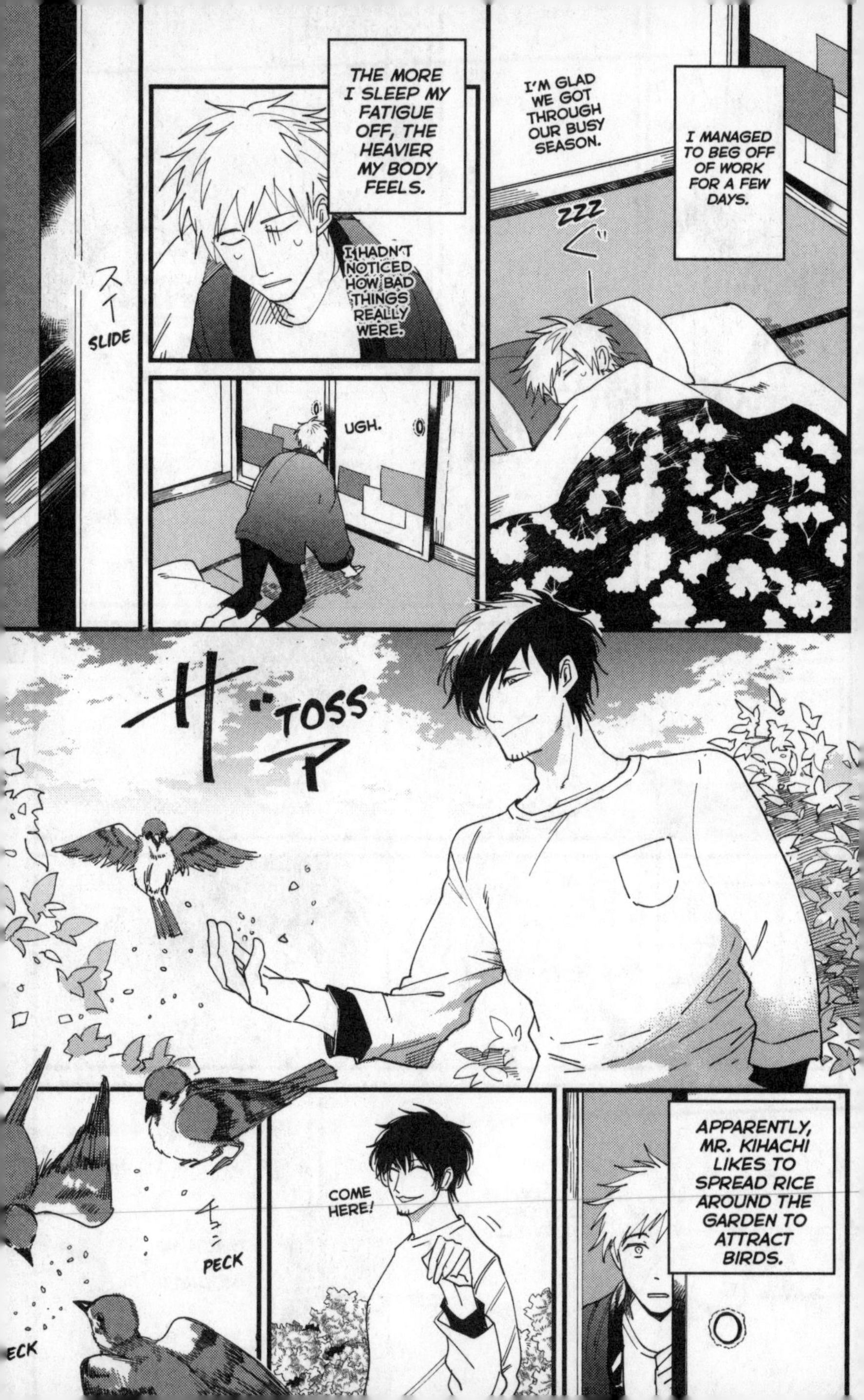
I MANAGED TO BEG OFF OF WORK FOR A FEW DAYS.
I'M GLAD WE GOT THROUGH OUR BUSY SEASON.
ZZZ
THE MORE I SLEEP MY FATIGUE OFF, THE HEAVIER MY BODY FEELS.
I HADN'T NOTICED HOW BAD THINGS REALLY WERE.
UGH.
SLIDE
TOSS
APPARENTLY, MR. KIHACHI LIKES TO SPREAD RICE AROUND THE GARDEN TO ATTRACT BIRDS.
COME HERE!
PECK
ECK

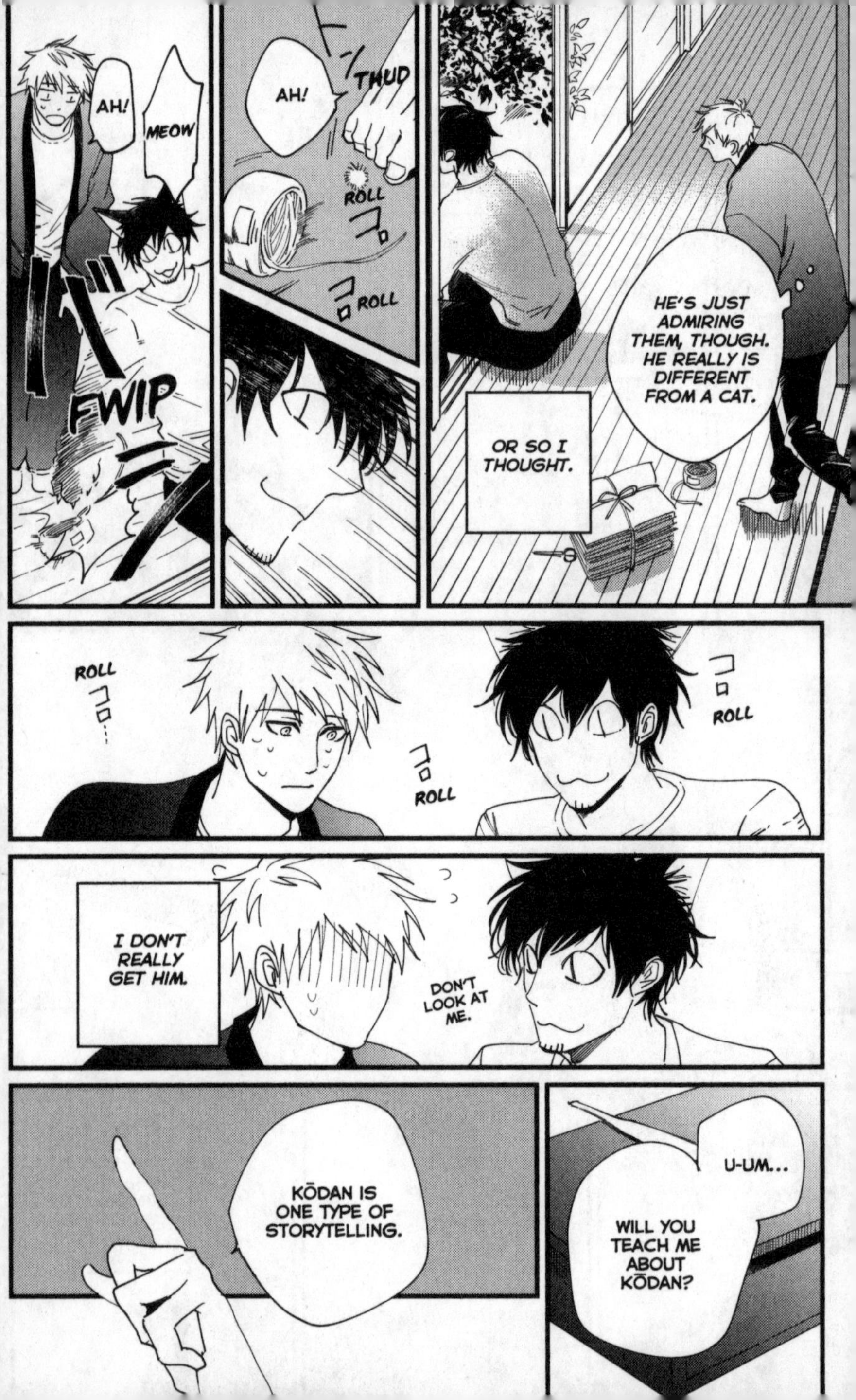

HE'S JUST ADMIRING THEM, THOUGH. HE REALLY IS DIFFERENT FROM A CAT.
OR SO I THOUGHT.
AH!
THUD
ROLL
コロ
コロ
ROLL
MEOW
AH!
FWIP
コロ
ROLL
コロ
ROLL
ROLL
コロ…
DON'T LOOK AT ME.
I DON'T REALLY GET HIM.
U-UM...
WILL YOU TEACH ME ABOUT KŌDAN?
KŌDAN IS ONE TYPE OF STORYTELLING.

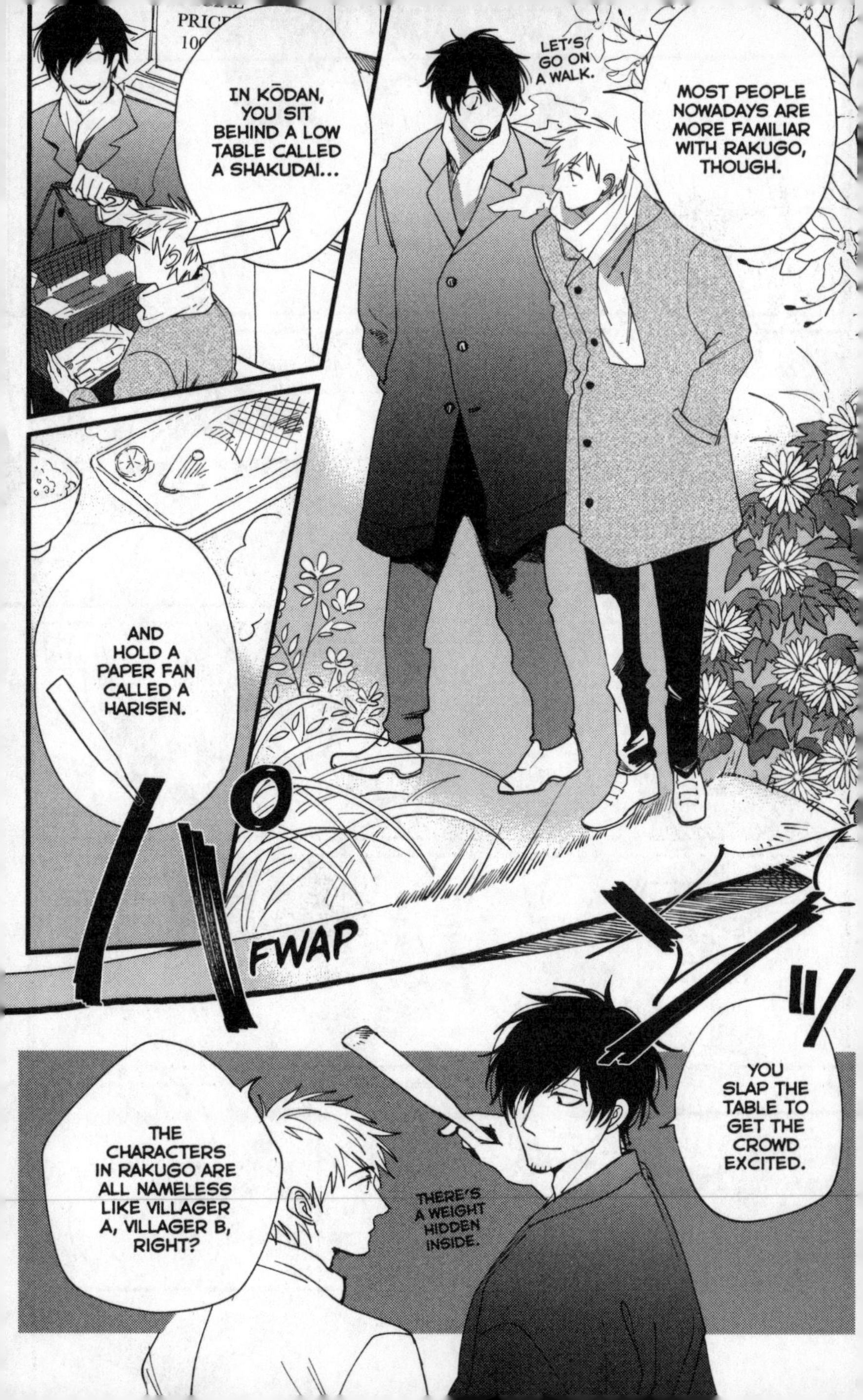
LET'S GO ON A WALK.
MOST PEOPLE NOWADAYS ARE MORE FAMILIAR WITH RAKUGO, THOUGH.
IN KŌDAN, YOU SIT BEHIND A LOW TABLE CALLED A SHAKUDAI...
AND HOLD A PAPER FAN CALLED A HARISEN.
FWAP
YOU SLAP THE TABLE TO GET THE CROWD EXCITED.
THERE'S A WEIGHT HIDDEN INSIDE.
THE CHARACTERS IN RAKUGO ARE ALL NAMELESS LIKE VILLAGER A, VILLAGER B, RIGHT?

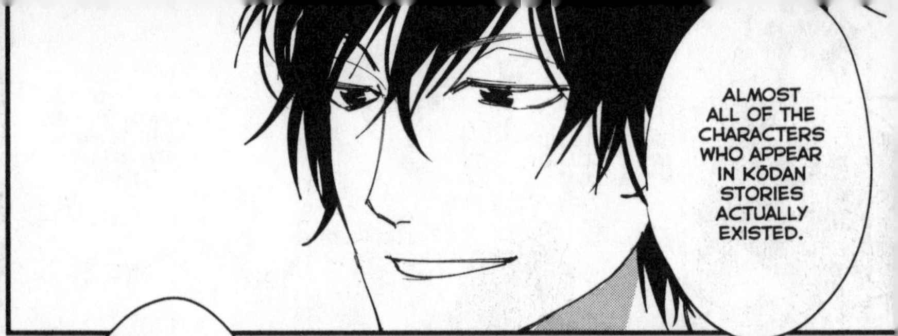
ALMOST ALL OF THE CHARACTERS WHO APPEAR IN KŌDAN STORIES ACTUALLY EXISTED.

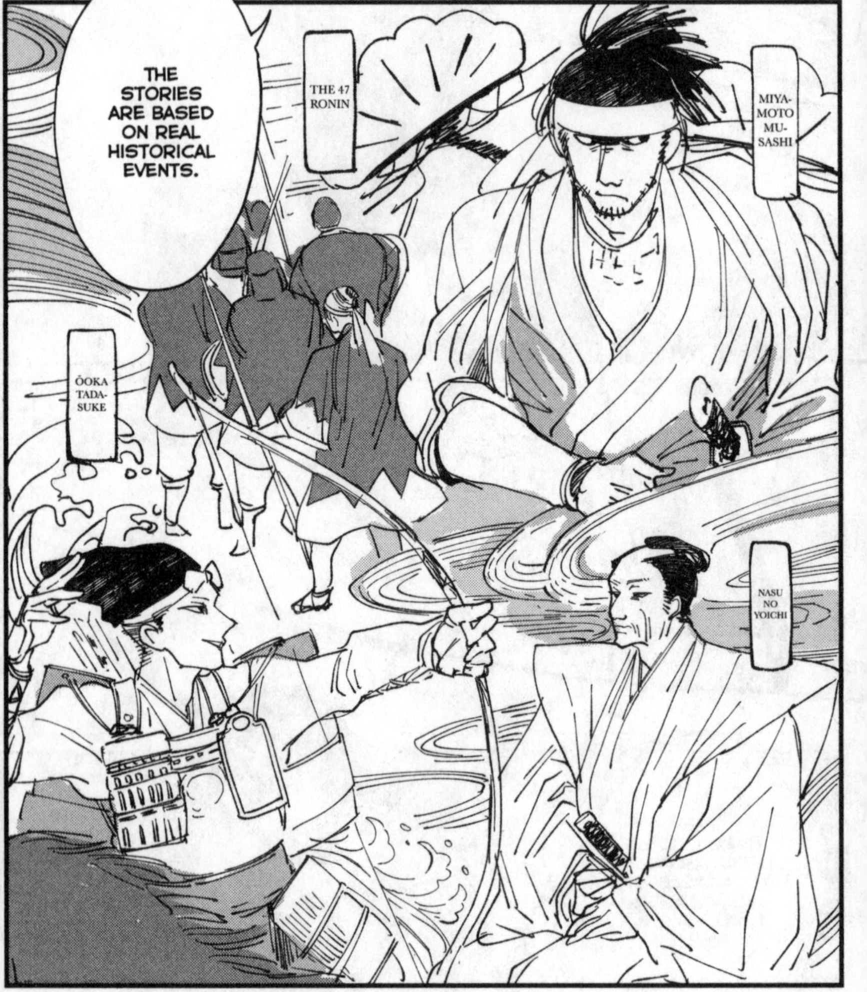
MIYAMOTO MUSASHI
THE 47 RONIN
THE STORIES ARE BASED ON REAL HISTORICAL EVENTS.
NASU NO YOICHI
ŌOKA TADASUKE

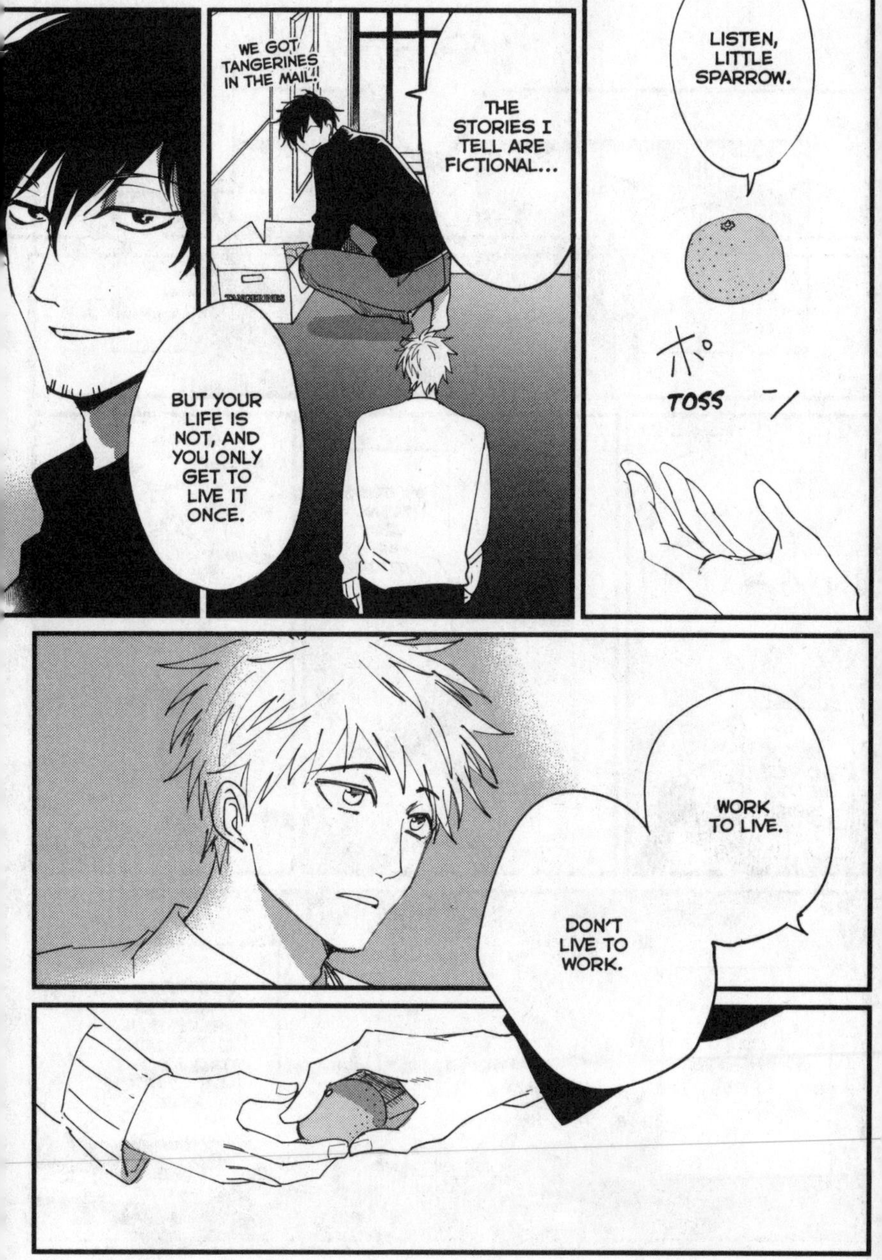
LISTEN, LITTLE SPARROW.
TOSS
WE GOT TANGERINES IN THE MAIL
THE STORIES I TELL ARE FICTIONAL...
BUT YOUR LIFE IS NOT, AND YOU ONLY GET TO LIVE IT ONCE.
WORK TO LIVE.
DON'T LIVE TO WORK.

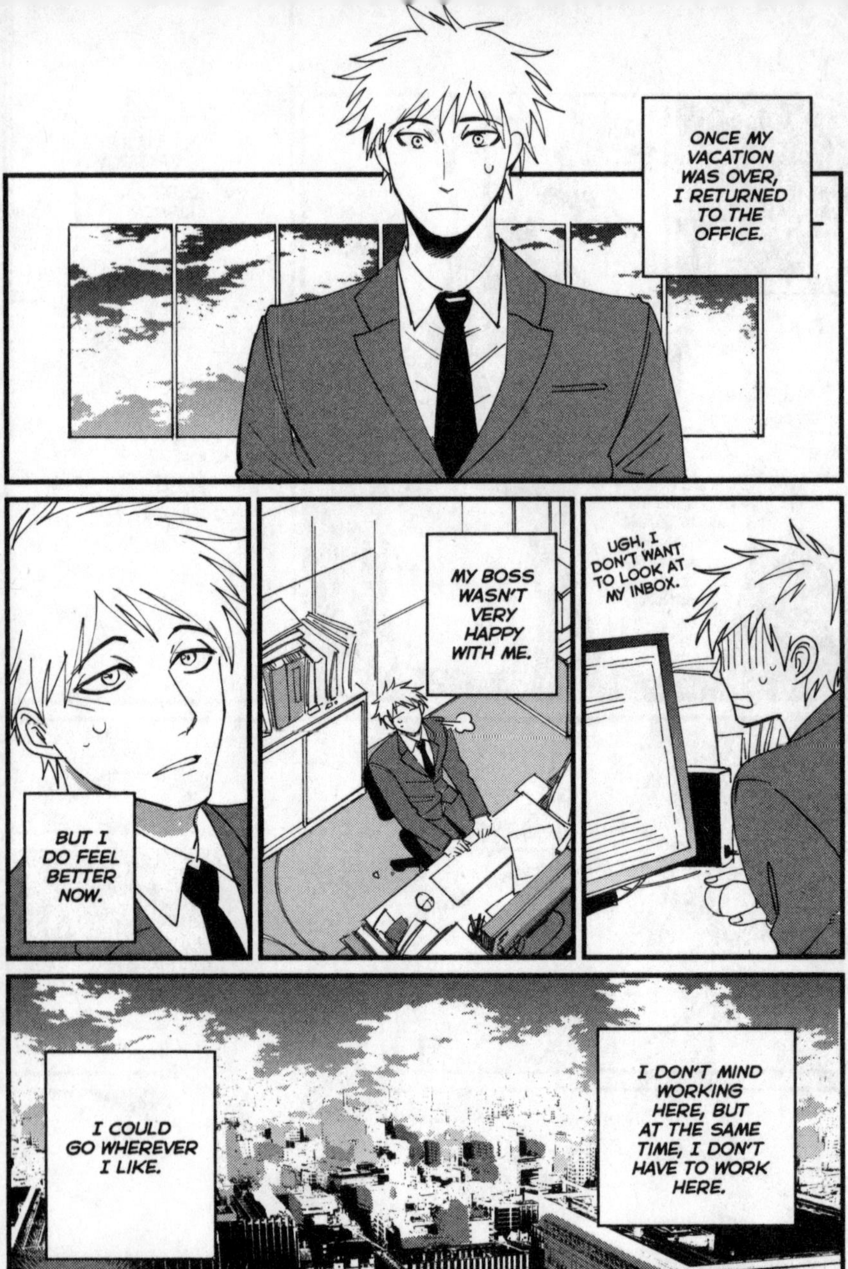
ONCE MY VACATION WAS OVER, I RETURNED TO THE OFFICE.
UGH, I DON'T WANT TO LOOK AT MY INBOX.
MY BOSS WASN'T VERY HAPPY WITH ME.
BUT I DO FEEL BETTER NOW.
I DON'T MIND WORKING HERE, BUT AT THE SAME TIME, I DON'T HAVE TO WORK HERE.
I COULD GO WHEREVER I LIKE.

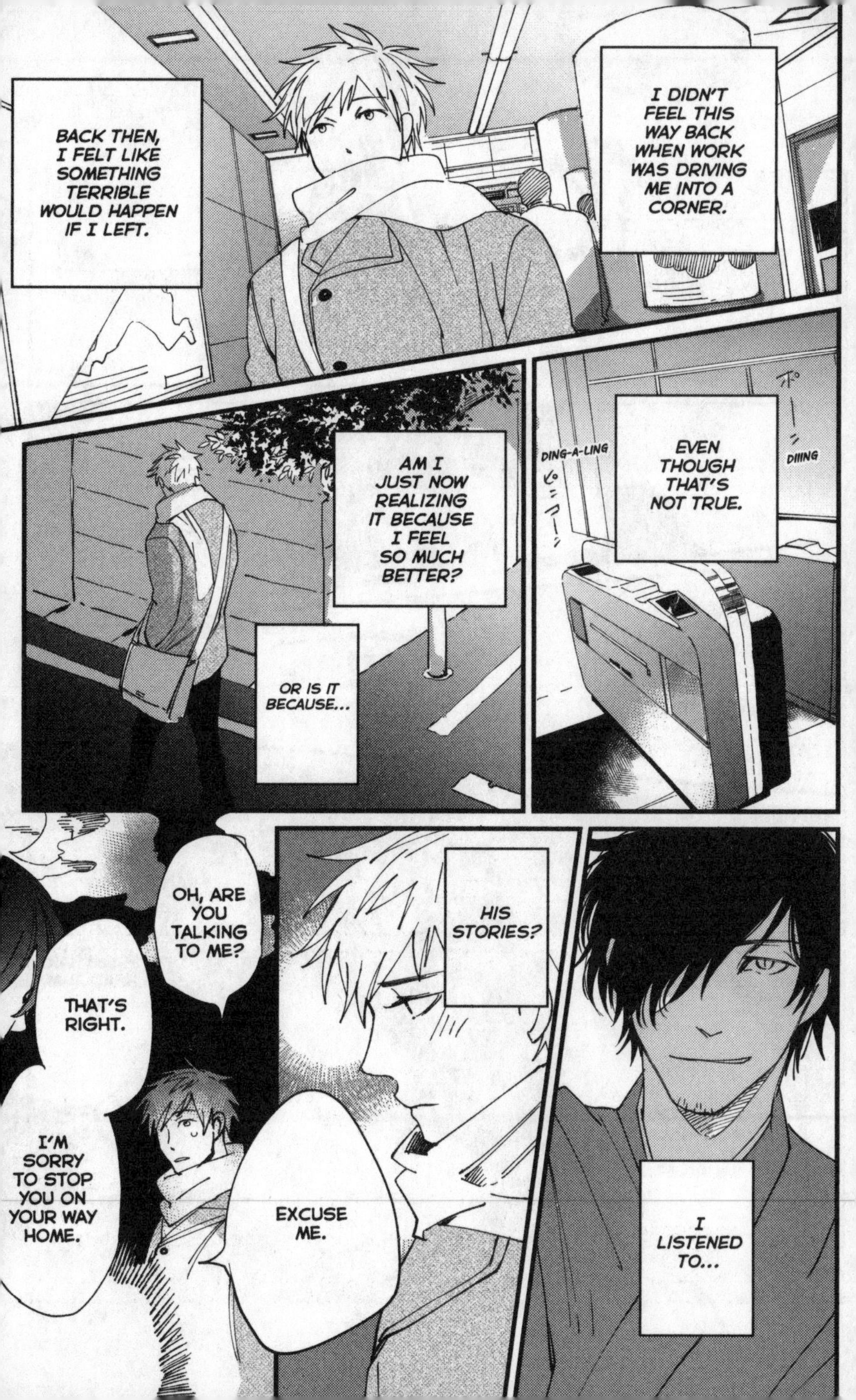
I DIDN'T FEEL THIS WAY BACK WHEN WORK WAS DRIVING ME INTO A CORNER.
BACK THEN, I FELT LIKE SOMETHING TERRIBLE WOULD HAPPEN IF I LEFT.
DIIING
EVEN THOUGH THAT'S NOT TRUE.
DING-A-LING
AM I JUST NOW REALIZING IT BECAUSE I FEEL SO MUCH BETTER?
OR IS IT BECAUSE...
I LISTENED TO...
HIS STORIES?
EXCUSE ME.
OH, ARE YOU TALKING TO ME?
THAT'S RIGHT.
I'M SORRY TO STOP YOU ON YOUR WAY HOME.

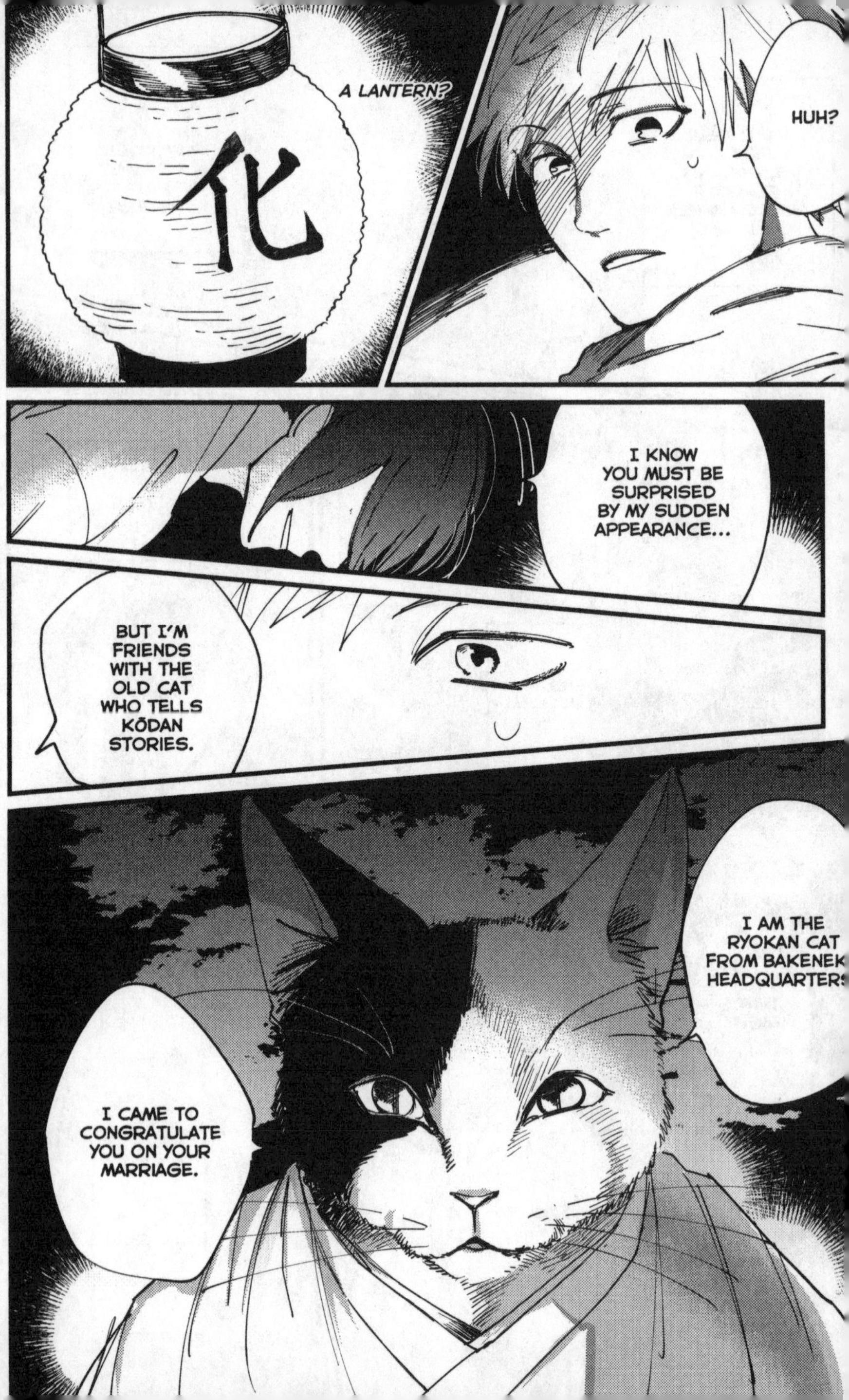
HUH?
A LANTERN?
化
I KNOW YOU MUST BE SURPRISED BY MY SUDDEN APPEARANCE...
BUT I'M FRIENDS WITH THE OLD CAT WHO TELLS KŌDAN STORIES.
I AM THE RYOKAN CAT FROM BAKENEK HEADQUARTER
I CAME TO CONGRATULATE YOU ON YOUR MARRIAGE.

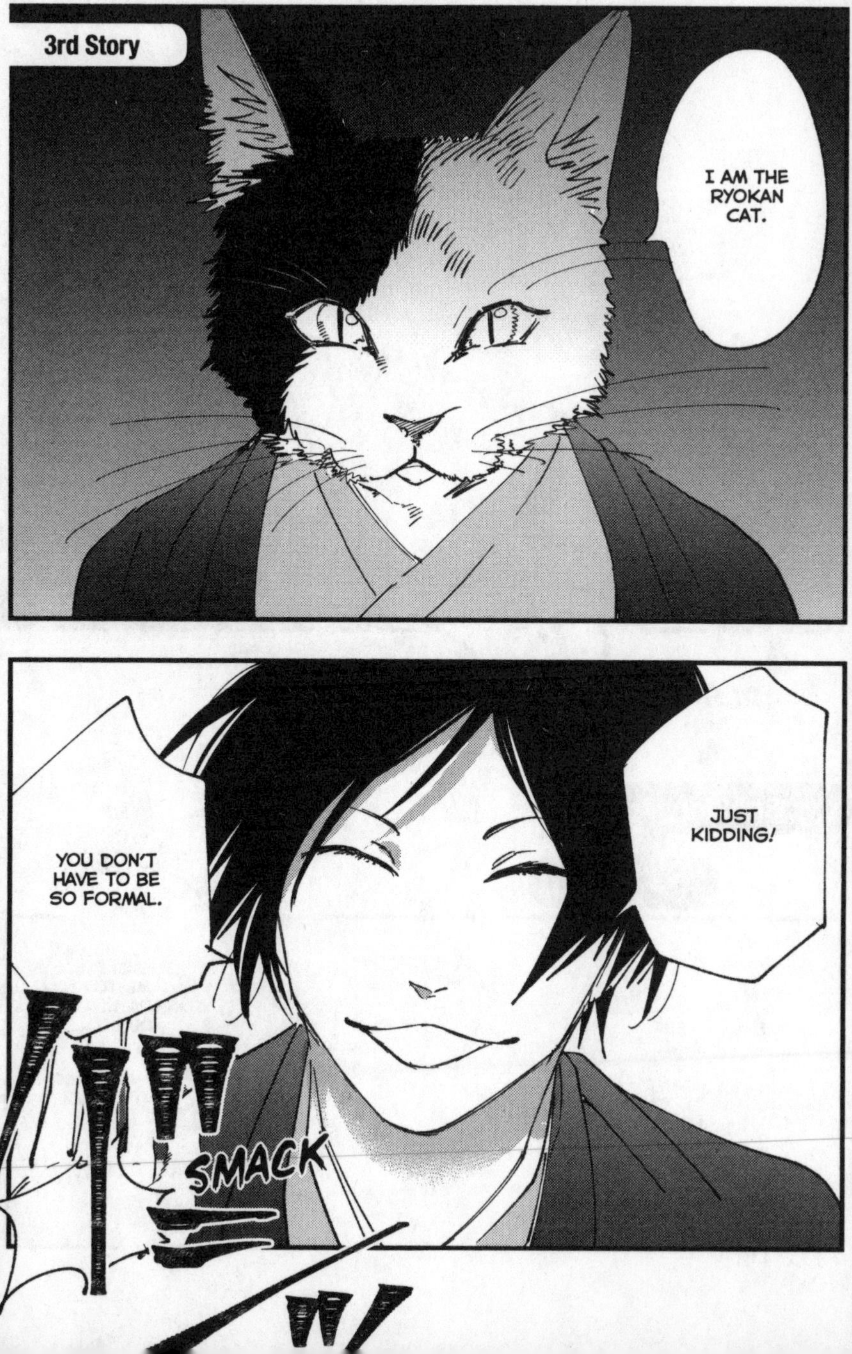
3rd Story
I AM THE RYOKAN CAT.
JUST KIDDING!
YOU DON'T HAVE TO BE SO FORMAL.
SMACK

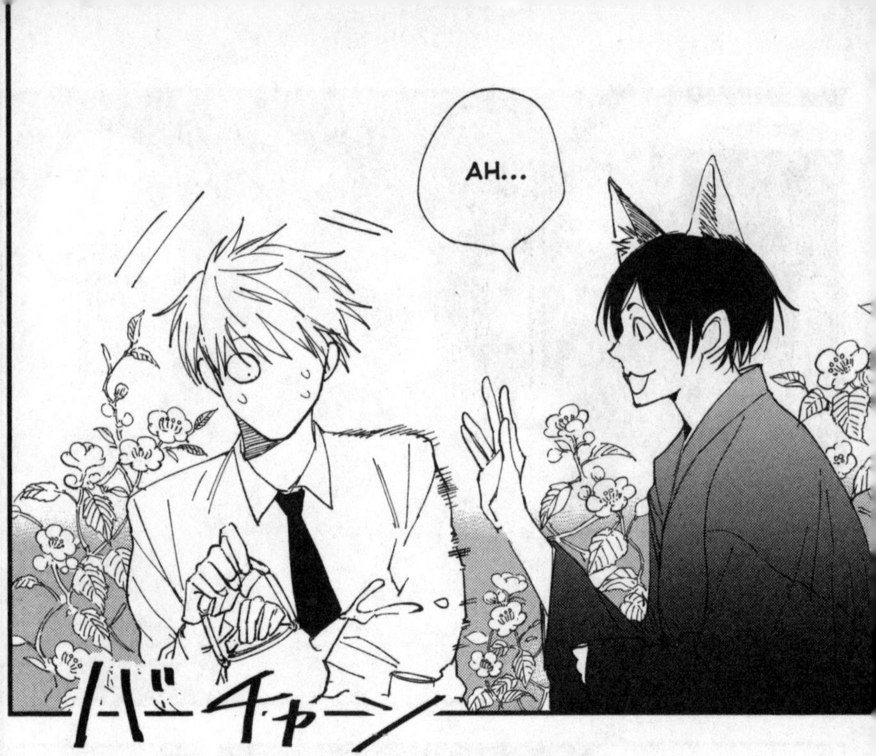
AH...
バチャーン
SPLASH

3rd Story

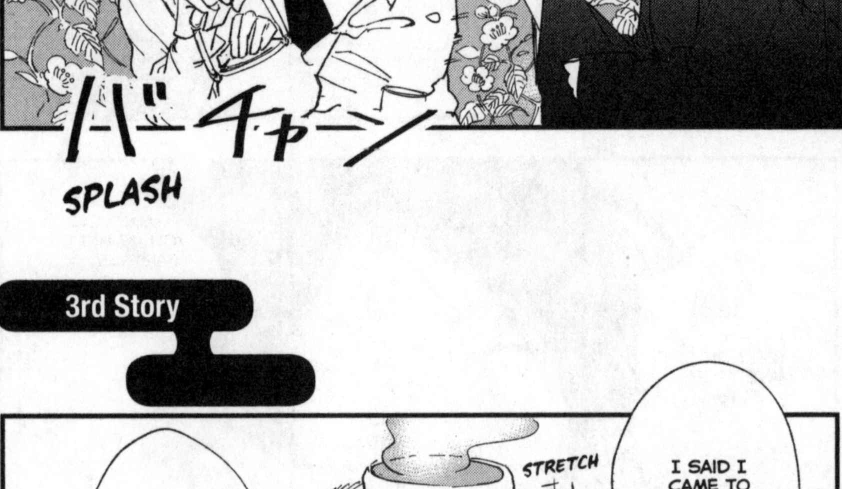
I SAID I CAME TO CONGRATULATE YOU...
STRETCH
むに
BUT REALLY, I JUST CAME TO SAY HELLO.

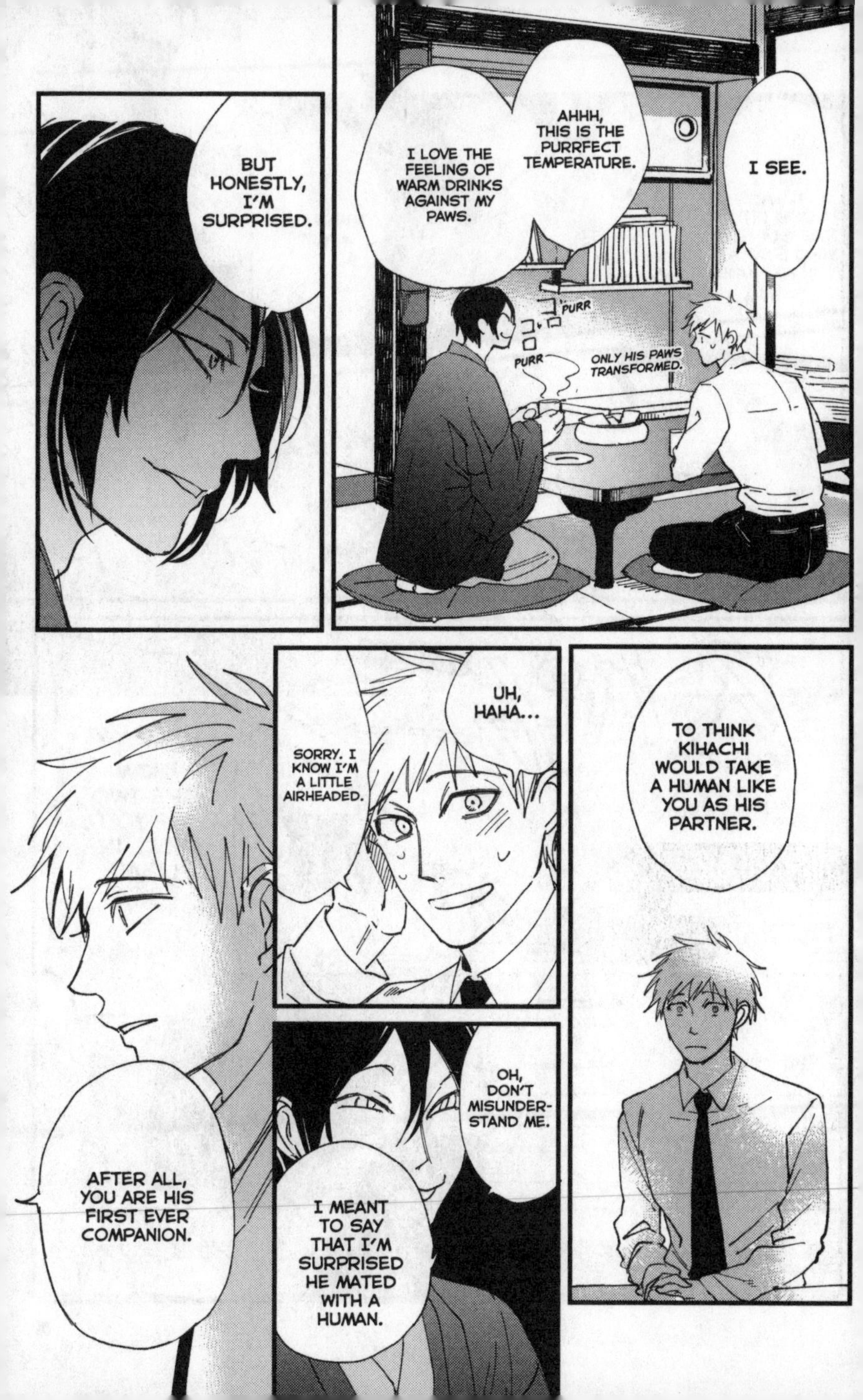
AHHH, THIS IS THE PURRFECT TEMPERATURE.
I LOVE THE FEELING OF WARM DRINKS AGAINST MY PAWS.
I SEE.
PURR
PURR
ONLY HIS PAWS TRANSFORMED.
BUT HONESTLY, I'M SURPRISED.
TO THINK KIHACHI WOULD TAKE A HUMAN LIKE YOU AS HIS PARTNER.
UH, HAHA...
SORRY. I KNOW I'M A LITTLE AIRHEADED.
OH, DON'T MISUNDER-STAND ME.
I MEANT TO SAY THAT I'M SURPRISED HE MATED WITH A HUMAN.
AFTER ALL, YOU ARE HIS FIRST EVER COMPANION.

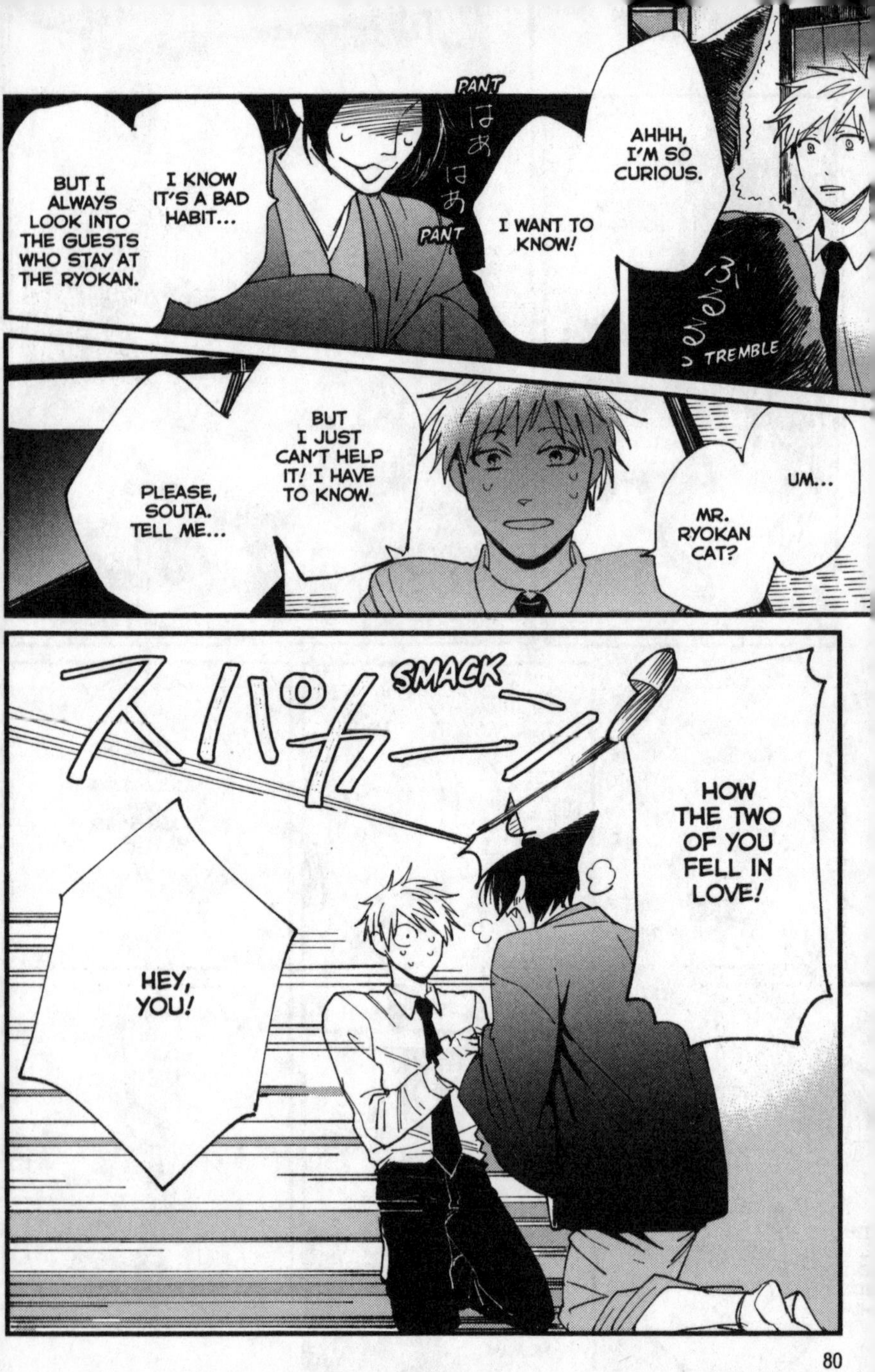

TREMBLE
AHHH, I'M SO CURIOUS.
I WANT TO KNOW!
PANT
はあはあ
PANT
I KNOW IT'S A BAD HABIT...
BUT I ALWAYS LOOK INTO THE GUESTS WHO STAY AT THE RYOKAN.
UM...
MR. RYOKAN CAT?
BUT I JUST CAN'T HELP IT! I HAVE TO KNOW.
PLEASE, SOUTA. TELL ME...
HOW THE TWO OF YOU FELL IN LOVE!
SMACK
スパーン
HEY, YOU!

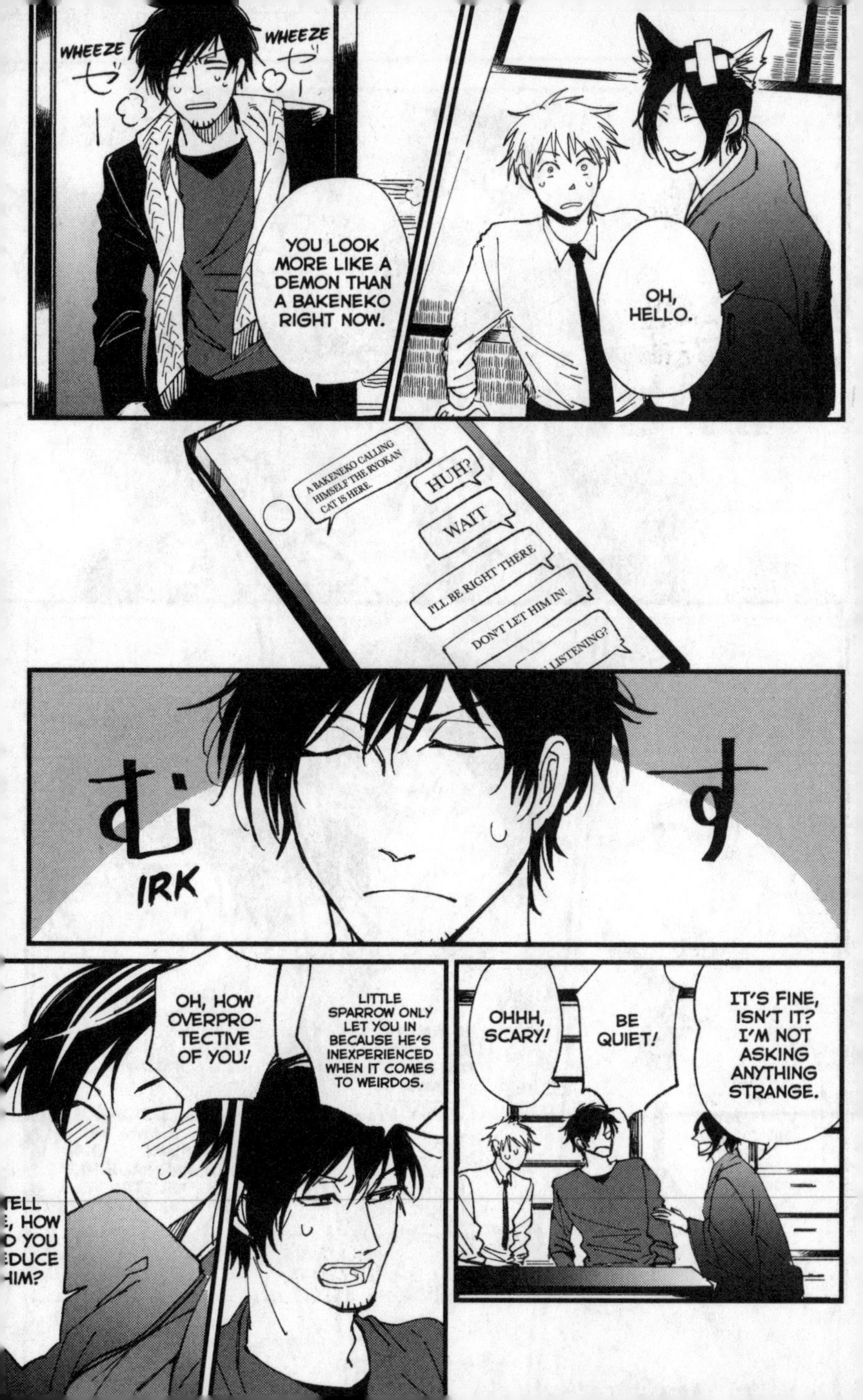
OH, HELLO.
WHEEZE
ゼ
WHEEZE
ゼ
YOU LOOK MORE LIKE A DEMON THAN A BAKENEKO RIGHT NOW.
A BAKENEKO CALLING HIMSELF THE RYOKAN CAT IS HERE.
HUH?
WAIT
I'LL BE RIGHT THERE
DON'T LET HIM IN!
LISTENING?
す
む
IRK
IT'S FINE, ISN'T IT? I'M NOT ASKING ANYTHING STRANGE.
BE QUIET!
OHHH, SCARY!
LITTLE SPARROW ONLY LET YOU IN BECAUSE HE'S INEXPERIENCED WHEN IT COMES TO WEIRDOS.
OH, HOW OVERPROTECTIVE OF YOU!
TELL E, HOW D YOU EDUCE HIM?

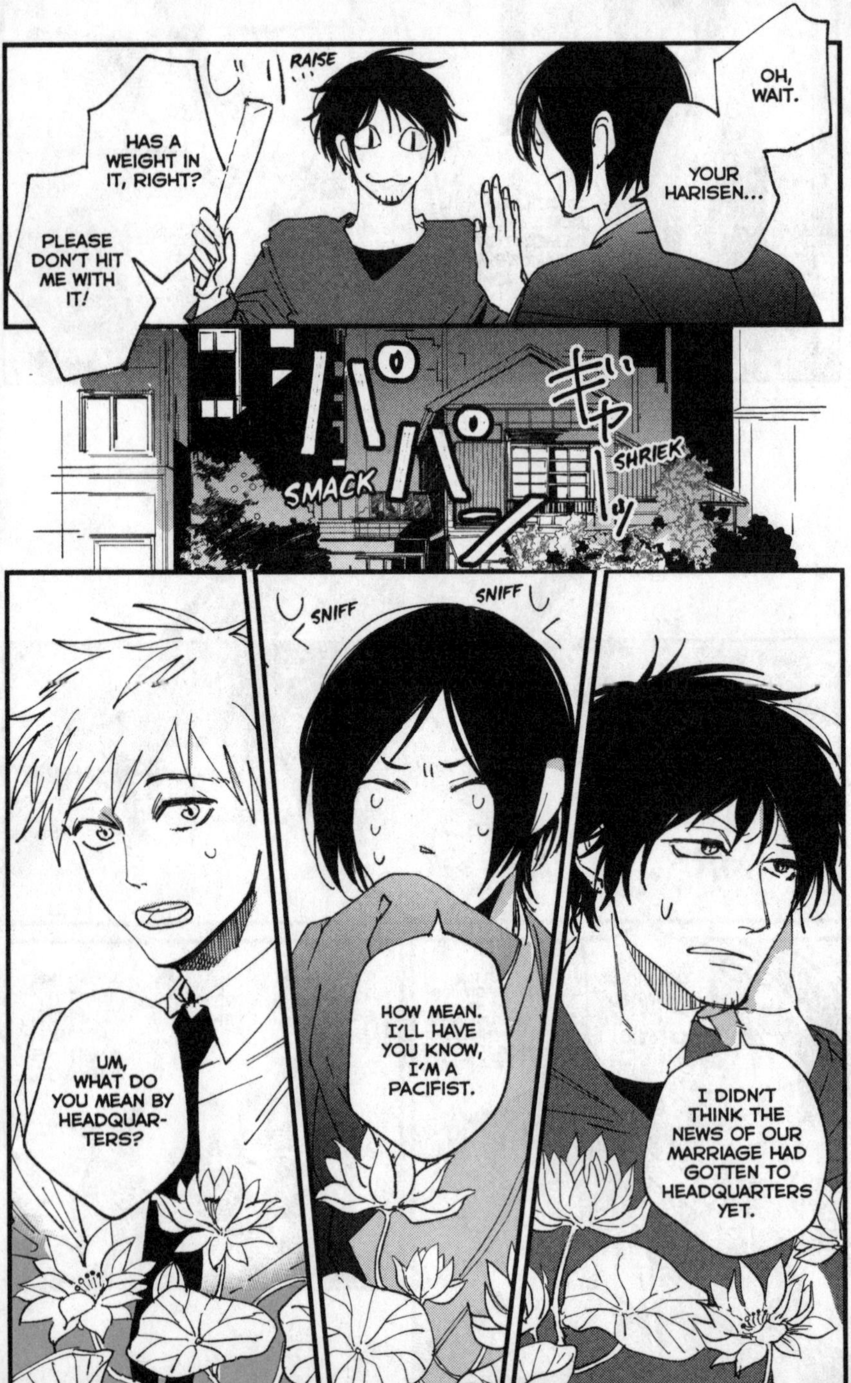
OH, WAIT.
YOUR HARISEN...
RAISE
HAS A WEIGHT IN IT, RIGHT?
PLEASE DON'T HIT ME WITH IT!
SHRIEK
SMACK
I DIDN'T THINK THE NEWS OF OUR MARRIAGE HAD GOTTEN TO HEADQUARTERS YET.
SNIFF
SNIFF
HOW MEAN. I'LL HAVE YOU KNOW, I'M A PACIFIST.
UM, WHAT DO YOU MEAN BY HEADQUAR-TERS?

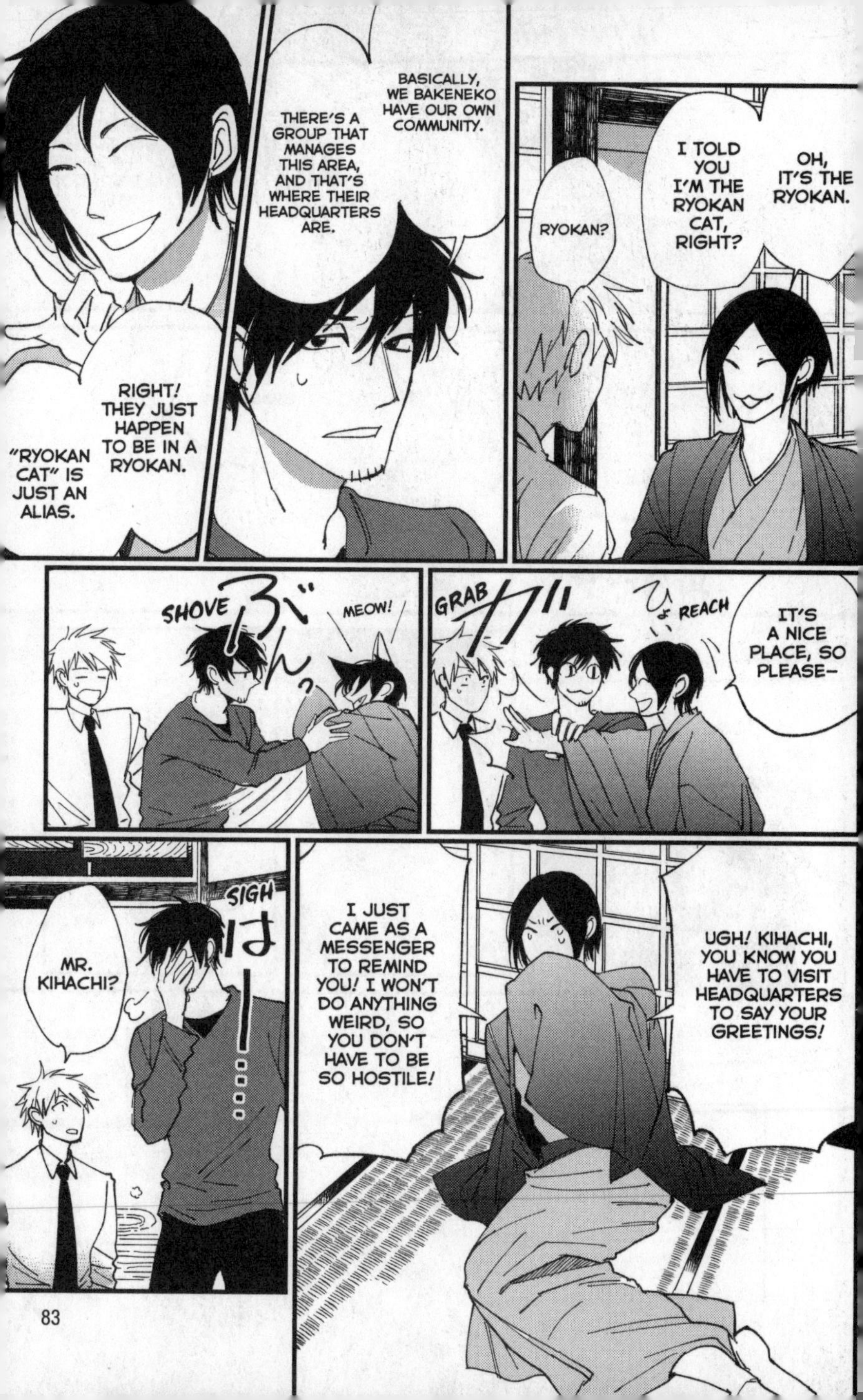

OH, IT'S THE RYOKAN.
I TOLD YOU I'M THE RYOKAN CAT, RIGHT?
RYOKAN?
BASICALLY, WE BAKENEKO HAVE OUR OWN COMMUNITY.
THERE'S A GROUP THAT MANAGES THIS AREA, AND THAT'S WHERE THEIR HEADQUARTERS ARE.
RIGHT! THEY JUST HAPPEN TO BE IN A RYOKAN.
"RYOKAN CAT" IS JUST AN ALIAS.
IT'S A NICE PLACE, SO PLEASE–
REACH
GRAB
MEOW!
SHOVE
UGH! KIHACHI, YOU KNOW YOU HAVE TO VISIT HEADQUARTERS TO SAY YOUR GREETINGS!
I JUST CAME AS A MESSENGER TO REMIND YOU! I WON'T DO ANYTHING WEIRD, SO YOU DON'T HAVE TO BE SO HOSTILE!
SIGH
MR. KIHACHI?

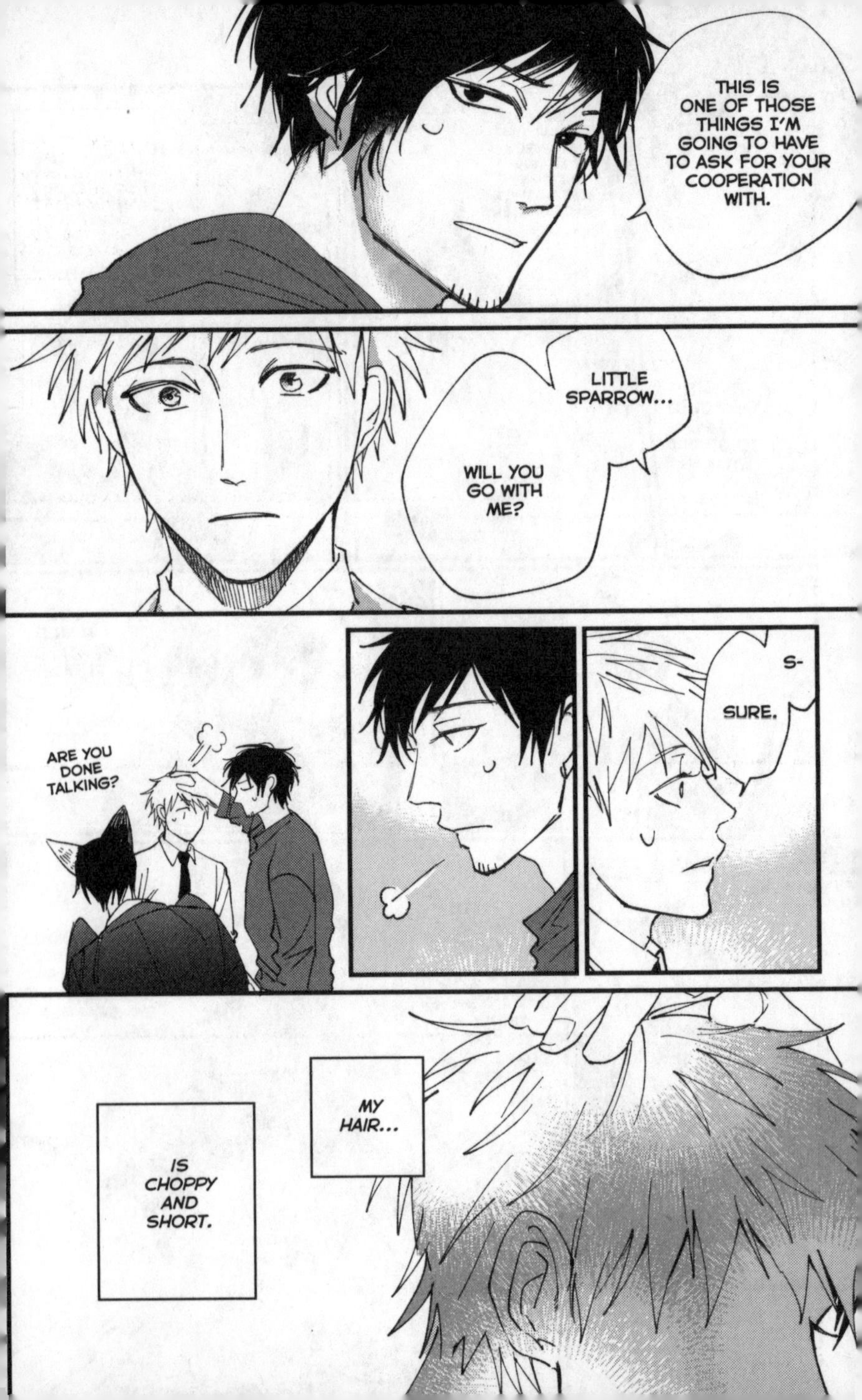
THIS IS ONE OF THOSE THINGS I'M GOING TO HAVE TO ASK FOR YOUR COOPERATION WITH.
LITTLE SPARROW...
WILL YOU GO WITH ME?
S-
SURE.
ARE YOU DONE TALKING?
MY HAIR...
IS CHOPPY AND SHORT.

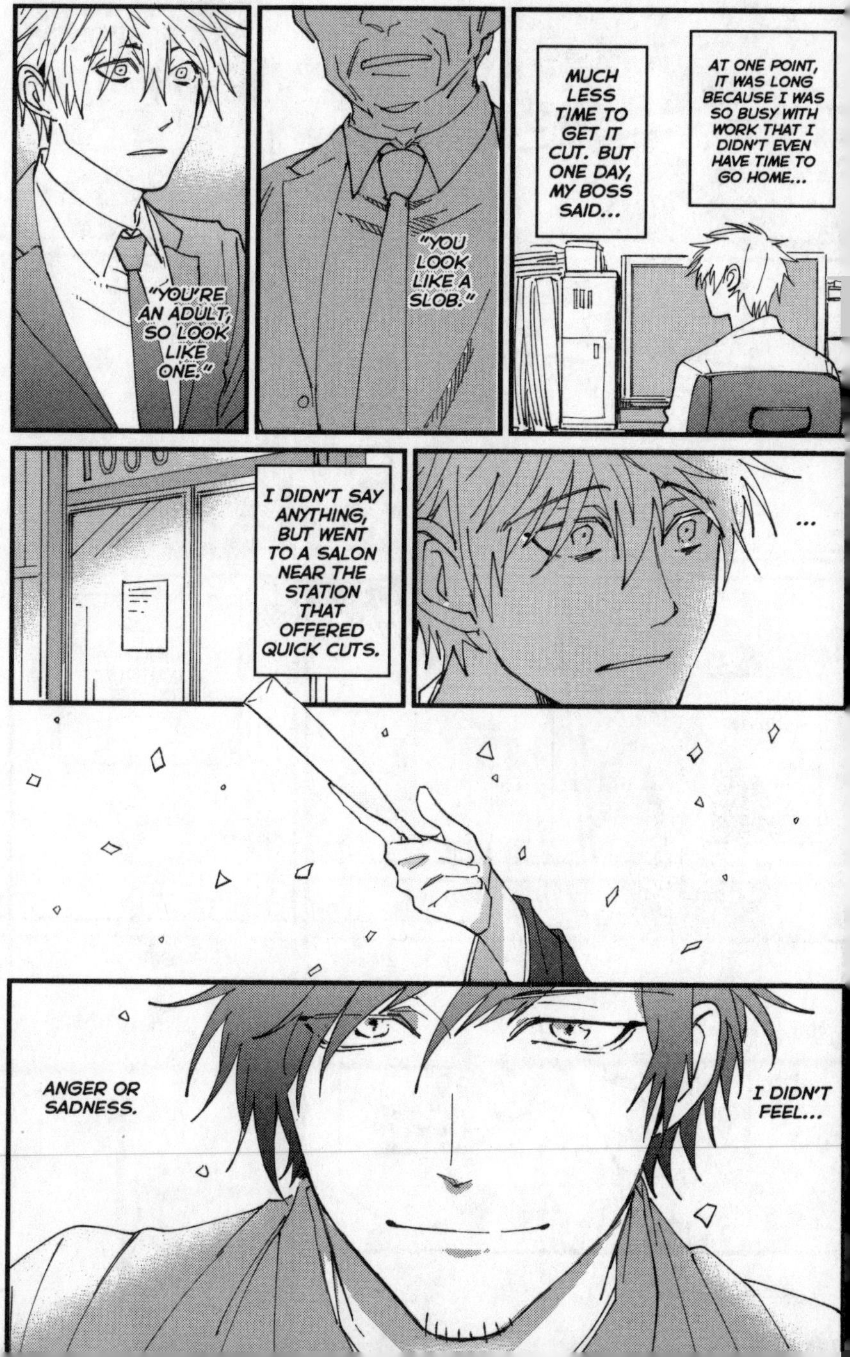
AT ONE POINT, IT WAS LONG BECAUSE I WAS SO BUSY WITH WORK THAT I DIDN'T EVEN HAVE TIME TO GO HOME...
MUCH LESS TIME TO GET IT CUT. BUT ONE DAY, MY BOSS SAID...
"YOU LOOK LIKE A SLOB."
"YOU'RE AN ADULT, SO LOOK LIKE ONE."
...
I DIDN'T SAY ANYTHING, BUT WENT TO A SALON NEAR THE STATION THAT OFFERED QUICK CUTS.
I DIDN'T FEEL...
ANGER OR SADNESS.

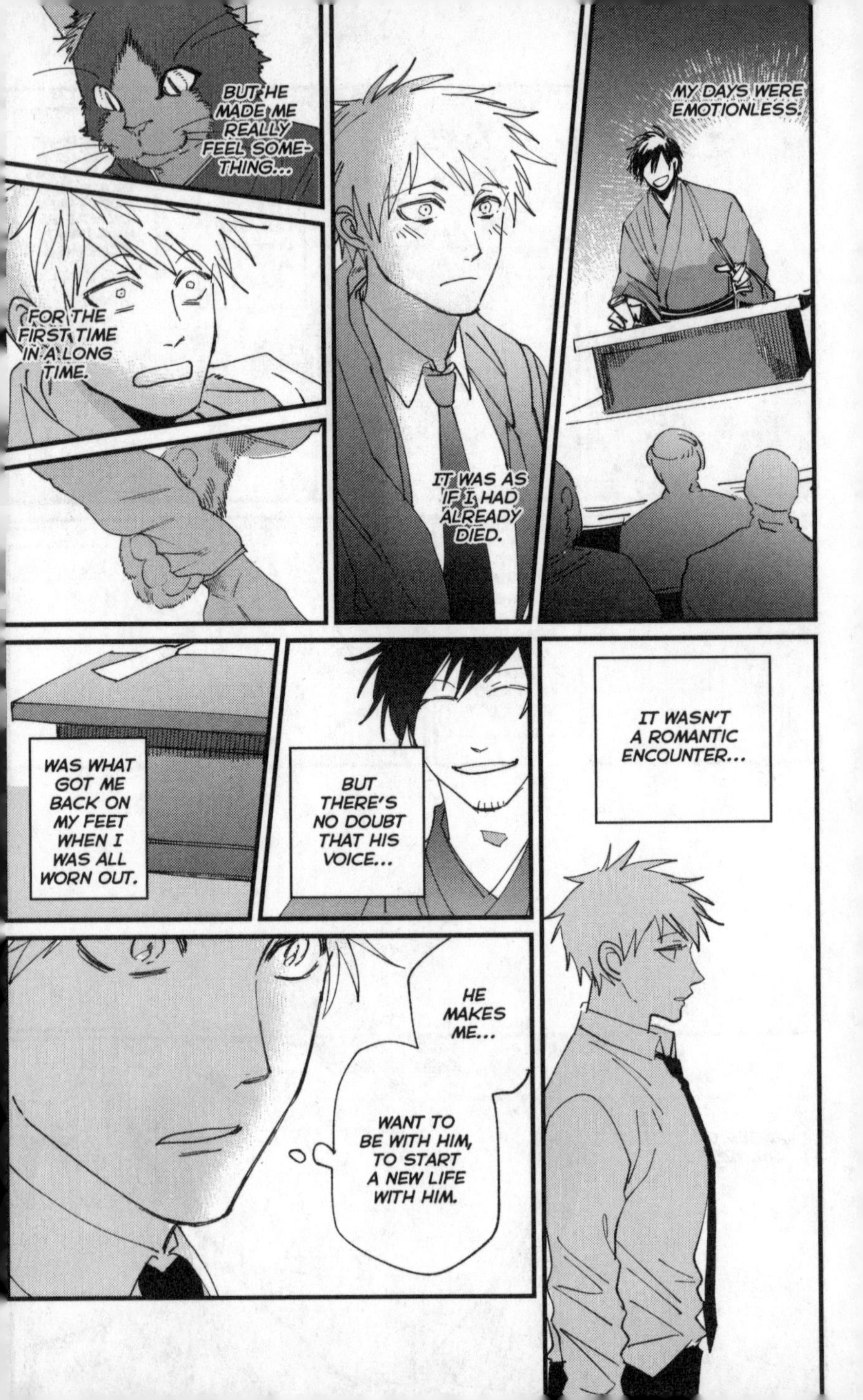
MY DAYS WERE EMOTIONLESS.
IT WAS AS IF I HAD ALREADY DIED.
BUT HE MADE ME REALLY FEEL SOME-THING...
FOR THE FIRST TIME IN A LONG TIME.
IT WASN'T A ROMANTIC ENCOUNTER...
BUT THERE'S NO DOUBT THAT HIS VOICE...
WAS WHAT GOT ME BACK ON MY FEET WHEN I WAS ALL WORN OUT.
HE MAKES ME...
WANT TO BE WITH HIM, TO START A NEW LIFE WITH HIM.

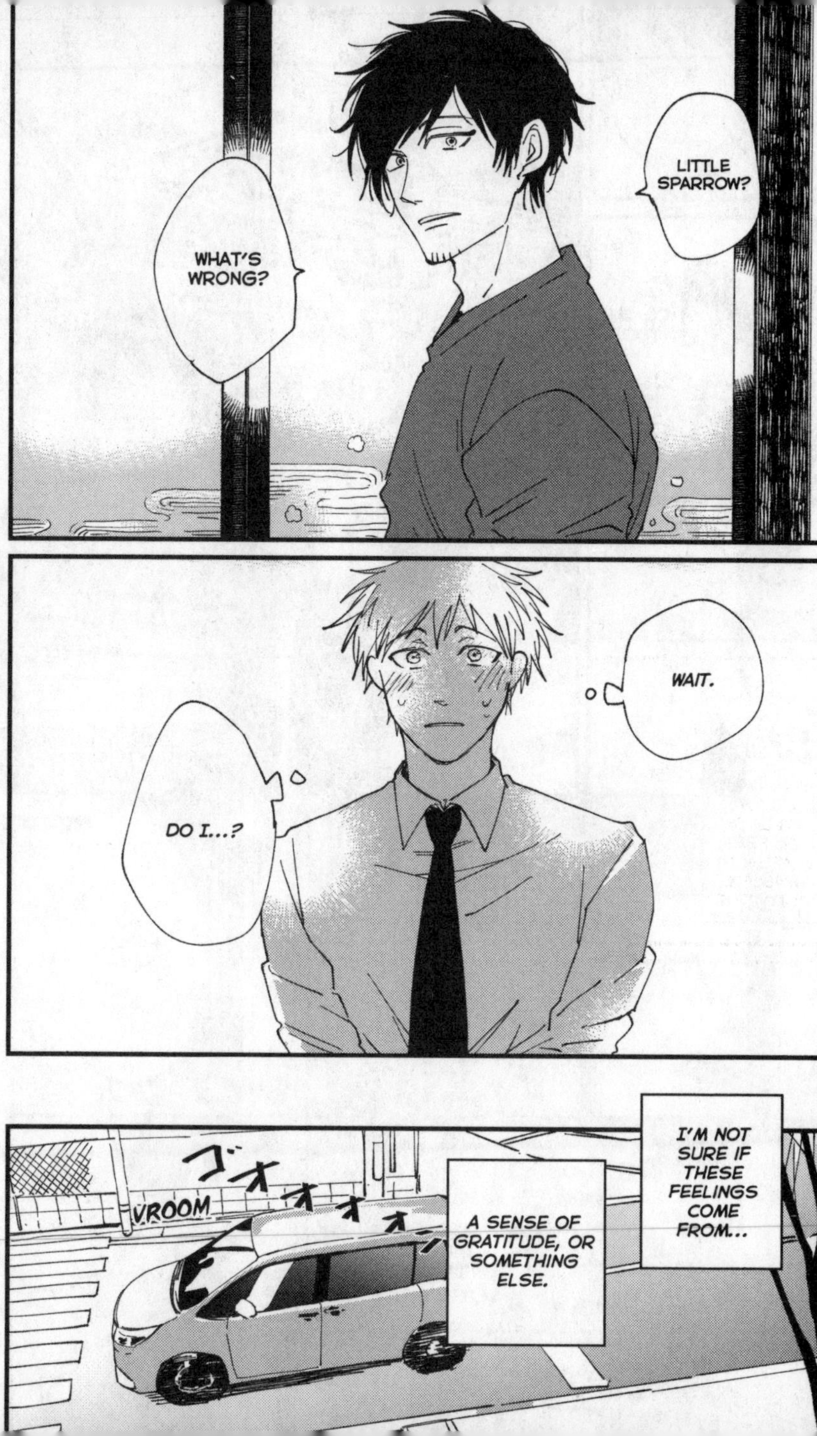
LITTLE SPARROW?
WHAT'S WRONG?
WAIT.
DO I...?
I'M NOT SURE IF THESE FEELINGS COME FROM...
A SENSE OF GRATITUDE, OR SOMETHING ELSE.
ゴオオオオ
VROOM

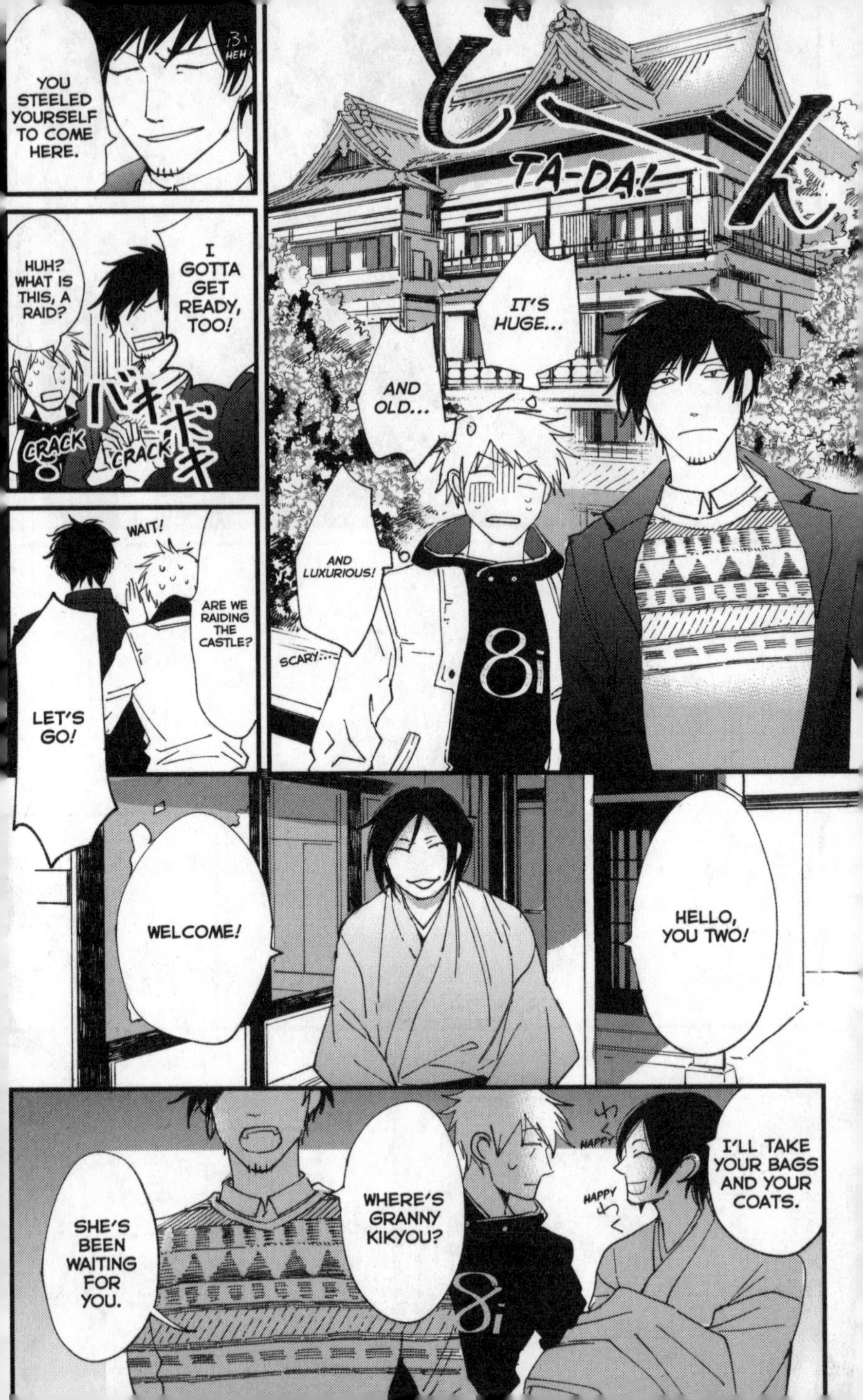
TA-DA!
IT'S HUGE...
AND OLD...
AND LUXURIOUS!
SCARY...
HEH
YOU STEELED YOURSELF TO COME HERE.
I GOTTA GET READY, TOO!
HUH? WHAT IS THIS, A RAID?
バキ ボキ
CRACK
CRACK
WAIT!
ARE WE RAIDING THE CASTLE?
LET'S GO!
HELLO, YOU TWO!
WELCOME!
I'LL TAKE YOUR BAGS AND YOUR COATS.
HAPPY
HAPPY
WHERE'S GRANNY KIKYOU?
SHE'S BEEN WAITING FOR YOU.

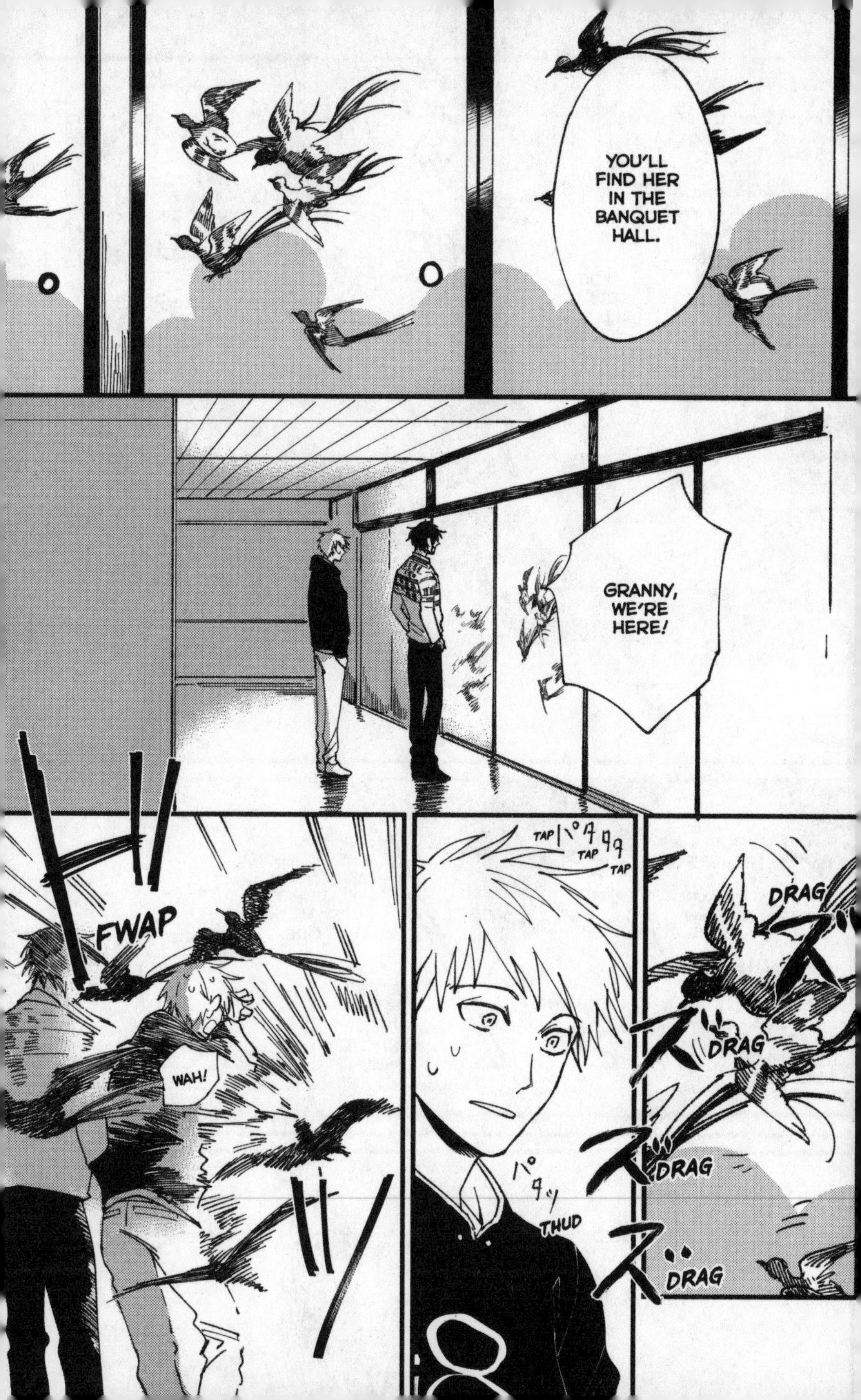
YOU'LL FIND HER IN THE BANQUET HALL.
GRANNY, WE'RE HERE!
DRAG
DRAG
DRAG
DRAG
TAP TAP TAP
THUD
FWAP
WAH!

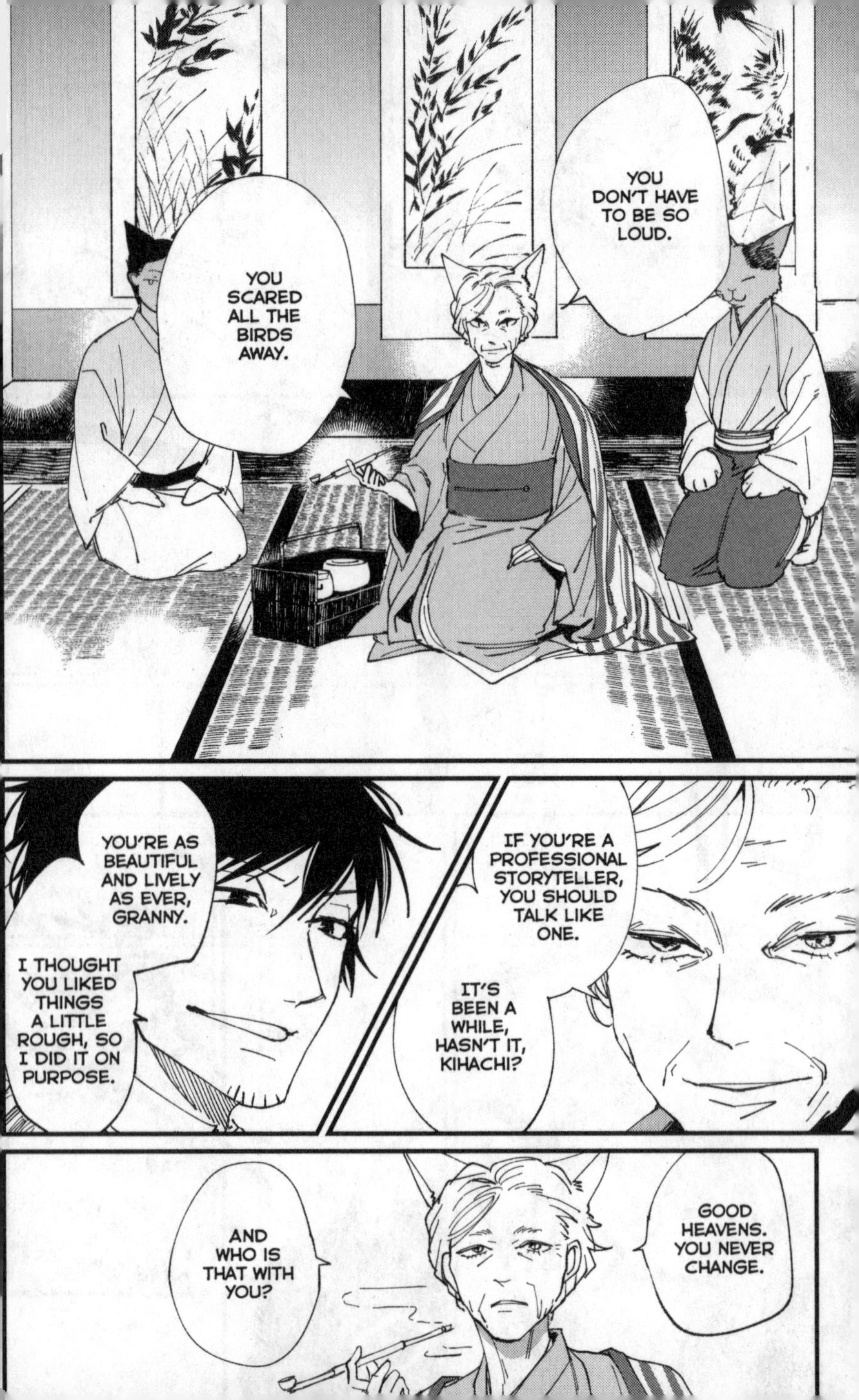
YOU DON'T HAVE TO BE SO LOUD.
YOU SCARED ALL THE BIRDS AWAY.
IF YOU'RE A PROFESSIONAL STORYTELLER, YOU SHOULD TALK LIKE ONE.
IT'S BEEN A WHILE, HASN'T IT, KIHACHI?
YOU'RE AS BEAUTIFUL AND LIVELY AS EVER, GRANNY.
I THOUGHT YOU LIKED THINGS A LITTLE ROUGH, SO I DID IT ON PURPOSE.
GOOD HEAVENS. YOU NEVER CHANGE.
AND WHO IS THAT WITH YOU?

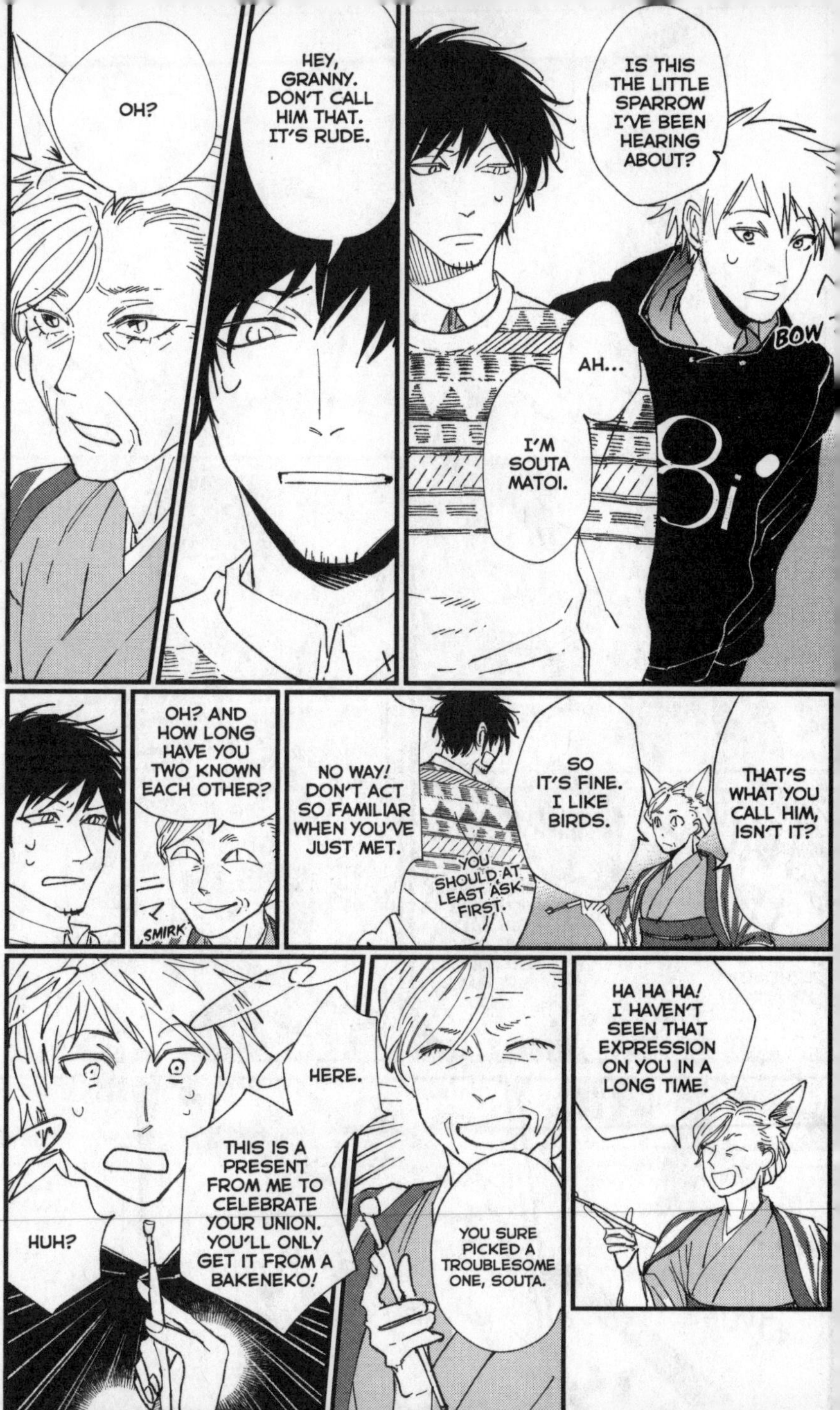
IS THIS THE LITTLE SPARROW I'VE BEEN HEARING ABOUT?
BOW
AH...
I'M SOUTA MATOI.
HEY, GRANNY. DON'T CALL HIM THAT. IT'S RUDE.
OH?
THAT'S WHAT YOU CALL HIM, ISN'T IT?
SO IT'S FINE. I LIKE BIRDS.
NO WAY! DON'T ACT SO FAMILIAR WHEN YOU'VE JUST MET.
YOU SHOULD AT LEAST ASK FIRST.
OH? AND HOW LONG HAVE YOU TWO KNOWN EACH OTHER?
SMIRK
HA HA HA! I HAVEN'T SEEN THAT EXPRESSION ON YOU IN A LONG TIME.
YOU SURE PICKED A TROUBLESOME ONE, SOUTA.
HERE.
THIS IS A PRESENT FROM ME TO CELEBRATE YOUR UNION. YOU'LL ONLY GET IT FROM A BAKENEKO!
HUH?

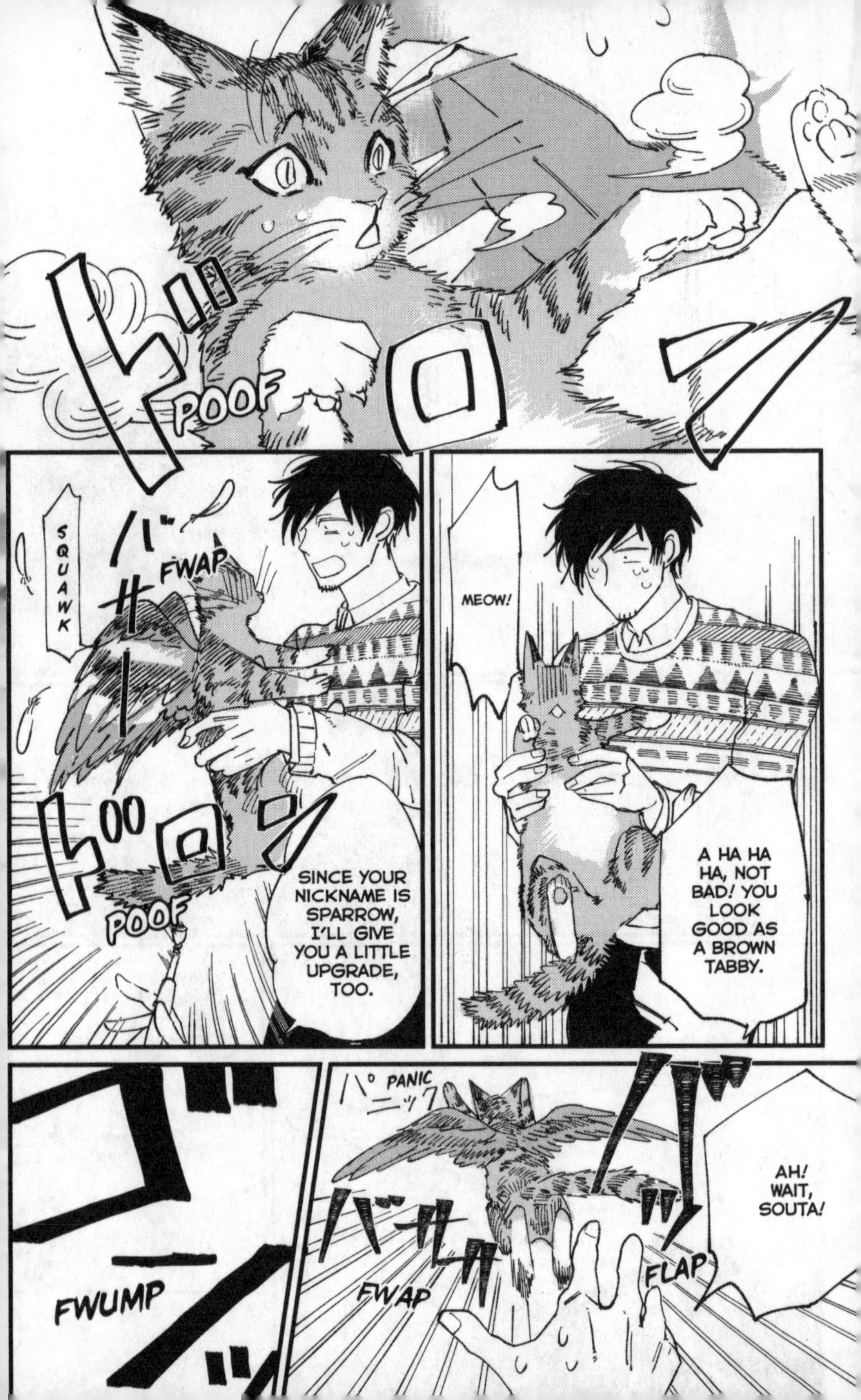
POOF
MEOW!
A HA HA HA, NOT BAD! YOU LOOK GOOD AS A BROWN TABBY.
SQUAWK
FWAP
POOF
SINCE YOUR NICKNAME IS SPARROW, I'LL GIVE YOU A LITTLE UPGRADE, TOO.
AH! WAIT, SOUTA!
パニック
PANIC
FLAP
FWAP
FWUMP

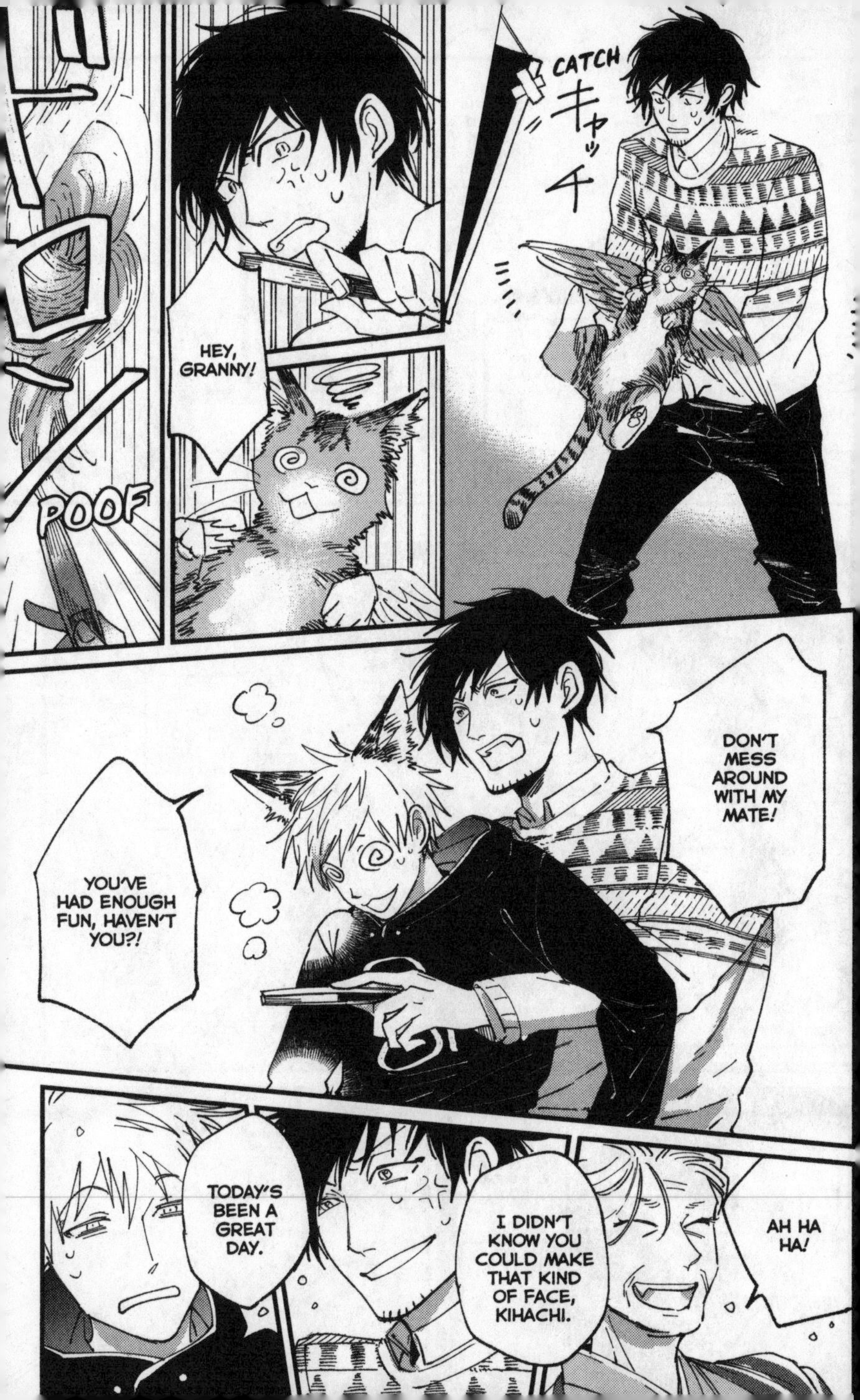
CATCH
キャッチ
HEY, GRANNY!
POOF
DON'T MESS AROUND WITH MY MATE!
YOU'VE HAD ENOUGH FUN, HAVEN'T YOU?!
AH HA HA!
I DIDN'T KNOW YOU COULD MAKE THAT KIND OF FACE, KIHACHI.
TODAY'S BEEN A GREAT DAY.

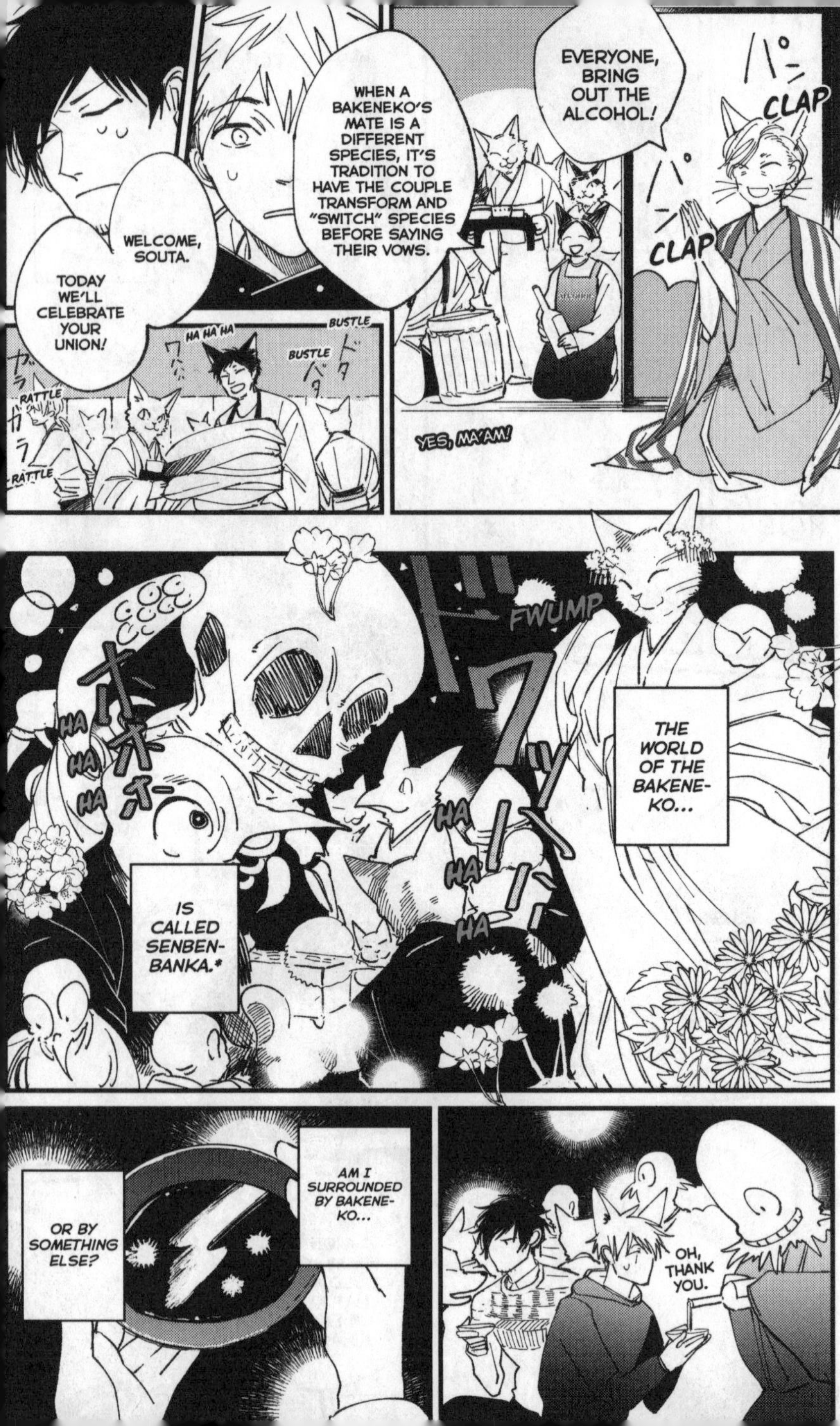
CLAP
CLAP
EVERYONE, BRING OUT THE ALCOHOL!
YES, MA'AM!
WHEN A BAKENEKO'S MATE IS A DIFFERENT SPECIES, IT'S TRADITION TO HAVE THE COUPLE TRANSFORM AND "SWITCH" SPECIES BEFORE SAYING THEIR VOWS.
WELCOME, SOUTA.
TODAY WE'LL CELEBRATE YOUR UNION!
BUSTLE
BUSTLE
HA HA HA
RATTLE
RATTLE
FWUMP
THE WORLD OF THE BAKENE-KO...
HA
HA
HA
HA
HA
HA
IS CALLED SENBEN-BANKA.*
OH, THANK YOU.
AM I SURROUNDED BY BAKENE-KO...
OR BY SOMETHING ELSE?

*LITERALLY, "TO TRANSFORM INTO MANY THINGS"

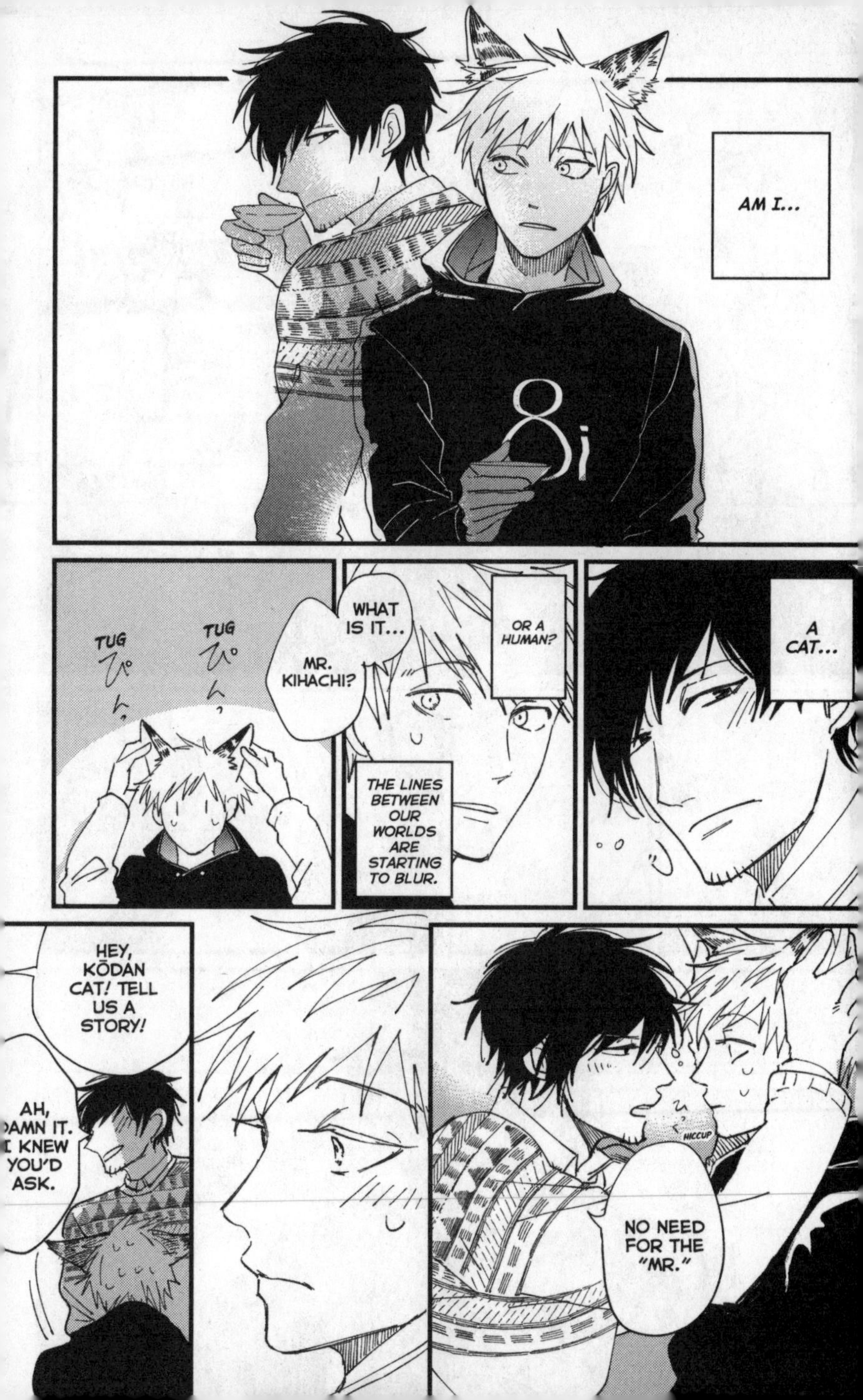
AM I...
A CAT...
OR A HUMAN?
WHAT IS IT... MR. KIHACHI?
THE LINES BETWEEN OUR WORLDS ARE STARTING TO BLUR.
TUG
ぴん
TUG
ぴん
HICCUP
NO NEED FOR THE "MR."
HEY, KŌDAN CAT! TELL US A STORY!
AH, DAMN IT. I KNEW YOU'D ASK.

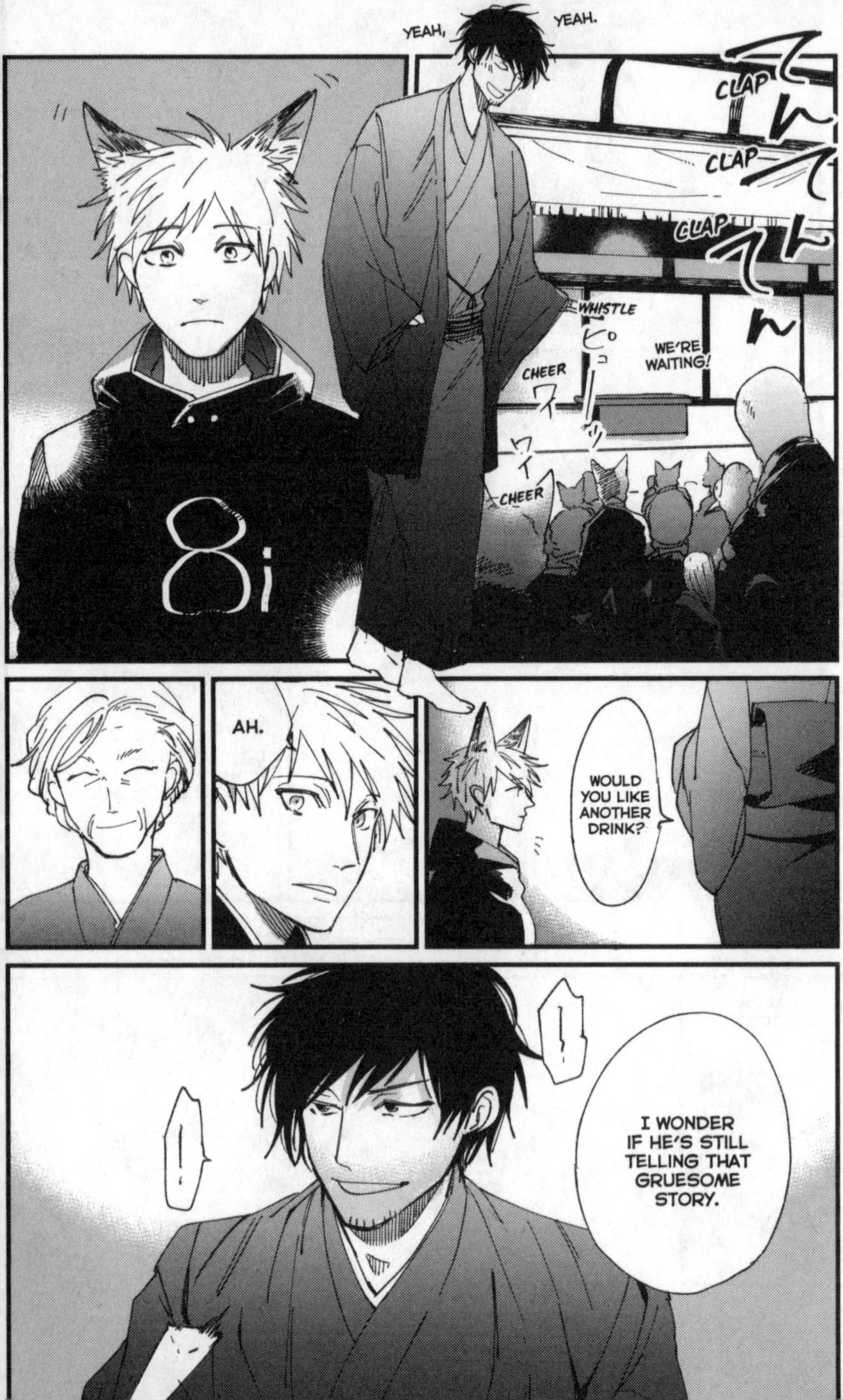
YEAH,
YEAH.
CLAP
CLAP
CLAP
WE'RE WAITING!
WHISTLE
CHEER
CHEER
WOULD YOU LIKE ANOTHER DRINK?
AH.
!
I WONDER IF HE'S STILL TELLING THAT GRUESOME STORY.
!

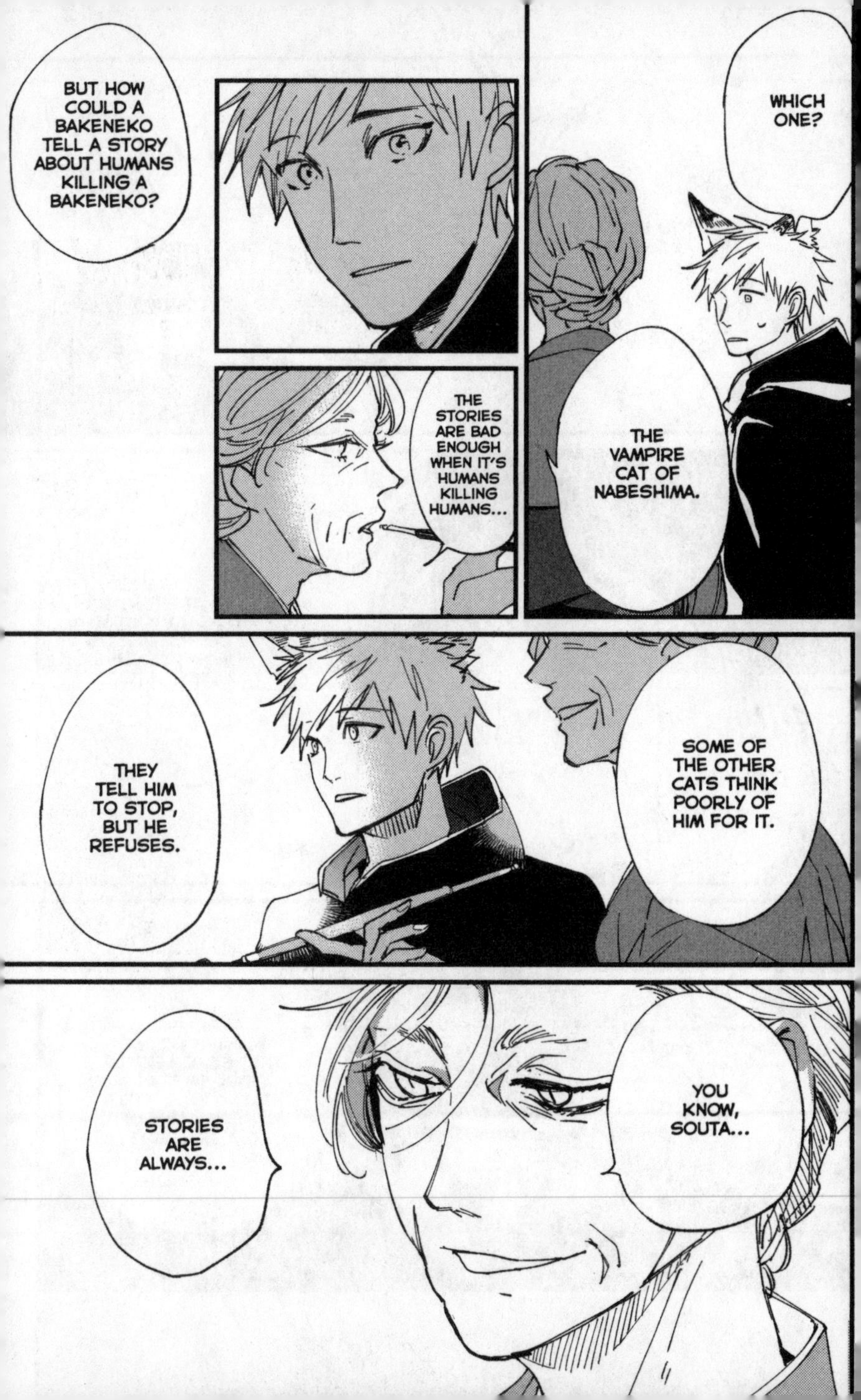
WHICH ONE?
THE VAMPIRE CAT OF NABESHIMA.
BUT HOW COULD A BAKENEKO TELL A STORY ABOUT HUMANS KILLING A BAKENEKO?
THE STORIES ARE BAD ENOUGH WHEN IT'S HUMANS KILLING HUMANS...
SOME OF THE OTHER CATS THINK POORLY OF HIM FOR IT.
THEY TELL HIM TO STOP, BUT HE REFUSES.
YOU KNOW, SOUTA...
STORIES ARE ALWAYS...

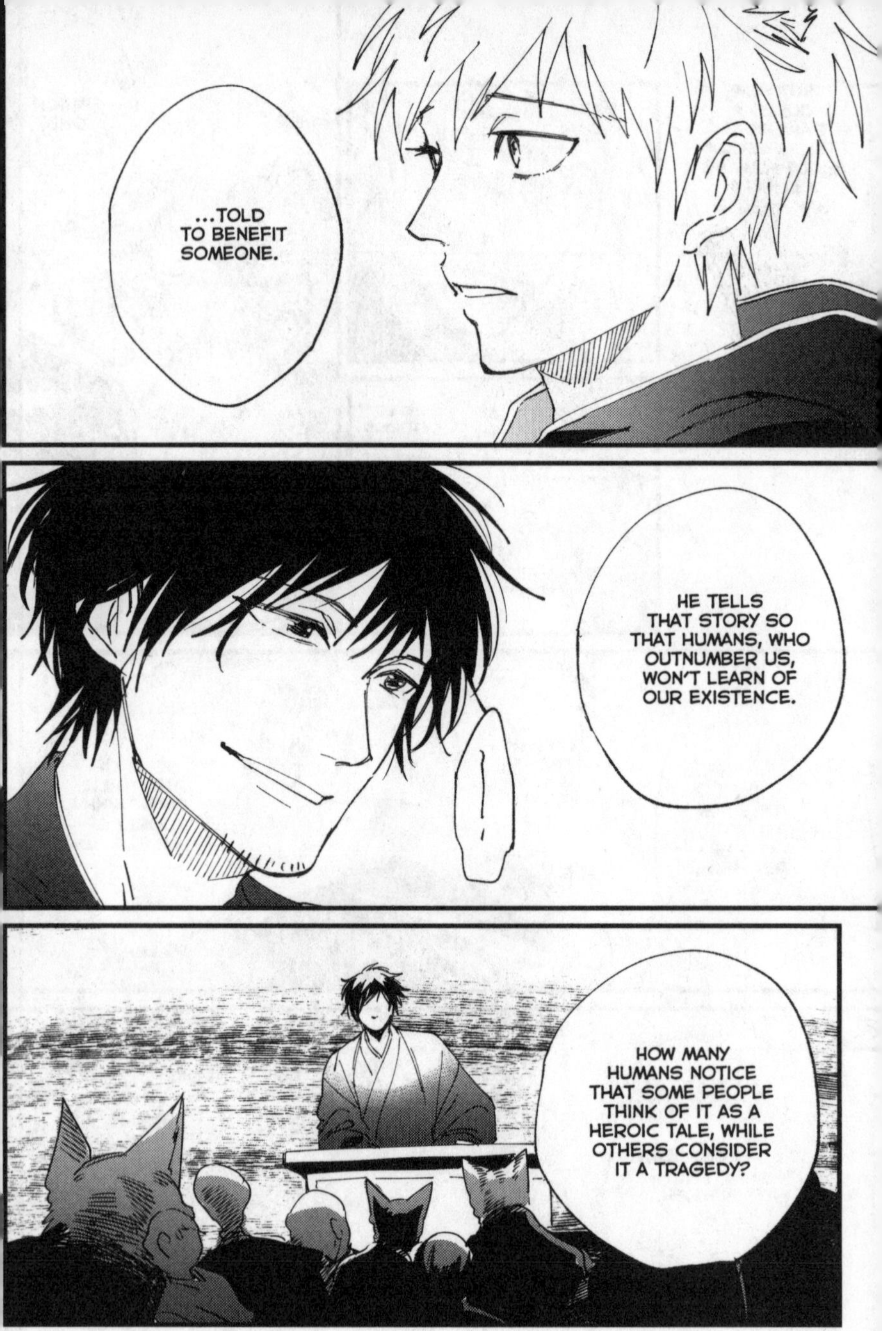
...TOLD TO BENEFIT SOMEONE.
HE TELLS THAT STORY SO THAT HUMANS, WHO OUTNUMBER US, WON'T LEARN OF OUR EXISTENCE.
HOW MANY HUMANS NOTICE THAT SOME PEOPLE THINK OF IT AS A HEROIC TALE, WHILE OTHERS CONSIDER IT A TRAGEDY?

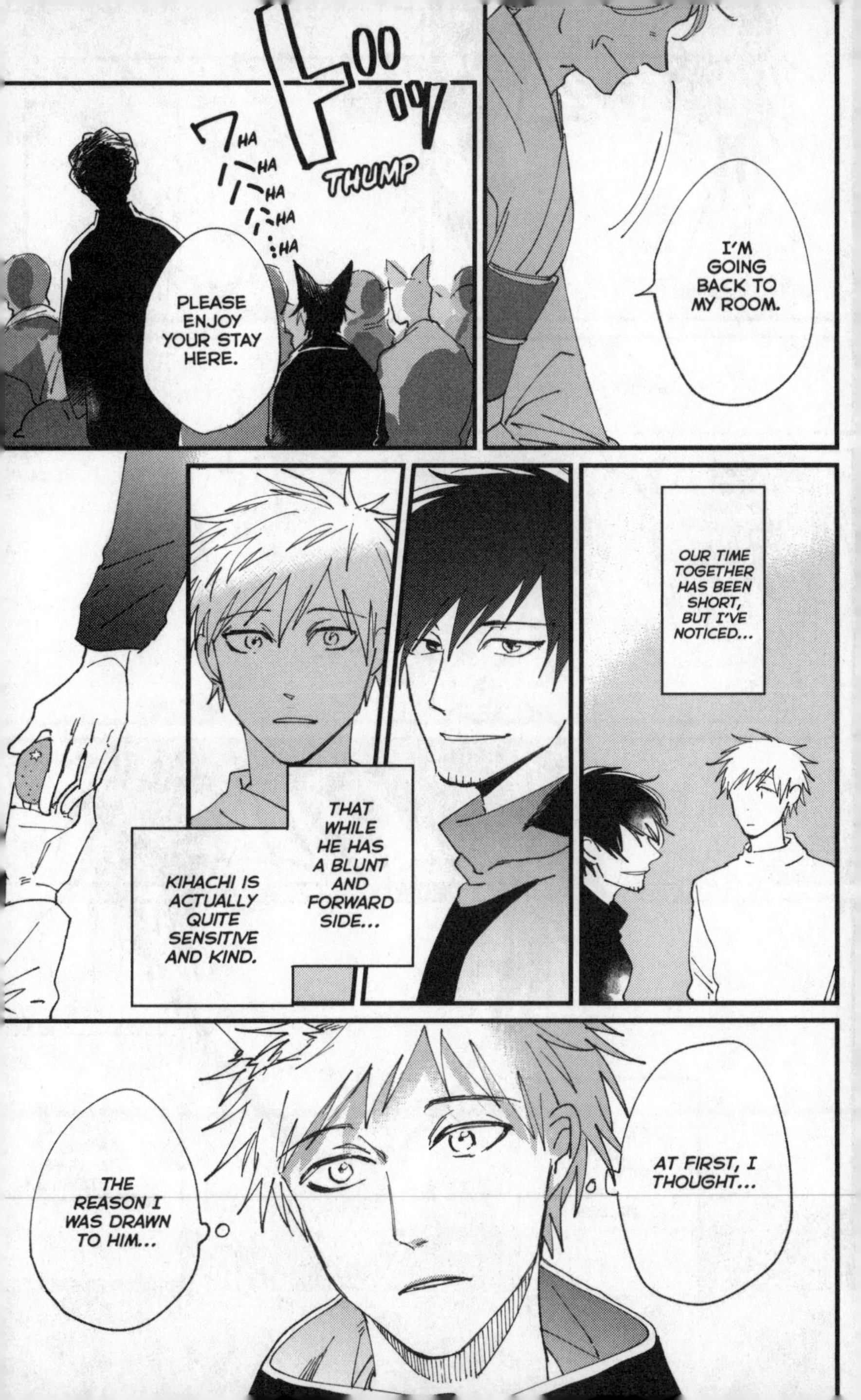
I'M GOING BACK TO MY ROOM.
THUMP
HA
HA
HA
HA
HA
PLEASE ENJOY YOUR STAY HERE.
OUR TIME TOGETHER HAS BEEN SHORT, BUT I'VE NOTICED...
THAT WHILE HE HAS A BLUNT AND FORWARD SIDE...
KIHACHI IS ACTUALLY QUITE SENSITIVE AND KIND.
AT FIRST, I THOUGHT...
THE REASON I WAS DRAWN TO HIM...

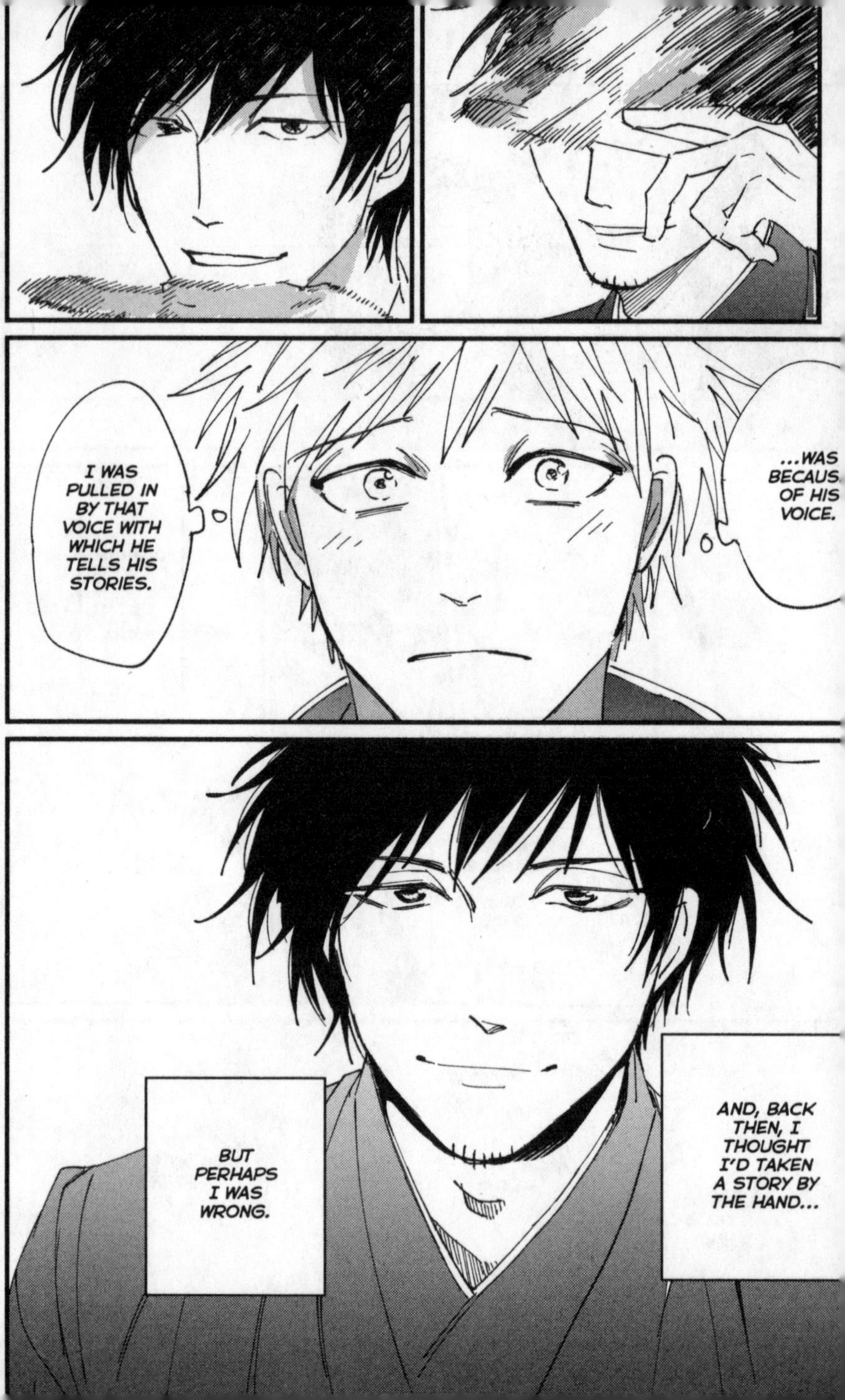
...WAS BECAUS OF HIS VOICE.
I WAS PULLED IN BY THAT VOICE WITH WHICH HE TELLS HIS STORIES.
AND, BACK THEN, I THOUGHT I'D TAKEN A STORY BY THE HAND...
BUT PERHAPS I WAS WRONG.

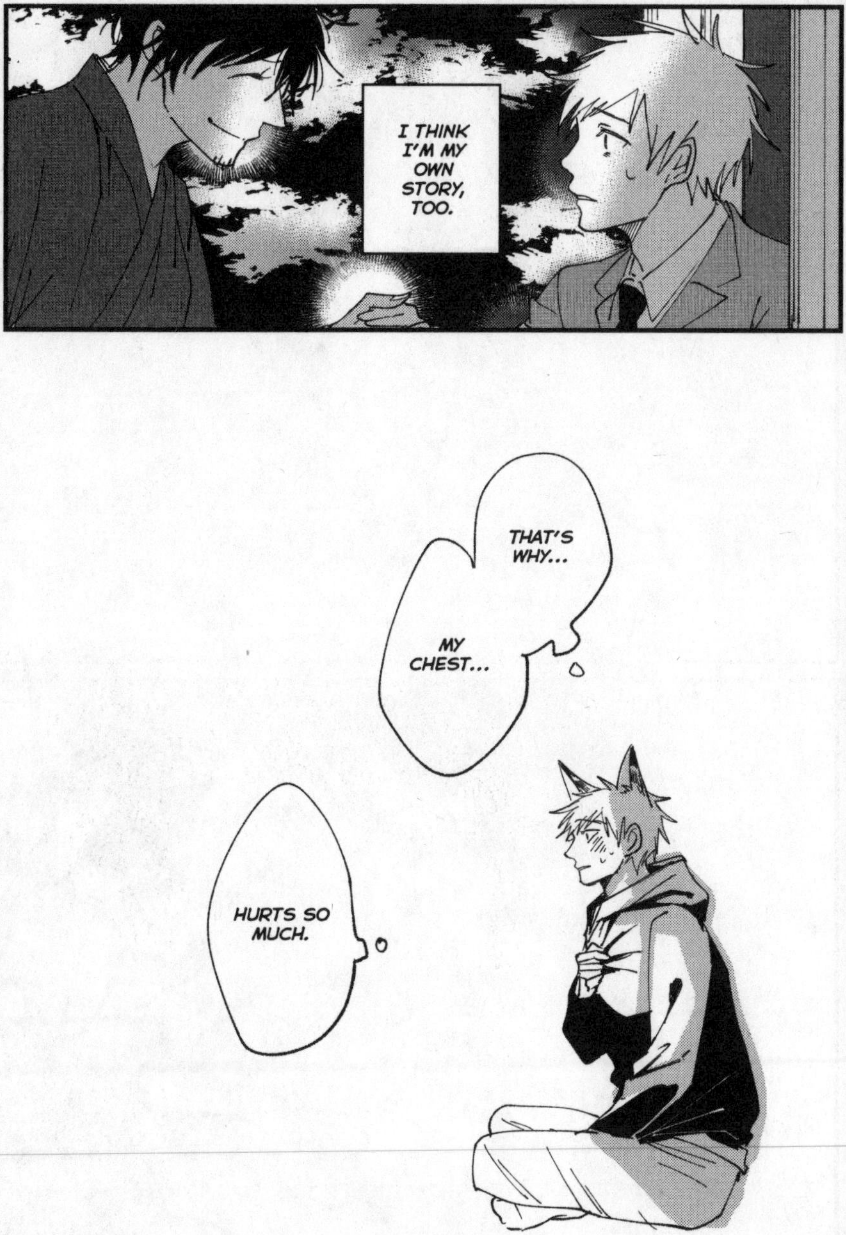
I THINK I'M MY OWN STORY, TOO.
THAT'S WHY...
MY CHEST...
HURTS SO MUCH.

4th Story

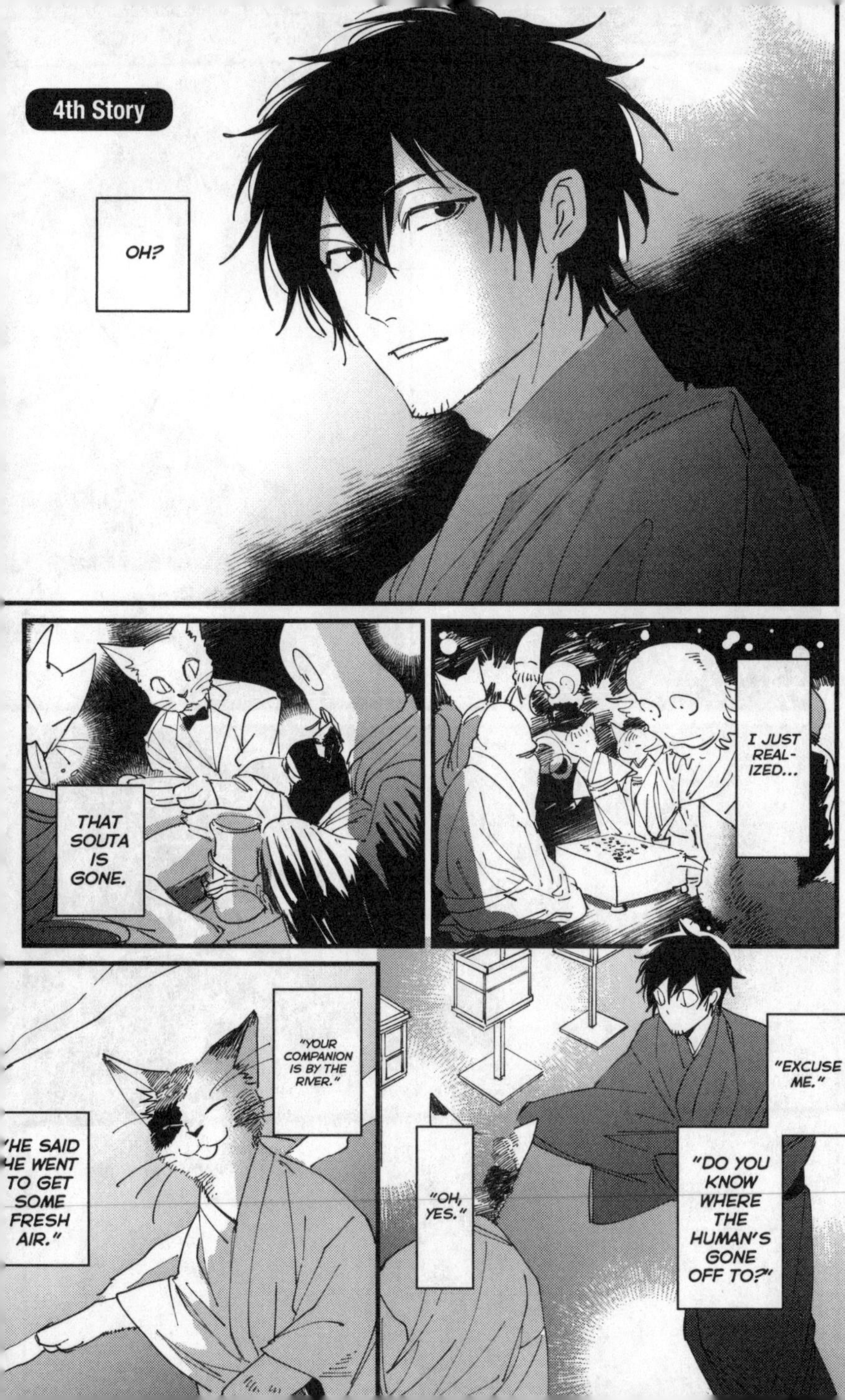
OH?
I JUST REAL-IZED...
THAT SOUTA IS GONE.
"EXCUSE ME."
"DO YOU KNOW WHERE THE HUMAN'S GONE OFF TO?"
"OH, YES."
"YOUR COMPANION IS BY THE RIVER."
"HE SAID HE WENT TO GET SOME FRESH AIR."

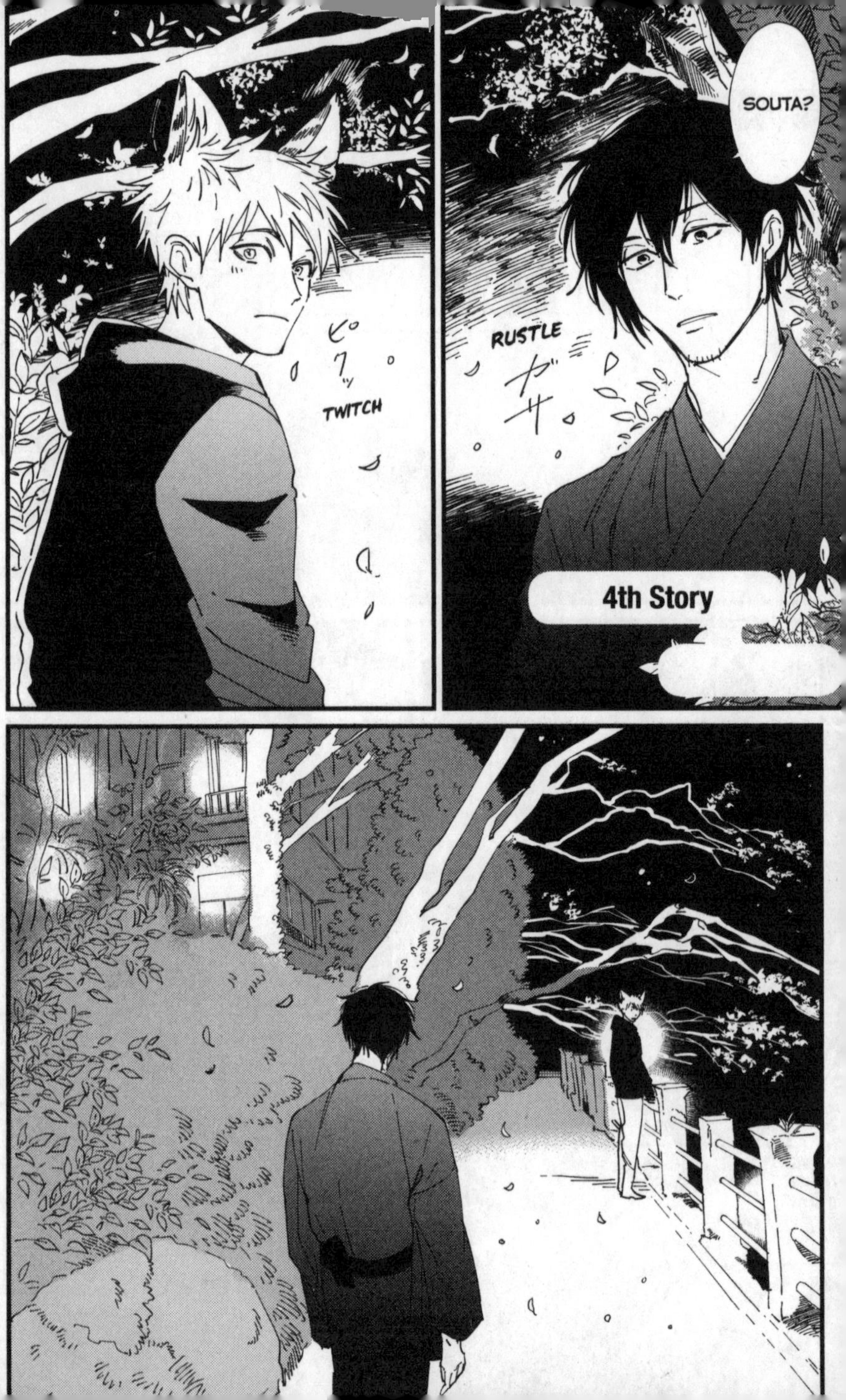
SOUTA?
RUSTLE
ガサ
4th Story
ピクッ
TWITCH

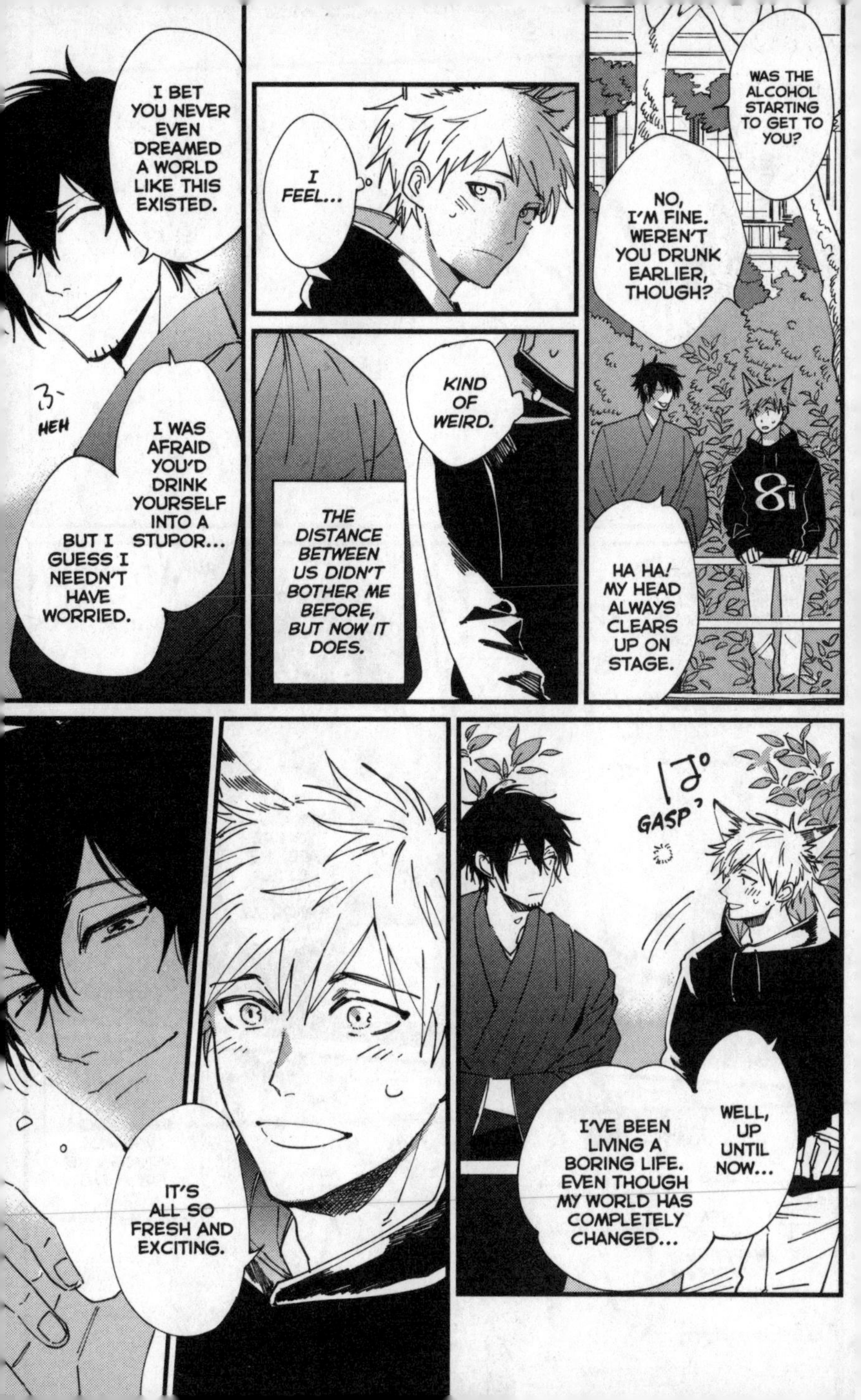
WAS THE ALCOHOL STARTING TO GET TO YOU?
NO, I'M FINE. WEREN'T YOU DRUNK EARLIER, THOUGH?
HA HA! MY HEAD ALWAYS CLEARS UP ON STAGE.
I FEEL...
KIND OF WEIRD.
THE DISTANCE BETWEEN US DIDN'T BOTHER ME BEFORE, BUT NOW IT DOES.
I BET YOU NEVER EVEN DREAMED A WORLD LIKE THIS EXISTED.
HEH
I WAS AFRAID YOU'D DRINK YOURSELF INTO A STUPOR...
BUT I GUESS I NEEDN'T HAVE WORRIED.
GASP
WELL, UP UNTIL NOW...
I'VE BEEN LIVING A BORING LIFE. EVEN THOUGH MY WORLD HAS COMPLETELY CHANGED...
IT'S ALL SO FRESH AND EXCITING.

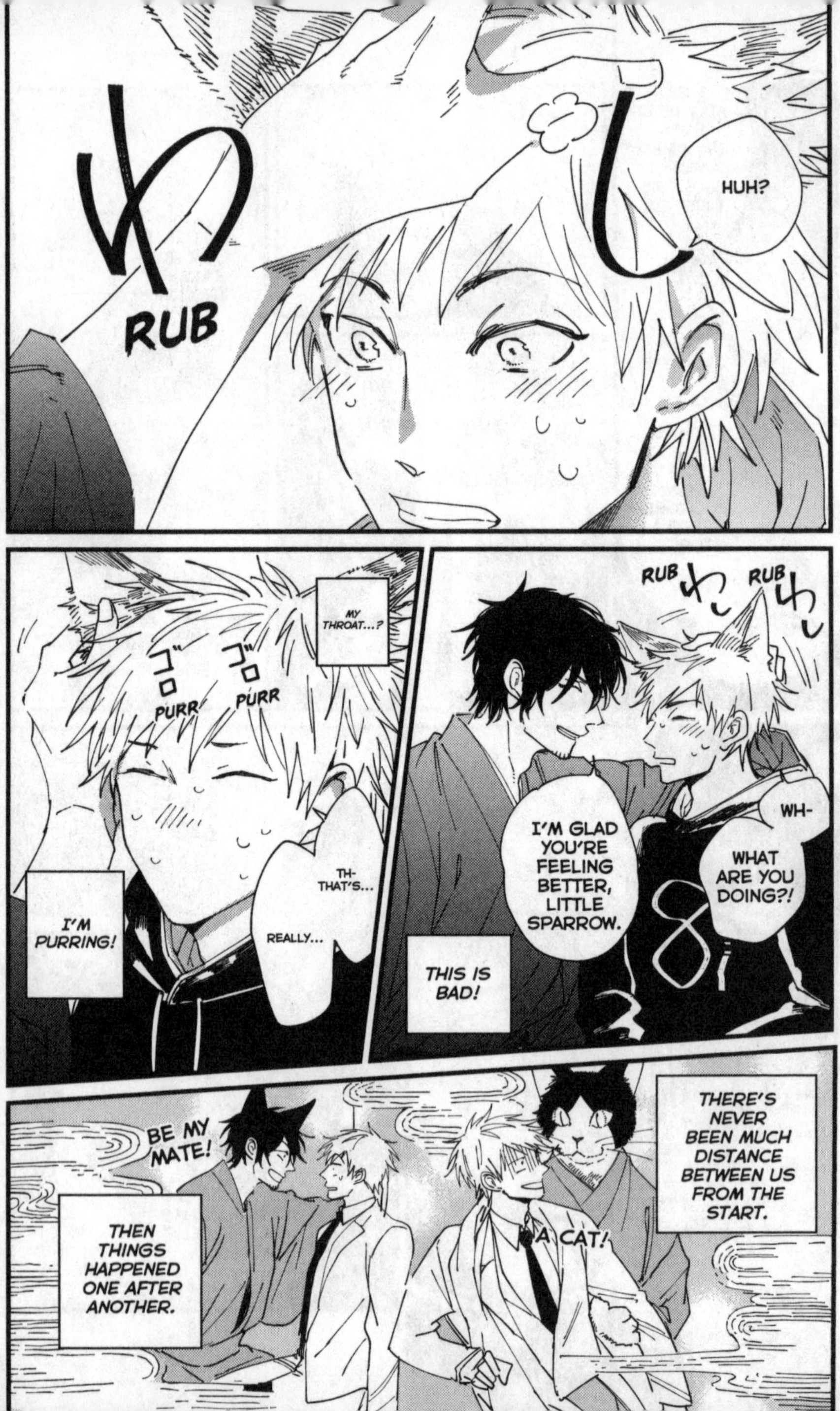

HUH?
わし
RUB
RUB わし RUB わし
WH-
WHAT ARE YOU DOING?!
I'M GLAD YOU'RE FEELING BETTER, LITTLE SPARROW.
THIS IS BAD!
MY THROAT...?
ゴロ PURR ゴロ PURR
TH- THAT'S...
REALLY...
I'M PURRING!
THERE'S NEVER BEEN MUCH DISTANCE BETWEEN US FROM THE START.
A CAT!
BE MY MATE!
THEN THINGS HAPPENED ONE AFTER ANOTHER.

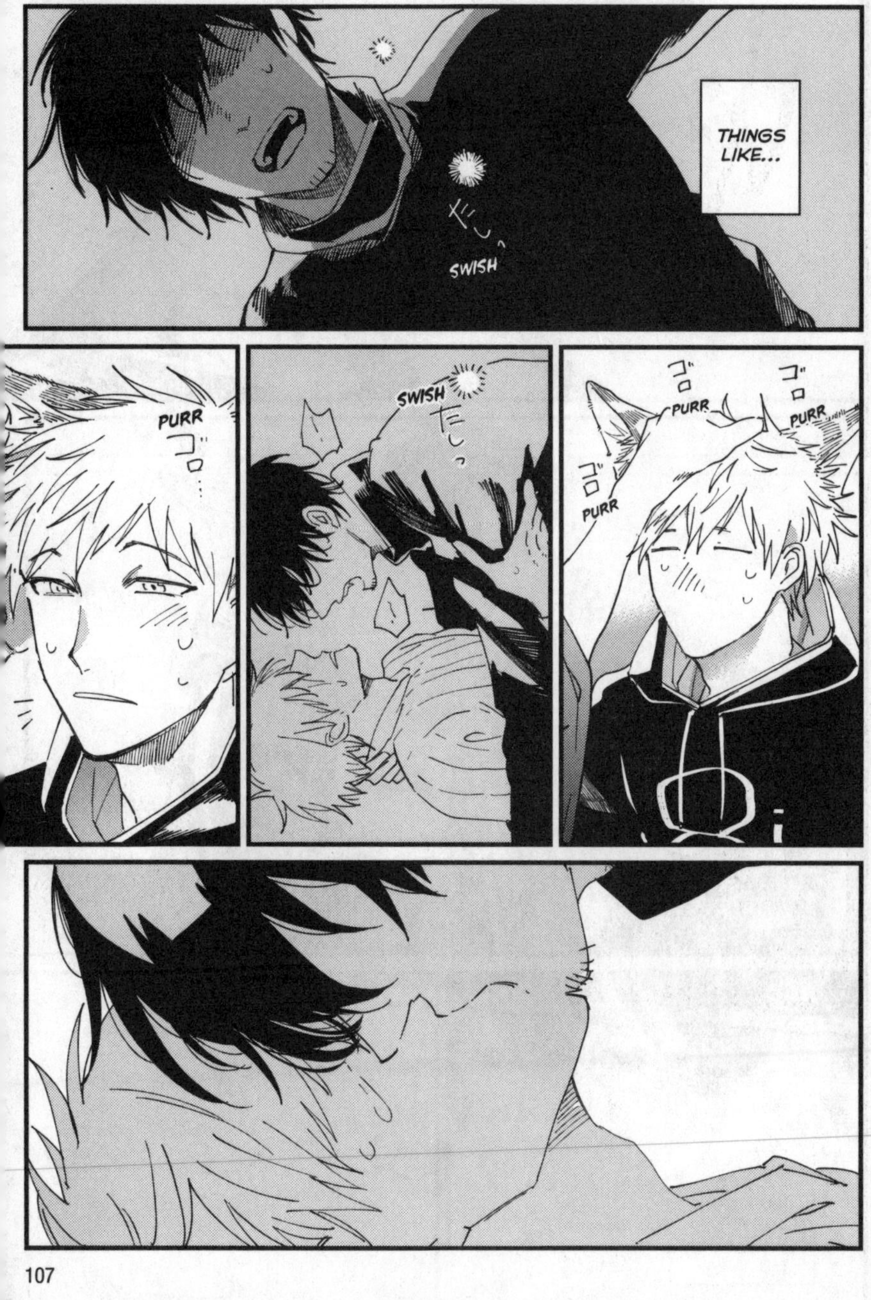
THINGS LIKE...
SWISH
ゴロ
PURR
ゴロ
PURR
ゴロ
PURR
SWISH
PURR
ゴロ...

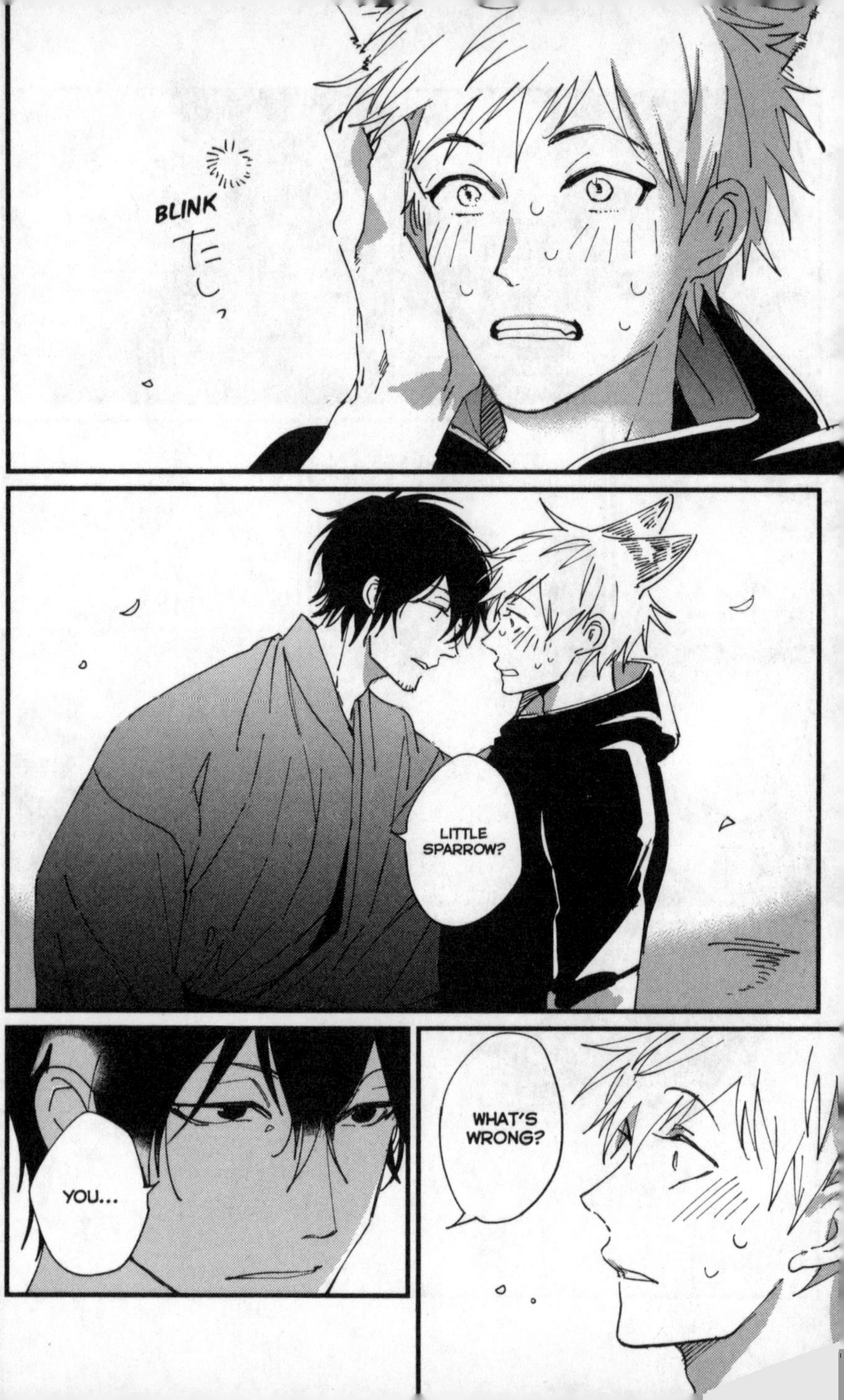
BLINK
LITTLE SPARROW?
WHAT'S WRONG?
YOU...

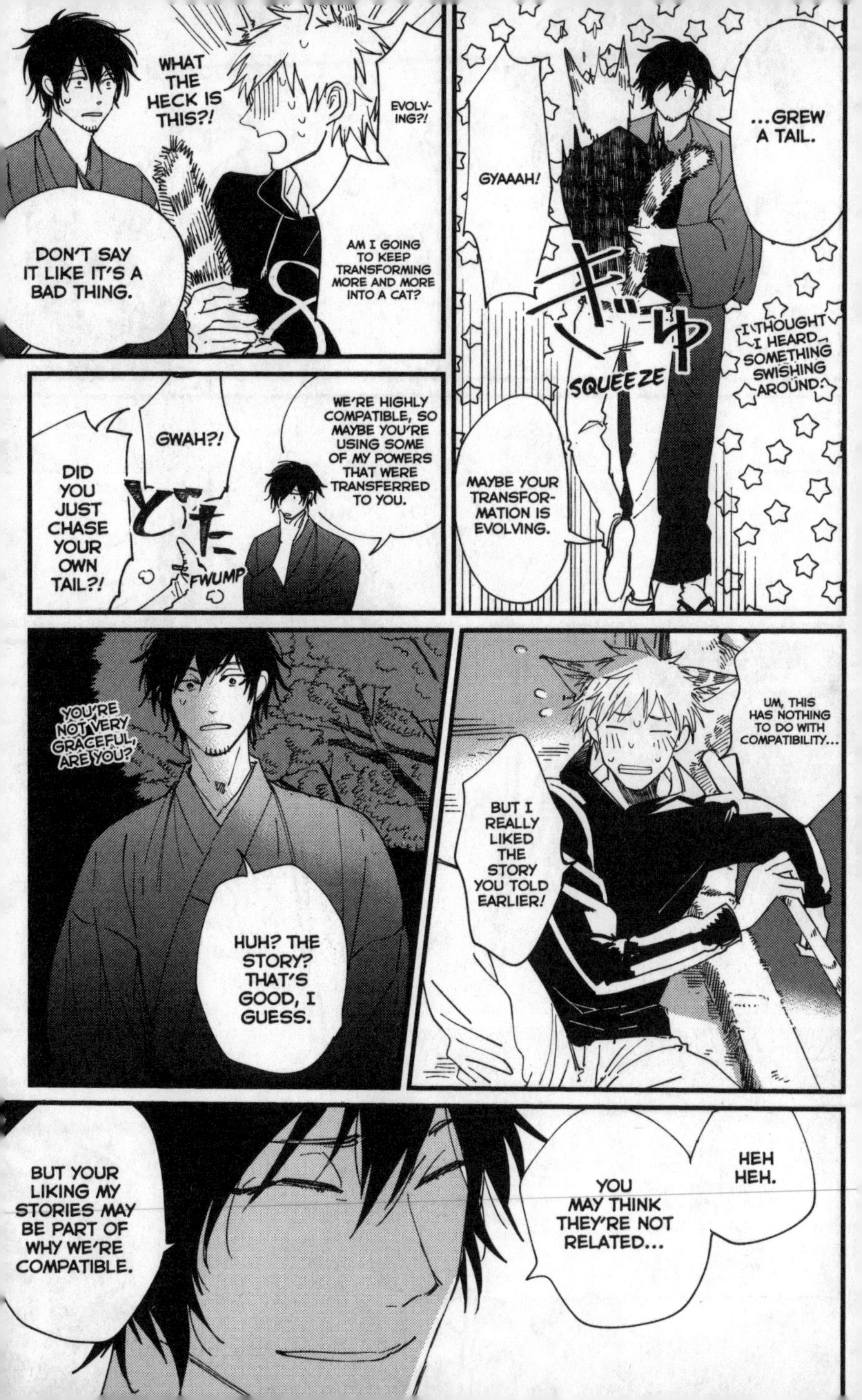
...GREW A TAIL.
GYAAAH!
I THOUGHT I HEARD SOMETHING SWISHING AROUND.
SQUEEZE
MAYBE YOUR TRANSFORMATION IS EVOLVING.
EVOLVING?!
WHAT THE HECK IS THIS?!
AM I GOING TO KEEP TRANSFORMING MORE AND MORE INTO A CAT?
DON'T SAY IT LIKE IT'S A BAD THING.
WE'RE HIGHLY COMPATIBLE, SO MAYBE YOU'RE USING SOME OF MY POWERS THAT WERE TRANSFERRED TO YOU.
GWAH?!
FWUMP
DID YOU JUST CHASE YOUR OWN TAIL?!
UM, THIS HAS NOTHING TO DO WITH COMPATIBILITY...
BUT I REALLY LIKED THE STORY YOU TOLD EARLIER!
YOU'RE NOT VERY GRACEFUL, ARE YOU?
HUH? THE STORY? THAT'S GOOD, I GUESS.
HEH HEH.
YOU MAY THINK THEY'RE NOT RELATED...
BUT YOUR LIKING MY STORIES MAY BE PART OF WHY WE'RE COMPATIBLE.

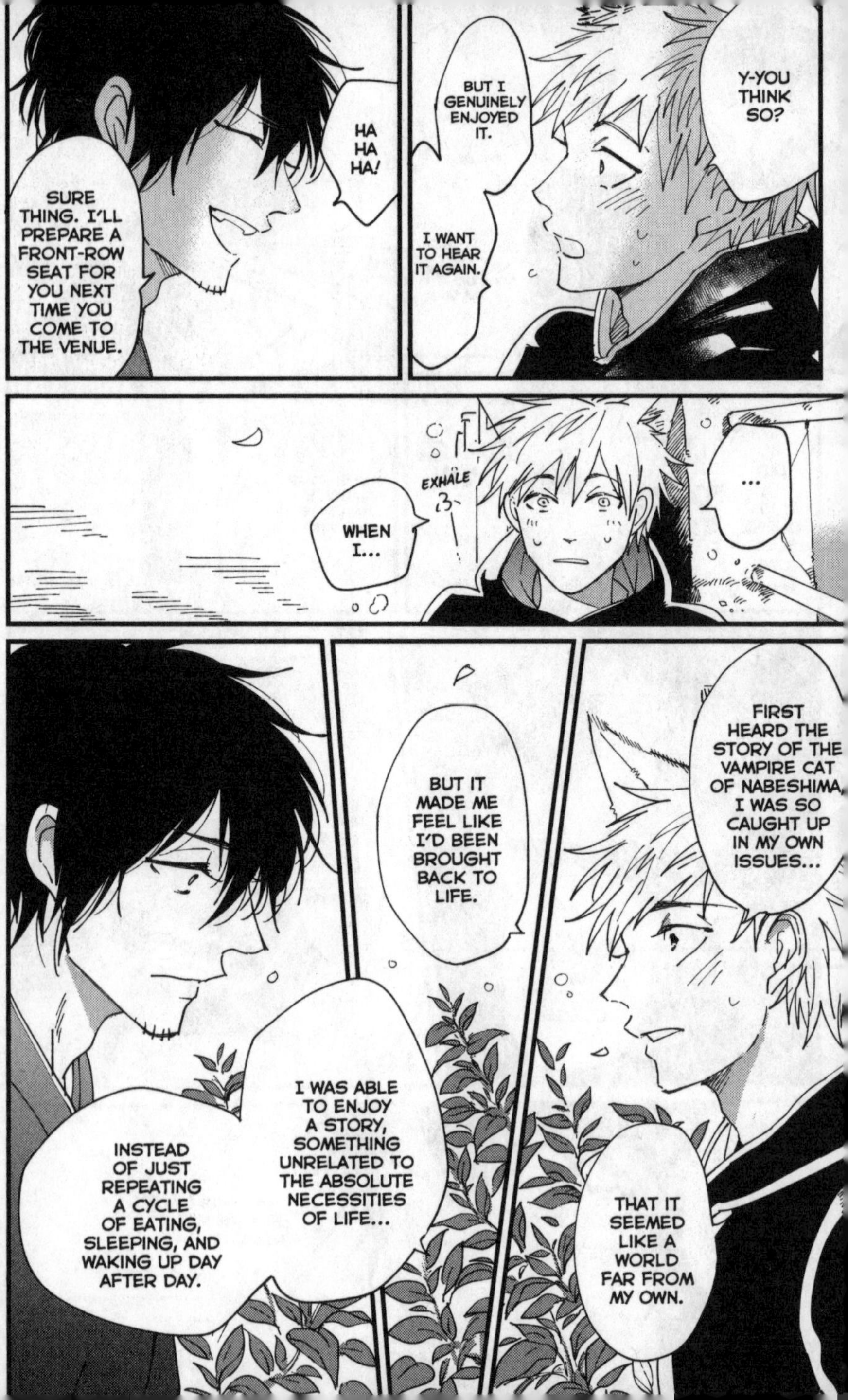
Y-YOU THINK SO?
BUT I GENUINELY ENJOYED IT.
I WANT TO HEAR IT AGAIN.
HA HA HA!
SURE THING. I'LL PREPARE A FRONT-ROW SEAT FOR YOU NEXT TIME YOU COME TO THE VENUE.
...
EXHALE
WHEN I...
FIRST HEARD THE STORY OF THE VAMPIRE CAT OF NABESHIMA, I WAS SO CAUGHT UP IN MY OWN ISSUES...
THAT IT SEEMED LIKE A WORLD FAR FROM MY OWN.
BUT IT MADE ME FEEL LIKE I'D BEEN BROUGHT BACK TO LIFE.
I WAS ABLE TO ENJOY A STORY, SOMETHING UNRELATED TO THE ABSOLUTE NECESSITIES OF LIFE...
INSTEAD OF JUST REPEATING A CYCLE OF EATING, SLEEPING, AND WAKING UP DAY AFTER DAY.

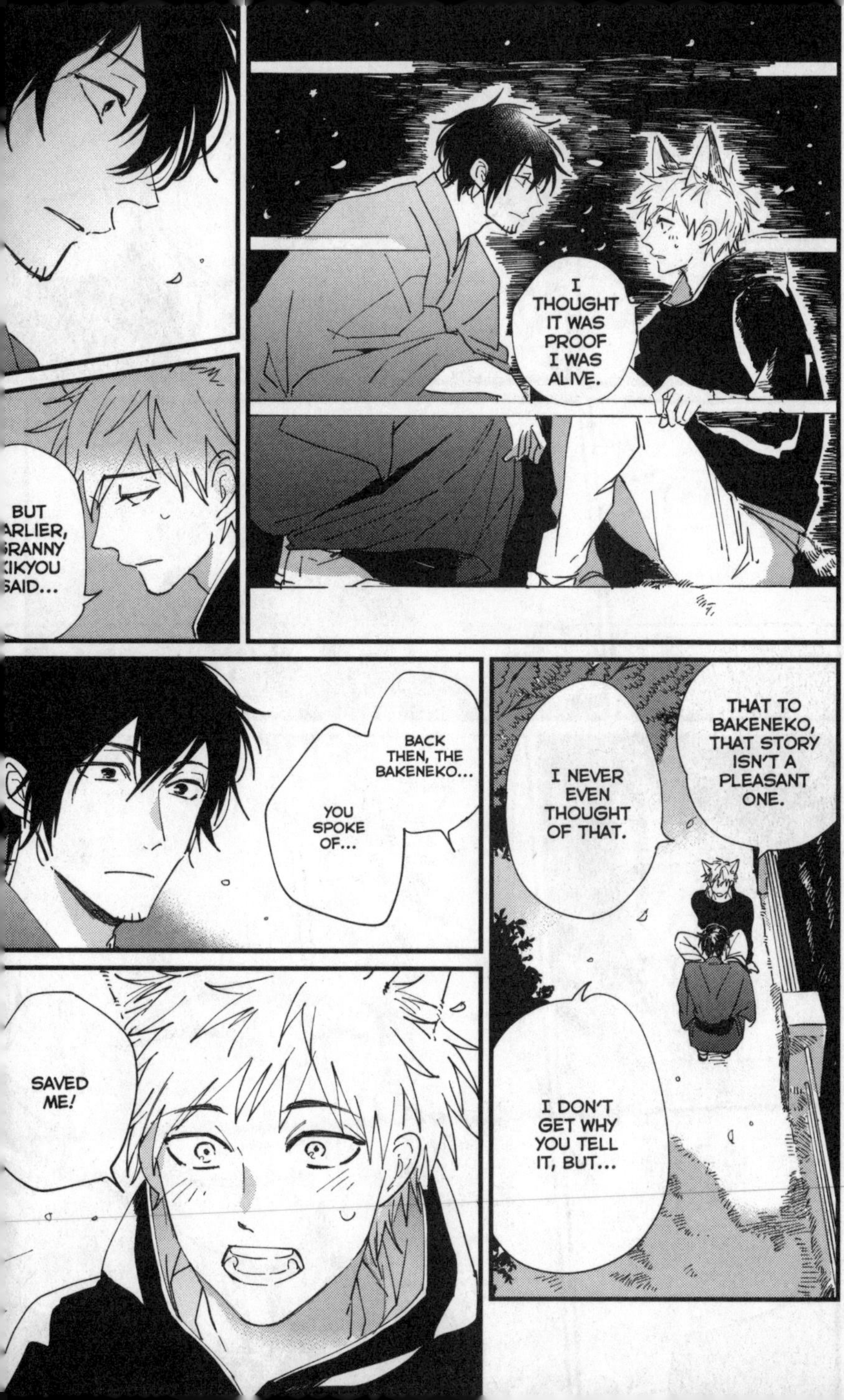
I THOUGHT IT WAS PROOF I WAS ALIVE.
BUT ARLIER, RANNY IKYOU SAID...
THAT TO BAKENEKO, THAT STORY ISN'T A PLEASANT ONE.
I NEVER EVEN THOUGHT OF THAT.
I DON'T GET WHY YOU TELL IT, BUT...
BACK THEN, THE BAKENEKO...
YOU SPOKE OF...
SAVED ME!

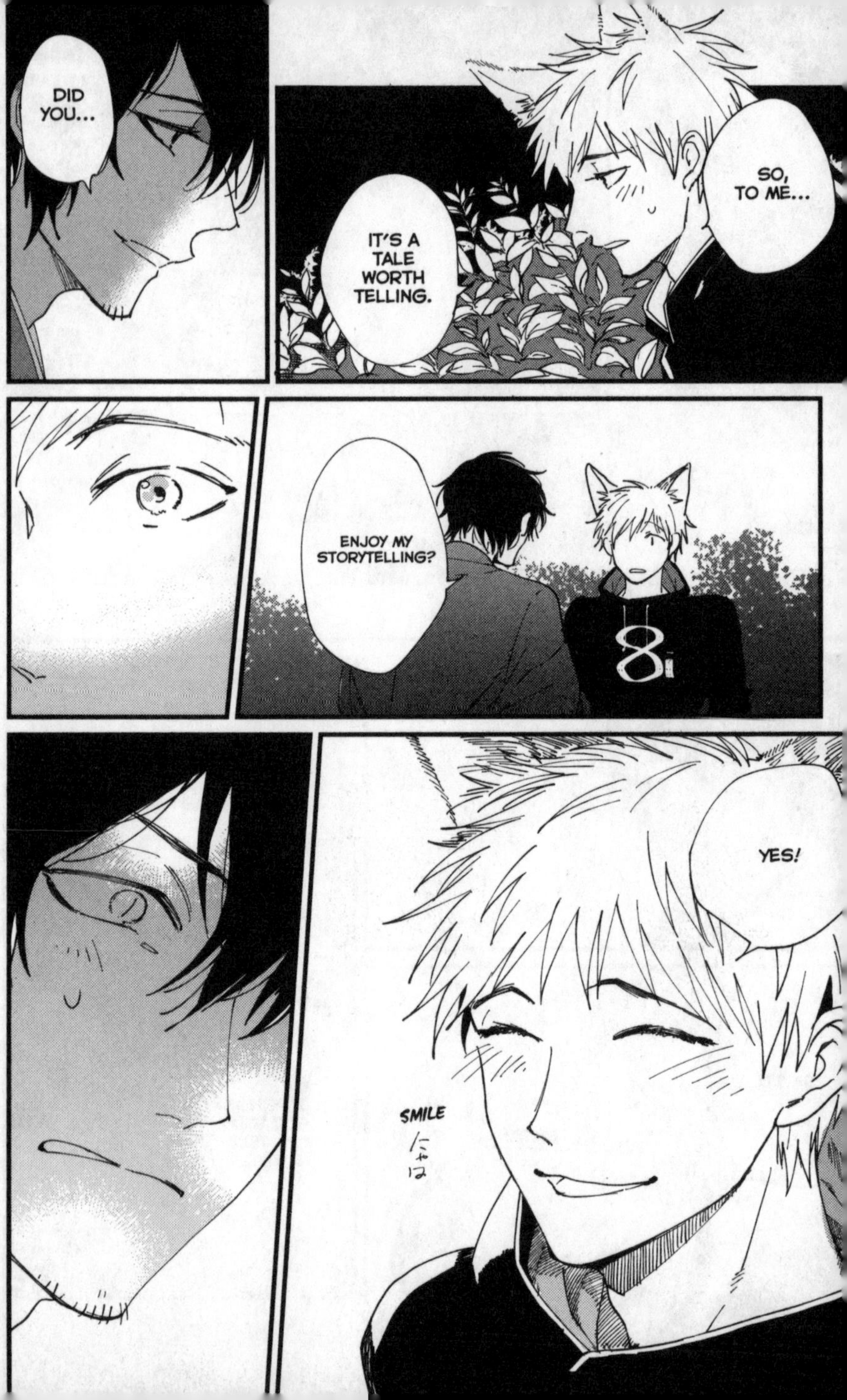
SO, TO ME...
IT'S A TALE WORTH TELLING.
DID YOU...
ENJOY MY STORYTELLING?
YES!
SMILE

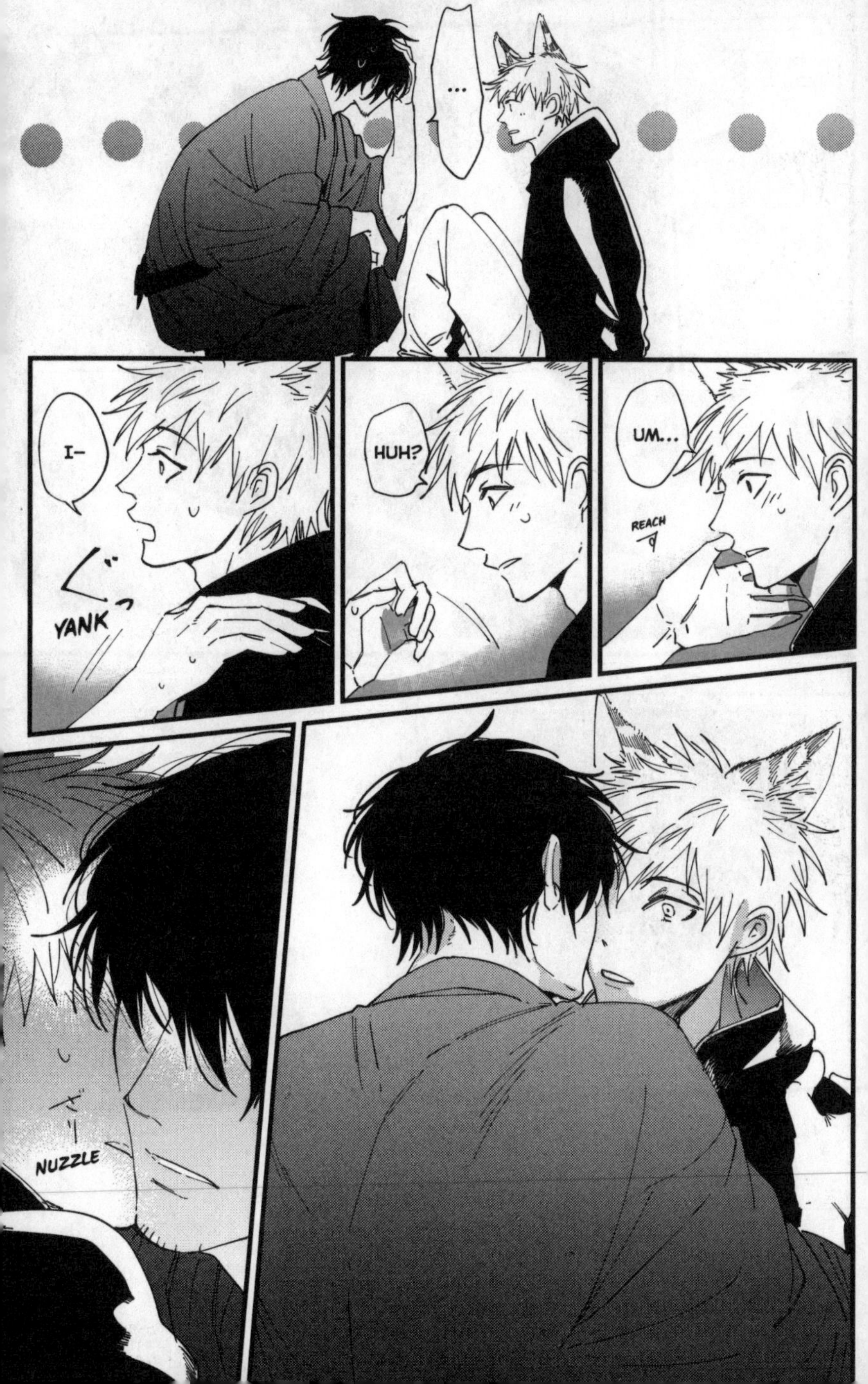
...
UM...
REACH
HUH?
I-
YANK
NUZZLE

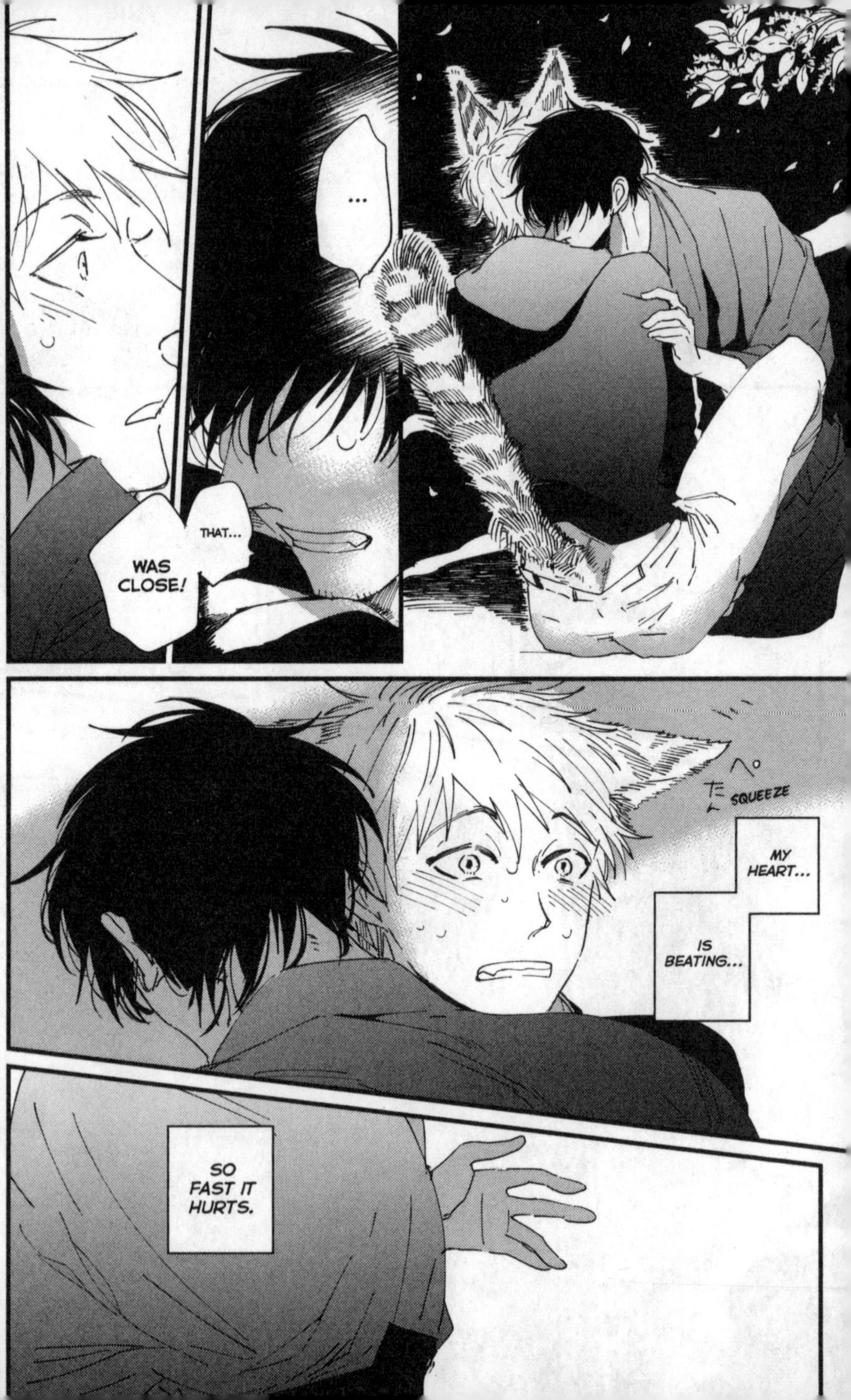
...
THAT... WAS CLOSE!
SQUEEZE
MY HEART...
IS BEATING...
SO FAST IT HURTS.

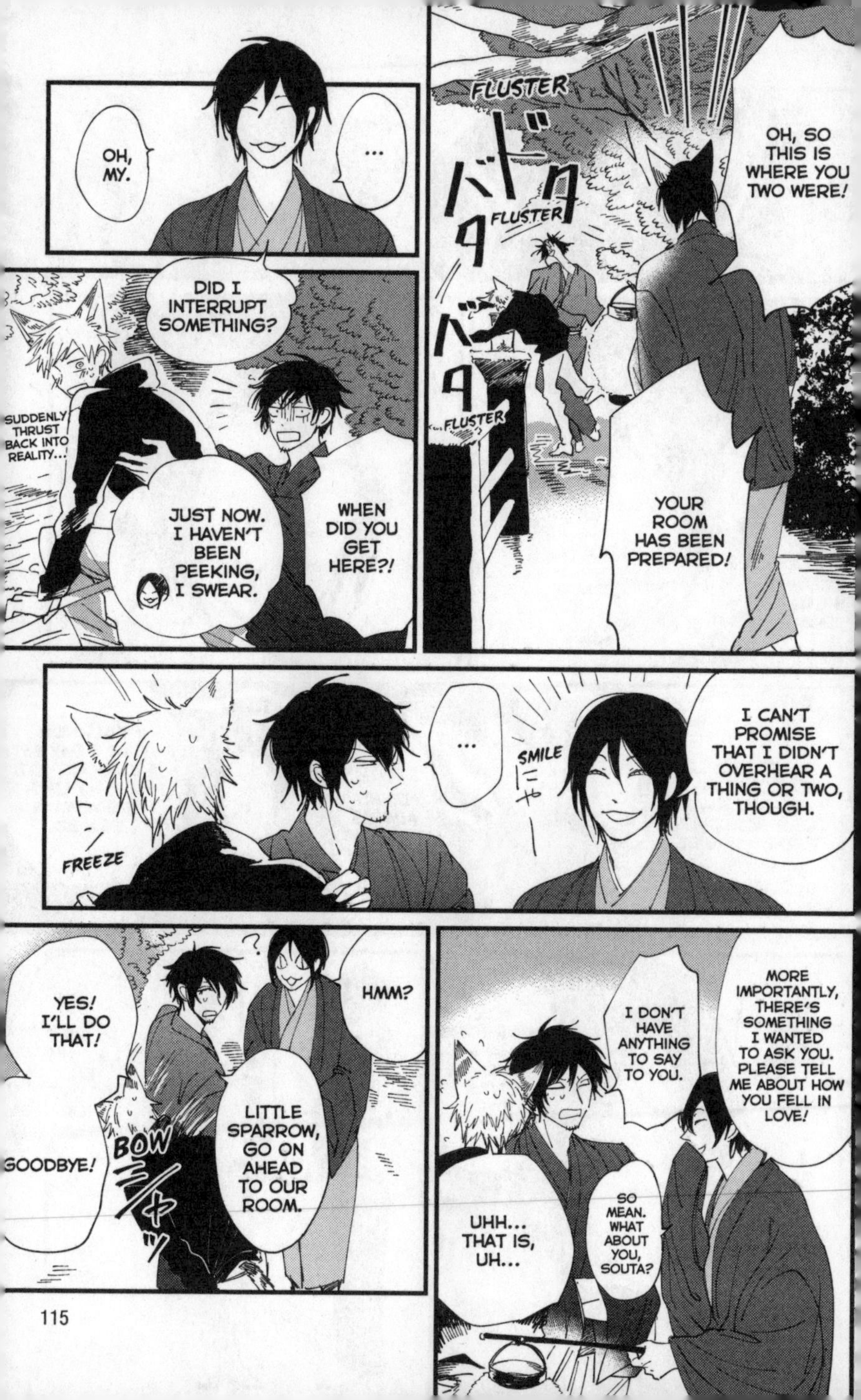

FLUSTER
FLUSTER
FLUSTER
OH, SO THIS IS WHERE YOU TWO WERE!
YOUR ROOM HAS BEEN PREPARED!
...
OH, MY.
DID I INTERRUPT SOMETHING?
WHEN DID YOU GET HERE?!
JUST NOW. I HAVEN'T BEEN PEEKING, I SWEAR.
SUDDENLY THRUST BACK INTO REALITY...
I CAN'T PROMISE THAT I DIDN'T OVERHEAR A THING OR TWO, THOUGH.
SMILE
...
FREEZE
MORE IMPORTANTLY, THERE'S SOMETHING I WANTED TO ASK YOU. PLEASE TELL ME ABOUT HOW YOU FELL IN LOVE!
I DON'T HAVE ANYTHING TO SAY TO YOU.
SO MEAN. WHAT ABOUT YOU, SOUTA?
UHH... THAT IS, UH...
HMM?
LITTLE SPARROW, GO ON AHEAD TO OUR ROOM.
YES! I'LL DO THAT!
BOW
GOODBYE!

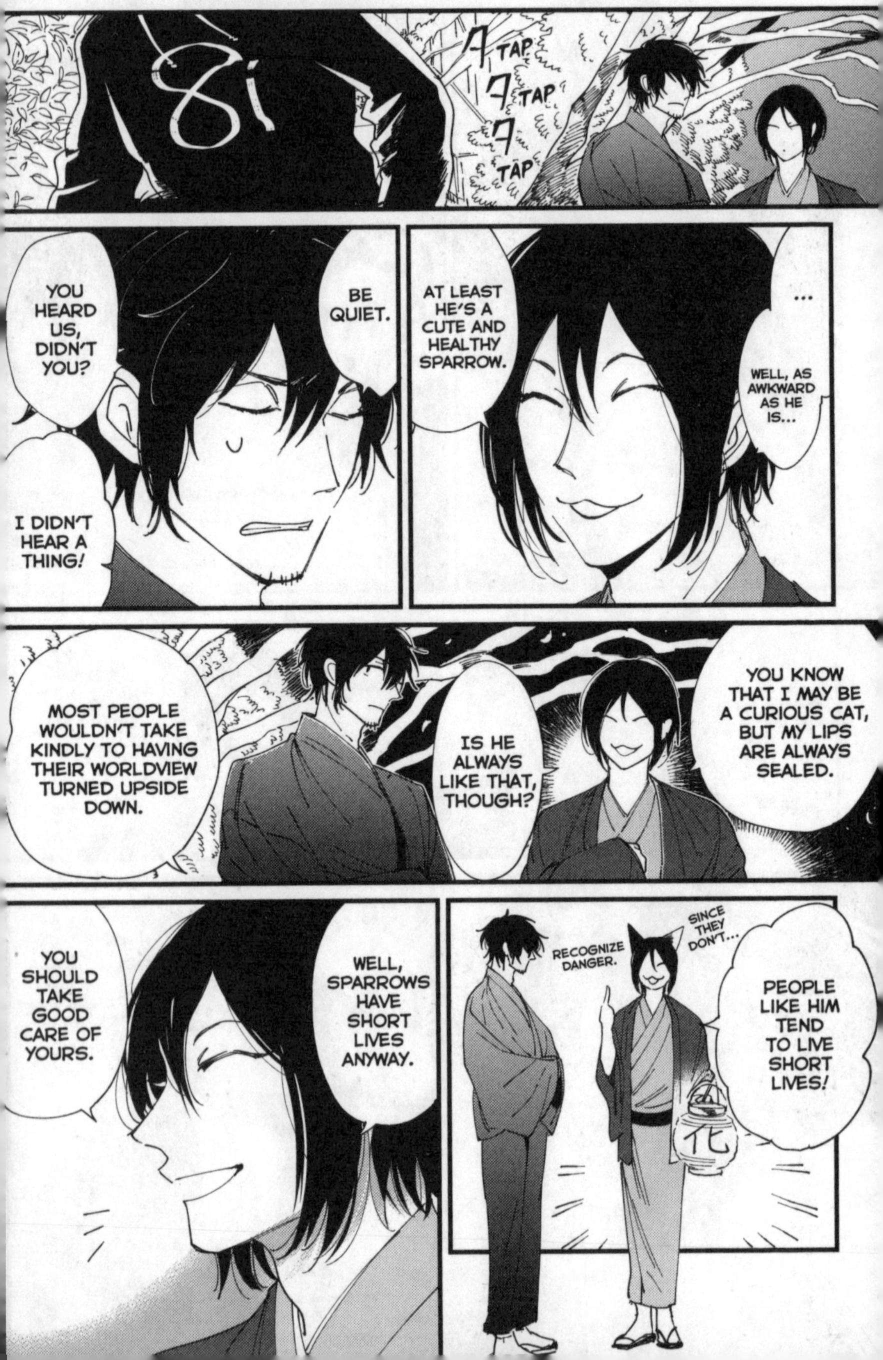
TAP
TAP
TAP
...
WELL, AS AWKWARD AS HE IS...
AT LEAST HE'S A CUTE AND HEALTHY SPARROW.
BE QUIET.
YOU HEARD US, DIDN'T YOU?
I DIDN'T HEAR A THING!
YOU KNOW THAT I MAY BE A CURIOUS CAT, BUT MY LIPS ARE ALWAYS SEALED.
IS HE ALWAYS LIKE THAT, THOUGH?
MOST PEOPLE WOULDN'T TAKE KINDLY TO HAVING THEIR WORLDVIEW TURNED UPSIDE DOWN.
PEOPLE LIKE HIM TEND TO LIVE SHORT LIVES!
SINCE THEY DON'T...
RECOGNIZE DANGER.
WELL, SPARROWS HAVE SHORT LIVES ANYWAY.
YOU SHOULD TAKE GOOD CARE OF YOURS.

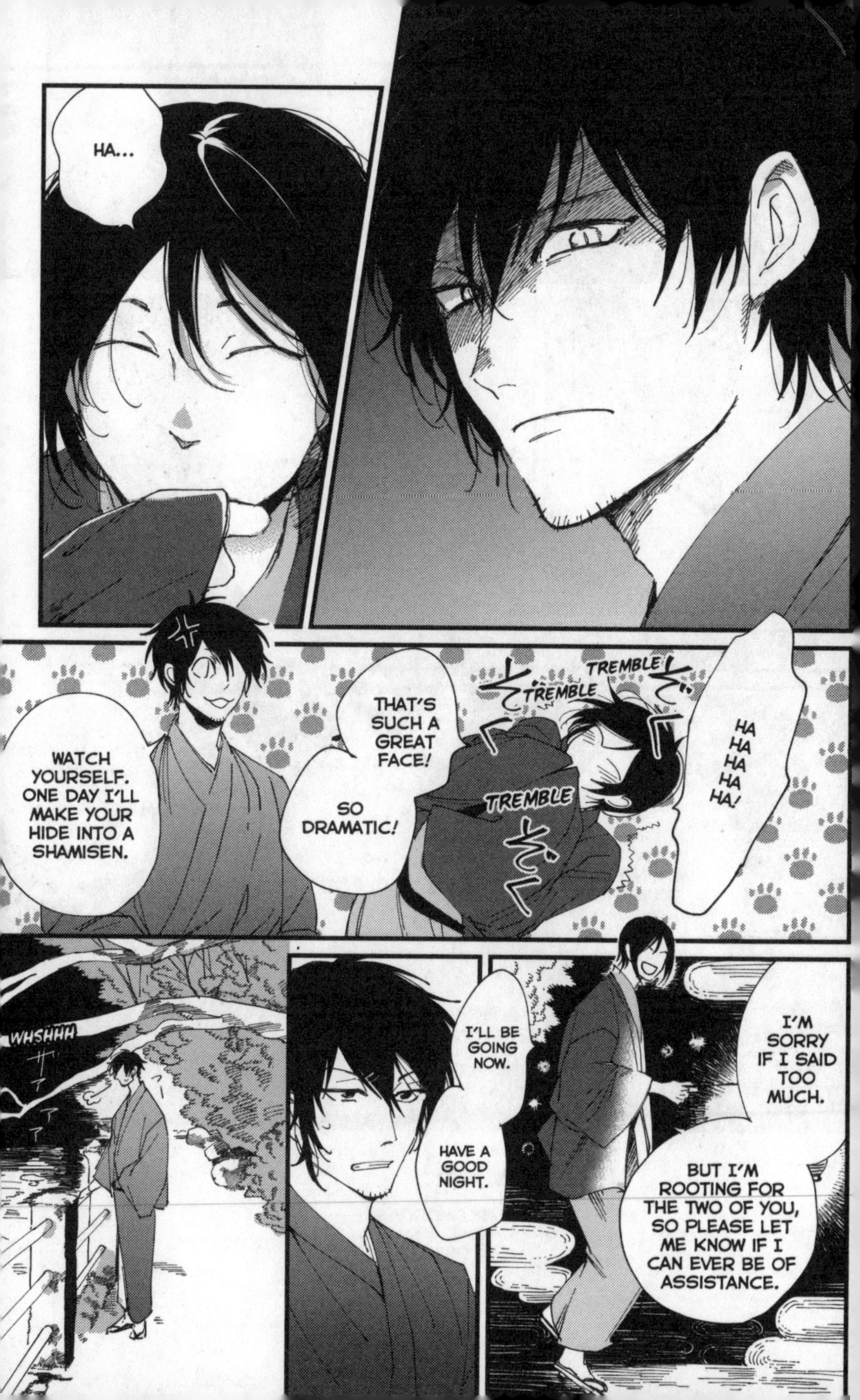
HA...
HA HA HA HA HA!
TREMBLE
TREMBLE
TREMBLE
THAT'S SUCH A GREAT FACE!
SO DRAMATIC!
WATCH YOURSELF. ONE DAY I'LL MAKE YOUR HIDE INTO A SHAMISEN.
I'M SORRY IF I SAID TOO MUCH.
BUT I'M ROOTING FOR THE TWO OF YOU, SO PLEASE LET ME KNOW IF I CAN EVER BE OF ASSISTANCE.
I'LL BE GOING NOW.
HAVE A GOOD NIGHT.
WHSHHH

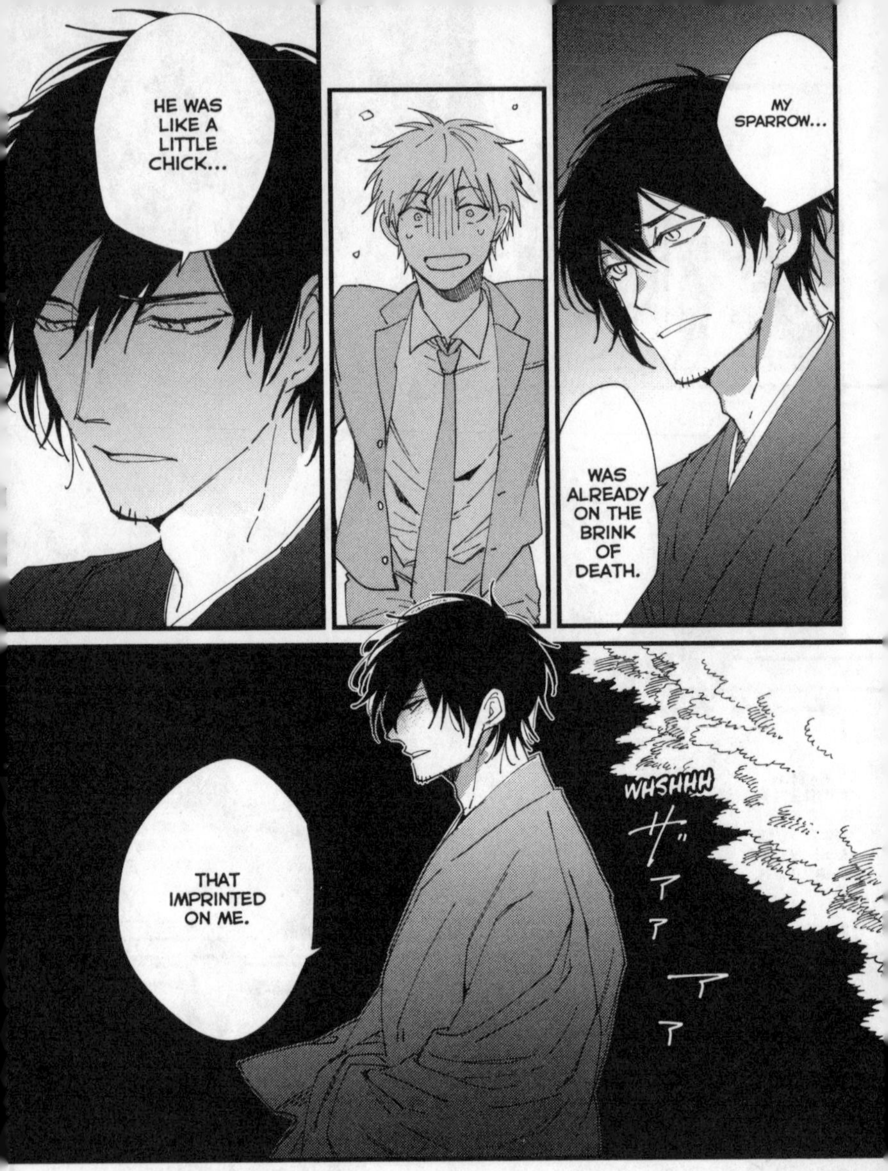
MY SPARROW...
WAS ALREADY ON THE BRINK OF DEATH.
HE WAS LIKE A LITTLE CHICK...
WHSHHH
ザァァァァ
THAT IMPRINTED ON ME.

MY EMOTIONS THAT WERE DEAD...

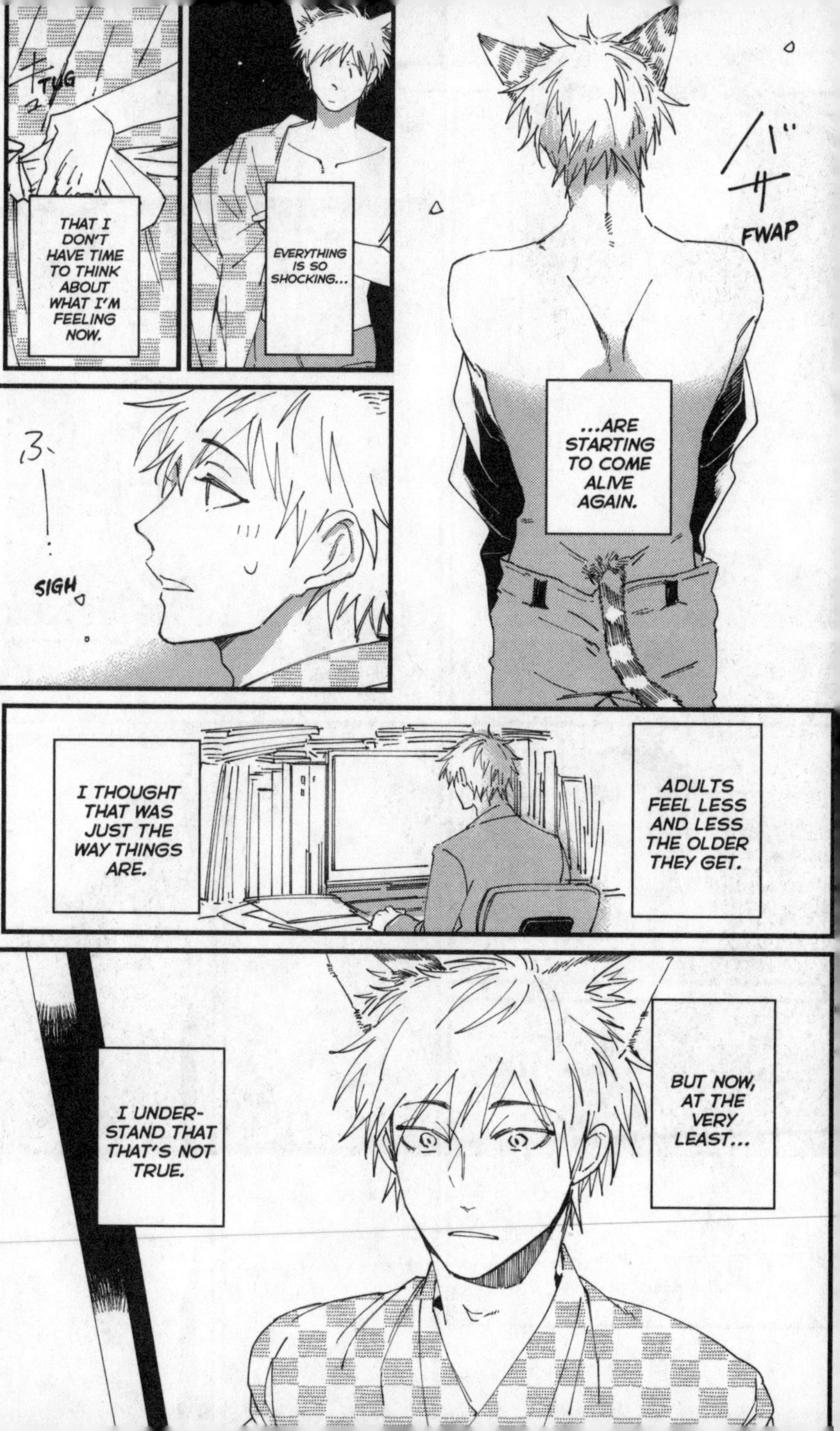
FWAP
...ARE STARTING TO COME ALIVE AGAIN.
EVERYTHING IS SO SHOCKING...
TUG
THAT I DON'T HAVE TIME TO THINK ABOUT WHAT I'M FEELING NOW.
SIGH
ADULTS FEEL LESS AND LESS THE OLDER THEY GET.
I THOUGHT THAT WAS JUST THE WAY THINGS ARE.
BUT NOW, AT THE VERY LEAST...
I UNDER-STAND THAT THAT'S NOT TRUE.

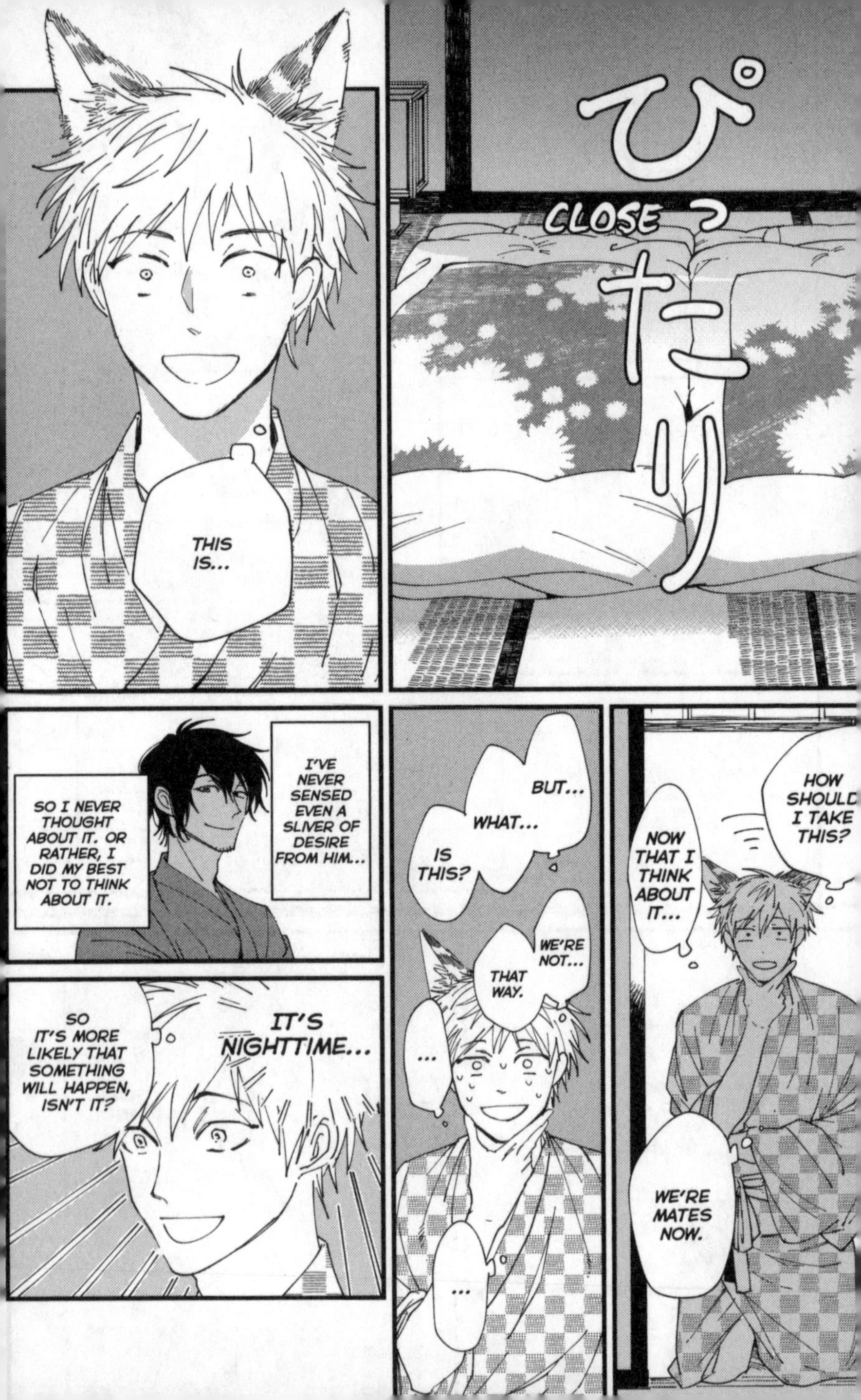
ぴ
CLOSE
つ
たーり
THIS IS...
HOW SHOULD I TAKE THIS?
NOW THAT I THINK ABOUT IT...
WE'RE MATES NOW.
BUT...
WHAT... IS THIS?
WE'RE NOT... THAT WAY.
...
...
I'VE NEVER SENSED EVEN A SLIVER OF DESIRE FROM HIM...
SO I NEVER THOUGHT ABOUT IT. OR RATHER, I DID MY BEST NOT TO THINK ABOUT IT.
IT'S NIGHTTIME...
SO IT'S MORE LIKELY THAT SOMETHING WILL HAPPEN, ISN'T IT?

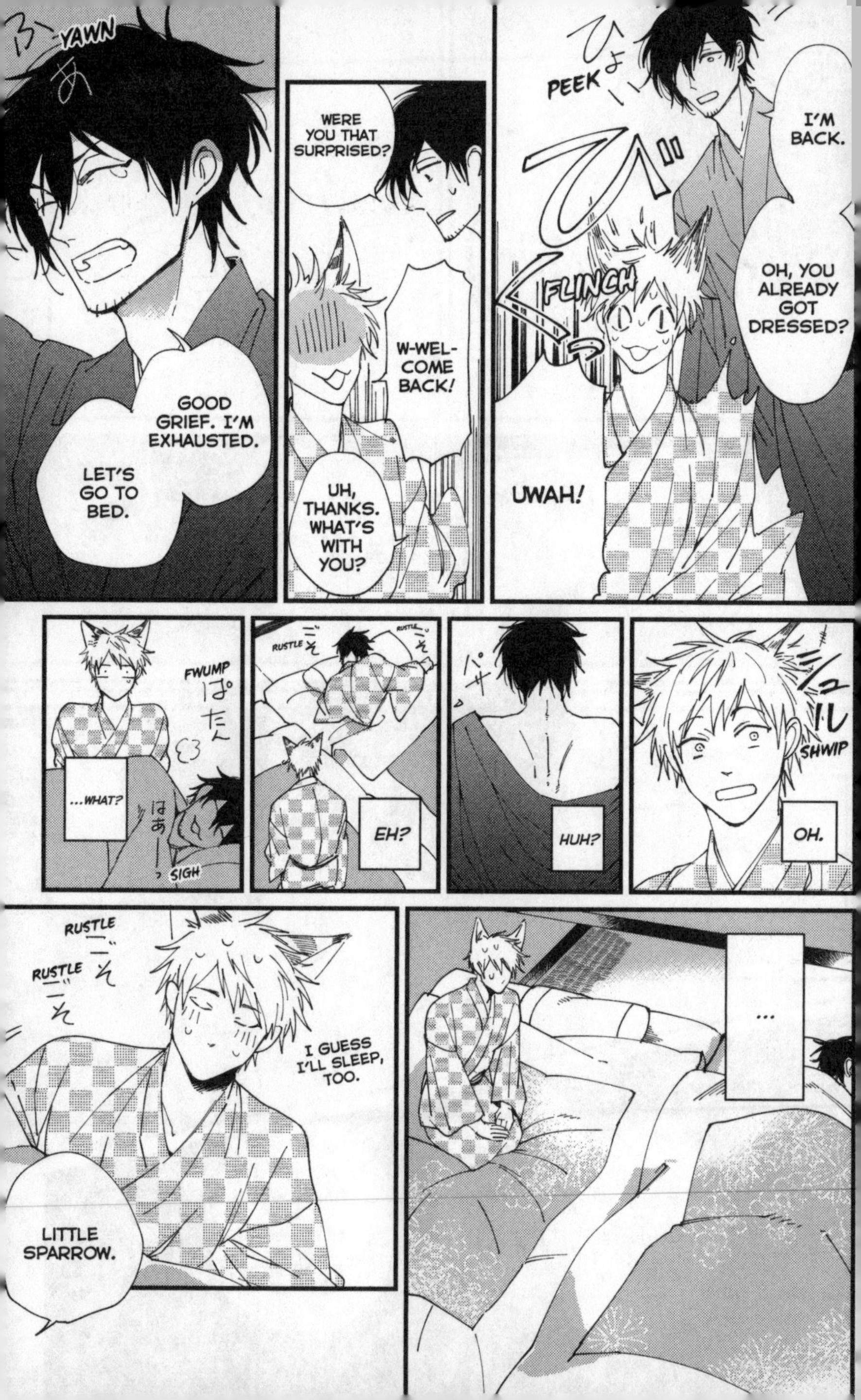
PEEK
I'M BACK.
OH, YOU ALREADY GOT DRESSED?
FLINCH
UWAH!
WERE YOU THAT SURPRISED?
W-WEL-COME BACK!
UH, THANKS. WHAT'S WITH YOU?
YAWN
GOOD GRIEF. I'M EXHAUSTED.
LET'S GO TO BED.
SHWIP
OH.
HUH?
RUSTLE ごそ
RUSTLE ごそ
EH?
FWUMP ぱたん
...WHAT?
はあー
SIGH
...
RUSTLE ごそ
RUSTLE ごそ
I GUESS I'LL SLEEP, TOO.
LITTLE SPARROW.

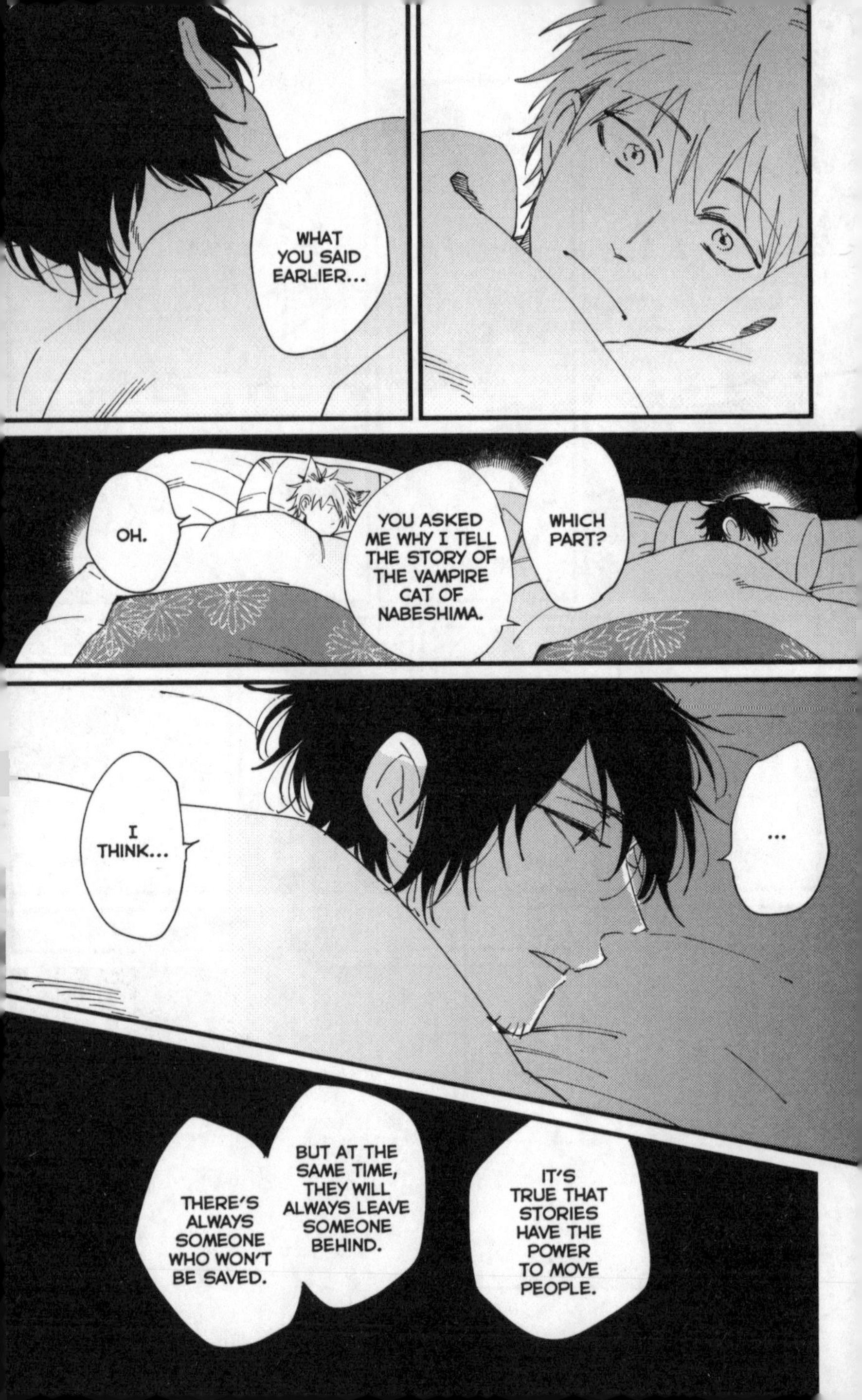
WHAT YOU SAID EARLIER...
WHICH PART?
YOU ASKED ME WHY I TELL THE STORY OF THE VAMPIRE CAT OF NABESHIMA.
OH.
...
I THINK...
IT'S TRUE THAT STORIES HAVE THE POWER TO MOVE PEOPLE.
BUT AT THE SAME TIME, THEY WILL ALWAYS LEAVE SOMEONE BEHIND.
THERE'S ALWAYS SOMEONE WHO WON'T BE SAVED.

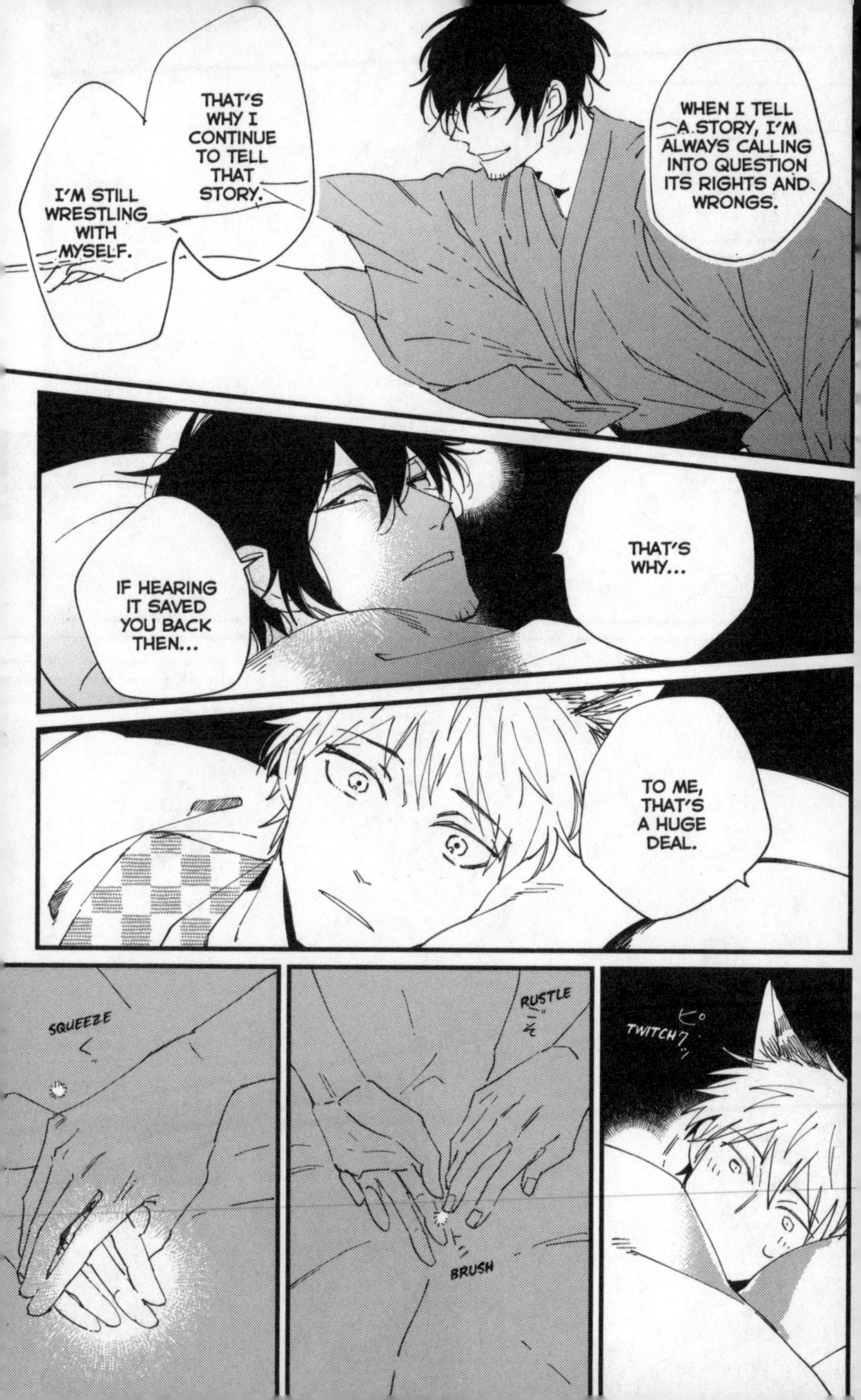
WHEN I TELL A STORY, I'M ALWAYS CALLING INTO QUESTION ITS RIGHTS AND WRONGS.
THAT'S WHY I CONTINUE TO TELL THAT STORY.
I'M STILL WRESTLING WITH MYSELF.
THAT'S WHY...
IF HEARING IT SAVED YOU BACK THEN...
TO ME, THAT'S A HUGE DEAL.
TWITCH
RUSTLE
BRUSH
SQUEEZE

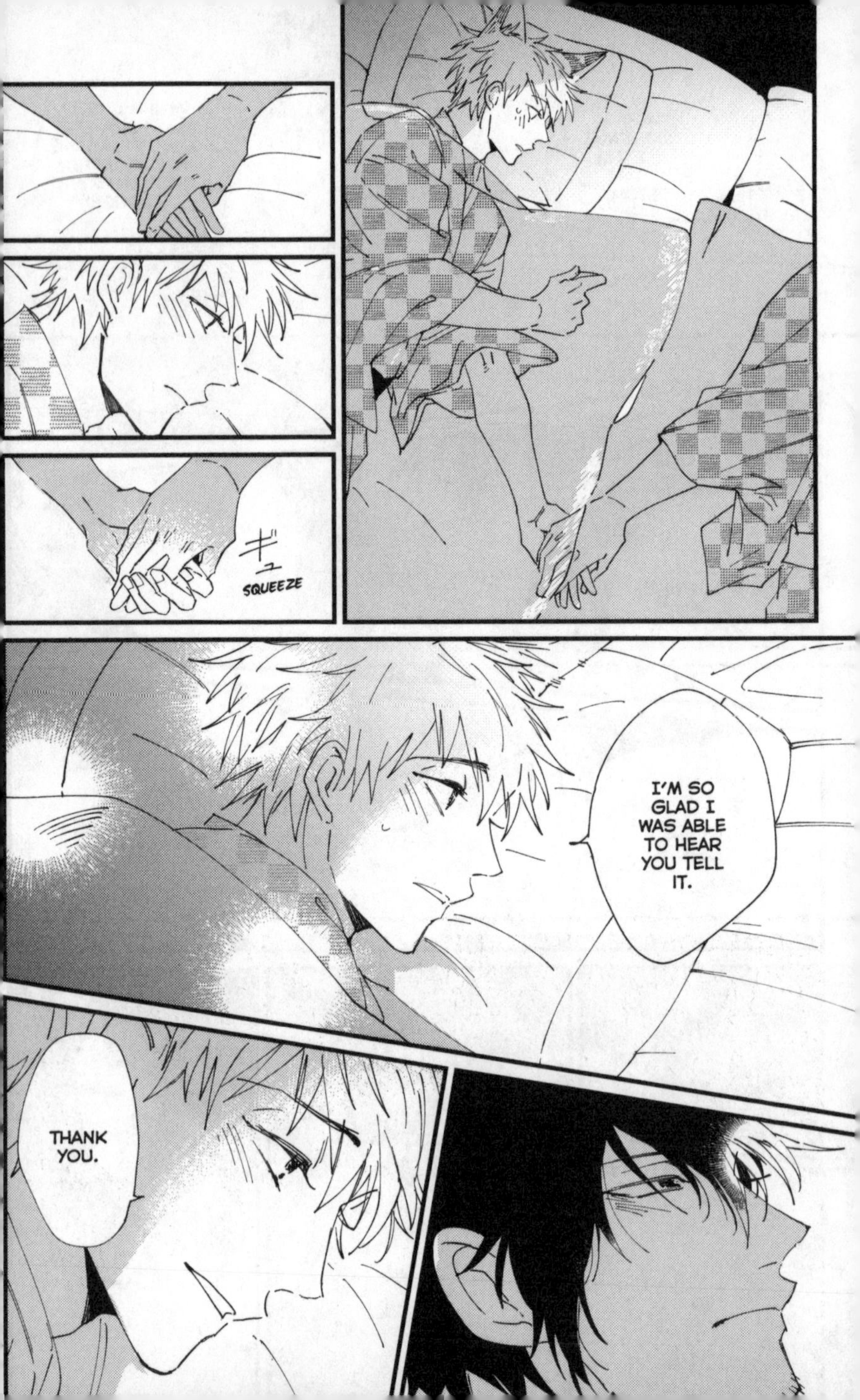
ギュ
SQUEEZE
I'M SO GLAD I WAS ABLE TO HEAR YOU TELL IT.
THANK YOU.

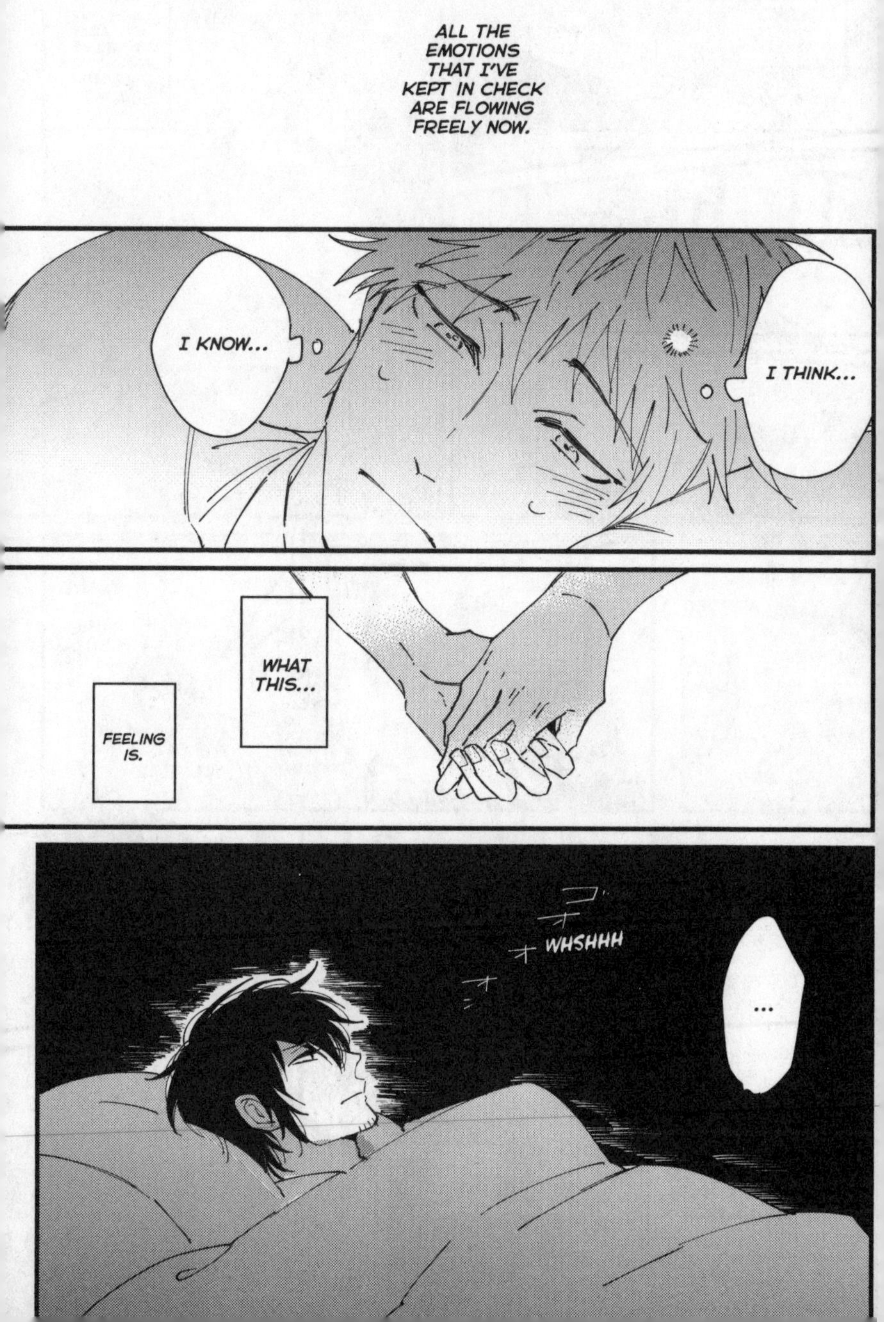
ALL THE EMOTIONS THAT I'VE KEPT IN CHECK ARE FLOWING FREELY NOW.
I THINK...
I KNOW...
WHAT THIS...
FEELING IS.
WHSHHH
...

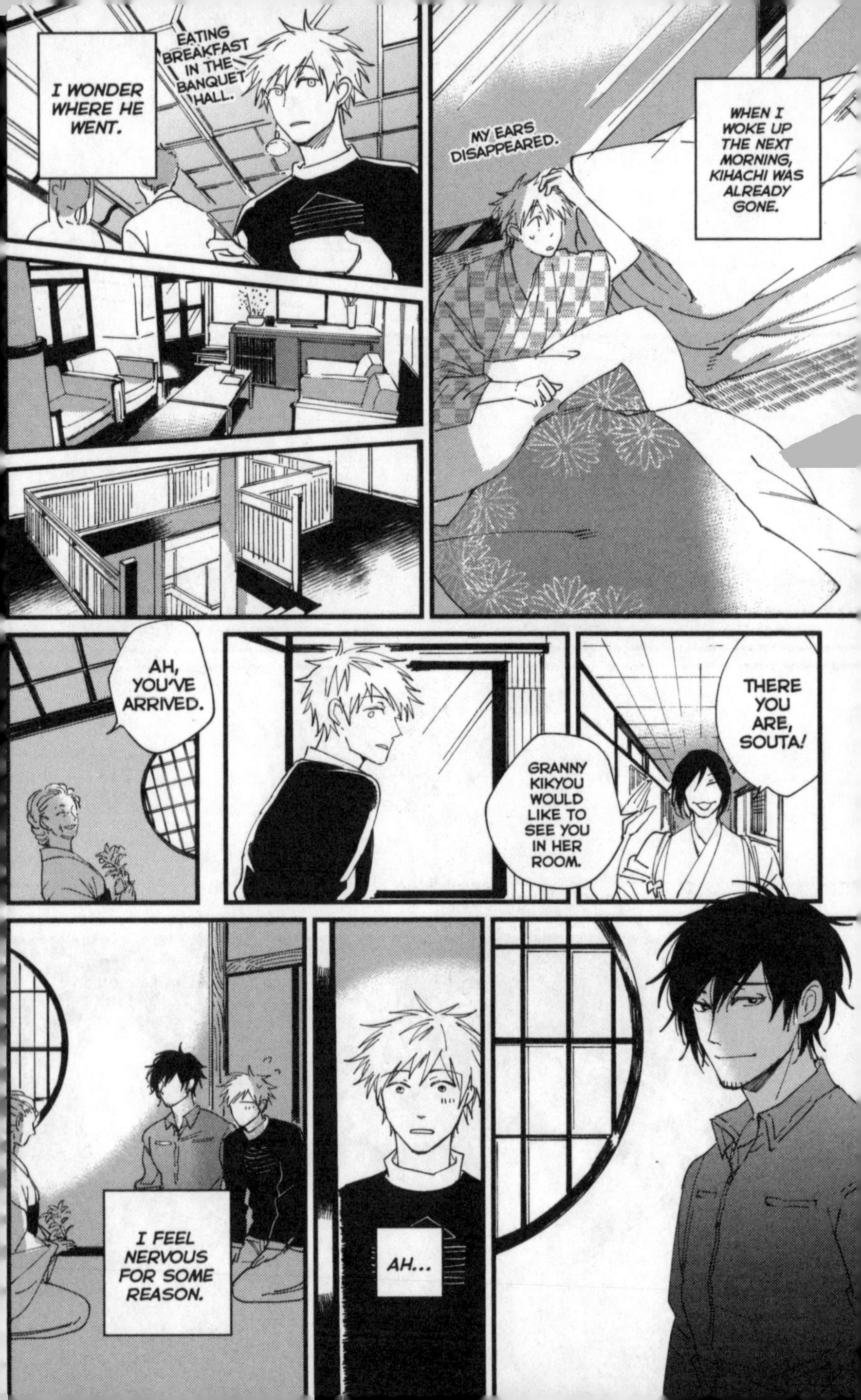
WHEN I WOKE UP THE NEXT MORNING, KIHACHI WAS ALREADY GONE.
MY EARS DISAPPEARED.
EATING BREAKFAST IN THE BANQUET HALL.
I WONDER WHERE HE WENT.
THERE YOU ARE, SOUTA!
GRANNY KIKYOU WOULD LIKE TO SEE YOU IN HER ROOM.
AH, YOU'VE ARRIVED.
AH...
I FEEL NERVOUS FOR SOME REASON.

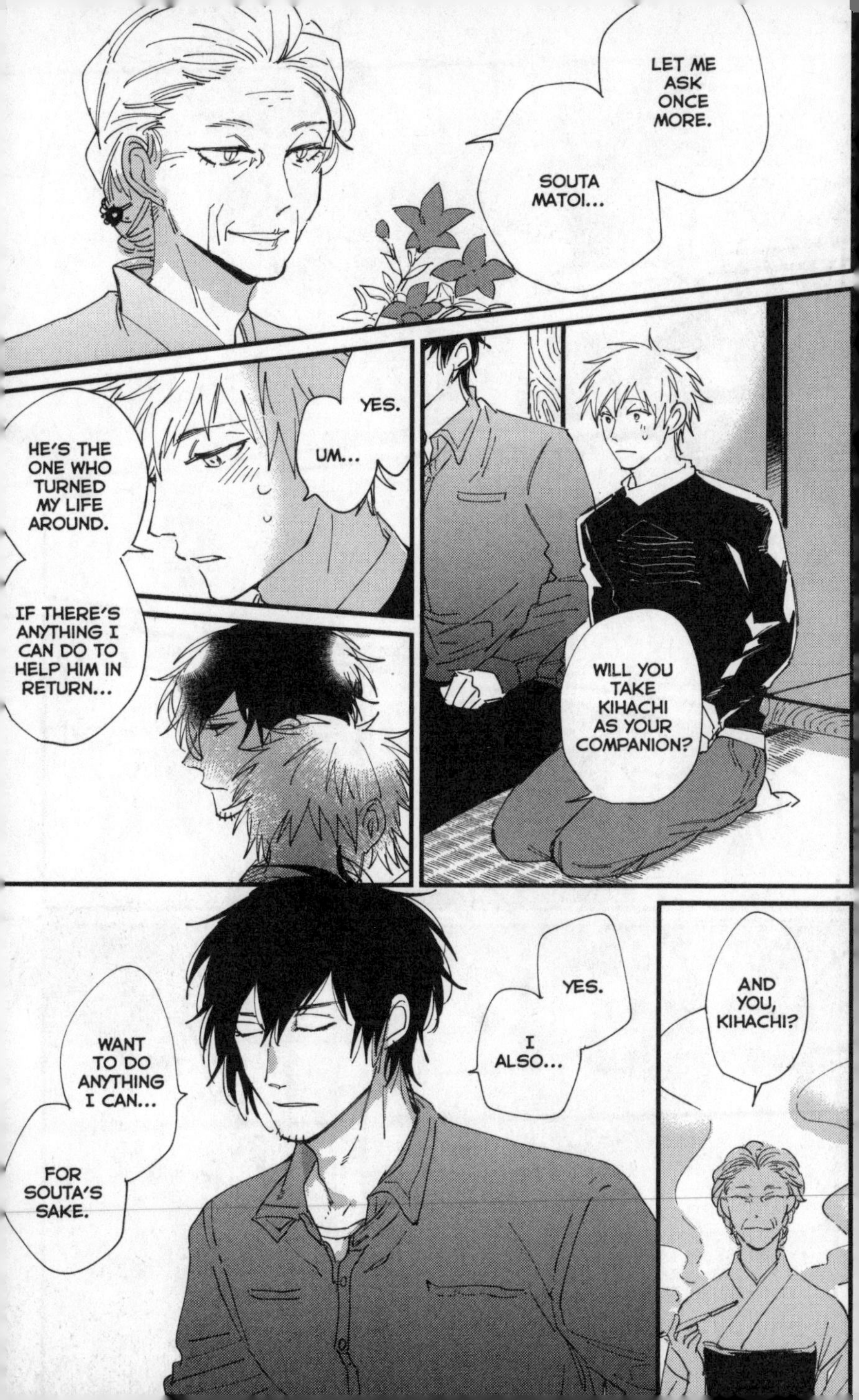
LET ME ASK ONCE MORE.
SOUTA MATOI...
WILL YOU TAKE KIHACHI AS YOUR COMPANION?
YES.
UM...
HE'S THE ONE WHO TURNED MY LIFE AROUND.
IF THERE'S ANYTHING I CAN DO TO HELP HIM IN RETURN...
AND YOU, KIHACHI?
YES.
I ALSO...
WANT TO DO ANYTHING I CAN...
FOR SOUTA'S SAKE.

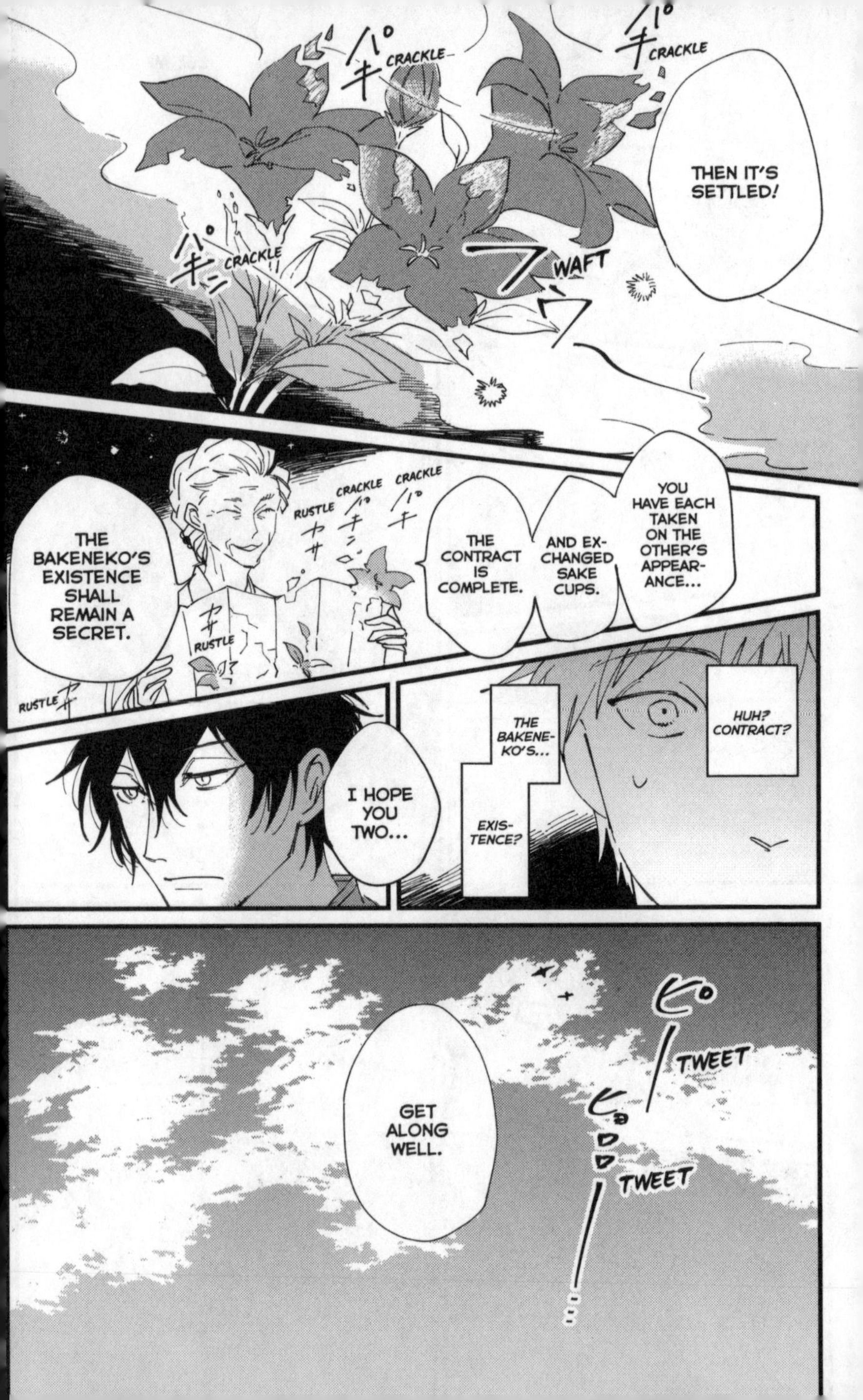
CRACKLE
THEN IT'S SETTLED!
CRACKLE
WAFT
CRACKLE
YOU HAVE EACH TAKEN ON THE OTHER'S APPEARANCE...
AND EXCHANGED SAKE CUPS.
THE CONTRACT IS COMPLETE.
CRACKLE
CRACKLE
RUSTLE
THE BAKENEKO'S EXISTENCE SHALL REMAIN A SECRET.
RUSTLE
RUSTLE
HUH? CONTRACT?
THE BAKENEKO'S...
EXISTENCE?
I HOPE YOU TWO...
TWEET
TWEET
GET ALONG WELL.

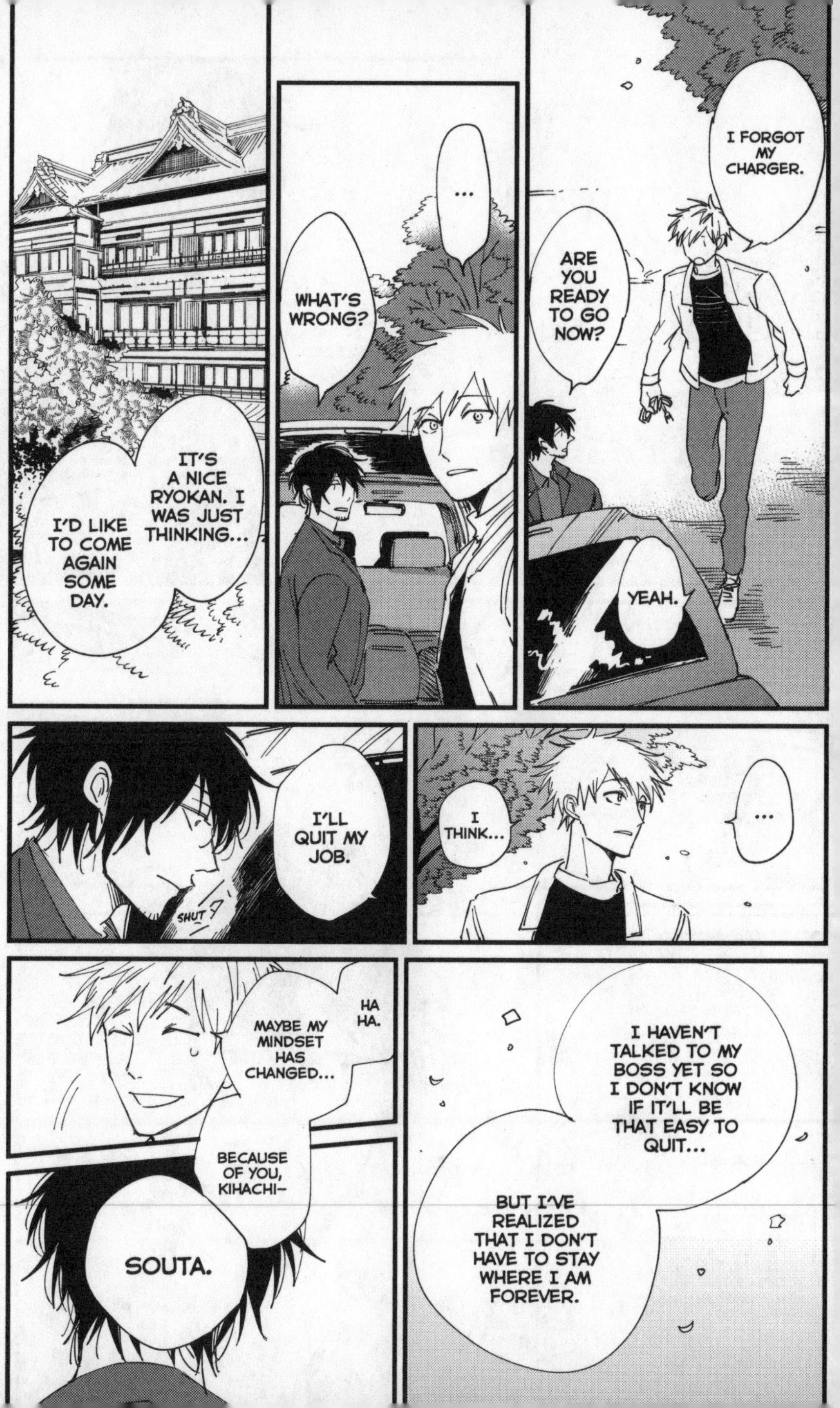
I FORGOT MY CHARGER.
ARE YOU READY TO GO NOW?
YEAH.
...
WHAT'S WRONG?
IT'S A NICE RYOKAN. I WAS JUST THINKING...
I'D LIKE TO COME AGAIN SOME DAY.
...
I THINK...
I'LL QUIT MY JOB.
SHUT
I HAVEN'T TALKED TO MY BOSS YET SO I DON'T KNOW IF IT'LL BE THAT EASY TO QUIT...
BUT I'VE REALIZED THAT I DON'T HAVE TO STAY WHERE I AM FOREVER.
HA HA.
MAYBE MY MINDSET HAS CHANGED...
BECAUSE OF YOU, KIHACHI–
SOUTA.

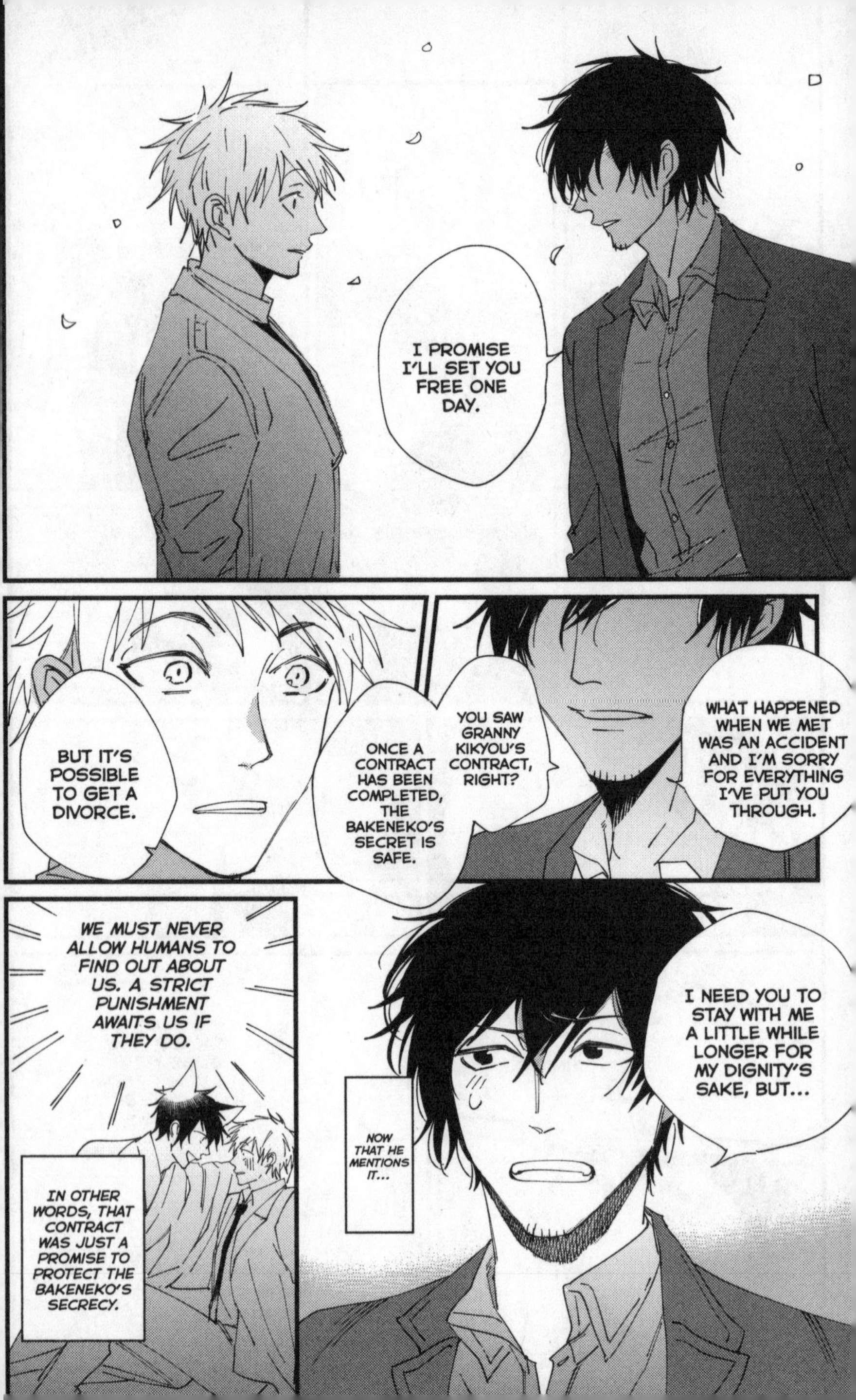
I PROMISE I'LL SET YOU FREE ONE DAY.
WHAT HAPPENED WHEN WE MET WAS AN ACCIDENT AND I'M SORRY FOR EVERYTHING I'VE PUT YOU THROUGH.
YOU SAW GRANNY KIKYOU'S CONTRACT, RIGHT?
ONCE A CONTRACT HAS BEEN COMPLETED, THE BAKENEKO'S SECRET IS SAFE.
BUT IT'S POSSIBLE TO GET A DIVORCE.
I NEED YOU TO STAY WITH ME A LITTLE WHILE LONGER FOR MY DIGNITY'S SAKE, BUT...
NOW THAT HE MENTIONS IT...
WE MUST NEVER ALLOW HUMANS TO FIND OUT ABOUT US. A STRICT PUNISHMENT AWAITS US IF THEY DO.
IN OTHER WORDS, THAT CONTRACT WAS JUST A PROMISE TO PROTECT THE BAKENEKO'S SECRECY.

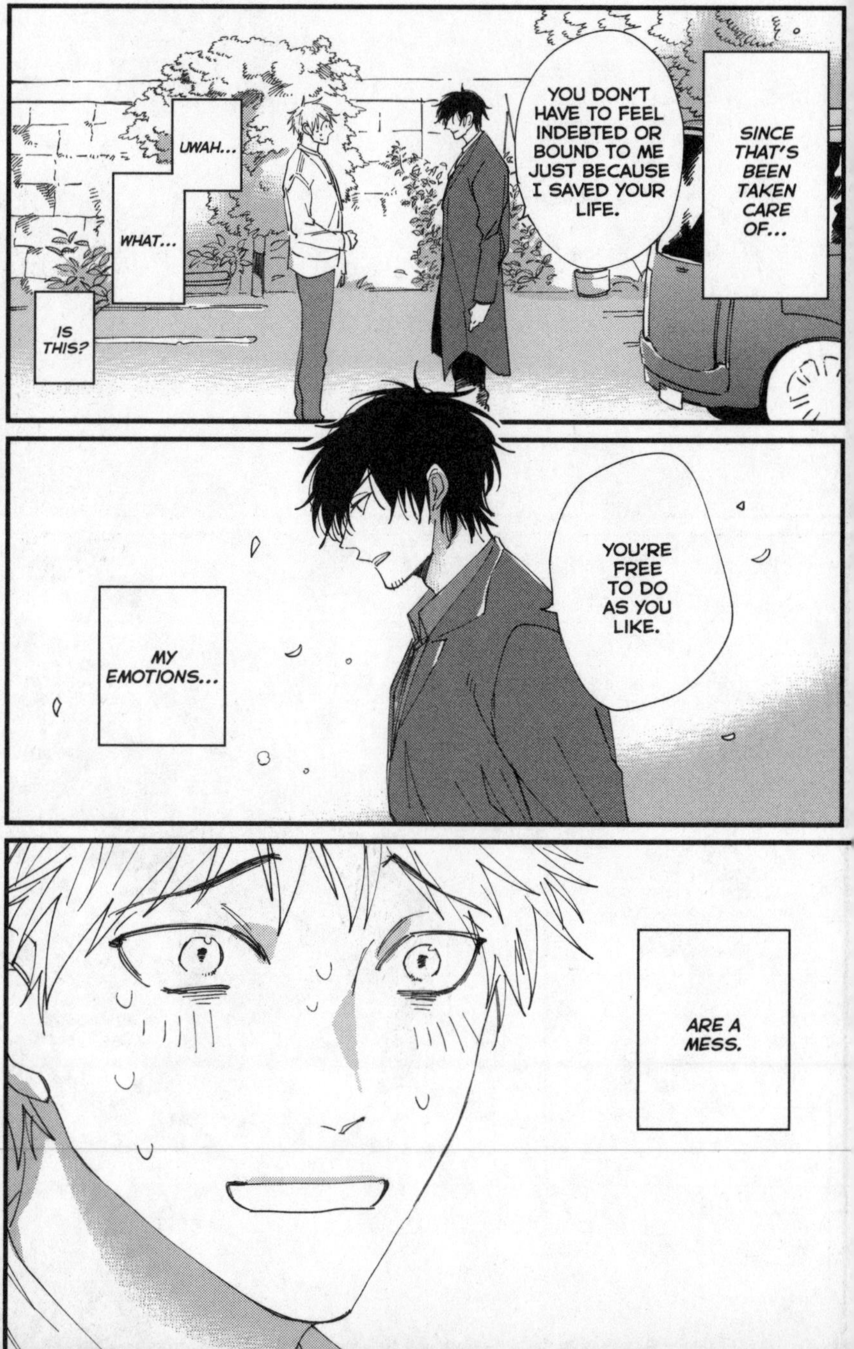
SINCE THAT'S BEEN TAKEN CARE OF...
YOU DON'T HAVE TO FEEL INDEBTED OR BOUND TO ME JUST BECAUSE I SAVED YOUR LIFE.
UWAH...
WHAT...
IS THIS?
YOU'RE FREE TO DO AS YOU LIKE.
MY EMOTIONS...
ARE A MESS.

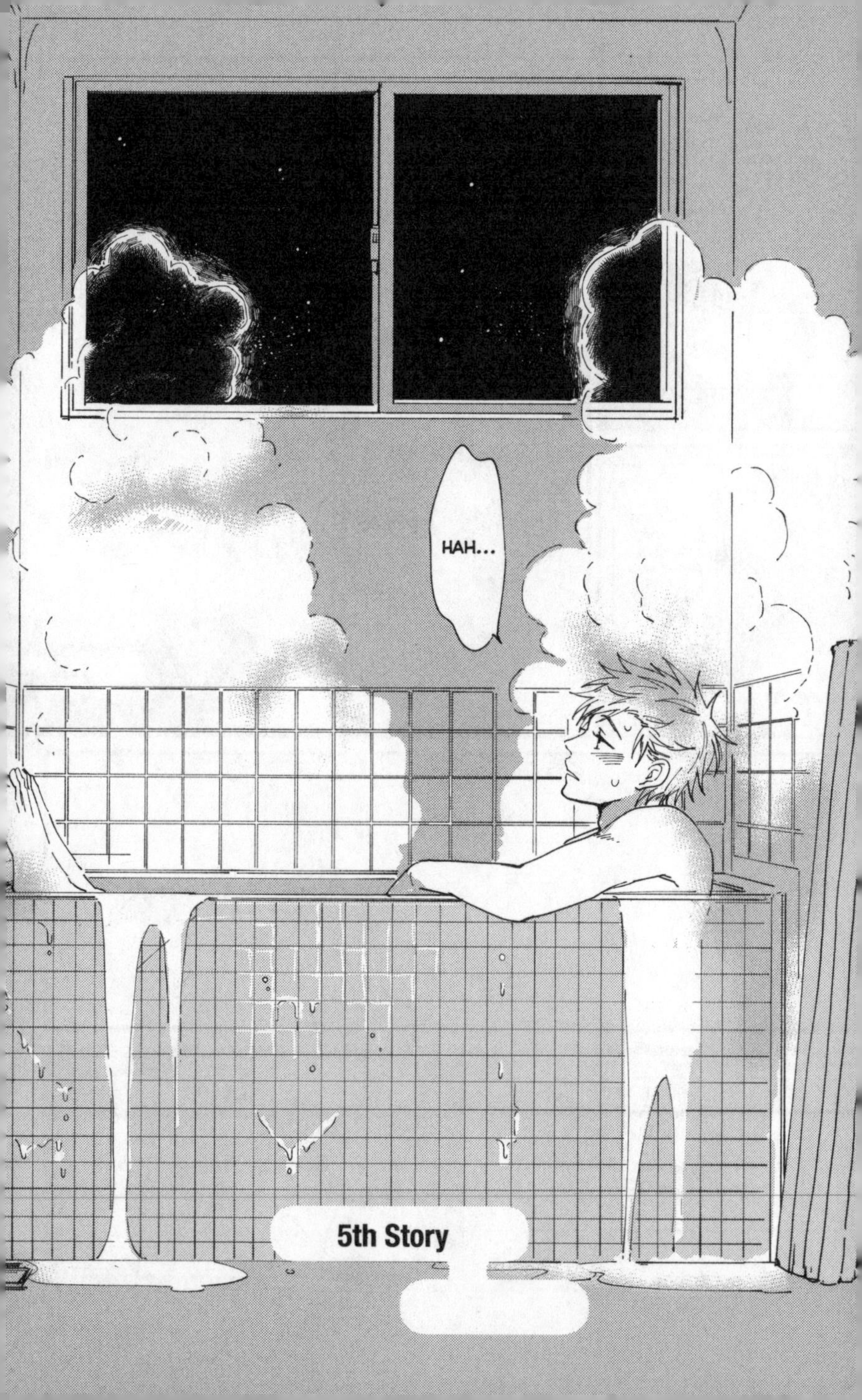
HAH...
5th Story

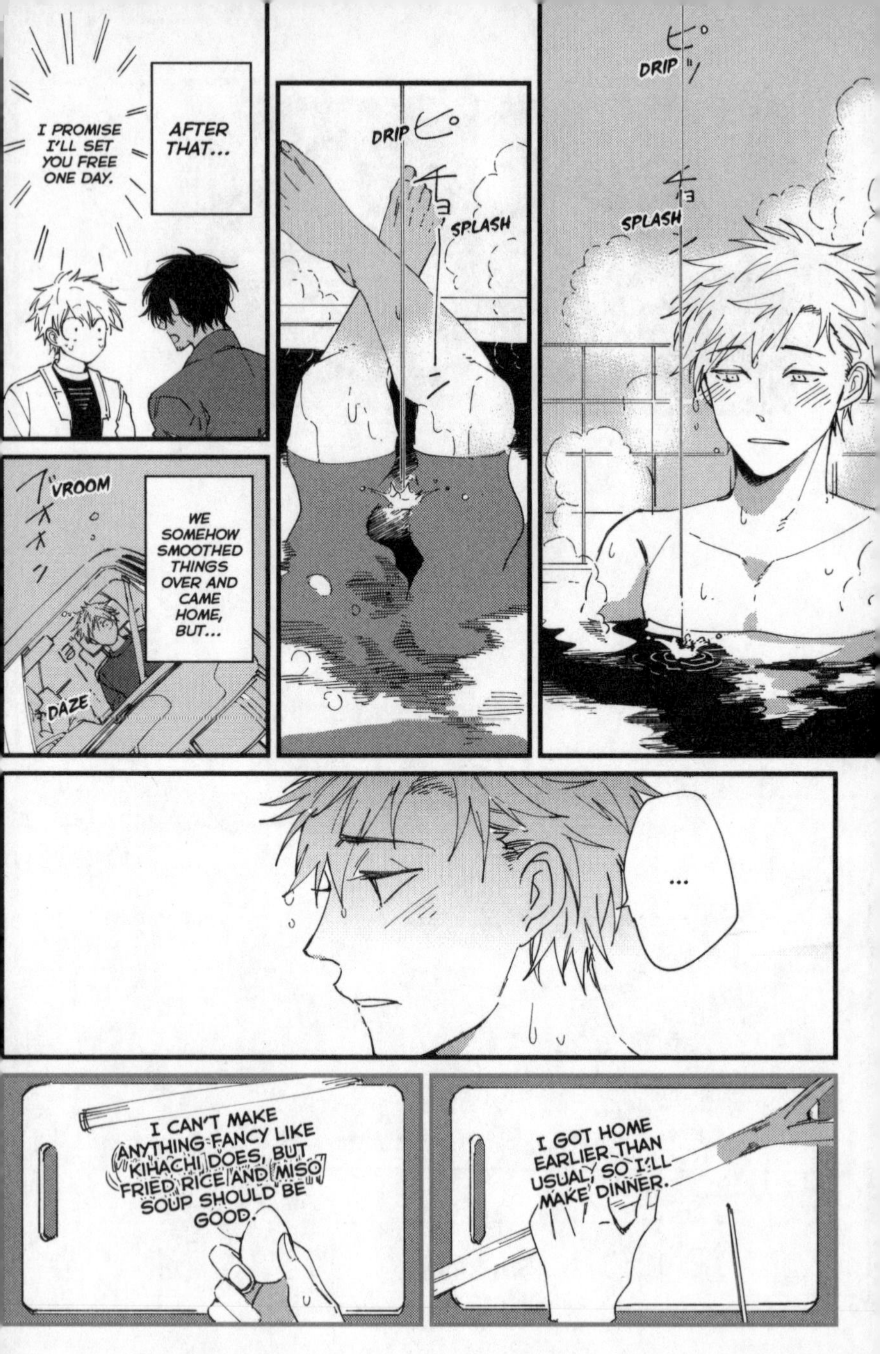
DRIP
SPLASH
DRIP
SPLASH
AFTER THAT...
I PROMISE I'LL SET YOU FREE ONE DAY.
VROOM
WE SOMEHOW SMOOTHED THINGS OVER AND CAME HOME, BUT...
DAZE
...
I GOT HOME EARLIER THAN USUAL, SO I'LL MAKE DINNER.
I CAN'T MAKE ANYTHING FANCY LIKE KIHACHI DOES, BUT FRIED RICE AND MISO SOUP SHOULD BE GOOD.

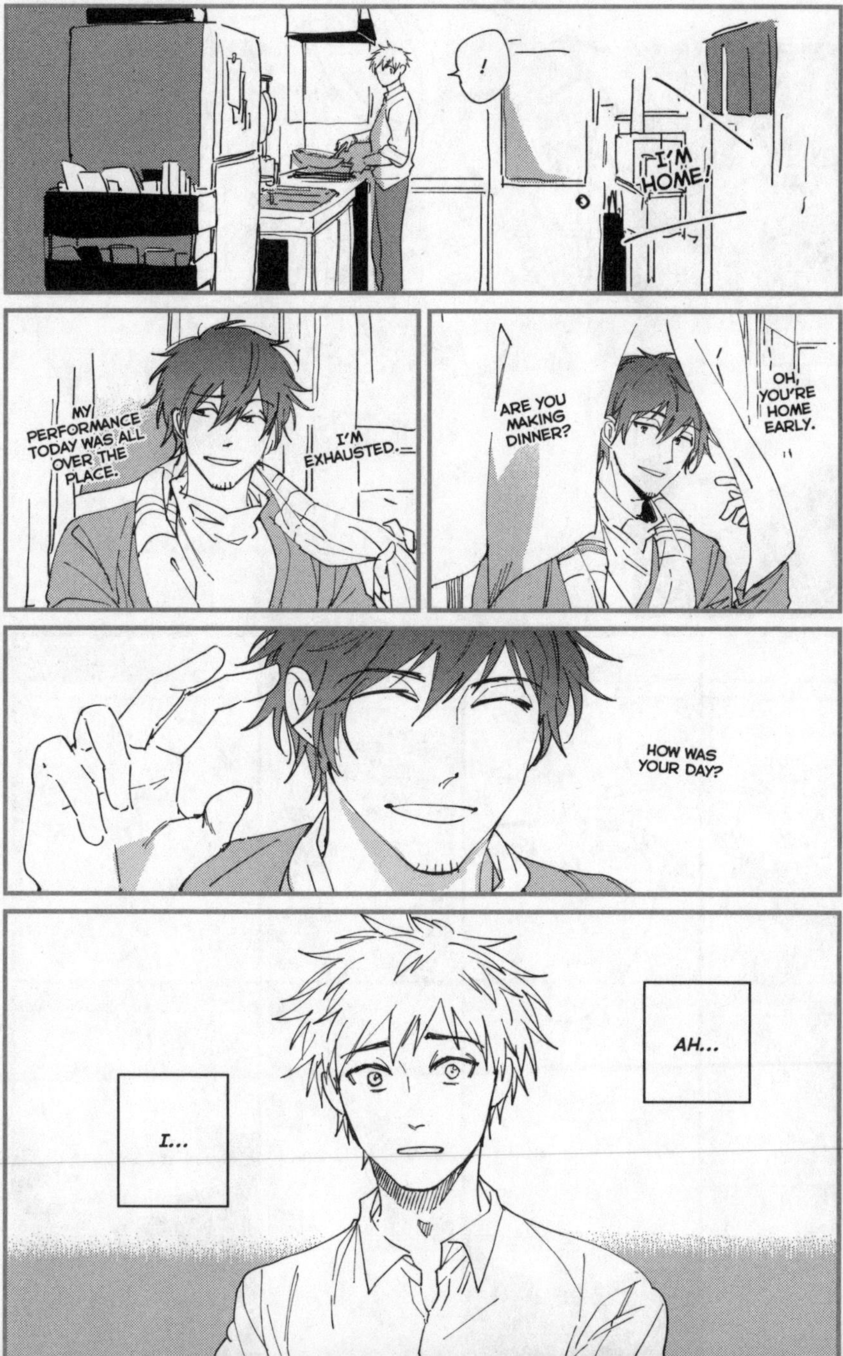
I'M HOME!
!
OH, YOU'RE HOME EARLY.
ARE YOU MAKING DINNER?
I'M EXHAUSTED.
MY PERFORMANCE TODAY WAS ALL OVER THE PLACE.
HOW WAS YOUR DAY?
AH...
I...

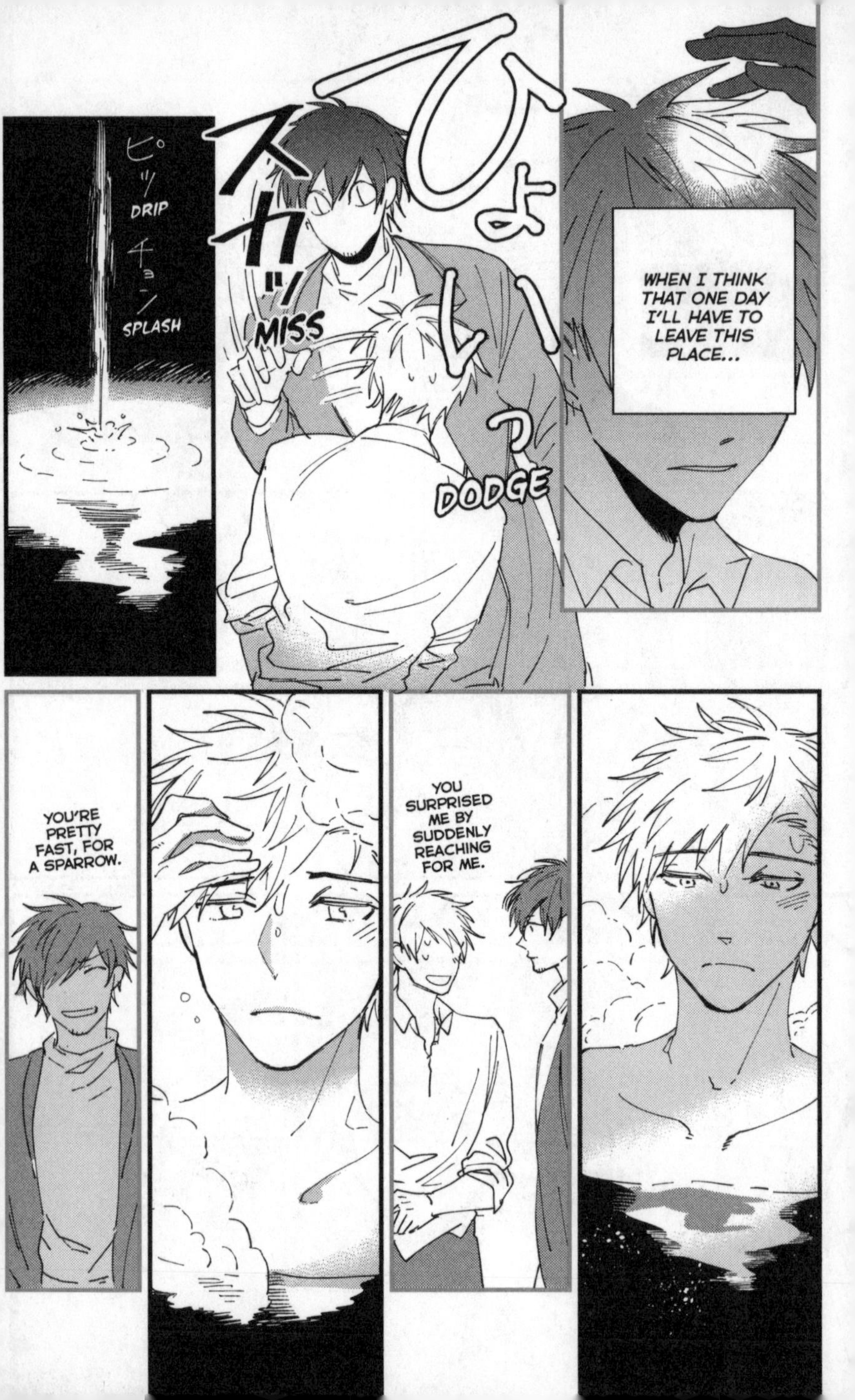
WHEN I THINK THAT ONE DAY I'LL HAVE TO LEAVE THIS PLACE...
ひょいっ
DODGE
スカッ
MISS
ピッ
DRIP
チョン
SPLASH
YOU SURPRISED ME BY SUDDENLY REACHING FOR ME.
YOU'RE PRETTY FAST, FOR A SPARROW.

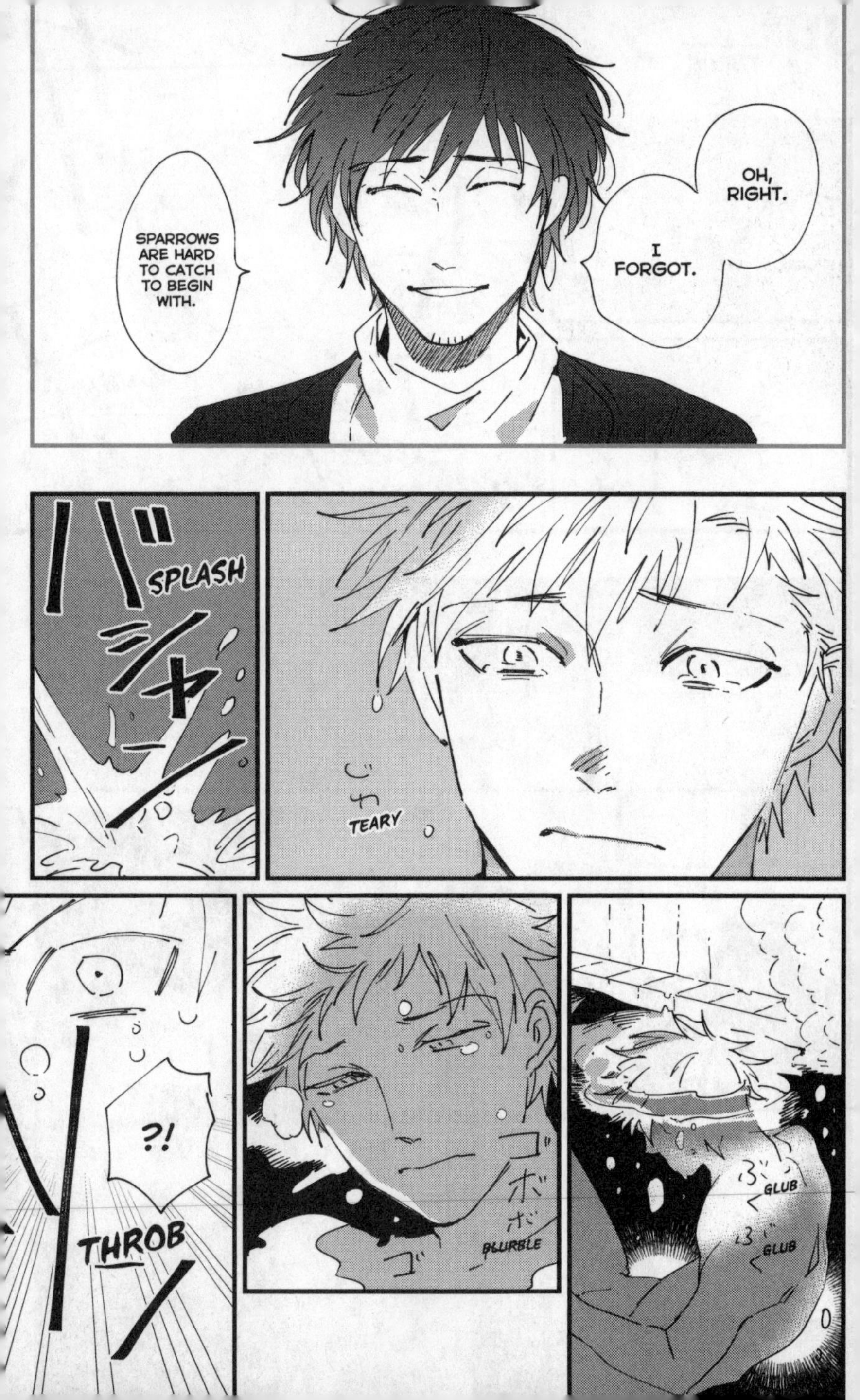
OH, RIGHT.
I FORGOT.
SPARROWS ARE HARD TO CATCH TO BEGIN WITH.
TEARY
SPLASH
GLUB
GLUB
BLURBLE
?!
THROB

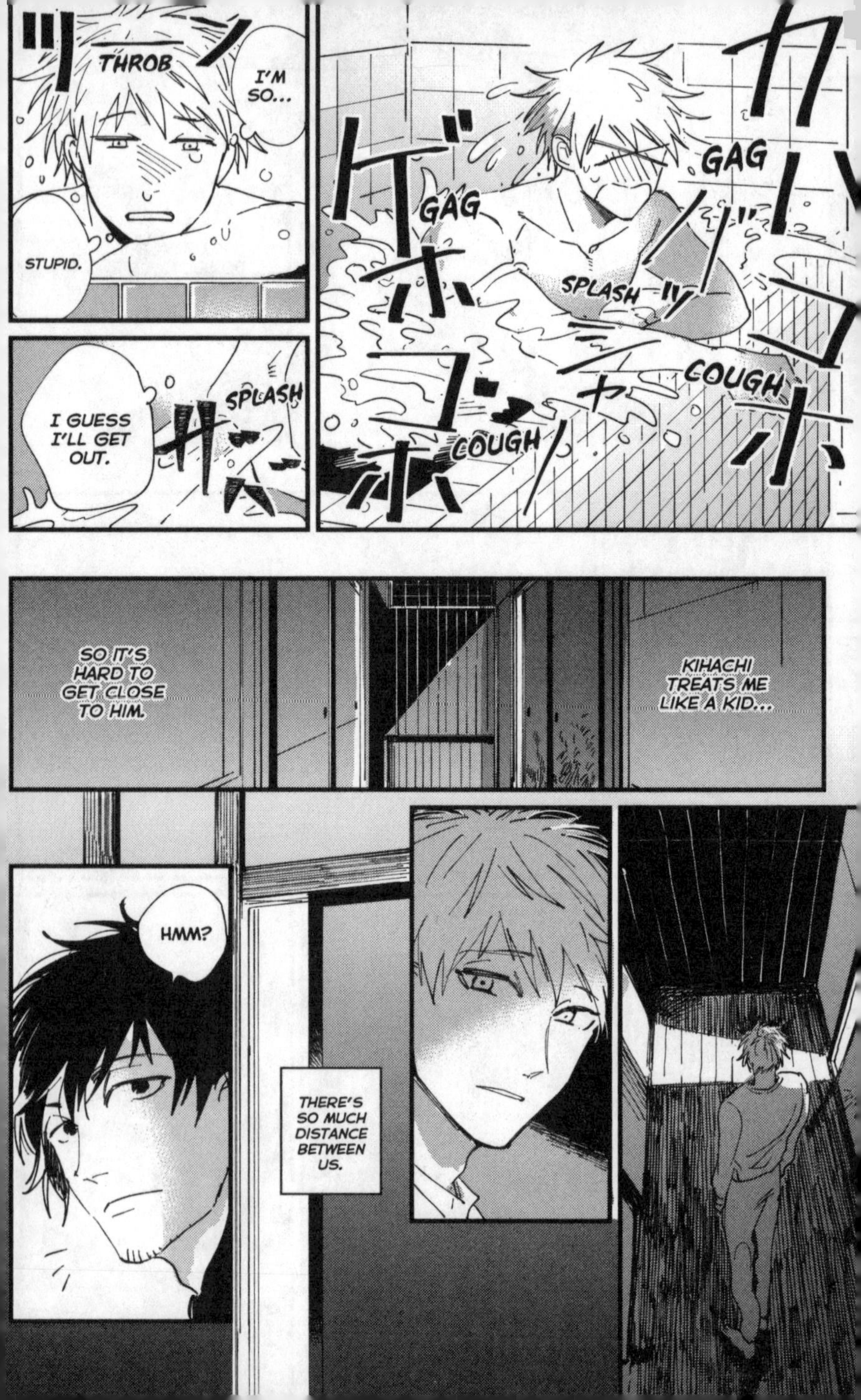
GAG
GAG
SPLASH
COUGH
COUGH
THROB
I'M SO...
STUPID.
SPLASH
I GUESS I'LL GET OUT.
KIHACHI TREATS ME LIKE A KID...
SO IT'S HARD TO GET CLOSE TO HIM.
THERE'S SO MUCH DISTANCE BETWEEN US.
HMM?

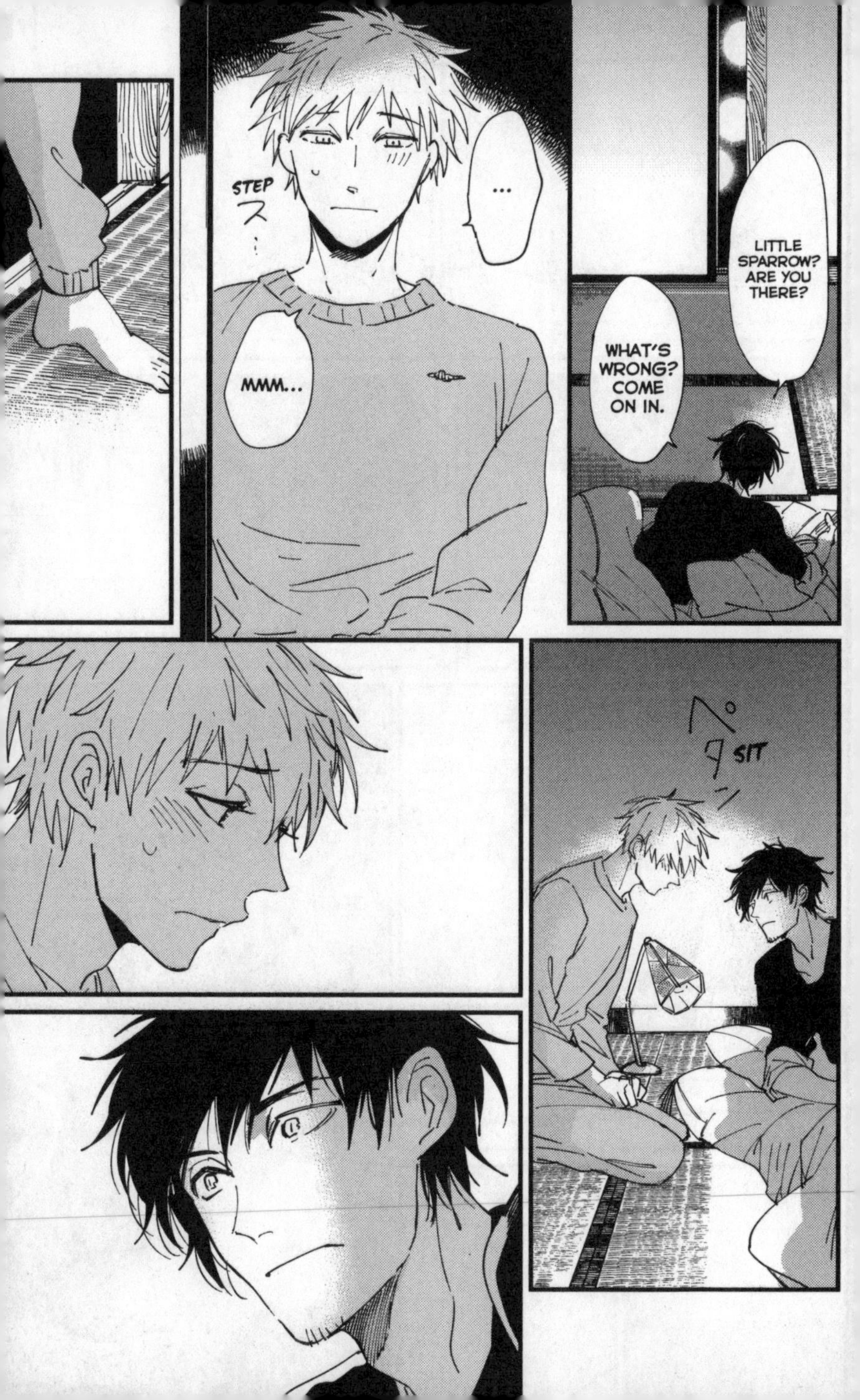
LITTLE SPARROW? ARE YOU THERE?
WHAT'S WRONG? COME ON IN.
...
STEP
ス…
MMM...
ペタン
SIT

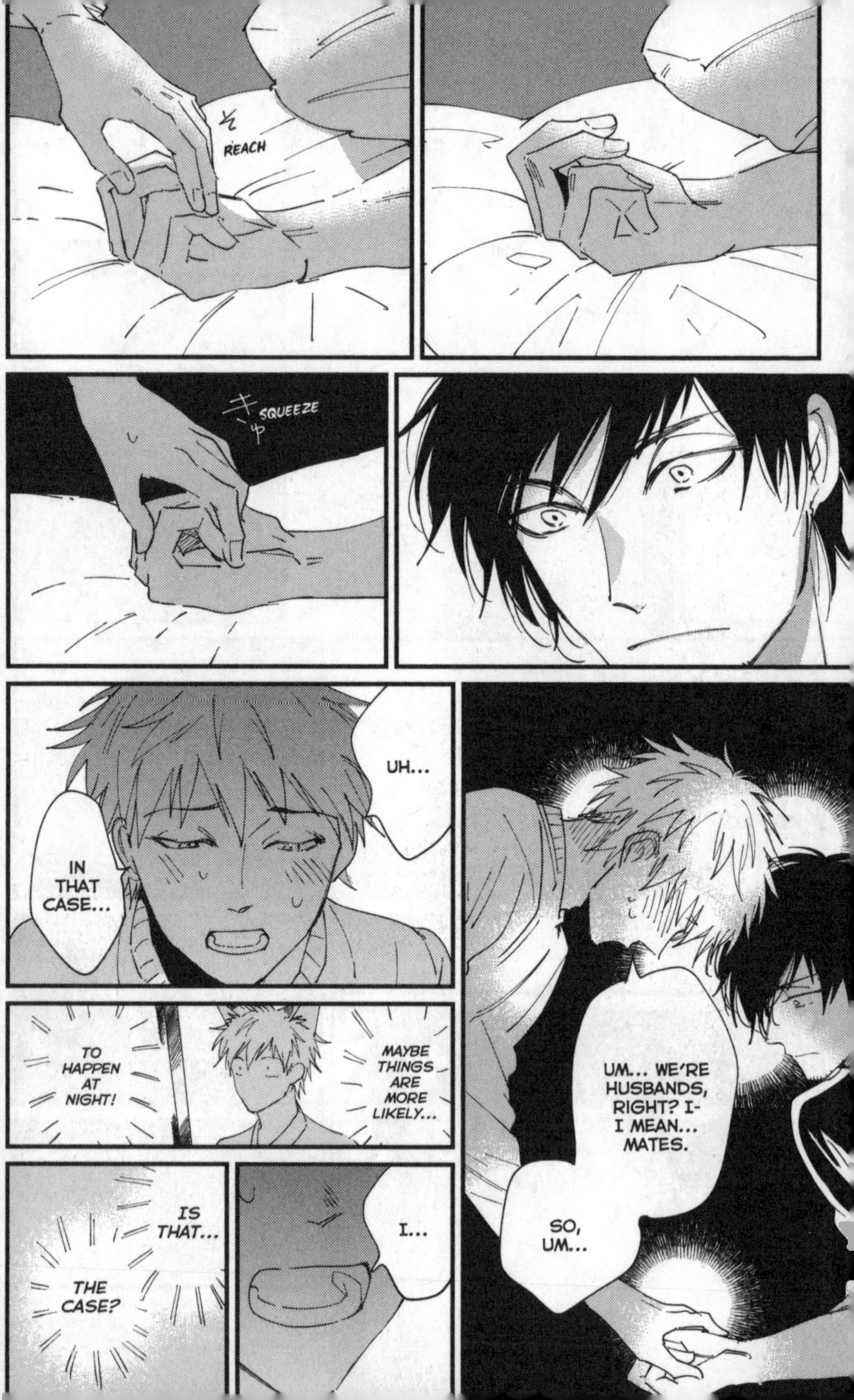
REACH
SQUEEZE
UM... WE'RE HUSBANDS, RIGHT? I- I MEAN... MATES.
SO, UM...
UH...
IN THAT CASE...
MAYBE THINGS ARE MORE LIKELY...
TO HAPPEN AT NIGHT!
I...
IS THAT...
THE CASE?

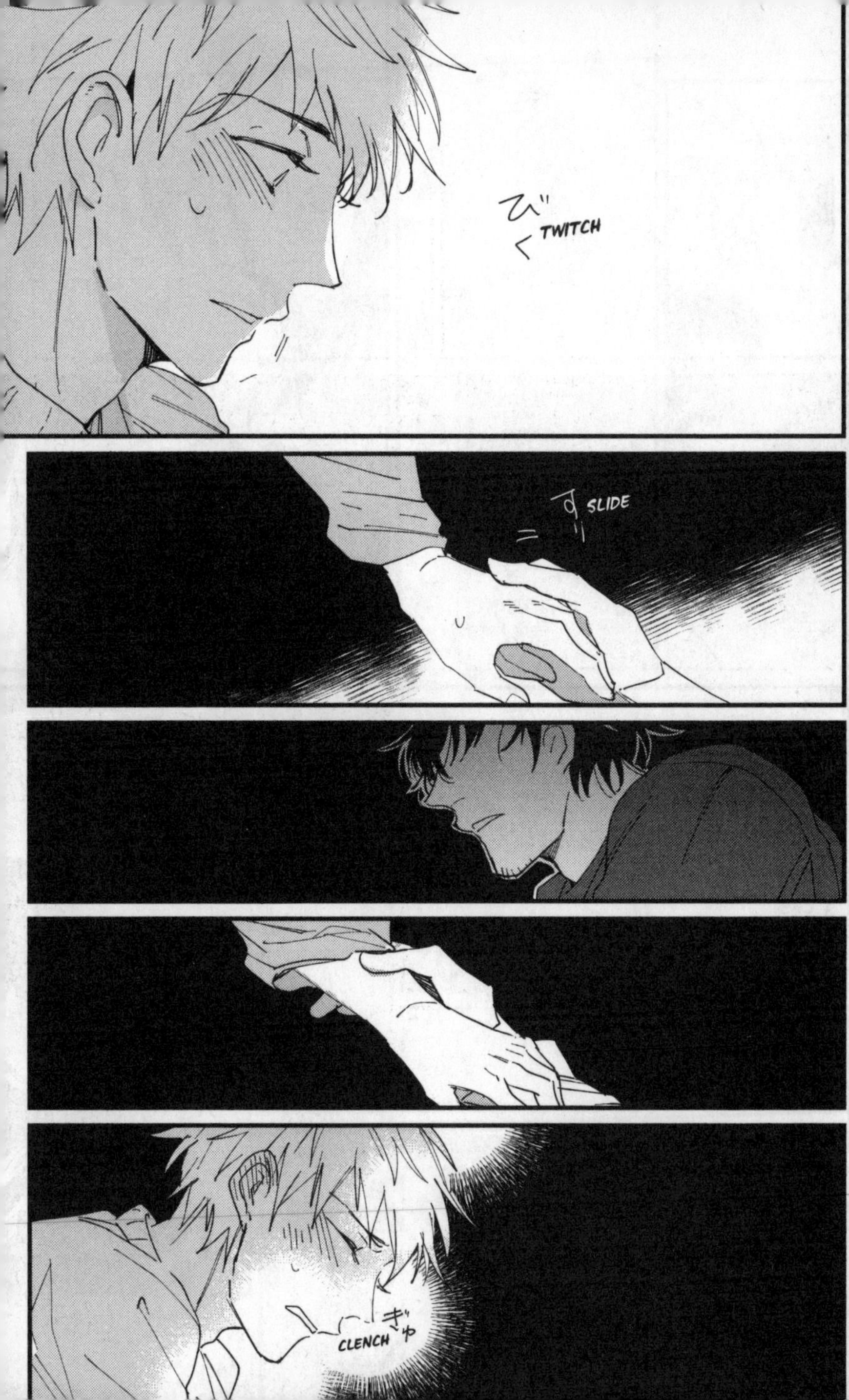
びく
TWITCH
す
SLIDE
ぎゅ
CLENCH

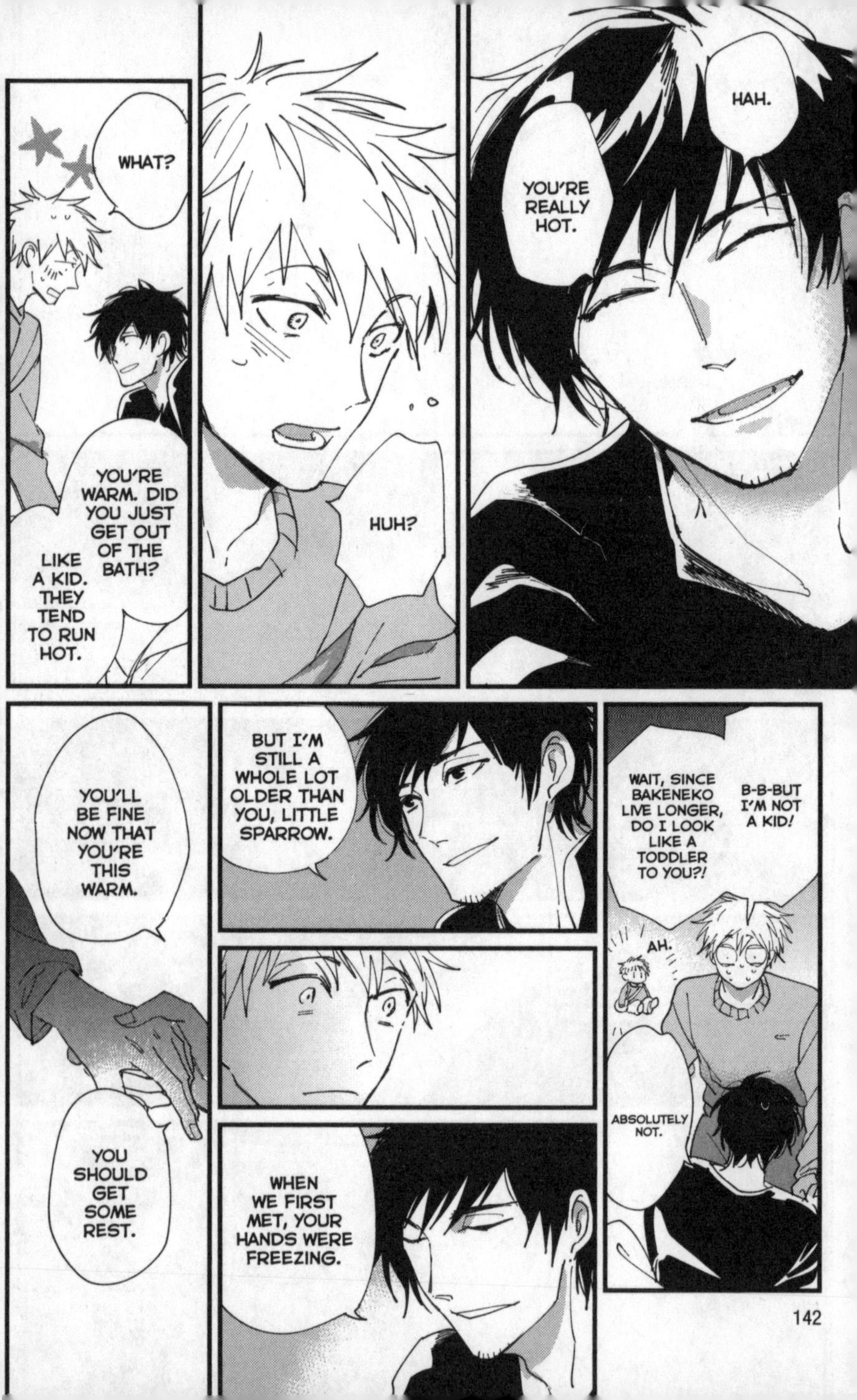
HAH.
YOU'RE REALLY HOT.
HUH?
WHAT?
YOU'RE WARM. DID YOU JUST GET OUT OF THE BATH?
LIKE A KID. THEY TEND TO RUN HOT.
B-B-BUT I'M NOT A KID!
WAIT, SINCE BAKENEKO LIVE LONGER, DO I LOOK LIKE A TODDLER TO YOU?!
AH.
ABSOLUTELY NOT.
BUT I'M STILL A WHOLE LOT OLDER THAN YOU, LITTLE SPARROW.
WHEN WE FIRST MET, YOUR HANDS WERE FREEZING.
YOU'LL BE FINE NOW THAT YOU'RE THIS WARM.
YOU SHOULD GET SOME REST.

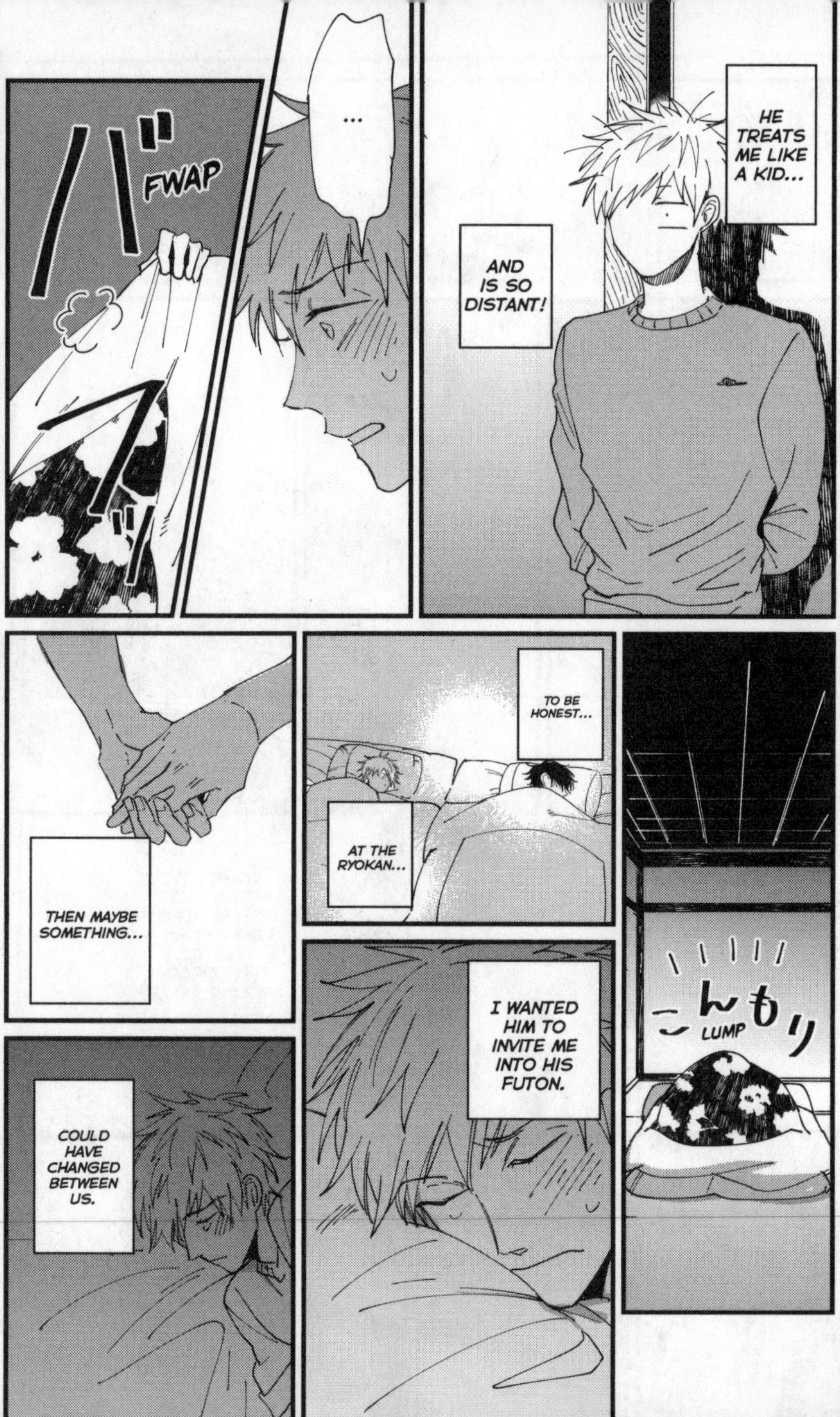
HE TREATS ME LIKE A KID...
AND IS SO DISTANT!
...
バッ
FWAP
こんもり
LUMP
TO BE HONEST...
AT THE RYOKAN...
I WANTED HIM TO INVITE ME INTO HIS FUTON.
THEN MAYBE SOMETHING...
COULD HAVE CHANGED BETWEEN US.

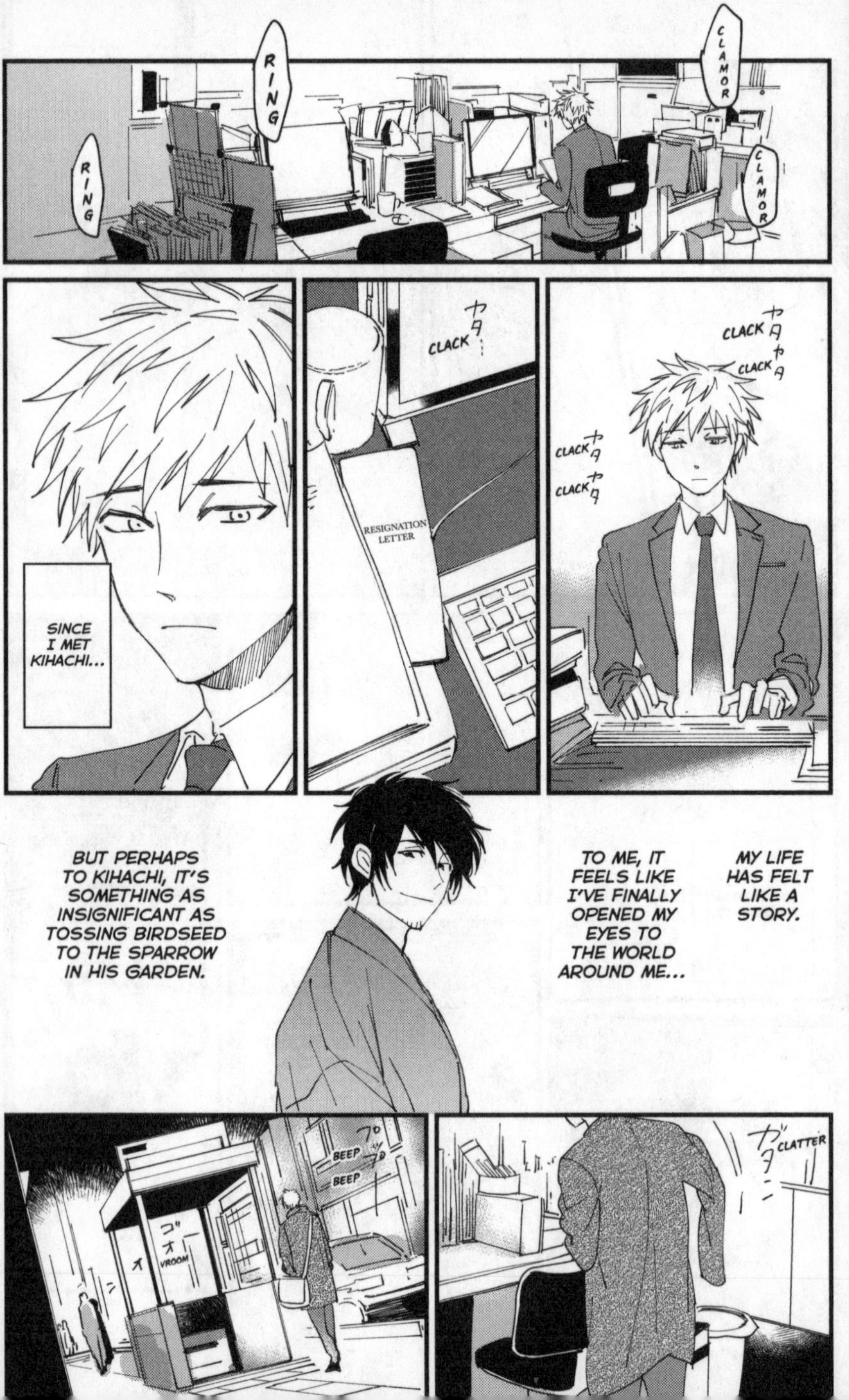
CLAMOR
CLAMOR
RING
RING
CLACK
CLACK
CLACK
CLACK
CLACK
RESIGNATION LETTER
SINCE I MET KIHACHI...
MY LIFE HAS FELT LIKE A STORY.
TO ME, IT FEELS LIKE I'VE FINALLY OPENED MY EYES TO THE WORLD AROUND ME...
BUT PERHAPS TO KIHACHI, IT'S SOMETHING AS INSIGNIFICANT AS TOSSING BIRDSEED TO THE SPARROW IN HIS GARDEN.
CLATTER
BEEP
BEEP
VROOM

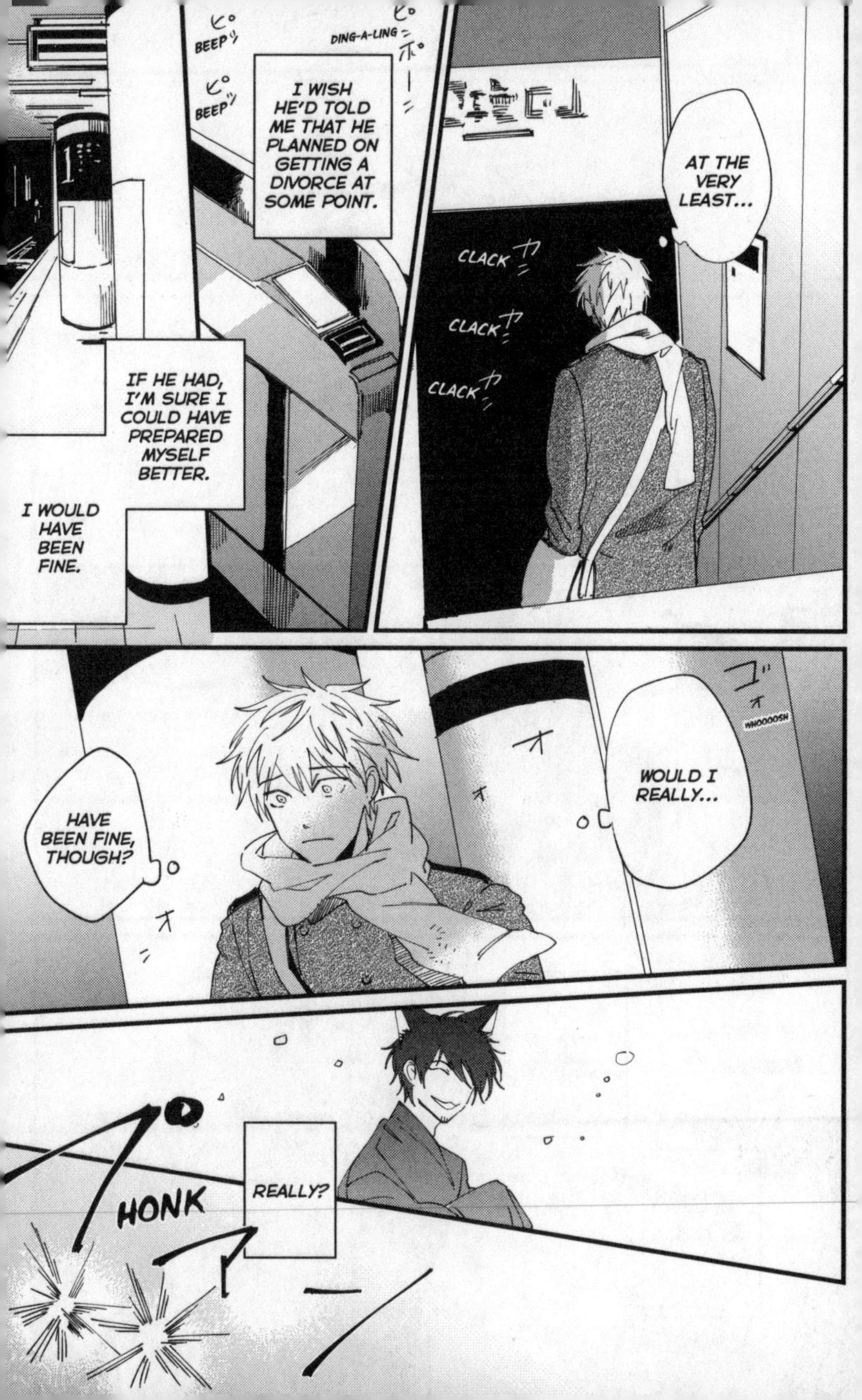
AT THE VERY LEAST...
CLACK
CLACK
CLACK
DING-A-LING
BEEP
BEEP
I WISH HE'D TOLD ME THAT HE PLANNED ON GETTING A DIVORCE AT SOME POINT.
IF HE HAD, I'M SURE I COULD HAVE PREPARED MYSELF BETTER.
I WOULD HAVE BEEN FINE.
WOULD I REALLY...
WHOOOOSH
HAVE BEEN FINE, THOUGH?
REALLY?
HONK

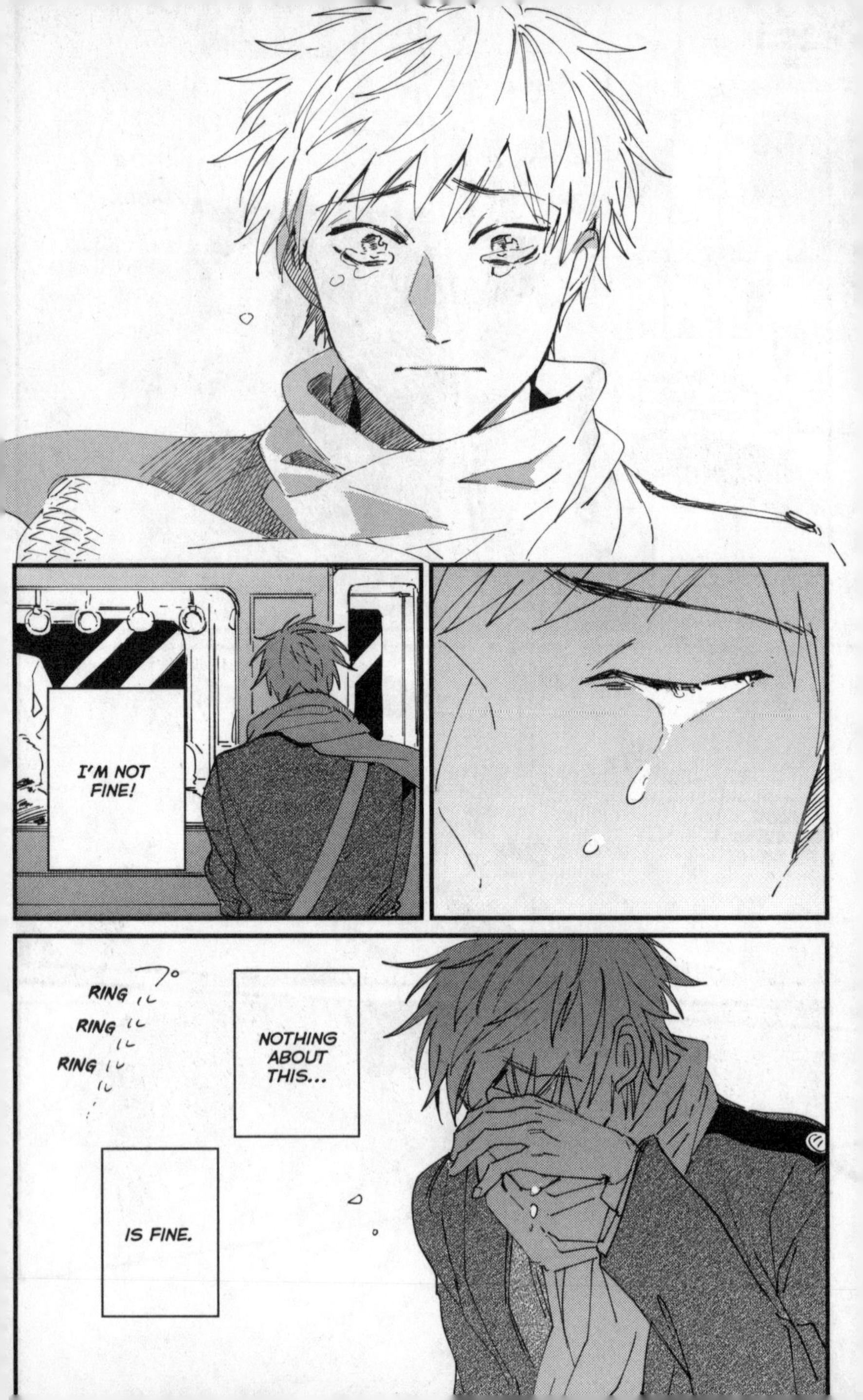
I'M NOT FINE!
NOTHING ABOUT THIS...
RING
RING
RING
IS FINE.

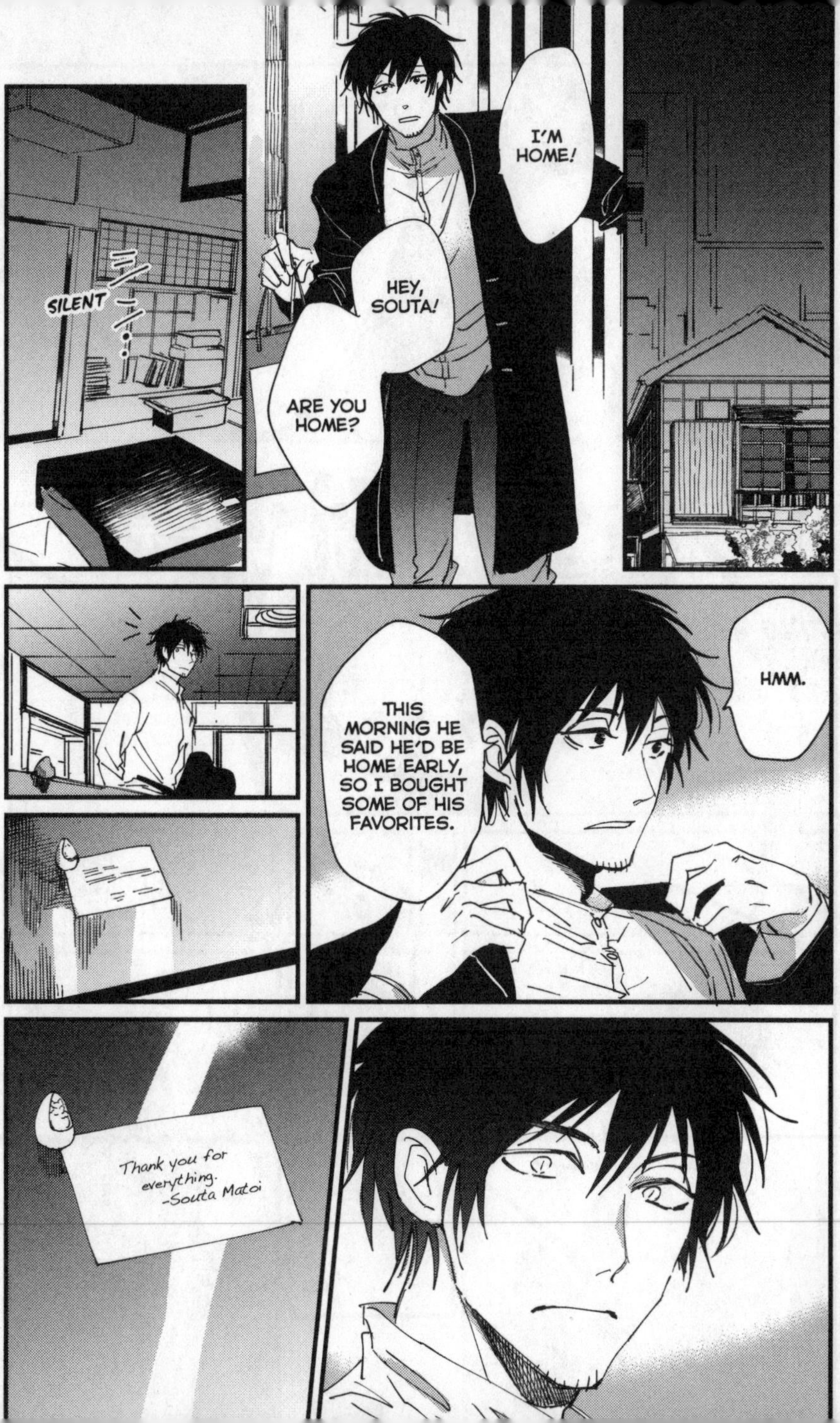
I'M HOME!
HEY, SOUTA!
ARE YOU HOME?
SILENT
HMM.
THIS MORNING HE SAID HE'D BE HOME EARLY, SO I BOUGHT SOME OF HIS FAVORITES.
Thank you for everything. -Souta Matoi

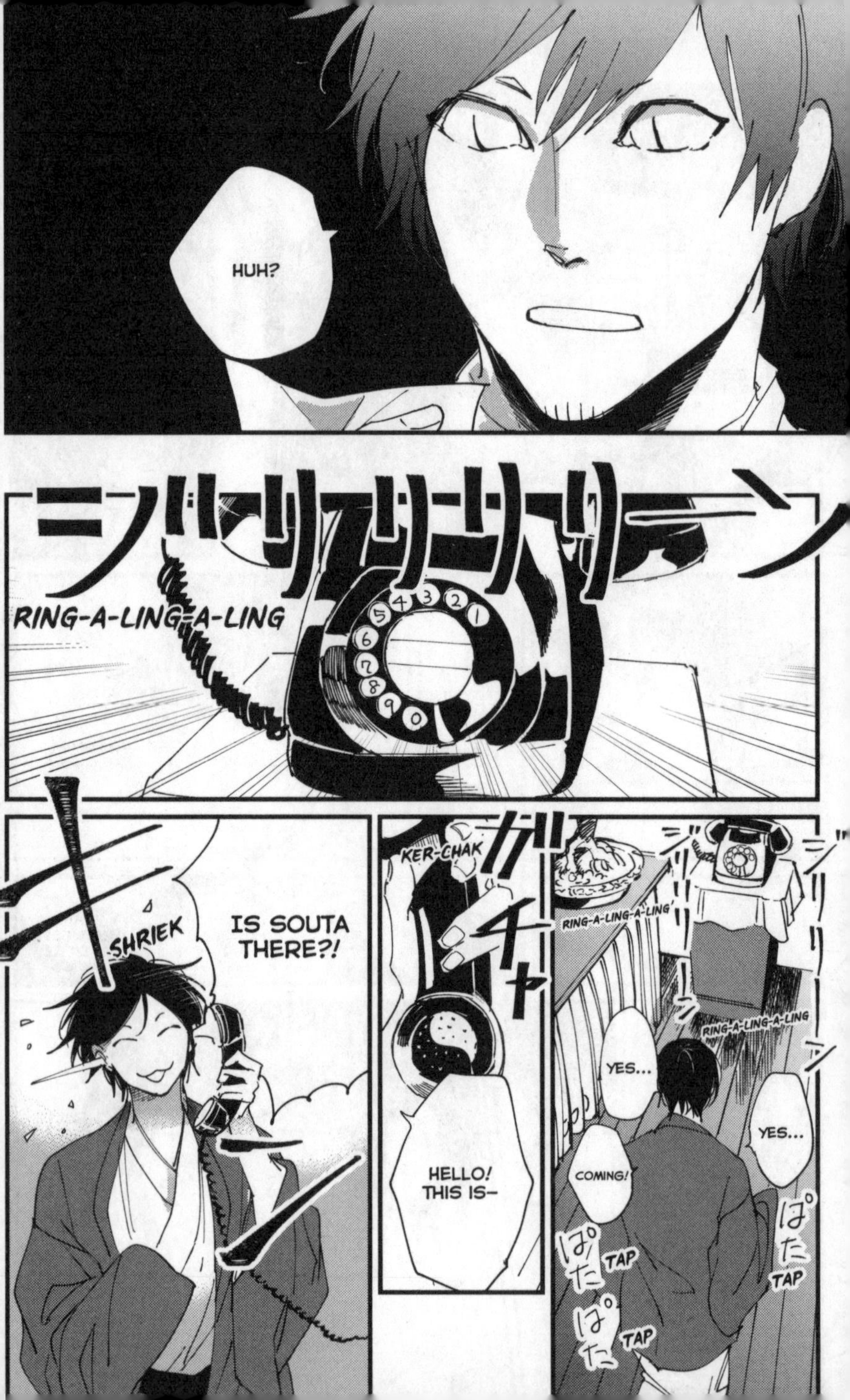
HUH?
RING-A-LING-A-LING
RING-A-LING-A-LING
RING-A-LING-A-LING
YES...
YES...
COMING!
TAP
TAP
TAP
KER-CHAK
HELLO! THIS IS–
SHRIEK
IS SOUTA THERE?!

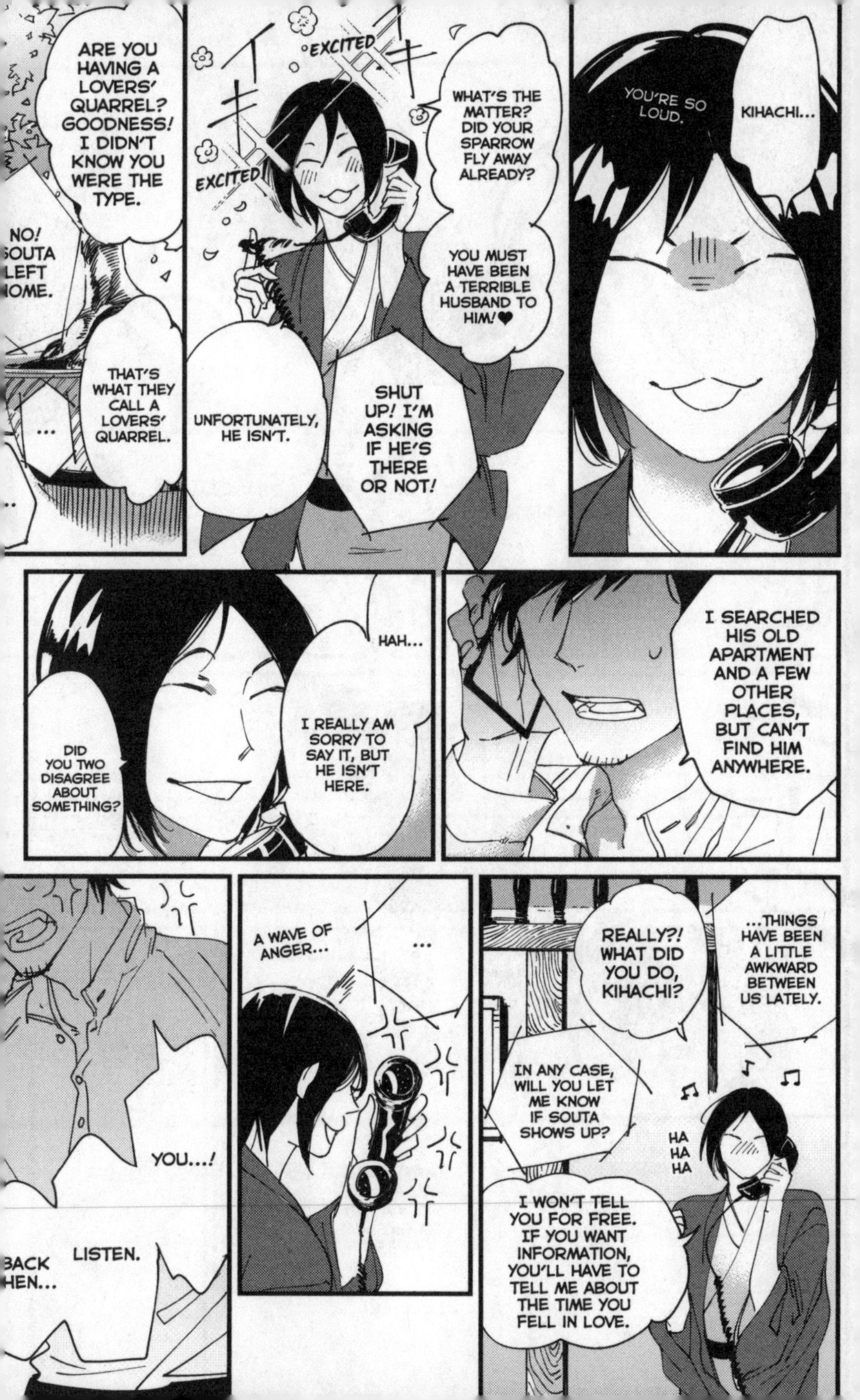
KIHACHI...
YOU'RE SO LOUD.
WHAT'S THE MATTER? DID YOUR SPARROW FLY AWAY ALREADY?
EXCITED
EXCITED
YOU MUST HAVE BEEN A TERRIBLE HUSBAND TO HIM!♥
SHUT UP! I'M ASKING IF HE'S THERE OR NOT!
UNFORTUNATELY, HE ISN'T.
ARE YOU HAVING A LOVERS' QUARREL? GOODNESS! I DIDN'T KNOW YOU WERE THE TYPE.
NO! SOUTA LEFT HOME.
THAT'S WHAT THEY CALL A LOVERS' QUARREL.
...
...
I SEARCHED HIS OLD APARTMENT AND A FEW OTHER PLACES, BUT CAN'T FIND HIM ANYWHERE.
HAH...
I REALLY AM SORRY TO SAY IT, BUT HE ISN'T HERE.
DID YOU TWO DISAGREE ABOUT SOMETHING?
...THINGS HAVE BEEN A LITTLE AWKWARD BETWEEN US LATELY.
REALLY?! WHAT DID YOU DO, KIHACHI?
IN ANY CASE, WILL YOU LET ME KNOW IF SOUTA SHOWS UP?
HA HA HA
I WON'T TELL YOU FOR FREE. IF YOU WANT INFORMATION, YOU'LL HAVE TO TELL ME ABOUT THE TIME YOU FELL IN LOVE.
...
A WAVE OF ANGER...
YOU...!
LISTEN.
BACK
HEN...

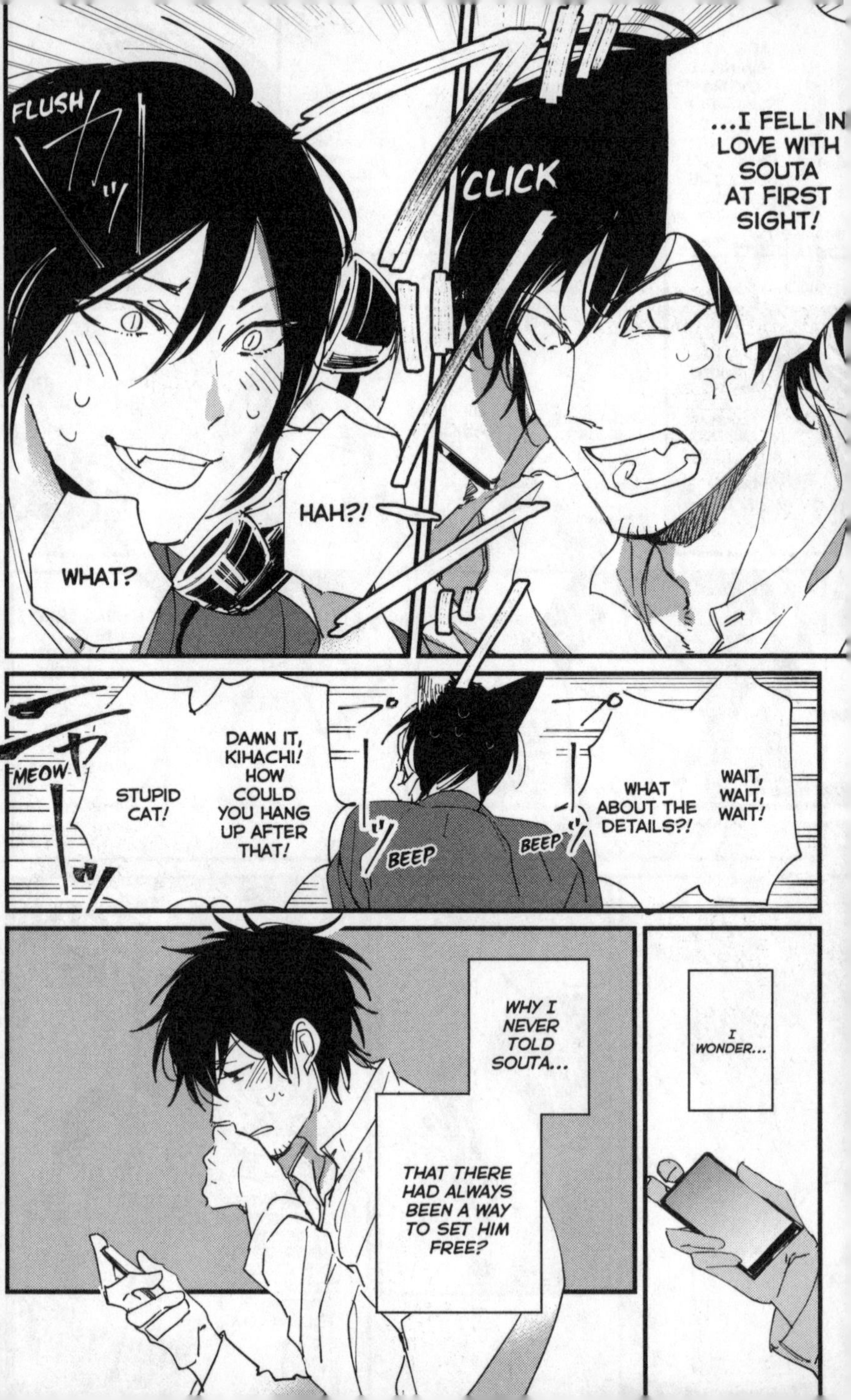
...I FELL IN LOVE WITH SOUTA AT FIRST SIGHT!
CLICK
HAH?!
FLUSH
WHAT?
WAIT, WAIT, WAIT!
WHAT ABOUT THE DETAILS?!
BEEP
BEEP
DAMN IT, KIHACHI! HOW COULD YOU HANG UP AFTER THAT!
STUPID CAT!
MEOW
I WONDER...
WHY I NEVER TOLD SOUTA...
THAT THERE HAD ALWAYS BEEN A WAY TO SET HIM FREE?

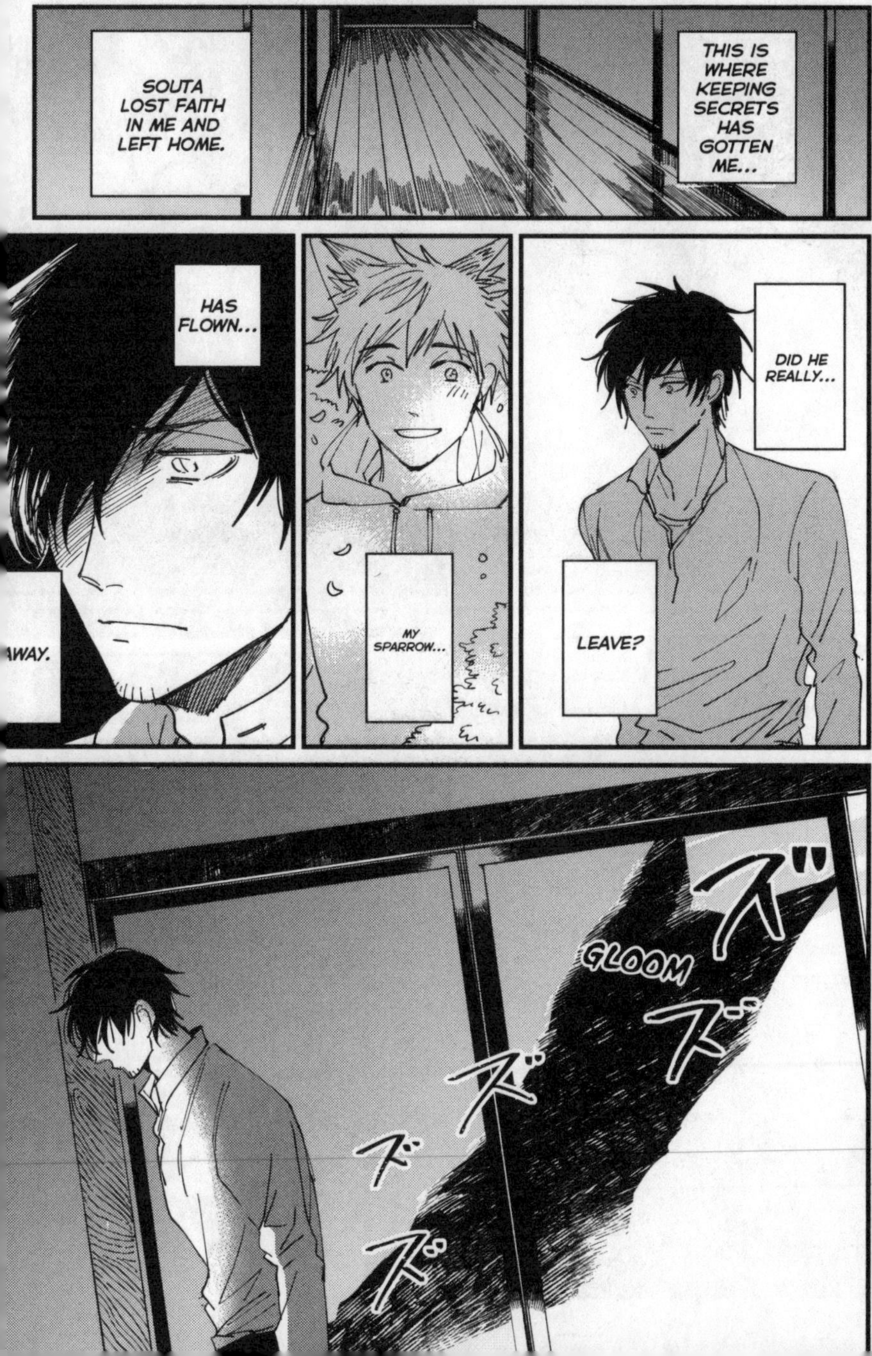
THIS IS WHERE KEEPING SECRETS HAS GOTTEN ME...
SOUTA LOST FAITH IN ME AND LEFT HOME.
DID HE REALLY...
LEAVE?
MY SPARROW...
HAS FLOWN...
AWAY.
ズズズズズ
GLOOM

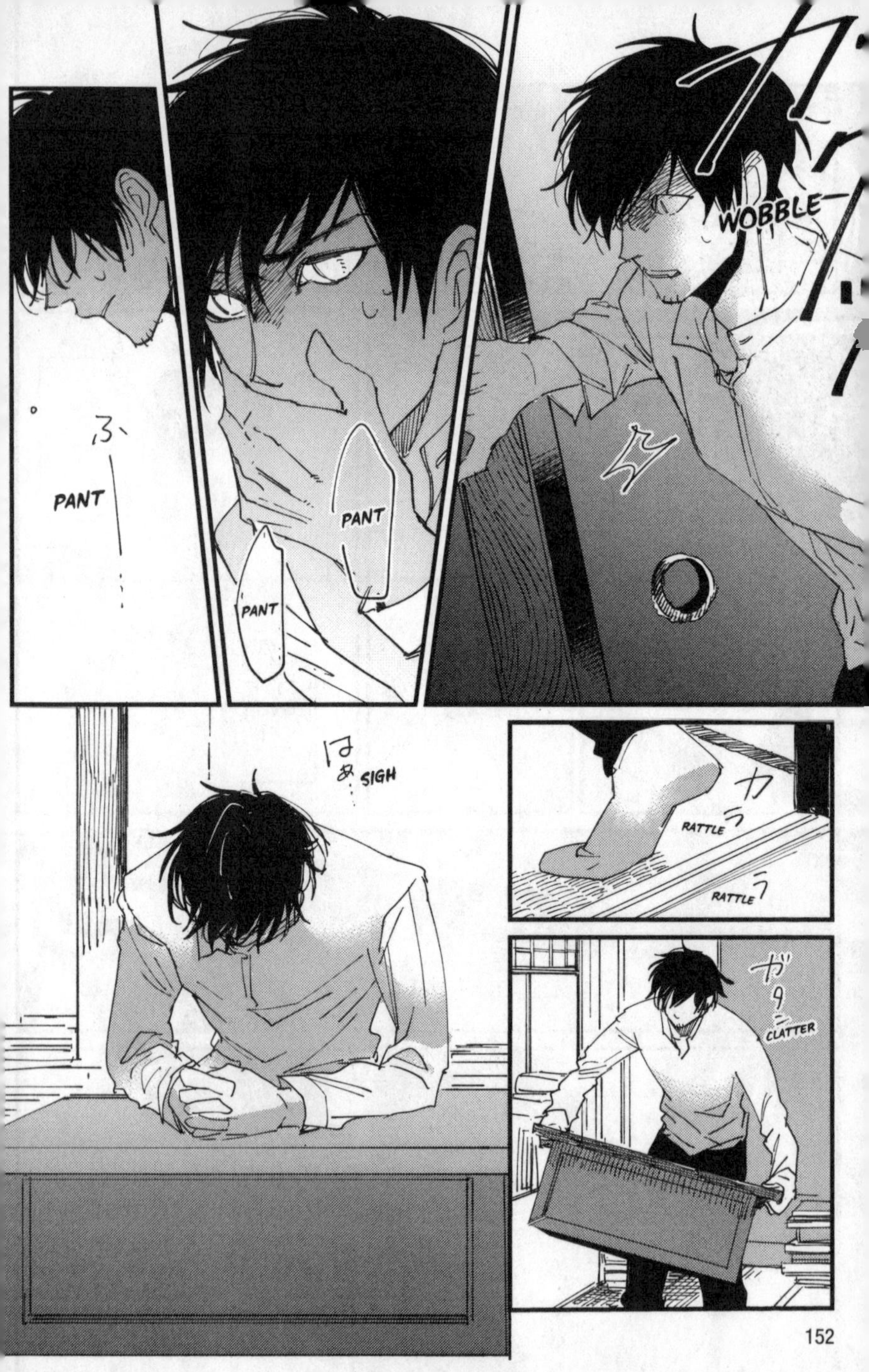

WOBBLE
PANT
PANT
ふ
PANT
カラ
RATTLE
ラ
RATTLE
ガタ
CLATTER
はぁ
SIGH

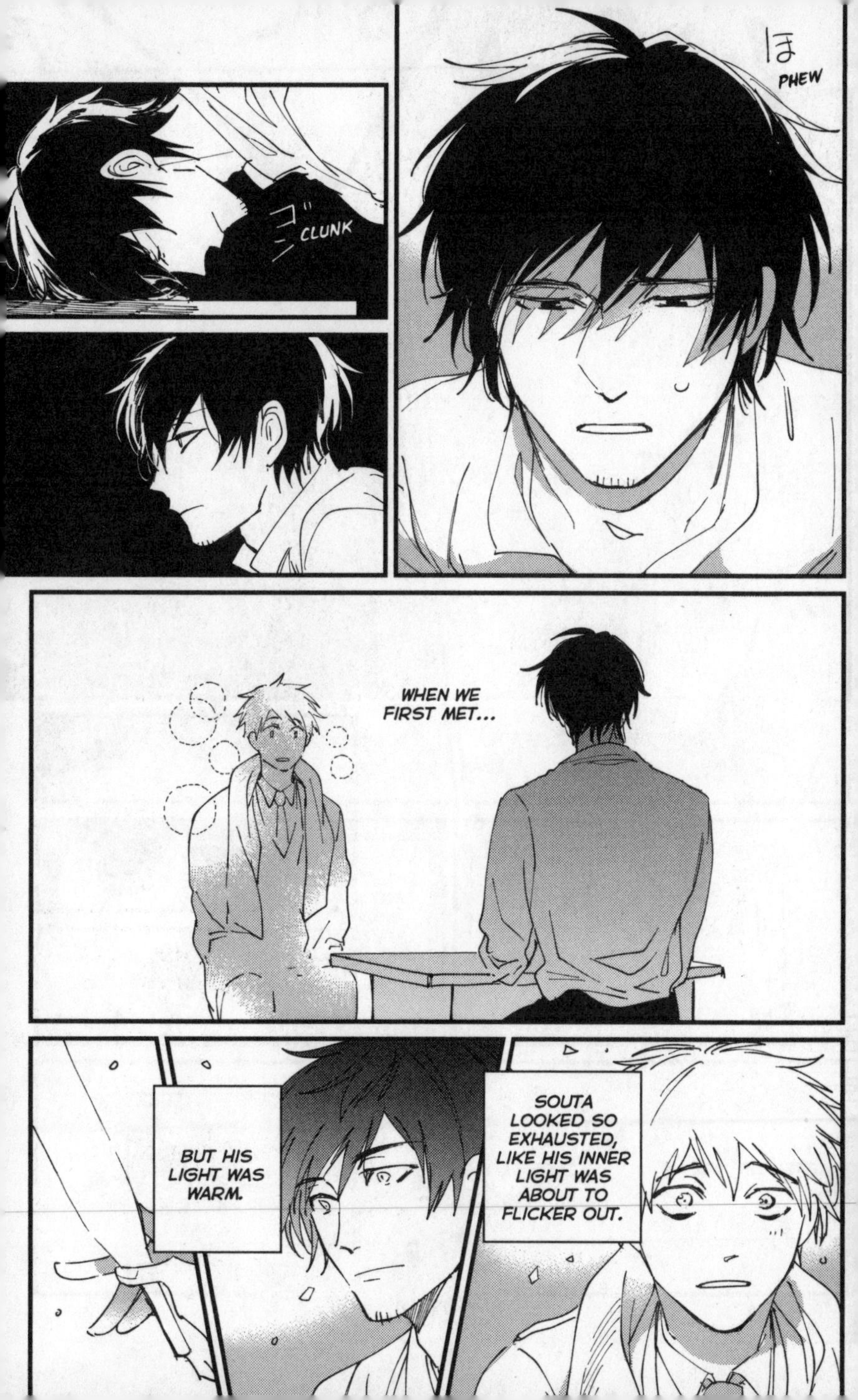
ほ
PHEW
ゴ
CLUNK
WHEN WE FIRST MET...
SOUTA LOOKED SO EXHAUSTED, LIKE HIS INNER LIGHT WAS ABOUT TO FLICKER OUT.
BUT HIS LIGHT WAS WARM.

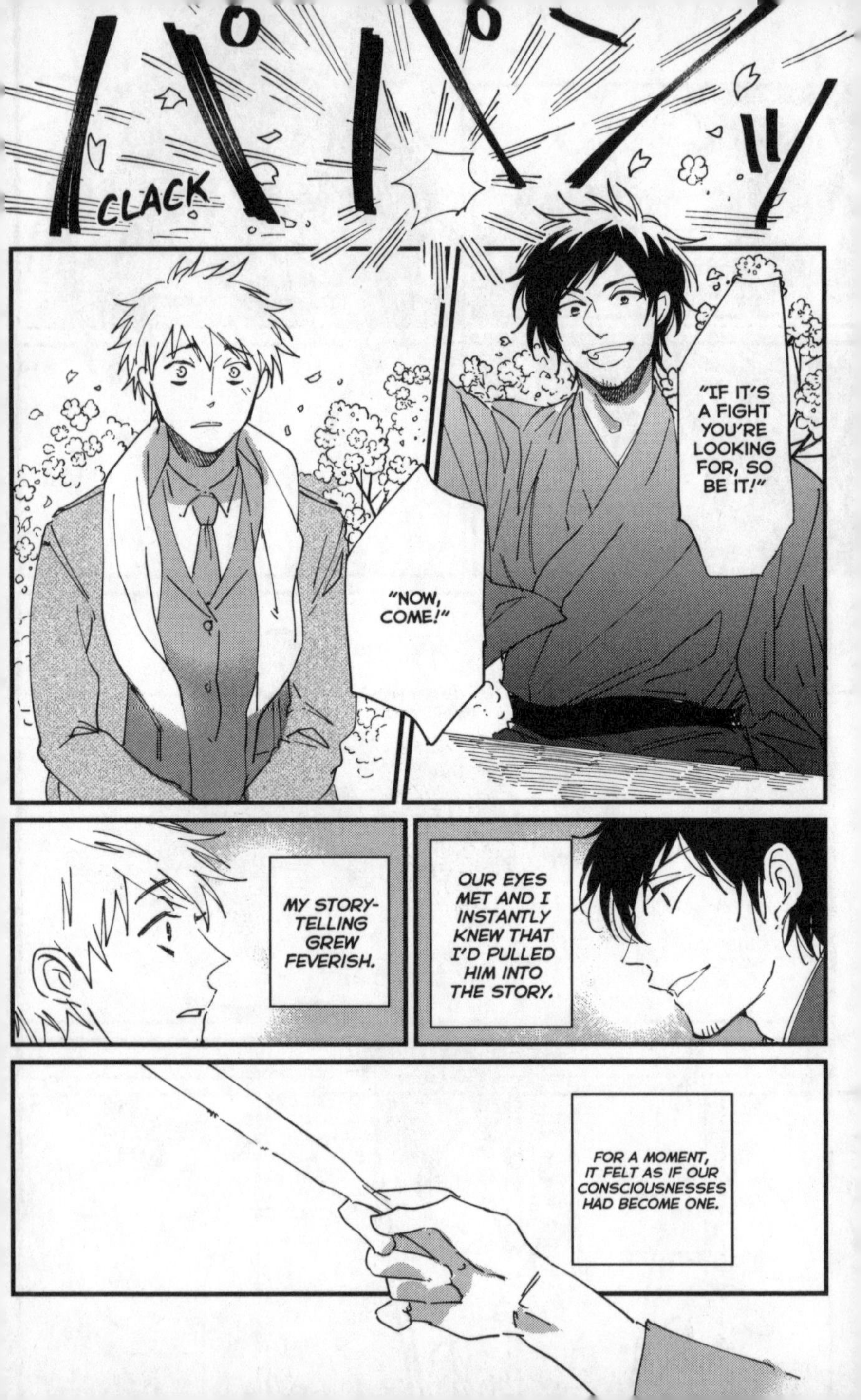
CLACK
"IF IT'S A FIGHT YOU'RE LOOKING FOR, SO BE IT!"
"NOW, COME!"
OUR EYES MET AND I INSTANTLY KNEW THAT I'D PULLED HIM INTO THE STORY.
MY STORY-TELLING GREW FEVERISH.
FOR A MOMENT, IT FELT AS IF OUR CONSCIOUSNESSES HAD BECOME ONE.

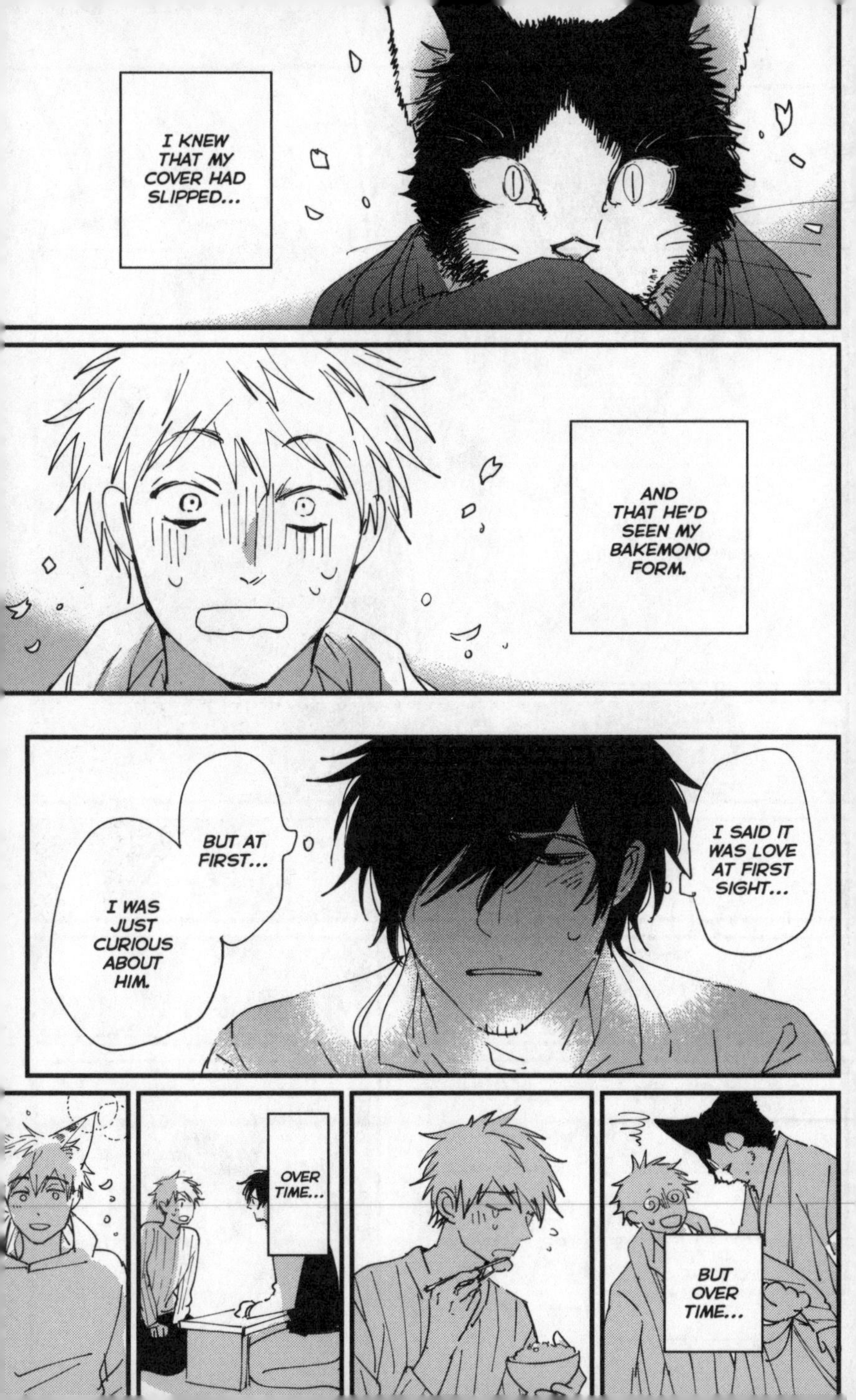
I KNEW THAT MY COVER HAD SLIPPED...
AND THAT HE'D SEEN MY BAKEMONO FORM.
I SAID IT WAS LOVE AT FIRST SIGHT...
BUT AT FIRST...
I WAS JUST CURIOUS ABOUT HIM.
BUT OVER TIME...
OVER TIME...

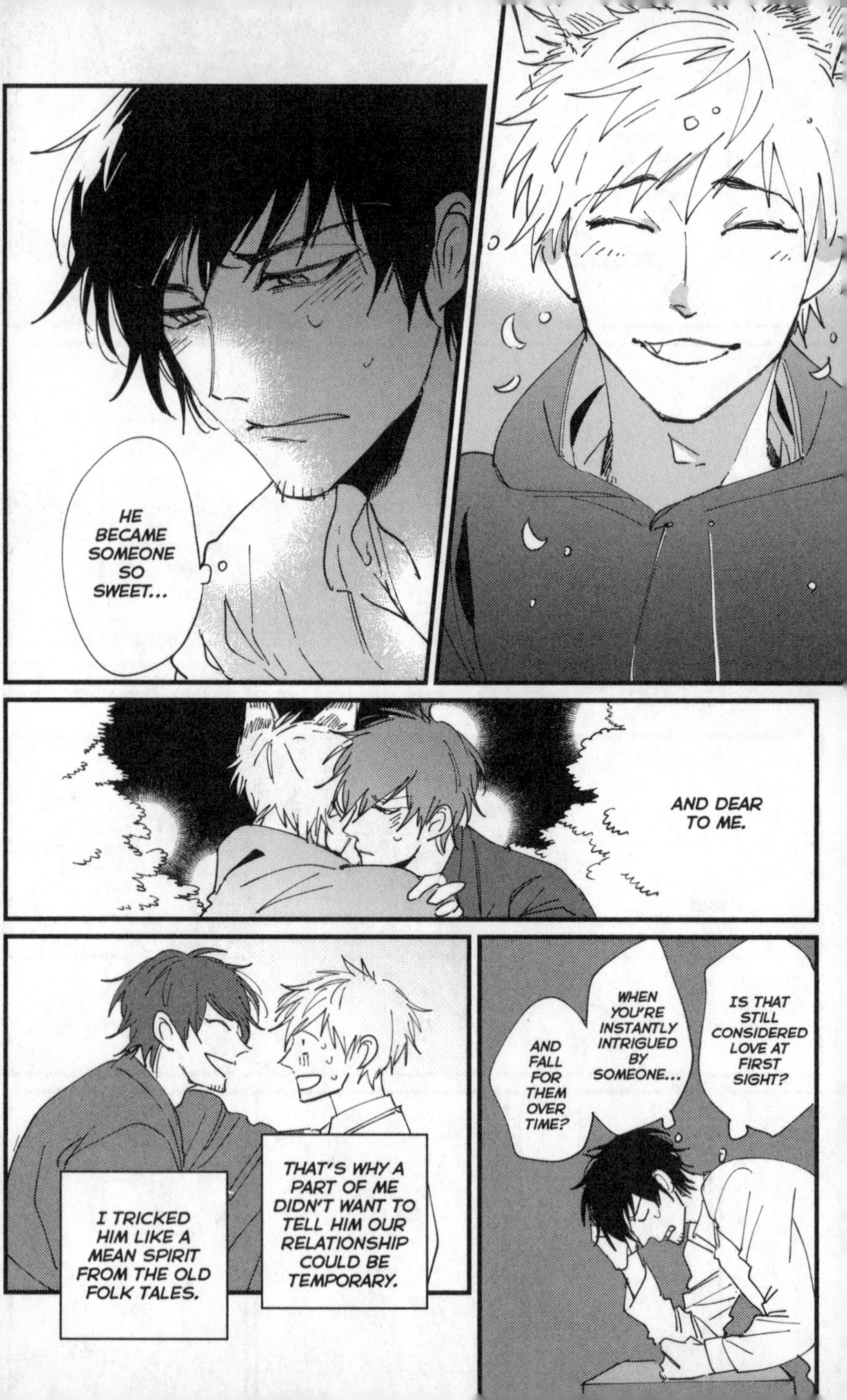
HE BECAME SOMEONE SO SWEET...
AND DEAR TO ME.
IS THAT STILL CONSIDERED LOVE AT FIRST SIGHT?
WHEN YOU'RE INSTANTLY INTRIGUED BY SOMEONE...
AND FALL FOR THEM OVER TIME?
THAT'S WHY A PART OF ME DIDN'T WANT TO TELL HIM OUR RELATIONSHIP COULD BE TEMPORARY.
I TRICKED HIM LIKE A MEAN SPIRIT FROM THE OLD FOLK TALES.

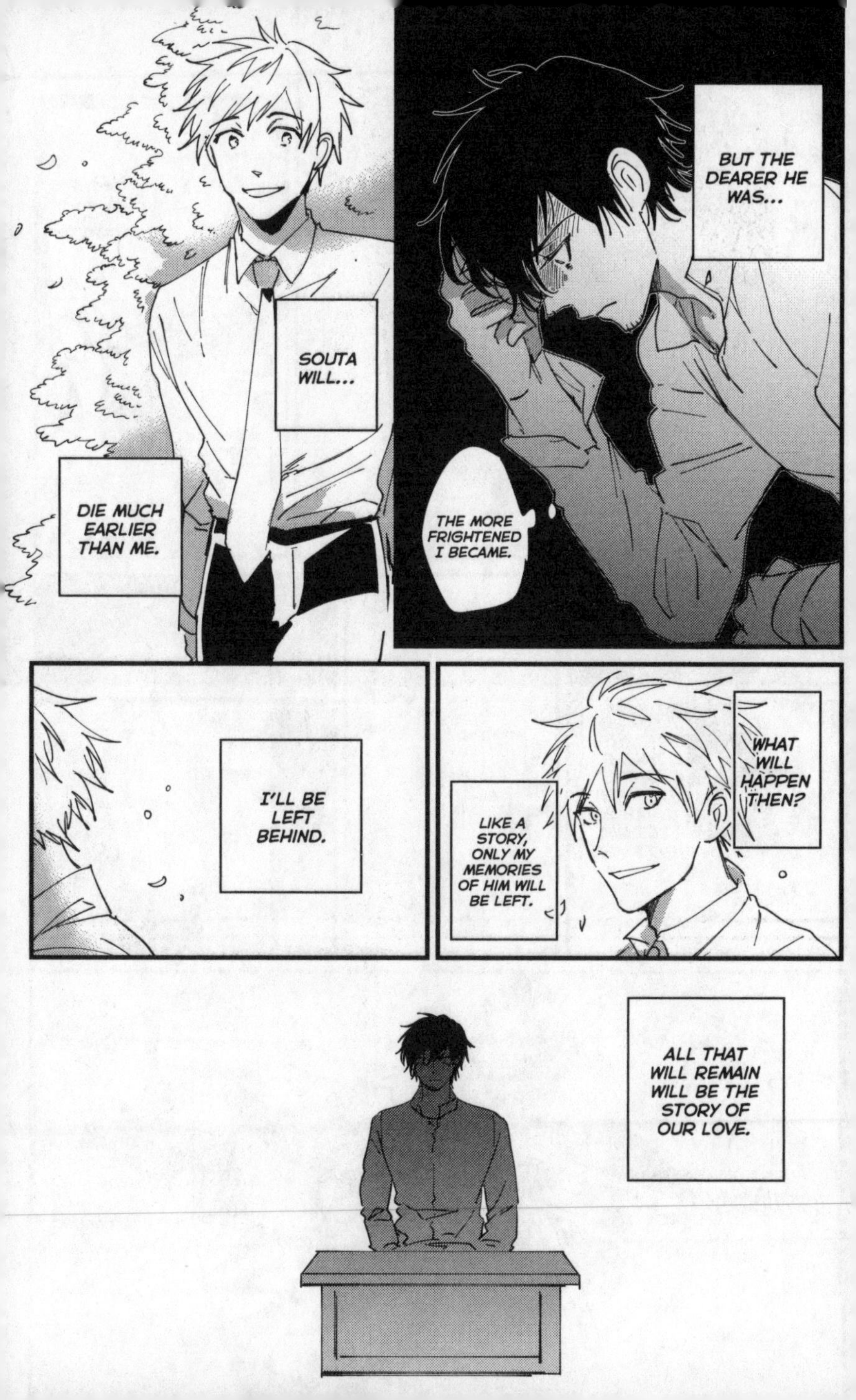
BUT THE DEARER HE WAS...
THE MORE FRIGHTENED I BECAME.
SOUTA WILL...
DIE MUCH EARLIER THAN ME.
WHAT WILL HAPPEN THEN?
LIKE A STORY, ONLY MY MEMORIES OF HIM WILL BE LEFT.
I'LL BE LEFT BEHIND.
ALL THAT WILL REMAIN WILL BE THE STORY OF OUR LOVE.

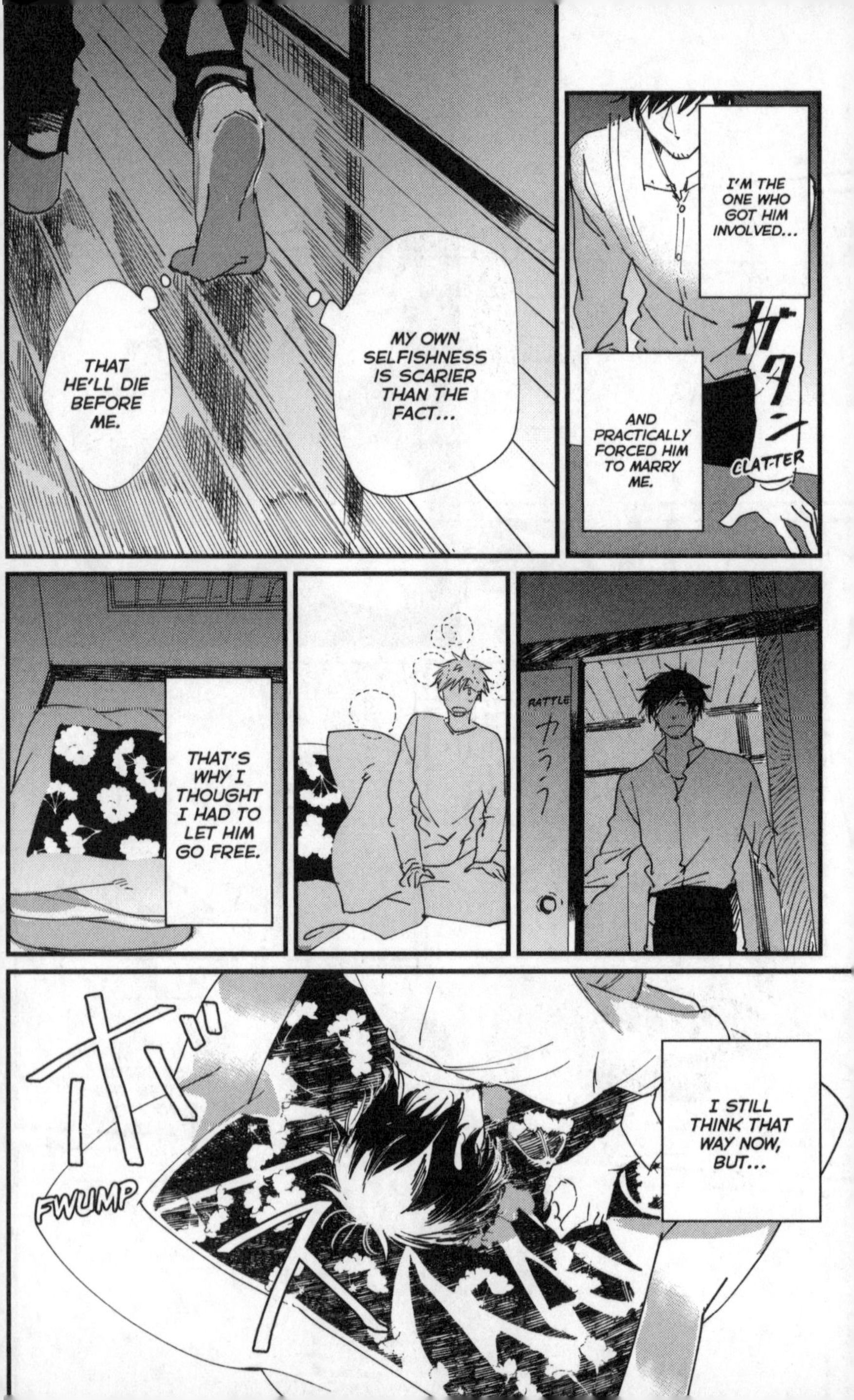
I'M THE ONE WHO GOT HIM INVOLVED...
AND PRACTICALLY FORCED HIM TO MARRY ME.
ガタン
CLAT-TER
MY OWN SELFISHNESS IS SCARIER THAN THE FACT...
THAT HE'LL DIE BEFORE ME.
RATTLE
カララ
THAT'S WHY I THOUGHT I HAD TO LET HIM GO FREE.
I STILL THINK THAT WAY NOW, BUT...
FWUMP

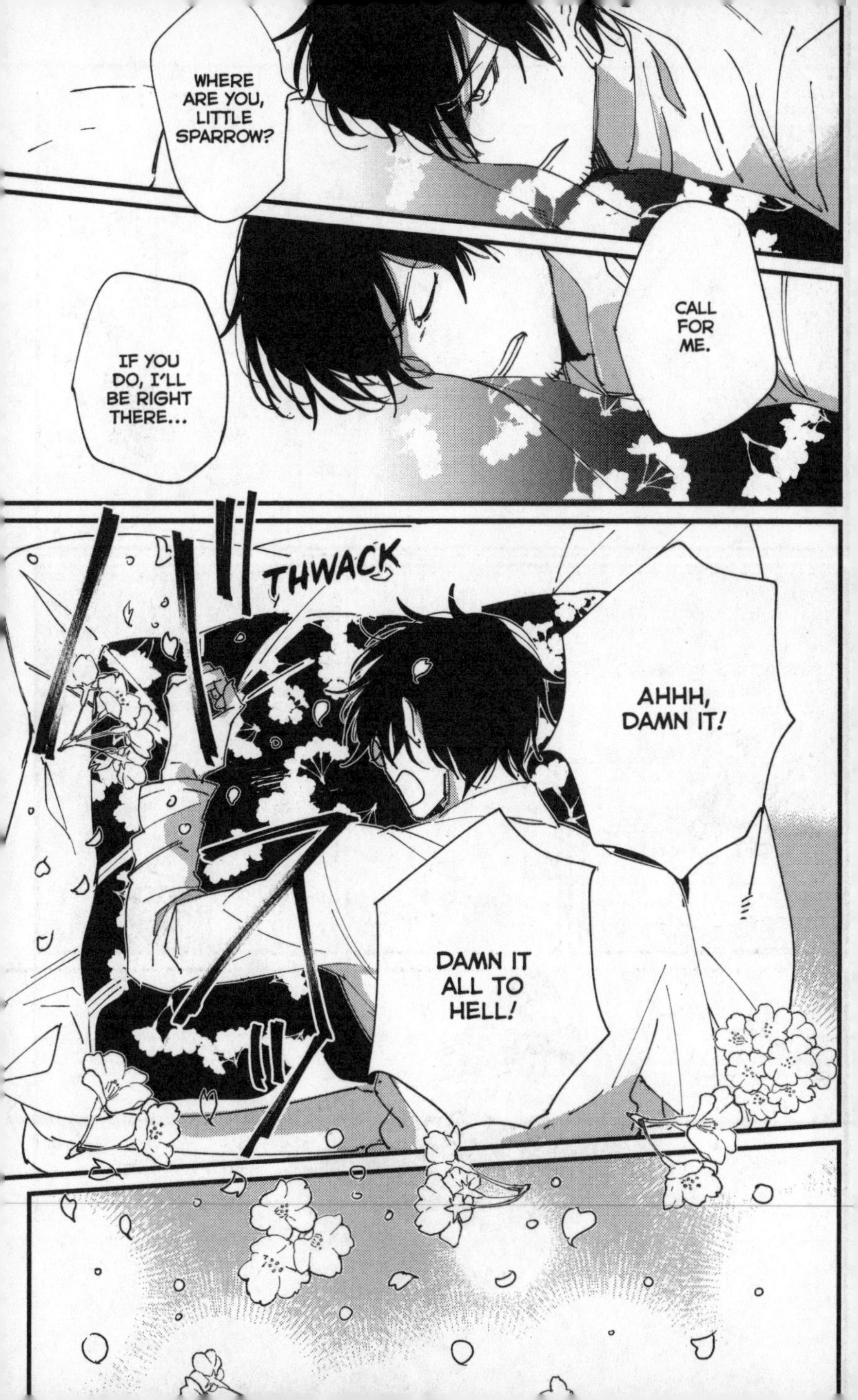
WHERE ARE YOU, LITTLE SPARROW?
CALL FOR ME.
IF YOU DO, I'LL BE RIGHT THERE...
THWACK
AHHH, DAMN IT!
DAMN IT ALL TO HELL!

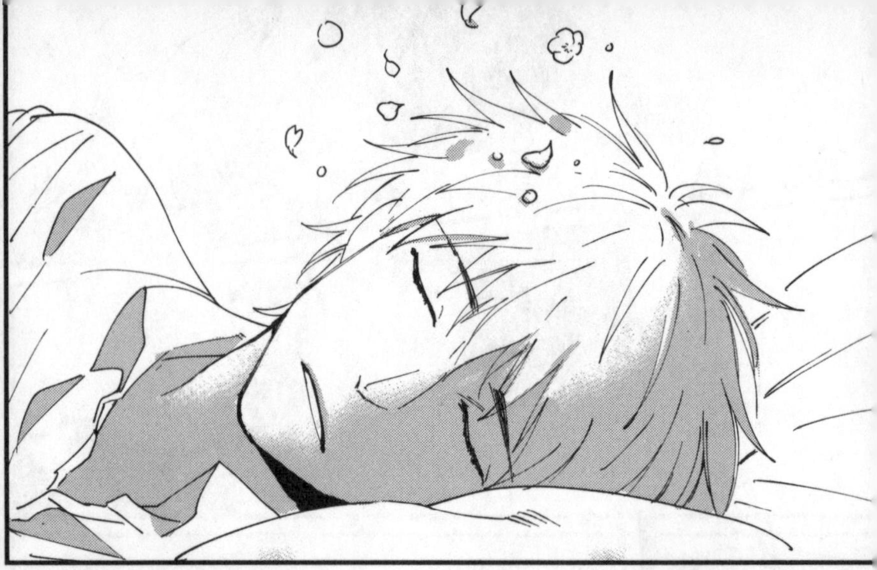

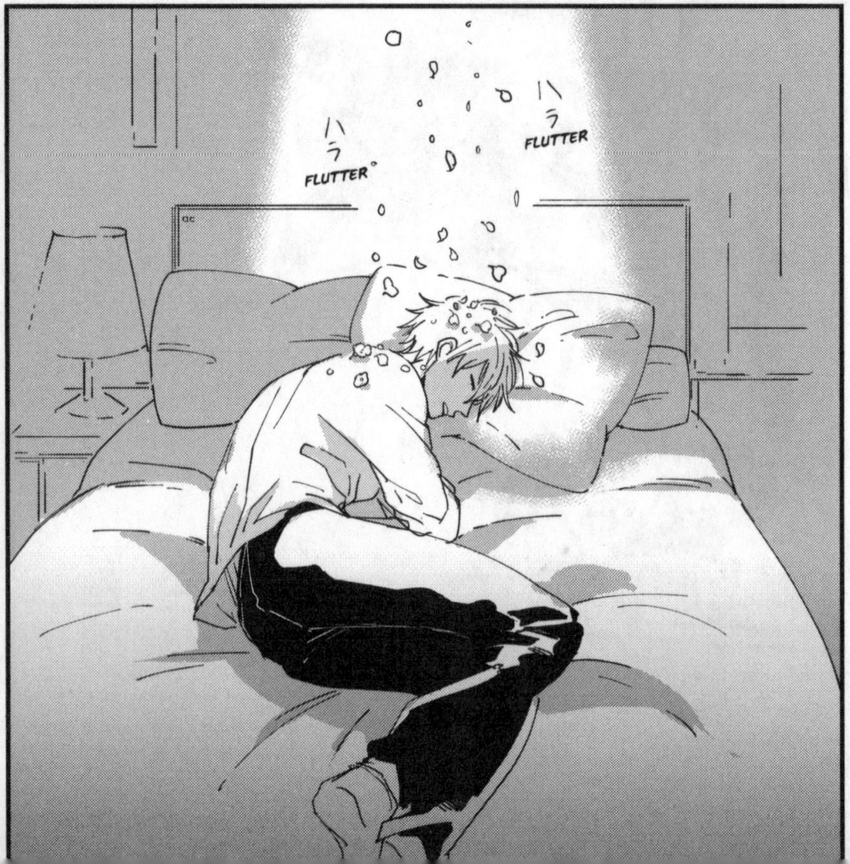
ハラ
FLUTTER
ハラ
FLUTTER

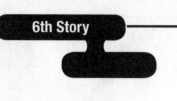

JUST BEFORE THE START OF THE MEIJI ERA, THE CITY OF EDO WAS IN A STATE OF DESTRUCTION.

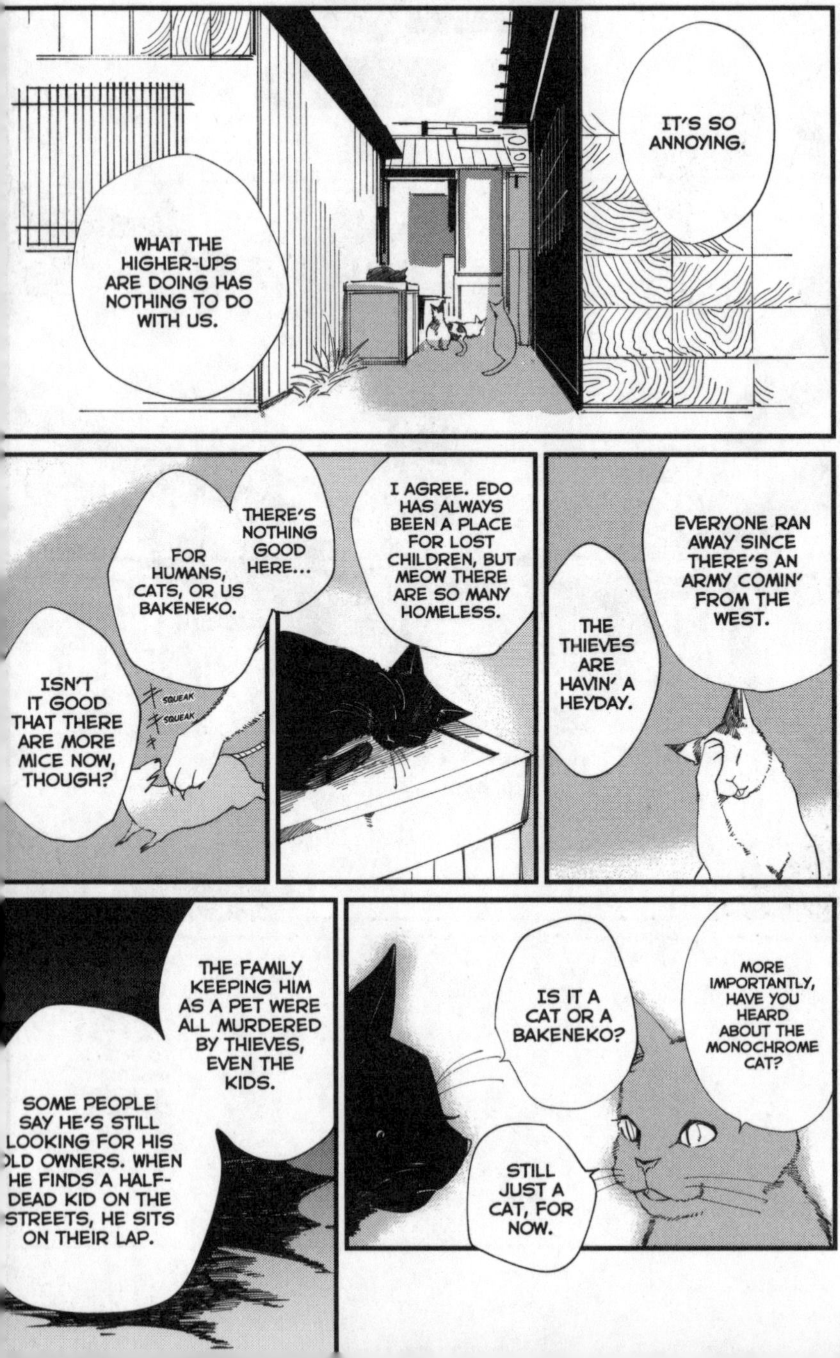
IT'S SO ANNOYING.
WHAT THE HIGHER-UPS ARE DOING HAS NOTHING TO DO WITH US.
EVERYONE RAN AWAY SINCE THERE'S AN ARMY COMIN' FROM THE WEST.
THE THIEVES ARE HAVIN' A HEYDAY.
I AGREE. EDO HAS ALWAYS BEEN A PLACE FOR LOST CHILDREN, BUT MEOW THERE ARE SO MANY HOMELESS.
THERE'S NOTHING GOOD HERE...
FOR HUMANS, CATS, OR US BAKENEKO.
SQUEAK
SQUEAK
ISN'T IT GOOD THAT THERE ARE MORE MICE NOW, THOUGH?
MORE IMPORTANTLY, HAVE YOU HEARD ABOUT THE MONOCHROME CAT?
IS IT A CAT OR A BAKENEKO?
STILL JUST A CAT, FOR NOW.
THE FAMILY KEEPING HIM AS A PET WERE ALL MURDERED BY THIEVES, EVEN THE KIDS.
SOME PEOPLE SAY HE'S STILL LOOKING FOR HIS OLD OWNERS. WHEN HE FINDS A HALF-DEAD KID ON THE STREETS, HE SITS ON THEIR LAP.

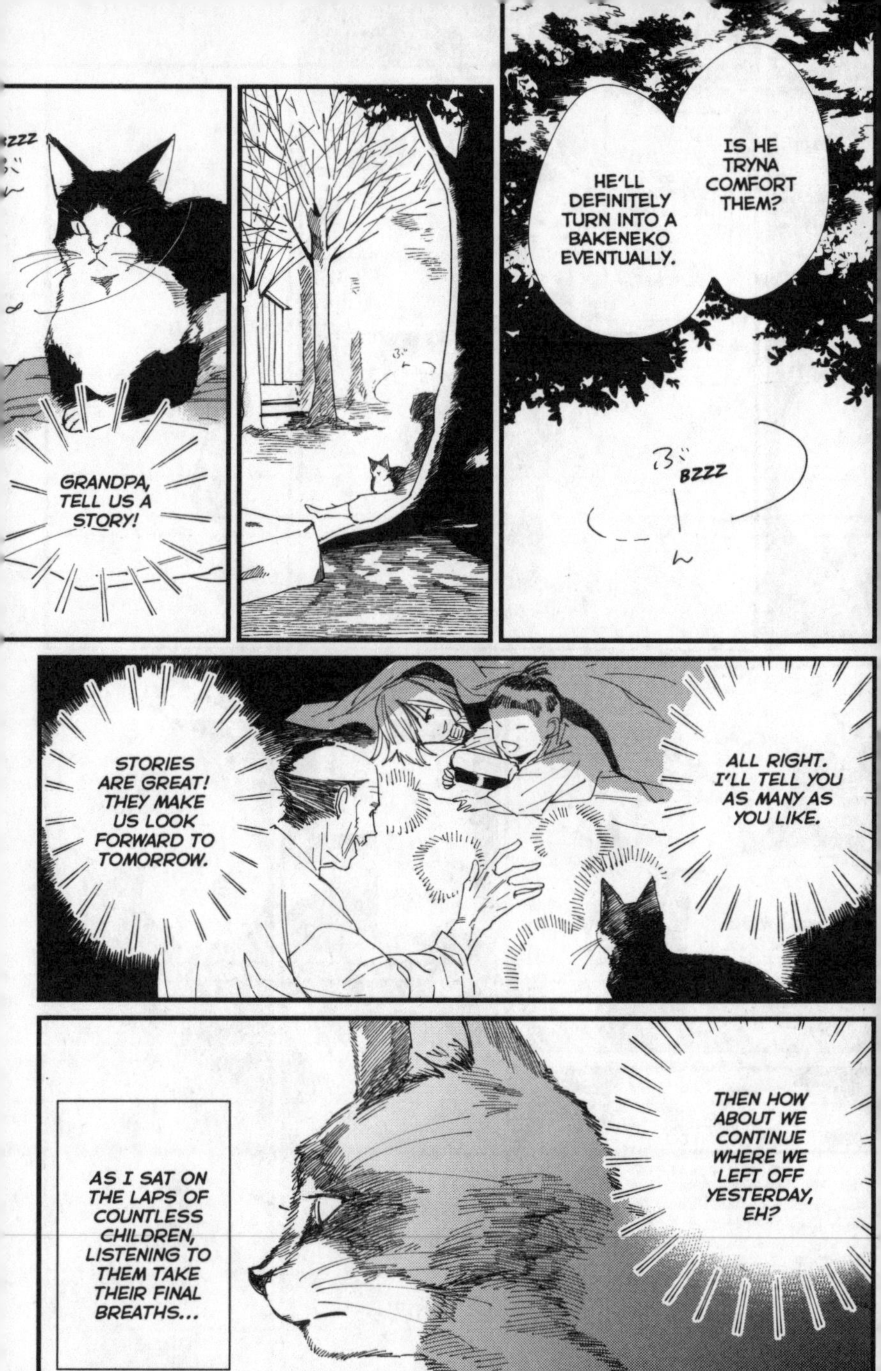
IS HE TRYNA COMFORT THEM?
HE'LL DEFINITELY TURN INTO A BAKENEKO EVENTUALLY.
BZZZ
BZZZ
GRANDPA, TELL US A STORY!
ALL RIGHT. I'LL TELL YOU AS MANY AS YOU LIKE.
STORIES ARE GREAT! THEY MAKE US LOOK FORWARD TO TOMORROW.
THEN HOW ABOUT WE CONTINUE WHERE WE LEFT OFF YESTERDAY, EH?
AS I SAT ON THE LAPS OF COUNTLESS CHILDREN, LISTENING TO THEM TAKE THEIR FINAL BREATHS...

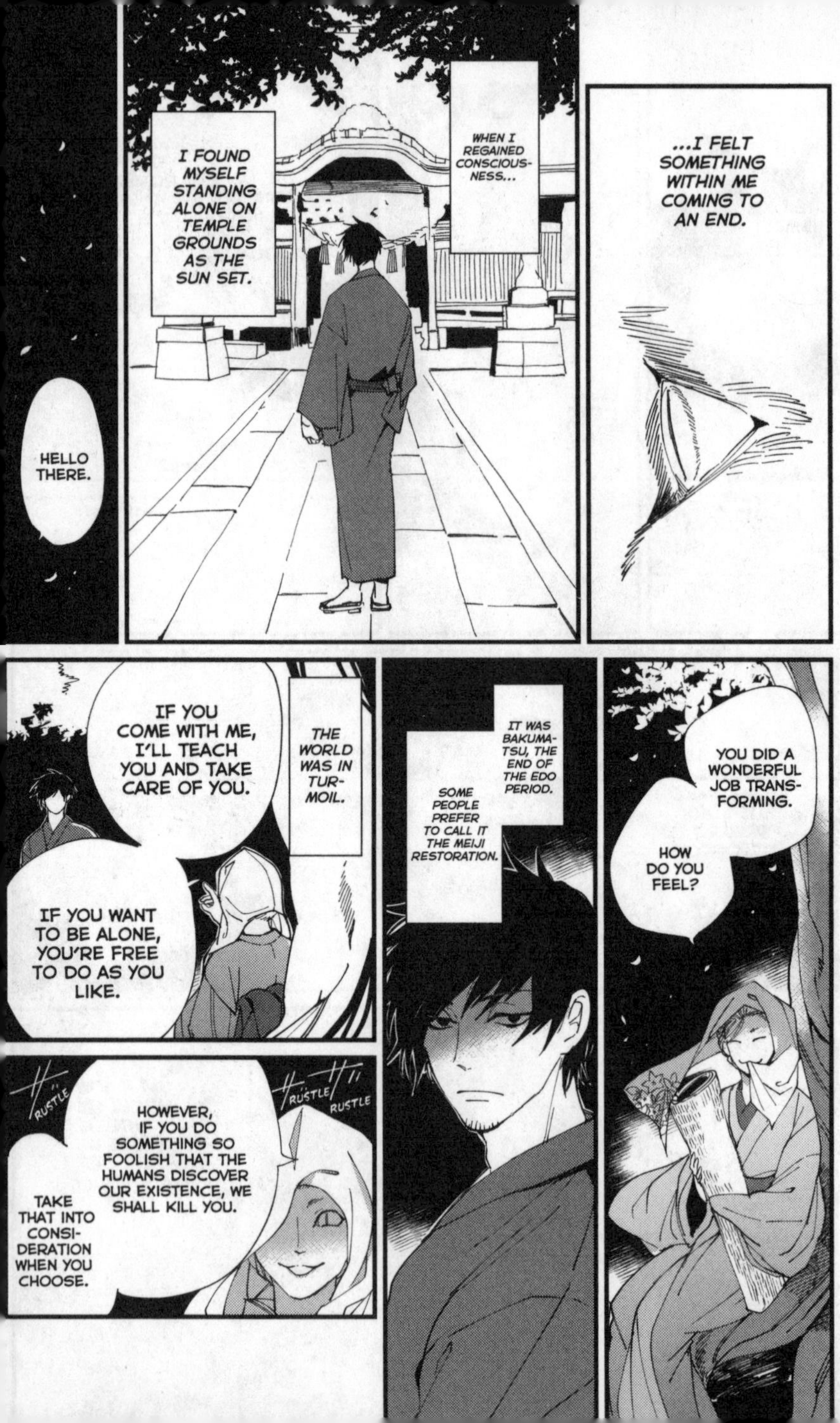
...I FELT SOMETHING WITHIN ME COMING TO AN END.
WHEN I REGAINED CONSCIOUS-NESS...
I FOUND MYSELF STANDING ALONE ON TEMPLE GROUNDS AS THE SUN SET.
HELLO THERE.
YOU DID A WONDERFUL JOB TRANS-FORMING.
HOW DO YOU FEEL?
IT WAS BAKUMA-TSU, THE END OF THE EDO PERIOD.
SOME PEOPLE PREFER TO CALL IT THE MEIJI RESTORATION.
THE WORLD WAS IN TUR-MOIL.
IF YOU COME WITH ME, I'LL TEACH YOU AND TAKE CARE OF YOU.
IF YOU WANT TO BE ALONE, YOU'RE FREE TO DO AS YOU LIKE.
RUSTLE RUSTLE
HOWEVER, IF YOU DO SOMETHING SO FOOLISH THAT THE HUMANS DISCOVER OUR EXISTENCE, WE SHALL KILL YOU.
TAKE THAT INTO CONSI-DERATION WHEN YOU CHOOSE.
RUSTLE

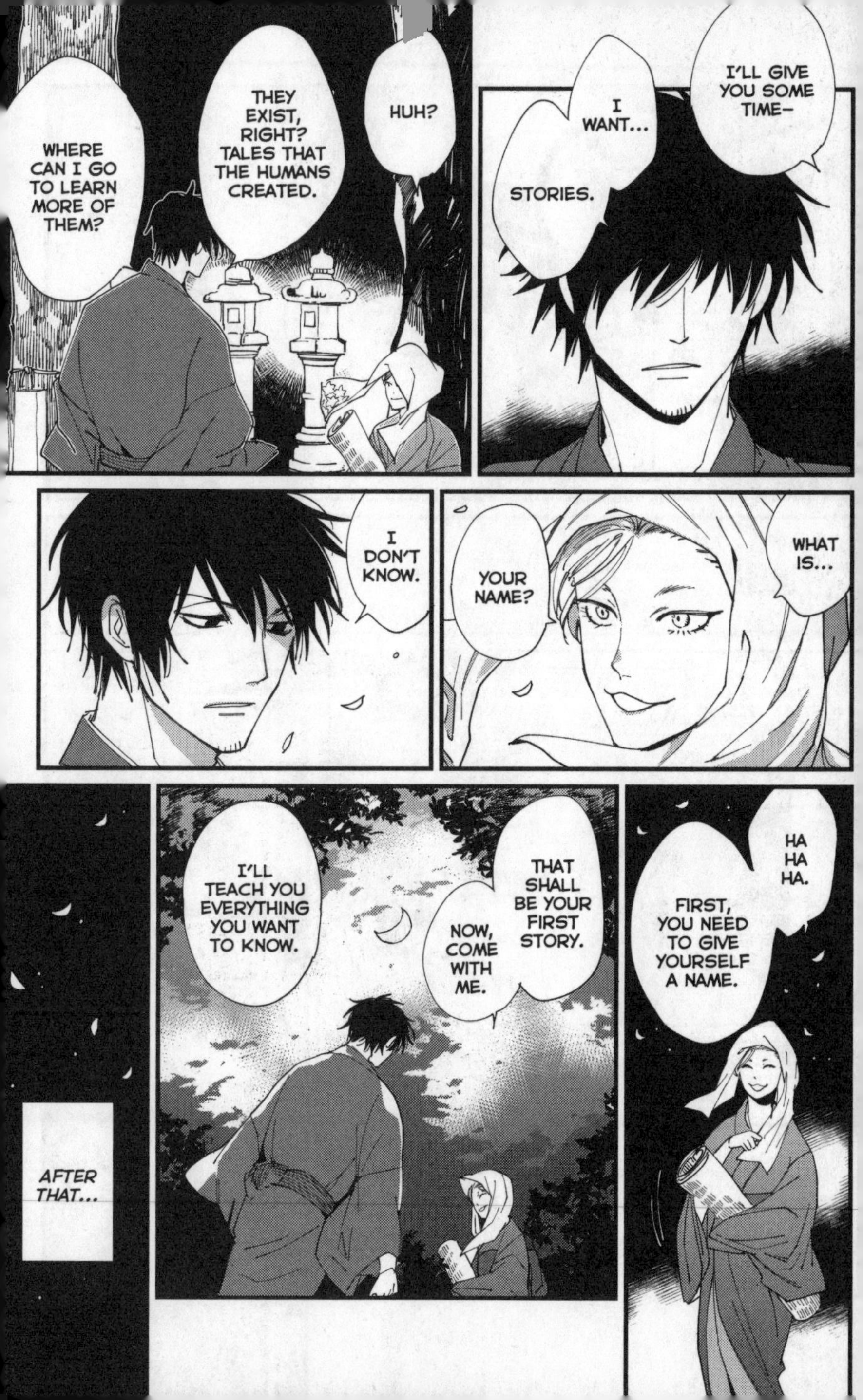
I'LL GIVE YOU SOME TIME–
I WANT...
STORIES.
HUH?
THEY EXIST, RIGHT? TALES THAT THE HUMANS CREATED.
WHERE CAN I GO TO LEARN MORE OF THEM?
WHAT IS...
YOUR NAME?
I DON'T KNOW.
HA HA HA.
FIRST, YOU NEED TO GIVE YOURSELF A NAME.
THAT SHALL BE YOUR FIRST STORY.
NOW, COME WITH ME.
I'LL TEACH YOU EVERYTHING YOU WANT TO KNOW.
AFTER THAT...

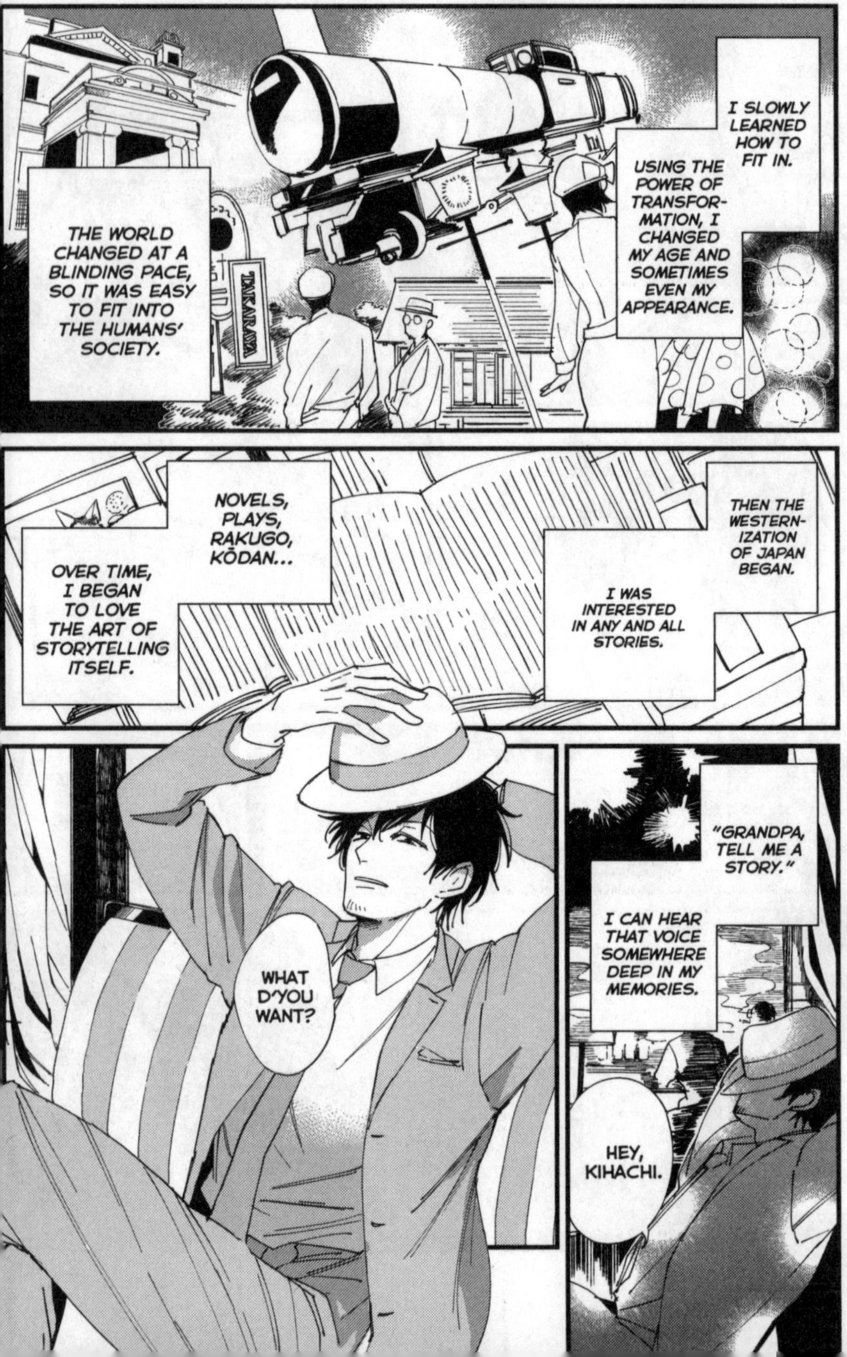
I SLOWLY LEARNED HOW TO FIT IN.
USING THE POWER OF TRANSFORMATION, I CHANGED MY AGE AND SOMETIMES EVEN MY APPEARANCE.
TAKARAYA
THE WORLD CHANGED AT A BLINDING PACE, SO IT WAS EASY TO FIT INTO THE HUMANS' SOCIETY.
THEN THE WESTERNIZATION OF JAPAN BEGAN.
I WAS INTERESTED IN ANY AND ALL STORIES.
NOVELS, PLAYS, RAKUGO, KŌDAN...
OVER TIME, I BEGAN TO LOVE THE ART OF STORYTELLING ITSELF.
"GRANDPA, TELL ME A STORY."
I CAN HEAR THAT VOICE SOMEWHERE DEEP IN MY MEMORIES.
HEY, KIHACHI.
WHAT D'YOU WANT?

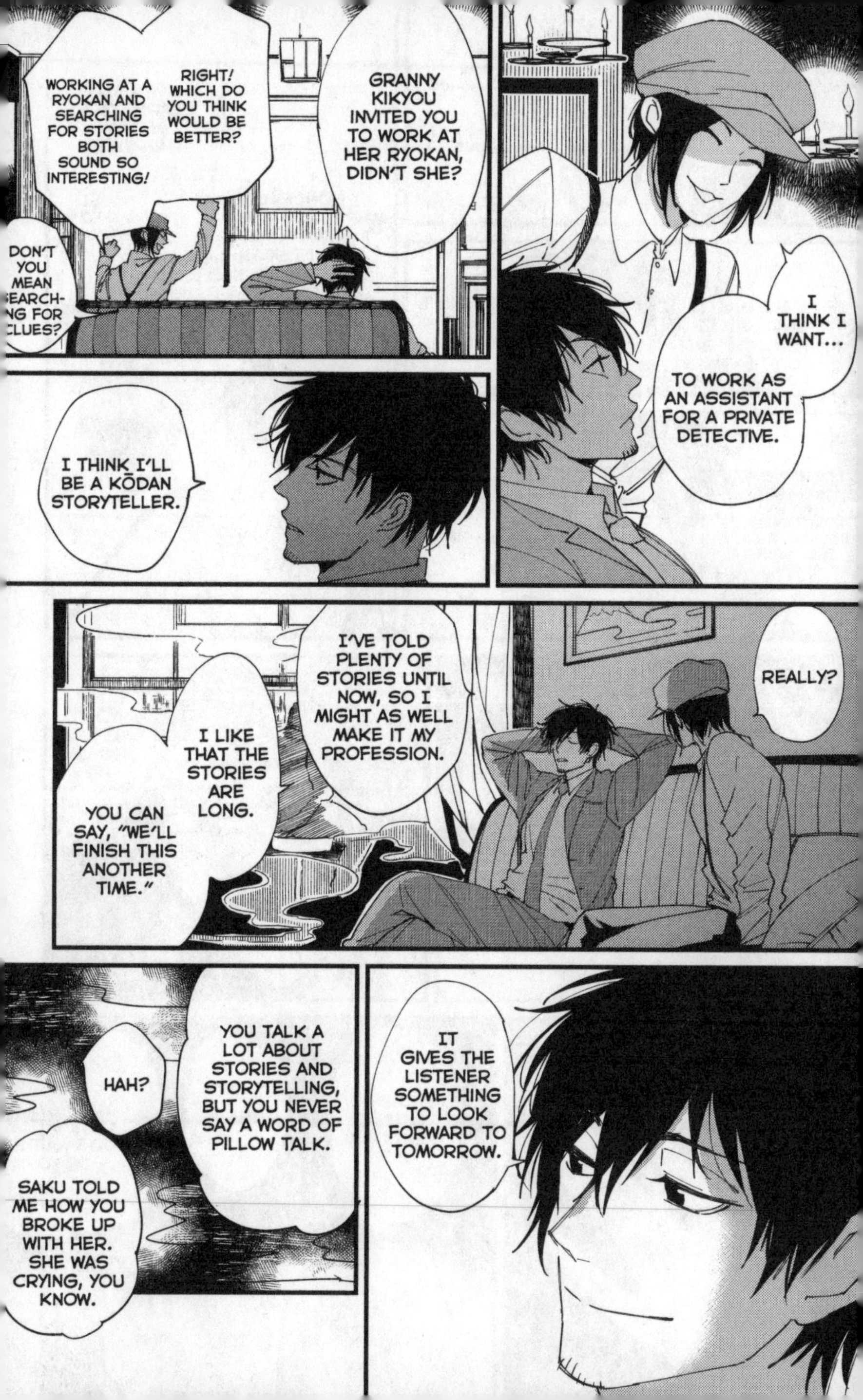
I THINK I WANT...
TO WORK AS AN ASSISTANT FOR A PRIVATE DETECTIVE.
GRANNY KIKYOU INVITED YOU TO WORK AT HER RYOKAN, DIDN'T SHE?
RIGHT! WHICH DO YOU THINK WOULD BE BETTER?
WORKING AT A RYOKAN AND SEARCHING FOR STORIES BOTH SOUND SO INTERESTING!
DON'T YOU MEAN EARCH- NG FOR CLUES?
I THINK I'LL BE A KŌDAN STORYTELLER.
REALLY?
I'VE TOLD PLENTY OF STORIES UNTIL NOW, SO I MIGHT AS WELL MAKE IT MY PROFESSION.
I LIKE THAT THE STORIES ARE LONG.
YOU CAN SAY, "WE'LL FINISH THIS ANOTHER TIME."
IT GIVES THE LISTENER SOMETHING TO LOOK FORWARD TO TOMORROW.
YOU TALK A LOT ABOUT STORIES AND STORYTELLING, BUT YOU NEVER SAY A WORD OF PILLOW TALK.
HAH?
SAKU TOLD ME HOW YOU BROKE UP WITH HER. SHE WAS CRYING, YOU KNOW.

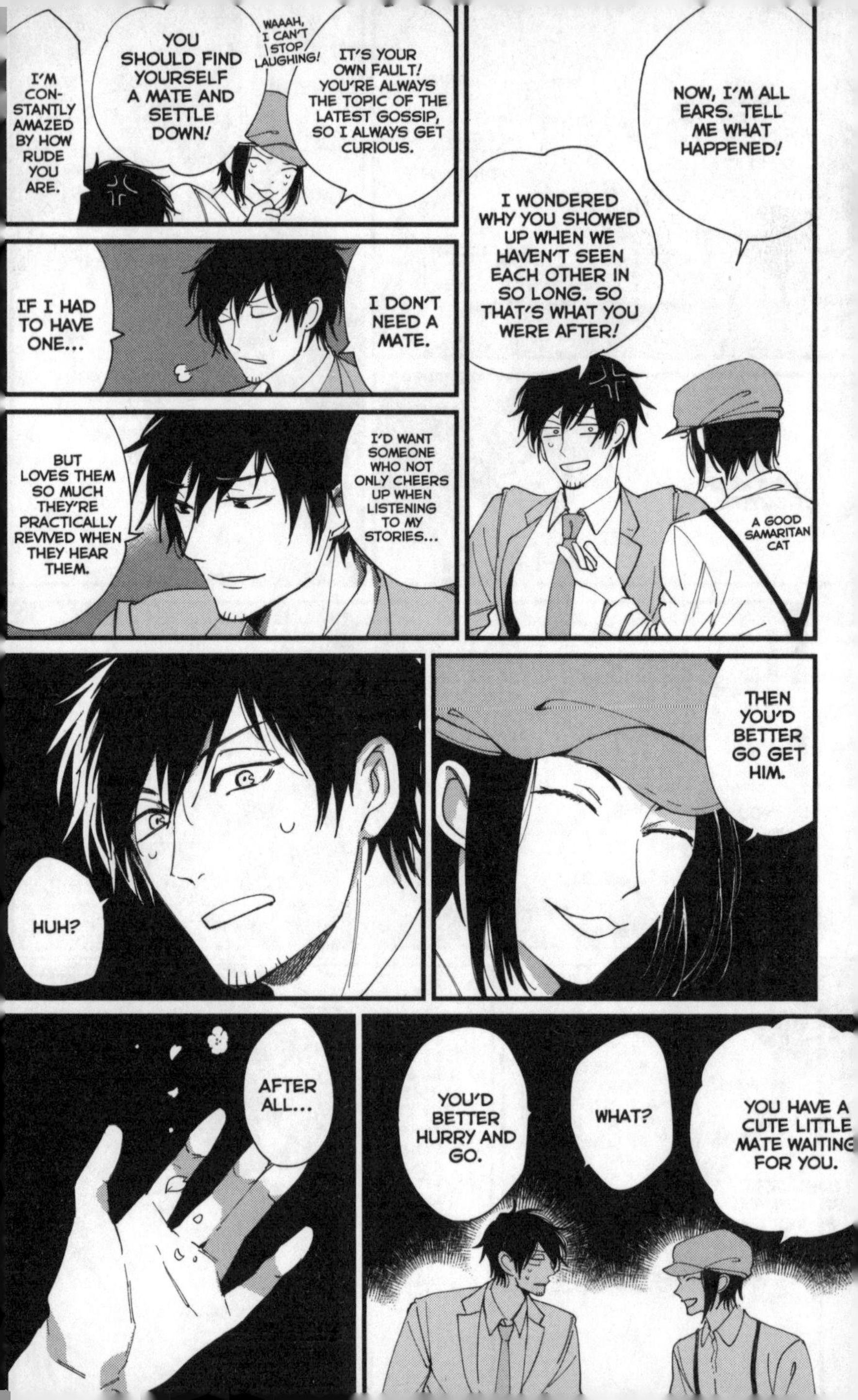
NOW, I'M ALL EARS. TELL ME WHAT HAPPENED!
I WONDERED WHY YOU SHOWED UP WHEN WE HAVEN'T SEEN EACH OTHER IN SO LONG. SO THAT'S WHAT YOU WERE AFTER!
A GOOD SAMARITAN CAT
IT'S YOUR OWN FAULT! YOU'RE ALWAYS THE TOPIC OF THE LATEST GOSSIP, SO I ALWAYS GET CURIOUS.
WAAAH, I CAN'T STOP LAUGHING!
YOU SHOULD FIND YOURSELF A MATE AND SETTLE DOWN!
I'M CON-STANTLY AMAZED BY HOW RUDE YOU ARE.
I DON'T NEED A MATE.
IF I HAD TO HAVE ONE...
I'D WANT SOMEONE WHO NOT ONLY CHEERS UP WHEN LISTENING TO MY STORIES...
BUT LOVES THEM SO MUCH THEY'RE PRACTICALLY REVIVED WHEN THEY HEAR THEM.
THEN YOU'D BETTER GO GET HIM.
HUH?
YOU HAVE A CUTE LITTLE MATE WAITING FOR YOU.
WHAT?
YOU'D BETTER HURRY AND GO.
AFTER ALL...

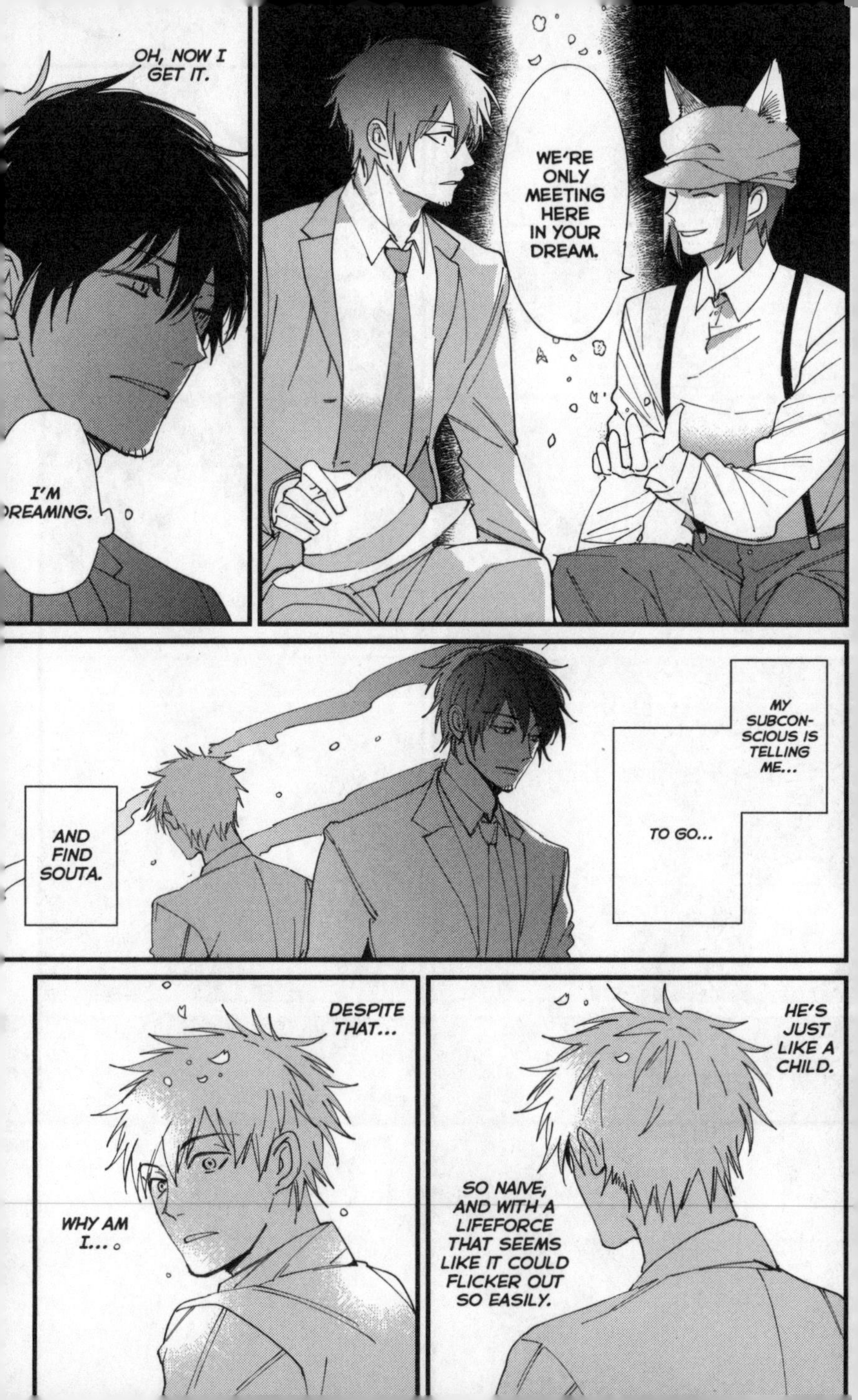
WE'RE ONLY MEETING HERE IN YOUR DREAM.
OH, NOW I GET IT.
I'M DREAMING.
MY SUBCON-SCIOUS IS TELLING ME...
TO GO...
AND FIND SOUTA.
HE'S JUST LIKE A CHILD.
SO NAIVE, AND WITH A LIFEFORCE THAT SEEMS LIKE IT COULD FLICKER OUT SO EASILY.
DESPITE THAT...
WHY AM I...

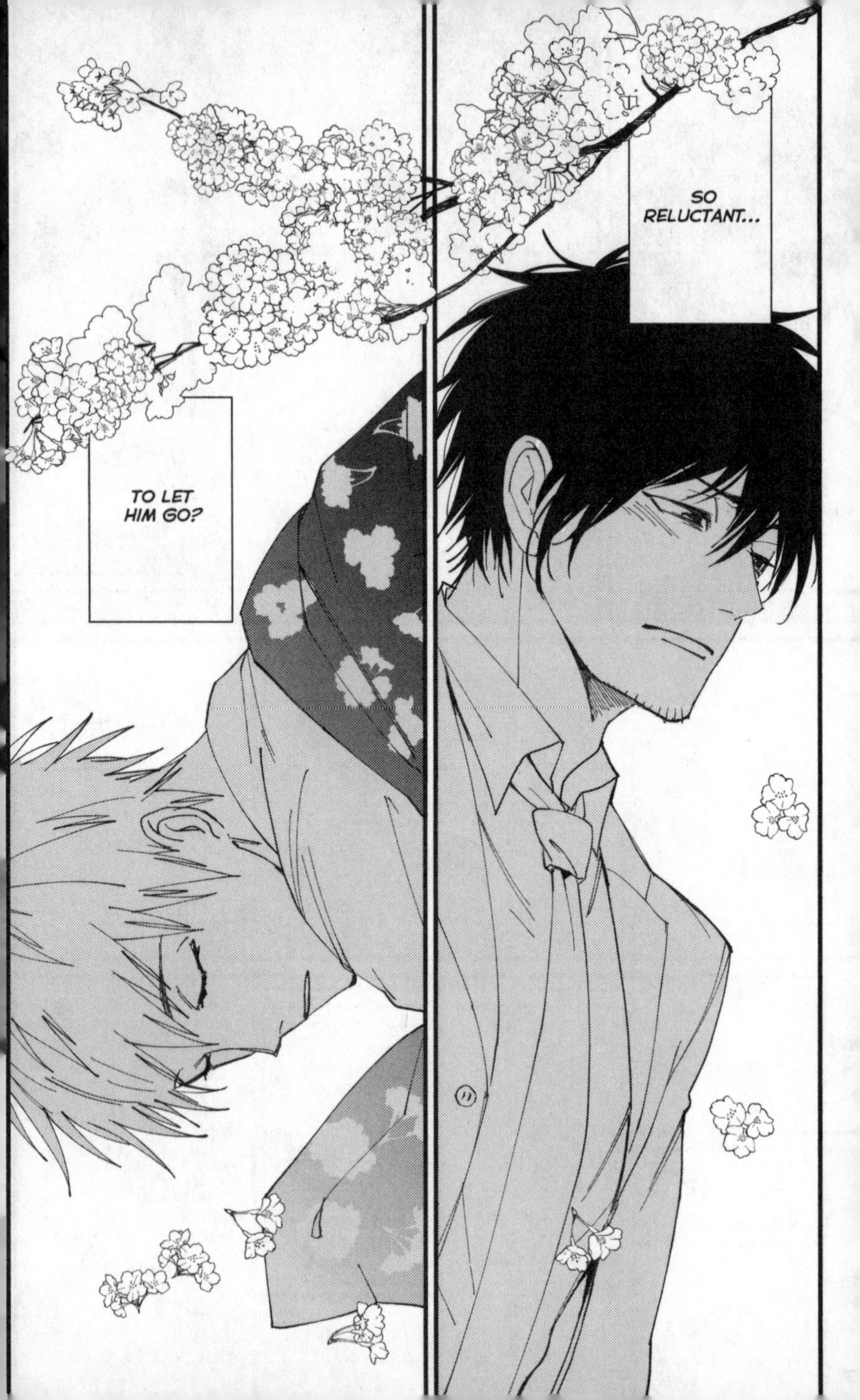
SO RELUCTANT...
TO LET HIM GO?

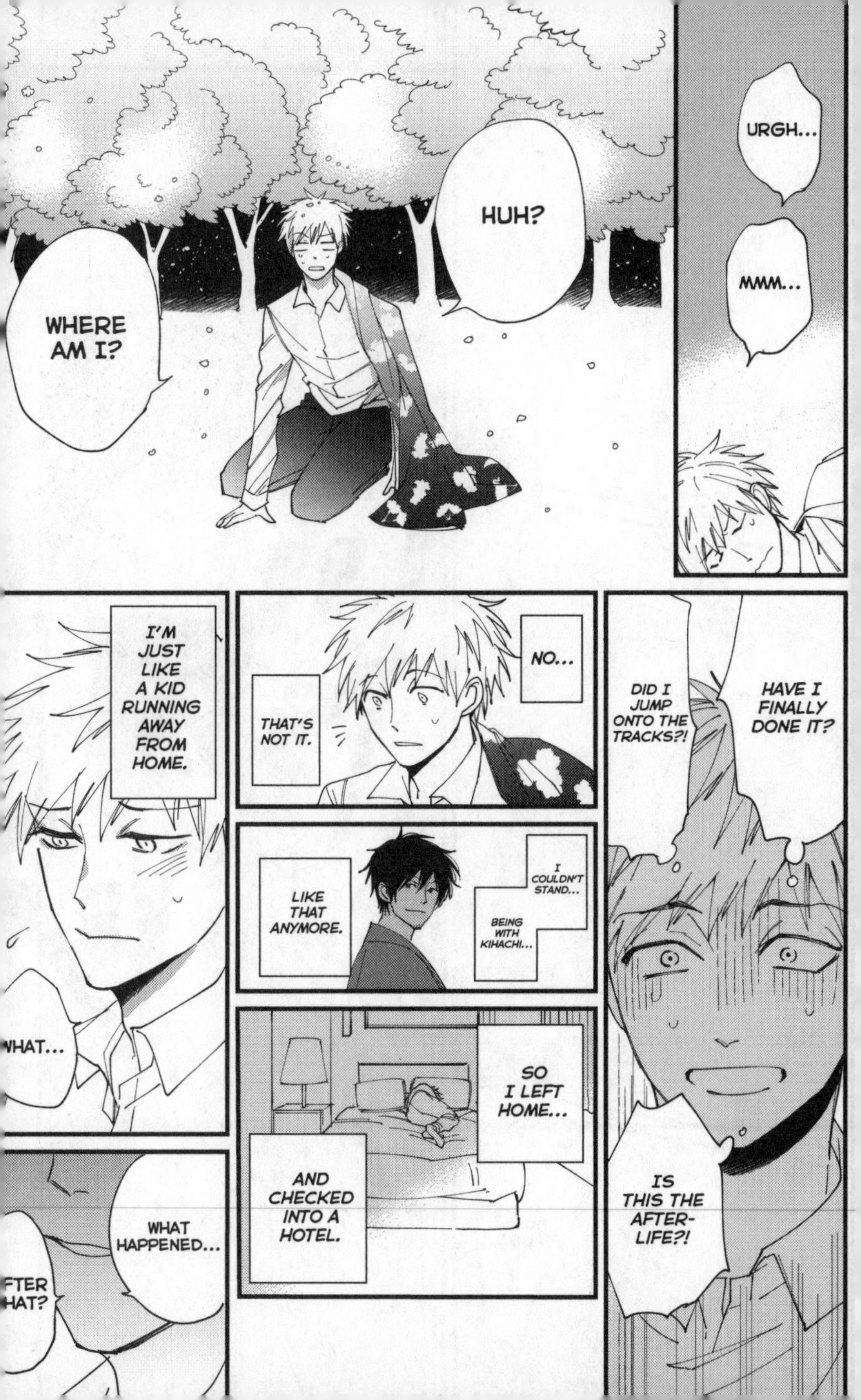
URGH...
MMM...
HUH?
WHERE AM I?
HAVE I FINALLY DONE IT?
DID I JUMP ONTO THE TRACKS?!
IS THIS THE AFTER-LIFE?!
NO...
THAT'S NOT IT.
I COULDN'T STAND...
BEING WITH KIHACHI...
LIKE THAT ANYMORE.
SO I LEFT HOME...
AND CHECKED INTO A HOTEL.
I'M JUST LIKE A KID RUNNING AWAY FROM HOME.
HAT...
WHAT HAPPENED...
FTER HAT?

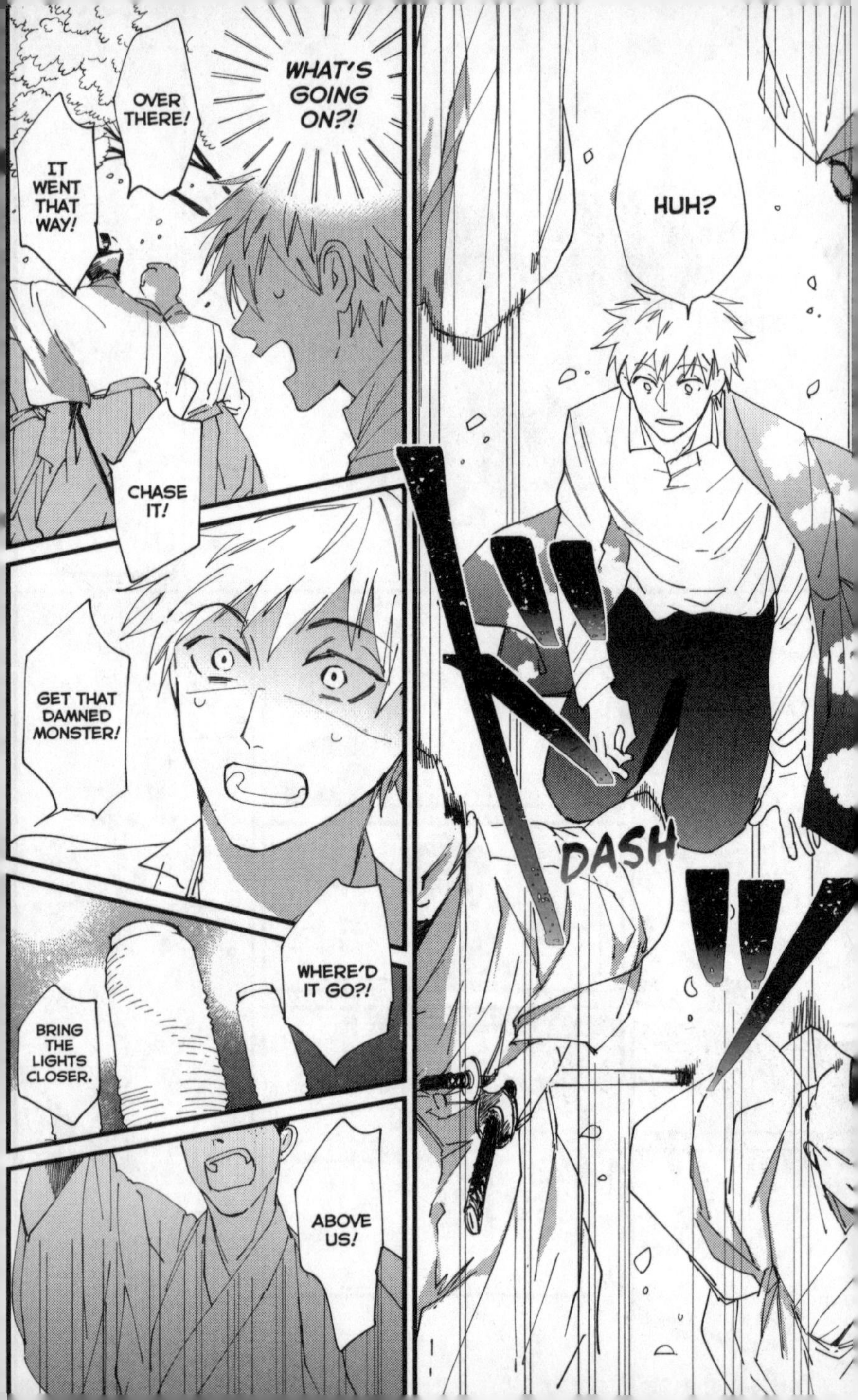
HUH?
DASH
WHAT'S GOING ON?!
OVER THERE!
IT WENT THAT WAY!
CHASE IT!
GET THAT DAMNED MONSTER!
WHERE'D IT GO?!
BRING THE LIGHTS CLOSER.
ABOVE US!

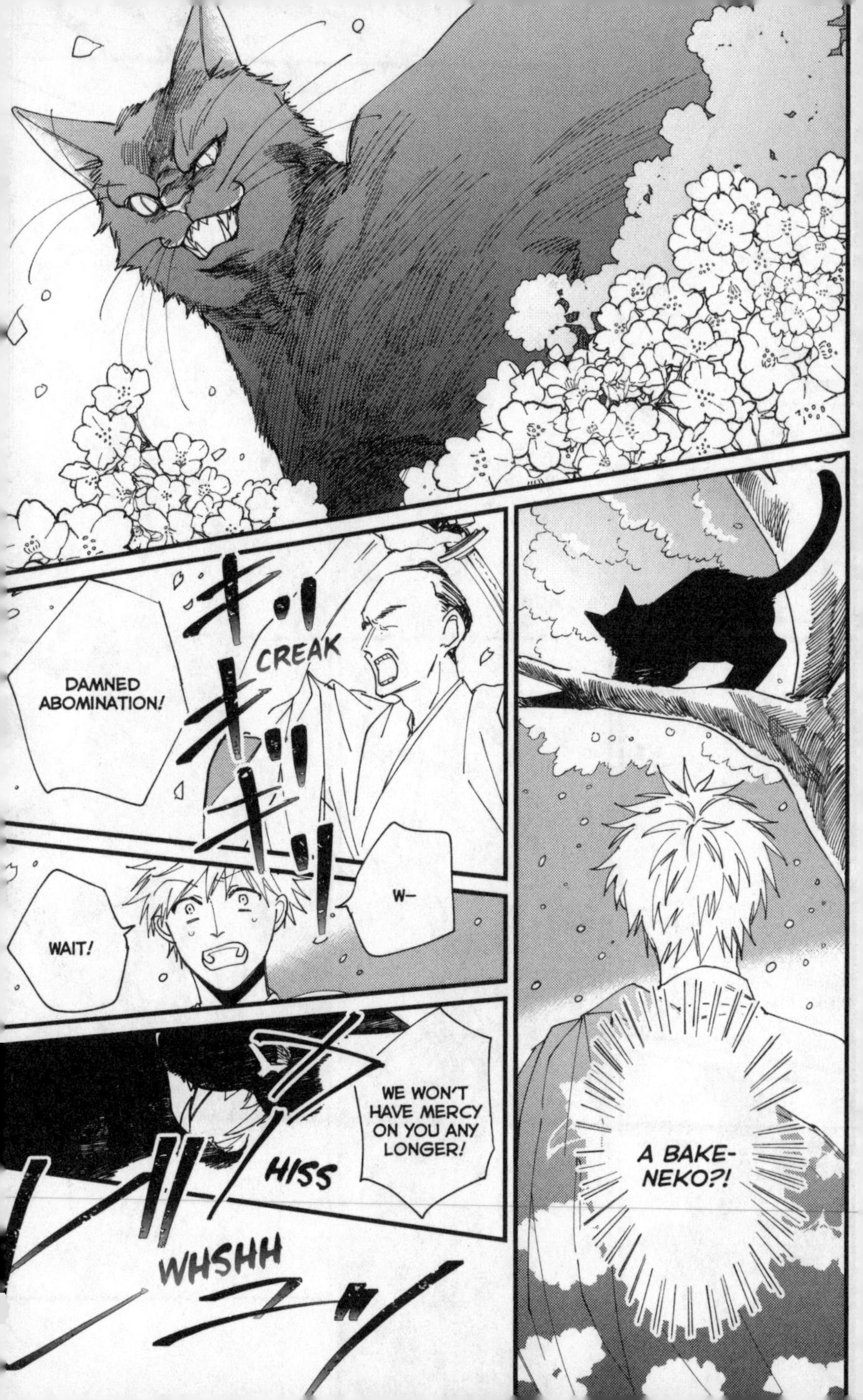
A BAKE-NEKO?!
DAMNED ABOMINATION!
CREAK
W—
WAIT!
WE WON'T HAVE MERCY ON YOU ANY LONGER!
HISS
WHSHH

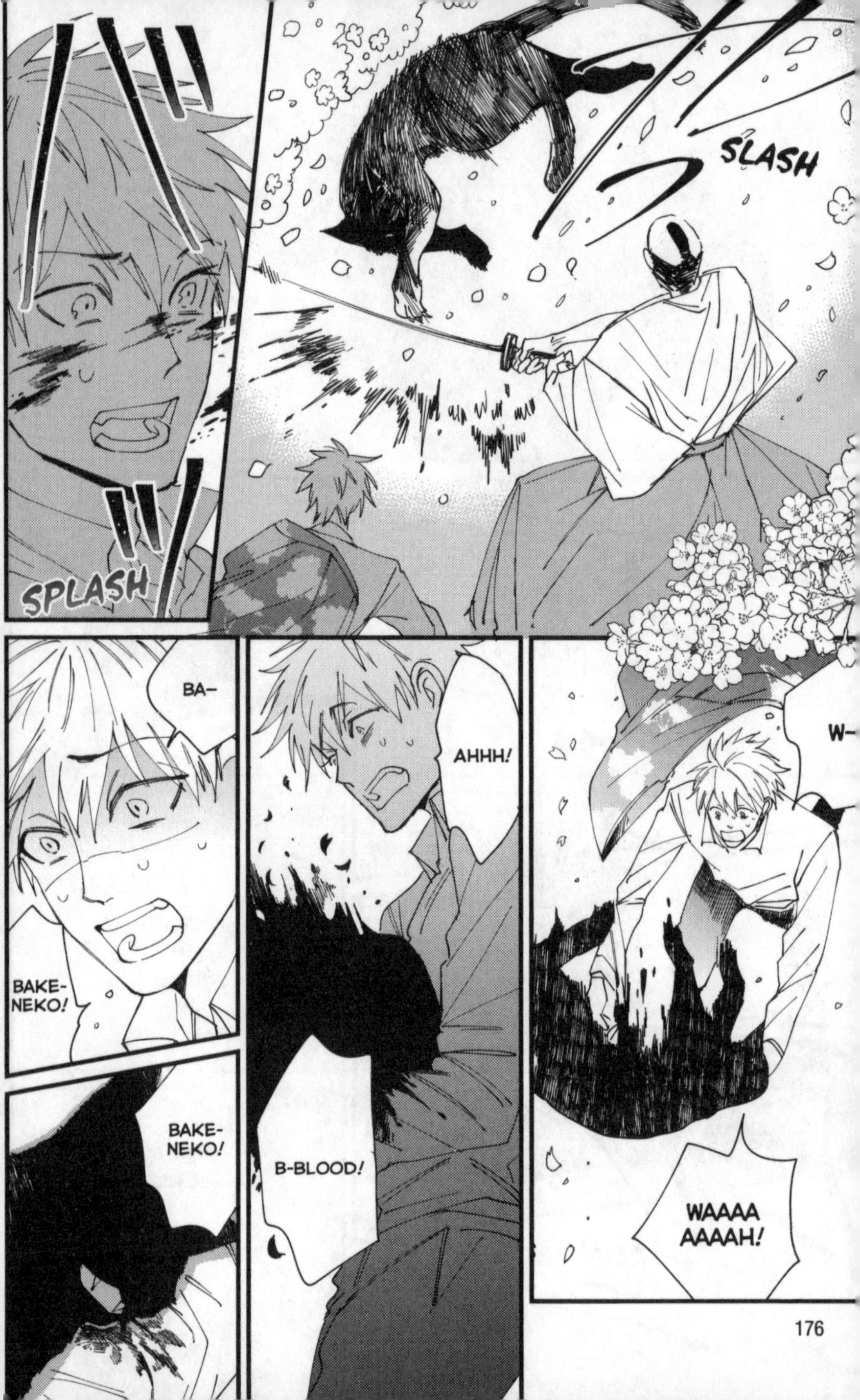

SLASH
SPLASH
W–
WAAAA AAAAH!
AHHH!
B-BLOOD!
BA–
BAKE-NEKO!
BAKE-NEKO!

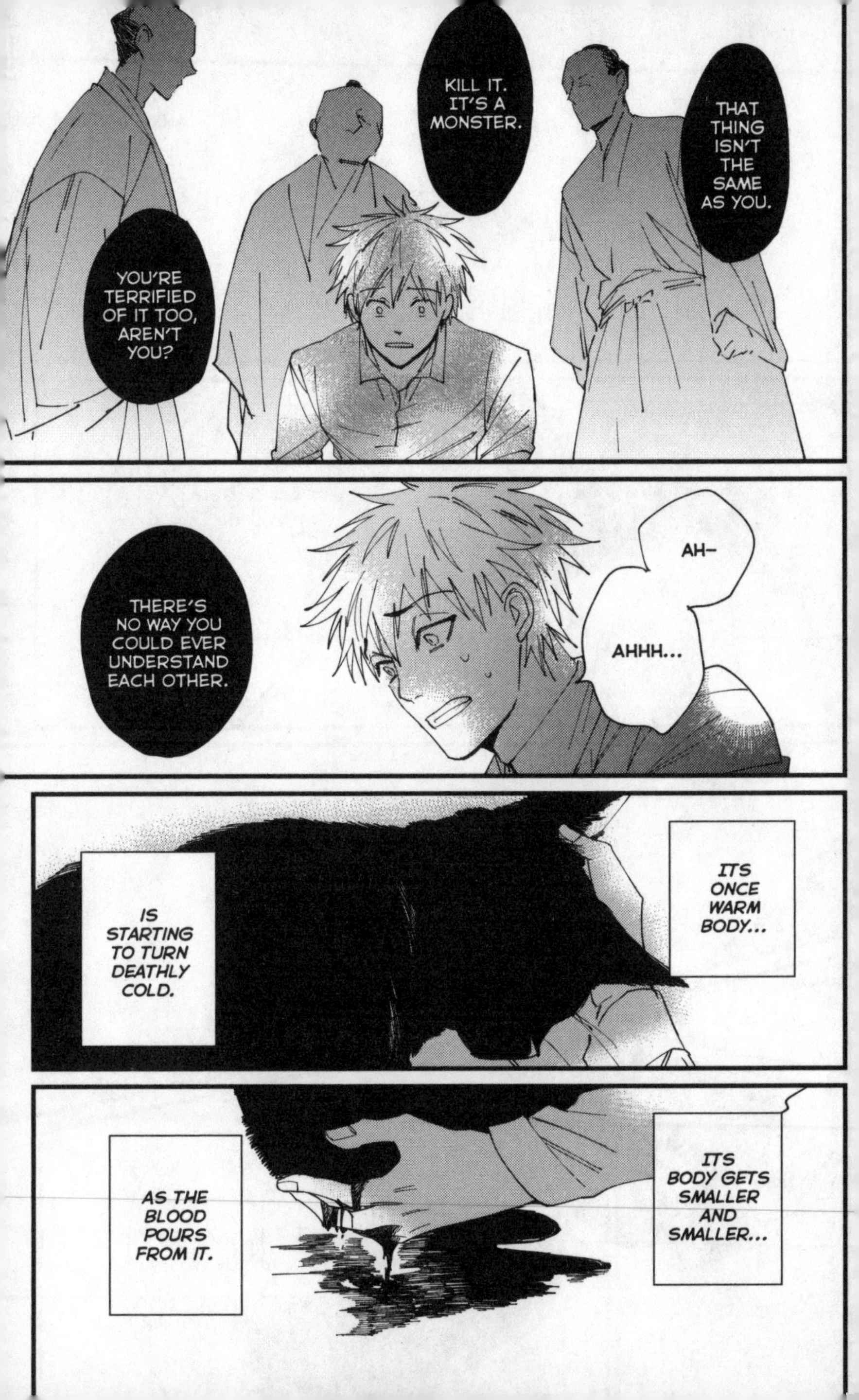
THAT THING ISN'T THE SAME AS YOU.
KILL IT. IT'S A MONSTER.
YOU'RE TERRIFIED OF IT TOO, AREN'T YOU?
AH-
AHHH...
THERE'S NO WAY YOU COULD EVER UNDERSTAND EACH OTHER.
ITS ONCE WARM BODY...
IS STARTING TO TURN DEATHLY COLD.
ITS BODY GETS SMALLER AND SMALLER...
AS THE BLOOD POURS FROM IT.

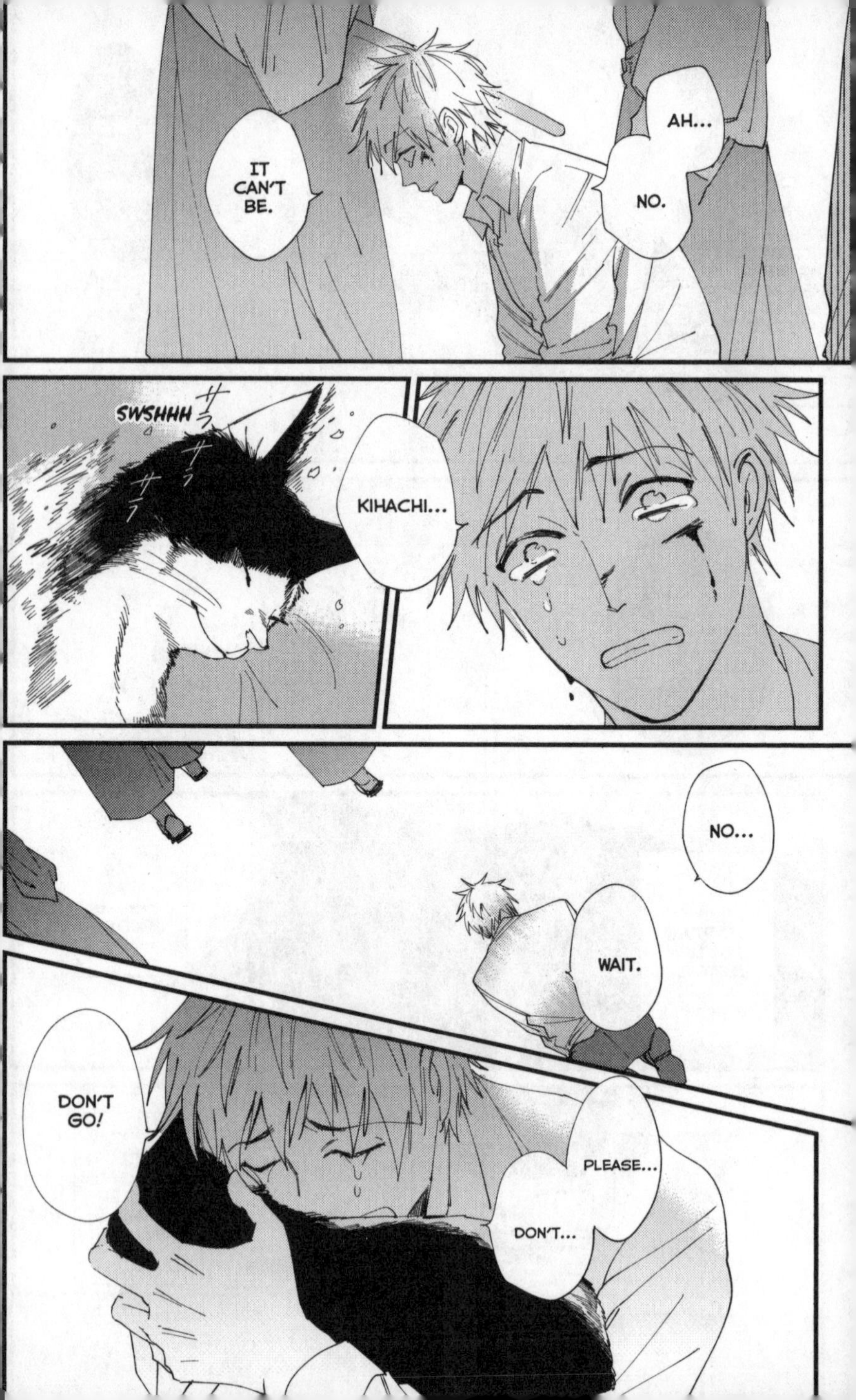
AH... NO.
IT CAN'T BE.
KIHACHI...
SWSHHH
サラ サラ サラ
NO...
WAIT.
PLEASE... DON'T...
DON'T GO!

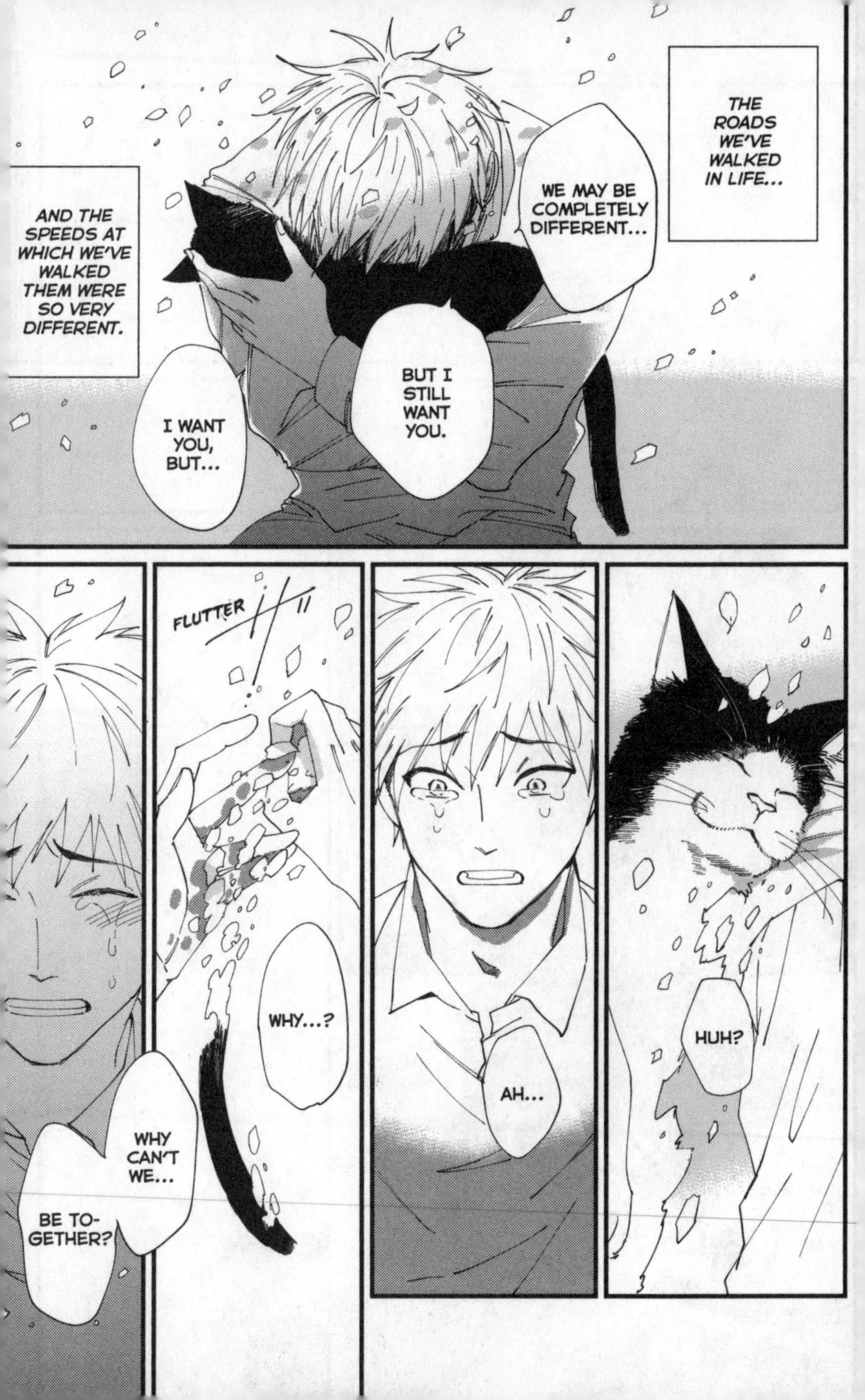
THE ROADS WE'VE WALKED IN LIFE...
WE MAY BE COMPLETELY DIFFERENT...
AND THE SPEEDS AT WHICH WE'VE WALKED THEM WERE SO VERY DIFFERENT.
BUT I STILL WANT YOU.
I WANT YOU, BUT...
HUH?
AH...
FLUTTER
WHY...?
WHY CAN'T WE...
BE TO-GETHER?

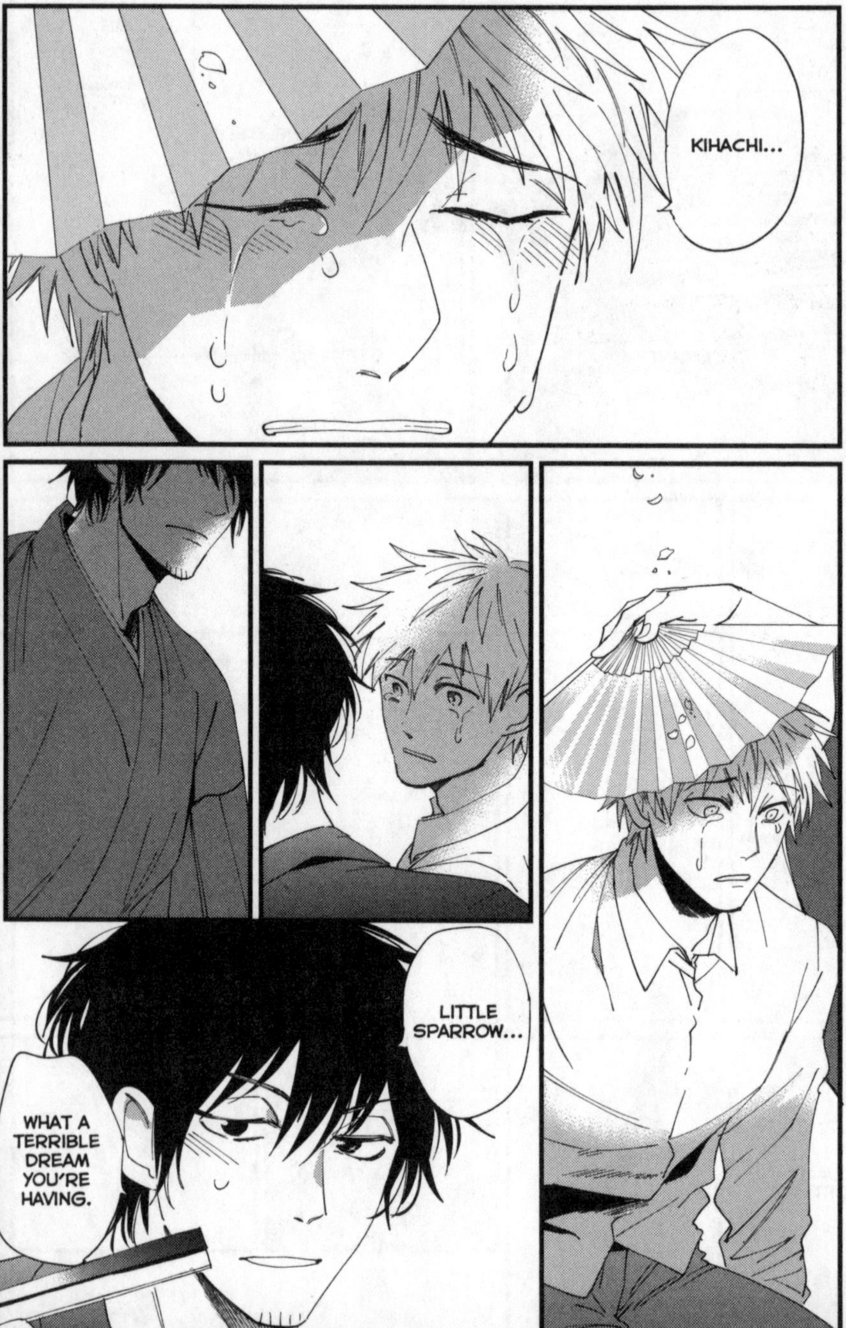
KIHACHI...
LITTLE SPARROW...
WHAT A TERRIBLE DREAM YOU'RE HAVING.

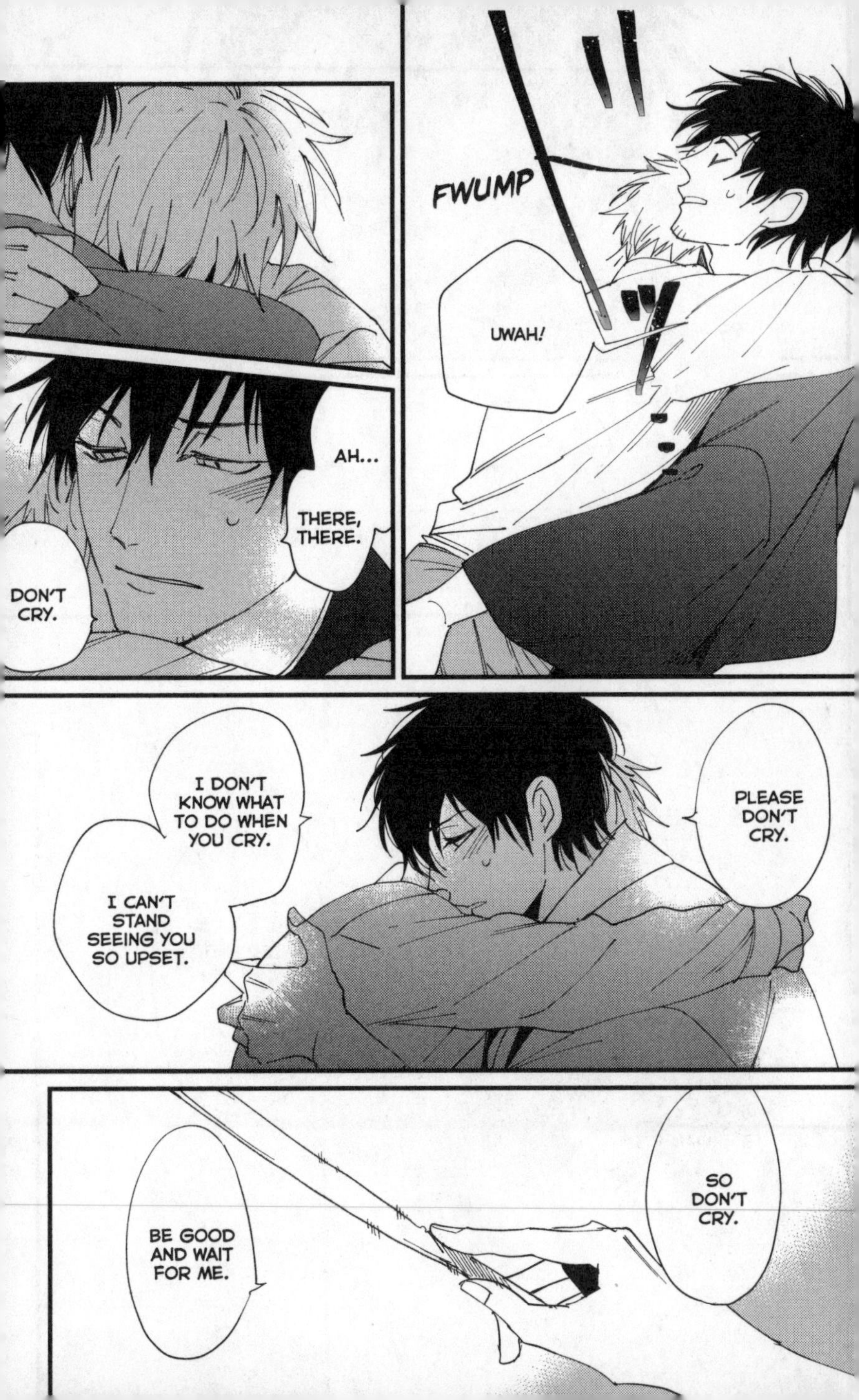
FWUMP
UWAH!
AH...
THERE, THERE.
DON'T CRY.
PLEASE DON'T CRY.
I DON'T KNOW WHAT TO DO WHEN YOU CRY.
I CAN'T STAND SEEING YOU SO UPSET.
SO DON'T CRY.
BE GOOD AND WAIT FOR ME.

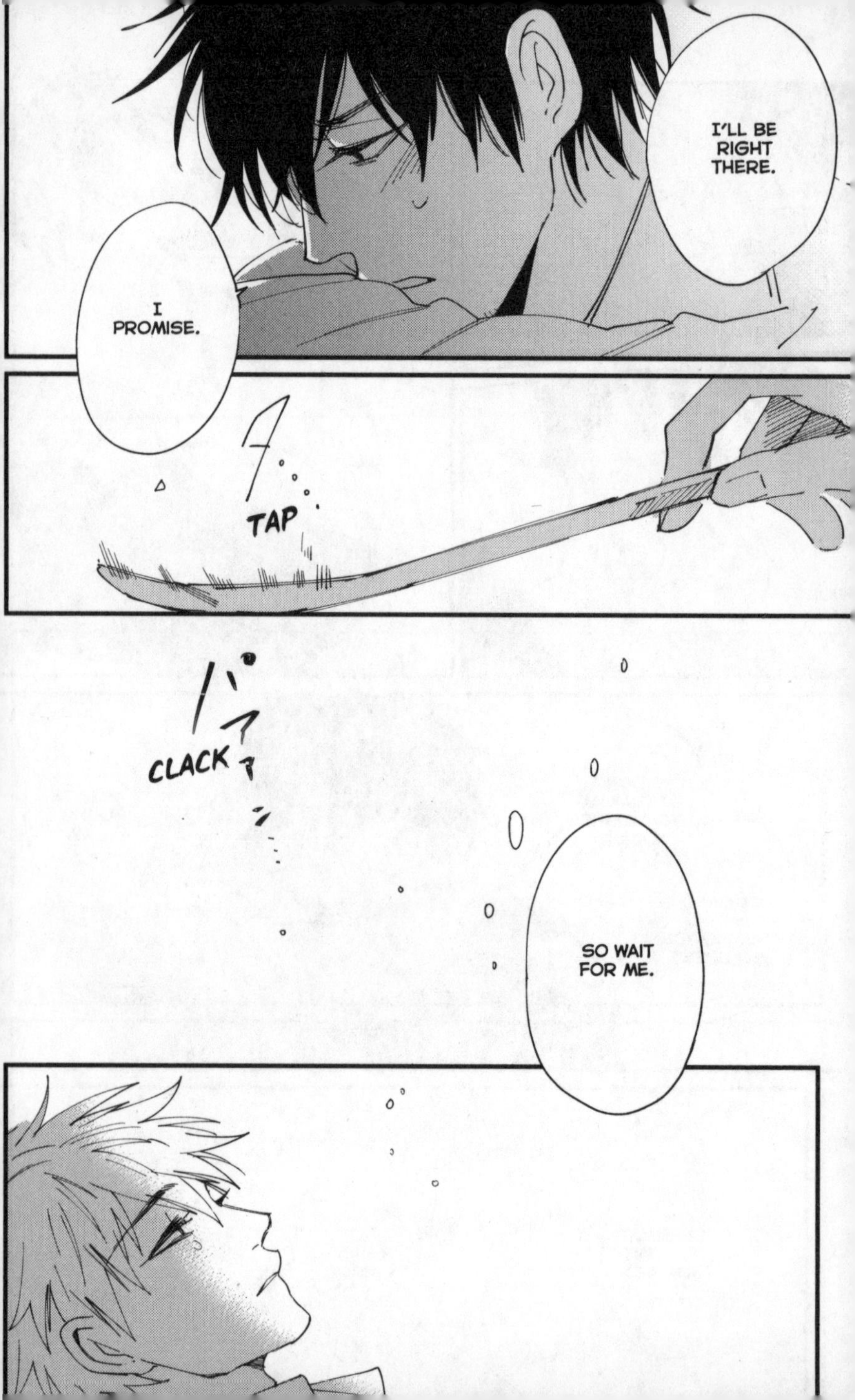
I'LL BE RIGHT THERE.
I PROMISE.
TAP
CLACK
SO WAIT FOR ME.

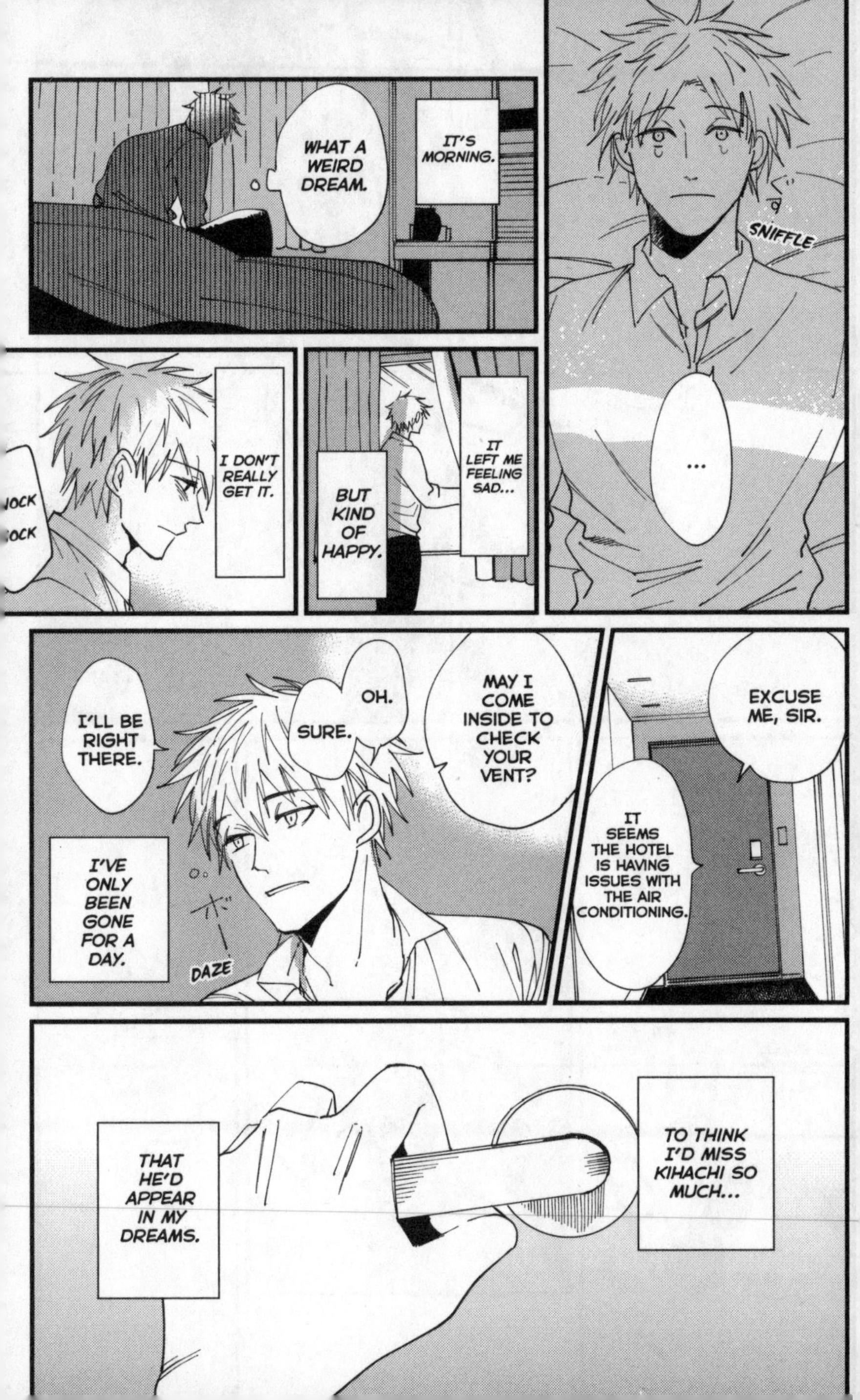
SNIFFLE
...
IT'S MORNING.
WHAT A WEIRD DREAM.
IT LEFT ME FEELING SAD...
BUT KIND OF HAPPY.
I DON'T REALLY GET IT.
EXCUSE ME, SIR.
IT SEEMS THE HOTEL IS HAVING ISSUES WITH THE AIR CONDITIONING.
MAY I COME INSIDE TO CHECK YOUR VENT?
OH.
SURE.
I'LL BE RIGHT THERE.
I'VE ONLY BEEN GONE FOR A DAY.
DAZE
TO THINK I'D MISS KIHACHI SO MUCH...
THAT HE'D APPEAR IN MY DREAMS.

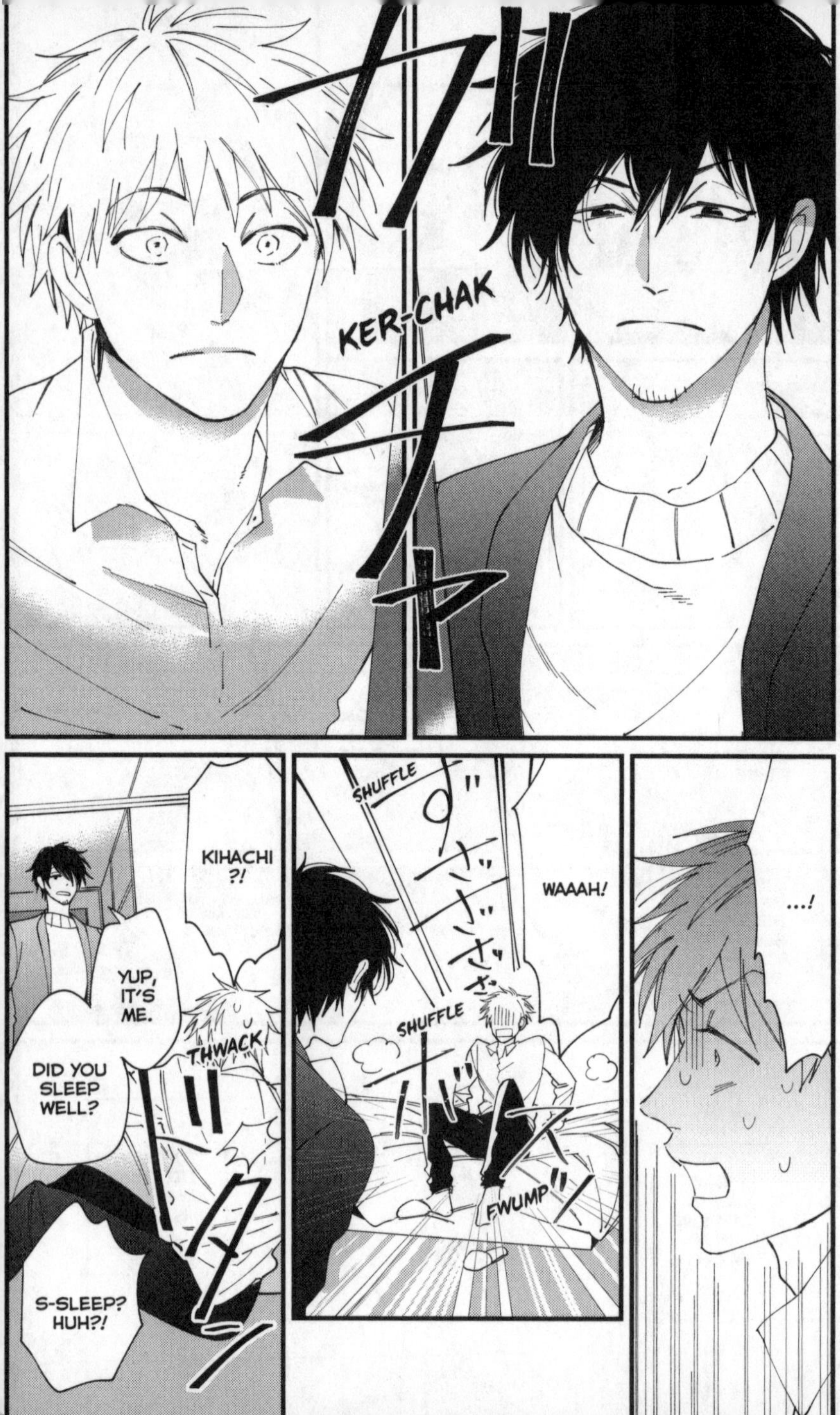
KER-CHAK
...!
SHUFFLE
WAAAH!
SHUFFLE
FWUMP
KIHACHI ?!
YUP, IT'S ME.
THWACK
DID YOU SLEEP WELL?
S-SLEEP? HUH?!

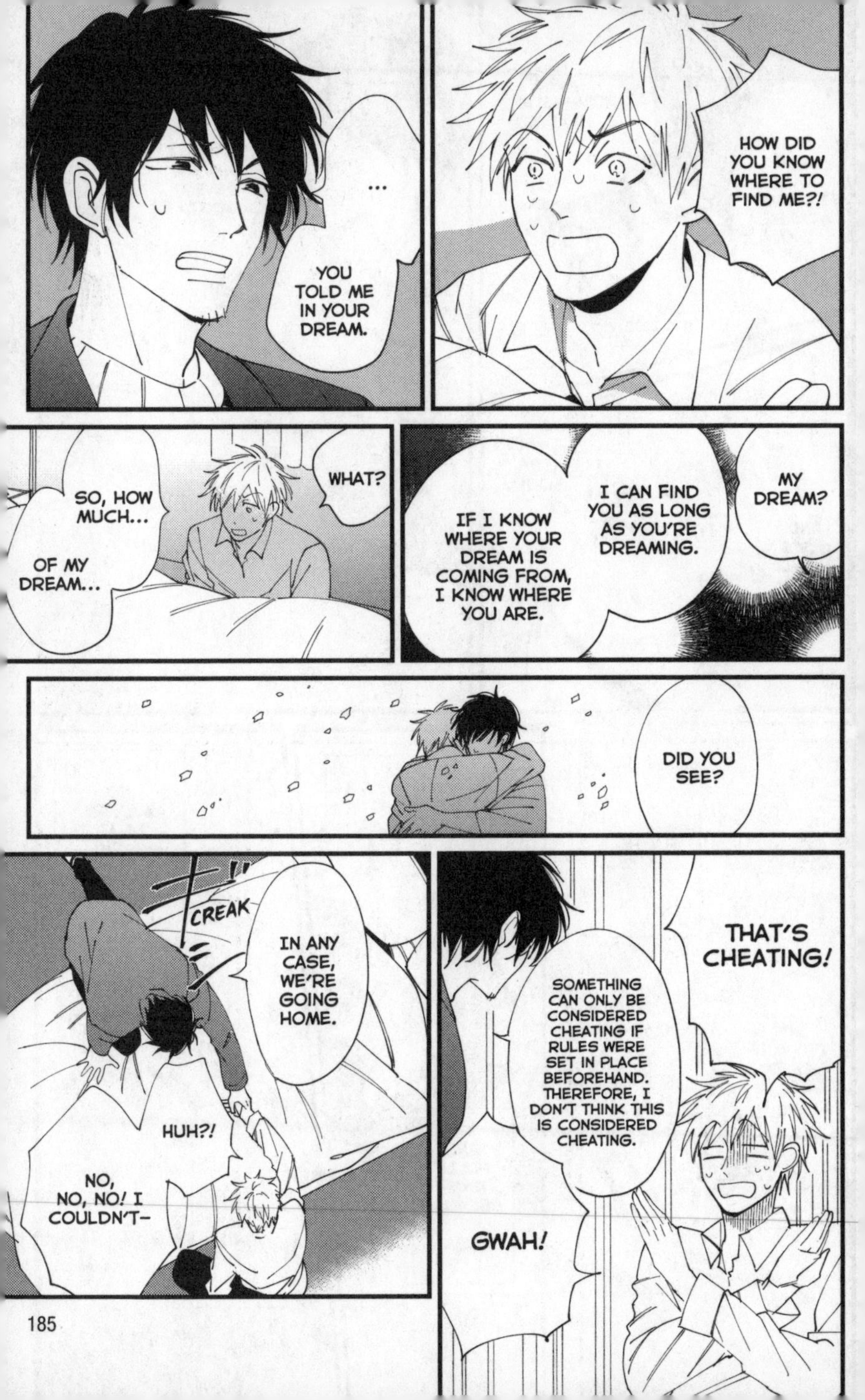
HOW DID YOU KNOW WHERE TO FIND ME?!
...
YOU TOLD ME IN YOUR DREAM.
MY DREAM?
I CAN FIND YOU AS LONG AS YOU'RE DREAMING.
IF I KNOW WHERE YOUR DREAM IS COMING FROM, I KNOW WHERE YOU ARE.
WHAT?
SO, HOW MUCH...
OF MY DREAM...
DID YOU SEE?
THAT'S CHEATING!
SOMETHING CAN ONLY BE CONSIDERED CHEATING IF RULES WERE SET IN PLACE BEFOREHAND. THEREFORE, I DON'T THINK THIS IS CONSIDERED CHEATING.
GWAH!
CREAK
IN ANY CASE, WE'RE GOING HOME.
HUH?!
NO, NO, NO! I COULDN'T–

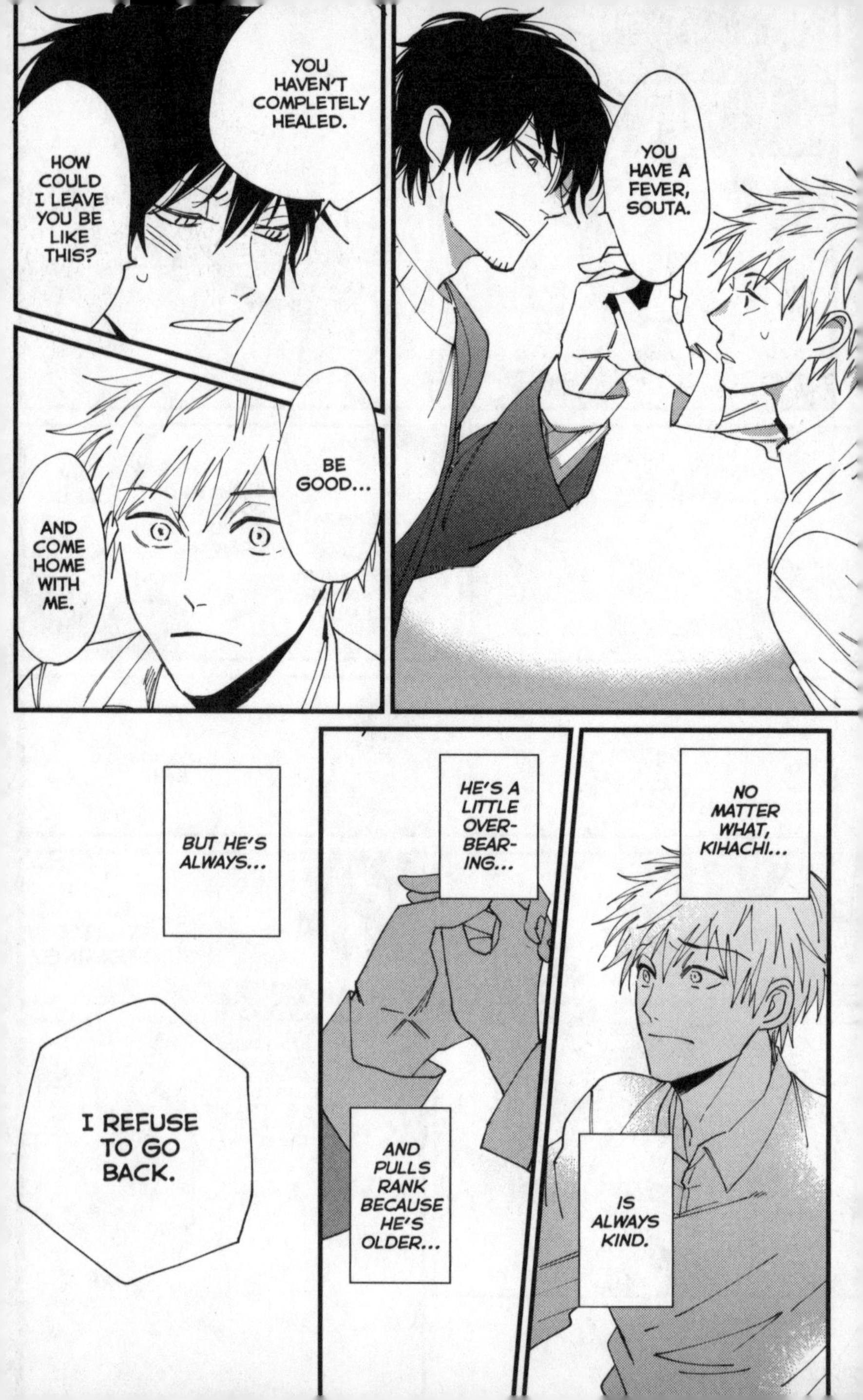
YOU HAVE A FEVER, SOUTA.
YOU HAVEN'T COMPLETELY HEALED.
HOW COULD I LEAVE YOU BE LIKE THIS?
BE GOOD...
AND COME HOME WITH ME.
NO MATTER WHAT, KIHACHI...
IS ALWAYS KIND.
HE'S A LITTLE OVER-BEARING...
AND PULLS RANK BECAUSE HE'S OLDER...
BUT HE'S ALWAYS...
I REFUSE TO GO BACK.

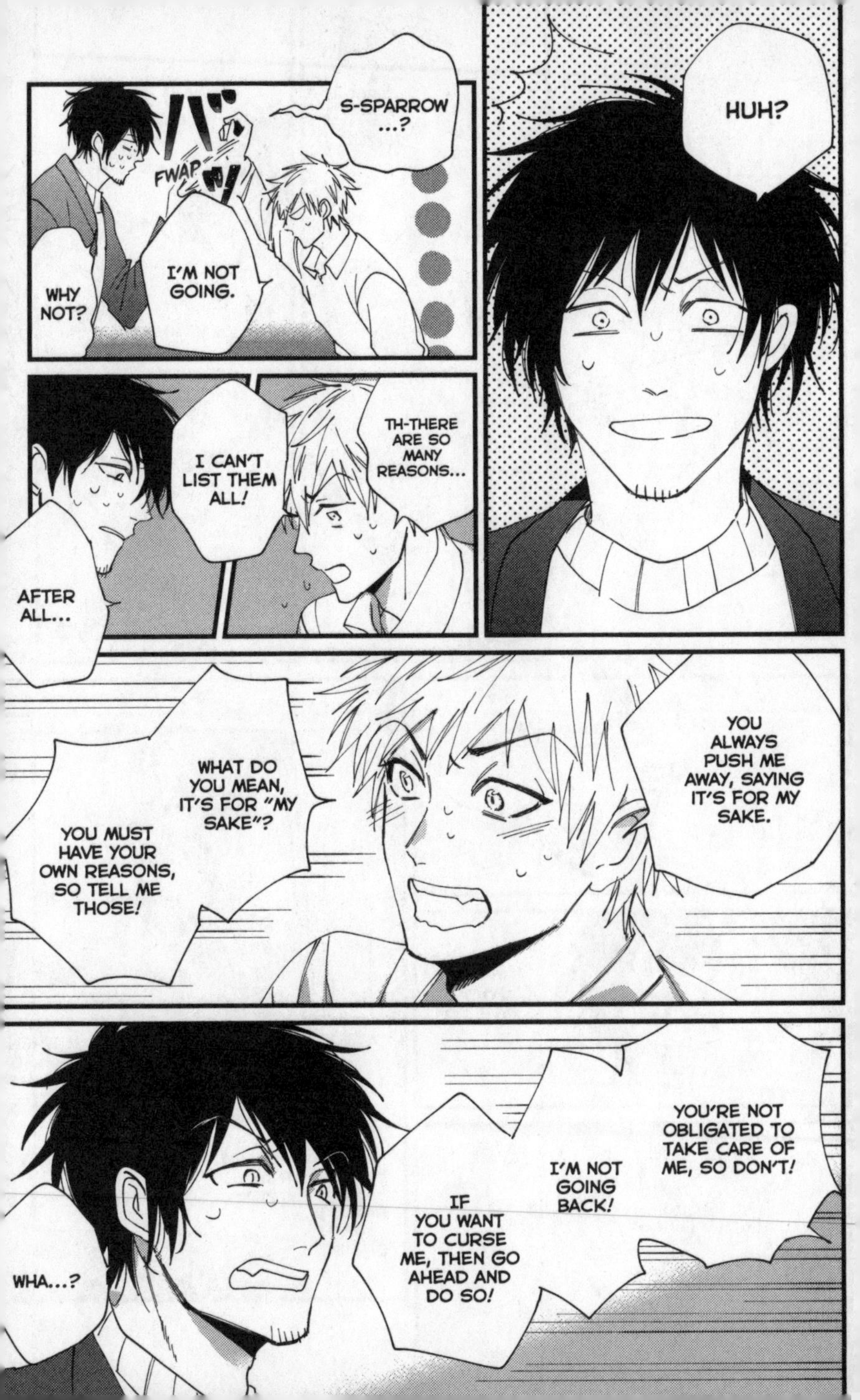
HUH?
S-SPARROW ...?
バ
FWAP
I'M NOT GOING.
WHY NOT?
TH-THERE ARE SO MANY REASONS...
I CAN'T LIST THEM ALL!
AFTER ALL...
YOU ALWAYS PUSH ME AWAY, SAYING IT'S FOR MY SAKE.
WHAT DO YOU MEAN, IT'S FOR "MY SAKE"?
YOU MUST HAVE YOUR OWN REASONS, SO TELL ME THOSE!
YOU'RE NOT OBLIGATED TO TAKE CARE OF ME, SO DON'T!
I'M NOT GOING BACK!
IF YOU WANT TO CURSE ME, THEN GO AHEAD AND DO SO!
WHA...?

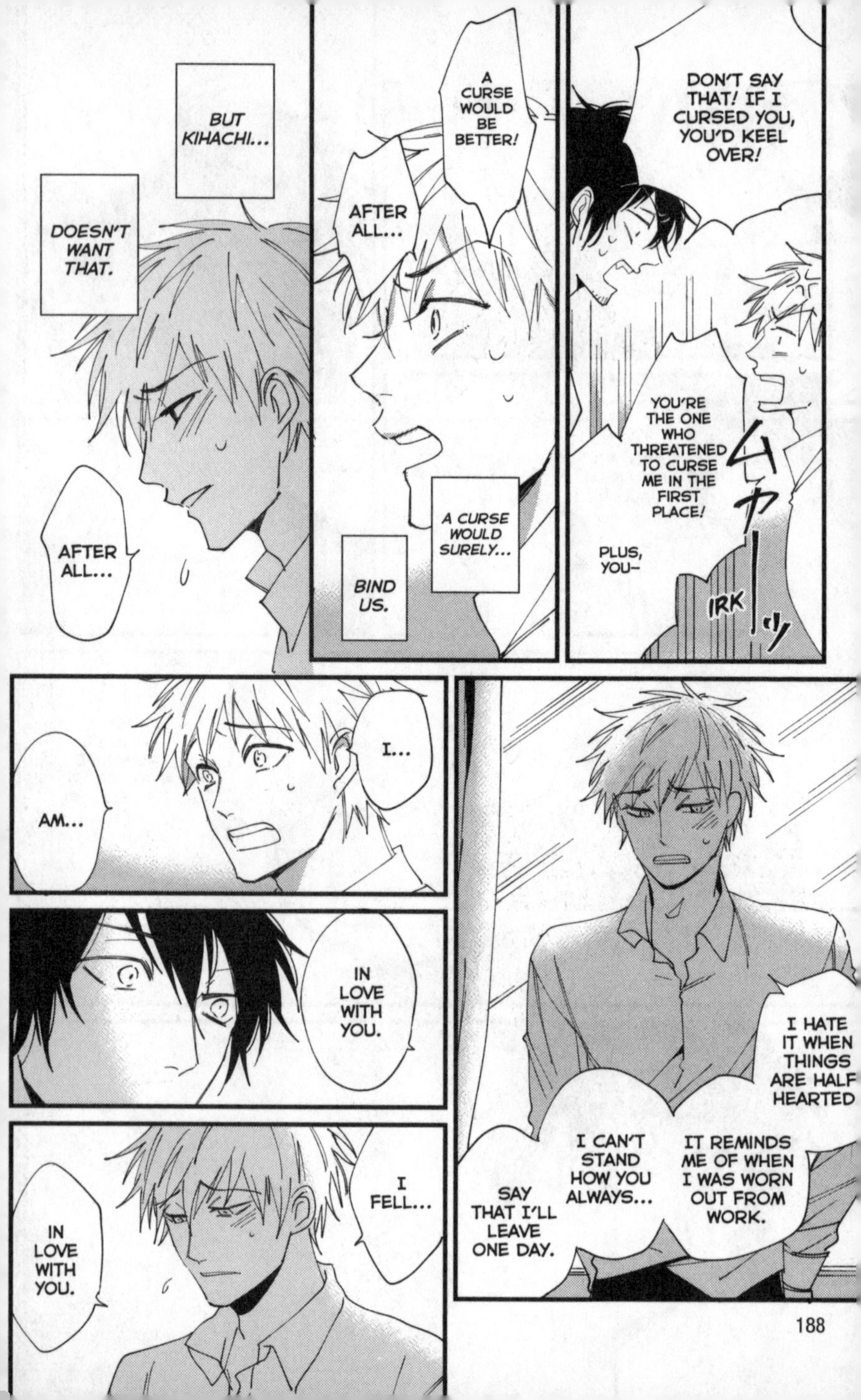
DON'T SAY THAT! IF I CURSED YOU, YOU'D KEEL OVER!
YOU'RE THE ONE WHO THREATENED TO CURSE ME IN THE FIRST PLACE!
ムカー
IRK
PLUS, YOU-
A CURSE WOULD BE BETTER!
AFTER ALL...
A CURSE WOULD SURELY...
BIND US.
BUT KIHACHI...
DOESN'T WANT THAT.
AFTER ALL...
I HATE IT WHEN THINGS ARE HALF HEARTED
IT REMINDS ME OF WHEN I WAS WORN OUT FROM WORK.
I CAN'T STAND HOW YOU ALWAYS...
SAY THAT I'LL LEAVE ONE DAY.
I...
AM...
IN LOVE WITH YOU.
I FELL...
IN LOVE WITH YOU.

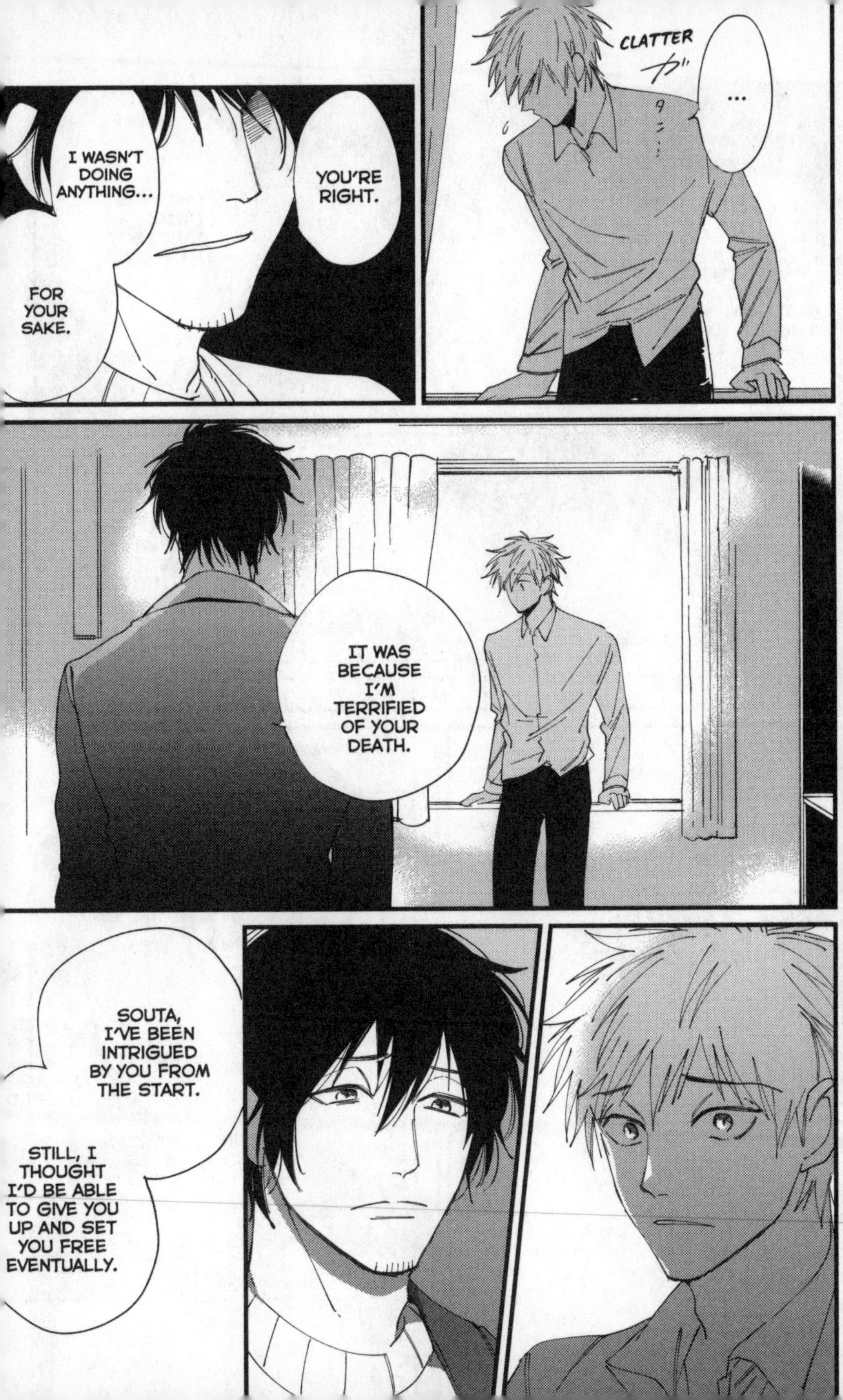
CLATTER
ガ
...
YOU'RE RIGHT.
I WASN'T DOING ANYTHING...
FOR YOUR SAKE.
IT WAS BECAUSE I'M TERRIFIED OF YOUR DEATH.
SOUTA, I'VE BEEN INTRIGUED BY YOU FROM THE START.
STILL, I THOUGHT I'D BE ABLE TO GIVE YOU UP AND SET YOU FREE EVENTUALLY.

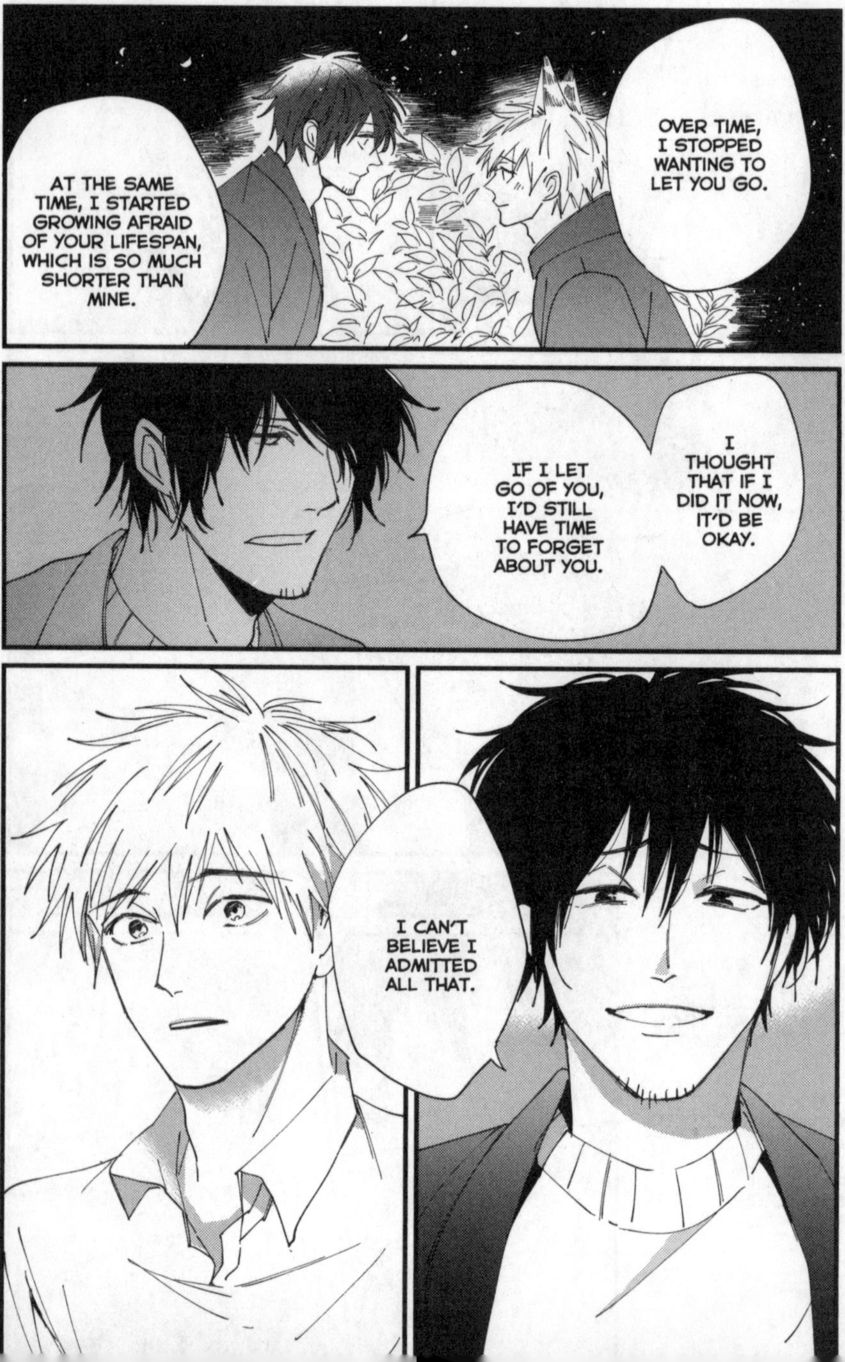
OVER TIME, I STOPPED WANTING TO LET YOU GO.
AT THE SAME TIME, I STARTED GROWING AFRAID OF YOUR LIFESPAN, WHICH IS SO MUCH SHORTER THAN MINE.
I THOUGHT THAT IF I DID IT NOW, IT'D BE OKAY.
IF I LET GO OF YOU, I'D STILL HAVE TIME TO FORGET ABOUT YOU.
I CAN'T BELIEVE I ADMITTED ALL THAT.

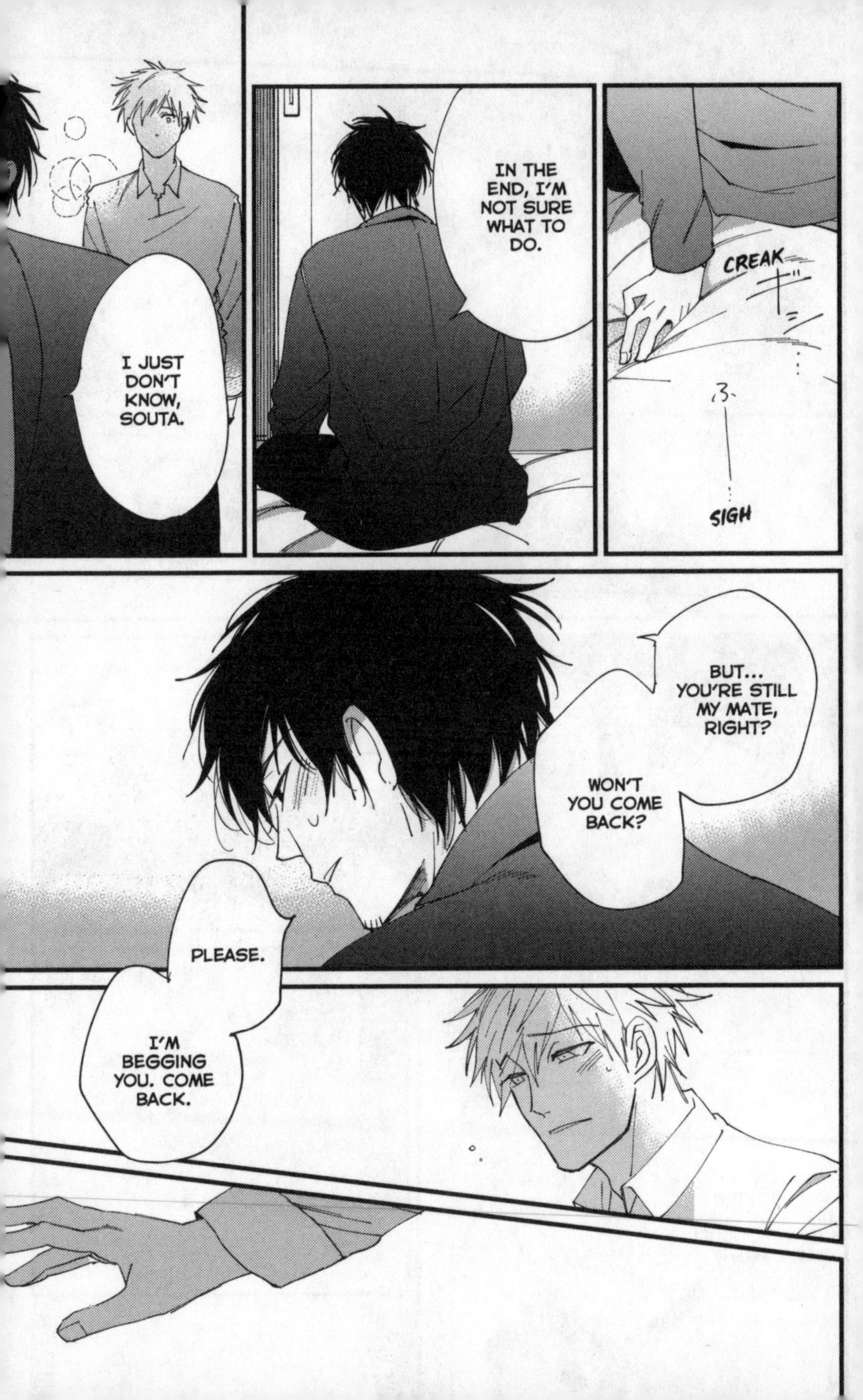
CREAK
SIGH
IN THE END, I'M NOT SURE WHAT TO DO.
I JUST DON'T KNOW, SOUTA.
BUT... YOU'RE STILL MY MATE, RIGHT?
WON'T YOU COME BACK?
PLEASE.
I'M BEGGING YOU. COME BACK.

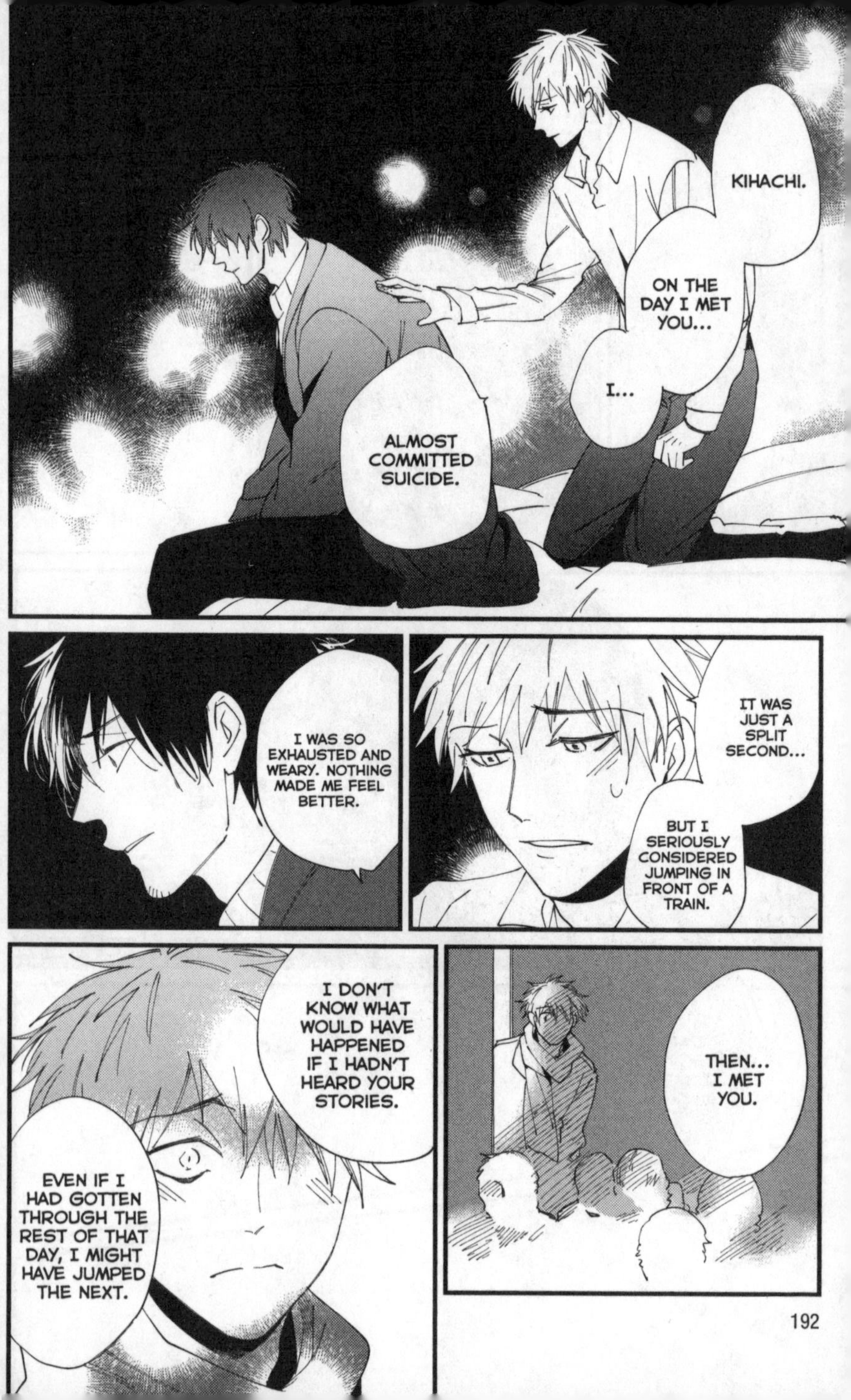
KIHACHI.
ON THE DAY I MET YOU...
I...
ALMOST COMMITTED SUICIDE.
IT WAS JUST A SPLIT SECOND...
BUT I SERIOUSLY CONSIDERED JUMPING IN FRONT OF A TRAIN.
I WAS SO EXHAUSTED AND WEARY. NOTHING MADE ME FEEL BETTER.
THEN... I MET YOU.
I DON'T KNOW WHAT WOULD HAVE HAPPENED IF I HADN'T HEARD YOUR STORIES.
EVEN IF I HAD GOTTEN THROUGH THE REST OF THAT DAY, I MIGHT HAVE JUMPED THE NEXT.

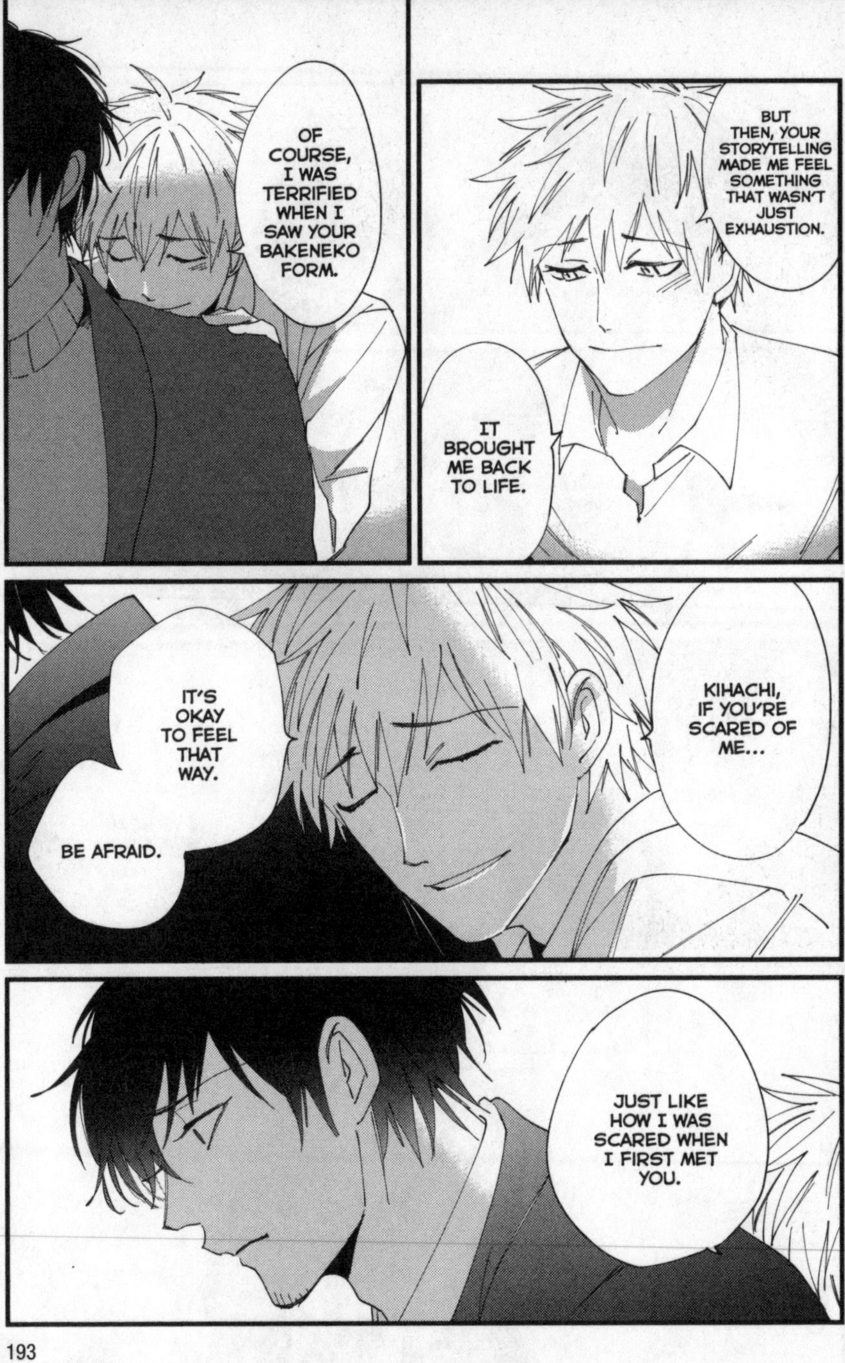
BUT THEN, YOUR STORYTELLING MADE ME FEEL SOMETHING THAT WASN'T JUST EXHAUSTION.
IT BROUGHT ME BACK TO LIFE.
OF COURSE, I WAS TERRIFIED WHEN I SAW YOUR BAKENEKO FORM.
KIHACHI, IF YOU'RE SCARED OF ME...
IT'S OKAY TO FEEL THAT WAY.
BE AFRAID.
JUST LIKE HOW I WAS SCARED WHEN I FIRST MET YOU.

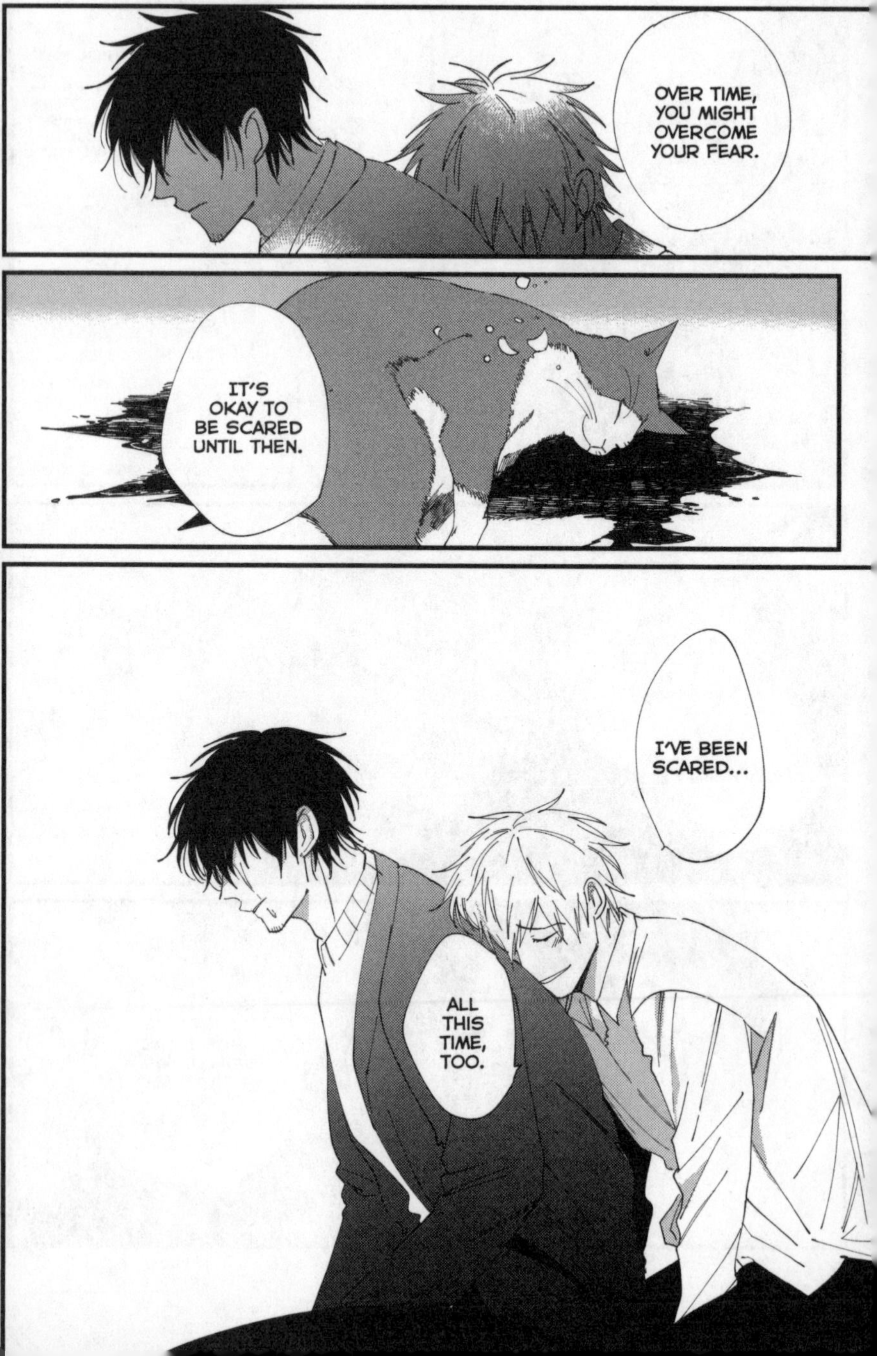
OVER TIME, YOU MIGHT OVERCOME YOUR FEAR.
IT'S OKAY TO BE SCARED UNTIL THEN.
I'VE BEEN SCARED...
ALL THIS TIME, TOO.

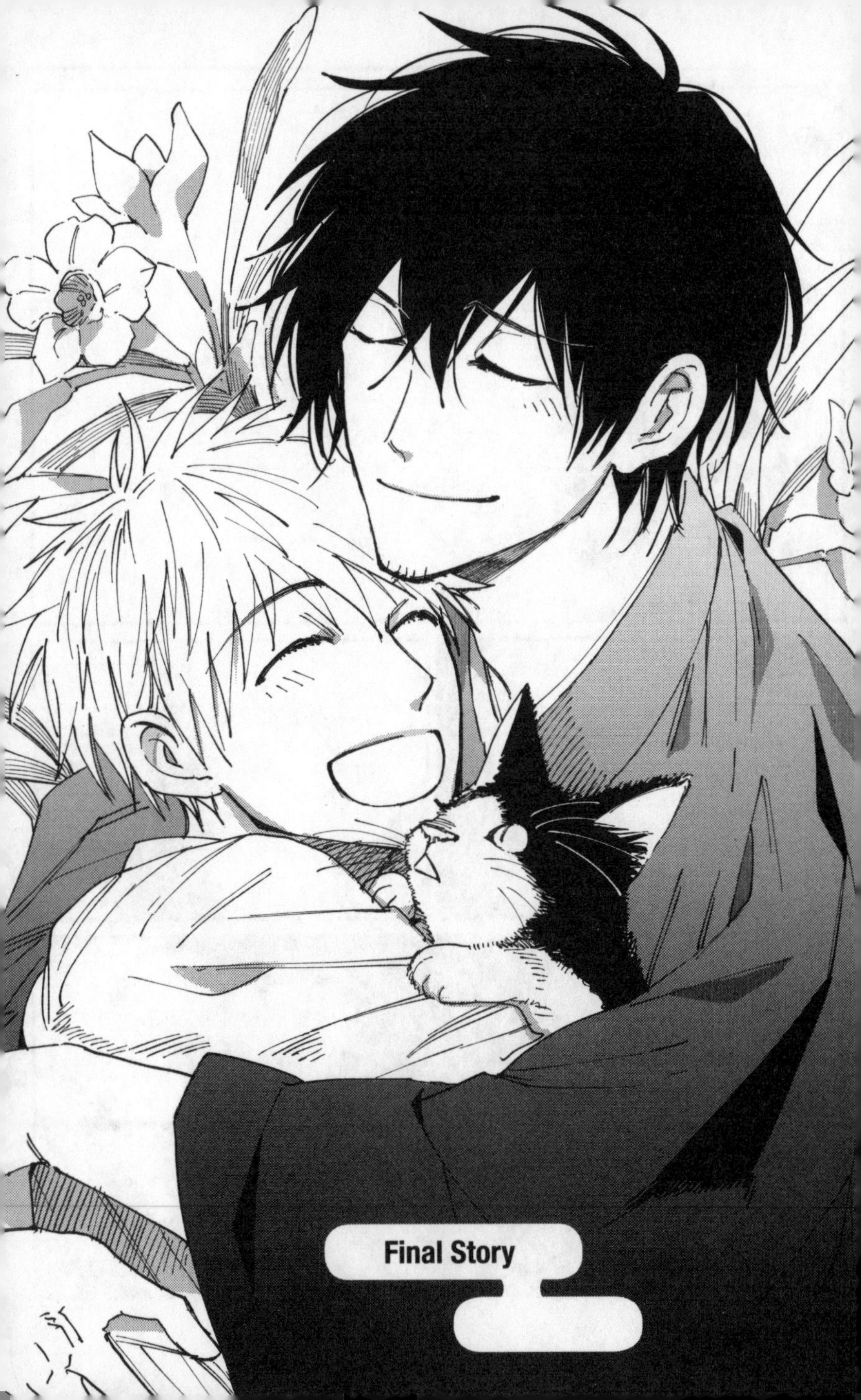
Final Story

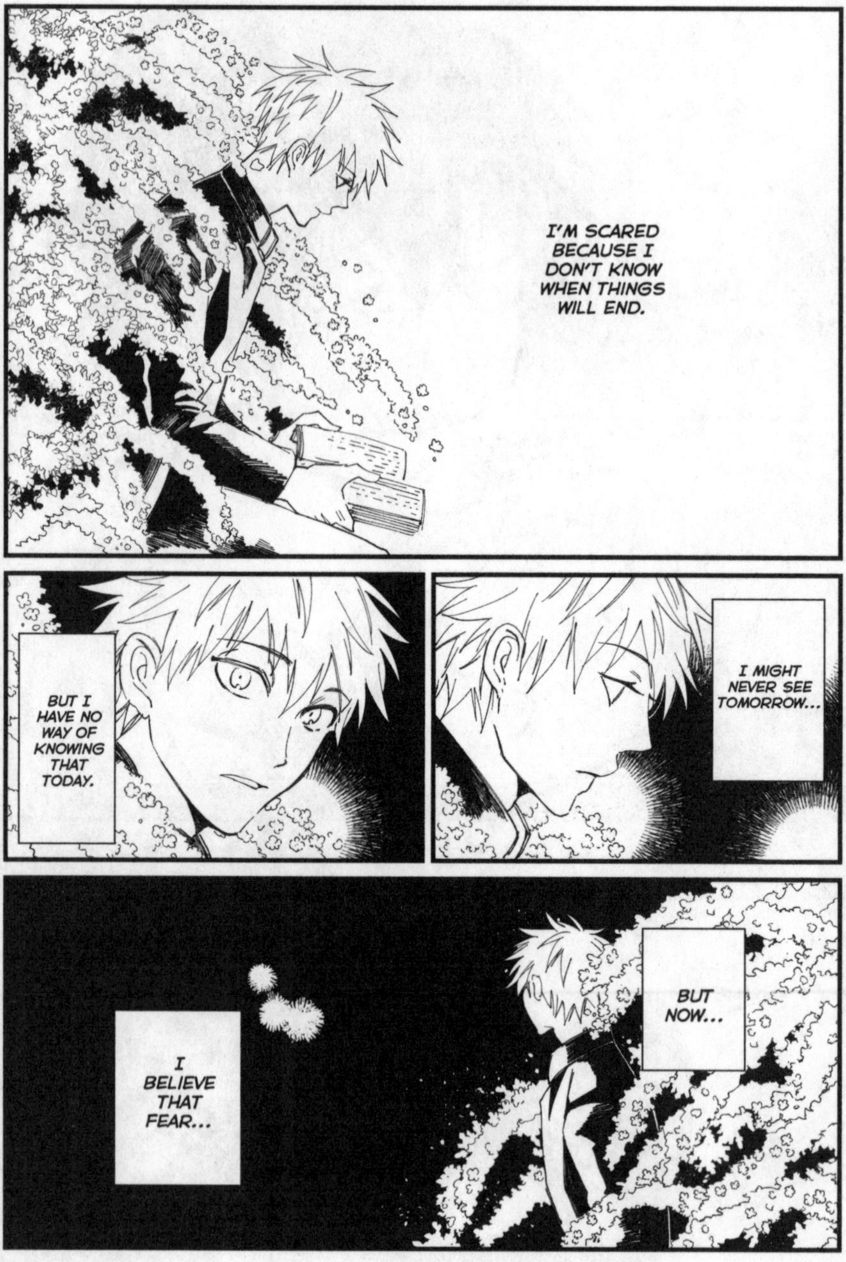
I'M SCARED BECAUSE I DON'T KNOW WHEN THINGS WILL END.
I MIGHT NEVER SEE TOMORROW...
BUT I HAVE NO WAY OF KNOWING THAT TODAY.
BUT NOW...
I BELIEVE THAT FEAR...

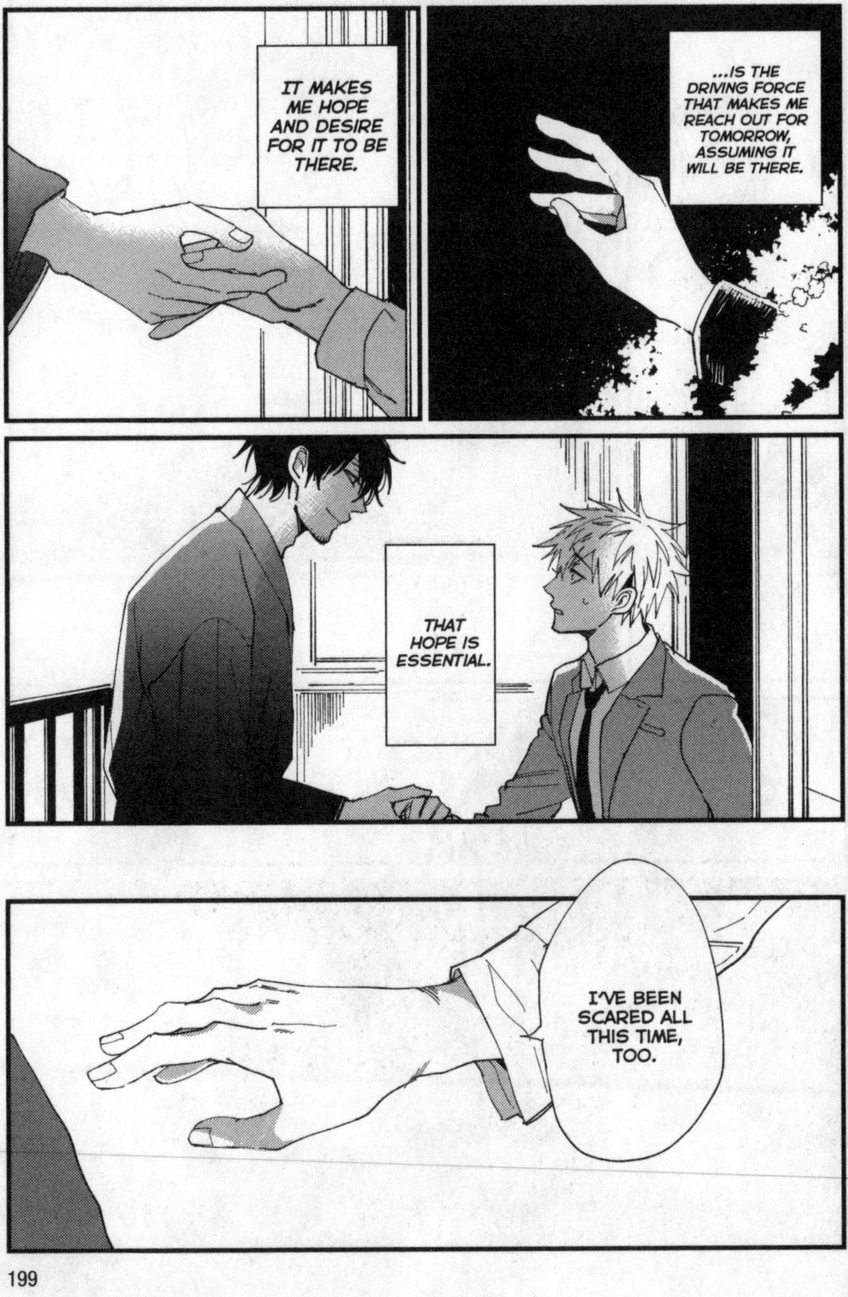
...IS THE DRIVING FORCE THAT MAKES ME REACH OUT FOR TOMORROW, ASSUMING IT WILL BE THERE.
IT MAKES ME HOPE AND DESIRE FOR IT TO BE THERE.
THAT HOPE IS ESSENTIAL.
I'VE BEEN SCARED ALL THIS TIME, TOO.

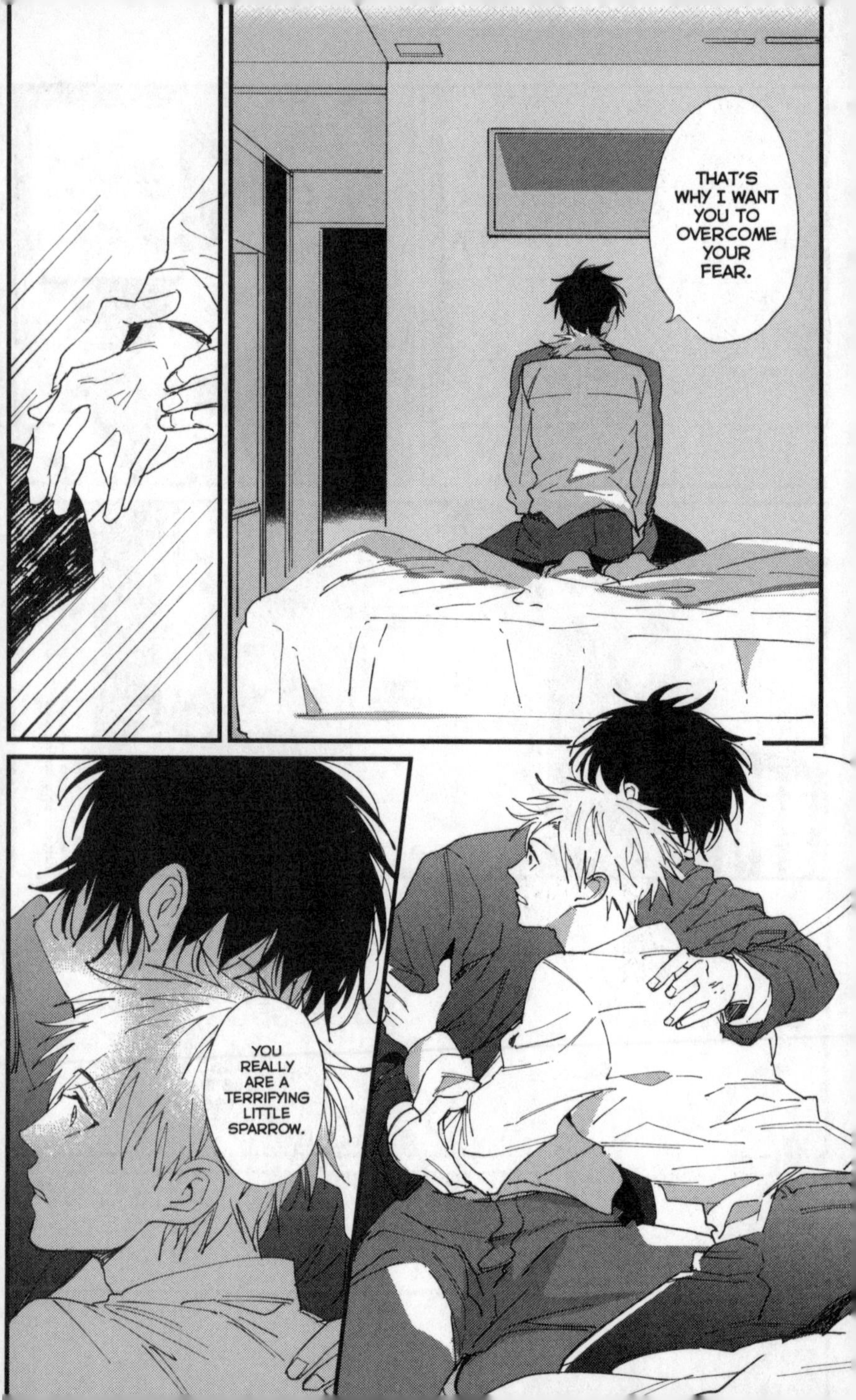
THAT'S WHY I WANT YOU TO OVERCOME YOUR FEAR.
YOU REALLY ARE A TERRIFYING LITTLE SPARROW.

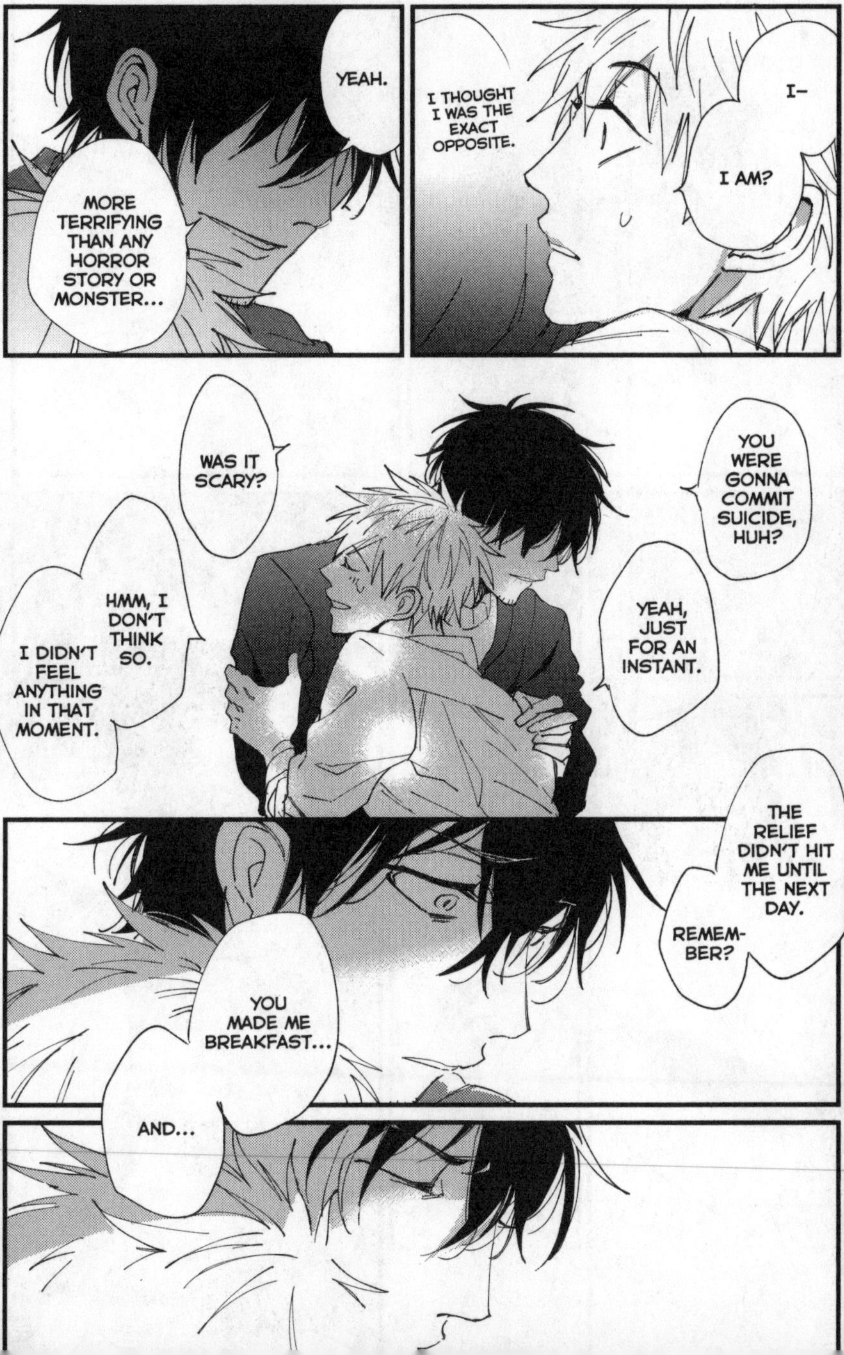

I—
I AM?
I THOUGHT I WAS THE EXACT OPPOSITE.
YEAH.
MORE TERRIFYING THAN ANY HORROR STORY OR MONSTER...
YOU WERE GONNA COMMIT SUICIDE, HUH?
YEAH, JUST FOR AN INSTANT.
WAS IT SCARY?
HMM, I DON'T THINK SO.
I DIDN'T FEEL ANYTHING IN THAT MOMENT.
THE RELIEF DIDN'T HIT ME UNTIL THE NEXT DAY.
REMEMBER?
YOU MADE ME BREAKFAST...
AND...

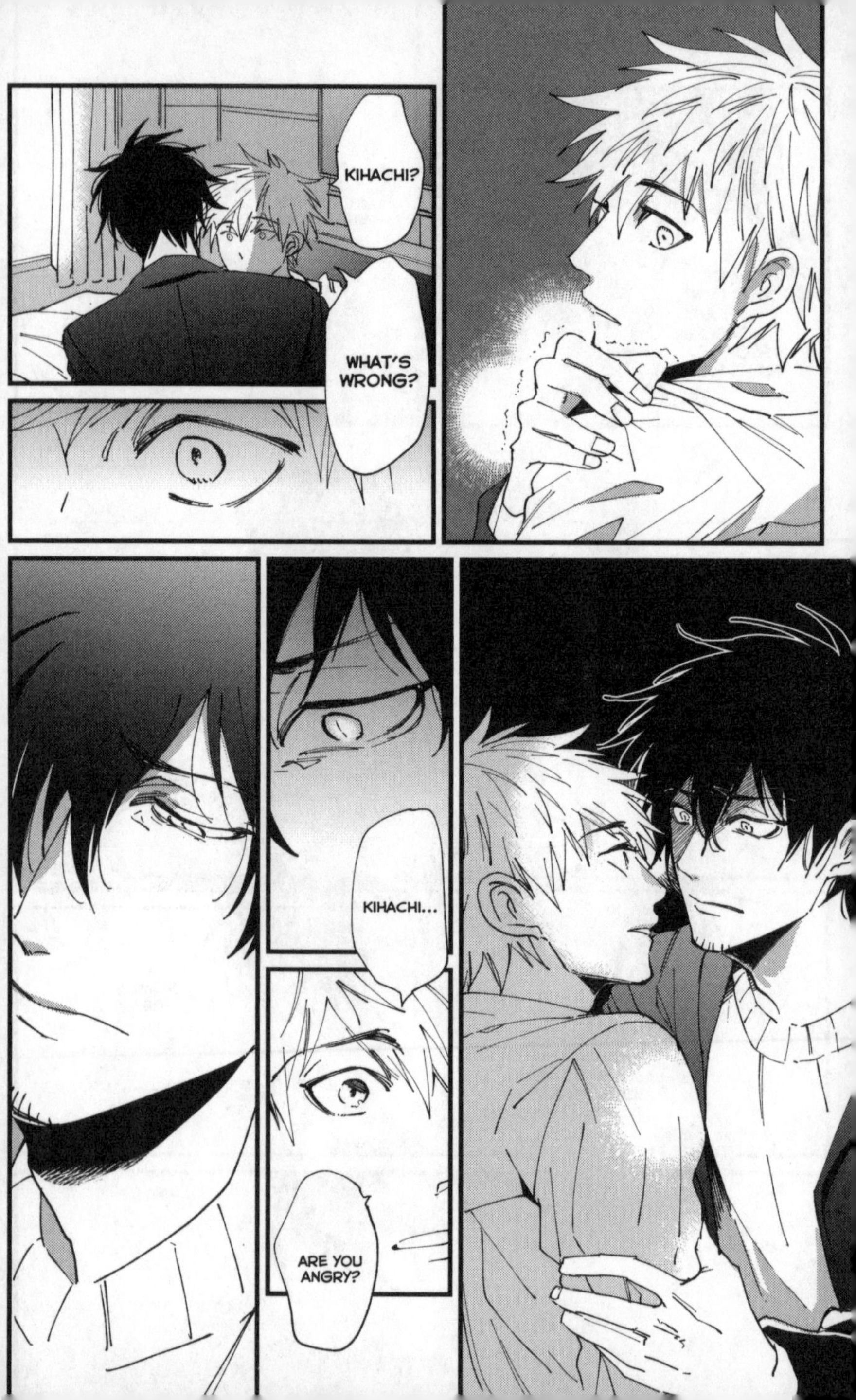
KIHACHI?
WHAT'S WRONG?
KIHACHI...
ARE YOU ANGRY?

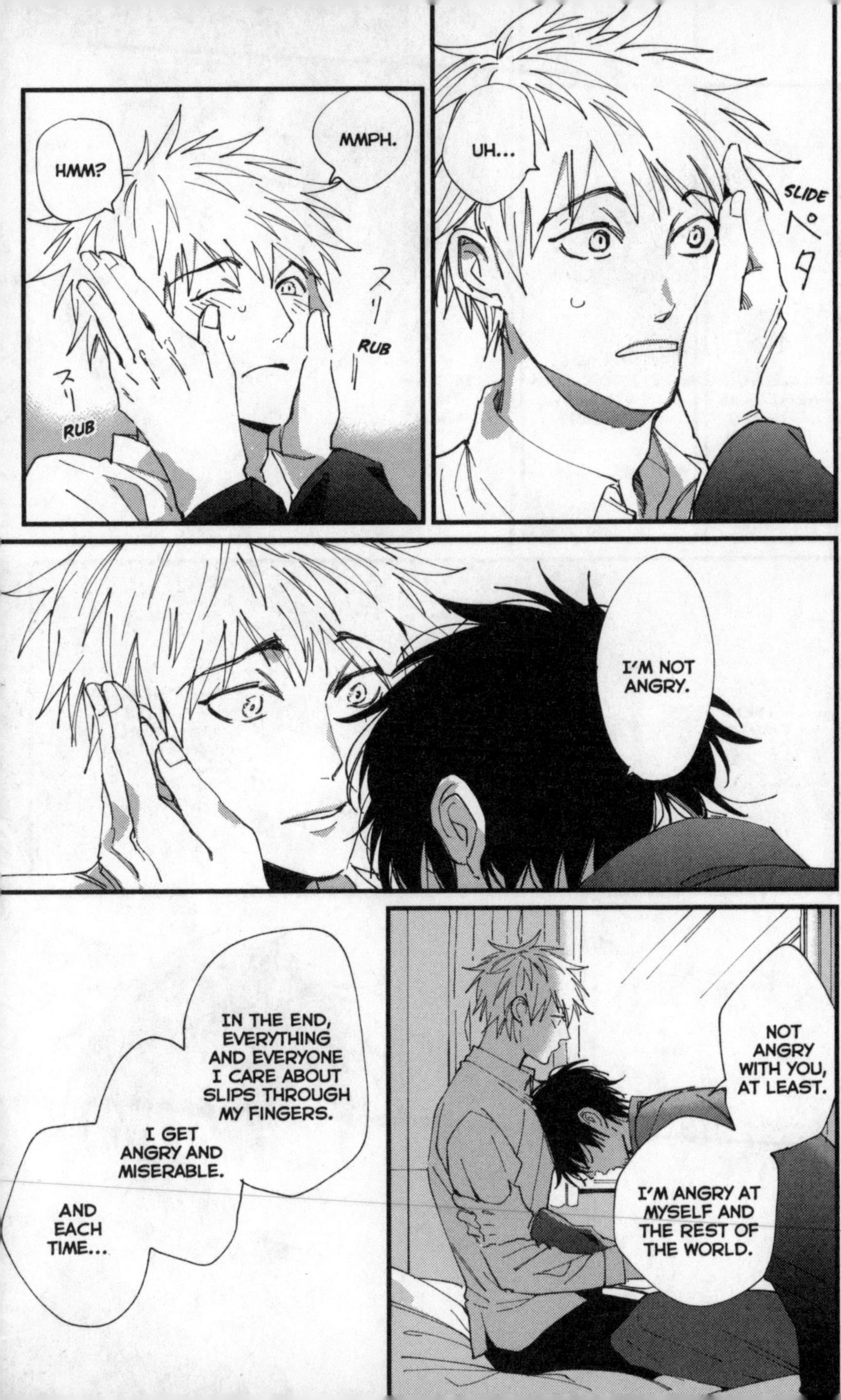
UH...
SLIDE
ペタ
MMPH.
HMM?
スリ
RUB
スリ
RUB
I'M NOT ANGRY.
NOT ANGRY WITH YOU, AT LEAST.
I'M ANGRY AT MYSELF AND THE REST OF THE WORLD.
IN THE END, EVERYTHING AND EVERYONE I CARE ABOUT SLIPS THROUGH MY FINGERS.
I GET ANGRY AND MISERABLE.
AND EACH TIME...

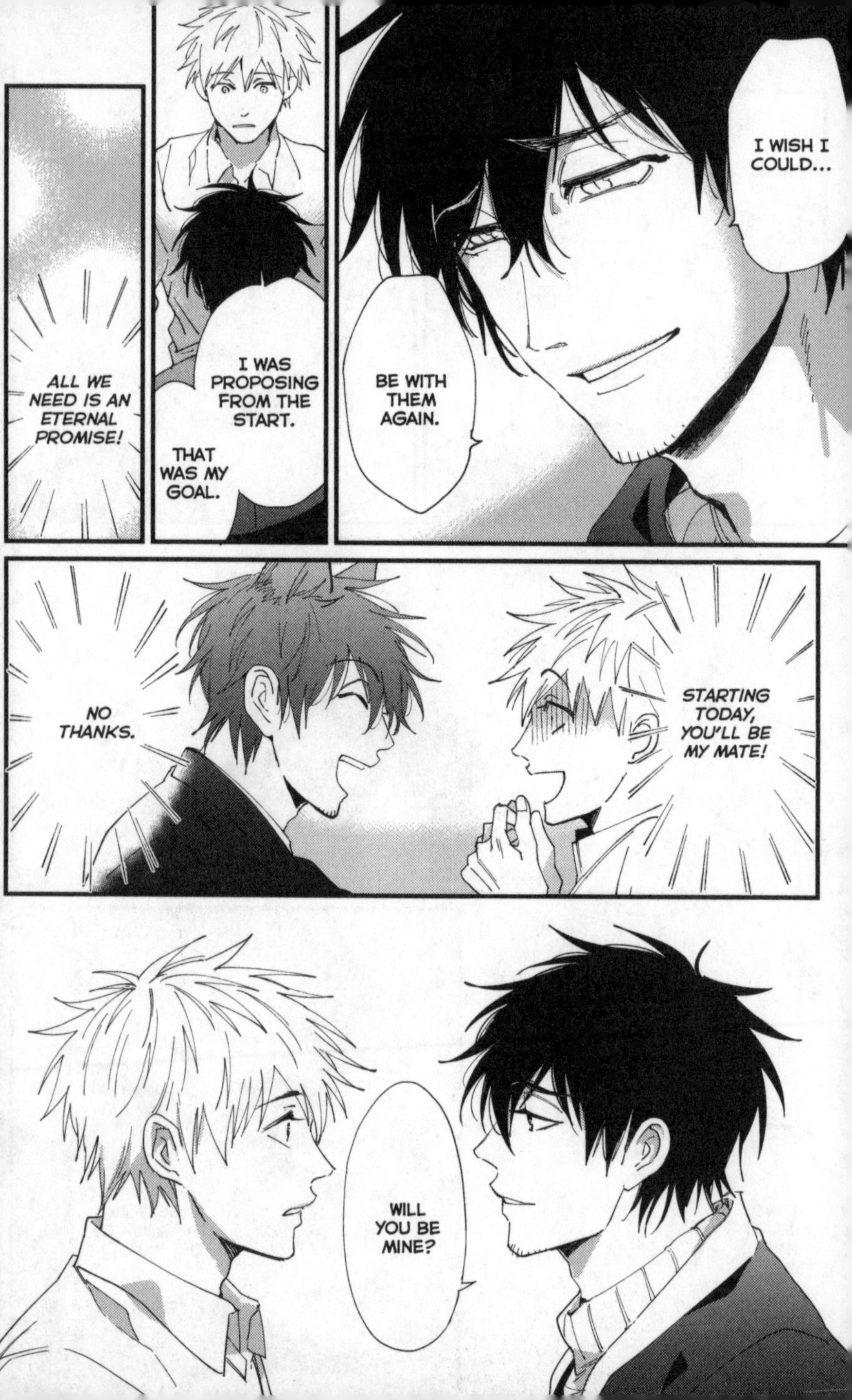
I WISH I COULD...
BE WITH THEM AGAIN.
I WAS PROPOSING FROM THE START.
THAT WAS MY GOAL.
ALL WE NEED IS AN ETERNAL PROMISE!
STARTING TODAY, YOU'LL BE MY MATE!
NO THANKS.
WILL YOU BE MINE?

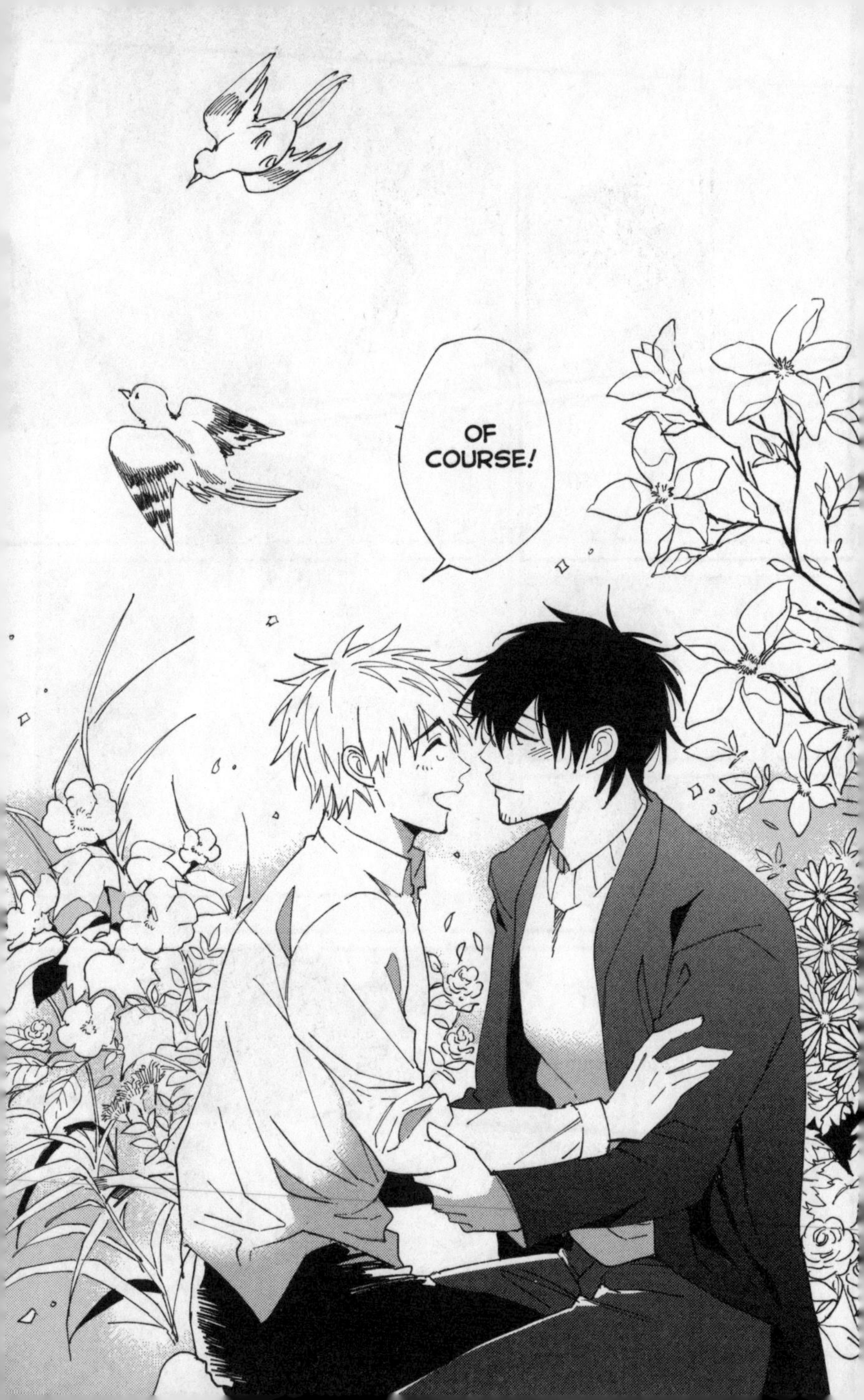
OF COURSE!

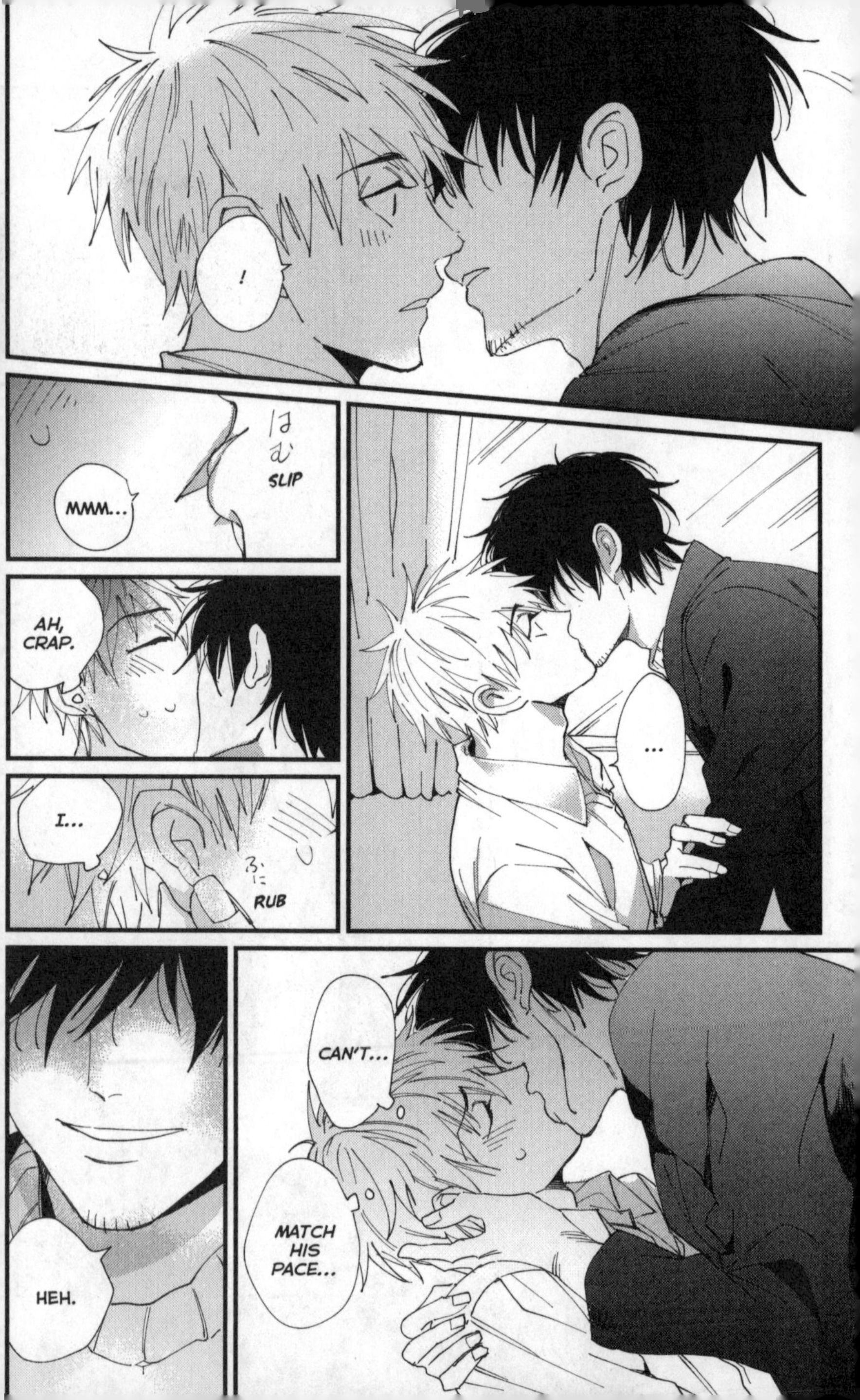
!
...
はむ
SLIP
MMM...
AH, CRAP.
I...
ふに
RUB
CAN'T...
MATCH HIS PACE...
HEH.

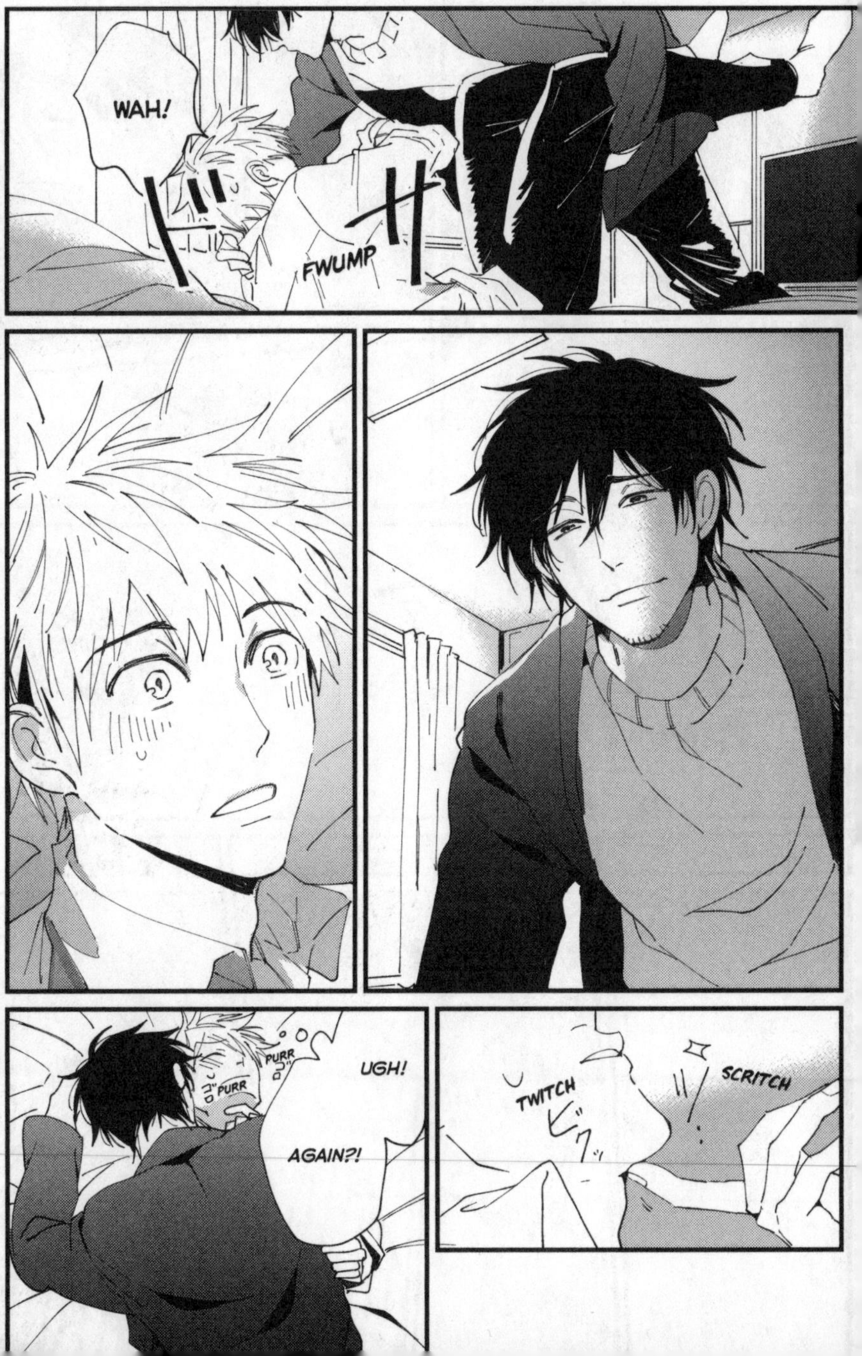
WAH!
FWUMP
SCRITCH
TWITCH
PURR
PURR
UGH!
AGAIN?!

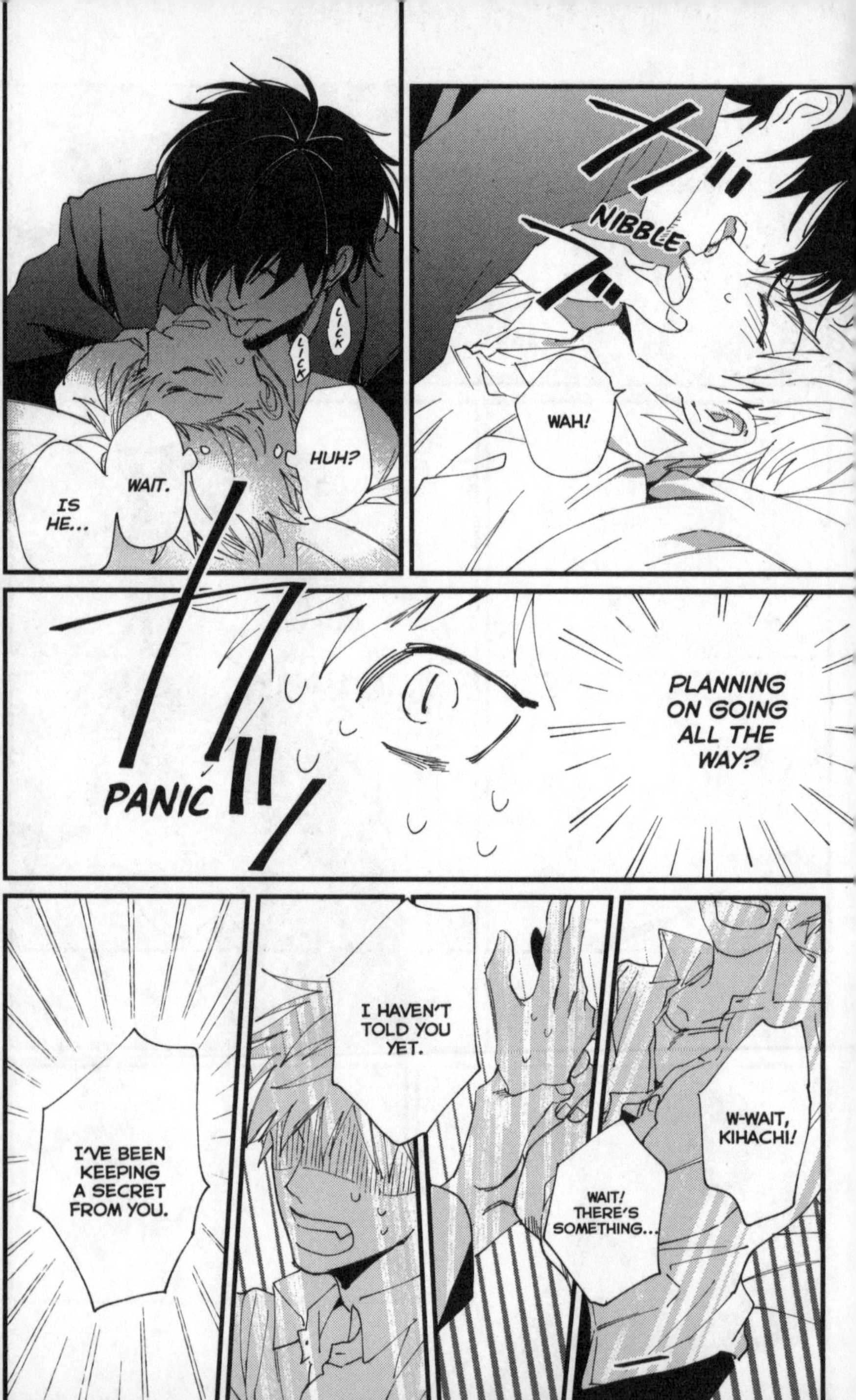
NIBBLE
WAH!
LICK
LICK
HUH?
WAIT.
IS HE...
PLANNING ON GOING ALL THE WAY?
PANIC
W-WAIT, KIHACHI!
WAIT! THERE'S SOMETHING...
I HAVEN'T TOLD YOU YET.
I'VE BEEN KEEPING A SECRET FROM YOU.

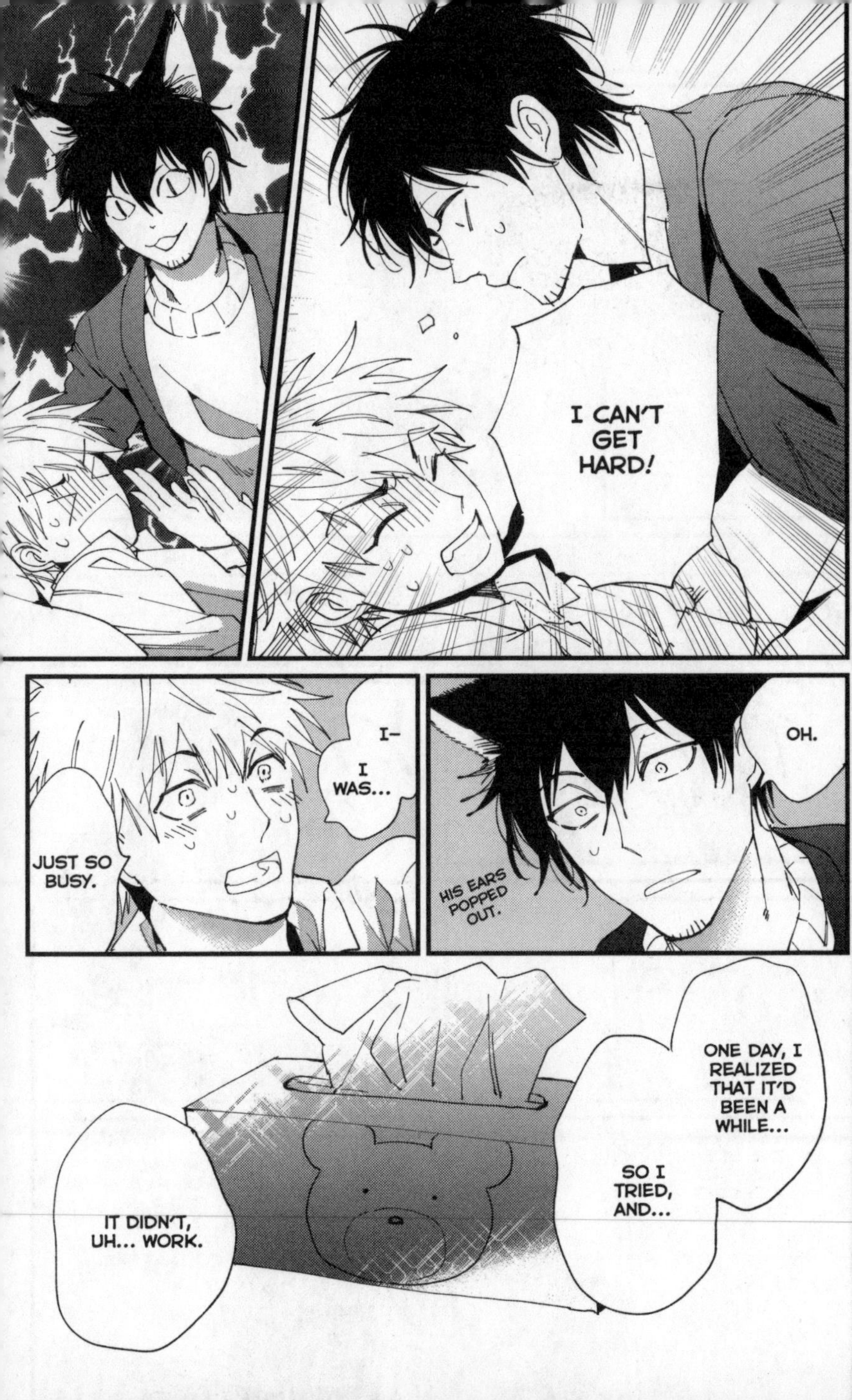
I CAN'T GET HARD!
OH.
HIS EARS POPPED OUT.
I— I WAS...
JUST SO BUSY.
ONE DAY, I REALIZED THAT IT'D BEEN A WHILE...
SO I TRIED, AND...
IT DIDN'T, UH... WORK.

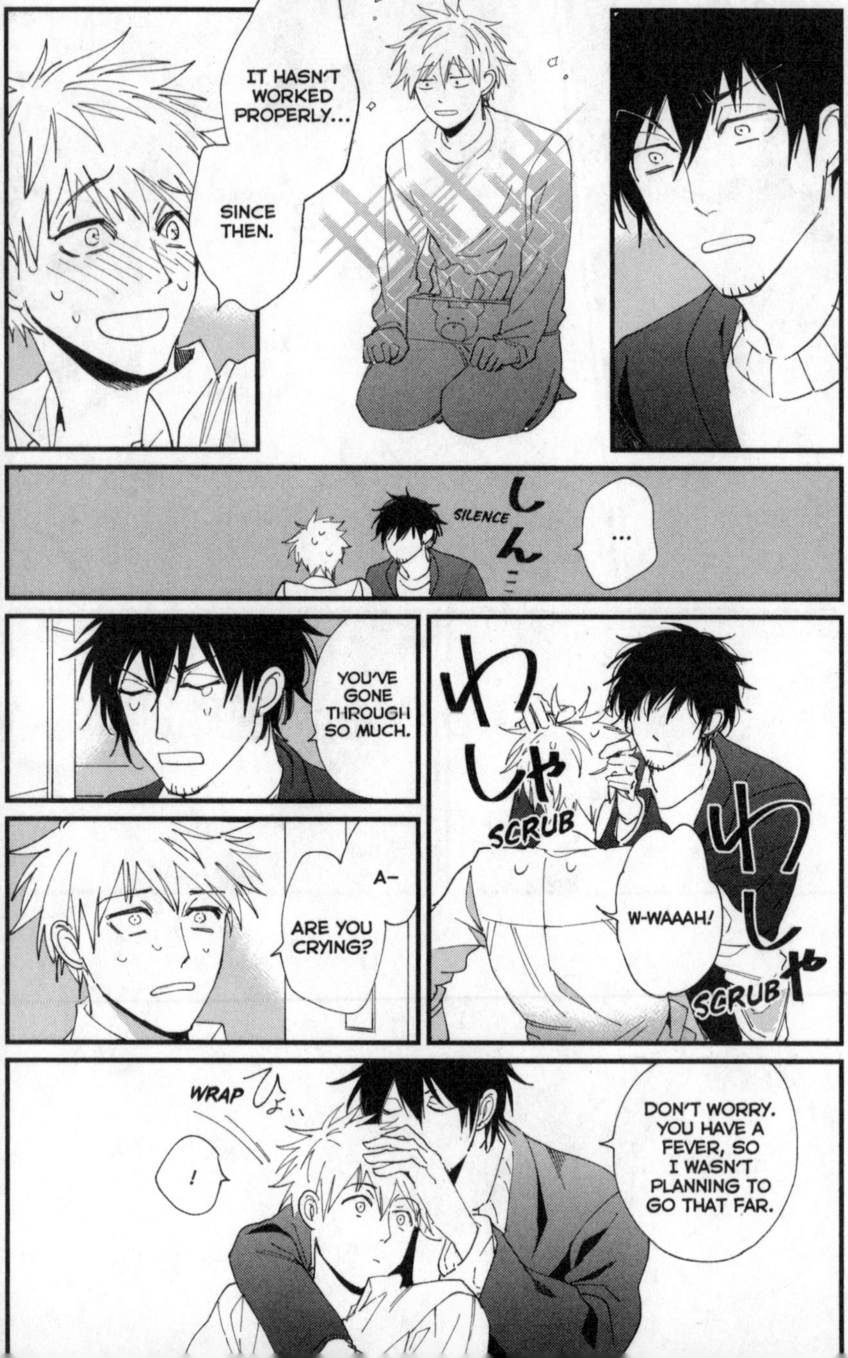
IT HASN'T WORKED PROPERLY...
SINCE THEN.
...
SILENCE しん
わしゃ SCRUB
W-WAAAH!
わしゃ SCRUB
YOU'VE GONE THROUGH SO MUCH.
A—
ARE YOU CRYING?
DON'T WORRY. YOU HAVE A FEVER, SO I WASN'T PLANNING TO GO THAT FAR.
WRAP ひょい
!

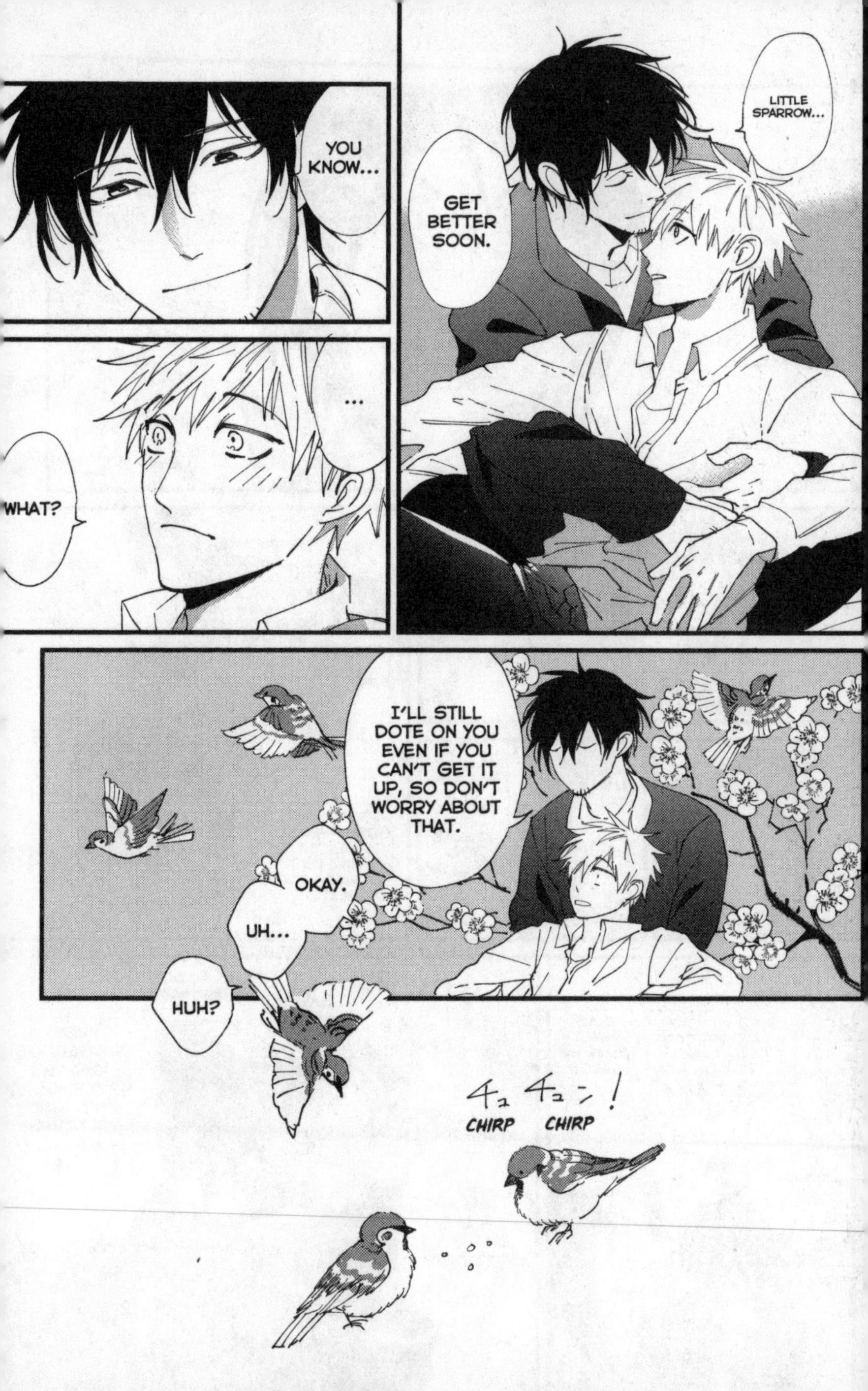
LITTLE SPARROW...
GET BETTER SOON.
YOU KNOW...
...
WHAT?
I'LL STILL DOTE ON YOU EVEN IF YOU CAN'T GET IT UP, SO DON'T WORRY ABOUT THAT.
OKAY.
UH...
HUH?
チュチュン!
CHIRP CHIRP

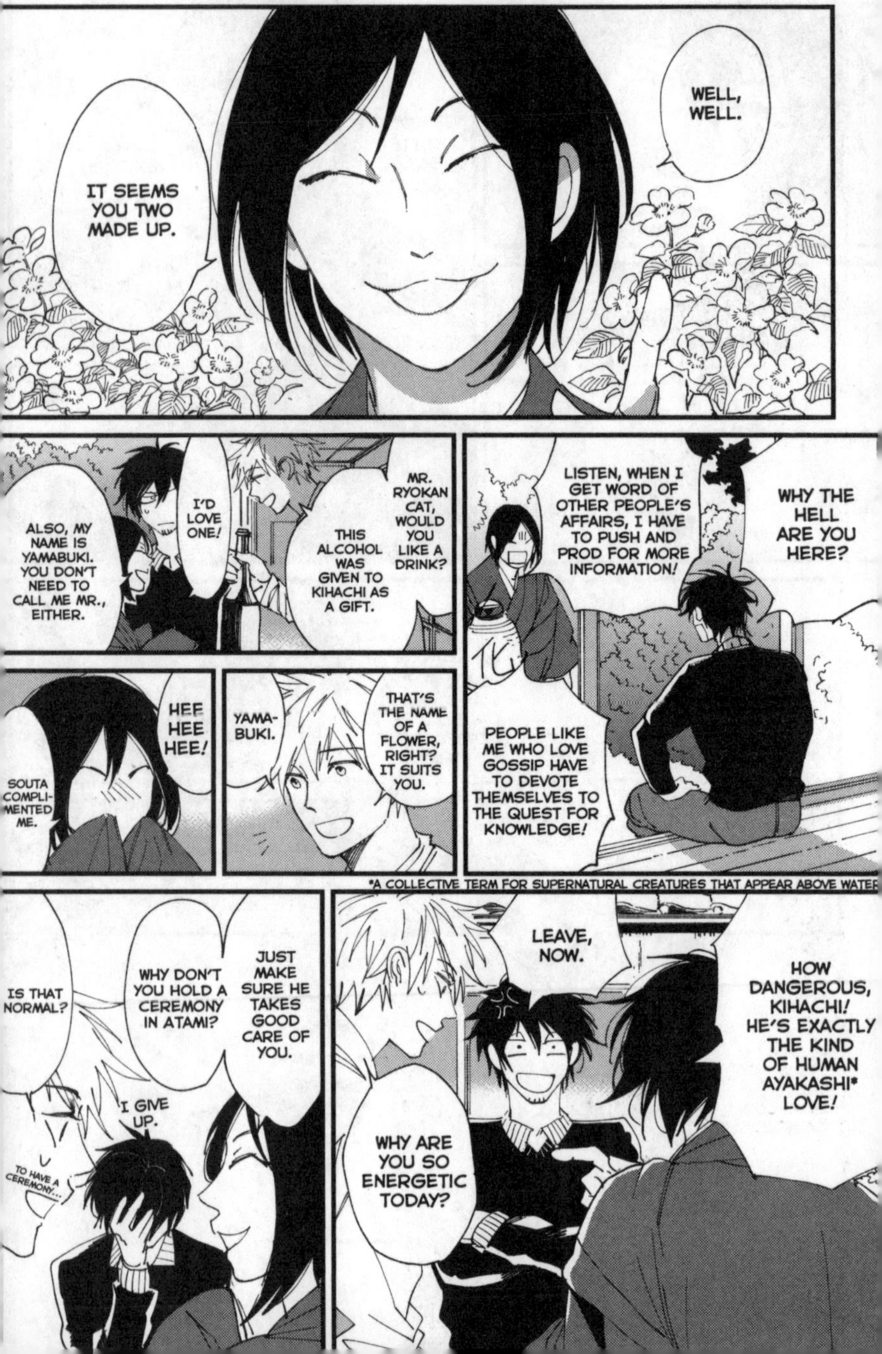
WELL, WELL.
IT SEEMS YOU TWO MADE UP.
WHY THE HELL ARE YOU HERE?
LISTEN, WHEN I GET WORD OF OTHER PEOPLE'S AFFAIRS, I HAVE TO PUSH AND PROD FOR MORE INFORMATION!
PEOPLE LIKE ME WHO LOVE GOSSIP HAVE TO DEVOTE THEMSELVES TO THE QUEST FOR KNOWLEDGE!
MR. RYOKAN CAT, WOULD YOU LIKE A DRINK?
THIS ALCOHOL WAS GIVEN TO KIHACHI AS A GIFT.
I'D LOVE ONE!
ALSO, MY NAME IS YAMABUKI. YOU DON'T NEED TO CALL ME MR., EITHER.
THAT'S THE NAME OF A FLOWER, RIGHT? IT SUITS YOU.
YAMA-BUKI.
HEE HEE HEE!
SOUTA COMPLI-MENTED ME.
*A COLLECTIVE TERM FOR SUPERNATURAL CREATURES THAT APPEAR ABOVE WATER
HOW DANGEROUS, KIHACHI! HE'S EXACTLY THE KIND OF HUMAN AYAKASHI* LOVE!
LEAVE, NOW.
WHY ARE YOU SO ENERGETIC TODAY?
JUST MAKE SURE HE TAKES GOOD CARE OF YOU.
WHY DON'T YOU HOLD A CEREMONY IN ATAMI?
IS THAT NORMAL?
I GIVE UP.
TO HAVE A CEREMONY...

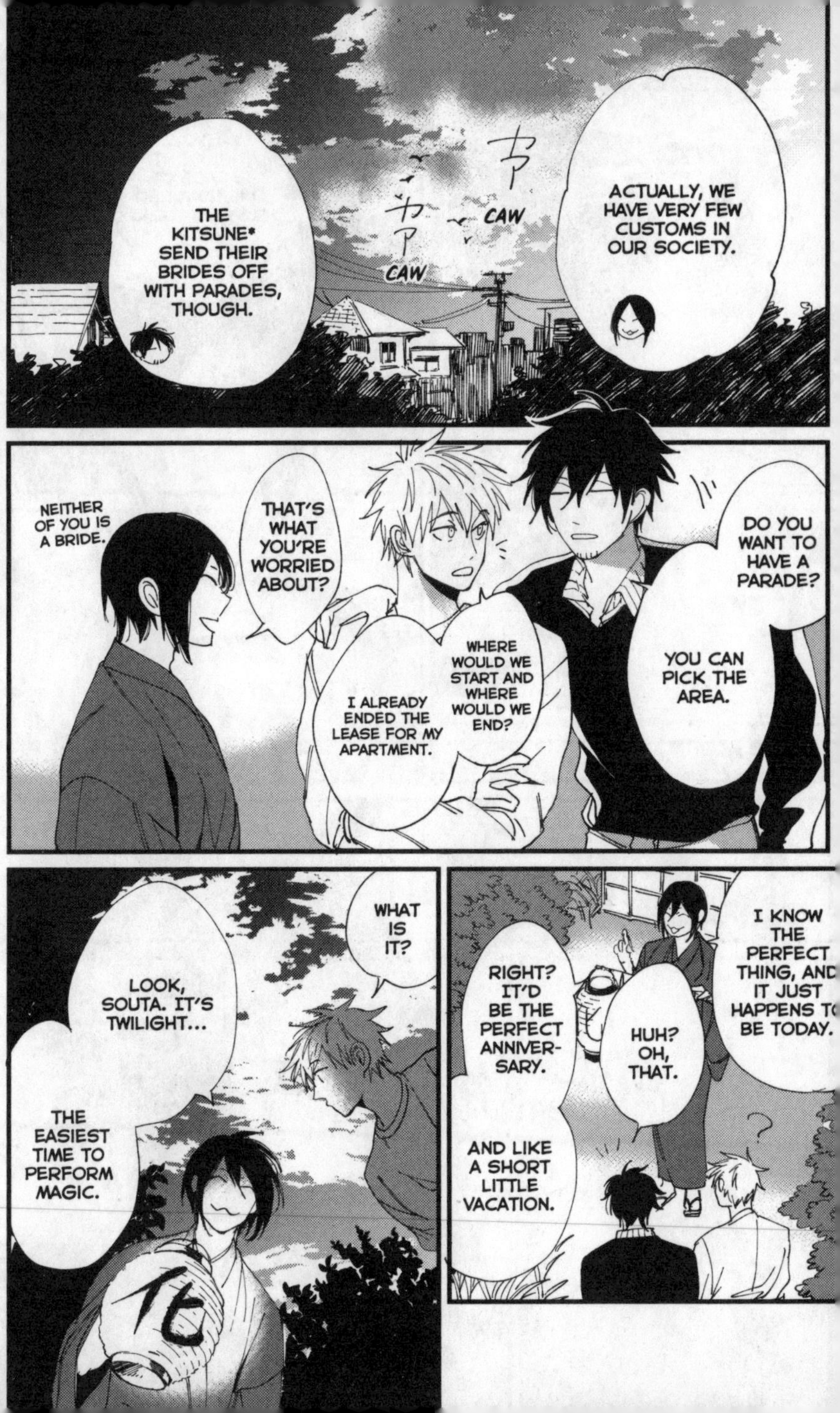
ACTUALLY, WE HAVE VERY FEW CUSTOMS IN OUR SOCIETY.
CAW
CAW
THE KITSUNE* SEND THEIR BRIDES OFF WITH PARADES, THOUGH.
DO YOU WANT TO HAVE A PARADE?
YOU CAN PICK THE AREA.
WHERE WOULD WE START AND WHERE WOULD WE END?
I ALREADY ENDED THE LEASE FOR MY APARTMENT.
THAT'S WHAT YOU'RE WORRIED ABOUT?
NEITHER OF YOU IS A BRIDE.
I KNOW THE PERFECT THING, AND IT JUST HAPPENS TO BE TODAY.
HUH? OH, THAT.
RIGHT? IT'D BE THE PERFECT ANNIVERSARY.
AND LIKE A SHORT LITTLE VACATION.
WHAT IS IT?
LOOK, SOUTA. IT'S TWILIGHT...
THE EASIEST TIME TO PERFORM MAGIC.

*FOXES WITH SUPERNATURAL POWERS AND THE ABILITY TO TAKE A HUMAN FORM

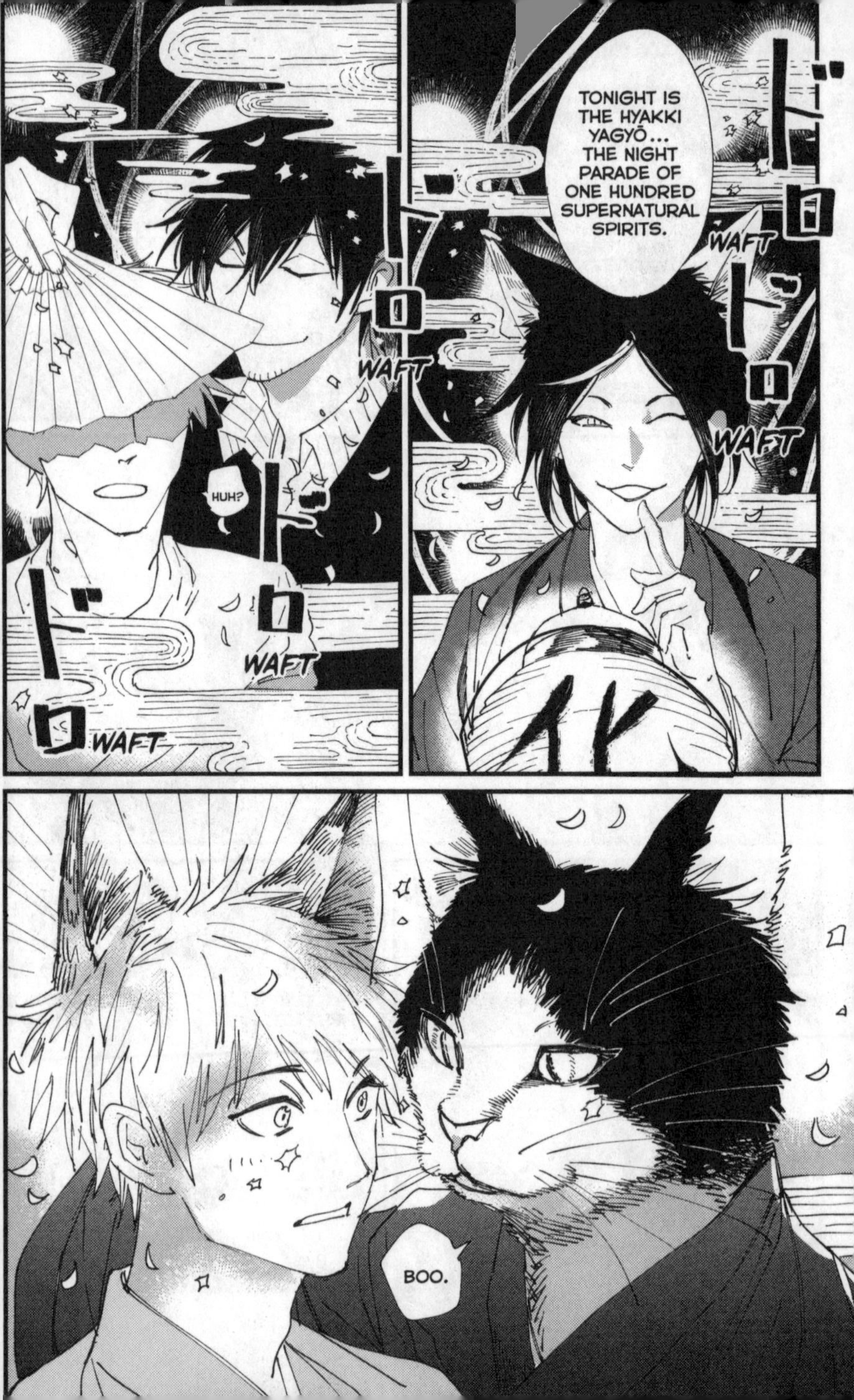
TONIGHT IS THE HYAKKI YAGYŌ... THE NIGHT PARADE OF ONE HUNDRED SUPERNATURAL SPIRITS.
WAFT
WAFT
WAFT
HUH?
WAFT
WAFT
BOO.

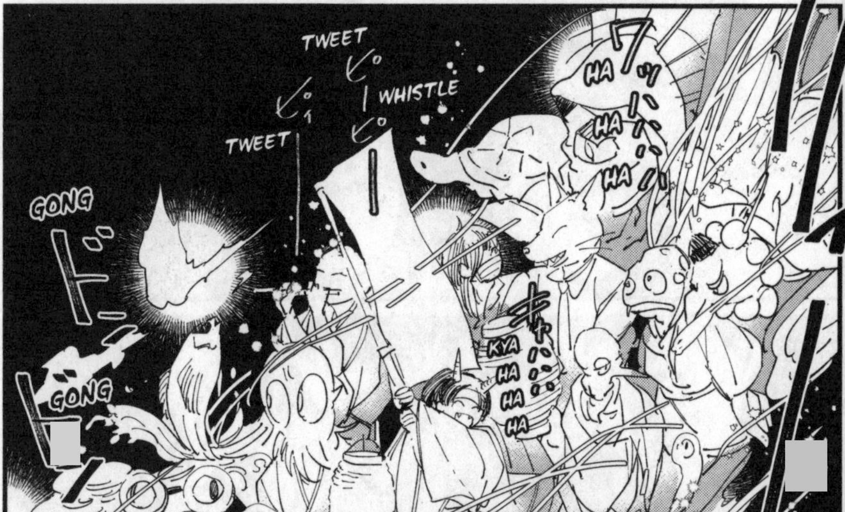
HA
HA
HA
TWEET
WHISTLE
TWEET
KYA
HA
HA
HA
HA
GONG
GONG
RIIING
HA
HA
HA

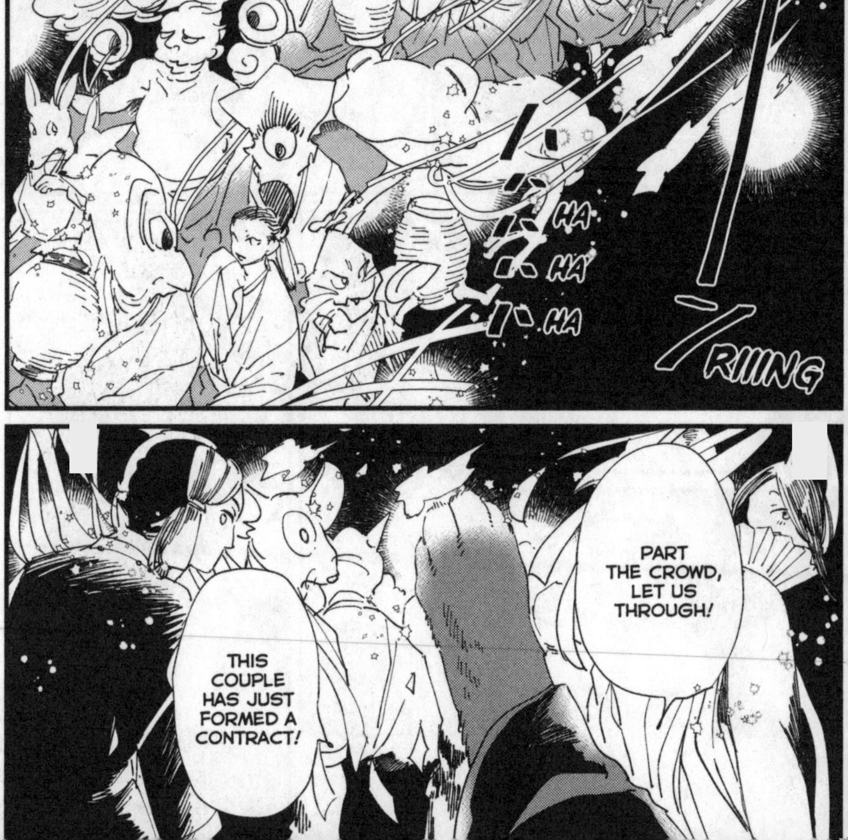
PART THE CROWD, LET US THROUGH!
THIS COUPLE HAS JUST FORMED A CONTRACT!

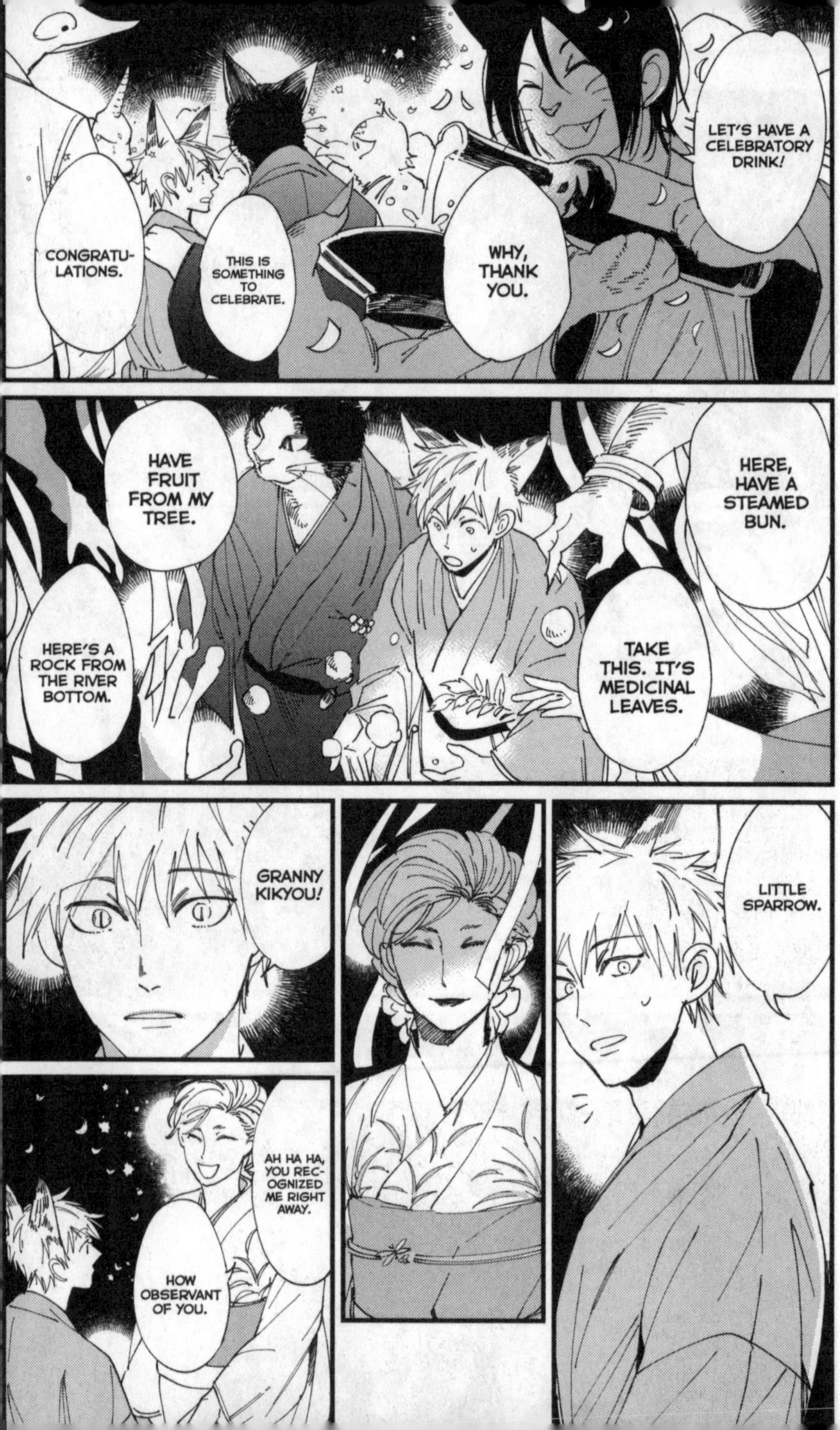
LET'S HAVE A CELEBRATORY DRINK!
WHY, THANK YOU.
THIS IS SOMETHING TO CELEBRATE.
CONGRATU-LATIONS.
HERE, HAVE A STEAMED BUN.
HAVE FRUIT FROM MY TREE.
TAKE THIS. IT'S MEDICINAL LEAVES.
HERE'S A ROCK FROM THE RIVER BOTTOM.
LITTLE SPARROW.
GRANNY KIKYOU!
AH HA HA, YOU RECOGNIZED ME RIGHT AWAY.
HOW OBSERVANT OF YOU.

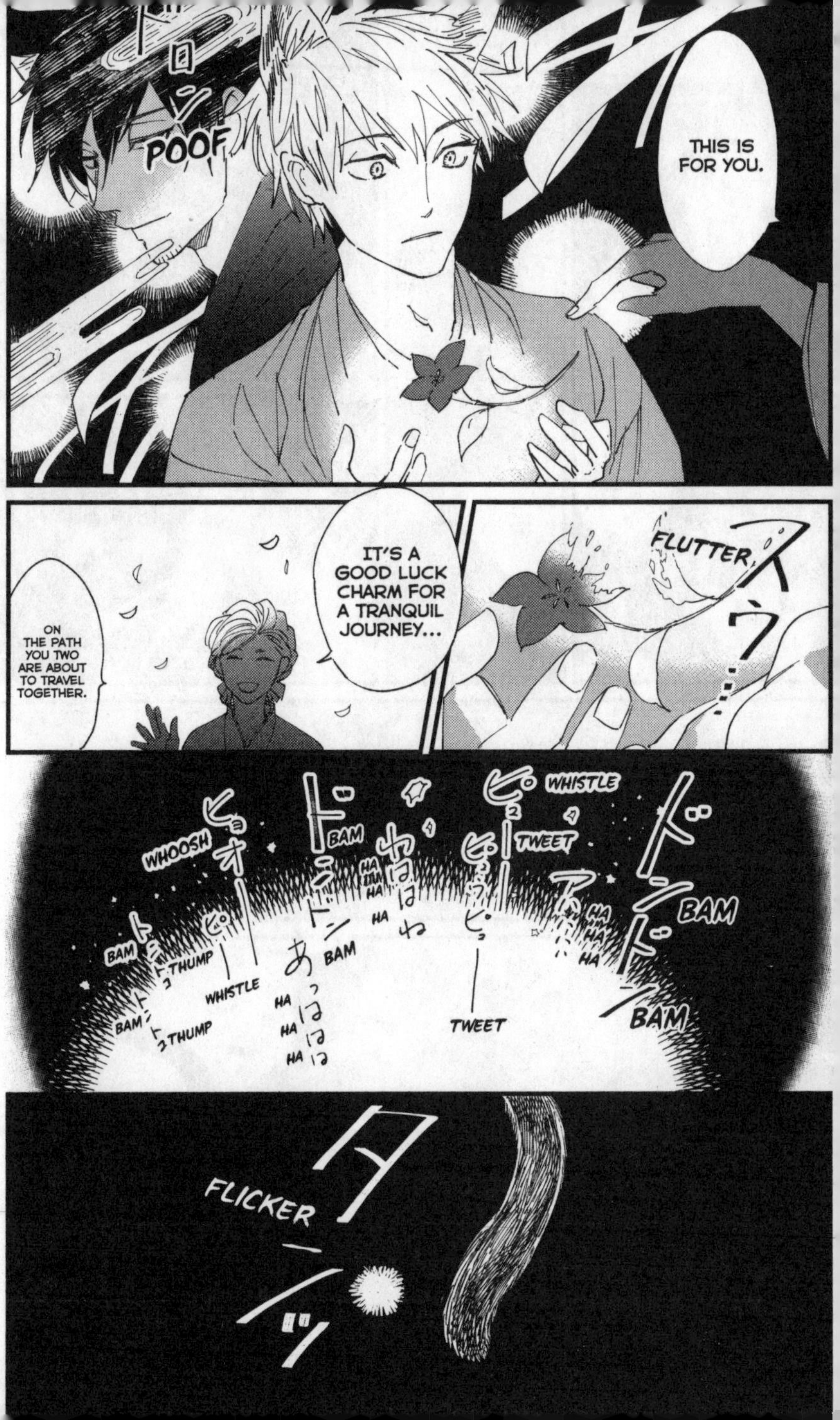
POOF
THIS IS FOR YOU.
FLUTTER
IT'S A GOOD LUCK CHARM FOR A TRANQUIL JOURNEY...
ON THE PATH YOU TWO ARE ABOUT TO TRAVEL TOGETHER.
BAM
BAM
HA HA HA
WHISTLE
TWEET
TWEET
BAM
HA HA HA
BAM
WHOOSH
WHISTLE
HA HA HA
BAM THUMP
BAM THUMP
FLICKER

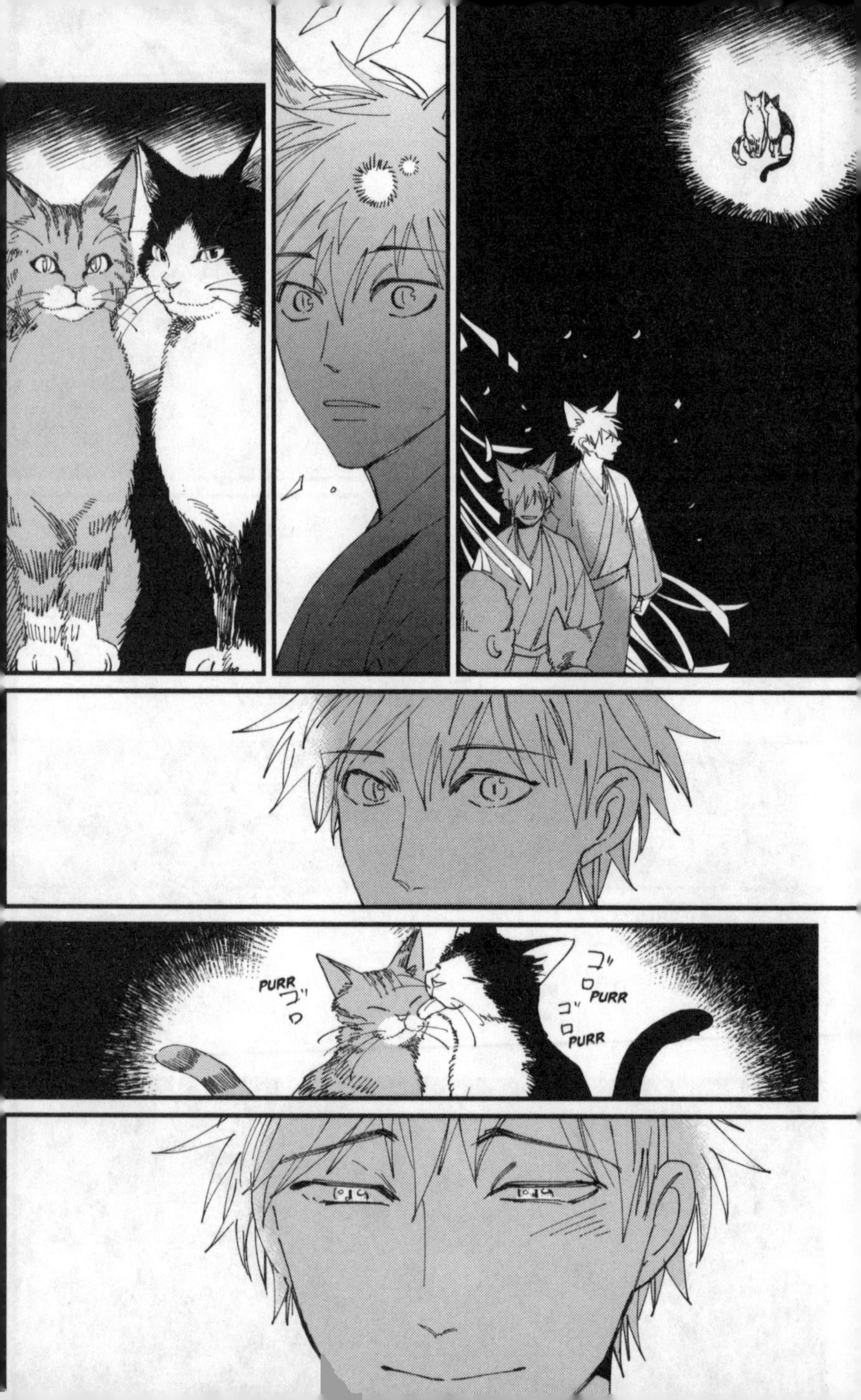
ゴロ
PURR
ゴロ
PURR
PURR
ゴロ

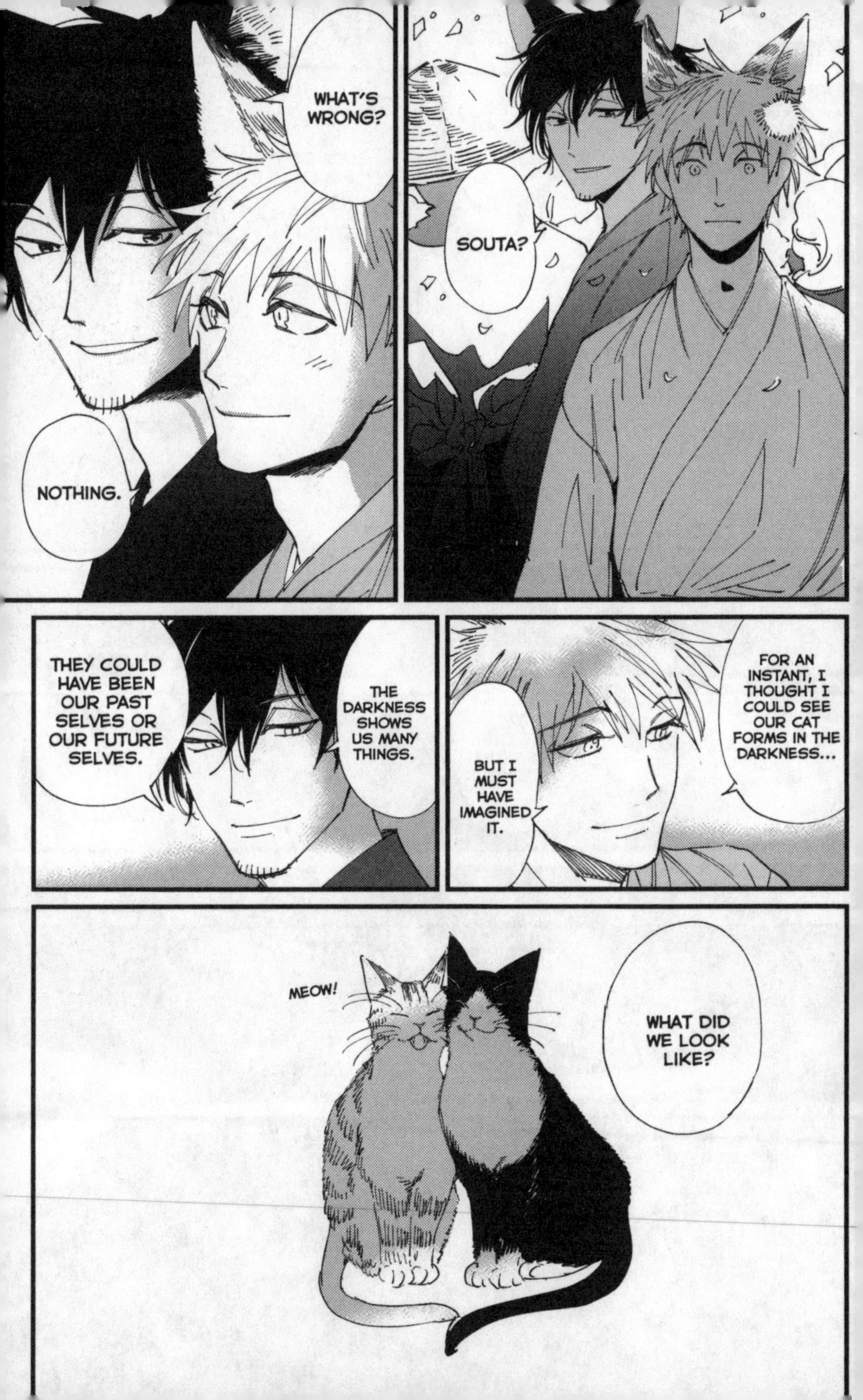
SOUTA?
WHAT'S WRONG?
NOTHING.
FOR AN INSTANT, I THOUGHT I COULD SEE OUR CAT FORMS IN THE DARKNESS...
BUT I MUST HAVE IMAGINED IT.
THE DARKNESS SHOWS US MANY THINGS.
THEY COULD HAVE BEEN OUR PAST SELVES OR OUR FUTURE SELVES.
WHAT DID WE LOOK LIKE?
MEOW!

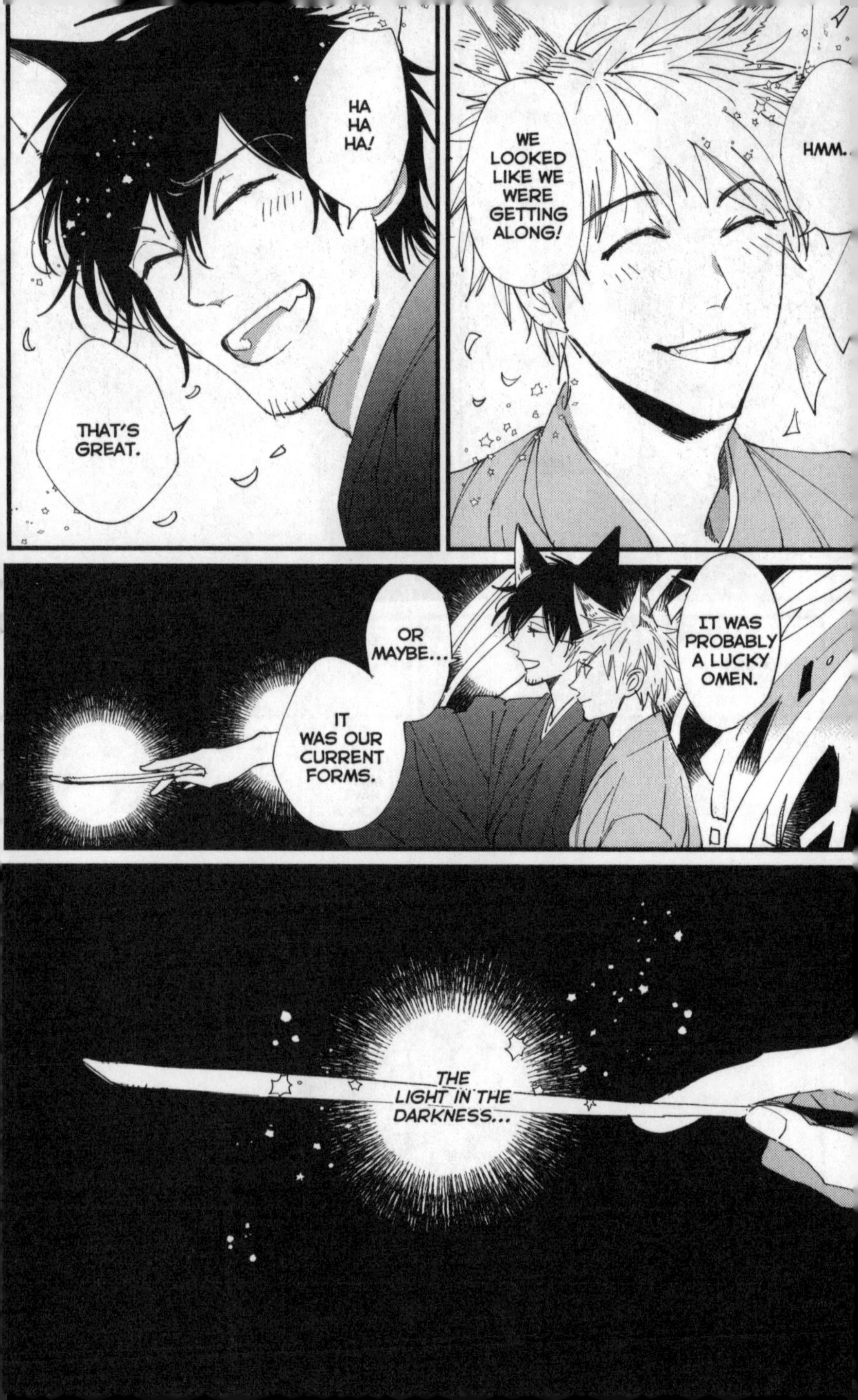
HMM.
WE LOOKED LIKE WE WERE GETTING ALONG!
HA HA HA!
THAT'S GREAT.
IT WAS PROBABLY A LUCKY OMEN.
OR MAYBE...
IT WAS OUR CURRENT FORMS.
THE LIGHT IN THE DARKNESS...

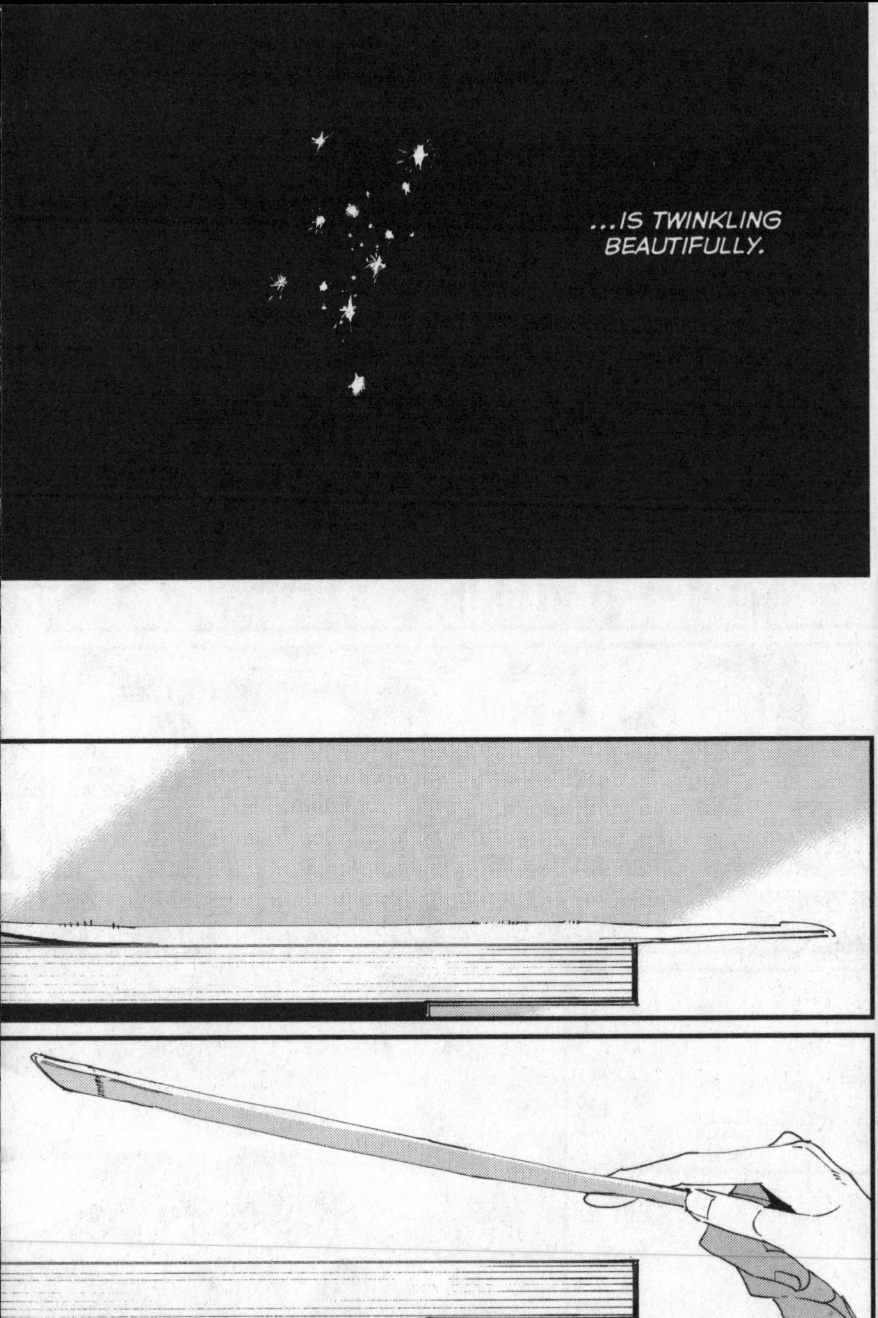
...IS TWINKLING BEAUTIFULLY.

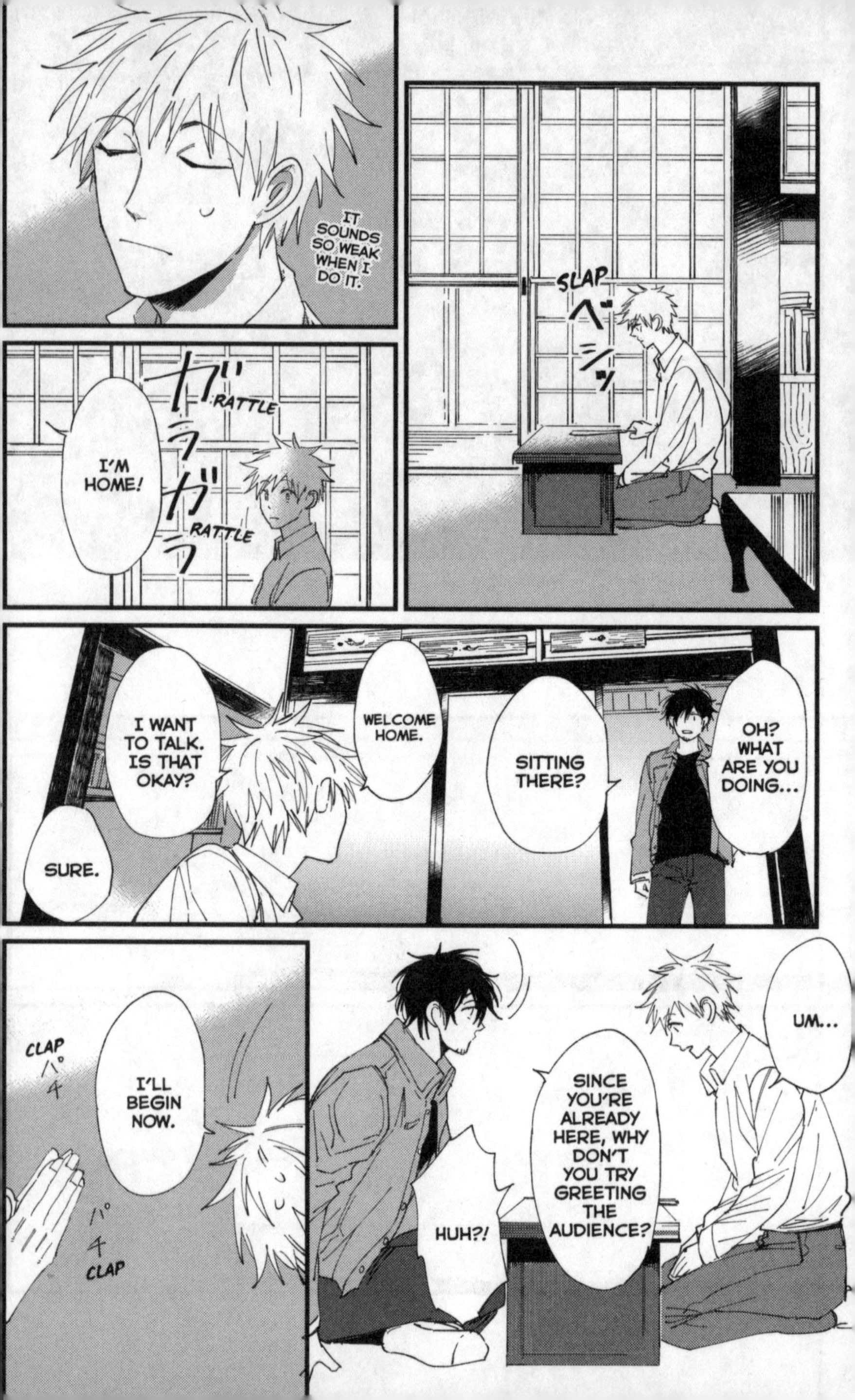
SLAP
べシッ
IT SOUNDS SO WEAK WHEN I DO IT.
ガラ RATTLE
ガラ RATTLE
I'M HOME!
OH? WHAT ARE YOU DOING...
SITTING THERE?
WELCOME HOME.
I WANT TO TALK. IS THAT OKAY?
SURE.
UM...
SINCE YOU'RE ALREADY HERE, WHY DON'T YOU TRY GREETING THE AUDIENCE?
HUH?!
I'LL BEGIN NOW.
CLAP パチ
パチ CLAP

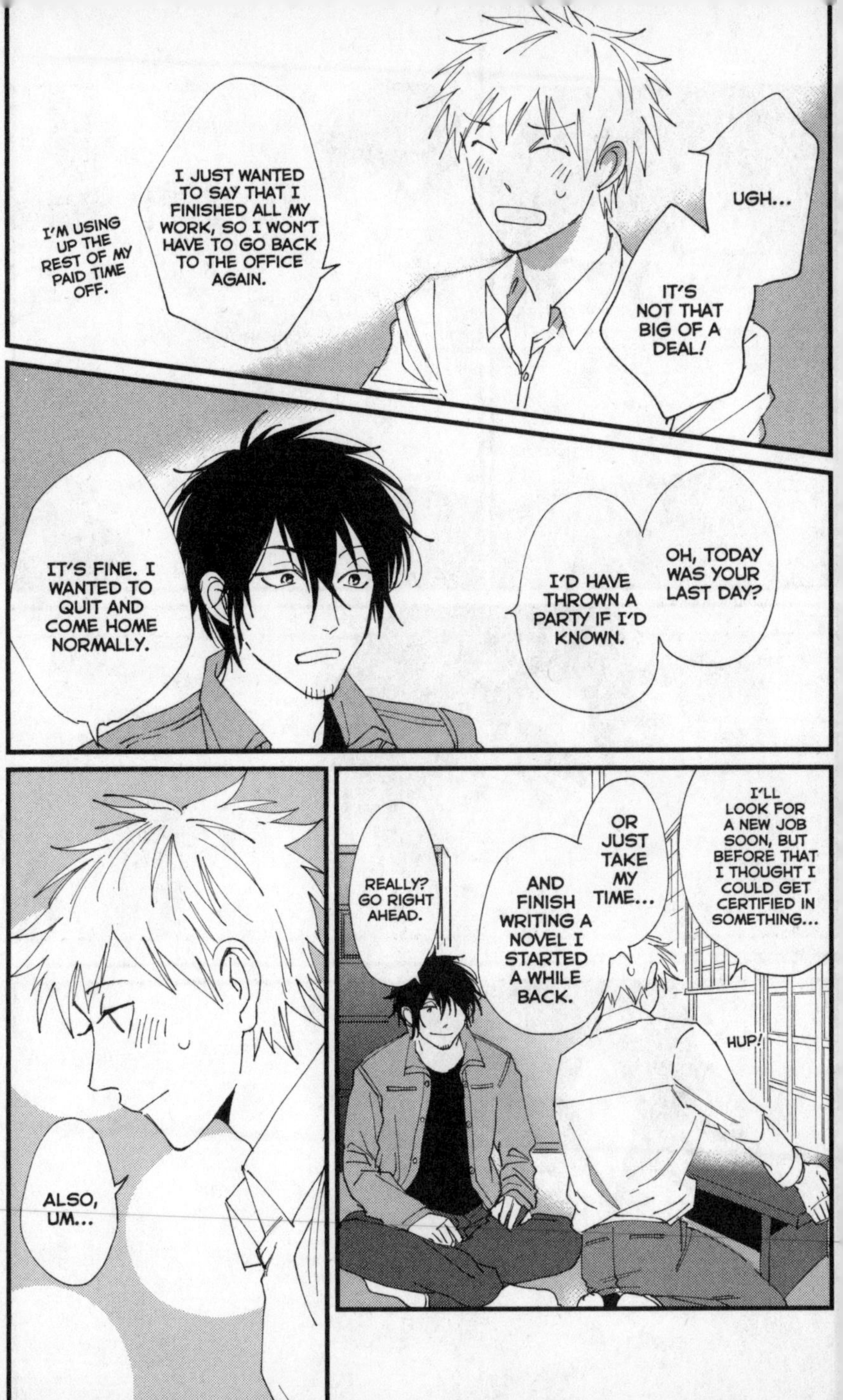
UGH...
IT'S NOT THAT BIG OF A DEAL!
I JUST WANTED TO SAY THAT I FINISHED ALL MY WORK, SO I WON'T HAVE TO GO BACK TO THE OFFICE AGAIN.
I'M USING UP THE REST OF MY PAID TIME OFF.
OH, TODAY WAS YOUR LAST DAY?
I'D HAVE THROWN A PARTY IF I'D KNOWN.
IT'S FINE. I WANTED TO QUIT AND COME HOME NORMALLY.
I'LL LOOK FOR A NEW JOB SOON, BUT BEFORE THAT I THOUGHT I COULD GET CERTIFIED IN SOMETHING...
OR JUST TAKE MY TIME...
AND FINISH WRITING A NOVEL I STARTED A WHILE BACK.
HUP!
REALLY? GO RIGHT AHEAD.
ALSO, UM...

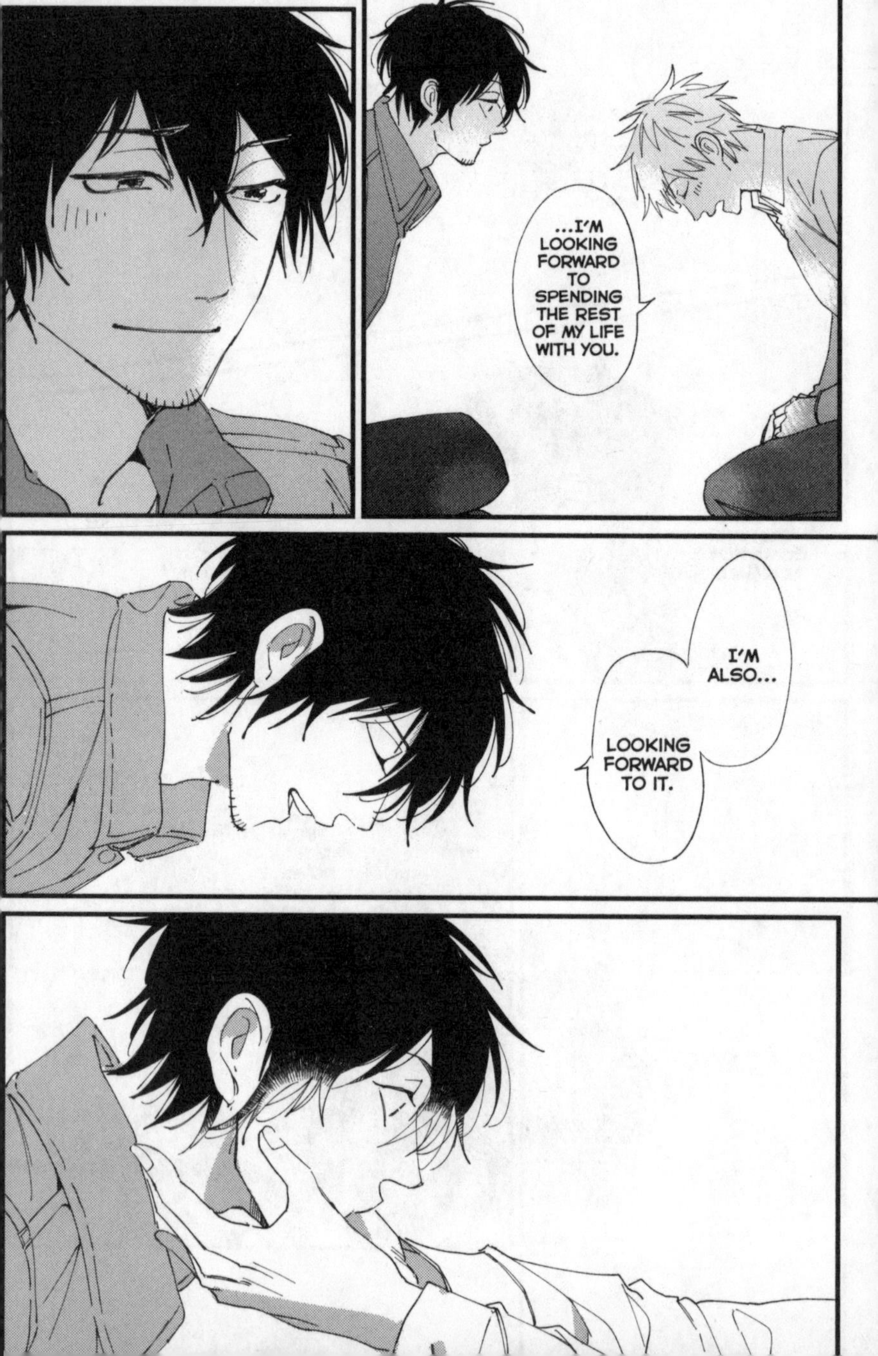
...I'M LOOKING FORWARD TO SPENDING THE REST OF MY LIFE WITH YOU.
I'M ALSO...
LOOKING FORWARD TO IT.

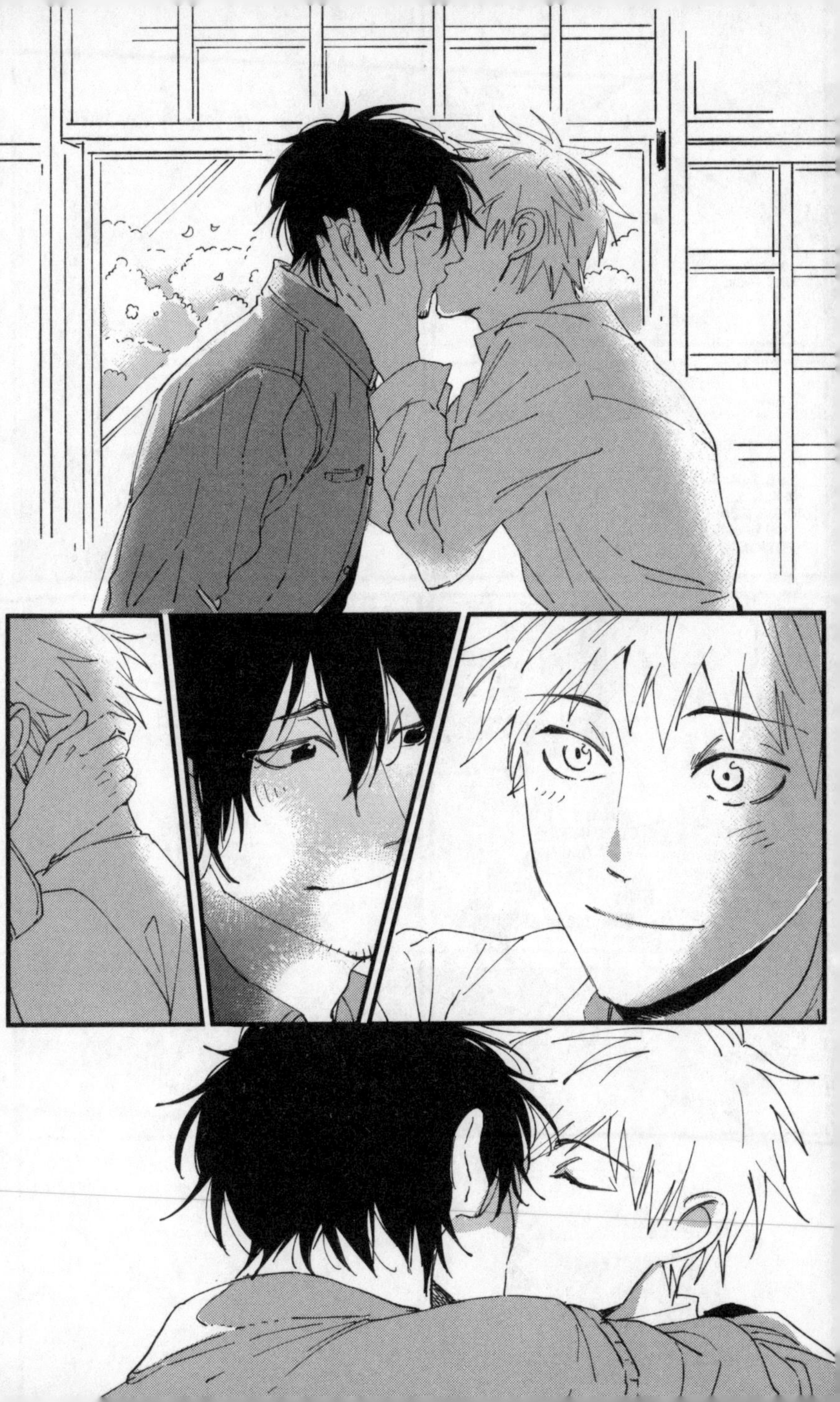

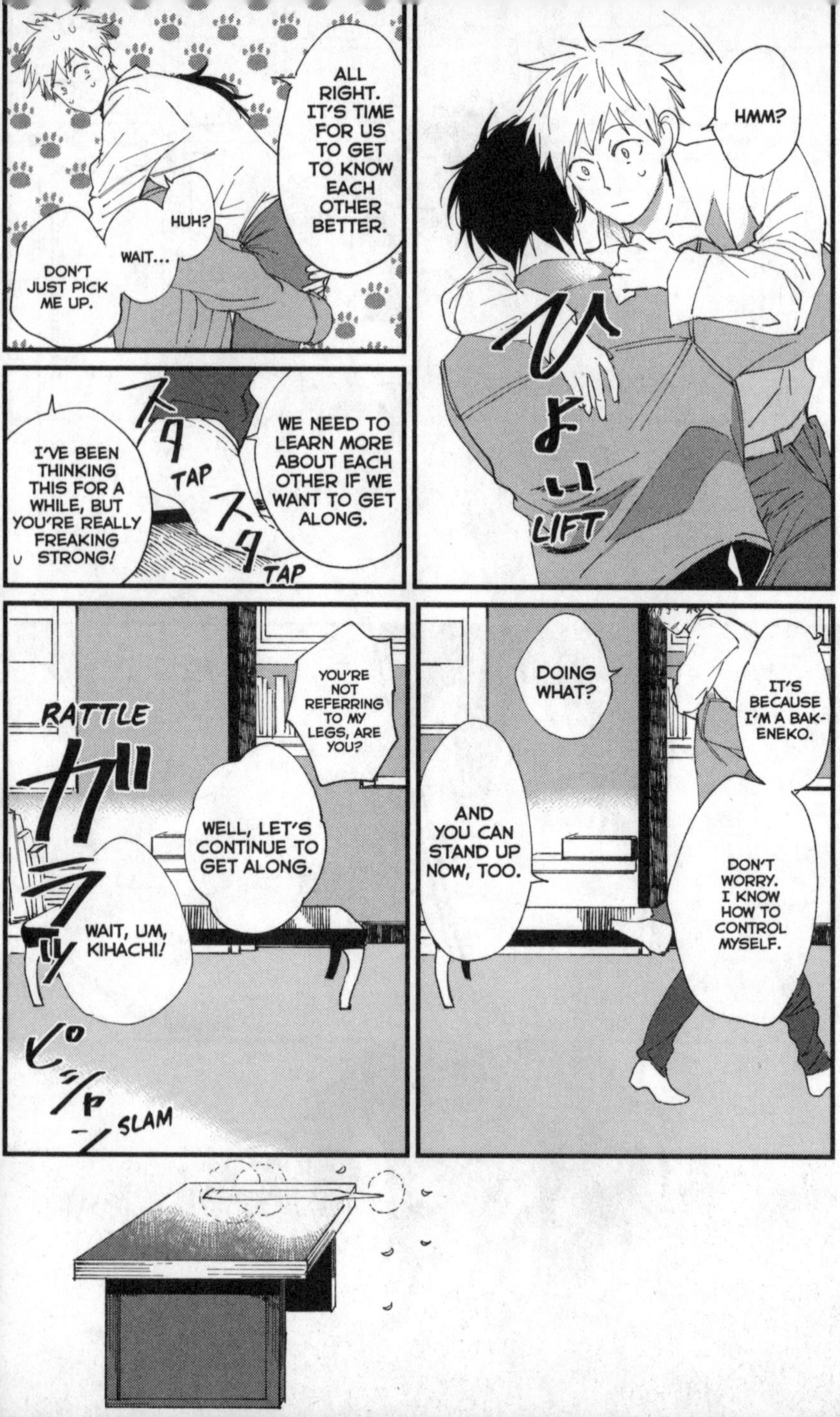
HMM?
ひょい
LIFT
ALL RIGHT. IT'S TIME FOR US TO GET TO KNOW EACH OTHER BETTER.
HUH?
WAIT...
DON'T JUST PICK ME UP.
WE NEED TO LEARN MORE ABOUT EACH OTHER IF WE WANT TO GET ALONG.
スタ
TAP
スタ
TAP
I'VE BEEN THINKING THIS FOR A WHILE, BUT YOU'RE REALLY FREAKING STRONG!
IT'S BECAUSE I'M A BAKE-NEKO.
DON'T WORRY. I KNOW HOW TO CONTROL MYSELF.
DOING WHAT?
AND YOU CAN STAND UP NOW, TOO.
YOU'RE NOT REFERRING TO MY LEGS, ARE YOU?
WELL, LET'S CONTINUE TO GET ALONG.
RATTLE
ガラッ
WAIT, UM, KIHACHI!
ピシャ
SLAM

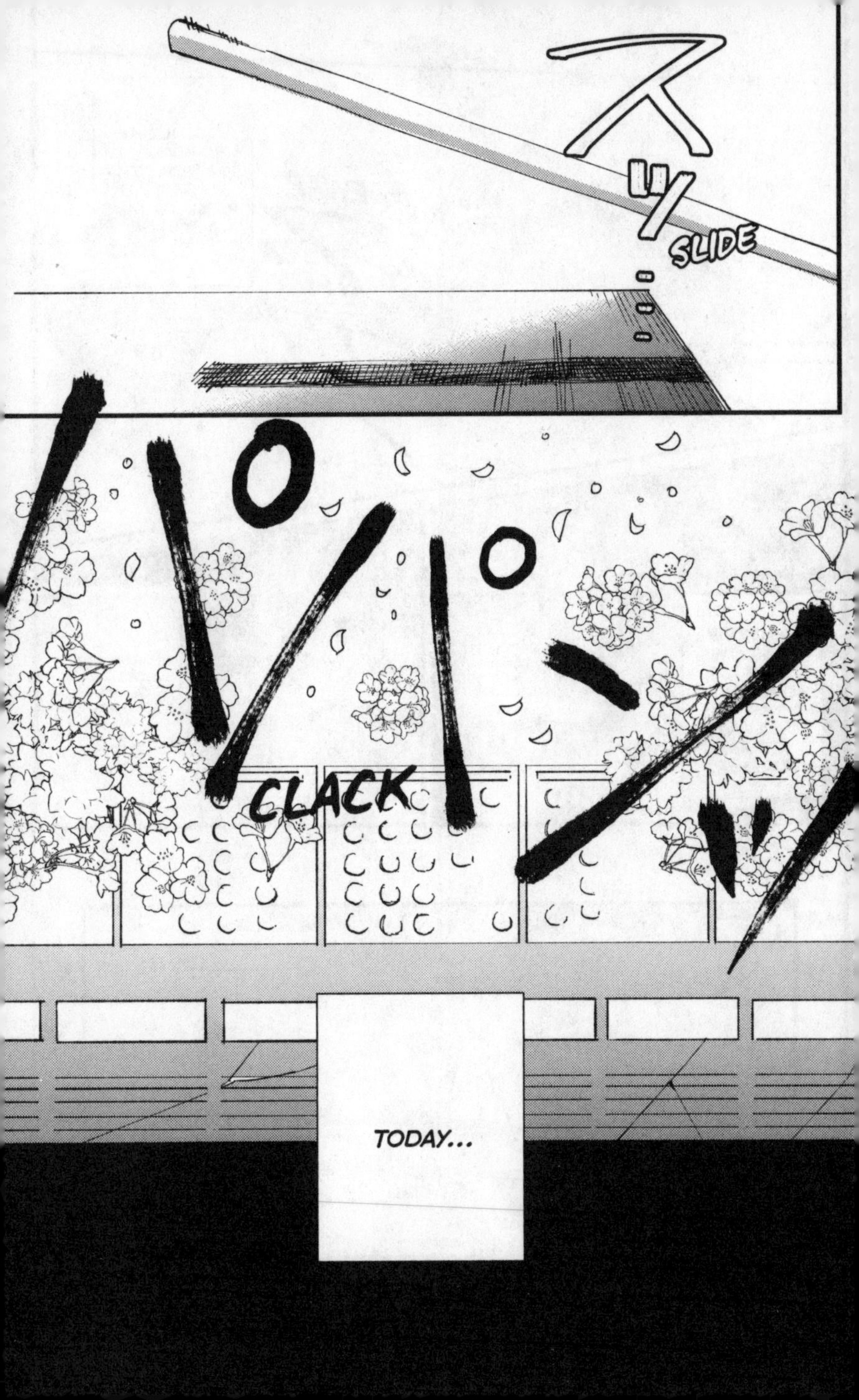
スッ
SLIDE
パンッ
CLACK
TODAY...

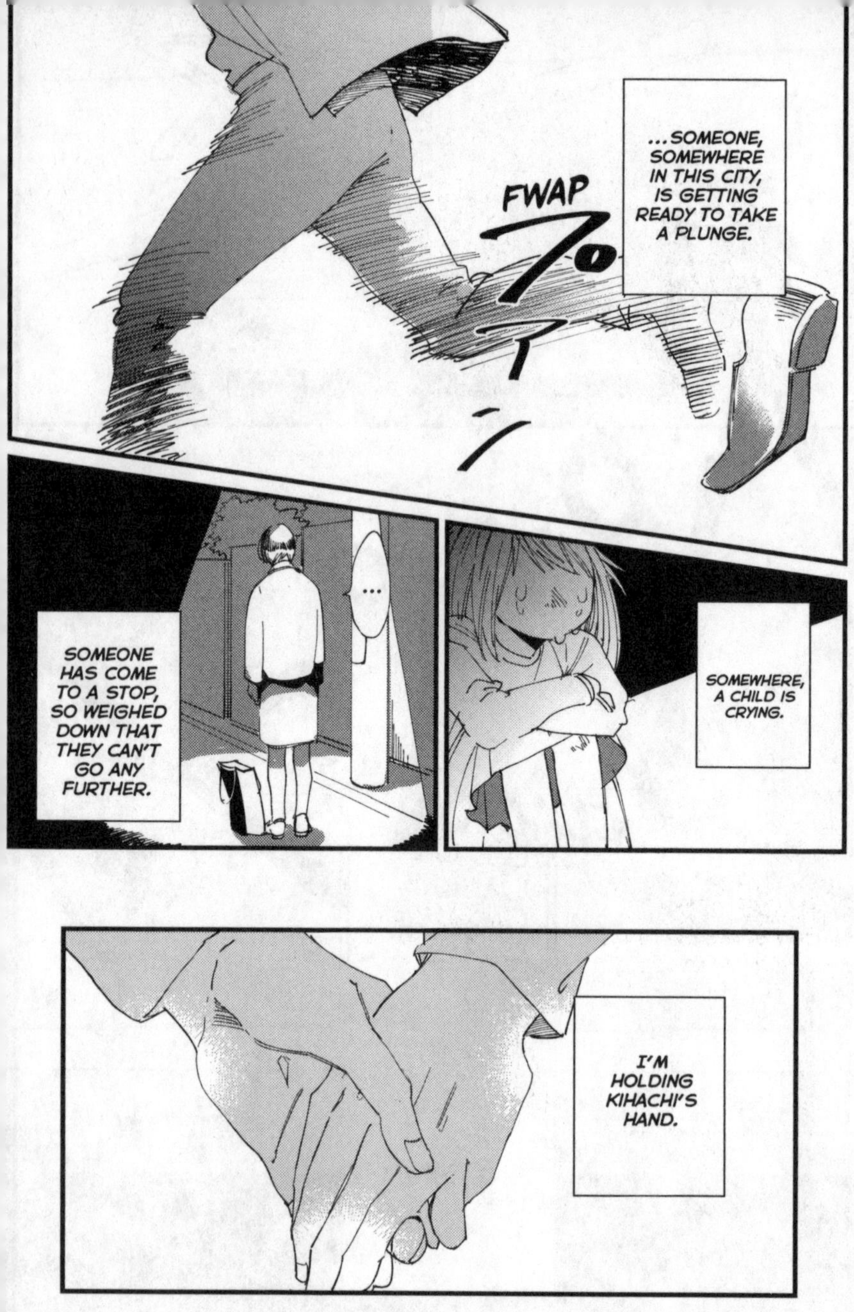
...SOMEONE, SOMEWHERE IN THIS CITY, IS GETTING READY TO TAKE A PLUNGE.
FWAP
SOMEWHERE, A CHILD IS CRYING.
...
SOMEONE HAS COME TO A STOP, SO WEIGHED DOWN THAT THEY CAN'T GO ANY FURTHER.
I'M HOLDING KIHACHI'S HAND.

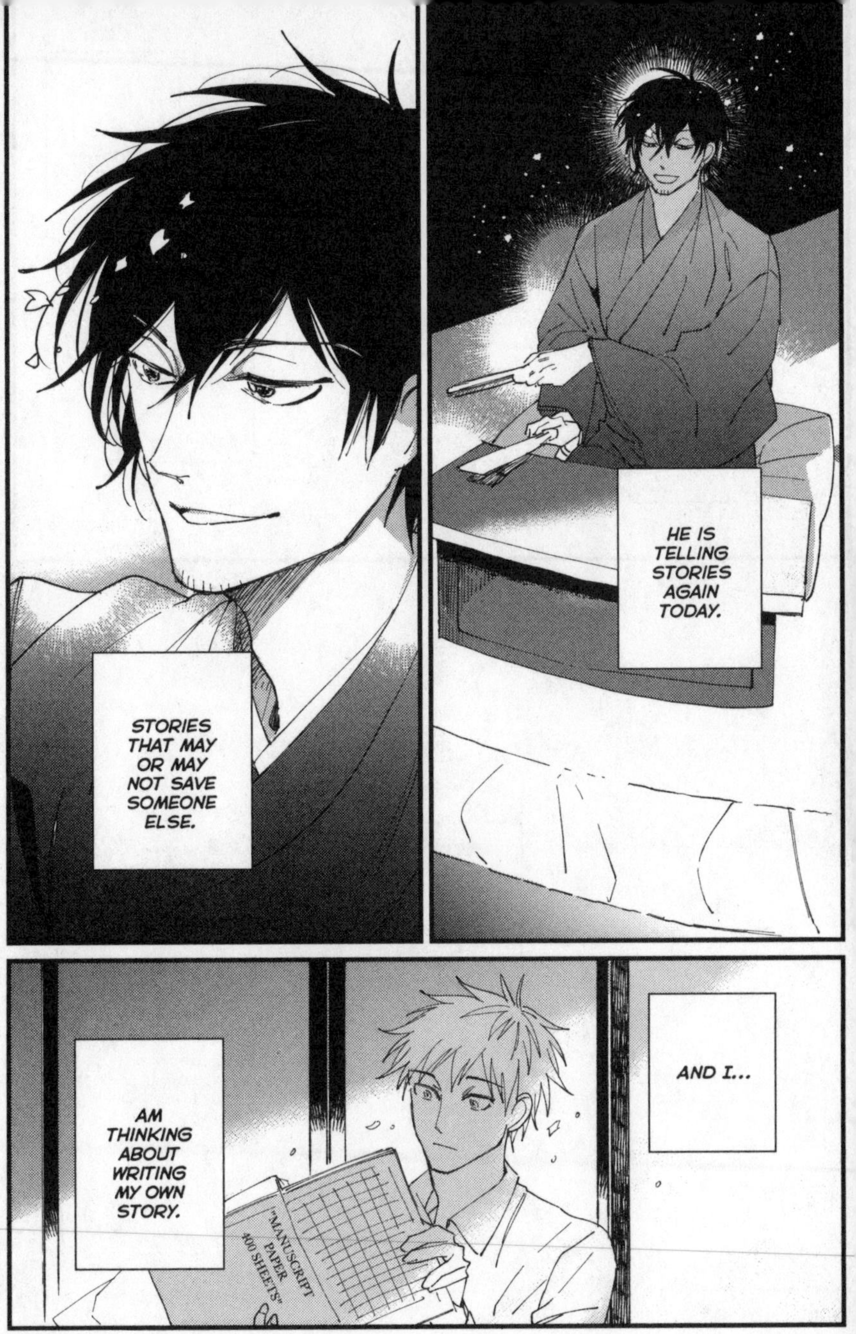
HE IS TELLING STORIES AGAIN TODAY.
STORIES THAT MAY OR MAY NOT SAVE SOMEONE ELSE.
AND I...
AM THINKING ABOUT WRITING MY OWN STORY.
"MANUSCRIPT PAPER 400 SHEETS"

I'LL START...

BY WRITING...

THE FIRST LETTER...

OF THE FIRST WORD.

The End

The Story of Their First Night Together

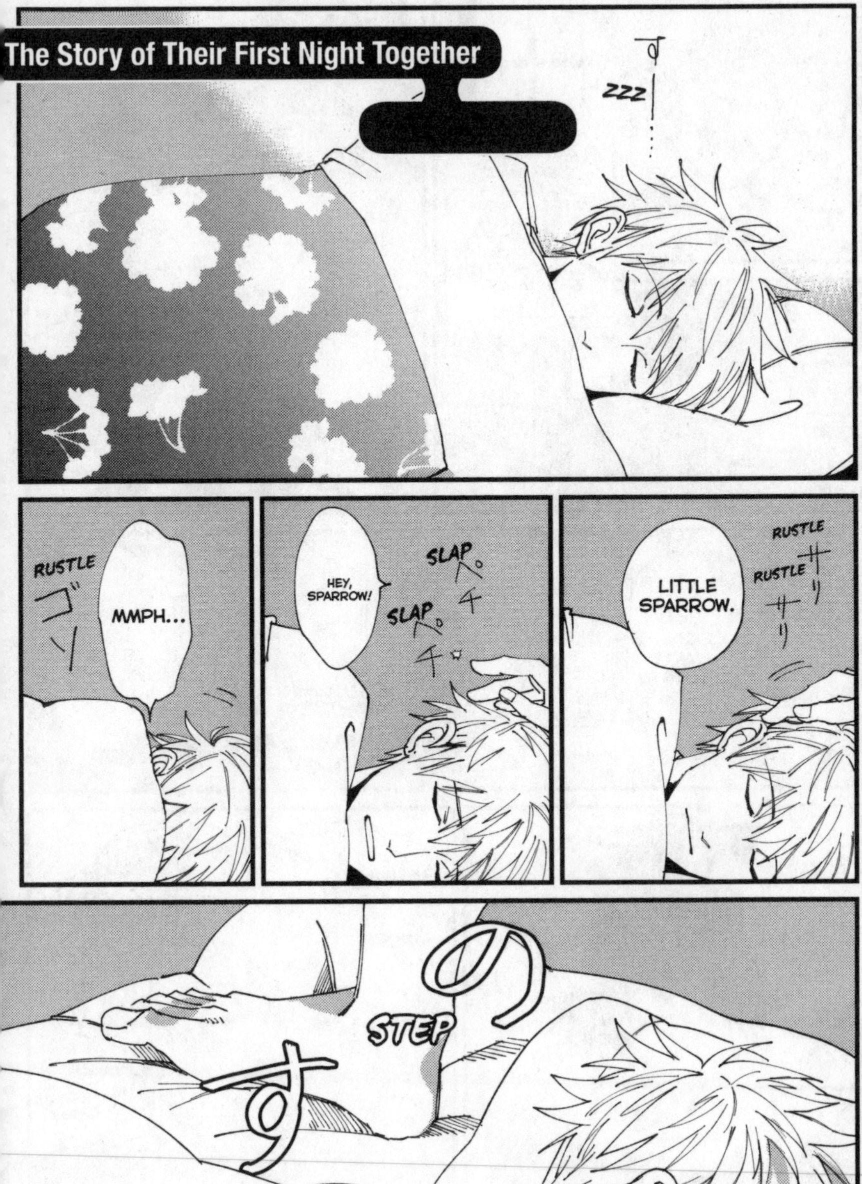
す
ZZZ
LITTLE SPARROW.
RUSTLE
サリ
RUSTLE
サリ
HEY, SPARROW!
SLAP
ペチ
SLAP
ペチ
MMPH...
RUSTLE
ゴソ
STEP
のす

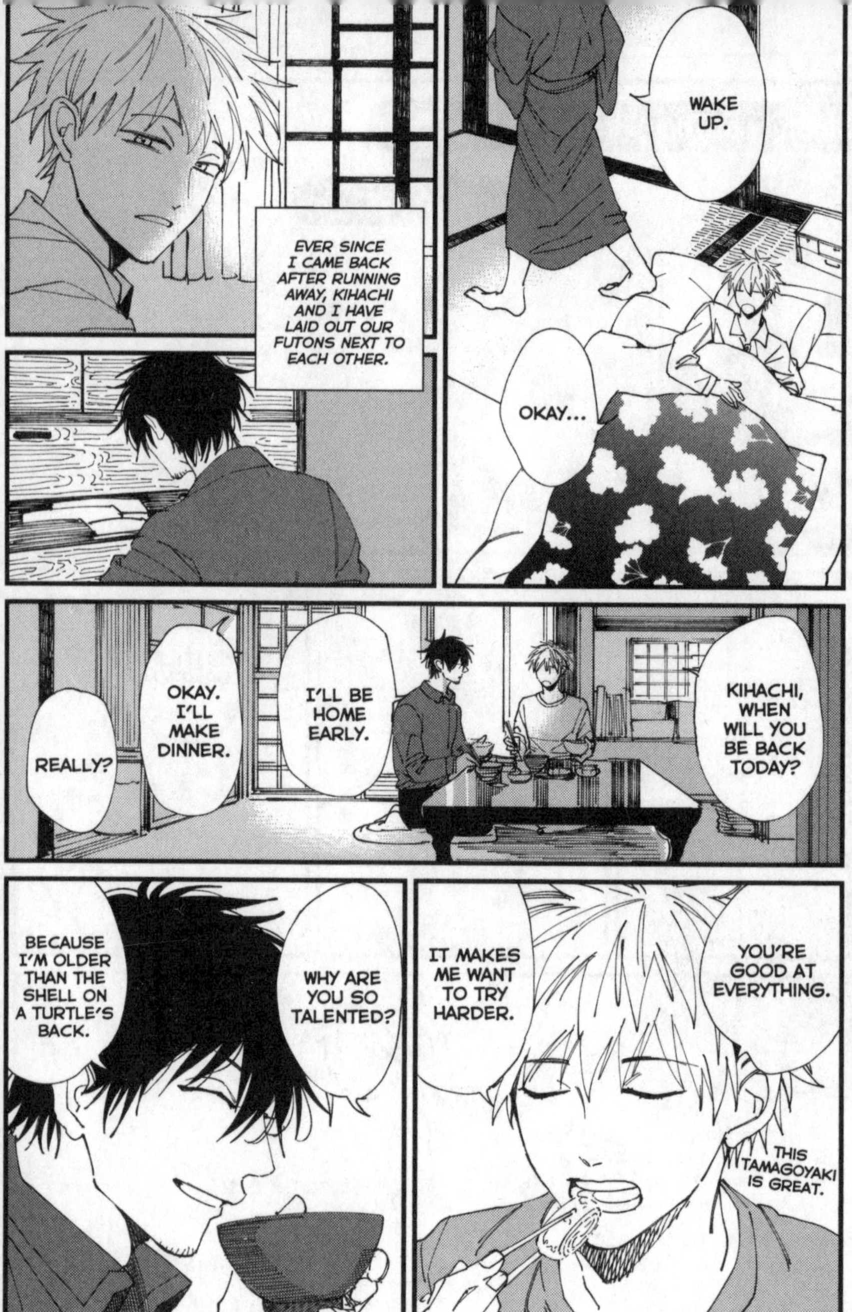

WAKE UP.
OKAY...
EVER SINCE I CAME BACK AFTER RUNNING AWAY, KIHACHI AND I HAVE LAID OUT OUR FUTONS NEXT TO EACH OTHER.
KIHACHI, WHEN WILL YOU BE BACK TODAY?
I'LL BE HOME EARLY.
OKAY. I'LL MAKE DINNER.
REALLY?
YOU'RE GOOD AT EVERYTHING.
IT MAKES ME WANT TO TRY HARDER.
THIS TAMAGOYAKI IS GREAT.
WHY ARE YOU SO TALENTED?
BECAUSE I'M OLDER THAN THE SHELL ON A TURTLE'S BACK.

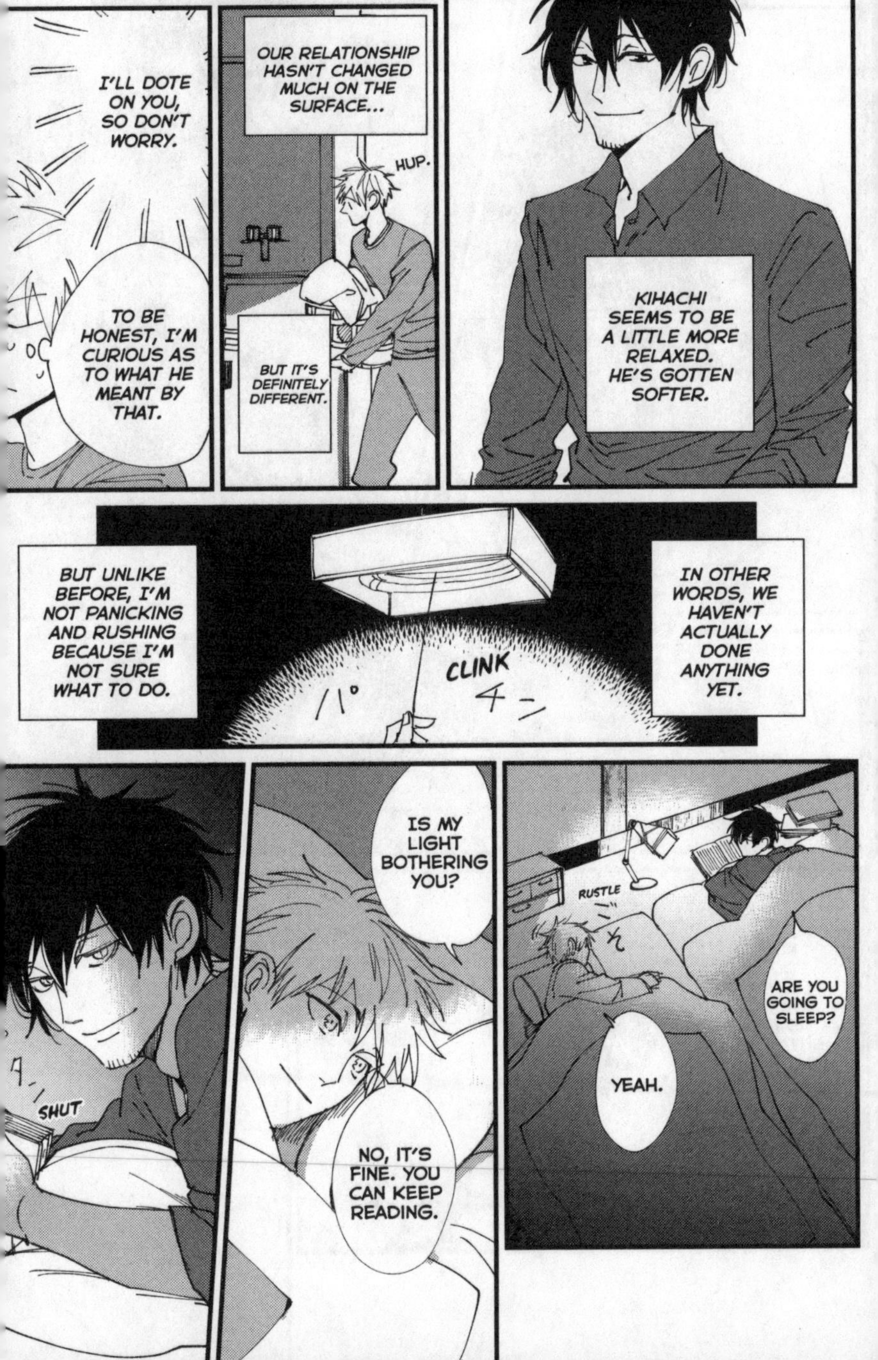
KIHACHI SEEMS TO BE A LITTLE MORE RELAXED. HE'S GOTTEN SOFTER.
OUR RELATIONSHIP HASN'T CHANGED MUCH ON THE SURFACE...
HUP.
BUT IT'S DEFINITELY DIFFERENT.
I'LL DOTE ON YOU, SO DON'T WORRY.
TO BE HONEST, I'M CURIOUS AS TO WHAT HE MEANT BY THAT.
IN OTHER WORDS, WE HAVEN'T ACTUALLY DONE ANYTHING YET.
CLINK
BUT UNLIKE BEFORE, I'M NOT PANICKING AND RUSHING BECAUSE I'M NOT SURE WHAT TO DO.
RUSTLE
ARE YOU GOING TO SLEEP?
YEAH.
IS MY LIGHT BOTHERING YOU?
NO, IT'S FINE. YOU CAN KEEP READING.
SHUT

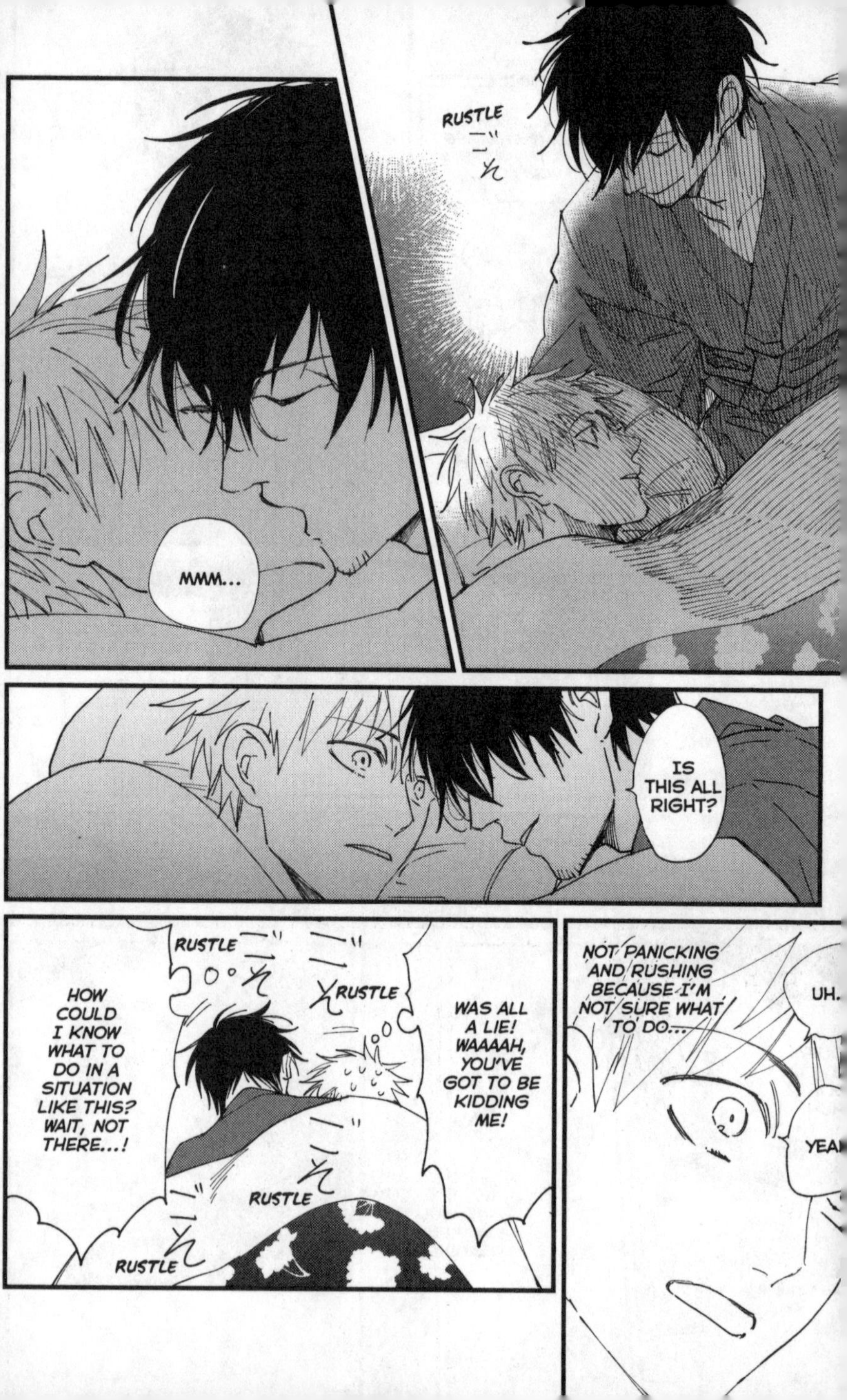
RUSTLE
MMM...
IS THIS ALL RIGHT?
UH.
NOT PANICKING AND RUSHING BECAUSE I'M NOT SURE WHAT TO DO...
RUSTLE
RUSTLE
WAS ALL A LIE! WAAAAH, YOU'VE GOT TO BE KIDDING ME!
HOW COULD I KNOW WHAT TO DO IN A SITUATION LIKE THIS? WAIT, NOT THERE...!
RUSTLE
RUSTLE

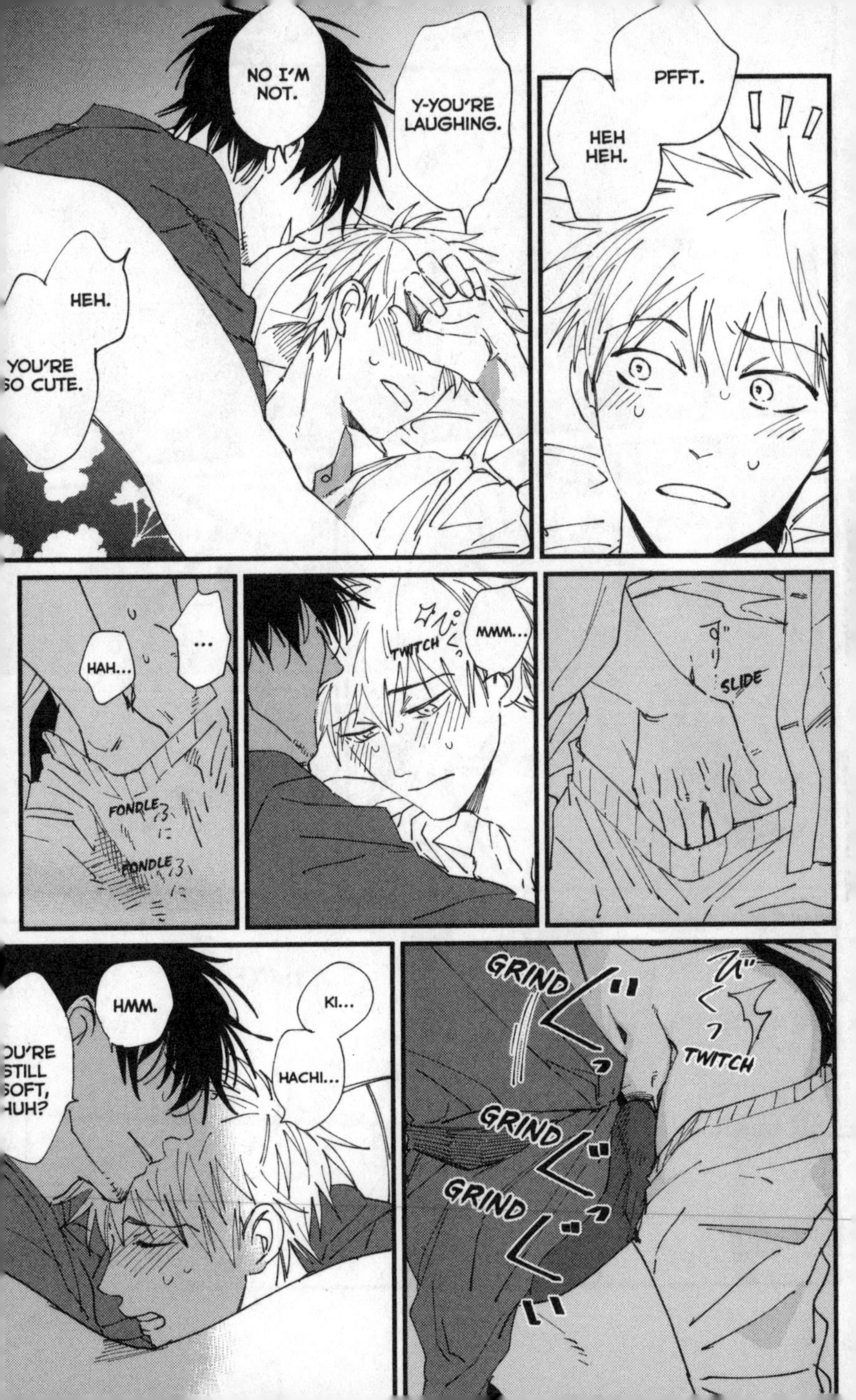
PFFT.
HEH HEH.
Y-YOU'RE LAUGHING.
NO I'M NOT.
HEH.
YOU'RE SO CUTE.
SLIDE
MMM...
TWITCH
...
HAH...
FONDLE
FONDLE
GRIND
TWITCH
GRIND
GRIND
KI...
HACHI...
HMM.
OU'RE STILL SOFT, HUH?

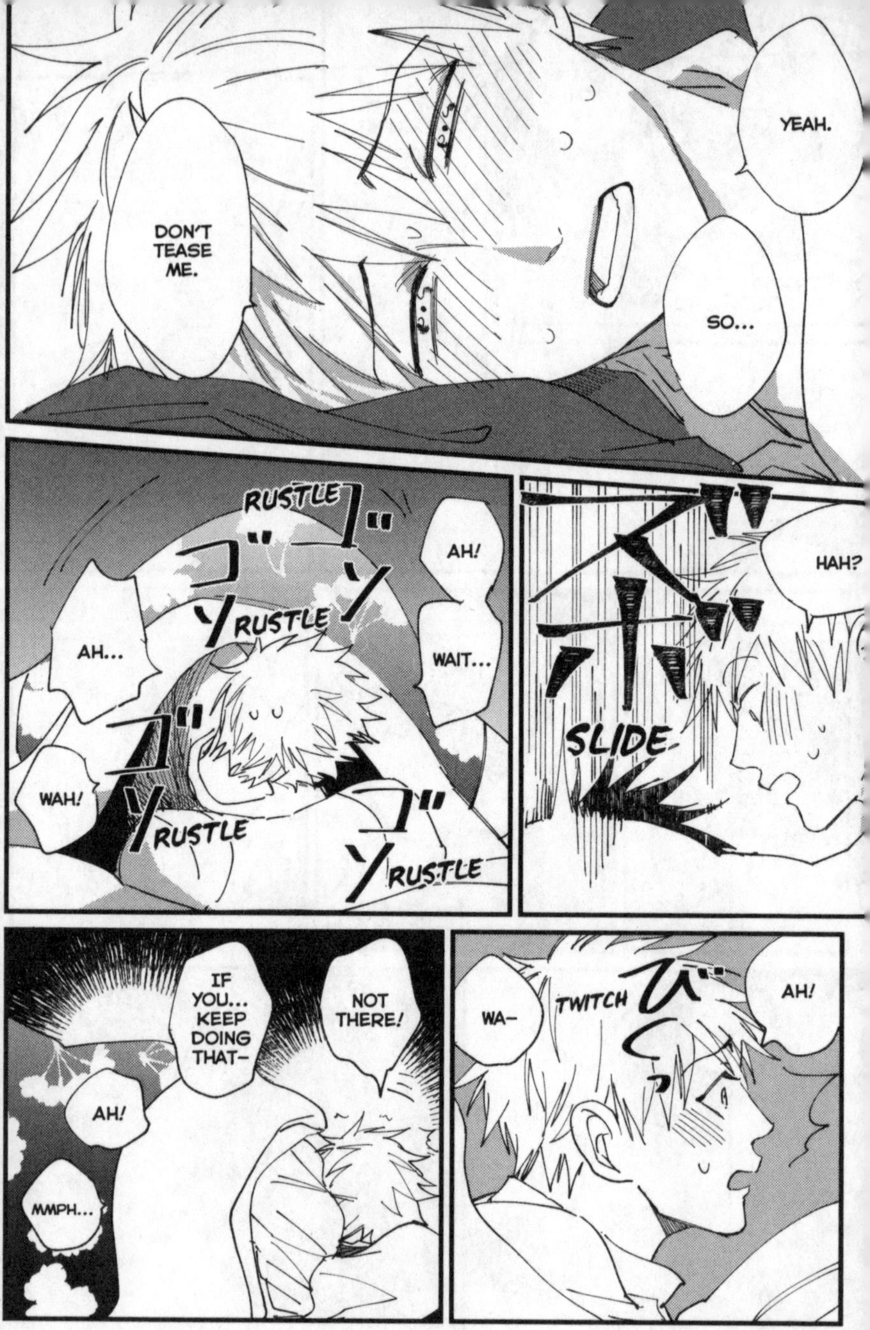
YEAH.
SO...
DON'T TEASE ME.
HAH?
SLIDE
AH!
WAIT...
RUSTLE
RUSTLE
AH...
WAH!
RUSTLE
RUSTLE
AH!
TWITCH
WA-
NOT THERE!
IF YOU... KEEP DOING THAT-
AH!
MMPH...

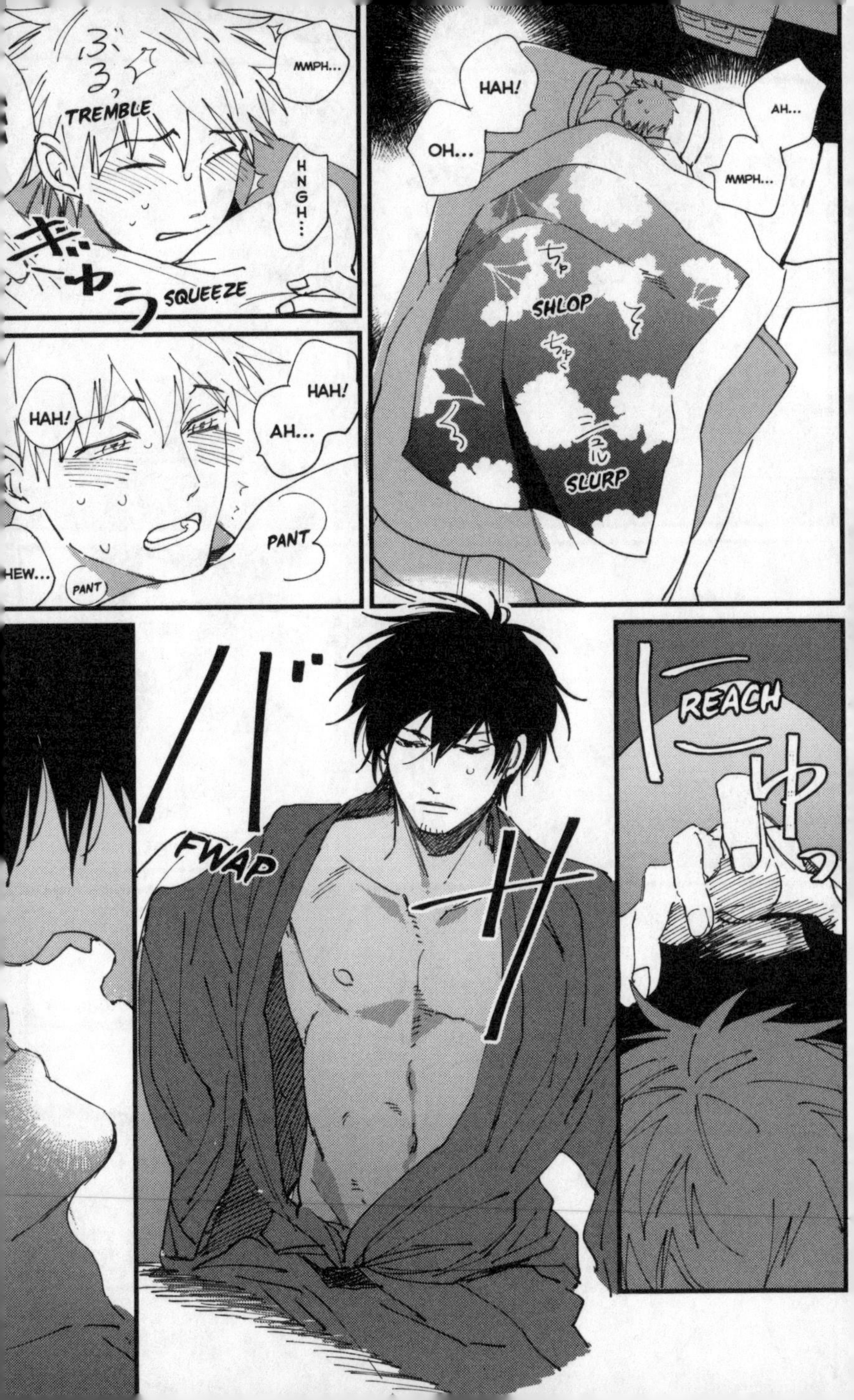
AH...
MMPH...
HAH!
OH...
SHLOP
SLURP
MMPH...
HNGH...
TREMBLE
SQUEEZE
HAH!
AH...
HAH!
PANT
PANT
HEW...
REACH
FWAP

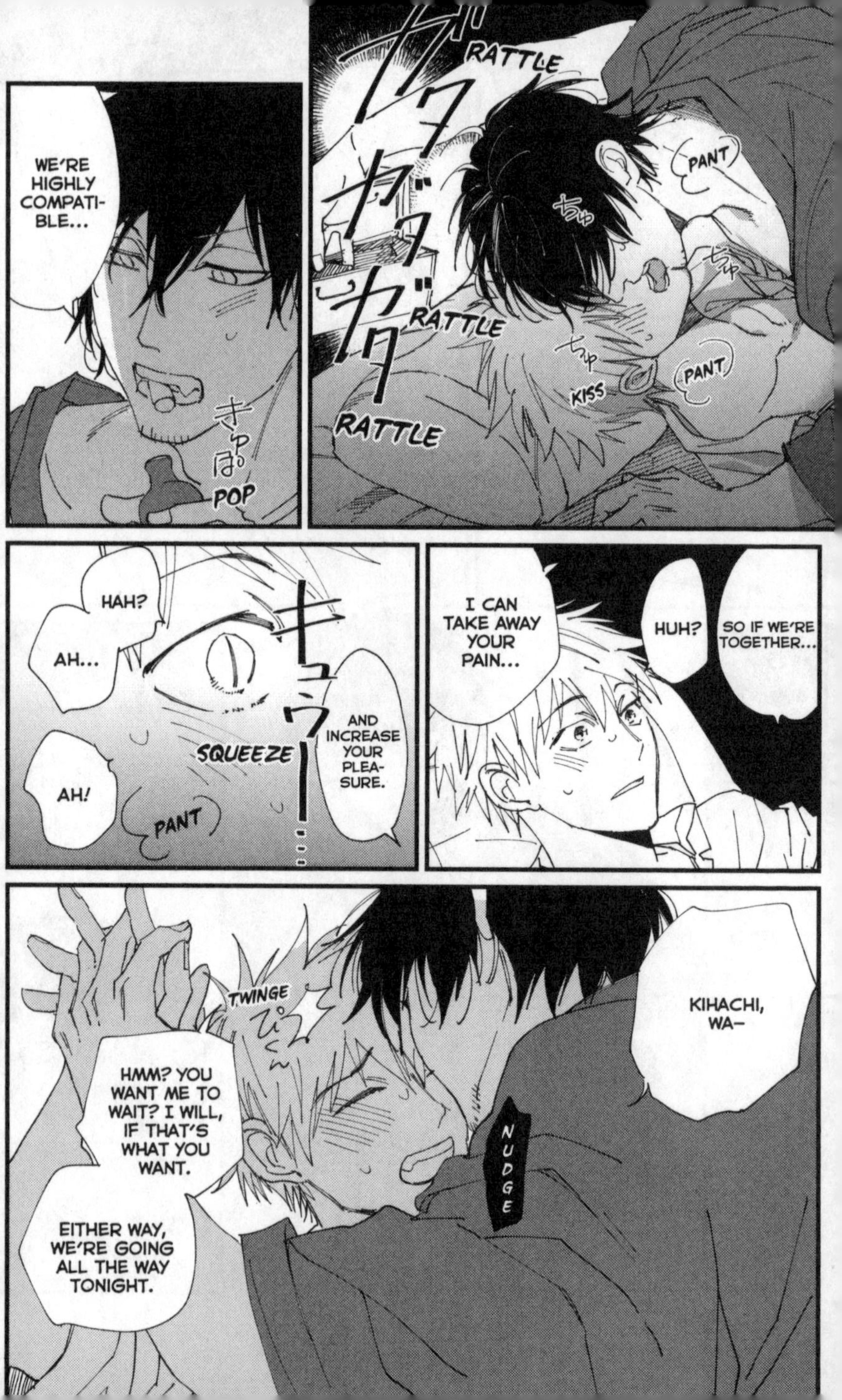
RATTLE
PANT
RATTLE
PANT
KISS
RATTLE
WE'RE HIGHLY COMPATI-BLE...
POP
SO IF WE'RE TOGETHER...
HUH?
I CAN TAKE AWAY YOUR PAIN...
AND INCREASE YOUR PLEA-SURE.
HAH?
AH...
SQUEEZE
AH!
PANT
KIHACHI, WA-
NUDGE
TWINGE
HMM? YOU WANT ME TO WAIT? I WILL, IF THAT'S WHAT YOU WANT.
EITHER WAY, WE'RE GOING ALL THE WAY TONIGHT.

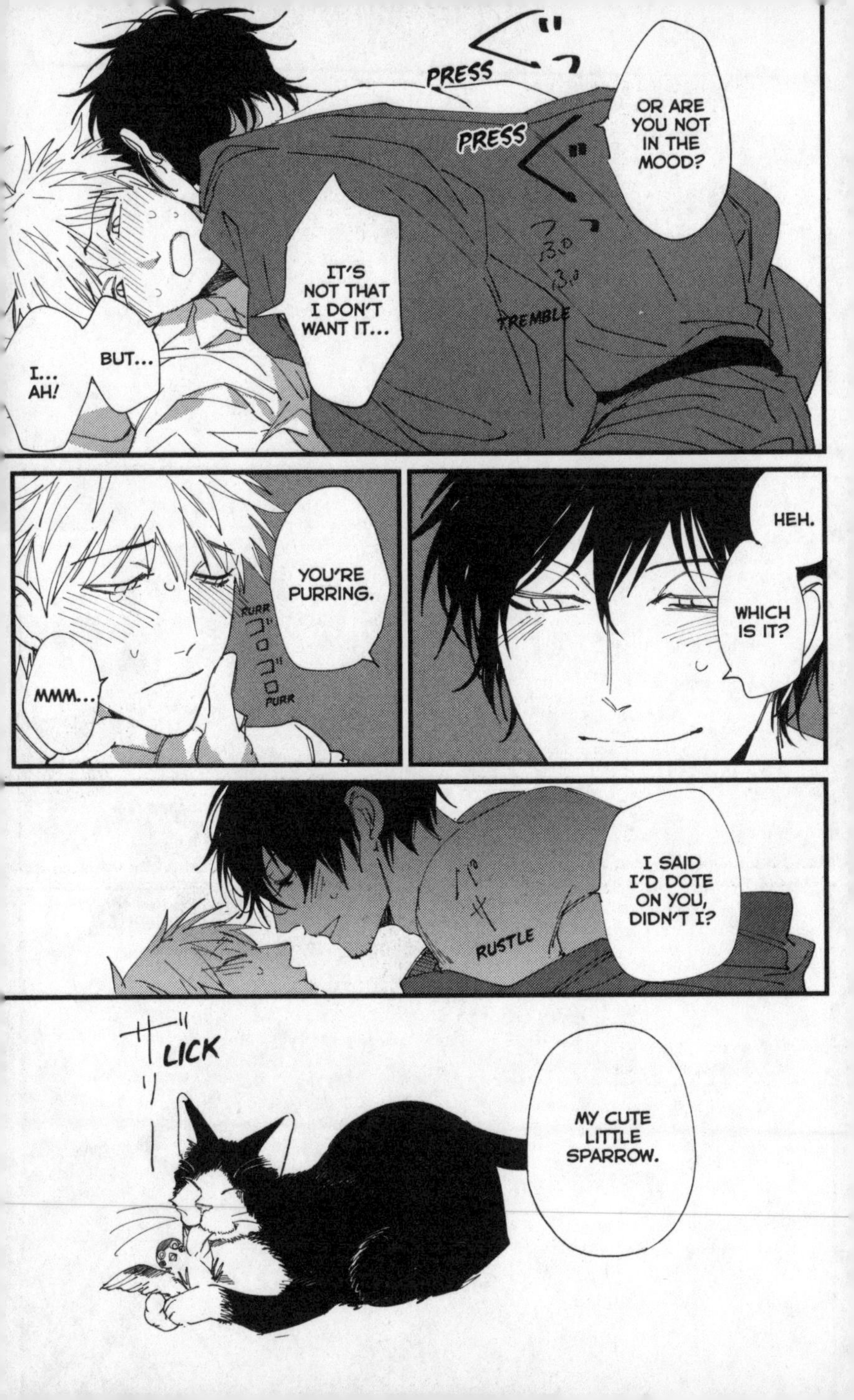
OR ARE YOU NOT IN THE MOOD?
PRESS
PRESS
TREMBLE
IT'S NOT THAT I DON'T WANT IT...
BUT...
I... AH!
HEH.
WHICH IS IT?
YOU'RE PURRING.
PURR
PURR
MMM...
I SAID I'D DOTE ON YOU, DIDN'T I?
RUSTLE
MY CUTE LITTLE SPARROW.
LICK

Thank you so much for reading! Horror kōdan stories are usually told only in summer, not in the winter, but I took some liberties when drawing this story.

Perhaps after this, Souta will become something inhuman. Perhaps he won't. Perhaps Kihachi will live a long life, and perhaps he won't.

In any case, I drew the ending hoping that they would enjoy the rest of their time together.

Greatest thanks to my editor, K-san.

Dento Hayane

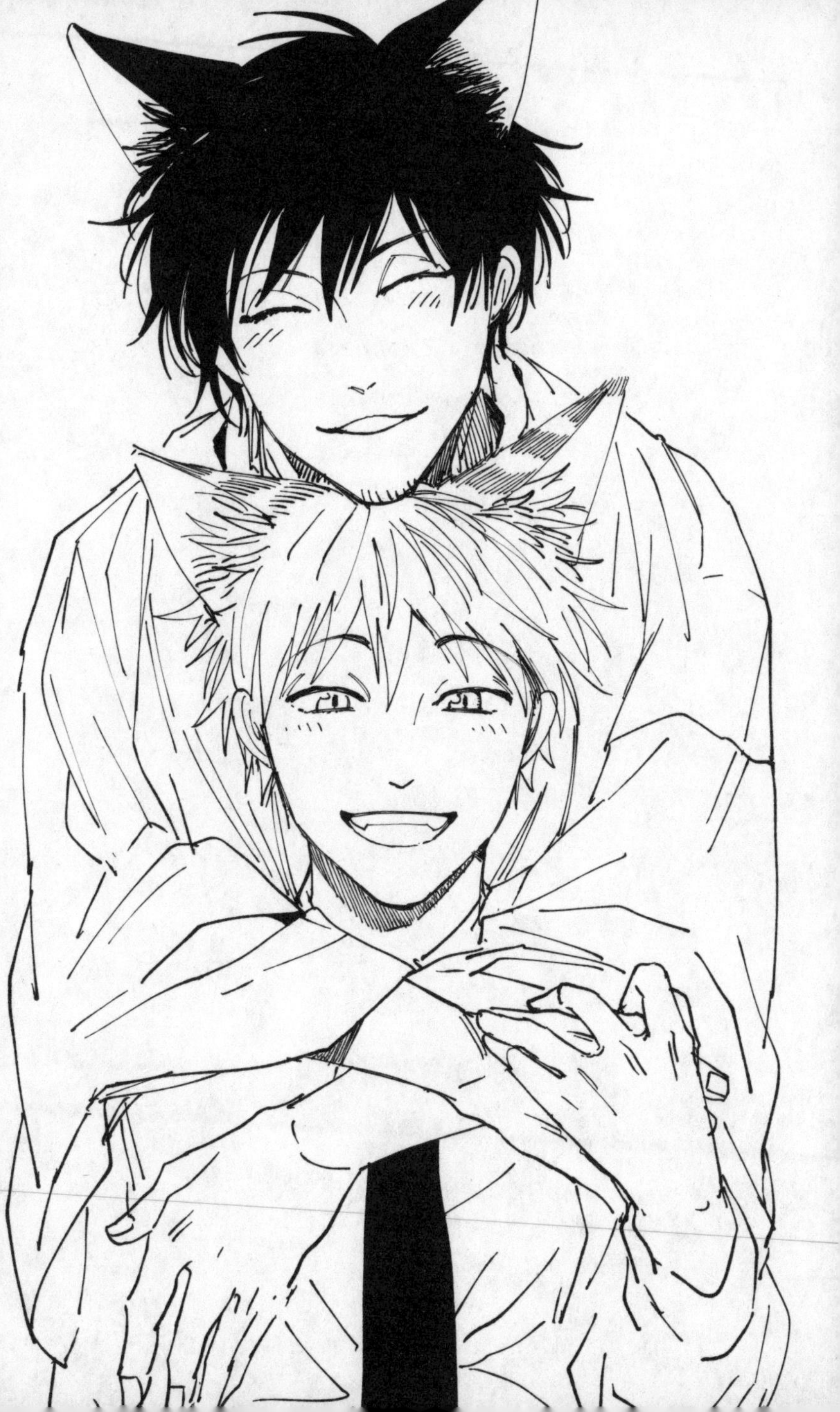

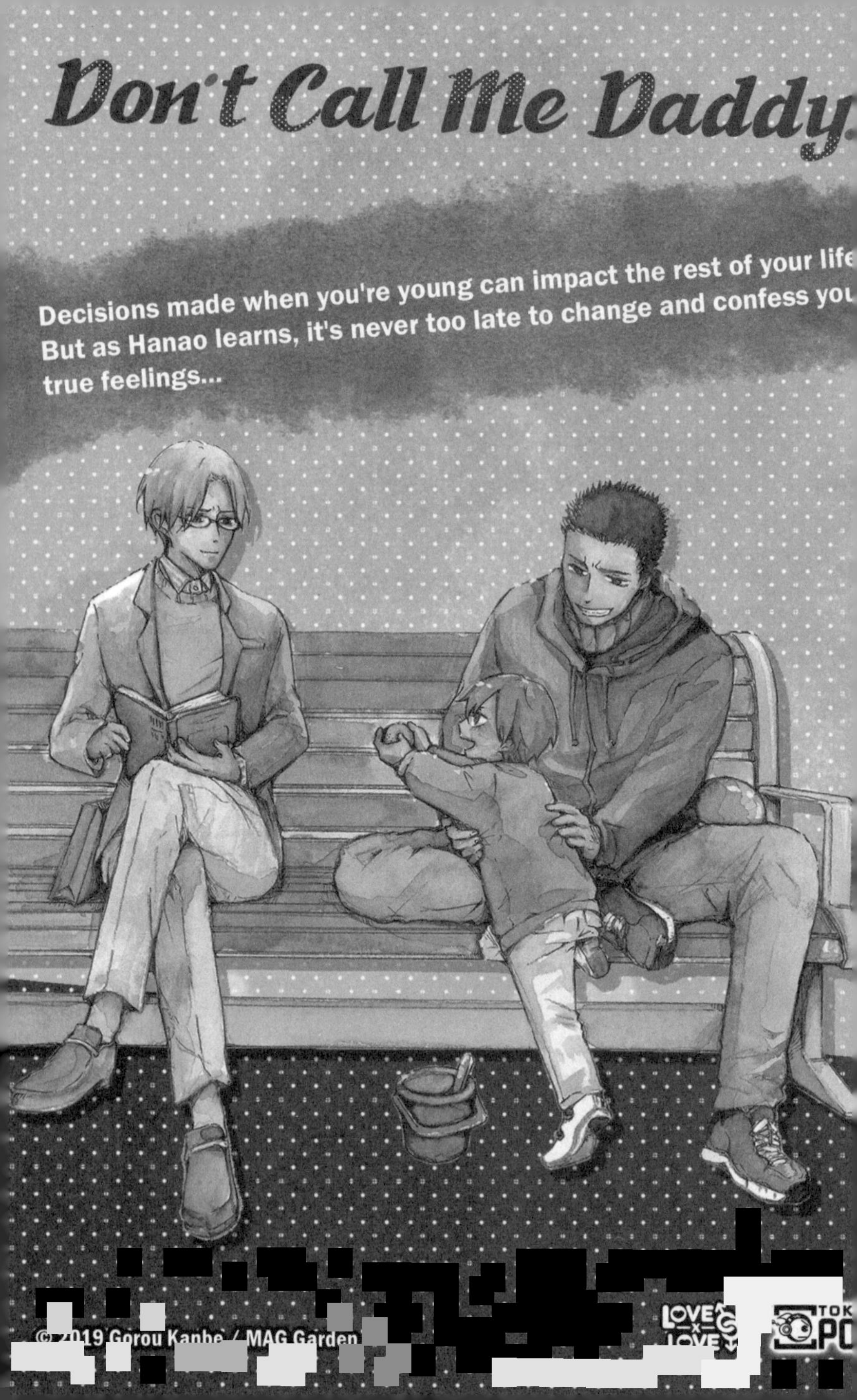
Don't Call Me Daddy
Decisions made when you're young can impact the rest of your life
But as Hanao learns, it's never too late to change and confess you
true feelings...
[redacted]

DON'T CALL ME DIRTY

houji is gay. Hama is homeless. Two men trying to make their way
a society that labels each of them as 'dirty' find a connection
ith one another — and a special relationship blossoms.

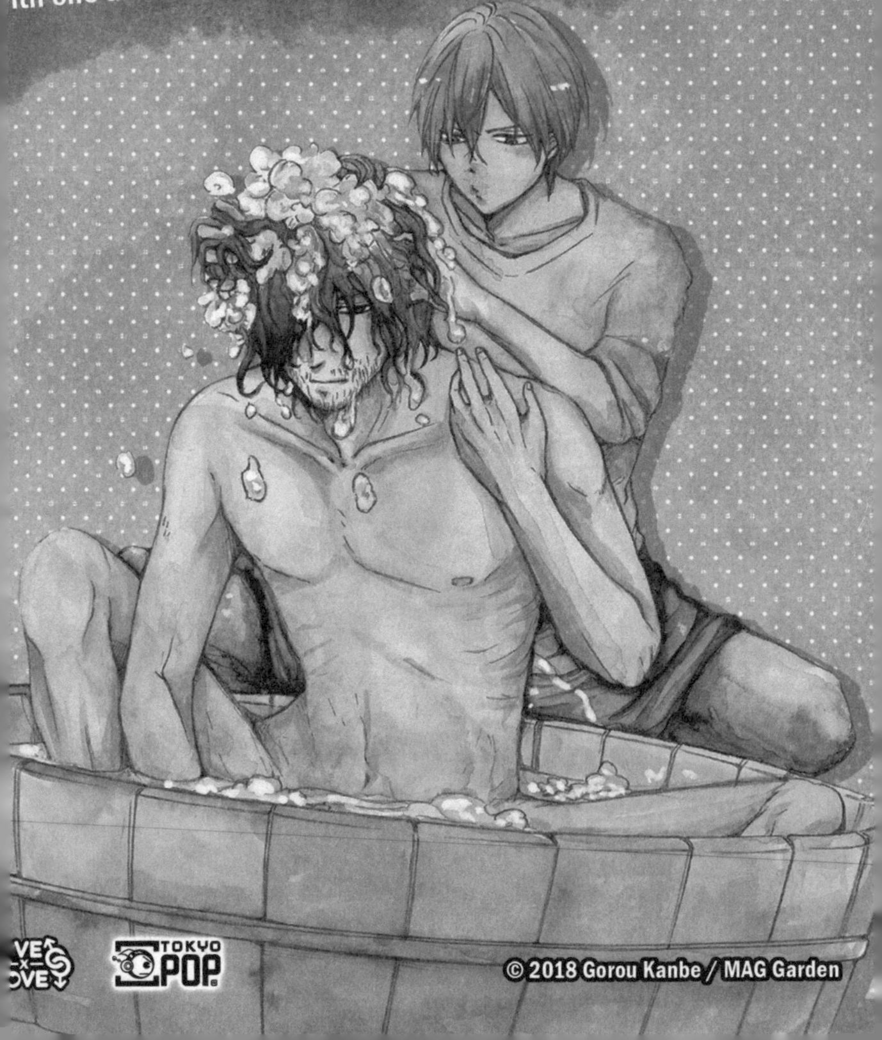

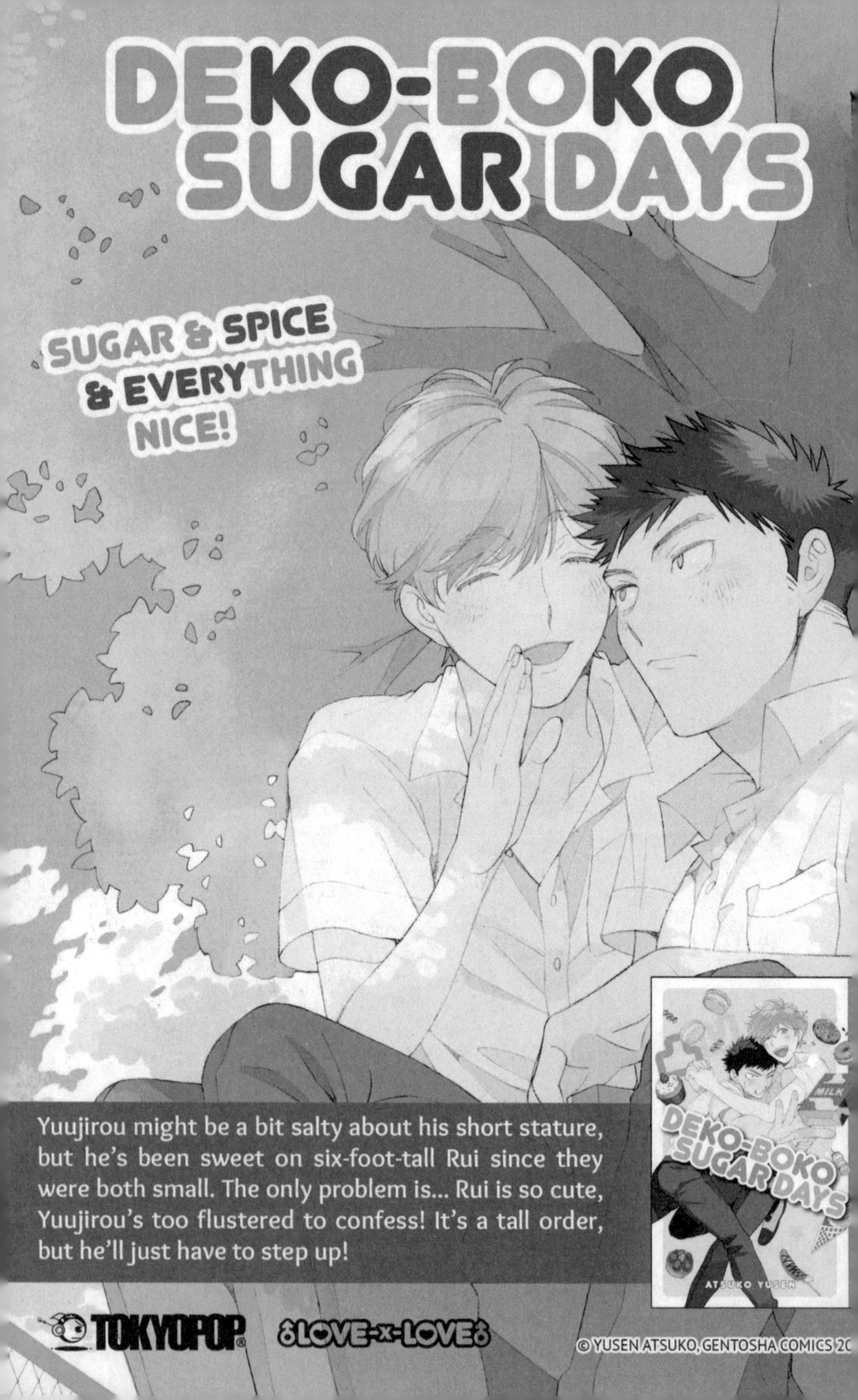
DEKO-BOKO SUGAR DAYS
SUGAR & SPICE & EVERYTHING NICE!
Yuujirou might be a bit salty about his short stature, but he's been sweet on six-foot-tall Rui since they were both small. The only problem is... Rui is so cute, Yuujirou's too flustered to confess! It's a tall order, but he'll just have to step up!
MILK
DEKO-BOKO SUGAR DAYS
ATSUKO YUSEN
TOKYOPOP®
LOVE x LOVE
© YUSEN ATSUKO, GENTOSHA COMICS 20

Servant & Lord

YEARS
AGO, MUSIC
ROUGHT THEM
TOGETHER...

AND THEN,
EVERYTHING
CHANGED.

TOKYOPOP

NTERNATIONAL
OMEN of MANGA

Lo / Lorinell Yu / TOKYOPOP GmbH

STAR COLLECTOR

By Anna B. & Sophie Schönhammer

A ROMANCE WRITTEN IN THE STARS!

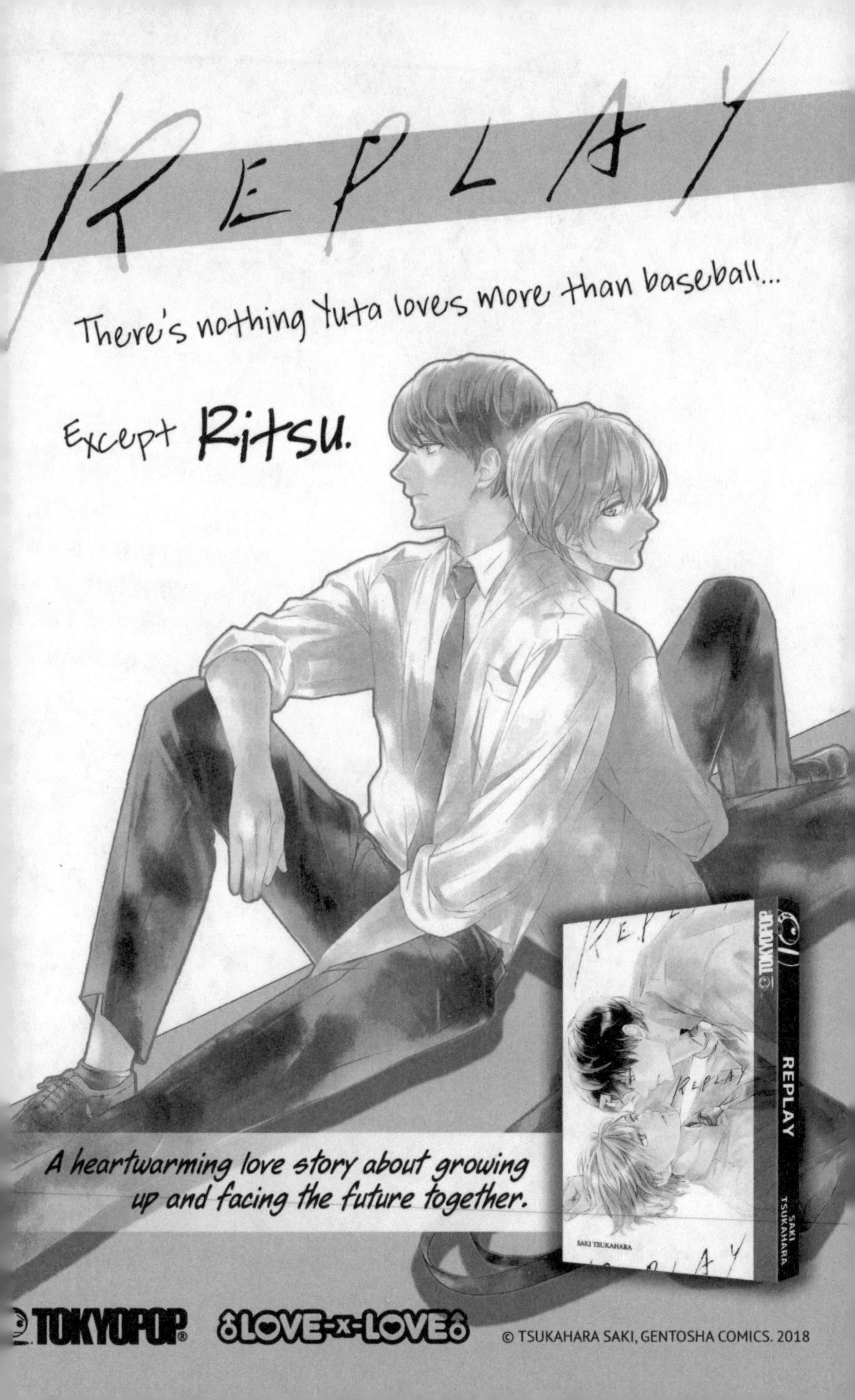
REPLAY
There's nothing Yuta loves more than baseball...
Except Ritsu.
A heartwarming love story about growing up and facing the future together.
REPLAY
SAKI TSUKAHARA
TOKYOPOP
LOVE-x-LOVE
© TSUKAHARA SAKI, GENTOSHA COMICS. 2018

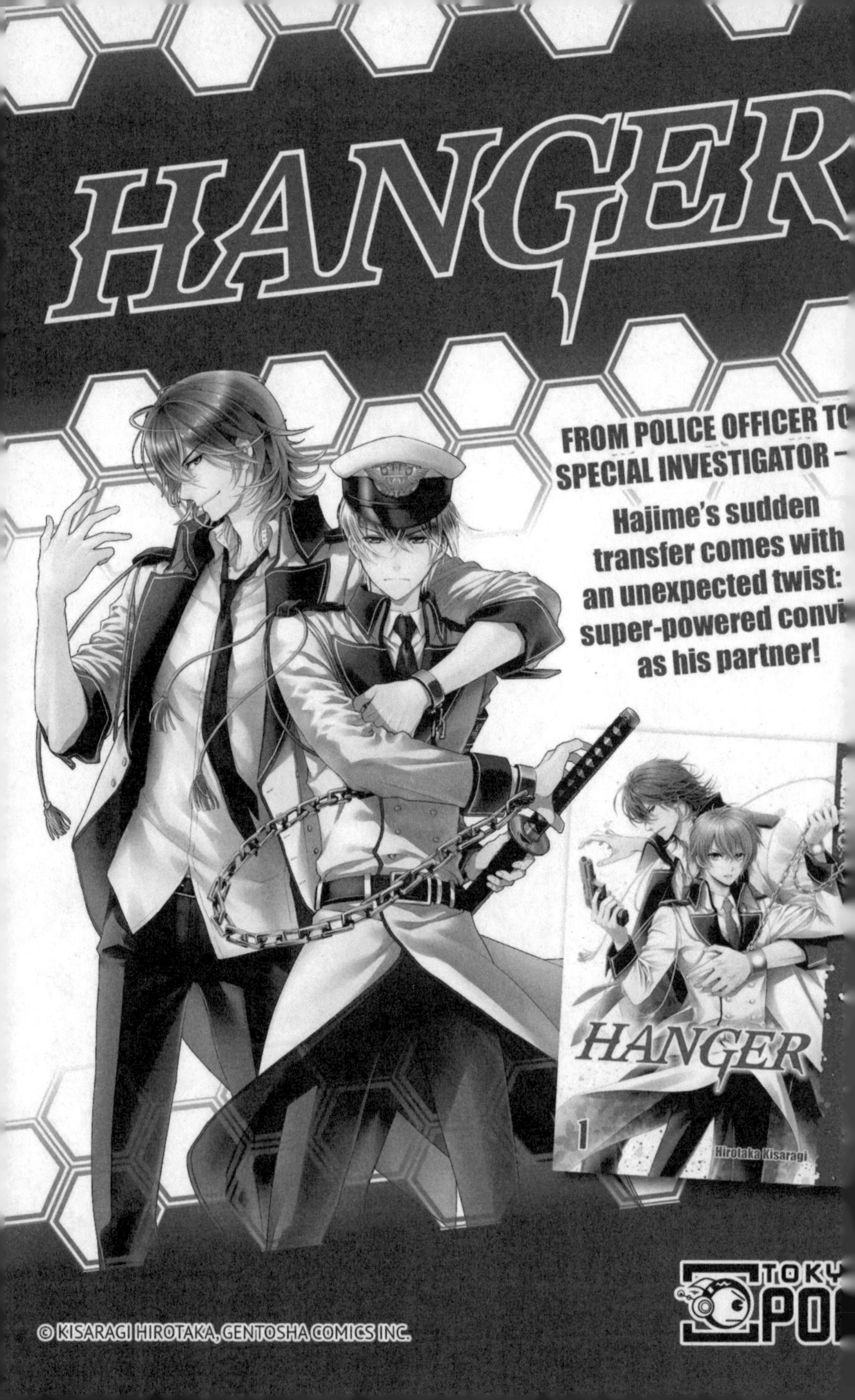
HANGER
FROM POLICE OFFICER T
SPECIAL INVESTIGATOR –
Hajime's sudden
transfer comes with
an unexpected twist:
super-powered convi
as his partner!
HANGER
1
Hirotaka Kisaragi
© KISARAGI HIROTAKA, GENTOSHA COMICS INC.

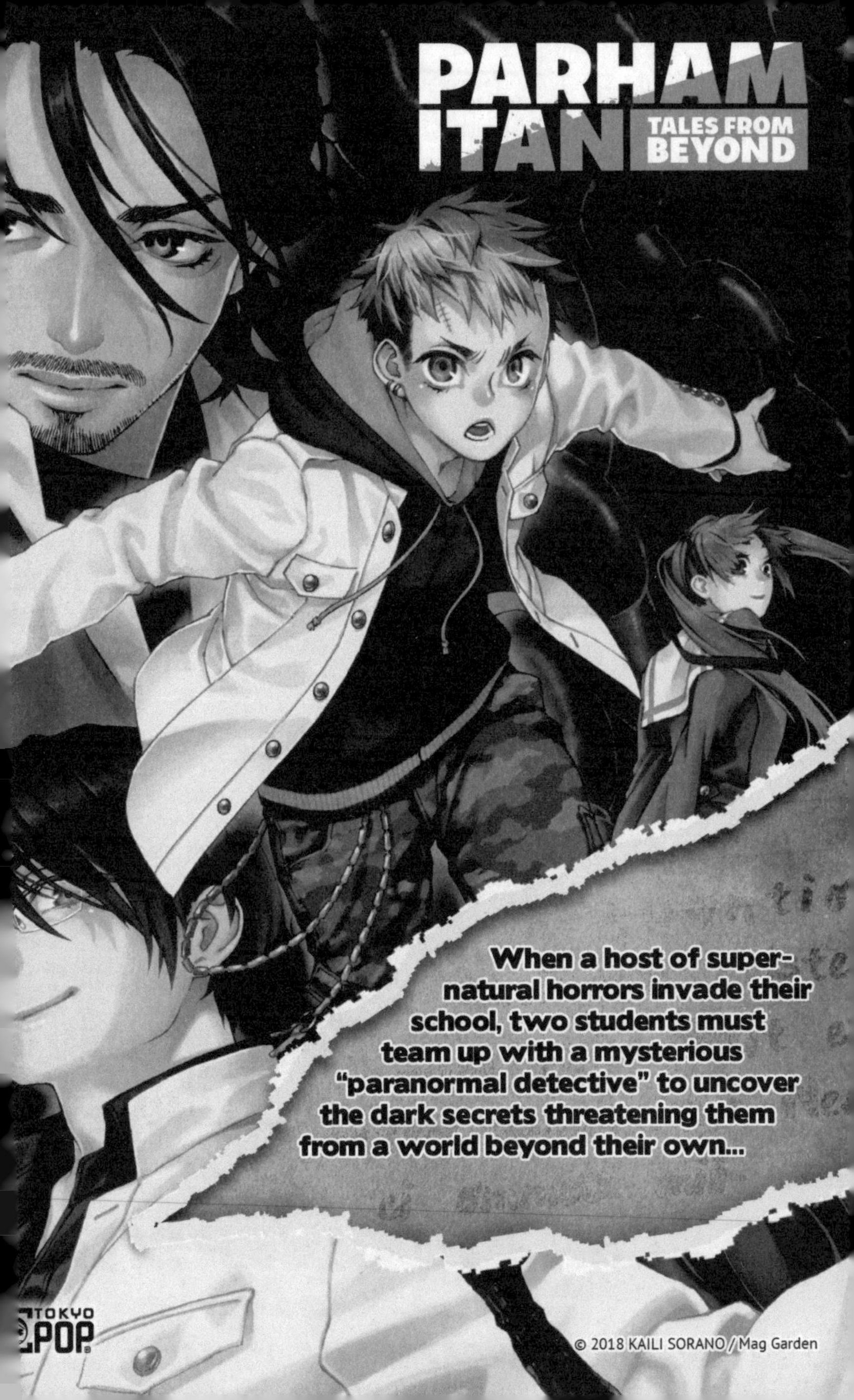
PARHAM ITAN
TALES FROM BEYOND
When a host of super-natural horrors invade their school, two students must team up with a mysterious "paranormal detective" to uncover the dark secrets threatening them from a world beyond their own...
TOKYOPOP
© 2018 KAILI SORANO / Mag Garden

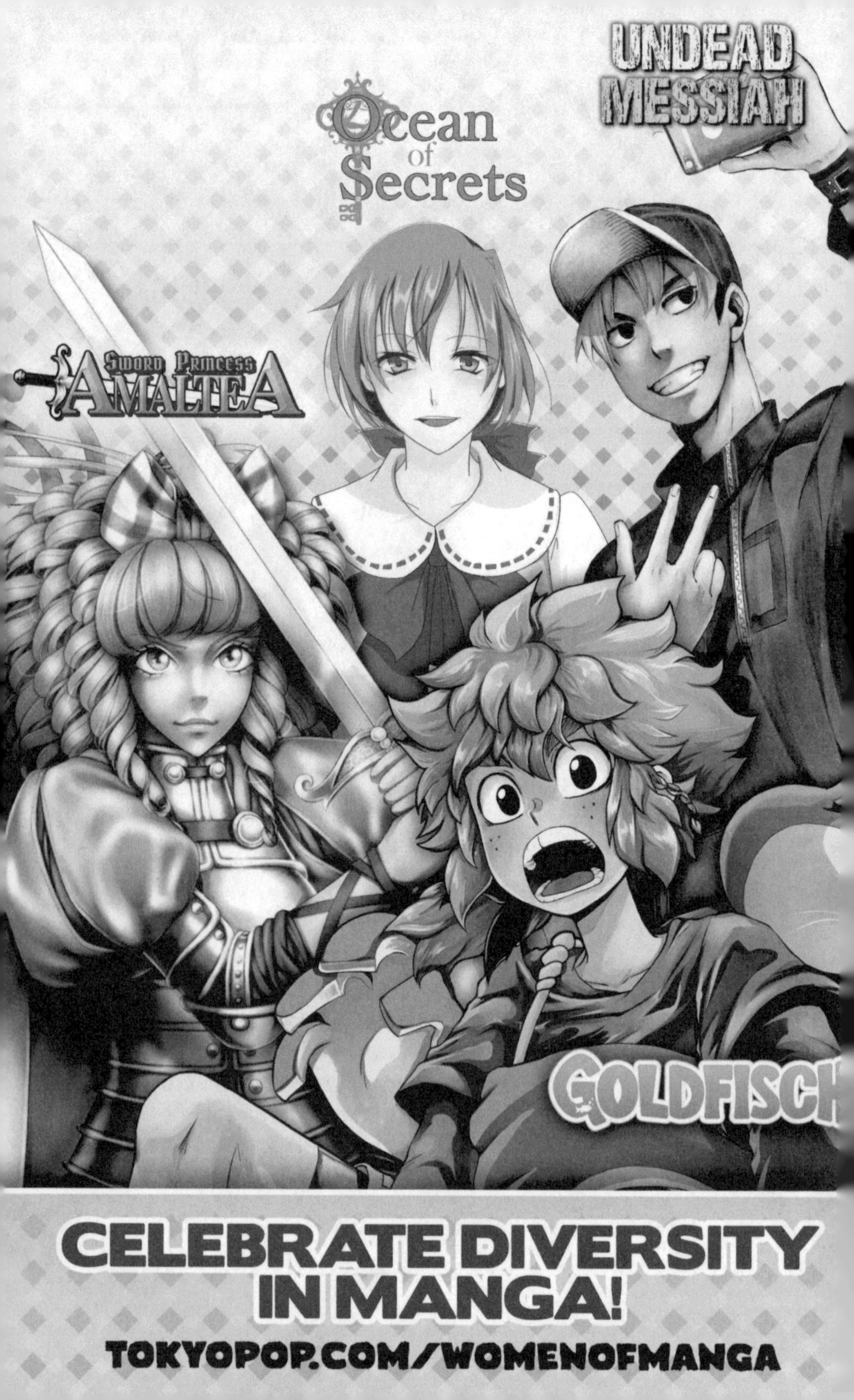
UNDEAD MESSIAH
Ocean of Secrets
SWORD PRINCESS AMALTEA
GOLDFISCH
CELEBRATE DIVERSITY IN MANGA!
TOKYOPOP.COM/WOMENOFMANGA

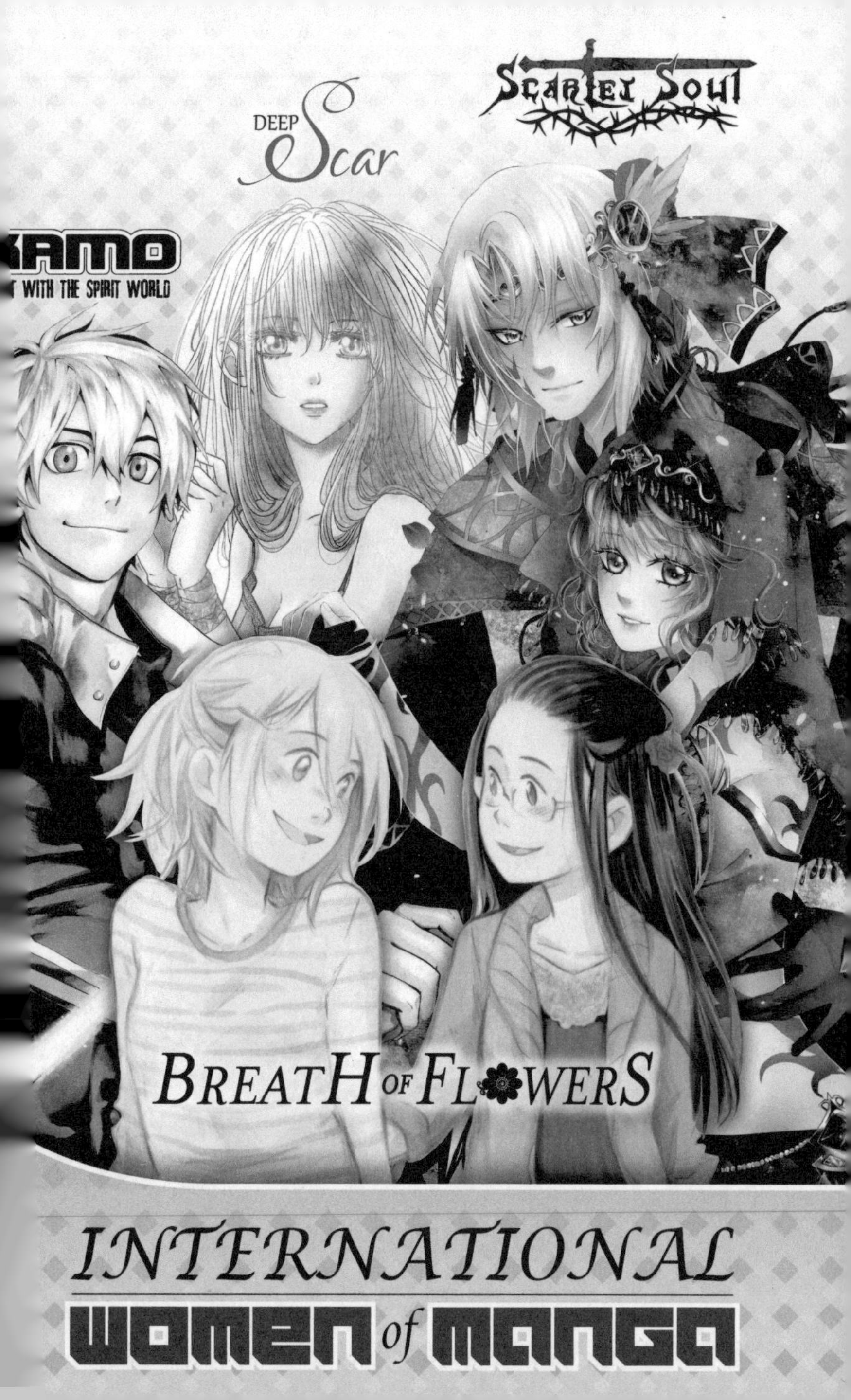
DEEP Scar
Scarlet Soul
KAMO
WITH THE SPIRIT WORLD
BREATH OF FLOWERS
INTERNATIONAL
WOMEN of MANGA

STOP

THIS IS THE BACK OF THE BOOK!

How do you read manga-style? It's simple! Let's practice -- just start in the top right panel and follow the numbers below!

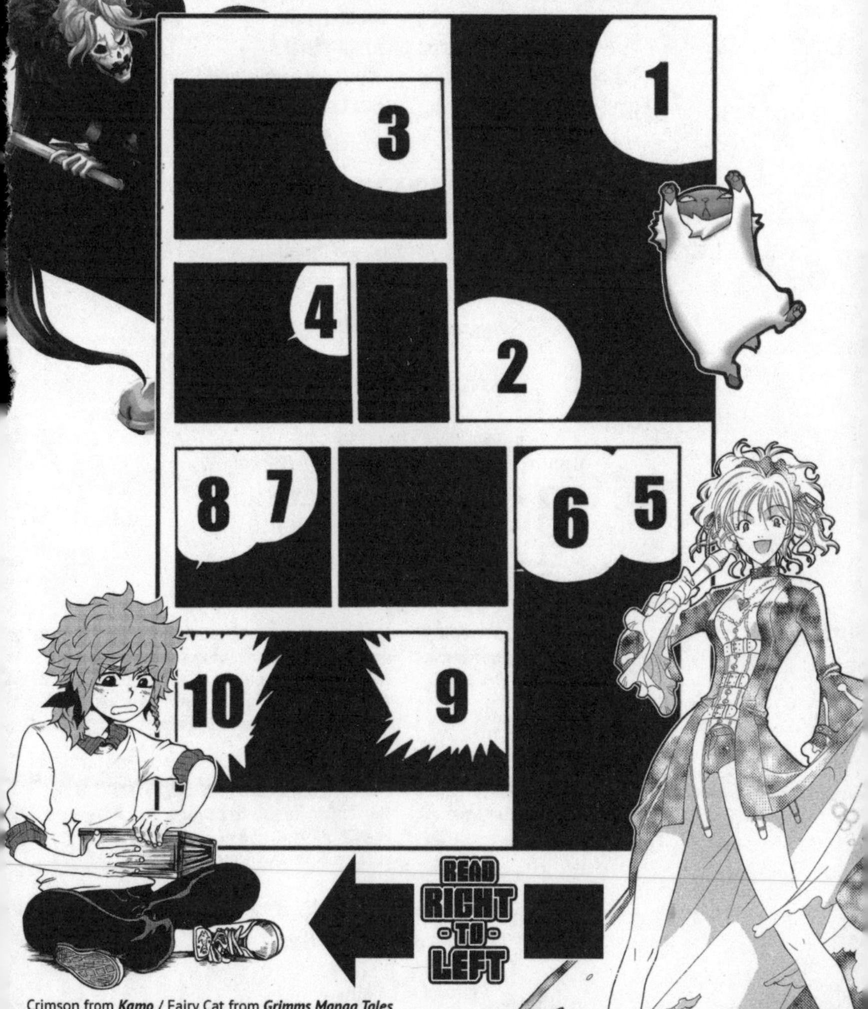
1
2
3
4
5
6
7
8
9
10
READ
RIGHT
-TO-
LEFT

Crimson from ***Kamo*** / Fairy Cat from ***Grimms Manga Tales***
Morrey from ***Goldfisch*** / Princess Ai from ***Princess Ai***

The Cat Proposed

Dento Hayane

Editor - Lena Atanassova
Marketing Associate - Kae Winters
Cover Design - Sol DeLeo
Translator - Katie Kimura
Copy Editor - M. Cara Carper
Proofreader - Caroline Wong
QC - Akiko Furuta
Licensing Specialist - Arika Yanaka
Retouching and Lettering - Vibrraant Publishing Studio
Editor-in-Chief & Publisher - Stu Levy

A TOKYOPOP® Manga

TOKYOPOP
5200 W Century Blvd
Suite 705
Los Angeles, CA 90045 USA

E-mail: info@TOKYOPOP.com
Come visit us online at www.TOKYOPOP.com

www.facebook.com/TOKYOPOP
www.twitter.com/TOKYOPOP
www.pinterest.com/TOKYOPOP
www.instagram.com/TOKYOPOP

Original Japanese edition published by FRANCE SHOIN
This English edition is published by arrangement with FRANCE SHOIN Inc., Tokyo
in care of Tuttle-Mori Agency, Inc., Tokyo.

ISBN: 978-1-4278-6748-3

First TOKYOPOP Printing: February 2021

10 9 8 7 6 5 4 3 2 1

Printed in CANADA

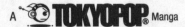